FAMILY MATTERS

FAMILY MATTERS

Child Welfare in Twentieth-Century New Zealand

Bronwyn Dalley

AUCKLAND UNIVERSITY PRESS

in association with the

HISTORICAL BRANCH, DEPARTMENT OF INTERNAL AFFAIRS

First published 1998

Auckland University Press
University of Auckland
Private Bag 92019
Auckland
New Zealand

© Crown Copyright, 1998

ISBN 1 86940 190 5

Printed by Publishing Press Ltd, Auckland

CONTENTS

ACKNOWLEDGEMENTS

I am pleased to have finished this history, a project which I have found challenging, interesting, and at times, difficult. Many individuals helped in one way or another to bring the work to completion.

I would like to thank first the supervisory committee which oversaw the history: Mike Doolan, Robin Wilson (who set up the project with Raoul Ketko), and especially Brian Manchester and Mary Todd. I have been privileged to have had the assistance and guidance of this group of current and former social workers who have been liberal with their time, gracious in their detailed comments on drafts of the manuscript, and willing to have a history which does not always show child welfare practices and policies in a favourable light. I thank each of them for their generosity and their open-mindedness. The Department of Social Welfare commissioned this project and allowed me a free hand in its conception and execution. Jock Phillips, at the time Chief Historian at the Historical Branch, Department of Internal Affairs, helped establish the project and supervised it; I thank him for his support. Thanks also to Claudia Orange, who assumed responsibility for the project in the Historical Branch and oversaw the production process.

I wrote the history while employed at the Historical Branch, and acknowledge the assistance of supportive colleagues there. Particular thanks for their encouragement and good cheer to Ian Dougherty, Bryan Gilling, Kathryn Hastings, Megan Hutching, and Malcolm McKinnon, who made useful comments on the Introduction and Conclusion. I appreciated the many stimulating conversations about social welfare with Margaret McClure, who commented on the Introduction and Conclusion, proof-read the text, and provided timely support. David Green edited the manuscript sympathetically and with skill, and has been an important colleague throughout the project.

A number of current and former social workers, in addition to the members of the supervisory committee, gave their time for interviews, commented on the text, and patiently explained the minutiae of 1980s' welfare policy. Thanks to Anne Caton, Lainey Cowan, Greg Putland, and Janet Worfolk. Bruce Asher kindly allowed me access to his taped interviews with former staff of the Child Welfare Division.

Several people read parts or all of the manuscript. Edward Dickinson offered valuable comments on Part I, and allowed me to read his draft history of child welfare in modern Germany, the bibliography of which I mined shamelessly. John Jensen made pertinent comments on an early draft of Part I. Margaret Tennant read the entire manuscript, asked challenging questions and made important suggestions – I am fortunate to continue to have the benefit of her scholarship and erudition.

I appreciated the assistance of staff at several libraries and archives: National Archives in Auckland, Christchurch and especially Wellington; the Alexander Turnbull Library; and interloans staff at the Department of Internal Affairs library. I owe particular thanks to the records and library staff at the Department of Social Welfare in Wellington: Bill Siddells arranged for me to work in the library and records area; Jalal Mayia and Evelyn Teo processed my requests for files with speed and good humour, and graciously shared their office space with me for several months; Gary Howat expedited access to departmental files, and allowed me to use his office.

Thanks also to those who allowed me to use their photographs and cartoons: Ron Crate; Eric Heath; Pat Lodge; John McCombe; Tom Scott; Malcolm Walker. Brenda Grant and Ron Fox of the *Evening Post* illustrations section were generous in their assistance, as were Carolyn Cameron at News Media and Sherwood Young of the New Zealand Police. Joan McCracken of the Alexander Turnbull Library's photographic section was resourceful in suggesting and locating images. Several people gave useful references: thanks to Peter Boston, Graeme Dunstall, Mary Gillingham, Ray Grover, Danny Keenan, Dugald McDonald, Kate Studholme, and Sue Upton.

Friends and colleagues tended to my welfare in various ways during the project. Thanks to John Barnes, Nick Clark, Susan Grogan, Charlotte Macdonald, Fiona McKergow, Tony Nightingale, and my sister, Lynette Quirk. Grant Phillipson listened patiently to numerous tales of woe; Kerry Taylor was always ready with a cup of coffee or a bottle of wine to discuss problems and pass the time of day. In this project, as in others of mine, Bronwyn Labrum has been confidante, support, sounding-board, critic, and dispenser of sensible (if ignored) advice about rest and recreation – I thank her for this, and for her friendship. Most of all, thanks to Rob Forlong.

Introduction

One day in November 1958, Mrs Wilson rang her local child welfare officers and asked them to take away her daughter, Deborah York.[1] Deborah had just returned from the Salvation Army Children's Home where she had spent her thirteenth birthday. Her mother had sent her there for being 'difficult' and for trying to run away. Mrs Wilson said that Deborah caused constant tension in the family by mixing with adolescents who were suspected of being 'sex delinquents'. Deborah appeared in the children's court later in the month charged with being delinquent, and was sent to a foster home. Mrs Wilson rang child welfare officers after one of Deborah's periodic visits home and claimed that she could no longer tolerate her. She complained that Deborah was deceitful and defiant, and had acted and dressed so precociously that she had developed a reputation for being 'cheap'. Child welfare officers removed Deborah to a Child Welfare Division family home in Wanganui. The foster parents there were soon also complaining of her conduct. She would not leave the boys alone, they said, and set out to make a conquest of any young man she met. Deborah returned home after six months, but was soon asked to leave, blamed now for causing marital discord between her mother and her stepfather. The couple subsequently separated, and Mrs Wilson asked for Deborah to come back home. By this time though, Deborah was feeling persecuted. Child welfare officers and psychologists had interviewed her for nearly two years to discern the causes of her behaviour; Deborah's only wishes were to be free of the Child Welfare Division and to be left alone.

This is just one of the stories that can be woven about Deborah's case. What we know of it comes from the child welfare officers who reconstructed Deborah's life through her case file; I have reconstructed it again, using pseudonyms rather than actual names, as I have done with all children and families in contact with the child welfare system after 1925.[2] Told from Mrs Wilson's perspective, the tale would have been different; expressed by Deborah herself, another portrayal would have emerged. If Deborah, her mother and her case workers were of another place, another time, another race, or male, other narratives and dramas would have unfolded.

In 1902, the year in which this history of child welfare begins, Deborah would have appeared before the magistrate's court for being 'uncontrollable' and for consorting with individuals detrimental to her welfare. She would have been admitted to the newly-opened Te Oranga Reformatory in Christchurch, a Department of Education residential institution for uncontrollable or criminal girls and young women. With 50 or 60 others, Deborah would have remained there until she was 21. She would have had no contact with her mother, apart from occasional letters. Deborah would not have spent all her time in the institution, however. Reintegration into society and a family environment was important for early twentieth-century child welfare workers, so she would have been sent to live with a family as their domestic servant, with wages paid to her. At the end of her institutional stay, Deborah would have been released into the surrounding community, whilst her only friends and sources of support were back in the reformatory.

Or take 1992, the year in which this history closes. Deborah would have most likely been male and Maori, categories over-represented in cases coming to the attention of the Department of Social Welfare, which now oversaw the welfare of children. Perhaps Deborah's teacher, friends or other family members had told social workers about her stepfather's ongoing sexual abuse of her, which accounted for her mood swings and general behaviour. The social workers would have consulted with the local care and protection resource panel and sexual abuse team before making any investigations. If these inquiries indicated that Deborah was in need of care and protection, the case would have been handed to a care and protection coordinator for a family group conference. While the Department of Social Welfare took a back seat, Deborah's family group of parents, grand-parents, aunts and uncles would have gathered to discuss the situation and work out their own solutions. The conference may have sent Deborah to stay with other family members for a time, or perhaps arranged counselling or education in parenting skills for her family at a local marae. Admitting Deborah to one of the few Social Welfare residences would have been one of the least likely outcomes.

This book seeks to explain the philosophies and practices of the child welfare services in twentieth-century New Zealand which responded to boys and young men, and to girls and young women such as Deborah. The history has been commissioned by the Department of Social Welfare, and its focus is on government services, as realised through the successive child welfare agencies: the Industrial Schools Section and Special Schools Section of the Department of Education, the Child Welfare Branch and Child Welfare Division of the same department, and then the Department of Social Welfare.[3] The book begins in 1902, when the Department of Education put the finishing touches to changes in the provision of children's welfare services. It closes 90 years later, in 1992, when the establishment of the New Zealand Children and Young Persons Service opened another chapter in the delivery of children's welfare. That story is still unfolding and awaits another historian. The work of the various government agencies clustered around several main areas: juvenile delinquency and youth offending, residential care, provision for ex-nuptial babies, adoption services, foster care, supervision and preventive policies, child neglect and child abuse. The eight chapters in this history expand on child welfare work in all of these areas, and trace changes and continuities in welfare philosophy and practice. Pairs of chapters traverse four separate periods corresponding to changes in the government agency responsible for children's welfare.

Important shifts have occurred around welfare matters and the most appropriate response to them in the course of the twentieth century. The variations in Deborah's story depict these shifts. Early in the century residential care was regarded as the best option for young offenders, and for young people who were considered to be out of control. Alternative forms of care, such as foster care with non-family members, were reserved for the least difficult children committed to the care of the state. The pendulum swung away from residential care as a first option from the late 1910s as foster care, and the supervision of children in their own homes, assumed importance. By the late 1950s, young people such as Deborah might experience a range of family care situations. Thirty years later, social workers and family members worked together to keep young people within the family grouping. Family-based care was the first option; non-kin foster care, family homes, and residential care followed in descending order of preference.

The nature of residential care itself changed markedly. Large institutions, separated from community and family, and housing both young offenders and children in need of 'care and protection', gave way to smaller and more varied units catering for distinct groups of young people. Public and professional criticism of institutional regimes for young people from the late 1970s led to a major reformulation of the place of institutions in child welfare services. Many of these institutions were closed from the mid-1980s as institutional care became reserved only for those young people considered to be in need of it.

As Deborah's case also indicates, child abuse and sexual abuse were at times recognised as significant social problems. Child abuse and neglect featured in early twentieth-century welfare work, when victims of abuse could be quickly removed from their homes and placed in residential care alongside young offenders. Public and professional interest in child abuse waned over most of the century until its rediscovery in the 1960s. Since that time, physical abuse, and then sexual abuse, have grown in importance as areas of social work, and increasingly, solutions to them are looked for within the family group.

Other child welfare issues and services have undergone shifts of emphasis. Tending to the welfare of children born outside marriage was a dominant issue over most of the century, but responses to ex-nuptial births have altered. Boarding children with other women was one option for single mothers unable to meet the costs of sole parenthood. Adoption became another option from the 1950s, as single mothers were encouraged to sever all ties with their babies. Both of these possibilities declined in importance from the 1970s, as the 'problem' of single motherhood dwindled. As with other areas of children's welfare, family links have been emphasised, and keeping children within biological family groups is now seen as of primary importance.

The client base of child welfare work has altered markedly. Males always outnumbered females, and Pakeha children and their families have formed the majority of those in contact with the child welfare system, but Maori have been an increasingly disproportionate minority in all areas of child welfare work since the 1950s. Pacific Island children and young people have constituted another disproportionate minority since the 1970s. This changing clientele forced a reassessment of children's welfare services, and the need to work in culturally appropriate ways has been a dominant force in the welfare profession since the early 1980s.

Definitions and interpretations of child welfare issues have altered over the century, in keeping with changing cultural, social and political contexts. Deborah's case mirrors these different contexts, as each interpretation of child welfare issues projected the fears and hopes of New Zealand society at particular moments. In 1902, there was the fear that sexually precocious young women such as Deborah would spread disease and moral degradation throughout society, endangering the well-being of the nation. The hope was that a period of isolation from society would enable her to become a useful woman, skilled in the domestic arts, a fit wife and mother; at the very least, the reformatory kept her off the streets. In 1958, there was the fear that, like other 1950s' teenagers, Deborah was set to become a sexual delinquent, fixated on dress, on boys, and on having a good time. The hope was that through temporary removal to a family home, part-way between an institution and private foster care, and through observation and interview, Deborah's problems could be overcome. In 1992, there was fear of the effects of sexual abuse on individual lives, and the knowledge that separating Deborah from her family supports could worsen those effects. There was the knowledge too that families, and Maori families especially, had been torn apart and disempowered through excessive welfare intervention in their lives. The hope was that by restoring mana and responsibility to families they would work through their own and Deborah's problems in the way that best suited them all, with social workers and the government assuming roles which would allow this to happen. Each of these interpretations of welfare issues, and their solutions, built on, and reacted to, those which had gone before. And each generation of policymakers was confident that both interpretation and solution were the right ones. As the Australian child welfare historian Robert van Krieken argues, an enduring tendency 'to see promising novelty where there is often recycling of old ideas and old recipes . . . disables us from perceiving long-term trends'.[4] Taking a long-term historical view encourages us to see the changes as successive loops in cycles of welfare provision. In twenty or 30 years' time, the policies and practices so carefully crafted in late twentieth-century New Zealand may no longer be valid.

Many of the developments in child welfare philosophy and practice stemmed from changes in attitudes to children and young people. The basis on which various child welfare policies developed suggests that there have been diverse constructions of childhood over the twentieth century.[5] Within these formulations, however, two strands project over child welfare policy and into practice. In New Zealand, as elsewhere, children and young people have been seen as victims of society or as threats to it, and sometimes as both at once.[6] The image of the vulnerable child always harboured the possibility of threats to social stability, secure family life, and the health of the nation. Indigent and neglected children had the potential to grow into criminals and miscreants, while cruelly-treated youngsters could develop into abusive adults. Such doubled perceptions of children meant that policies towards the two 'groups' were never too far apart. For their own good, and that of the nation, indigent, neglected or abused children could all be located with foster families, or placed in residential institutions; for their own good, and that of the nation, delinquent and criminal children too could be placed in foster care or residential homes. Mutually sustaining issues of welfare and justice pervaded the entire spectrum of social policies for children over most of the century.

This dual construction lay behind the notion of sex delinquency and the admission of such young people, mainly girls, to residential institutions. It also enabled young offenders to be detained or supervised for long periods while attempts were made to find in a damaged past the underlying causes of behaviour. Policies in the 1980s and 1990s have endeavoured to break down the perceptions of abused and neglected children as potentially dangerous, and of young offenders as victims in need of treatment rather than punishment. The long persistence of such representations among welfare workers and the public suggests that the task will be difficult and ongoing.

Changes in child welfare policy and practice mask continuities in philosophy and approach. The major continuity and central theme traced in this history is the core role of the family in child welfare. At all times and in all social contexts, child welfare policymakers enunciated the importance of a domestic, family environment as the best site for ensuring children's welfare. Definitions of that 'best' environment changed over the century, as Deborah's stories suggest, and the practice of resolving children's welfare through the family departed from the philosophy at many points. Nonetheless, a form of family-based care was held up as the ideal situation for children and young people from the late 1910s: foster care or supervision in a young person's home was supplemented by family homes from the 1950s, and by family-based care and kin networks from the 1980s.

The centrality of a family life for children enabled child welfare agencies at times to display a flexible attitude towards family forms. While some in society heaped opprobrium on single mothers in the 1920s, or stressed the advantages said to accrue to a child through adoption in the 1950s, child welfare agencies provided assistance to enable the single mother to keep her child. Extended family forms were recognised as well. Before the widespread urbanisation of Maori after the Second World War, child welfare agencies endeavoured to keep Maori children with their families or in their own tribal area, perhaps in the hope that out of sight was out of mind.

Families themselves frequently preferred a form of family-based care, and often approached child welfare agencies with requests or demands for assistance. Harassed mothers asked child welfare officers to sort out troublesome children they could no longer handle; others petitioned the courts to commit their children to a residential institution; some called on the agencies to halt the abuse their children suffered. Families took an active part in relationships with child welfare agencies, perhaps seeing intervention as a way to resolve generational conflicts or to assert their status in domestic power relations. They negotiated and compromised with child welfare authorities, invited them into their homes, or succeeded in downplaying the presence of welfare workers in their children's lives.[7]

Working through families to maintain child welfare inevitably turned a spotlight on family situations. Because of the belief that healthy and well-adjusted families formed the basis of an ordered society, any supervision or observation of a child outside an institutional setting also entailed the supervision and observation of his or her family. Sometimes the supervision and observation were overt, with entire families placed on the agencies' caseloads. At other times, they were a by-product of working with children and young people. Whether overt or not, and whether invited or not, intervention, once initiated, could be very hard for families to stop. They could find themselves drawn into a relationship with child welfare agencies that lasted months or even years. Not until the 1980s was such ongoing involvement reassessed, and acknowledged to create as many difficulties as it set out to ameliorate.

A further theme of this history, although not a focus, is one of government child welfare services forging and breaking alliances with other welfare groups. Throughout the twentieth century, the government was only one among a number of organisations working in the area of children's welfare.[8] Some of these organisations provided institutional services; the Salvation Army, for example, ran children's homes of the type to which Deborah was sent in the 1950s. Several of these institutions preceded government services, but with both funding and legislative authority on its side the government was arguably the most important child welfare agency. At times, government agencies eschewed other providers as less important and offering facilities less rigorous than their own. Official attempts to 'go it alone' were short-lived, however, as experience taught that working towards the welfare of children, young people and their families was a task in which the entire community had a stake.

Government agencies, families, and the community collectively constituted a network spun to enunciate, to maintain and to structure children's welfare, within what one historian has dubbed the 'mixed economy' of welfare.[9] The parameters of that relationship have shifted as families and community groups have sought greater involvement in child welfare services, sometimes on sufferance. Overall, the boundaries of the state became increasingly porous during the twentieth century, as more and more community-based welfare organisations were recognised as having a role in ensuring children's welfare; but power over and responsibility for child welfare have never resided in the state alone.[10] The path-breaking Children, Young Persons, and Their Families Act 1989 revealed significant movement by formally recognising the mixed economy of child welfare that had operated informally since the nineteenth century.

The children and young people in whose name child welfare policies and practices developed were seldom part of the welfare network. Another theme of this history is the role played by children and young people themselves. It was a performance conducted largely in the abstract, for as a number of scholars have argued, the ethos and practice of child welfare has more to do with adult perceptions of children and their needs than with the children and young people themselves.[11] I do not suggest that children and young people were silent participants in child welfare work. Their voices come through loudly at times, displaying a breadth of emotions and responses to their families and to child welfare services. I have tried to bring these voices and these perceptions to the foreground of the story, but this book is a history neither of children nor of childhood, and it is not told from the perspective of those at the heart of child welfare philosophy and practice. Children and young people enter this history as they entered child welfare services: as 'figures in that familiar landscape of adult reform programmes'.[12]

New Zealand shared in an international interest in child welfare from the late nineteenth century. Its use of overseas models and the development of indigenous responses to welfare matters constitute a further theme of this history. In this as in other areas of welfare and social policy, New Zealand has periodically led the world. New Zealand's first major child welfare legislation, the Child Welfare Act 1925, was based on practices occurring elsewhere, but its implementation was viewed with interest around the globe. New Zealand continued to look to other countries – Britain, Australia, Scandinavia and North America – picking up some ideas, rejecting others, and devising indigenous programmes to meet child welfare needs particular to this country. The Children, Young Persons, and Their Families Act 1989 lifted New Zealand to the forefront internationally in child welfare policy and practice, and this Act and the resulting system have been models watched and followed by other nations. This legislation captured a fundamental rethinking of the entire framework of child welfare, in enabling families to take the central role in making decisions about children's welfare, and in emphasising the importance of cultural heritage and cultural practice.[13]

The final theme of this history is the light that New Zealand's child welfare history sheds on welfare services and the development of its welfare state more generally. As the historian David Thomson points out, much of New Zealand's 'welfare state' was developed early in the twentieth century; child welfare services were a part of that development, although they have largely been ignored in discussions of welfare in New Zealand, thus obscuring their importance.[14] Indeed, government child welfare initiatives predated most other state welfare schemes. The Neglected and Criminal Children Act 1867, which authorised residential institutions for such children, was one of the earliest state welfare provisions. The Child Welfare Branch of the Department of Education, established in 1925 and operational from 1926, was the first semi-autonomous section of a government department devoted exclusively to welfare matters. From early on, child welfare services incorporated particular types of welfare that had little to do with the various benefits and pensions which characterised other areas of the welfare state, and which have largely dominated welfare history in this country. Child welfare was predicated on casework and investigation, inquiry and observation, supervision and non-monetary assistance. Such services meant the development of relationships with children, young people and their families in ways that were complex and challenging for all parties. Examining these services invites a way of looking at our welfare history in which the practice of the policies is as important as the policies themselves.

Child welfare has long been a significant issue in New Zealand. Government responsibility for providing child welfare services, and for working to improve children's welfare, has seldom been questioned. The form and extent of these services have been debated frequently, and the balance between government, community and family obligations has always been a matter for negotiation and reassessment. This discussion and reformulation of child welfare services underscores their continued importance to New Zealand society. Securing the welfare of New Zealand's children and young people remains as vital in the 1990s as it was in the 1900s.

PART I

'Humanity and national efficiency':

the emergence of a child welfare system,

1902–1925

Introduction

In his annual report of 1901 William Walker, the Minister of Education, wrote approvingly of the changes in New Zealand's industrial schools for delinquent and neglected children over the previous two years. 'The success that has attended industrial school work in New Zealand, despite imperfections and drawbacks that the [Education] Department is now endeavouring to remove, has not escaped the notice of authorities outside the colony', he trumpeted. He went on to cite the praises New Zealand's system had merited in a paper read before the British Royal Statistical Society which declared its industrial school system to be among the best in the world. This good slot in the international rankings – a much-prized status still – had evaporated by the time of the First World War, with New Zealand commentators characterising the system as 'chaotic, unco-ordinated, [and] handicapped by inexperienced staff'. In the interests of 'humanity and national efficiency', the entire scheme of dealing with children committed to the care of the state should be reviewed, concluded a new Minister of Education imbued with a zeal to fashion a new post-war society.[1] These assessments initiated a series of changes from 1916 culminating in the Child Welfare Act 1925, which guided the official administration of child welfare in New Zealand for the next 50 years.

Over the late nineteenth and early twentieth centuries, industrialisation, the growth of towns and cities, emergent political and labour structures and an expanding bureaucracy combined to form the basis of modern New Zealand society. Demographic and population changes altered the social structure, particularly that of Pakeha society, which lost its 'frontier' aspect as the population aged, more immigrants arrived and the sex ratio became more even. Declining mortality and rising fertility in Maori society dispelled portents of a 'dying race', while declining fertility in Pakeha society fuelled the spectre of 'race suicide'.[2] The First World War's toll accentuated such perceptions and inflamed an already intense public and political interest in the quality, as well as the quantity, of the populace.

Developments in public health, and in particular from the late 1890s in welfare and income provision, created a network of 'social services' as the state played a greater role in the lives of its citizens and the country carved out an international reputation as a 'social laboratory'. Hospitals, a charitable aid system providing assistance to the destitute, and pensions for the aged and widows were available, alongside existing provision by religious and other voluntary philanthropic organisations.[3] Social service, motivated both by altruism and by a desire to forge an orderly and ordered society, was also predicated on notions of racial fitness and national efficiency. Fears about the creeping evils of the degenerate in society, such as the criminal, the brazenly pauper, the mentally unsound and the generally unfit, ensured that assistance would never be too generous nor too freely available, to discourage the proliferation of the undesirable. Eugenics, the science of racial fitness through correct breeding and a healthy environment, gained currency in New Zealand, as elsewhere, around the turn of the century, and provided an ideological context for much contemporary social policy.[4] Anxieties about the declining Pakeha birth rate aroused an intense interest in maternal health. Early twentieth-century society reified motherhood and women's maternal role, particularly as it became clear that women (and men) were taking steps to limit the size of their families. Individuals such as Plunket Society founder Frederic Truby King and groups such as the Women's Christian Temperance Union emphasised the importance of childrearing and motherhood. The Plunket Society, among other groups, fostered notions of scientific childrearing and instructed mothers on how best to nurture the small makers of the country's future.

A fit society also meant an efficient and prepared society, ready to meet local and imperial emergencies, and to guard itself against an Asian menace suspected to be eyeing the country from afar. In the first decade of the twentieth century, the notion of national efficiency focused increasingly on fashioning a fighting stock. New Zealand's military prowess, the reputation of which was reaching mythic proportions both at home and abroad, took on the mantle of a national ideal with the First World War. The years before the war had witnessed a proliferation of militaristic pursuits: cadet corps for children and youth, and regimented organisations such as the Boy Scouts and Girl Guides. The war enhanced martial skill further, and even though the selection of troops indicated that the nation was not, in fact, in the pink of health, the failing only emphasised more strongly the need for a vigorous population.

The changes in the Pakeha population, the interest in national health and efficiency, and the spread of social services coalesced in a focus on the welfare of children as the source of the nation's future. Safeguarding and regulating children's health and welfare almost captured New Zealand social policy before 1930; as the historian Margaret Tennant has argued, needy, abused, or neglected children aroused public sentiment in a way few other social groupings could.[5]

In many western nations during the nineteenth century, religious, scientific, philanthropic, cultural and political influences combined to construct a state of childhood which was perceived as a time of innocence and vulnerability. Historians have suggested that the period between the 1870s and the 1930s witnessed the development of the conditions of 'contemporary' childhood: a state which was 'legally, legislatively, socially, medically, psychologically, educationally and politically institutionalized'.[6] One historian has dubbed this perception the 'welfare child', distinguished by the expansion of initiatives to prevent ill-treatment, to regulate the hours and form of children's labour, and to provide for children's health and welfare.[7] The child who, in the view of some, should not labour outside the home, should attend school, and should be surrounded with a raft of protective legislation, had become 'economically "worthless" but emotionally "priceless"'.[8]

Child-protection and child-saving movements epitomised much of the effort being made towards securing children's well-being. Already influenced by a general anti-cruelty movement sweeping middle-class society, child-protection groups, such as the English National Society for the Prevention of Cruelty to Children, founded in 1889, and the American societies founded in the 1870s, built upon an image of childhood innocence and fostered the notion that children should be protected. Primary goals of these organisations were to remove children from 'unsavoury' or 'dangerous' backgrounds, and to take action to prevent abuse and neglect. It was from such groups, in conjunction with government initiatives, that organised official child welfare policies emerged in most western nations in the later decades of the nineteenth century.[9]

The flip-side of the concept of helpless children in need of protection from adult society was that of the child as potentially dangerous. Sentimentalised perceptions of children as unsullied by the temptations of the world allowed little scope for youthful pranks and naughtiness; the concept of the juvenile delinquent emerged as an almost inevitable corollary of childhood innocence. Actions previously tolerated or accepted as youthful high spirits became redefined as delinquencies in most western societies, and institutions established to protect children embodied a reformative, punitive function as well.[10] Delinquent and criminal children whose behaviour and presence threatened society received as much attention as their neglected and vulnerable siblings.

Nineteenth-century Pakeha New Zealand shared many of these changing attitudes towards children, the 'social capital' of the future.[11] Colonial childhood was increasingly hedged around with requirements which defined it as separate from the world and experience of adults. As the historian Jeanine Graham shows, there were extensive legislative initiatives for children's welfare in the later nineteenth century: children received education (from 1877), legislation enacted from the 1860s limited the hours they could work in factories, and those who were neglected could be provided for by the government (from the 1860s).[12] Philanthropic and religious agencies also enunciated the importance of child life, and established orphanages, children's homes and welfare groups from the mid-nineteenth century.[13]

Children's 'value' embodied economic dimensions too. The exigencies of a frontier society placed a premium on labour and made essential the contribution of children to the family economy. With child labour sufficiently important to allow parental rights to remain beyond the orbit of external regulation or intervention, the child could be regarded as a chattel, a vital asset on the road to prosperity.[14] Some areas of child life continued to lie outside the scope of protective legislation. With politicians and social reformers showing a marked reluctance to intervene too closely in domestic arrangements, the regulation of child labour ignored children who worked on family farms or in family businesses.

Residential institutions formed the basis of government social services for children in nineteenth-century New Zealand. The increase in the number of children left destitute following the 1860s' gold rushes led to calls on central government to make provision for homeless and neglected youngsters. The Neglected and Criminal Children Act 1867 enabled Provincial Councils to establish 'industrial schools' to which the courts could commit neglected, indigent or delinquent children. These institutions were empowered to detain children and young people until the age of 21 and to provide them with a combination of education and vocational ('industrial') training, with an emphasis on the latter, to enable them to rise above their criminal or indigent past and become useful citizens. Their punitive aspects were strong, and institutional life was grim and lonely for many of the residents who lost contact with family and friends. Training continued beyond the institution, with residents licensed out to service positions with employers – farm labouring for boys and domestic work for girls. Industrial schools, along with church-run institutions, were large dormitory-like barrack structures, often located on the outskirts of towns to keep recalcitrant youngsters away from public view.[15]

New Zealand was also influenced by a growing international alarm over juvenile delinquency which characterised the last two decades of the nineteenth century. Perhaps in response to changing patterns of youth culture and work, public attention in Britain, North America and Australia focused on the conduct of older children.[16] The 'larrikin nuisance', as aspects of juvenile (mis)behaviour were frequently termed in New Zealand and Australia, dominated debates over adolescent conduct from the 1880s. The presence of larrikins – gangs of children and young people wandering the streets, harassing respectable citizens and acting as public nuisances – suggested a breakdown of family life and a threat to social order. The solution was seen to lie in greater regulation of children's activities, and from the 1880s the number of children and adolescents committed to industrial schools for juvenile forms of misbehaviour increased dramatically.[17]

In 1880 the Department of Justice relinquished jurisdiction over industrial schools to the Department of Education, which continued to administer all matters pertaining to child welfare until 1972. The Industrial Schools Section of the Department oversaw the administration of the various functions until in 1909 it was renamed the Special Schools Section, a name it retained until the appearance of the Child Welfare Branch in 1926. The relocation from an agency primarily concerned with penal and judicial matters to one which focused on education represented a shift in the perception of industrial schools from being primarily punitive to more reformative institutions. The change of terminology from Industrial Schools to Special Schools further symbolised this shift. These steps were in keeping with a growing sentimentalisation of child life, and signalled that children should be assisted and treated, reformed rather than only punished.

The Industrial Schools Act 1882 gave the Education Department control over all institutions which had been gazetted as government schools. Private and religious schools remained beyond this control until 1902. The Department had the power to appoint staff, control the discharge of residents, and arrange for the inspection of institutions. But this authority was more apparent than real. Uniformity of practice was rare, and individual managers exercised considerable power, sometimes to the detriment of the residents. Both the 1867 and the 1882 Acts stipulated that indigent or neglected children should be kept separate from those with 'criminal tendencies'. In practice, no distinction was made and all ages, both sexes and those committed for a variety of causes were confined together in the same institution. This lack of classification hampered institutional management, and was compounded by the inability of official regulations and inspections to direct the administration or oversee the welfare of residents.

The Industrial Schools Act introduced the practice of boarding out industrial school residents with foster parents. In exchange for either maintenance payments from the government or the labour services of the children, foster parents supplied children with a family environment. Institutional managers conducted periodic checks on the children's welfare, although their thoroughness was dubious, given the duties expected of residential staff. Boarding out was a radical departure from the British-based policies which had hitherto guided the administration of children's welfare. Developed in Britain, boarding out rapidly became a feature of the child welfare programmes of South Australia and New South Wales, where its use exceeded that in Britain.[18] New Zealand officials continued to look outwards to other international developments in child welfare throughout the period before 1925, focusing particularly on the United States and Canada for ideas about juvenile justice. The introduction of boarding out also suggested that large residential institutions did not necessarily provide the best method of caring for destitute or neglected children. Instead, their needs were seen as being best served in a family environment where care devolved upon the community rather than the government, for whom it was a cheaper option than residential care in any form. Boarding out also reinforced the ideologies of racial fitness and national efficiency. The more personal, family-type care potentially to be gained in a respectable foster home, under the guidance of a full-time mother, could be a way to transform the children of the streets into useful little citizens.

By the turn of the century, public and departmental criticism of the industrial school system was mounting. The number of young people committed in the wake of the depressed economy of the 1880s and 1890s made institutions dangerously overcrowded and taxed their capacity to the full, as admissions jumped from approximately 800 in 1880 to 1700 in 1900. Such growth far outweighed that of children as a proportion of the total population.[19] It was in an effort to counter this growth and to stem the tide of juvenile delinquency that the Education Department completely overhauled the system between 1899 and 1902. Taking advantage of institutional developments overseas, George Hogben, the Inspector-General of Schools, planned to ensure an effective separation between those with a delinquent background, and those committed through no fault of their own.[20] The latter group was detained in industrial schools, such as those at Caversham (Dunedin) and Auckland, both of which received girls of all ages and boys under ten or twelve. Those deemed to be 'viciously uncontrollable' or who had been convicted of an offence were accommodated in the Canterbury reformatories of Burnham, for males, and Te Oranga, for females, from

1900. Receiving homes in Wellington and Christchurch provided temporary accommodation prior to placement in another institution or boarding out.

Hogben also extended centralised control over all institutions through greater inspection. Roland Pope, who had experience in managing institutions, became the first Assistant-Inspector of Industrial Schools in 1901. Thomas Walker and Jessie Stewart, both of whom had experience with the welfare of school-age children, joined him the following year. Inspectors could visit institutions unannounced and report to the Department their findings on all aspects of the administration and the welfare of the residents. Official visitors appointed directly by the Minister of Education complemented inspectors by acting as an informal check on the management, although without full rights of inspection and recommendation.

Other forms of provision for children's welfare were added to the Education Department's portfolio between 1900 and 1925; these provisions, together with changes in industrial schools and boarding out, form the focus of Chapter One. Responsibility for administering adoptions and for the welfare of infants maintained apart from their parents, and for the incipient children's courts and juvenile probation, extended the Department's oversight of children's welfare and the number of children coming to its attention. The enlarged responsibility necessitated a growing range and number of staff. Fewer than 2000 children were in contact with the state system in 1900; by 1925 the figure had reached more than 7000.[21] Joining the residential staff and inspectors from 1907 were female District Agents, who were responsible for checking on the welfare of infants in foster homes; male probation officers were appointed from the time of the First World War. The gendered division of labour would remain for many years, with women staffing residences for females and working with girls, boys aged under ten or twelve, and all infants, while male officers took responsibility for older boys and staffed male institutions alongside female domestic staff. Welfare practices also began to change as staff adopted casework methods and an individualised approach to state wards.

Hogben was one of the two key individuals working in children's welfare during the early twentieth century, and his system was one of the two reformulations of welfare services for children before 1925. John Beck, who was to become the first Superintendent of Child Welfare in 1926, assumed Hogben's reforming mantle. Beck's approach differed markedly from Hogben's, and from 1916 he dismantled and reassembled the entire child welfare system. The changes Beck wrought by 1925 are the focus of Chapter Two. Later child welfare officials described Beck as 'a genius. He had vision and he was really years ahead of his time. . . . no greater single contribution has been made by anyone else to Child Welfare in this country'.[22] Hogben and Beck exemplified the power that public servants could wield in early twentieth-century New Zealand. Like officials in other areas, they initiated and drove through changes which did not always garner political support at the outset.

Child welfare lay at the intersection of policies and practices in welfare, education, policing and justice. By the beginning of the twentieth century, provision for neglected, destitute and delinquent children was an established part of state and voluntary activity in New Zealand. Many accepted the idea that there could and should be intervention in the domestic sphere to regulate the welfare of its most vulnerable, and potentially most difficult, members. The extent and form of this intervention, the balance between welfare and justice, and the tension between state duties and parental responsibilities were issues that were less easy to resolve.

CHAPTER 1

Control, reformation and protection: the basis of child welfare

Between 1900 and the First World War many of the core features of New Zealand's child welfare system were defined. The nineteenth-century inheritance of residential institutions and boarding out continued, and, in the case of institutions, changed in practice and structure. The outlines of a juvenile justice system emerged in children's courts, and a fledgling juvenile probation system took shape. Work with children outside institutions expanded, as those who were not committed to the care of the state, such as infants in foster homes and adopted children, came to public attention. Much child welfare work focused on children within some form of family, as family-based care was posited as the ideal – for children, for families, and ultimately for the good of a society nurturing its future.

'Advancing the general well-being of the community': industrial schools and reformatories

In 1900 members of the Nelson Charitable Aid Board paid a surprise visit to St Mary's Orphanage at Stoke. Opened in 1874, the residence was run by the Roman Catholic French Marist order, and was home to more than 100 boys. The Board members found much to alarm them: insufficient food and bedding for the overworked residents, excessive punishments, and the use of secret, dark cells.

George Hogben rushed to the institution on a special and covert visit, crossing Cook Strait under an assumed name to avoid detection, or so the story goes.[1] The subsequent Royal Commission into the management of the orphanage supported most of the Board's findings. The Commission recommended the replacement of the staff of single male religious by men of a more 'cheerful' disposition, and urged that all institutions employ at least two women officers, in the belief that women's 'natural' maternalism would not tolerate the 'unnatural' treatment of children. The excessive punishments were clear illustrations of what could happen when institutions were exempt from central control, as such private institutions were. Accordingly, the Commission recommended the implement-ation of regulations to guide the management of all residential institutions, private and government.[2] Conditions at St Mary's did not markedly improve despite the regulations issued in 1902. Claims by some residents that they had been punished inappropriately – '[Mr McFadden] began to punish me by strapping me on the soles of my feet. He said it was what the Turks did' – led to a departmental investigation in 1904. Roland Pope found some of the charges to be

The Roman Catholic St Mary's Orphanage at Stoke in 1909, three years before the Education Department took over its administration. NATIONAL ARCHIVES, CW 1, 40/3/39

groundless, including the one cited above, but noted that staff had not followed the regulations in administering discipline. He concluded that Stoke was 'distinctly the most unsatisfactory industrial school in the colony'.[3]

The ongoing saga of St Mary's symbolised the problems which beset the entire industrial school system before the First World War. Institutional managers who acted without authority – or with too much authority – excessive punishments, forlorn and frightened residents, unpleasant conditions, and sometimes incompetent staff were not just a feature of privately-run homes. Education Department staff may have congratulated themselves that government institutions were far superior to private institutions, but this was certainly not the case. For reform-minded public servants, the system was well overdue for a radical reassessment.

Hogben's scheme of receiving homes, industrial schools, and reformatories for the more 'uncontrollable' and delinquent children and young people formed the basis of the industrial school system until 1916. The 1902 regulations marked the final stage of his plans, and addressed all aspects of administration and the welfare of residents of the institutions, and of those in service positions or boarded out. In addition to the schools in operation by 1902, several new institutions were gazetted on the assumption that they would be an 'increasingly powerful means of advancing the general well-being of the community'.[4] To the industrial schools at Auckland and Caversham were added two schools for boys: the Boys' Training Farm at Weraroa (Levin) in 1905, and the former Stoke Orphanage, which the Department assumed control of in 1912. The Christchurch reformatories of Te Oranga and Burnham admitted those with 'dangerously sensual and criminal tendencies'. Another receiving home opened in Nelson in 1915 to complement those at Wellington and Christchurch. A further 'special needs' school joined those at Sumner, for deaf children, and Auckland, for blind. The Otekaike Special School for Boys, near Oamaru, opened in 1908 for those classed as 'feeble-minded'. Its establishment reflected anxieties about racial health which took the form of a growing concern in New Zealand and elsewhere about the extent of mental defects in the population and the most efficacious treatment for the 'subnormal'.[5]

Four private Roman Catholic industrial schools existed alongside the state system, as well as a network of other private and religious children's homes and orphanages. With the exception of one or two cottages or smaller units at Weraroa and Otekaike, industrial schools were large, dormitory-like structures catering for up to 100 residents and sprawling across acres of farmland. Nearly all were converted from existing buildings rather than being purpose-built. Unlike private religious children's homes, government institutions endeavoured to separate or classify residents into various divisions, on the basis of behaviour, age or reason for committal, and to house them in separate parts of an institution under distinctive regimes.

The number committed to institutions increased over the first two decades of the century at a rate which outstripped the growth in the child population. Six hundred and forty-one children and young people resided in institutions at the end of 1901; by 1916 the number had risen to 1009. Figure 1 shows the changes in the residential population between 1901 and 1916, and also in the numbers boarded out.[6] The number passing through institutions each year was, of course, much higher, as new residents entered and others were discharged. Usually between 400 and 500 residents were outside the homes in service on farms and in private houses. Maori children formed a tiny minority of the residential population. The residents ranged from young babies at receiving homes to adults at the Te Oranga and Burnham reformatories, with the majority aged twelve and above. Children and young people could remain in institutions, or under residential jurisdiction through being licensed out to service, until they reached 21. For most, this meant a period of detention of about seven years.[7]

Those young people deemed to pose a particular danger to the moral fibre of society could remain institutionalised for many years. Illustrating the influence of eugenic thought on Education Department policy, legislation passed in 1909 and 1910 extended institutional control indefinitely for those defined as morally

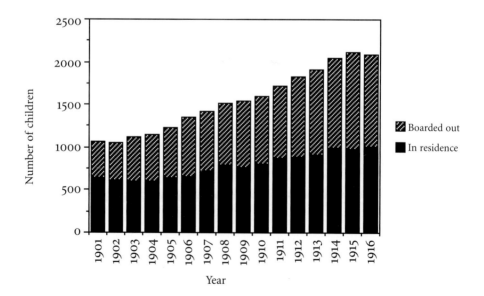

FIGURE 1 *Number in residence and boarded out, 1901–1916*

degenerate or a danger to the community, or whose mental state made their release inadvisable. With judicial approval, four-year extensions could be granted, enabling lifelong detention if necessary. Within three years, nine adults had been confined under the Industrial Schools Amendment Act 1909, and eight under the Education Amendment Act 1910. By the end of 1915, 32 were held under the former legislation alone.[8] On this issue the Department participated in a wider public debate over the inherited nature of feeble-mindedness. That much of the discussion emphasised the deleterious effects of morally degenerate women as particular sources of corruption suggests that there were deep-seated anxieties over the role of women in society.[9] The vast majority of those detained under the legislation – 27 of the 32 – were women, illustrating the gendered nature of the eugenic debate, which held women to be potentially the more dangerous sex.

Welfare and women's groups as well as public commentators supported the legislation, with some interpreting it as 'the first step in a crusade against the propagation of the unfit'.[10] The *New Zealand Times* challenged the 'quaint notion' that individuals aged over 21 should not have their freedom taken away, suggesting that liberty hardly seemed legitimate for 'one of those perverts whose presence in society is a permanent menace to law and an outrage upon decency'. With mounting enthusiasm – and use of metaphor – it claimed that the provision would be welcomed by all who hoped to see the 'social gutter' cleansed:

> Victims of a bad hereditary, of imperfect chemical processes, of an evil environ-
> ment, or one of those obscure cerebral lesions which baffle surgical skill, these
> poor degenerate specimens of humanity are a poison to every race. . . . As
> society advances it will awake to the wisdom of turning into the desert the murky
> tributary now flowing into the bloodstream of life.[11]

Sensational as this language may have been, it pointed to a wider concern that would continue to be expressed into the 1930s.

Children and young people entered the Department's institutions for a variety of reasons defined in the Industrial Schools Act 1882. Being destitute or homeless, neglected or maltreated, living in undesirable surroundings or with unsavoury companions, being uncontrollable or mischievous, or committing an offence could all be grounds for committal. Magistrates had the power to order children under sixteen, if destitute, neglected or convicted of an offence, or under eighteen, if convicted of an offence only, to an institution. Distinctions between matters of care and protection – children who were abused or neglected, for example – and juvenile justice – children who committed offences – were not rigid, as conceptions of children as victims and as threats overlapped. Nevertheless, the criteria for committal to a reformatory tended towards the 'worst'-behaved children and young people, whether or not they had been convicted of an offence.

By far the largest category of committals was related to destitution, and included parental indigence or neglect, begging, and having no home or visible means of support. These comprised almost half of all committals until 1912, after which they declined to about a quarter by 1916. Rather than representing a real decline in poverty or destitution, however, the change was due to a more intense focus on the youthful behaviour which had been evident since the earlier anxieties over the larrikin nuisance in the 1880s. The number of children and young people committed for being 'uncontrollable' rose from about 1 per cent of the total in 1901 to over 30 per cent by 1916. The term 'uncontrollable' encompassed a myriad of behaviours and activities, from stealing fruit to 'giving cheek', from running away from home to loitering on the streets. Such activities would now be regarded as minor, if they were remarked upon at all, and not considered suitable grounds for a court appearance, let alone detention in an institution. But for a society which put stock in its national fitness, and which focused closely on child health and welfare, they were signs of both potential and actual danger.[12]

The categories for committal ostensibly distinguished between offences, the (mis)behaviour of children, and inadequate home conditions. In fact, most of the residents of industrial schools and reformatories were committed on moral or behavioural grounds. The gendered nature of committals and of behavioural expectations for girls and boys was also clear, and would continue for much of the history of juvenile residential institutions. Girls and young women comprised most of those committed for being uncontrollable or for associating with disreputable persons, but less than 10 per cent of those charged with an offence. Admission to institutions for sexual precocity or signs of 'unhealthy' sexuality was a pattern repeated elsewhere, and was a feature of the confinement of adult women in New Zealand and other nations. As a number of historians have suggested, the morality-based nature of female confinement points to a more widespread anxiety about the role of women in society, an anxiety which portrayed female sexuality as something to be channelled into the most appropriate avenues.[13] It was safer to keep potential propagators of the unfit off the streets and to focus their activities in more wholesome directions. Girls and young women made up about 40 per cent of committals before 1925 – a higher proportion than in subsequent years – which suggests that this aim may have been realised.

Anxiety over male sexuality was not nearly as common as a cause for committal, reflecting distinctive expectations of male and female behaviour, and perhaps a greater acceptance of male sexual activity. Rather than focusing on the sexual behaviour of boys and young men – apart from masturbation or same-sex relationships – public attention centred on the prankish, socially annoying features of boy and youth culture. Forming gangs, being cheeky, lurking on street corners, as well as petty theft, were the most common causes for the admission to institutions of boys and young men.

The reasons for committal suggest that the institutions served a range of purposes. In confining those convicted of theft or assault, they acted as places of punishment and detention. Clearing the streets of troublesome, dangerous or morally offensive youths was also important. Public fears over the larrikin nuisance, or the forward, brash behaviour of girls and young women warranted action. Placing these children in residences, pointing out the error of their ways and seeking to mould them into useful citizens afforded social protection on many fronts.

The industrial school system was not necessarily an imposition on an unwilling community. Families, their children, and the Education Department formed a 'triangulated network of struggles and negotiations' over children's welfare. It was an unequal network, for despite the degree of agency parents and families could display in initiating welfare assistance, considerable power remained in the hands of state officials. In such a relationship, of course, the children and young people themselves were usually the least powerful actors.[14] Many families welcomed or sought assistance for their children, particularly in the absence of other forms of large-scale public relief. Institutions could be both a form of control of and a help to beleaguered families and communities. Institutionalisation could mean the opportunity to reform family relationships by bolstering parental authority over recalcitrant youngsters. Some parents 'willingly' committed their children to care. The number of these committals was never large, and usually less than 5 per cent of the total between 1902 and 1916. These parents often cited an inability to control their offspring. Mrs McAlaster of Timaru, who had cared for her granddaughter since she was a baby, found that she had become very stubborn and needed 'a strong hand to keep her down'. Her own poor state of health, she claimed, was made worse by her granddaughter, who was 'continually making me ill with her cheek and abuse'. Others used the institutions as temporary shelters for their children until their circumstances improved. Mrs Harwood of Auckland wanted her children committed to an industrial school until she obtained a divorce from her husband. Some women utilised the institutions as a means of removing their children from a father's authority. Mrs Sampson of Palmerston North asked the Department to admit her son Ernest to Weraroa, where he would be away from the bad influence of his father. Although separated, Mr Sampson frequently visited the family home to inform Ernest that he 'would learn him to grow up and curse his mother'.[15]

The gendered nature of such requests may conform to a wider pattern of women seeking out welfare assistance for their families. Mothers were more likely

Physical jerks formed an important – and gendered – part of industrial school training. While residents of the Otekaike Special School for Boys indulged in acrobatics (above), those at the Richmond Special School for Girls participated in more decorous activities (opposite).
DEPARTMENT OF SOCIAL WELFARE

than fathers to apply for charitable relief from hospital boards or voluntary groups. The number of women's welfare organisations in New Zealand may attest to a highly gendered pattern of both need and need provision. Historians elsewhere have noted women's and especially single women's use of children's courts and welfare agencies as means to exert authority over their children or to shift the balance of power in family relationships; similar strategies were employed by New Zealand women.[16]

At an official level, the object of confining children was reformation. This is, of course, a loaded term, one which suggests control, policing and instruction in appropriate behaviour. Rightly or wrongly, the Department believed that its industrial school residents needed 'persuasive' correction to turn them away from their former habits, and the instruction provided was directed towards crafting good citizens. On a visit to the Burnham Reformatory in 1909, George Fowlds, the Minister of Education, informed the residents, in an address long on the advantages of order and discipline, that when they left the home it would be as 'young men of good character, who would so fill their places in the world that Burnham would have no reason to be ashamed of them'. With even greater gusto he stressed that 'they should endeavour to go from Burnham clean in body and

mind, determined to do the best they could, and to do it all the time'; with some irony, perhaps, the assembled residents greeted the end of the address with 'hearty cheers'.[17]

Educational and vocational training formed the basis of instruction at industrial schools and reformatories. Schooling to ensure proficiency in reading, writing and arithmetic was complemented by nature study, science or civics. Religious and moral training, health lessons, and military drill (for boys) completed the curriculum. Most institutions emphasised industrial rather than educational training, however. The Otekaike Special School stressed the value of manual skills, such as basket-making, as a way of keeping the boys occupied and enhancing their dexterity and mental ability.[18] At the reformatories, industrial training incorporated a punitive function, and education could be a minor consideration. Inquiries into Burnham (1906) and Te Oranga (1908) revealed instances of residents pulling up tree-stumps and farming unyielding land. Teachers in these homes sometimes considered their role to be pointless. Ada Harrison of Te Oranga complained that girls were frequently removed from class for domestic duties. She believed that the other staff, particularly the manager, Ellen Branting, had 'no sympathy with . . . [the] school-work'. For her part, Branting reminded Harrison that the curriculum of the school should equip the residents with a 'useful knowledge for life'; arithmetic would always be 'much more important' than the plays of Shakespeare.[19]

Industrial training was divided along gender lines. In Caversham and Te Oranga, the girls were taught domestic chores, including cooking, sewing, and laundry work. Boys received instruction in manual trades such as small-scale carpentry, or more usually, farm work. The gender boundary was not necessarily rigid, as Te Oranga used its residents to clear gorse from the property and maintain the garden.[20] The larger purpose of the labour, however, was more explicit, as both girls and boys were to fill niches: domestic servants or farm labourers. Little attempt was made to broaden their career horizons until after the changes to the entire industrial school system of 1916.

Suitably behaved residents who had passed the school-leaving age and achieved a proficiency in work skills were licensed out to employers as a prelude to their complete discharge into the community. Here the young men and women were expected to display the skills they had learnt. Still under the nominal control of the institution, those in service were midway between junior employees and institutional residents. This could be an anomalous and difficult role for young women and men, who often found their situation circumscribed by the disadvantages of both positions.

A comprehensive set of instructions to guide residents in service, first issued in 1905, stipulated the conduct that was expected. These guidelines exhorted the young man to 'cheerfully obey his employer, and do his best to serve him faithfully at all times'. (Girls and young women, deemed to be more in the habit of accepting personal direction and guidance, were not considered to need such notes.) He should remember to attend church on a regular basis, 'keep from using foul or coarse language; never go to hotels for drink, nor idle about hotels, billiard-rooms, and other places of the kind'.[21] A service contract for both male and female residents drawn up between the manager of the institution and the employer required all wages to be paid to the Department, leaving only a small personal allowance. This allowance was gradually increased, until by the time of a resident's discharge she or he was in full control of her or his wages.

As well as reducing the cost of institutional care, placement gave residents a chance to live in a family environment. Service relationships could be abusive ones. Some employers paid very low wages, overworked the residents, and felt under no obligation to provide further training. Kathleen Masters, Manager of the Christchurch Receiving Home, wrote scathingly of Mrs Sorrenson, an 'exacting mistress' who worked Ivy Parker particularly hard. Five adults lived in Mrs Sorrenson's house, and Ivy had no assistance with any of the work. She did not receive the usual weekly half-holiday accorded live-in servants, but laboured thirteen days out of every fourteen. If Ivy's work was so essential to the household, Masters suggested, she should receive more than 11s a week, which was considerably less than other servants received. Not surprisingly, perhaps, Ivy was described by Mrs Sorrenson as a 'little difficult to manage' and possessed of a 'sulky temper'.[22] Physical and sexual abuse could also occur. An employer on a farm at Rakaia to which Georgina Shore had been licensed considered her to be 'fair game'; the Department's officers returned her to Te Oranga.[23]

The conditions experienced in service were not necessarily new to these young women and men. Institutional life was often grim, as the reality of institutional management frequently fell short of the theory. Regulations did not guarantee either efficient management or the fair treatment of the children. The interpretation of the regulations rested with often harassed and overworked managers who took matters into their own hands, or who ruled over their domain in an autocratic manner. Harriette Petremant, who was outspoken, partial, dictatorial and sometimes callous in her management of the Caversham Industrial School, was asked to resign in 1909 following a drawn-out inquiry into her administration.[24] Stubborn, unruly or unhappy residents could provoke exasperated or cruel staff into acting outside the regulations by inflicting excessive or unusual punishments. Staff at Caversham and Te Oranga used corporal punishment and solitary confinement extensively, and employed shaming punishments, such as sitting residents at a specially-designated thieves' or 'fibbers'' table, or forcing them to wear unusual clothing. The Caversham staff assigned extra scrubbing as a disciplinary measure, which made the residents unable to discriminate between work as punishment and as a 'natural and proper condition of life', according to Secretary of Education Edward Gibbes.[25]

Public and departmental inquiries alike testified to the difficulties that staff and residents experienced, sometimes on a daily basis amidst the tedium of institutionalised life. The inquiries into Burnham and Te Oranga showed the inadequate classification of residents to be a major problem hindering the smooth management of both institutions. According to Helyar Bishop, who conducted the inquiry into Te Oranga, 'the difficulties of management . . . are almost overpowering'; it was 'practically impossible' to keep separate the different groups of residents.[26] The excuse of inadequate classification of residents between and within institutions was a recurring refrain which was frequently chanted as a cover for more pervasive and insidious management problems.

The rapid turnover of untrained staff caused many difficulties and misunderstandings. Meagre salaries generated the 1906 inquiry into Burnham, which lost the services of seven officers between March and May that year; pay was generally acknowledged as insufficient to induce reliable people to remain in the job. In many instances, the positions were seen as only temporary while officers searched for something better. The isolated rural location of homes such as Otekaike was a major drawback to staff who felt themselves to be as confined and restricted as the residents. Hot in summer and freezing in winter, Otekaike was far from any recreational amenities, and the close and constant proximity of staff to each other heightened any personal differences.[27]

Staff were constantly on call if they lived in the institution – as most did – and were frequently overworked and tired. Anna Cox of the Christchurch Receiving Home attributed the repeated illnesses of several of her staff to overwork. Inadequate cooking and sleeping facilities there took their toll: one officer was anaemic and suffered from 'nervous exhaustion', another had a serious 'inflammation' of the leg, and a third had three bouts of bronchitis in as many months in the winter of 1910.[28] The increasing number of admissions also strained institutional management. Building programmes had been initiated in some homes, but many residents were jammed into already overcrowded and inadequate accommodation. Institutions such as the Caversham Industrial School, described as insanitary, rambling and shabby, remained in a poor state throughout the period, and the theme of overtaxed and unsuitable conditions ran through the inspection and annual reports of most institutions.[29]

For staff whose only training was on the job, the difficulties must have seemed unsurmountable at times, and the behaviour of some of the residents too much. Management problems certainly provided a context for – but did not justify – the treatment of residents at some institutions. Some staff were clearly unsuitable. A military influence pervaded Burnham, which employed a

Lumpy beds and bare floors in the sparse dormitory of the Boys' Training Farm at Weraroa, Levin. DEPARTMENT OF SOCIAL WELFARE

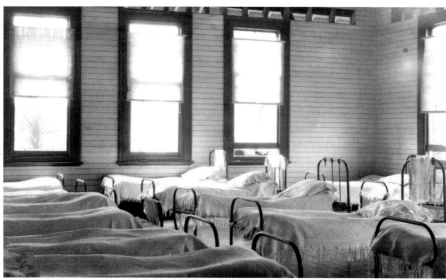

former British Sergeant-Major to drill the residents.[30] Other staff exploited their positions of authority and power through physical and sexual abuse. The retreat of the Marist Brothers from the Stoke Orphanage in 1912 amidst charges of sexual molestation of the young boys was not necessarily an isolated or exceptional occurrence, although such abuse was almost never reported. The Education Department sought to keep to a minimum contact between female residents and male staff. From 1900 men were prohibited from holding office in homes for girls, except as gardeners or odd-job men. A suggestion that Otekaike house both sexes aroused considerable consternation among officers who knew of the potential problems of detaining boys and girls of all ages – and male and female staff – in the one institution. 'Bitter experience', Pope contended, should alert the Department to the folly of such a move. Gibbes was more explicit: he informed the Director of Education that with two exceptions (who remained with the Department), the male officers in charge of each of the institutions in the nineteenth century had been implicated 'to a greater or less extent' in offences against female residents.[31]

That many institutional problems centred on punishment was indicated by the inquiry into Te Oranga in 1908, which focused on the corporal punishment and shaming rituals used on adolescent girls. An inspection of the Caversham Industrial School in the same year uncovered a heavy reliance on physical means of maintaining discipline. Harriette Petremant took umbrage at Inspector Walker's criticisms, angrily informing the Department that:

> corporal punishment is the only punishment that tells. [The residents] have neither brains nor consciences for any other form of punishment to have effect. They have no sense of honour to appeal to. They rather enjoy being sent to bed than otherwise. The things they do I am sure no normal child would either think of or dare to do. I should like to propose that Mr Walker come and live here and see if matters can be improved.

Her comments and methods earned her a sharp rebuke from Gibbes, along with a reminder that the Department expected her to be 'one who is above all things the child's friend and defender'.[32]

It would be wrong to portray the Department's institutions as completely without regulation, with frightened and submissive residents at the mercy of uncaring staff who treated them as automatons, their needs subservient to the running of a prison-like institution.[33] The writings of former residents such as John A. Lee (in *Delinquent Days)* convey an impression of an institutional experience marked by pain, unhappiness and abuse. Lee described the Burnham Reformatory as a 'sterilising hell', and wondered why the Commission of Inquiry in 1906 found that 'all was well'. 'Some people', he noted, 'only become aware of injustice when the blood spatters their clothing.'[34] Other former residents remembered happier times, during which they enjoyed good relationships with staff and returned to the institutions for holidays or for companionship in the absence of family perhaps lost as a consequence of their committal.[35] Both impressions of institutional life are equally valid, illustrating the complexity of institutions which fulfilled a variety of social needs.

The voices of residents rarely made themselves heard beyond the institutions, however. Contact with friends and family was tightly circumscribed, with mail censored and visits infrequent, if not impossible because of the removal of many children to locations far from their home. Visitors were not always aware of the problems residents faced. 'One day I must read that Royal Commission report [of 1906] to find out why good men were blind and deaf', Lee recalled of the Burnham inquiry.[36] Young children, in turn, may have been too intimidated by adults and officialdom to seek out visitors to the homes. While residents' voices do emerge through official and departmental inquiries, they were structured by the medium of the event. The recorded answers to questions in inquiries such as that into Te Oranga could be formulaic, as residents responded to queries rather than offering their own perceptions of institutional life.

An unhappy alliance: the Education Department and private institutions

The Education Department had an ambivalent attitude to the private industrial schools and church homes which existed alongside its own institutions. Officers such as Hogben, Pope and Gibbes recognised that the government could not provide for all destitute and neglected children. Private and religious work was clearly necessary or the state system would be overloaded. The management of private institutions caused alarm, however, and was nearly always seen as inferior to that in government schools.

Two policies guided the Department's approach to private institutions: a refusal to gazette them as industrial schools entitled to government subsidy, and the inspection of all orphanages, children's homes and other institutions which provided long- or short-term residential care. The Industrial Schools Act 1882 had made provision for the gazetting of private schools, but only four had been granted this status by 1900.[37] All were Roman Catholic institutions, and their status as private industrial schools may have been part of the broader provision of separate education for Catholic children. Repeated applications from other groups, including the Roman Catholic Mt Magdala Asylum in Christchurch, fell on deaf ears. Despite the rapid growth of private homes from the turn of the century, the Education Department remained firm in its refusal to approve any further gazettals.

The failure of most of these homes to board out children was a central reason for the Department's position. Officials frequently informed private institutions of the desirability of boarding out, and the disadvantages of confining children together in large groups. With few exceptions, most chose to continue policies of institutionalisation. Many church homes resisted boarding out because of its questionable ability to provide, in their view, the correct moral and religious context for children. Within the walls of church homes, church authorities could be confident their charges were receiving the religious instruction they deemed a necessary part of life. In such circumstances, the Department declared itself to be under no obligation to make the work of maintaining the schools any easier by granting or increasing capitation payments if the homes took in state wards. The parlous financial state of some of the institutions was another concern for departmental officers, who believed that the need to obtain monetary assistance motivated most applications to be gazetted.[38]

At the heart of the Department's position was the belief that these institutions were badly managed and provided care of dubious and irregular quality. The specific instances of poor management revealed in the inquiry into St Mary's Orphanage in 1900 led the Department to look closely at the administration of private institutions. In Hogben's opinion, 'bitter experience has shown that it is almost impossible to obtain from such schools such results as may be reasonably expected from Govt. Industrial Schools.'[39] All private institutions were subject to a stringent inspection and reporting process, and most were found to be wanting. At the Parnell Orphan Home in 1906, Hogben found 35 of the 53 children to be suffering from ringworm. He was at a loss to explain how such a 'loathsome disease' could spread, 'except through neglect from gross ignorance or care-lessness'. He concluded that the children would probably be better off in the poorest-equipped public institution than 'in this private home supported by benevolent people with the best intentions'.[40] Educational provisions were considered poor in other institutions. Gibbes informed the management of St Mary's, Auckland, that it was a matter for regret that they did not take a more liberal view of the education of their charges, 'handicapped as they are in most cases by early neglect and other drawbacks'. He requested that the head teacher be relieved of all the other duties which interfered with her teaching role.[41] The quality of the staff also attracted adverse comment. The departmental officer Mrs Scales reported in 1914 that the Heni Materoa Creche in Gisborne had considerable difficulty getting suitable employees, describing the Matron as kind, but with no experience in the management of institutions or the care of children.[42]

The financial difficulties under which many private institutions operated prompted some to launch emotive campaigns for funds, such as that of the St Saviour's Orphanage, Christchurch, in 1915. THE *PRESS* (CHRISTCHURCH) COLLECTION, ATL, G-8691-1/1

Like their government counterparts, private and church-run homes often functioned despite immense difficulties. Staff were untrained and poorly paid (if they were paid at all), buildings could be ramshackle and overcrowded, and financial solvency frequently rested on the uncertain basis of charitable contributions and fund-raising. The plight of needy or neglected children may have had the emotive pull on the discretionary pound of the benevolently minded that groups like the elderly lacked, as Margaret Tennant suggests, but church and private homes were often in straitened circumstances.[43] Reflecting on the state of his institution's finances in 1924, one private school administrator noted ruefully that the residence had been operating on an overdraft for a 'very long time'.[44]

Whether the conditions in private institutions were markedly worse, or better, than those in government schools is a moot point, but the Education Department gleaned evidence to support its view of its own superiority. In Pope's opinion, the private institution 'cuts at the very root of our organisation for the uplifting of these poor children whose lives, before coming under State care, have

Pah Farm, Onehunga, was used by the Roman Catholic St Mary's Orphanage in the 1910s.
NATIONAL ARCHIVES, CW 1, 40/3/34

been such as to demand the strongest pity'.[45] The Department was nevertheless willing to use private services when the need arose. The Managers of the Te Oranga Reformatory found that Mt Magdala could play a useful role by taking in their most recalcitrant residents. Twelve Protestant girls, 'more or less lawless and reckless, uninfluenced by any restraints of reason and amenable only to the sternest exercise of authority and compulsion' were removed there following a fire at Te Oranga in 1915.[46]

A similarly ambivalent and at times vexed relationship existed between the Education Department and the hospital and charitable aid boards which contributed to the support of destitute children in government schools, boarded out children, or, more rarely, maintained their own institutions. The Department was eager to ensure that boards continued to foster children and to contribute to the upkeep of destitute children in their own families. It was less supportive of the management of their institutions. The Southland Hospital and Charitable Aid Board's Lorne Farm attracted particular criticism. To George Benstead, Manager of the Otekaike Special School, Lorne Farm was 'to all intents and purposes . . . an

Institutional life could be highly regimented: residents of the Salvation Army Boys' Home at Eltham line up to salute a visitor to the institution in the 1890s. R. STANDISH COLLECTION, ATL, F-44824-1/2

Old Country Workhouse under a kinder name'. He declared himself 'very much surprised to find that such a system of dealing with the education of the children of the State was countenanced in this progressive and democratic country'.[47] The agreement of the Inspector-General of Hospitals, Thomas Valintine, that it was undesirable to confine young and old in one institution led to concerted efforts on the Board's part to rid itself of all responsibility for maintaining children. The difficulties between the Education Department and charitable aid boards were not resolved until the early 1920s, when boards limited their attention to providing assistance to children in poor families.[48]

A 'fatherly chat' and a 'judicious friend': children's courts and juvenile probation

The extension to children and young persons of special rights in the judicial process became a feature of child welfare systems towards the end of the nineteenth century. Special courts or arrangements for children date from the 1870s, when American states made distinct provision for young offenders, enabling cases against them to be separated from those against adults. There was a rapid expansion of children's courts as a discrete part of the judicial system following the establishment of the first in Illinois in 1899. By 1925, nearly all American states had introduced them, and other countries, including New Zealand, had followed suit.[49]

During the nineteenth and early twentieth centuries children committed to the care of the state in New Zealand passed through the regular adult court system, normally the magistrates' court. Cases of child neglect, indigency, mis-behaviour and desertion, as well as offences, were heard in open court, and the judicial proceedings were the same as those for adults. This practice came under increasing criticism from the beginning of the twentieth century. According to the politician Frederick Baume, attendance at magistrates' courts compelled children 'to look upon sights and hear things which were occasionally of a most disgusting character, and showed depraved human nature in its worst form'. Children neither respected nor feared these courts, and worst of all, they became schools of crime for the young.[50] He and others envisaged instead a more private place, away from prying eyes, where magistrates could have a fatherly chat with a child, and give timely advice to both children and parents.

Some New Zealand magistrates, perhaps aware of international develop-ments, had begun to hear cases involving young people separately by 1905. Christchurch's Helyar Bishop and Dunedin's Howell Young Widdowson either used their own chambers for children's cases, or cleared the court. Notes on their methods were circulated to all magistrates in 1906. The Juvenile Offenders Act 1906 picked up the practice, and empowered magistrates to schedule a special time at which to hear all cases involving those aged sixteen years and younger. If necessary, the court could be cleared, leaving only counsel, journalists and members of appropriate institutions or welfare groups. The magistrate also gained the choice of either admonishing a child or entering a conviction.[51]

The establishment of these 'children's courts' mirrored changing attitudes towards children. Greater recognition of childhood as a phase of life which should be shielded from the harsher aspects of the adult world had facilitated the development of separate institutions for children; separate judicial facilities now followed. Not coincidentally, children's courts arose at the same time as a more intensive policing of the behaviour of young people developed from the late nineteenth century in the wake of the scares about juvenile delinquency and the larrikin nuisance.[52]

The combination of changing conceptions of childhood and children's special place in the country's future allowed children's courts to incorporate specific notions of justice. Reformation and treatment, rather than punishment, became the prerogative of these courts, promising as they did an opportunity to shape the character of young lives. The welfare focus of the courts turned attention away from the offence or complaint which had brought an individual before the court and onto the family background. Normal rules of judicial evidence and procedure could be, and were, suspended as magistrates sought out underlying reasons for children's actions to enable them to prescribe the most appropriate treatment. Personal circumstances and personal history were paramount; offending and misbehaviour were regarded as symptomatic of a poor environment or 'bad breeding'. Close inquiry into the life of child and family was thus imperative, whether undertaken by social workers, court officials, medical officers or those conversant with the emerging specialism of psychology.[53]

Some supporters of children's courts, imbued with knowledge of procedures in the United States, called for a fully-fledged children's court system. William

Larrikins in the making? In what appears to be a posed shot, a group of boys lounge and play in a ramshackle urban setting. ATL, G-10529-1/1

Reece, an official visitor to industrial schools, toured England, Germany and the United States during 1909, inspecting institutions and court facilities. Particularly impressed with the children's courts of North America, he advocated on his return that a similar system be created here. New Zealand was following a 'forward policy' with its incipient children's courts, he noted, but could go further by holding cases right away from other courts, under specially-appointed magistrates or justices, and by according no publicity to the proceedings.[54]

The New Zealand system was not extended – then at least – along these lines. Instead, magisterial and Education Department attention turned to a more preventive approach to juvenile delinquency through the introduction of juvenile probation, under which young people would be ordered to undergo a period of court-ordered supervision under the direction of specially-assigned officers. Juvenile probation had emerged in other nations as part of the children's court system, and had particular currency in the United States. Reece had commented

A more idealised and genteel image of children at play. G. LESLIE ADKIN COLLECTION, MUSEUM OF NEW ZEALAND TE PAPA TONGAREWA, B.022884

favourably on its use there, and other individuals and welfare groups supported it as a way both to reduce the number of children entering institutions and to effect change in children's home environments.

Education Department officials developed the principles of a fledgling probation system in the early 1910s. This action was in part precipitated by an apparent change in the background of the institutional population. The Department routinely assembled information on the parents of committed youngsters, characterising them as 'good', 'bad', or 'undesirable', a classification which suggests more about those making the assessments than those being assessed. A rise in the number of boys committed whose parents were classed as of good character forced the Department to reconsider the origins of delinquency. Depraved or bad parents, or heredity had been the traditional explanations for the phenomenon, but in the face of this apparent change in parental character in the 1910s, explanations turned to poor parenting skills and a lack of parental control. Supervising a child in his or her own home would enable departmental staff to influence the parents for good, whereas incarceration denied the opportunity for direct intervention into the domestic circumstances of children committed to the care of the state. As soon as a boy showed any delinquent tendencies, suggested Pope, he should be 'taken in hand' and placed under the supervision of a specially-appointed officer. This 'judicious friend' would help to retrain the boy and his parents to their proper responsibilities in the natural surroundings of their own home. The objective was to supplement weak parental control but avoid committal, 'which implies the breaking of the family tie, the lessening of parental responsibility, and an upbringing in conditions that can never take the place of a good home, no matter how high a level of sympathetic and enlightened administration is attained'. If neither parents nor boy were amenable and willing to open their doors to officialdom, the child could be committed to an institution.[55]

Private organisations and individual magistrates were experimenting with similar schemes at the same time, and the Department probably drew on these. Reverend Axelsen of the Dunedin Presbyterian Support Services Association, for example, provided a probation service to the town's courts. The local magistrate Howell Young Widdowson sometimes made it a condition of not committing a boy that he remain at home, subject to Axelsen's supervision. At other times, Axelsen placed the boys in districts away from their former associates. Widdowson gave Axelsen full endorsement, suggesting only that he would be more successful if supported by greater authority in the matter of guardianship of children.[56]

A case in the Christchurch 'juvenile court' in December 1912 clearly influenced the direction of the Department's scheme. Rather than cautioning or convicting

Inadequate space for healthy recreation, and unsupervised play, were considered to be causes of child delinquency. Here Wellington children fossick around the derelict hulk of the Maori *at Pipitea Street.* J. N. TAYLOR COLLECTION, ATL, F-104803-1/2

five boys for the theft of toy pistols and whistles from a local store, the magistrate, V. G. Day, ordered that they should not go out after dark, that they should regularly attend school, and that they should not attend the cinema. In Day's view, the last condition was particularly important. After attending a screening of *The Wild West*, the boys could not, apparently, resist the temptation of acting it out in real life, 'and the theft of so many toy pistols seemed to denote the presence of a large number of would-be desperadoes, eager to follow in the footsteps of Ned Kelly and his famous gang'.[57]

The Department implemented its juvenile probation scheme first in Auckland, where, Pope argued, the need was most urgent. No private organisations offered a probation service in the city, and the Department sought to fill this obvious gap by complementing, rather than replicating or replacing, private services. This initial limitation of its service, and its tacit support of private schemes in other centres, further illustrated the ambivalent response of officialdom to private philanthropic enterprise. The Department was caught between a need to use private arrangements, and a desire to control the operation and extent of those arrangements. Its scheme, like the private ones, would apply 'almost entirely' to boys. Few girls, apparently, could be dealt with 'successfully' by close personal supervision in their own homes. This gendered pattern of probation derived from the wider gendered nature of juvenile delinquency, in which the particular danger posed by female sexual delinquency to society's future and well-being led to a greater emphasis on incarceration than on supervised liberty.

Frederick Shell, who had previously been a missioner to seamen in Wellington and was recommended by Pope, began his work at the beginning of 1913. His position was as an agent to the managers of the Department's institutions, but under direct departmental control. To reassure institutional staff that the office was not a threat to their authority, the Department emphasised that Shell's assistance would be invaluable in maintaining the influence of the managers: 'the essential to success is co-operation', it stressed.[58]

Local magistrates and the Department alike hailed the scheme as a success. After two years of its operation, John Beck, a senior officer in the Special Schools Section, reported that the Auckland magistrates relied a great deal on Shell's supervision.[59] Shell, too, considered his work to be successful. His probation rules – not to be outdoors after dark unless in the company of an adult, to attend church on Sundays, and to report when instructed – led to gratifying outcomes. Only three of the 22 probationers in 1913 had 'misconducted' themselves and been admitted to institutions. To emphasise further his success, he noted that some parents themselves had approached him, requesting that their child be placed under his supervision. The scheme had passed the 'experimental stages', he believed, and become 'an indispensable factor in the prevention and correction of delinquency among children'. There were financial savings, too; he estimated that he had saved the government over £3200 in institutional maintenance.[60]

There were also difficulties, however, arising particularly from Shell's dubious legal standing. By law, he could not assume the guardianship of children, and magistrates consequently sometimes refused to assign cases to him. The Department partially rectified this in 1915 by vesting in Shell the guardianship of all boys in the Auckland district who had been placed on probation. He sometimes found his awkward status and authority challenged in court, and requested that he be granted the position of Special Constable.[61] The Department's inability to expedite this request brought home to it some of the problems of continuing to base probation on shaky legal foundations.

Probation held out many advantages both to the Education Department and to the wider society. Re-educating children in their own families was increasingly considered, both internationally and in New Zealand, to be an ideal method of lowering the rate of juvenile delinquency and keeping children out of costly institutional care. It complemented, to some extent, the imperatives which promoted an expansion of the boarding out of children from institutions into family environments. Yet juvenile probation went further in making an explicit attempt to re-educate parents and families as well as the children concerned. The adoption of the system from 1913 suggested an increased willingness to interpret children's problems as a consequence of parental and family deficiencies. Although the child's environment had long been held as crucial to his or her make-up, the Education Department now for the first time made the leap to tackling that environment itself by intervening within the family and directing its attention towards other family members. Nominally, the child or young person was under supervision; in practice, the whole household experienced its effects.

Boarding out: the mark of a civilised community

The opportunity to influence family arrangements was inherent in boarding out or fostering residents from industrial schools. As Margaret Tennant has suggested, boarding out enabled intervention into two sets of families: the family with whom a child was boarded, and the family to which the child, in theory a missionary now imbued with the knowledge and skills gained through committal, would return, or which she or he would later form.[62]

Confining children in large institutions – 'herding' them together was the favoured description – had come under sustained criticism over the last two decades of the nineteenth century. The cost of institutional care, the stigma accompanying committal to a residence, and a growing emphasis on the nurturing potential of the family swung the pendulum of child welfare away from an exclusively institutional focus. New Zealand accompanied Australia in moving towards boarding out, first to complement institutional care, and then in preference to it.[63] The Education Department maintained that boarding out children allowed them to 'acquire habits of self-reliance that cannot be formed in the seclusion of an institution which is a kind of prison. They come to look upon their foster-parents as their natural guardians, protectors, and counsellors, and the home becomes a starting point and a rallying point for them as they enter naturally into the ordinary relations of common every-day life.'[64] Boarding out, in sum, signified an enlightened and civilised community.

Boarding out continued to grow in importance in the early twentieth century. As Figure 1 shows (p. 24), both the number of children and the percentage of the industrial school population boarded out increased before the First World War. Around 400 children, approximately 30 per cent of the total committed to state care, were boarded out in 1902; by 1916 the figure had grown to over 1000 children, or 40 per cent of the total.[65] Boarding out was preferred for infants, young children, and industrial school residents who were less than fourteen years old, the age at which board payments ceased. The Burnham and Te Oranga reformatories, with their older and supposedly more difficult populations, boarded out only a tiny minority of their residents.

Comprehensive regulations surrounded the practice of boarding out. The managers of industrial schools and receiving homes, assisted by paid and unpaid local visiting officers and lady officers – known as boarding-out officers – were charged with making regular visits to all homes in which children were boarded. The 1902 regulations provided extensive guidelines for the conduct of foster parents: children were to be treated with care and kindness, they were to be trained in habits of diligence and usefulness, school attendance was mandatory, punishment was regulated, only children aged over twelve could work, and restrictions were placed on the type and amount of work they could perform.[66]

The practice was not without its detractors. Women's and welfare groups were in the vanguard of the criticism which escalated following publicity given to the deaths of infants in foster homes. Public conferences on boarding out in 1907 and 1908 registered strong disapproval of it and suggested that the Department look more closely at the use of the smaller 'cottage home' system that was in vogue elsewhere. As they were the most advanced method, it was only fair, it was suggested, that cottage homes be employed in place of boarding out, 'for the children of the poor have an absolute right, not to "poor homes," but to the best science and love can give them'.[67] Comprising members of such groups as the Canterbury Children's Aid Society and the Women's Christian Temperance Union, these conferences identified several deficiencies, including the dearth of suitable homes which compelled the Education Department to take whatever it could get, the difficulties of adequate inspection, and the likely effect of introducing the children of 'depraved' parents into the home of respectable citizens. It was regarded, furthermore, as unrealistic to expect a woman to care for the boarded-out child as she would for her own. Betraying their own privileged position, several women's groups claimed that most foster mothers were ignorant about the 'scientific methods of dealing with children suffering from hereditary taint and specially bad environment'. To these shortcomings was added a further catalogue: boarding out was totally inappropriate for the physical, mental and moral development of children; classification, the supposed panacea for institutional ills, was impossible; and there was little scope for harried foster mothers to provide individual training.[68]

The Department was sensitive to any criticism of its methods in the wake of the 1906 inquiry into the Burnham Reformatory. Gibbes invited boarding-out officers to address the criticisms, to comment on the merits and disadvantages of boarding out, and to offer suggestions for its improvement or replacement. Perhaps not surprisingly, all supported boarding out, seeing it as a sure way to improve the opportunities for children committed to care. 'After sixteen years' experience', wrote Anna Cox, ' I maintain that it is very successful in bringing up neglected and destitute children to be a gain, instead of a burden to the country'. Officers sketched an idyllic environment for fostered children in rural areas: 'There is always a garden, and generally a dairy and some poultry. The children share the duties and the pleasures too'. For some, there could be no other option: 'It follows the Divine plan of the child in the environment of home and family. For the well-being of the State it is essential that the idea of the family should be fostered. It is fundamentally right, and, being a natural law, may only, I believe, be disregarded at our peril'. Cottage homes – 'merely institutions on a small scale' – were dismissed on the grounds of cost and the difficulty of obtaining suitable staff.[69]

With such unanimous endorsement, and the Department's faith in the system given added credence, opposition was disregarded. To emphasise further the pre-eminence of the method, the Department printed its officers' responses in its annual report for 1909. And as if to underscore the point that New Zealand was in the forefront of international developments, the report included a detailed account of the 1909 North American 'White House Conference' on the care of dependent children, which had given its complete approval to boarding out.

The Department promoted boarding out by pointing to the calibre of foster families. It did not collect information on these families, but scattered case notes and letters from foster mothers suggest that they were not generally well off financially. Board payments, albeit small, were a vital source of income to some poorer households, although the Department was careful to assert that financial motives played little part in the decision to foster. Ella Dick, who supervised the welfare of children around Wellington, considered there was a general public impression that 'the question of £.s.d.' ruled boarding out, and that little justice was done to the 'high and pure' motives that influenced many women – or to the happiness that the children brought to their lives. She spoke of foster mothers in glowing, almost messianic terms, citing the example of one experienced foster mother, Mrs Clark:

In the Industrial School work one's womanly sympathies and righteous indignation are both aroused by the treatment that the children have received from those to whom they belong. The character of a woman like Mrs Clark with her unfailing love and goodness to the children helps one, and keeps alive one's belief in human nature. . . . She is a woman blessed with that wonderful power of control which so many mothers of the last generation possessed and so few of the present! Mrs Clark never seems to have to scold or punish the children, they obey her in a wonderful way.[70]

Boarding out was not only important for children, it seems, but was a means of reaffirming to women the importance of motherhood and child-raising.

Not all foster parents were like Mrs Clark, but problems were never sufficiently serious to dislodge the Department's faith in the system. Obtaining suitable homes at the rate of payment offered was the major difficulty, as it would remain throughout the century; it was, in fact, too low to allow financial motives to intrude too overtly. Boarding-out officers pointed this out to senior officials in 1908–9 when they were given the opportunity to comment publicly on the system. Thomas Archey, the Manager of Burnham, felt 'bound to urge that a larger weekly payment should be offered to foster-parents. I am convinced that we should in this way have an abundant reward in the higher class of persons we should secure for our young children.'[71] Most officers echoed these sentiments, acknowledging that they could find homes, but that obtaining suitable homes was another matter.

The Department had increased its rates in 1903 in the first change since 1883: 7s a week for children under twelve and 6s for older children was about the same sum as the daily wage, without board, of an agricultural labourer or domestic servant.[72] Payments ceased when children turned fourteen, the age at which the Department expected them to leave school and earn their own keep. These rates continued until 1912, when complaints compelled the Department to act. Boarding-out officers in Wellington and Canterbury especially found that not only were the rates no longer attracting desirable foster parents, but children were being returned when they reached twelve and the rates declined. Gibbes now acknowledged that applications for an increase in the rates had been staved off so frequently that they could no longer be opposed. On his recommendation, new rates were set and the practice of paying more for infants was made official.[73]

The First World War led to demands for a further increase. Ella Dick had ten foster children returned on a single day in October 1916, eight because of the high cost of living and low rate of payment. Mrs Payne of Masterton returned her foster children with regret, stating that she was unable to cook and sew for them on the amount given, as the 8s provided would only go as far as 5s had before the war. Her husband was less reluctant to part with the children: he 'wanted me to send them back since they came in fact he did not want me to take them in the first place.'[74] Boarding-out officers found boys in Christchurch clad in neither shoes nor socks due to the low rates paid, and one officer had, to her horror, a foster mother boasting that she could ' "keep a boy on next to nothing" '.[75] The Department refused to approve a further increase despite these hardships.

A significant attraction of boarding out to the state was, of course, its relative cheapness. For a Department mindful of expenditure, this was a significant advantage. Maintaining children in residences involved considerable outlay, in

Staff and young residents of Gisborne's Heni Materoa Creche. The Education Department had little success in persuading private institutions to board out children. NATIONAL ARCHIVES, CW 1, 40/6/42

both staffing and building costs. Boarding out, on the other hand, involved minimal staffing costs, and the rates of payment to foster parents were never generous. Safeguarding the future of the nation by keeping children in family groups and checking periodically on the welfare of both child and family was even more attractive when it could be done on the cheap.

A limit on the number of children any foster home could receive introduced in 1916 proved contentious. Problems of overcrowding and poor conditions in foster homes which took in a large number of children prompted the Department to restrict the number in any one home to five. Previously, provided the homes were roomy and clean, and there was suitable domestic help (not

Foster mother Mrs Mills and her daughter – both of whom look exhausted – display the infants they cared for at the 1917 Dunedin Baby Demonstration. NATIONAL ARCHIVES, CW 1, 40/25/22

provided by the Department), foster mothers could take in any number of children. Many boarding-out officers criticised this step, with Wellington's Ella Dick the most outspoken. She was also, she believed, the most affected, as she had long relied on large foster homes for those for whom she was unable to find other accommodation. Dick interpreted the move as a further attack on foster parents, 'at a time when they need every consideration'. She predicted that the restriction would pose serious difficulties for women who had altered their lifestyles to take in more children, and that there would be great difficulty in boarding out children in future. It was a decision, she believed, that had been made in haste by officials who had no knowledge of either the foster mothers or their capabilities: 'These good women of ours who take the children as infants and care for them are real mothers and doing splendid work for New Zealand. They deserve more help and praise than they are getting lately.' 'Does not the Department approve of large families?', she asked.[76] It proved difficult to implement the limitation, and officers like Dick found sufficient special grounds on which to make exceptions.

Boarding out was also a significant point of dispute between government and private or religious institutions, which negotiated over children's welfare in this area as in others. Despite the Department's support of boarding out as the pre-eminent method, it drew the line at compelling private or religious groups to use it, and they remained free to continue with institutionalisation. Private groups which boarded out were rare enough in this period to warrant special mention in departmental reports. In 1903 Pope visited the St Vincent de Paul's Orphanage in Dunedin, finding it to be one of the best-conducted Roman Catholic schools and noting approvingly that the Sisters had boarded out all of the babies.[77]

Whether or not private and church homes adopted boarding out, the Education Department's faith in the practice suggests that it had a growing belief in the importance of the best environment for children. Children from morally suspect backgrounds, whose parents were classed as 'bad' or 'depraved', could be placed in 'better' households which would impart ideas about clean living and good citizenship. Ideas about poor heredity would remain current in New Zealand for some time to come, but it was accepted that even bad breeding could be influenced for the better by a sound environment.

Stamping out the 'fearful slaughter of the innocents': infant life protection

The Infant Life Protection Act 1907 assigned to the Education Department the inspection of all licensed foster homes where infants under six years of age were maintained away from their birth families. Most of these children had been born outside marriage and placed by women who paid for their support but were unable to keep them. This measure expanded considerably the Department's responsibilities for children's welfare, and brought it into close contact with infant health and welfare groups such as the Plunket Society at a time when infant welfare issues were assuming national importance. Unlike children in institutions, at service, or boarded out in private homes, these infants had not been committed to the care of the state. They were the first of the various groups of 'non-state' children for whom the Education Department would be respon-sible over the course of the century. They also constituted the first group in relation to which the Department took a broadly preventive approach: inspecting foster homes for infants sought to ensure their welfare and prevent future social problems.

New Zealand, like other countries, had experienced an alarm and panic over 'baby-farming' in the late nineteenth century.[78] The lack of government assistance for single mothers led some to hand over their babies to women who, for a fee, cared for the infants. This may have been a legitimate business transaction, but in the public mind the process was more sinister, and a means for mothers to rid themselves of unwanted children. Baby-farmers were commonly depicted as callous women, who took the money and left the child unattended, or worse. The image of babies left to die slowly or murdered by their caregivers provided the impetus for infant life protection legislation in New Zealand and elsewhere.

The passage of New Zealand's Infant Life Protection Act in 1893 was a response to alarm at the alleged growth of baby-farms from the mid-1880s; the Commissioner of Police claimed that there were twenty such homes in Christchurch alone.[79] All homes in which children aged under two years were kept apart from their birth parents for more than three consecutive days in return for payment were required to be registered as foster homes with the police, who could visit and inspect them at any time. The execution of Minnie Dean, the 'Winton baby-farmer', in 1895 for the murder of two children in her care led to a review of the legislation. Police powers of inspection were extended under an 1896 Act which also raised the upper age limit to four years.[80]

Even with this facility for greater police inspection, the administration of infant life protection work was fraught. Police officers were not necessarily those best suited to overseeing the welfare of infants. One politician sketched a ludicrous picture of police inspection: 'All that he [the police officer] can do is to go to the house of the keeper, and probably be shown into the front room; then the home-keeper will bring him the child. He will look at it, and probably be rather frightened of it than otherwise, and then will go away. Inspection means a great deal more than that.'[81] Visiting foster homes constituted a minor part of police duties, and many officers had neither the time nor the resources to conduct thorough or regular inspections. The Christchurch Police Matron was expected to visit 60 homes in addition to performing her regular duties; this workload was only brought to light after the death of an infant.[82]

The move to Education Department jurisdiction was presented as a means of improving children's welfare by placing infant life under the control of the most appropriate, and most experienced, government agency.[83] As with much other social policy, particularly that which focused on children's welfare, debate surrounding the 1907 Act was couched in terms of rectifying the country's declining birth rate and boosting its (white) population. There was, nevertheless, a suspicion that protective legislation could enable the 'wrong' population to prosper by enabling single mothers to offload their responsibilities, thereby encouraging vice and undermining the family. 'The home is the basis of the whole of our civilisation and country', James Allen reminded his parliamentary colleagues, and foster homes should not usurp the place of the natural father and mother.[84] Ella Dick was even more explicit. She argued that it was the children of the 'girls' of the more intelligent classes of society who were worth saving as future citizens, not those of the sort the Department usually assisted.[85]

The legislation came into effect at the beginning of 1908. Exemplifying the contemporary interest in infant welfare, it advanced from four to six years the upper age limit of children for whose care a licence was required. Unless licensed as foster parents, and thereby subject to inspections, women could now not legally take infants from birth parents for payment for a period of more than seven days. Exemptions to the provisions of the Act were enunciated more clearly: close relatives and institutions supported by the government or public subscription could apply for exemption from being licensed, on condition that the homes were first inspected by departmental officials and that consent was given before infants were removed from them.[86]

Most importantly for the Education Department, the Act made provision for the appointment of officials to enforce its requirements. In addition to their regular duties, the women in charge of the two receiving homes and of two of the industrial schools were gazetted as District Agents: Sarah Jackson (Auckland), Ella Dick (Wellington), Anna Cox (Christchurch), and Harriette Petremant (Dunedin).[87] Smaller centres were assigned sub-agents. Visiting officers, who were either trained nurses or women experienced in the care of young children, assisted each District Agent. Unpaid honorary local visitors were also appointed to visit foster homes. In contrast to the previous system of police inspection, Education Department inspection was carried out by a network of experienced or trained officials, some of whom worked full-time in the area.

District agents were expected to be conversant with current philosophies of infant welfare and feeding, including those being promulgated by the Plunket Society. The belief that women should be, but were no longer, familiar with the basic principles of childrearing had become almost commonplace as New Zealand's Pakeha birth rate fell. Agents would be a means of instructing women in the latest methods of infant feeding and childrearing; their work was thus a corollary to similar attempts being made to professionalise motherhood in girls' education and other areas. The cornerstone of the instruction was 'scientific' feeding and the avoidance of artificial foods. The Department's detailed *Feeding of Infants*, which was supplied to all foster mothers, expressed this philosophy of things scientific. Adopting Plunket Society notions, the instructions incorporated advice on the type and correct quantity of food, including 'humanised' milk, as well as recommended feeding times. Different schedules were provided for different age groups. Infants of three weeks, for example, were to be fed a precise mixture (using the measured medicine spoon provided) of boiled cow's milk, cream, boiled water, sugar of milk, and lime water. A miscellany of advice on other aspects of infant health and welfare was also included: 'The sucking of "dummy teats" is harmful, and should not be allowed'; 'Do not feed a baby just to keep it quiet'; 'A child should have as much fresh air as possible'.[88]

Tried and true remedies died hard amongst some agents, suggesting that despite the official rhetoric of a scientific approach to infant welfare, traditional methods remained strong. Sarah Jackson prescribed alternate meals of egg-white mixed with brandy and barley water for one fostered infant who was suffering from thrush, a condition she attributed to the use of humanised milk.[89] The outspoken Harriette Petremant informed the Secretary of Education that 'notwithstanding the excellent results obtained by Dr King', she had found cases where the substance 'did not agree', and could even lead to death if the infant remained on it. She reminded Gibbes of her 'vast experience' of infant nursing in New Zealand and elsewhere; she was 'not at all ignorant' on the matter. Aware of the Department's endorsement of the milk and of the Plunket Society in general, she confirmed that she would do all she could to make the mixture popular, but would have no hesitation in seeking other methods and advice if she found it to be unsuitable.[90]

The Department's relationship with the Plunket Society itself was not always cordial. Infant life protection work brought the two groups into close contact, and at times an uneasy rivalry simmered below the surface. In 1910 Bella King, the wife of Plunket founder Truby King, issued a stinging critique of the Department's administration. She expressed her disappointment that the Society had been 'shut out' of a role in the administration of the legislation, and referred to the Society's 'complete, cruel and immediate' disillusionment with the Department's attitude. In her opinion, an 'unfortunate and utterly unlooked for spirit of official exclusiveness and opposition' had characterised the Department's approach. She also pointed to the lack of qualifications and training (specifically Karitane training, provided exclusively by the Society) of the officers appointed under the legislation, some of whom were not even mothers – a charge frequently used to denigrate the skills of women working in the area of children's welfare. The officers were, she maintained, imbued with a spirit of distrust towards those who could assist them in the field.[91]

The Education Department knew that its officers were unable to cover the whole sphere of infant life protection work, and welcomed the extra assistance provided by Plunket nurses. The extent to which it accepted Plunket Society aid in its own work is more difficult to define, and the boundaries between the work of district agents and of Plunket nurses remained blurred. Pope preferred Department and Society to work separately, but in accord, towards the same end of enhancing children's chances in life.[92] In practice there was not always co-operation, and no doubt the views of some district agents over the merits of humanised milk soured relations.

The Plunket Society promulgated the necessity of proper infant feeding, with the correct foods consumed in suitable surroundings. It would most likely have deemed this feeding situation unsuitable, despite the child's chubby limbs. E.M.F. COPELAND COLLECTION, ATL, F-27091-1/4

The Society frequently asked the Department to establish closer links and allow it a broader role in infant life protection. Amy Carr, the Society's President in 1910, asserted that great benefits would accrue if government inspectors and Plunket nurses worked in tandem.[93] Plunket's criticisms of the Department's selection of foster homes led to the suggestion that the Society's officers assist with the inspection of homes. Pope noted that while there had been many useful instances of cooperation, innovations which assigned Plunket an official status would be another matter, and could lead to unfriendliness and 'cross-pulling' between the two.[94] An offer of six months' free Plunket training for the Department's Dunedin officers received a mixed reception. In informing the Dunedin District Agent of the offer, Gibbes intimated that the Department was not putting any pressure on officers to accept, although he acknowledged that any extra training would be valuable. Perhaps it was Truby King's direct criticism of the Department's work which disturbed Gibbes: King's conviction that the benefits of Plunket training would enable the Department's officers to see how satisfactory it was 'to work understandingly instead of groping along by mere rule of thumb' was both heavily underlined and had a large exclamation mark inserted in the margin of the Department's copy. Not until the late 1920s could the Department's agents claim that they had 'no difficulty acting in unison' with the Society.[95]

Plunket was not alone in its criticisms of the Department's administration. The 1907 conference which had so condemned boarding out also passed judgment on the administration of infant life protection, claiming that licences (under police administration) had been granted capriciously.[96] The cottage home system, touted as a better method than either institutionalisation or boarding out, was similarly lauded in relation to the care of infants. Only in a cottage home, argued the social reformer Eveline Cunnington, could administrators be 'in closer touch with the advanced thought of the day, as regards the training of the infant mind – body and soul'.[97] In 1910 Ella Dick claimed that there was no longer 'strong opposition' to the Department's infant life protection work; instead, criticism may have been subsumed within more general critiques of boarding out.[98]

The Education Department defended its infant life protection work in the same manner that it upheld the general principle and practice of boarding out: fostering children exposed them to the beneficial effects of family life, and was preferable to confining them indiscriminately in institutions. It was deemed particularly important for very young babies, who required specialised care which only a devoted mother was believed to be able to give. The effects on the women who took in infants was an additional advantage of the system, which became a means of re-initiating women in the role of motherhood. 'The women are delighted to show us that the little limbs are getting rounded and the little faces rosy, and look so pleased when we praise their love for, and care of the children', Ella Dick wrote in 1910. 'Some of the women are amazingly unselfish and loving to the fragile, ailing little creatures under their care.' Young babies could even melt the hearts of women who had initially taken them because of the financial remuneration – even though the Department consistently claimed that there were no such women: 'Happily, the helplessness of infancy is its defence; and many a child finds a home in the arms of the woman who admits that financial necessity alone opened her door to the stranger.'[99]

There were difficulties in the administration of infant life protection nevertheless. Obtaining suitable homes for infants was a perennial problem, as it was for foster care more generally. In Invercargill in 1908, only seventeen from a list of 45 foster homes earned the complete approval of the visiting officer in terms of cleanliness, desirability of location, and quality of care provided. The officer was philosophical about the remainder, clearly aware that perfection was not to be obtained, and that even some of the 'less desirable' homes and foster mothers displayed redeeming features. Janet Byfield, for instance, was 'a slatternly woman: untidy house but [in] essence [a] good nature'; Jane Niven's was an 'untidy home [which] might get better by teaching'.[100] These examples suggest some of the negotiations and trade-offs which took place between foster mothers and departmental officials. The latter may have visited homes and commented on the cleanliness of the surroundings, but they often turned a blind eye to less than pristine conditions if the women were attending well to the children's welfare.

Some women were reluctant to take very young or sick babies due to the extra care they needed, and some district agents had difficulty placing such infants. Others were wary that birth parents would default on maintenance payments and leave them raising someone else's child for free. After 1908 the costs of payments for such infants who were technically destitute fell on charitable aid boards, but that arrangement tended to be honoured only in the breach. In consequence, Sarah Jackson argued, women who might otherwise have given babies a good home would not run the risk of being left without payment or redress.[101] Under such circumstances, the Department was sometimes compelled to take on less 'suitable' homes. Agents such as Ella Dick freely admitted that mistakes were made in issuing licences. Most of the trouble she ascribed to the effects of drink:

> we suddenly get a hint that a foster-mother whom we like and trust is addicted to drink, although her house is clean and well kept, and the baby is thriving; but, knowing how the drink habit grows, and the danger of a woman under its influence caring for a baby . . . we feel great anxiety until we are sufficiently certain to be able to withdraw the license. Of course, it is only women who are drinkers at home secretly who can deceive us even at first.[102]

In 1916 the neighbours of foster mother Mrs Kiernander reported that she was 'not very temperate', regularly partaking of a glass of beer. The District Agent visited and found the child well, but asked Mrs Kiernander to relinquish her licence when she admitted drinking. Her husband was not as compliant, demanding to know the names of the 'dirty slanderers who have no character of their own'. He invited the agent to come to his house any evening to 'talk temperance with her'.[103]

Licences could be denied or recalled on a number of grounds, including ill-treatment of an infant, poor conditions, or misconduct by the foster parent. Mrs Quintal of Ponsonby, for example, was acknowledged to be a good mother to her own six young children, but her six-roomed, partly furnished and untidy house suggested to the agent that she was not in a position to take in a foster child. Mrs

Powell of Auckland embodied much of what the Department objected to in a foster parent: she was living apart from her husband, she could give no character reference and did not have a respectable appearance, she was only 25 years old, and she had taken in a male boarder.[104] For such women, the small amount they could earn through fostering infants may have been vital to their livelihood.

Departmental officers also had to inspect foster homes and institutions which had been granted exemptions under the Act. Some of these were the homes of relatives of the infants, and could pose difficulties for departmental staff when kinship ties were considered to override other considerations. Mrs Powdrill of Warkworth looked after her unmarried daughter's toddler, who was a 'fine sturdy boy', according to the visiting officer, and evidently well cared for. Mrs Powdrill herself was a 'superior looking woman', and the agent had no hesitation in granting her an exemption. Mrs White of Auckland, on the other hand, was out of the house all day while nominally in charge of her grandchild. The child's mother worked as a waitress at the Dominion Tea Rooms, and the elder Mrs White left the toddler with an eight year old.[105]

Institutions granted exemptions were another matter. The fact that they were institutions ran contrary to the departmental policy of boarding out wherever possible. For infants in particular, institutionalisation was viewed as especially harmful if they were kept with children of other ages. The establishment of Mother Aubert's St Vincent de Paul's Foundling Home in Auckland in 1910 aroused particular concern. Unlike other maternity and infant institutions, St Vincent's admitted very young babies and made no attempt to forge a bond between mother and child. Despite Mother Aubert's justification of her work, the Department believed the practice encouraged vice, screened men from publicity and financial responsibility, and deprived young women of the experience of feeding their babies, which was seen as the most effective way of their redeeming themselves. Sarah Jackson warned that the home would need to be very carefully watched lest it did more harm than good, and the Department's officers maintained a scrutiny of its management. To their dismay, they found a higher infant death rate than in other homes, and they attributed this to institutional life itself rather than to the poor condition of the babies that Mother Aubert admitted. The closure of the home in 1916 by episcopal decree served only to confirm all the Department's forebodings about institutionalising babies.[106]

The debates over the Foundlings Home illustrate a response to single motherhood which went beyond wholesale condemnation of the women concerned. Single women were ineligible for the government assistance provided to other women living alone, such as widows, and they often experienced moral censure when applying for charitable relief. Historians have commented on this intolerance, but the Department's infant life protection policies and practices suggest the need for a more complex reading of attitudes towards ex-nuptial births.[107] Some commentators and departmental officials were more sympathetic to the situation of single mothers and aware of the need to provide for the welfare of their children. The high death rate among the infants of single mothers in New Zealand probably influenced this attitude – ex-nuptial babies were two or three times as likely to die within their first year as those born in marriage.[108] The *New Zealand Herald* counselled policymakers that the illegitimate child should not be given advantages over the children of the 'hard-working and industrious', but stressed that New Zealand's honour demanded that the 'fearful slaughter of the innocents which disgraces our modern society' should be stamped out.[109]

Outright vilification of single mothers was rare amongst infant life officers, with most exhibiting an ambivalence towards single motherhood and the cases that came within their view. The Department's espousal of the necessity of a family environment for children extended to the desirability of establishing bonds between mothers and their babies, whether or not they had been born in marriage. According to Jackson, institutions such as Mother Aubert's which broke that bond lost sight of the fact that the 'tendency of the age is to attach less and less importance to moral reputation' and more importance to preserving infant life.[110] While Jackson clearly disregarded her own 'moral stance' on many issues, other agendas were at work here, particularly notions of re-educating women to motherhood and halting the decline in the birth rate. Because of an awareness that these policies could be seen as encouraging the least suitable sections of society to reproduce – 'so much so that the old law of the survival of the fittest will soon cease to operate to the advantage of the race' – less charitable options also emerged. Jackson, in the established tradition of providing a solution to single motherhood, recommended the establishment of a reformatory institution for women in which they would cease to be a 'menace' to the wider community.[111]

Child life itself, rather than the conditions under which it was brought about, was the central issue of infant life protection work. The Department measured its 'success' in the area in terms of the number of deaths in its foster homes and associated institutions. Between 1908 and 1915, the death rate of infants in foster homes fell from 2.56 per cent to 0.98 per cent, a result with which the Department was 'well satisfied'. The rate in exempted institutions was higher, fluctuating between 5.23 per cent in 1911 and 1.08 per cent in 1915.[112]

For the parents, normally the mothers, of the infants, the 'success' or 'benefits' could be quantified in other ways as well. Between 1908 and 1915, the Department had an average of about 1200 infants in registered homes. These homes provided one option for women who may have had few others when faced with an illegitimate child. Anna Foley, who was in the Salvation Army Home in Auckland to give birth, placed her child with Mrs Gordon, and later took the baby to the

Home of Compassion in Island Bay, Wellington. Her parents, who lived in Blenheim, knew nothing about Anna's pregnancy or the child.[113] Women's use of the system also illustrates the role that kin or neighbourhood networks could play in childcare. Martha McGee placed her son Leonard with her kinswoman Rosa Williams, while George Harrington looked after his granddaughter on behalf of her fifteen year old mother.[114] Some men also turned to the Department's services when faced with caring for their children alone. Fred Trane's wife, 'much addicted to drink', had left her husband to care for their four children, and while he did not know her whereabouts and had no desire to find out, he did wish to find homes in which to place the children. A carter by trade, he was away from his home for most of the day, leaving his mother to tend to the children. After making some inquiries, Sarah Jackson was able to take the infants and place them out.[115]

Infant life protection services also signalled an advancing intervention into the lives and futures of families, and placed a focus on the primacy of family care. Nonetheless, the education and re-education of mothers, and adoption of the newest techniques to ensure infant health, revealed some of the more deep-seated reasons driving children's welfare in this period. The motivation to act early to prevent future problems – for children's welfare and for society more generally – was paramount in the proliferation of the infant welfare services provided by the Department of Education.

The baby market: monitoring adoption

The provisions of the Infant Life Protection Act 1907 also applied to the adoption of infants when the birth parents paid a sum, or premium, to the adoptive family. In such cases district agents inspected and licensed the home of the adoptive parents, just as for any other home in which an infant was maintained away from the birth family. Like infant life protection work, this role in monitoring adoption practices extended the Department's involvement in the lives of 'non-state' children.

New Zealand had passed its adoption legislation in 1881, becoming the first country in the British empire to regulate the legal adoption of children. Previously, adoption had had no legal status, and simply involved the 'transfer' of a child from one family to another, with all the loss of rights that entailed. Adoptions in the nineteenth and early twentieth centuries among Pakeha families frequently included the payment of a premium to the adoptive families.[116] Paid in either a lump sum or instalments, the premium was a recognition of the costs of raising a child during its first few years. To many observers, this practice was more akin to baby-farming, and this was indeed sometimes the case. Paying others to 'adopt' their babies probably appealed to single women who had few other choices.

The baby-farming scare of the late nineteenth century may have prompted moves to regulate the payment of premiums. The 1907 legislation followed closely on the heels of the Adoption of Children Amendment Act 1906, which forbade the payment of premiums without the express approval of a court. Problems remained nevertheless. According to the Education Department, there was still a temptation for adoptive parents to 'get rid' of the child as soon as the premiums were paid.[117]

Screening all application orders for adoption by inspecting the homes of prospective adoptive families was intended to counter this danger. Some district agents were very enthusiastic and thorough in their inspections. One Christchurch solicitor informed Pope that some of his clients were disturbed by the inspection of their homes under the provisions of the Infant Life Protection Act; they had wished to regard themselves as the parents of the children, not as baby-farmers.[118] The Education Department maintained that investigation alone

The Christchurch City Council capitalised on the veneration of motherhood and child life in this 1918 advertisement to enable the extension of electrification. CANTERBURY MUSEUM, 692

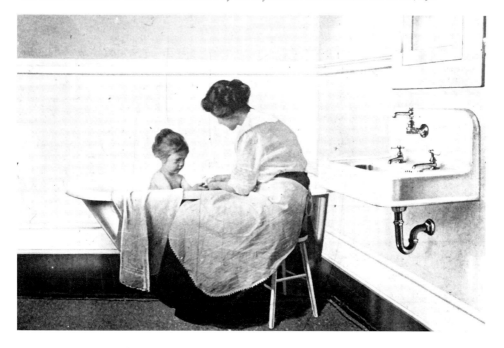

was insufficient, and recommended a probationary term of supervision for all adoption orders, during which its officers would regularly inspect all cases to ensure their continued suitability, much as it did with the adoption of industrial school children. Only through supervision, the Department suggested, could problems be checked. While magistrates could cancel adoption orders, the Department argued that 'much suffering may be endured by an adopted child before any neglect or ill-treatment to which it may be subjected becomes so patent as to call for public interference'. To support its case, it cited a short catalogue of unsatisfactory adoptions during 1908 in which abuse or other problems had occurred. Seven week old James Coulter had been adopted by the Todd family of Wellington for a £20 premium. A subsequent call on the Todds found James to be in a neglected state, and he was admitted to the Island Bay Home of Compassion. Other children were shuttled around from one adoptive situation to another. Five year old Robert McCabe was adopted by an Auckland family for no premium in July 1908. Perhaps realising that they could not keep the child, the family passed him, again without a premium, to a family living on Waiheke Island.[119]

The Department's suggestions for further monitoring of adoption practices were not always welcomed by magistrates, who at times resented its 'intrusion' into their domain. Magistrates sometimes ignored the recommendations of the officers who had investigated the applications, making orders despite advice to the contrary. Mrs Bugden of Gisborne applied for a licence as a foster mother in 1908, but was declined when the District Agent found her to be unsuitable; a magistrate later granted her application to adopt six week old Annie Soloman.[120] The Education Department was not the only agency to have its advice disregarded. The Wellington branch of the Society for the Protection of Women and Children, for example, had ventured to make suggestions on an adoption case in 1905, only to receive a stern rebuke from the local magistrate. He pointed out, somewhat acidly, 'that the Magistrate is in a much better position to judge of the circumstances of a case than is your committee, and that he is not going to be influenced by any extraneous body no matter how good its intentions may be'.[121]

There were, of course, occasions when magistrates did act on advice. Some expressly asked district agents to take a more active role in supervising adoptions. Auckland magistrate Charles Kettle recommended that the District Agent supervise the welfare of Rachel Goodart, who was adopted by Joseph and Fanny Atkin in 1913, as she was a truant and a local church social worker had reported that she was becoming difficult to control; a prohibition order served on Ernest Cantell in 1912 was sufficient inducement for the magistrate to order the supervision of the child he and his wife had adopted.[122] Such instances of cooperation tended to be rare. A lack of common purpose and professional dialogue between magistrates and departmental officials characterised the regulation of adoption, and would continue throughout the twentieth century.

The essential features of the Department's child welfare system and philosophy were in place by 1916. It had expanded considerably its jurisdiction over children's welfare as interest in child health and welfare escalated. From administering only to those committed to the care of the state, either in residential institutions or boarded out, the Department had also gained a preventive focus in overseeing the welfare of young children in private homes. Juvenile probation had a preventive focus, too, and like other features of the child welfare system symbolised a growing involvement of state officials in the lives of New Zealanders. Tending to the welfare of children in family situations facilitated this involvement, but it also meant much more. Pursuing child welfare through family welfare emphasised family and community responsibility for children; the 'partnership', however uneven, between the state, the family and the community was a way of nurturing the country's welfare.

CHAPTER 2

Towards the Child Welfare Act 1925

The Education Department recast New Zealand's child welfare system between 1916 and 1925, when the Child Welfare Act was passed. The increasing number of admissions to industrial schools during the 1910s exposed major shortcomings in the system which had formed the basis of state care for 50 years. In keeping with a belief in the centrality of family life for children, the Department set about closing industrial schools and placing their residents in service positions or foster homes. The probation system was also extended on this principle, as post-war changes consolidated earlier developments. In a climate of wartime population loss, childhood and child life assumed a new importance as the nation rebuilt itself, and the changes in child welfare formed part of a cluster of state initiatives to enhance child health and well-being. Greater concern facilitated greater control, as these changes intensified state involvement in New Zealanders' family lives.

To save a 'small army of children': a philosophy of change

In 1916, Minister of Education Josiah Hanan tabled in Parliament a special report positing a new emphasis for the education system. The war, he claimed, had tested the country's national resources, 'revealing our strength and our weakness', and it was in education and training that New Zealand possessed 'the greatest reconstructive agencies at our disposal for the repair and reorganization of national life'. As one of those 'reconstructive agencies', the industrial school system occupied a special place in the agenda for rebuilding the nation. The 'small army of children' in the care of the state required particular attention if New Zealand were to prosper and utilise all its human resources.[1]

By the end of 1916 the 'small army' was 4000 strong, dispersed among institutions and foster homes, under probation and in homes governed by the infant life protection legislation. An increase of 200 in the last two years was 'of such pressing importance that it should cause grave concern, not only on account of the darkened and unhappy condition of so many handicapped lives, but on account of the national loss resulting from this threatened wastage of human resources'. Hanan suggested a range of causes for the growth in numbers, but blamed inadequate parenting above all. Incapacity, ignorance and weak home influences were not the prerogative of one social class; he saw a general '"dragging up" of ill-disciplined, ill-nourished, and ill-educated children'.[2]

Baby shows were common in 1910s' New Zealand. Mrs Rangitiki, Mrs Irving and Mrs Goss display their sons in 1914. CANTERBURY MUSEUM, 7493

The early cementing of bonds between mother and child was believed to be one way of guarding against later neglect or delinquency. G. LESLIE ADKIN COLLECTION, MUSEUM OF NEW ZEALAND TE PAPA TONGAREWA, B.022799

Hanan enunciated a multi-pronged solution to combat the expanding number of state children and to promote better care of those who remained in the community. He advocated the extension of boarding out, with institutionalisation seen as a last resort. For children and young people deemed to be unsuitable for boarding out under 'ordinary conditions', a reclassification of institutions and their residents would be effected. Future policy would be guided by the adage that prevention was better than cure; influencing parents, as well as their children, through more probation and preventive work was an integral part of this strategy.[3]

As the title of one history of English child welfare suggests, war was 'good' for babies and other young children in that it accorded a new rationale for health and welfare developments. The First World War provided the context and stimulus for changes in health and welfare policy across the Western world, as safeguarding maternal, infant and child well-being assumed new meaning.[4] A slew of health and welfare initiatives targeted at children accompanied the changes to the child welfare system in New Zealand: the school medical and dental services were expanded, children's health camps began in 1919, and the reorganisation of the health system in 1920 led to the formation of divisions for Dental Hygiene, School Hygiene, and Child Welfare, the last under the leadership of Truby King.

In an illustration of the power and initiative which could be invested in senior public servants in the late nineteenth and early twentieth centuries, many of the developments between 1916 and 1925 were due to the determination and vision of one individual. John Beck, like George Hogben before him, was a vital catalyst for change, both in industrial schools and in the entire programme for dealing with delinquent and neglected children. Most of the changes implemented from 1916 originated with Beck, who studied international precedents and then endeavoured to convince others of the utility of his proposals. He was not always successful in winning over colleagues and superiors, and many of the changes occurred in spite of political opposition, and sometimes without a firm legal basis. Getting his proposals into legislation that would provide a legal footing for child welfare work was as important as the developments themselves.

Of Scottish birth, Beck emigrated with his parents to New Zealand in the 1880s. He had wanted to pursue an engineering career, but instead joined the Department of Education as a cadet – the lowest rung on the civil service ladder – in September 1899. Financial considerations may well have influenced his choice of career. Later in life he recalled his move to Wellington:

> Preparations for my future life were simple. On the old family sewing machine (it made a noise like a chaff-cutter) my mother made down my elder brother's overcoat so that it fitted me – in parts. Out of my father's weekly salary of £2.11.0 he produced a pound for me. As neither suitcase nor portmanteau was available, a 'wee kist' was rummaged up from among the family lumber, into which box were packed my few possessions. Thus proudly equipped for my new life, at sixteen I crossed the straits for the first time, to land, a complete stranger, on the wharf at Wellington.

As assistant to Roland Pope, Beck visited all the industrial schools and reformatories. In 1907 he toured children's courts and child welfare institutions in New South Wales. As with his later trip to Canada and North America in 1925, this exposure to other child welfare systems would provide him with ideas relevant to his work in New Zealand.[5]

Happy, healthy family life was the right of all children, according to child welfare agencies, and especially important for rebuilding the population after the loss of life during the First World War.
G. LESLIE ADKIN COLLECTION, MUSEUM OF NEW ZEALAND TE PAPA TONGAREWA, A.006390

Beck's visits to state and private industrial schools gave him valuable first-hand knowledge of the system. Looking back on his experiences, he suggested that only those 'versed in the inner workings' of institutions could be aware of the 'grave abuses which undoubtedly existed, abuses which were all the more difficult to combat because of the diversity of types [of residents] admitted'. 'Slowly, but very definitely,' he asserted, rather self-importantly:

> the realisation was borne in upon me that these institutions, belonging as they did to a past era, were long outmoded, and that drastic changes in the system were an urgent necessity. And with the realisation grew a mounting ambition that I should be the one chosen to undertake this humanitarian reform.[6]

Hanan's 1917 report may have been the first major public indication that changes were afoot in the industrial school system, but Beck had mooted the proposals within the Department some months earlier when he took over from Pope as head of the Special Schools Section.[7] Between 1917 and mid-1920 Beck issued a steady series of statements which outlined the rationale for change, described the proposals in detail, and reported on the developments enacted.

Economically and socially, reframing the industrial school system seemed to make good sense. As human capital and social assets, children were investments for the future and the wellspring of continued racial health. It was with these sentiments in mind that the child welfare system was overhauled in three key areas: the industrial school population was reduced by reclassifying residents and making greater use of boarding out; the probation system was extended; and legislation to provide a foundation for these and other changes was enacted.

A 'systematic purging': the demise of the industrial schools

The Child Welfare Act 1925 expunged the term 'industrial school' from the Education Department vocabulary. This terminological expulsion marked the final stage of a reorganisation of the institutions which began in 1916 and involved the closure of some homes and the refocusing of others. As with the second round of institutional closure and reorganisation which occurred from the mid-1980s, the changes between 1916 and 1925 were difficult to implement. Opposition was strong as some officers in the Department, seemingly 'ahead' of public opinion, gave practical force to their belief in the value of family life for children and young people.

Changes in the industrial school system occurred alongside continuities in other aspects of the state care of children and young people. The practice of infant life protection work, adoption and boarding out remained largely unaltered; the Education Department maintained its ambivalent relationship with private welfare groups, disparaging the system of private institutions but calling on voluntary aid for assistance in probation work. The modifications in the system around these services nevertheless had an impact on them. Boarding out and probation both became central to the new child welfare system, and this centrality meant that there was greater cooperation with families, and with religious and community groups which were enlarging their own spheres of social work.

The industrial school system had become increasingly overloaded by the time Beck assumed control in 1916. The number of children and young people under the Department's charge increased from the beginning of the First World War, a rise in the residential population of 300 in three years reflecting an overall increase in the number committed to the care of the state and matching a drop in the proportion boarded out from institutions.[8] The consequent overcrowding in rundown facilities placed a strain on already inefficient classification systems; according to Beck, some institutions were 'overflowing'.[9] These pressures coincided with a wartime reduction in staffing numbers and curtailment of expenditure. Many years later Beck recalled the level of financial stringency operating within the industrial school system at this time. The expenditure of £100 to repair the lighting at Te Oranga was refused. Unable to install a new system, the institution had to make do with a gas-fired arrangement powered by a system of water wheels, a small motor and pulleys, attended to daily by the gardener, whose task it was to wind the pulleys. Under such circumstances the reorganisation of industrial schools became a matter of necessity.[10]

The Department's time-honoured and traditional response was to increase the availability of accommodation at the institutions. Initially it suggested augmenting the facilities at Burnham, Te Oranga and the Auckland Industrial School, and building a completely new institution. The high cost of doing this, estimated at about £36,500 in capital expenditure and an annual upkeep of £10,500, was sufficient to shelve the proposal.[11] Whether such plans were considered seriously is unlikely, given the trend in New Zealand and internationally away from large institutions.

From the beginning of 1917, Beck extended further the idea that institutionalisation was the least desirable response to most of the children committed to the care of the state. He allowed that institutions occupied a 'valuable and necessary' place for children of 'vicious' habits and those who could not be immediately boarded out. For the normal healthy child, however, boarding out was the closest approximation to a regular home life. 'Only those who have come in close contact with the institution-bred child', he argued, 'can realize the tremendous handicap with which he begins life in the outside world.'[12]

Beck embarked on what he termed a 'systematic purging' of the industrial schools. Proceeding on the principle that many residents were in institutions through no fault of their own, but because of destitution or parental neglect, he argued that they required only the opportunity to 'prove' themselves. Beck visited most institutions early in 1917, identifying those fit for service or boarding out and removing them. He took issue with the detention of residents for any longer than was necessary. Not only did this affect a young person's chances for rehabilitation by leaving him or her 'completely institutionalised', it could also cause anguish for families. 'Later . . . I was to meet many a parent embittered by the fact that their son had been returned too late to be successfully re-absorbed into the family', he noted.[13]

The residences for boys and young men at Weraroa and Stoke, the Auckland Industrial School, and the Te Oranga and Burnham reformatories came in for particular scrutiny. Beck cut a swathe through each, reducing their population dramatically by reclassifying the residents to other homes, sending them to service, or authorising their boarding out. The combined population of Weraroa and Stoke was halved, from more than 400 to 190; and the Auckland Industrial School's list of 50 children deemed unsuitable for fostering was reduced to three after Beck re-examined their case histories. During 1917 and 1918 Beck reduced the population of other institutions. From about 1000 industrial school residents in December 1916, the number had fallen to around 500 by December 1918, as Figure 2 indicates. By the end of 1918 the reduction enabled the closure of the Te Oranga and Burnham reformatories, and the reclassification of the Auckland Industrial School as a receiving home.[14]

The Department's most recent institution, the Special School at Otekaike, also came in for rigorous inspection, and was found wanting. No expert in the treatment of the 'feeble-minded', Beck concluded that Otekaike housed too many boys of 'obviously . . . low-grade mentality' who could not profit by the training. Its staff were inexperienced; one was characterised as drunken and lazy, while another was rude to the residents; and the farm had been badly neglected. Beck blamed the Manager, George Benstead, who had been allowed several years of 'over indulgence' in running the institution with a free hand. Faced with the choice of having his administration subjected to a full inquiry or resigning,

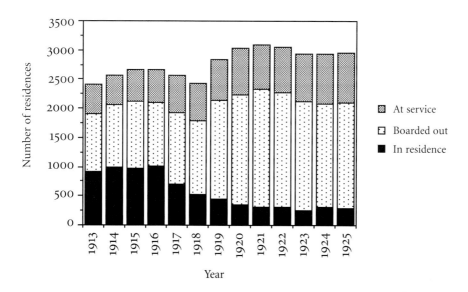

FIGURE 2 *Number of young people in residence, boarded out and at service, 1913–1925*

Benstead took the latter option. Beck remained at the home for a month, during which the parents of 'the mongols and cretins, epileptics and low-grade spastics' were asked to move their children elsewhere, and the institution was thereafter able to admit only boys classed generally as 'backward'.[15]

Most of those removed from departmental institutions were boarded out or placed at service; probation was reserved for those newly before the courts and for 'approved' residents of the institutions. Boarding out children had become more difficult during the war years as the Department refused to increase the rates of payment, expecting foster parents to put up with the low rates 'as a matter of course' as part of wartime privations. The need to reduce the number of industrial school residents forced the Department to reassess its stance on the issue, and in mid-1917 it raised the rates for children under twelve. A more generous clothing allowance was granted, and the boarding-out rates were increased again during the 1919 financial year. More frequent inspection of homes also became possible thanks to the appointment of additional women as boarding-out officers from 1917, and in the long-neglected provincial and rural areas from 1919.

The Department used the extension of boarding out as a further opportunity to castigate private and religious institutions for their continued refusal to adopt it to any serious extent. Beck claimed that by allowing church and other social service groups to continue with large-scale institutionalisation – 'which has been abandoned even in England for some years' – the state was enabling them to 'exploit and experiment with' the young life of New Zealand.[16] The growing number of children's homes and particularly orphanages was also anathema to the Department's officers, who had the power to inspect them, but not to enforce their recommendations for boarding out. 'To put the matter briefly,' Beck thundered:

> the State has allowed private enterprise under the guise of benevolence to step in and handle the children of the State under a system that is obsolete, without any Government supervision either as regards the establishment of institutions, the selection of children who are admitted to these institutions, or the training and ultimate destiny of the children so dealt with.[17]

These were strong words and cannot have eased the sometimes tense relationship between the Department and private services.

The Department experienced few difficulties in placing other residents in service positions. In some respects its policy of removing employable young people from the industrial schools helped satisfy the wartime demand for labour. Beck could find little justification for keeping the residences 'full to overflowing' when there was 'a cry from one end of the country to the other for farm workers and domestic servants'.[18] During 1917 and 1918 the Department increased the proportion of those under its authority at service from 16 to over 20 per cent, with most placed in either farm work or domestic service.

The reorganisation of the industrial school system proceeded amidst criticisms; Beck later identified 'officialdom, and public opinion' as the two principal opponents of his scheme.[19] Departmental criticisms came from older officers such as Roland Pope, Sarah Jackson and Thomas Archey, the Manager of Burnham. These officials had been trained under an older system and disagreed with the scope of deinstitutionalisation. Pope and Jackson remained unconvinced of the merits of widespread boarding out. 'Normal' children, each claimed, would respond well to boarding out with suitable foster parents, but pernicious results could be expected if this was done indiscriminately or in unsuitable cases.[20]

Extending boarding out sometimes provoked adverse comment in the districts where the children and young people were maintained. Residents of the Auckland suburbs of New Lynn and Henderson took exception to boarded-out children attending local schools. Howard Ellis, the Principal of the New Lynn School, claimed that former industrial school residents lowered the average mental capacity of the pupils and 'contaminated' the other children. Rather than jeopardise his plans, Beck agreed to notify Ellis of the particulars of all the boarded-out children, in exchange for Ellis's undertaking that he would treat them 'humanely' and sympathetically. Less than a year later, however, Ellis threatened to hold an 'indignation meeting' unless the Department removed the children from his school.[21]

The closure of the Te Oranga and Burnham reformatories generated the greatest controversy in public, and the bitterest quarrels within the Department. Beck had long been concerned about the mixing of neglected, destitute and delinquent young men and boys at Burnham. Many 'big boys' over school age, he believed, had been sent to the institution merely as punishment, without any attempt being made to change their behaviour. Beck had not initially intended to close Burnham, but devised plans for the removal of its 'incorrigible' residents as a means of reducing the problems of the institution. He changed his mind and recommended its complete closure after a visit in late 1917.[22]

Beck found much to fault in the staff, too, and considered the Manager and Matron honest in their intention to assist those under their charge, but too old to change their methods. He condemned the Manager's practice of 'roaring' at the boys and publicising their misdemeanours to the other residents. 'Boyish pranks' were treated too severely, the detention yard was used with frequency for trivial matters, and the Deputy Manager's tendency to grant favours to residents who informed on their fellows was criticised. Beck was also concerned that the

Vocational training, such as basket-making, had different meanings in boys' and girls' institutions. The small dainty items – useful for storing knitting – of the Richmond Special School for Girls (above) contrast with the sturdy chairs made in the Otekaike Special School for Boys (opposite).
DEPARTMENT OF SOCIAL WELFARE

residents received only a smattering of practical training, being taught to repair boots, for instance, but not to make them. In all, he pronounced, the residents were made to feel more like prisoners than 'industrial school boys'.[23]

The number of residents was reduced steadily during the last months of 1917, but matters came to a head over the placement of 25 who had been at the home for as long as nine years. These, Beck noted, were 'the incorrigibles who were detained in the detention house under prison conditions, the Manager considering that none of them was fit to be allowed out'. No doubt to suit his own agenda that the administration of Burnham required wholesale change, Beck preferred to identify these residents as 'the unfortunate products of an effete system' who had been 'stranded' at the reformatory with little chance of making good.[24] This may well have been the case, but Beck used the opportunity to exert his authority over industrial school staff whom he considered to be out of step with modern trends in childcare. In opposition to the Manager at Burnham, who believed that eight of the 25 should remain there, Beck transferred all of them to Weraroa. Placed under a 'modified control' with considerable freedom as a prelude to their release into the community, the young men may have exercised

an unintended influence on their new residence; within a year, Weraroa's Manager complained of an 'epidemic' of absconding.[25] Beck's actions earned a sharp rebuke from the Minister, who learned of the transfer only after it had taken place. Normally an ally of Beck, Hanan took a dim view of such a flagrant disregard for procedure, and of Beck's failure to clear the transfer with himself or follow the Department's policy that changes be made cautiously, with each stage reviewed carefully.[26] The episode was indicative both of the power Beck could assume as a reform-minded public servant, and of the tenuous authority on which many of the changes were made.

Plans for the closure of the Te Oranga Reformatory arose relatively late in Beck's institutional proposals. Initially Beck and Hanan had considered that if most difficult young women were removed, the home could function smoothly. Beck imagined it as a Christchurch Training School for Girls, which would take in young women who required domestic training; later, he thought it could be utilised as an institution for boys, or handed over to the Prisons Department. A visit to the home in 1917 changed his views. Beck found the home, in a 'grim building' surrounded by a twelve-foot-high fence, to be in a 'chaotic state'. Frequent changes of manager had left the institution leaderless and the staff at liberty to act as they pleased in administering discipline.[27]

Te Oranga's closure caused little departmental comment but generated considerable community concern. Beck later reflected that he was aware that the

The Te Oranga Reformatory for Girls is shown before the removal of bars and wire-netting from the windows. DEPARTMENT OF SOCIAL WELFARE

closure would be 'worse even than the struggle over Burnham, for situated as the buildings were on the outskirts of a city, public opinion, I felt sure, would be a potent force against me. In this surmise I was correct.'[28] The number in residence fell from 40 to five, and the home closed in November 1918. Nearly all the residents were placed in service positions in and around Christchurch, and although Beck expected a number of them to 'fail' – presumably meaning that they would reoffend – few did.[29] Local people were not enthusiastic about the sudden presence in their midst of a large number of female 'sexual delinquents'. Women's, religious and welfare groups met during 1918 to protest against the decision. Wanting to safeguard the well-being of the community by detaining young women whose sexual activities were regarded as inappropriate, these groups asked the Department to reassess its turning loose of 'wayward' young women to wreak havoc in the community. According to Beck, the atmosphere in the meetings was hostile and the speeches against the Department bitter: 'One well-known Christchurch minister, pointing at me an accusing finger, stated that no decent lad would be safe in the community!'[30] Throughout the early 1920s local groups petitioned that the home be reopened, claiming that it would be a deterrent against 'immorality' and single motherhood.[31] Burnham's residents,

'The Rosebuds', Caversham 'Receiving Home' – a photographic tableau presented to John Beck in the mid-1920s. DEPARTMENT OF SOCIAL WELFARE

while perhaps equally 'incorrigible' and difficult, were evidently not as 'immoral'. The closure of that reformatory did not attract equivalent local condemnation, and the sexual behaviour of its residents aroused scant comment.

The major changes to the industrial school system had been effected by 1920. Receiving homes operated in Auckland, Hamilton, Napier, Wellington, Nelson and Christchurch, taking in young children and screening others before placement. The Boys' Training Farm at Stoke was reserved for younger feeble-minded boys, and Otekaike for the older ones; the Richmond School for Feeble-minded Girls, opened in 1916, continued much as before. Only two longer-term residential institutions remained: Caversham for girls, young women and young boys, and Weraroa for older boys and young men. Both acted as central institutions for those who were believed to require special training before being placed out to service or with foster parents. All the other institutions had been closed or reclassified. None of the homes was now known officially as an industrial school.

In 'natural surroundings': the extension of probation services

Extension of the fledgling probation system was, according to Beck, the cornerstone on which all of the changes to the industrial schools rested.[32] As Hanan noted, probation's central merit was its preventive rather than punitive nature; it 'has for its object the strengthening of character in these children in the natural surroundings of their own homes'.[33] The expansion of probation before 1920 was focused on three main areas: the appointment of probation officers for both boys and girls in the main centres; the establishment of short-term probation homes; and the enhancement of the power of probation officers and placing of their work on a solid legal basis. From 1920 the Department consolidated and extended these changes, and adopted newer forms of probation, including assistance to new private probation schemes, an informal probation whereby a magistrate adjourned a case for a fixed period while the young person was placed under supervision, and an even more informal system which bypassed the courts entirely.

Beck outlined the extended system in early 1917. Probation homes would be established along the lines of the makeshift 'home' which Frederick Shell had operated from his own premises in Auckland since 1913. These homes would be small institutions, initially for boys, providing temporary accommodation for those whom magistrates deemed to require a short period in an institution rather than longer-term admission to Weraroa. Boys being transferred from one institution to another, or between service positions, would also use the probation home instead of being detained temporarily in police stations. The specially-appointed probation officers who would run the homes would have an extensive supervisory role over the boys both when they were with their families and when they were at service. The homes would differ physically from the earlier industrial schools by providing individual cubicles in place of the large or small dormitories or cottages of other institutions.[34]

The Statute Law Amendment Act 1917 provided the legal machinery for the introduction of both probation officers and the homes. The first probation officers were gazetted from April 1918: they were Frederick Shell and Caroline Brooke for the Auckland region; John Dineen for Wellington, Marlborough and the West Coast; Alexander Bissett for Canterbury and the West Coast; and William Fullarton for Otago and Southland. Others followed as the scheme was expanded into provincial areas such as Whangarei, Hamilton and Nelson from 1920, and Napier, Invercargill, Palmerston North and Greymouth from 1921. All women boarding-out officers and managers of receiving homes were gazetted as juvenile probation officers from 1921. Probation homes – all for boys – had been opened in the four main centres by 1920.[35]

The 1917 legislation also clarified the anomalous standing of the probation officer. Shell had earlier drawn attention to problems with his quasi-legal status, and in 1916 Beck had sought to remedy this. It was 'absolutely necessary', he argued, that something be done to give Shell – and future probation officers – the correct power to deal with young offenders.[36] From 1917 probation officers were given the powers, protection and privileges of police constables in the execution of their duties. This meant they could conduct full inquiries into each case, provided them with an official status in court, and enabled them to cooperate with the police in passing on to magistrates relevant information about cases. Most importantly, they now had the legal power to deal with children and young persons without having them committed to institutions or nominally to the control of the managers of the homes. Shell had experienced problems with institutional staff who had considered probationers to be under their jurisdiction. The new power of probation staff enabled them to do away with the awkward fiction of committal to a residence.

The varied work of probation required officers with a range of skills. Training was provided on the job as officers learnt by experience, trial and error. Even so, the successful officer needed 'exceptional qualifications': 'he must possess initiative, be sympathetic though firm, and must at all times be prepared to devote the whole of his time to his work. For the man who carries out his duties properly there can be no fixed hours – he must be prepared to respond at all times to any call for assistance or advice.'[37] Given these requirements, it is perhaps not surprising that the Department had some difficulty in recruiting suitable men and women.

Probation involved a varied and significant daily round of duty. 'From a social point of view', Beck claimed, 'probation may be said to be a process of educational guidance through friendly supervision. Mere surveillance is not probation. Probation is an intimate personal relationship which deals with all the factors of a child's life – particularly his home.'[38] Probation officers were empowered to investigate cases as soon as they became aware of them, either through information provided by the police or as a result of their own inquiries. They did so by visiting homes, schools or workplaces to interview family, friends and employers, and to check on the conditions in which young people lived and worked.

The relationship with the young person and his or her parents was critical, especially for periods of supervision lasting a year or more. Gaining the confidence of parents and child, the first step in this relationship, required probation staff to be fully conversant with family and home circumstances. Once an officer had got to know the child and family, a plan of supervision could be devised as he or she set about re-educating them. Parents were informed of their responsibilities towards their children and the need to set a good example; chats with the child emphasised the need to 'stand loyal to all good principles' in life and to 'do right'.[39] Child re-education took a tangible turn: library and recreation club membership, suitable employment, advice on banking and purchasing, and a correspondence and home visiting regime.

The changes to the industrial school system between 1916 and 1918 added significantly to the responsibilities of all probation officers, particularly as more children and young persons of both sexes were being placed on probation. Only fourteen young people were on probation in Auckland in 1914; four years later the number had soared to 207. By the middle of 1920, Beck estimated that about 85 per cent of those appearing before the courts were placed on probation. His figures were a little optimistic. Of 818 children and young people before the courts in 1919, 224 were placed on probation, 166 were admonished and discharged, and 253 were sent to institutions; the remainder were either fined, or the cases were adjourned or withdrawn. The caseloads of officers could be onerous. Less than a year after the appointment of officers in each of the four main centres and assistant officers in Auckland and Wellington, Beck called for more personnel. Using as a benchmark the United States, where 40 was

Encouraging young people to join clubs, such as this Boy Scout troop which is preparing for a hike, was a cornerstone of the probation system. S. C. SMITH COLLECTION, ATL, G-46850-1/2

considered to be the maximum caseload, Beck argued that New Zealand officers were overloaded and the success of the scheme was threatened: in a combination of formal and informal probation, the two Auckland officers shared 268 cases, the two in Wellington shared 397, and the sole officers in Christchurch and Dunedin had 110 and 119 cases respectively.[40]

While home visiting and supervision formed the core of a probation officer's activities, there were other aspects to the work. Probation officers assumed some of the tasks of the managers of residential institutions, whose work was increasingly restricted to the administration of the homes, perhaps because many of them had neglected their institutions in favour of visiting children in the community. Probation officers were expected to supervise all residents at service, to collect maintenance money from the parents who contributed to their child's upkeep, and to provide assistance in finding employment for ex-residents and those taken off probation. Magistrates, or parents, could also call on the officers to administer a 'thrashing' to unruly youngsters.[41]

From 1919, the Department experimented with its range of probation services. In that year it enabled parents who were having difficulty with their children to bypass the courts and seek the assistance of probation officers privately. Supervision could be arranged for 'uncontrollable' children who required firmer discipline. Beck claimed this service was particularly useful to women, on whom fell the task of controlling children while their husbands were absent from home. Such preventive probation work became increasingly important; in 1925, probation officers assisted 283 families and 526 children in this way.[42]

The Department interpreted these figures as proof of the success and community acceptance of its work, and in many respects this may have been the case. Parents previously faced with the prospect of having their child incarcerated, often far from home, for a long period may have welcomed the introduction of probation as a way of maintaining their household. Others may have found the visits from probation officers a relief from their own burden of childcare, a chance to discuss their child's well-being and future, or an opportunity to assert their authority over their offspring. As many may have experienced probation as an intrusion into their lives, and tolerated only grudgingly and superficially the advice dispensed.

Community 'acceptance' of the scheme also involved greater community participation, and from the early 1920s the Department embraced the assistance with probation provided by voluntary and religious organisations which had increased their social work during the first two decades of the century. In an uncharacteristically charitable response towards any type of voluntary social work, Beck waxed lyrical about the merits of one scheme, the Big Brothers of the YMCA:

This movement may . . . be regarded as the most important contribution on progressive lines that has been made of recent times by private effort to the community welfare work of the Dominion, and marks the beginning of a system providing for sympathetic and practical co-operation between the Department's welfare officers and members of social organizations, a beginning that it is hoped will develop and extend in the direction of providing in the incipient stages for the friendly supervision, guidance, and assistance by private effort of the whole of the small army of young people who through the indifference of the parents, improper home conditions, or lack of proper environment are likely to develop along antisocial lines or become liabilities instead of assets to the State.[43]

By the 1920s, of course, the demands of the probation services were exerting considerable pressure on a Department which found itself unable to respond to all cases. Enlisting the aid of private and church groups eased the burdens on departmental staff, who could farm out some of their less difficult cases.

Of the various forms of church and private social work, that provided by the YMCA Big Brother movement was the most significant for probation. Other groups, such as the Presbyterian Social Services Association and the Salvation Army, provided probation assistance on a smaller scale. The Big Brother movement was formed in 1922 to supervise boys and young men whom the Department had recommended for probation. The scheme started in a small way in Auckland with four boys, but grew steadily until by mid-1924 almost 100 had been supervised. Only five of these were deemed failures and subsequently committed to an institution. Each probationer was assigned a Big Brother, normally a successful young man who was not so far removed from his own youth as to have forgotten 'what it feels like to be a boy'.[44] Like the Department's staff, the Big Brothers paid regular visits to the homes or workplaces of their 'little brothers', persuading them to join the YMCA or cultivating a 'healthier interest' in life by encouraging them to join sports teams or night classes. A Roman Catholic version began in 1923, and in 1924 the YMCA scheme was extended to the other main centres, as well as Wanganui and Palmerston North.

The Department had no doubts about the importance, implications, or success of the extended probation system; the involvement of private groups was further evidence of the system's success. Within months of inaugurating the system, the Department claimed a 97 per cent 'success rate', which it reiterated throughout the 1910s and 1920s; only a minority of probationers 'failed' and were committed to an institution. This type of 'success' could be measured in financial terms as well. Probation was a cheaper option than institutionalisation, and Beck was fond of pointing out the savings that had accrued since 1917. By the time most

People living in isolated rural districts, such as this Maori family, had little contact with the child welfare system, which was predominantly urban until the 1920s. ATL, G-7840-1/1

of the changes had been initiated in 1920, he estimated the gross savings to be over £67,000 in capital expenditure and £60,000 in annual maintenance costs.[45]

Not everyone was convinced of the merits of probation. Roland Pope and Sarah Jackson, who were dubious about extending boarding out, also expressed doubts about expanding probation. Pope suggested that the Department instead use groups like Dunedin's Presbyterian Social Services, which had provided supervision since 1913 at no cost to the government. Extending probation to girls and young women was as problematic as closing Te Oranga had been. Worry about the deleterious consequences of placing female sexual delinquents in the community led to condemnations of this option for young women.[46] A group of residents of suburban Auckland protested vehemently, but unsuccessfully, against the attendance at the local school of children from the Mount Albert Probation

Home. The probationers, some of whom 'had not only been convicted, but were morally deficient', were seen to pose a 'serious menace' to the moral well-being of the other pupils, and some parents were contemplating removing their children from the school.[47] Newspapers alleged that probation was a soft option for young offenders. 'A right good thrashing is a pretty fair corrective for many a juvenile side-stepping', *Truth* claimed, lamenting that magistrates could order a 'mental tonic and a straightening up of that old-fashioned kind' only upon conviction or with parental consent.[48] Beck addressed such criticism in his 1925 report, suggesting that probation was being regarded less and less as mere discharge, or 'letting off' young people too easily.[49]

The probation system was presented as – and indeed was – the major means at the Department's disposal for saving and influencing the post-war generation. Beck expressed clearly the necessity for this:

> In view of the drain on the resources of the Dominion during the period of the war, and of the need now to increase our productive powers, it is essential that the country should protect and foster its children, that it should utilize the most effective means of conserving the health of the young of the nation, and should so train them that they will be strong and vigorous to carry on not only the vocations of peace but also the practice of war if that be required.[50]

Preventing children from becoming burdens on the state was the recurring motif in the Department's rhetoric. This had advantages which could be portrayed financially and socially, but also had far deeper resonance in post-war society. Not only was it the state's duty to prevent the burden of dependency, Beck argued, 'it is much more economical in the end – to ensure that the destitute neglected and dependent children and juvenile delinquents are given a fair chance in decent surroundings to grow up healthy and vigorous and law abiding in order that they may become future assets, instead of permanent burdens on the community in the form of paupers and criminals'.[51] Probation provided the Department's officers with a unique opportunity to influence parents as well as children in a way that boarding out could not. As Beck noted, home visiting enabled probation officers to insist on changes on the part of the parents and in home conditions as part of the probationer's reformative programme.[52] In this respect, the extension of probation signalled a new direction in state intervention in family life. Officials now entered homes in greater numbers and with more frequency than before, seeking to influence domestic arrangements as a means of reforming both children and parents, rather than extricating children from the family environment. In the process, dependency on the state could be reinforced, rather than removed.

On a proper footing: a legal basis for the changes

The permutations involved in establishing a workable nationwide probation system exposed the disadvantages of proceeding on shaky legal foundations. Giving legislative effect to the new mode of working for children's welfare had become a matter of urgency by the early 1920s, when most of the changes to the industrial school system and the care of committed children had been enacted. Children's courts continued to operate in an ad hoc fashion as they had for nearly two decades, but it was clearly desirable to have the system formalised and made uniform; this would also keep New Zealand abreast of international developments.

Beck mooted the idea of introducing legislation to encompass the changes in the first months of 1917, and Hanan repeated the suggestion in his special report on the industrial school system later that year.[53] Both men envisaged the establishment of a legal basis for probation homes, better protection for neglected and deserted children, the reorganisation of industrial schools, provision for the inspection of private homes, and the implementation of a special children's court system. Beck's staff collected material on overseas child welfare legislation from mid-1917, and prepared drafts of legislation shortly thereafter. By late 1920 they had prepared a 'children's code' which outlined the legislative requirements.[54] Despite almost yearly promises in Parliament that the child welfare legislation would be introduced 'this session', no bill was introduced until 1925. Beck later recalled: 'With the passing of the Child Welfare Act of 1925 ... I had a feeling of great relief and satisfaction that the long struggle against the – at times – baffling indifference of the authorities both in and out of the Department and the resentment of the old-timers, who lacked the vision to see the necessity of progression, was nearing an end. For nearly ten years the lone-handed struggle had gone on.'[55]

Never one to shirk his claim to an idea, Beck was nevertheless perceptive in his assessment of this 'baffling indifference'. He could dismiss the criticism of retired or junior officers, but opposition or inactivity from his superiors was another matter. Beck had never been on good terms with his immediate superior, the Assistant-Director of Education, John Caughley, preferring to deal with the Director, William Anderson. Caughley's elevation to the position of Director in 1920 eroded the relationship further. Beck now chose to bypass the Director and to go straight to his Minister, whom he informed verbally of new policy directions and other changes.[56]

Caughley's rise came shortly after the departure from Cabinet in August 1919 of the Liberal Josiah Hanan when the wartime National ministry was dissolved. This deprived Beck of one of his staunchest allies; Hanan's replacement, Francis

Dillon Bell, remained as Minister of Education for only a few months, not long enough to push through the desired legislation. Bell's successor, James Parr, had a strained relationship with Beck, with whom he crossed swords over a number of matters in the early 1920s.[57] While Beck is a vivid example of the power public servants could wield in early twentieth-century New Zealand, he also exemplifies some of the difficulties they faced in doing so. Without firm and enduring political supporters prepared to legislate for policy changes, proposals could be stymied and left to wallow in legal uncertainty.

The delays in having a child welfare bill introduced in Parliament led Beck to pen an impassioned demand for action in his official report for 1920. Claiming that it was difficult to perceive any more important function of government at the time than the care of future citizens, he angrily condemned the existing regime. He described the Industrial Schools Act as almost obsolete, and criticised the tendency to treat young offenders as adults because of the failure to establish a separate children's court system. 'In nearly every enlightened country in the world', he argued, 'it has been realized that the methods adopted for the punishment of adult offenders cannot be applied in the case of children.' This report and the 'fierce storm of criticism' which followed, Beck alleged, caused Parr to retreat from introducing legislation in 1920 or 1921.[58]

Although there was a degree of community disquiet about the changes taking place in the industrial school system and the use of probation, there were also demands for further change. Various community, religious and welfare groups advocated a child welfare bill that would give recognition to the changes and introduce new measures such as children's courts.[59] From the early 1920s Beck utilised this community support to exert pressure for the enactment of his proposed legislation. In particular, he relied on the efforts of the Auckland Community Welfare Council. The Council, a coalition of more than twenty welfare societies, was formed in Auckland in the early 1920s to discuss child welfare issues. Using information supplied by Beck, the YMCA and other societies within the Council had drawn up a 'children's charter', which outlined the need for legislative changes, children's courts and extended probation. The charter also borrowed from the League of Nations' Children's Charter, promulgated in Geneva in 1924, which stated, among other things, that the 'delinquent child must be reclaimed'.[60] Following deputations from this and other groups, Parr accepted the charter as the basis for legislative change. Once before the house, the Child Welfare Bill proceeded smoothly and quickly. First read in July 1925, it was passed in October and came into effect in April 1926.[61]

A long delay between the first plans for new legislation and the passage of a bill was to be characteristic of child welfare legislation in the twentieth century.

The pattern begun with the Child Welfare Act 1925 would be repeated for the Children and Young Persons Act 1974, and the Children, Young Persons, and Their Families Act 1989. Each piece of legislation was recast and reworked, with new policies included and others discarded. Part of the delay in each case was due to attempts to incorporate as much as possible in the legislation. In addition to changes in institutions, boarding out, probation and juvenile justice, Beck sought also to include in the Child Welfare Act limitations on child labour, an expansion of child health and medical services, and greater coordination of social welfare initiatives for children.

Of these issues, the regulation of children's labour was the most significant and potentially far-reaching. The Department had identified work such as street trading and employment in places of entertainment as primary causes of delinquency among boys and young men. Beck estimated that between 60 and 85 per cent of those committed to the care of the state had been engaged in street trading of some sort, be it selling newspapers of an evening or purveying confectionery and tickets at picture theatres.[62] To combat the 'pernicious influence' of casual trading, he proposed to enhance the powers of probation officers by giving them the authority to supervise all street traders. This would be complemented by a system of regulation and the licensing of those youths for whom it could be proved that work would not endanger their physical and moral welfare, or their attendance at school.[63]

Children's street labour had been a matter of public attention for some time, with responsibility for it laid squarely at the feet of parents. Lack of parental control, monotonous or 'sordid' home conditions, insufficient domestic comforts and the failure of parents to retain their children's attention all contributed to producing youths for whom 'the streets are the evening schools'.[64] Richard Seddon's Liberal government had prohibited children under twelve from trading in the streets, while the Protection of Children Act 1906 restricted the type of public entertainment children could perform. Further restrictions exposed the ambivalence of attitudes towards children's labour. As the sociologist Viviana Zelizer has argued, the issue was not one of whether or not children should work, but what constituted acceptable work.[65] After all, children in industrial schools and reformatories worked in the institutions and on the farms attached to them, and were sent out to service at a young age to earn their keep. Economic arguments were also important. Responding to Hanan's call for greater legislative protection for children, Reform Party Prime Minister William Massey claimed that if the government prevented boys from earning pocket money, it would probably cause hardship to many families. Children's street labour could be legitimated as inculcating habits of independence and business skills which would stand them in good stead later in life.[66]

The objections that were raised to children's street labour and work in picture theatres focused primarily on moral dangers rather than the nature of the work. The streets and places of public entertainment were presented as undesirable spaces for unchaperoned children. Beck claimed in 1920 that 200 children were charged before the courts each year for offences they had committed mainly because of ideas and suggestions they had picked up though viewing picture shows.[67] There is an echo here of the earlier anxiety over the larrikin nuisance. The solution, for Beck and a range of organisations, was more censorship of films, and general restrictions on the types and places of entertainment which children could attend, and the hours during which they could do so.

Moral implications could be perceived from physical appearances. Street traders, according to Beck, were 'easily distinguishable from the other residents in the majority of cases by their poor physique and miserable appearance generally'.[68] Tired and overworked children could not concentrate on their

This Wanganui girl looks cheerful enough as a walking advertisement for Durodown Mattresses, but child welfare reformers claimed that such street employment led to child delinquency and moral decay. ATL, G-21114-1/1

studies. Thirteen year old James Cotton of Dunedin, for example, rose at 4 a.m. to meet the milk-cart and work until school began at 9. Immediately after school he delivered milk again before going to the 'vaudeville', where he made up packets of sweets to sell, arriving home at 11 p.m. During the day he was so weary that he was 'quite unable' to attend to his lessons, and was 'naturally more inclined *to sleep*'.[69]

Restrictions on neither street trading nor the attendance of children at places of public entertainment appeared in the Child Welfare Act. Instead, the legislation allowed for the issuing of regulations to deal with these matters. Parr suggested that his Department would find it preferable to deal with cases of street trading as they arose, rather than by proscribing all activities.[70] Children's labour, and street trading in particular, remained issues throughout the 1920s and 1930s, but no regulations were introduced.

There was a similar reluctance to incorporate in the legislation the health or medical services which Beck and Caughley advocated. In early 1919 Beck sketched a scheme to enhance considerably the work of the Department's infant life protection staff. He suggested that they liaise closely with the Plunket Society, to ensure there was a plentiful supply of humanised milk in each centre and to run milk depots and baby centres where infants could receive regular health checks. He also suggested that the Department establish cottage homes to which a woman could send children to convalesce or while she was giving birth, and refuges for the children of single mothers.[71]

Beck framed these proposals in terms of national efficiency and the saving of child life. Because of the wastage of human life during the war, he argued, everything possible should be done to protect and foster infants and young children.[72] He also presented these innovations as a means of coordinating under the Education Department the disparate services provided for children's welfare. The notion of the Department as a coordinating agency was novel, but the desire to define its sphere of influence with respect to other departments or social service groups harked back to an earlier period. As before, the Department sought to establish the parameters of its relationship with the Plunket Society. The teaching of mothercraft skills to those whose children were born within marriage should be left to the Plunket Society, Beck explained; it carried out work of national importance. Illegitimate children and unfit parents, however, were better off under the expert guidance of state officials.[73]

Beck condemned the 'haphazard' manner of caring for destitute and dependent children; there was no controlling authority, and 'an utter lack of cooperation even between Government Departments'.[74] Rather than taking over the work of voluntary agencies, Beck and Caughley suggested, the Education Department should oversee greater cooperation between agencies. Caughley argued that the Department should not only deal with the aspects of child welfare work which had been assigned to it, but should act as a central agency, making the services of other organisations more efficient, proffering advice, and preventing overlapping effort.[75] As the central child welfare agency, the Education Department would have carved out a powerful niche for itself, enabling it to control the expanding policy sphere of infant and child well-being. No doubt Beck saw this also as an opportunity to bring into the fold the various private children's homes which refused to adhere to his notions of child welfare.

With the exception of provision for convalescent homes for children, the final legislation contained none of the recommendations concerning health and medicine, nor the coordinating role. There was already a plethora of health and medical initiatives for children and infants under the guidance of Truby King in the Child Welfare Division of the Department of Health, and there may well have been a desire on the government's part to avoid a duplication of effort. The drawbacks of giving too prominent – and influential – a role to the Education Department was also a consideration. Parr had expressed anxiety about the authority to stop street trading which the Department would be able to assume by issuing regulations under the Child Welfare Act. This invested too much power in one Department, he believed, and a coordinating child welfare role for the Department would afford it equivalent powers and more.[76] The government and senior officials in the Education Department continued to decline similar demands from Beck and welfare groups during the later 1920s and 1930s.

Beck's legislative plans had encompassed a panoramic sweep of responsibilities for the new Child Welfare Branch; the final result was somewhat less than he had anticipated. Most of the provisions of the Act were not new, but consolidated existing practices and, most importantly, placed them on a legal foundation. Nonetheless, the significance of the Child Welfare Act should not be under-estimated. The enshrining in statute of the changes which had taken place over the previous decade marked a clear break with the philosophy which had guided children's welfare since the nineteenth century. A new ideology of child welfare had emerged well before the mid-1920s, however; the Child Welfare Act caught up with, rather than set, the new policy for children.

PART II

'Social readjustment':

the work of the Child Welfare Branch,

1925–1948

Introduction

Economic depression and a world war marked New Zealand society between the 1920s and the late 1940s. The depression was uneven in its effects across society and exposed significant inequalities. Those already poor became even more destitute, and the families of working people swelled their ranks as unemployment hit the lower and middle socio-economic groups. The marginality of Maori to Pakeha worlds, both geographically and socially, was intensified by economic depression. The first Labour government which swept to power in 1935 espoused a vision of a decent society which provided for the needs of its citizens. Welfare services which had expanded slowly during the 1910s and 1920s now received a boost, but the Second World War shattered the rosy mood of the late 1930s. This conflict was a test of the national efficiency for which New Zealand society had striven over the years, and the regulations which engulfed the nation during the 1940s attest, perhaps, to the 'success' of the quest.

Depression and war focused social policy more firmly on the family, and children's health and welfare, so much the target of early twentieth-century social policy, receded into the background. The payment of family allowances began in 1926, and from 1938 various forms of assistance supported family life: sickness and unemployment benefits, subsidised medical care, state housing schemes, mortgage relief, and later a universal family benefit. The Child Welfare Act of 1925 in some respects marked the apogee of children's health and welfare matters, in that it consolidated a philosophy which had gained ascendancy over the course of the early twentieth century. In other ways, however, it was their swansong. Children's health and welfare would remain important during the mid-century decades, as the value of child life continued to have salience, but this value would be expressed more cogently within a wider context of policies relating to the family.

The Child Welfare Act set the agenda for child welfare policy and practice in New Zealand for more than half a century. Through a network of child welfare officers, the Child Welfare Branch of the Department of Education increased markedly the scope of its work with children and, through them, families. The Act consolidated two decades of change and proclaimed the primacy of non-institutional care. Only in 'exceptional cases', the parameters of which were decided by the Superintendent of Child Welfare, would children live permanently in institutions. Between 1926 and 1948, there were usually fewer than 300 children in the Department's institutions at any time, and their average length of detention was two or three years.

The Act created a separate system of juvenile justice through children's courts for those aged under sixteen, and made provision for those under eighteen to have their cases transferred there. Children's courts were held in premises away from other courts, and presided over by specially-appointed magistrates. Court associates, women and men of good standing who had an interest in children's welfare, could be appointed to assist children and advise magistrates. Court attendance was also limited: the proceedings were not to be published, and only individuals associated with the case, or representatives of welfare groups, could be present. Child welfare officers could investigate all cases brought to the court, and were given the opportunity to present written or verbal reports on them. They could also lay informations against children or their parents in order to bring cases to court. Previously the prerogative of the police, this new right intensified the investigative powers of the Education Department.

Children's courts picked up ideas which guided the administration of juvenile justice elsewhere. John Beck had always kept abreast of overseas developments in child welfare, and his 1925 visit to North America involved inspecting courts in the United States and Canada. Although he had devised New Zealand's system well before this visit, the tour confirmed the path that New Zealand would follow. Special magistrates and separate court facilities for children were common in the United States, and associates, or 'referees', were a feature of most of the courts.[1]

In practice, children's courts focused on treatment and reformation, rather than punishment. The new power of magistrates to order committal to the care of the Superintendent of Child Welfare or to an institution, without laying down the details of either the form of care or type of institution, symbolised this change. Chapter Three examines the practice of children's courts, and traces some of the policies for dealing with children who were passed through them to the care of the Superintendent. This chapter also explores discussions over juvenile delinquency and youthful misbehaviour, which were regarded as significant social problems and believed to contribute to a growth in the number of children coming to official attention.

Significant aspects of the work of the Child Welfare Branch were not rooted directly in the legislation. With one of its central responsibilities being to 'prevent wastage in child-life', traditional child welfare functions were expanded to encompass all aspects of a child's social welfare, and to provide any form of assistance.[2] By 1948, the Branch had taken on an impressive array of duties: practical assistance to large or needy families, inspecting all private children's institutions, supervising Pacific Island children resident in New Zealand, overseeing the welfare of British children evacuated to New Zealand during the Second World War, checking on the welfare of children when marriages broke down, and investigating applications for various pensions. New duties brought new forms of intervention and assistance: advice on budgeting and childrearing, grants in aid, cash grants, and relief in kind.

Such extended responsibilities and new forms of assistance transformed the Child Welfare Branch from an agency of child welfare into one of social welfare. Indeed, its establishment led to calls for the development of a general Department of Social Welfare. Beck's North American tour had convinced him of the merits of such a department. His report on the visit recommended that all government welfare agencies be brought under one central welfare department. Less than a year after the passage of the Child Welfare Act, welfare organisations and child welfare officers demanded that the Branch be separated from the Education Department, as its work was more concerned with welfare than with education.[3] These demands remained unsatisfied, but the Child Welfare Branch became a social welfare department in all but name. Child welfare policies, and the Branch in general, occupied a crucial place in the development of New Zealand's welfare state, and one which has been largely overlooked. State intervention into society and family life expanded markedly in the period between the wars, and the Branch was one vehicle of this; in practice it was the forerunner of the Department of Social Welfare created in 1972.

The Child Welfare Branch most clearly manifested its broad welfare focus through the preventive policies which assumed importance after 1925. The Branch increasingly sought to prevent problems without having recourse to the court system and the subsequent process of committing a child to the state. Keeping preventive options out of the court system was a clear intention of those who framed the legislation. 'Constructive' child welfare programmes, it was considered, should be developed by the Branch and child welfare officers outside the judicial system.[4] Preventive supervision schemes, which were approved by the Superintendent of Child Welfare rather than the courts, enabled child welfare officers to supervise a child for a set period, but lacked the legal standing of probation. Chapter Four traces the development of the preventive policies which had their genesis outside the system of children's courts and which applied to children who had not been committed to the care of the Superintendent of Child Welfare. It particularly focuses on the rise of preventive supervision for children and their families, and the targeted provision of assistance to needy families in the 1940s.

The expansion of probation and preventive work required the cooperation of private welfare groups. The Department of Education moved from accepting, on sufferance or with restrictions, the assistance of a few select church and voluntary groups, to increasingly encouraging their participation. Ensuring the welfare of the nation's children was considered to be a community responsibility in which all groups had a role to play. By the late 1930s, both Beck and Jim McClune, his successor as Superintendent, emphasised the importance of the community in dealing with issues of child welfare, with the Branch acting in an advisory capacity.[5]

The enlarged parameters of policy after 1925 led to significant changes in the Child Welfare Branch. The first three Superintendents of Child Welfare, John Beck (1926–38), Jim McClune (1938–46) and Charlie Peek (1946–64), increased the number of child welfare officers from the twenty gazetted in the mid-1920s to nearly 100 by the mid-1940s, just over half of whom were women.[6] The Branch extended its work by opening offices in provincial and rural districts, and by the late 1940s officers were operating throughout the country. More than 250 unsalaried honorary child welfare officers worked in areas without a resident Branch officer, and in other rural and urban settings.

The Branch maintained a gendered division of employment between officers. Women conducted all work involving girls of any age, infants, and boys under ten. In practice, this meant that women undertook all the work relating to adoptions, infant life protection, the supervision of girls and young women, and checks on girls and younger boys boarded out. They also investigated the circumstances of all ex-nuptial births, as stipulated by the Child Welfare Act, inquiring into the condition of mother and child and notifying the Superintendent if the child's well-being was in any way threatened. Men undertook all the work associated with older boys and young men. The titles assigned to women and men reflected their different spheres of work. Women were called child welfare officers in recognition of their more general tasks, while men were designated as boys' welfare officers; unless referring to specific officers, I use the generic term child welfare officer to refer to both women and men.[7]

A child welfare officer's duties were varied, involving court appearances, supervision, inspections of foster homes and private institutions, and investigations into the details of family life. Training was still gained on the job, through trial and error and advice from colleagues. More specialist instruction would not come until the 1950s, even though Beck had signalled its importance following his tour to North America, and McClune reiterated the need for training during the 1930s.[8] The Branch set 25 years as the minimum entry age for officers, thereby hoping to gain experienced staff, and favoured teachers, nurses, and those who had worked for private welfare agencies.

The growing network of officers and the expansion of all aspects of child welfare work brought more children and young people to the Branch's attention. The number of cases investigated annually rose from 3908 in 1925 to a peak of 8543 during the Second World War before falling to 7267 in 1947. This growth far outstripped that of the population aged under twenty. The number of cases investigated rose from 74.36 per 10,000 under twenty year olds in 1925 to 134.3 in 1947, peaking at 157.88 in 1943/4.[9] For the first time, Maori children and adolescents comprised a noticeable number of cases, due in part to the new presence of child welfare officers in Maori communities, and to the wartime drift into towns of Maori youths seeking employment.

More staff and new policies accounted for only some of the expansion in the work of the Child Welfare Branch. A rising incidence of petty theft and other forms of delinquent behaviour, along with a general anxiety about juvenile delinquency, contributed to the growth. Young women in particular were considered to be a problem group. The Branch believed that public perceptions of juvenile delinquency, especially towards the end of the war, were more alarmist than well-founded, but the readiness to regard a range of youthful activities as delinquent indicated a growing intolerance of certain forms of behaviour, especially during the years of depression and war.

The desirability of 'social adjustment' lay at the core of the policies enunciated in the Child Welfare Act, and the terms 'adjustment' and 'readjustment' were frequently invoked to describe the work of the Branch. The personal casework expected of child welfare officers expanded from the 1920s. Their range of investigative duties, whether in making ex-nuptial birth inquiries, writing court reports or preparing for supervision, emphasised getting to know a child as a prelude to devising the best possible form of 'treatment'. Background, home conditions and character were seen as vital, whether a child had committed an offence, was delinquent, or was neglected. This type of approach placed a premium on welfare, rather than on questions of justice or due process, for those who appeared in the children's courts, and helped to erode the distinctions between delinquent children and those who were neglected. Courts may have symbolised adjustment and reformation, but those terms embodied punishment as well, and in practice, adjustment and punishment were never far apart. Merging offenders and non-offenders heightened this association and also blurred the already murky distinctions between children who could be regarded as threats to society and those who could be seen as its victims.[10] In terms of the philosophy of adjustment, children could indeed be both at the same time.

The concept of adjustment also incorporated psychology and a more scientific approach to behaviour which focused on investigating the child's environment as a causal factor. Heredity, once lauded as an explanation for social ills, faded from view as creating the right living conditions became paramount. Internationally and in New Zealand, psychology established itself as a science between the wars, and across social policy areas, including health and justice, it gradually replaced the earlier emphasis on eugenics and racial science. In terms of child welfare, psychological methods often incorporated the mental testing of children, for both 'sub-normality' and 'normality'. The Special School at Otekaike used a range of such tests in the 1920s to measure intelligence and to map out educational and vocational programmes for the residents; probation homes also tested the 'mental condition' of their residents before sending them to other homes or back into the community.[11]

New Zealand's first psychological laboratory had opened at Victoria University College in 1908. Following its incorporation into the tertiary curriculum from 1916, the discipline of psychology expanded into the areas of health, education and social policy. The 1924 Committee of Inquiry into Mental Defectives and Sexual Offenders, on which Beck served, illustrated its growing influence. Some of those who gave evidence used the opportunity of discussing mental defect and feeble-mindedness to expand on the more general application of psychology.[12] Beck's North American tour introduced him to the extensive use of psychological assessments of children, and he recommended that facilities be provided in the four main centres for the psychological examination of 'problem cases'.[13] From the later 1920s, the Branch made use of psychological assessments in cases coming before the children's courts, relying at first on the services of psychologists employed by the Mental Hospitals Department, and later on the psychological clinics associated with university colleges.

Psychological assessments were expanded during the superintendency of Jim McClune with the support of Clarence Beeby, who became Assistant-Director of Education in 1938 and Director in 1940. McClune advocated the appointment of a psychologist who would specifically assist child welfare officers, rather than continued reliance on staff attached to other departments or to the child guidance clinics which had been established by 1936. The Department's first psychologist, James Caughley, was appointed in 1945, and by 1948 there were psychologists in the Department's offices in the main centres. Beeby, who previously had been the Director of the Council for Educational Research, had a doctorate in psychology and had been greatly influenced by Cyril Burt, a leading English authority on child guidance and delinquency in the inter-war period. Burt's works formed part of the Department's library, and in the mid-1940s the Branch arranged to have them placed on semi-permanent loan to child welfare officers. Residential institutions increasingly brought in psychologists for case conferences, such as those introduced at the Girls' Training Centre (the former Te Oranga) during the 1940s.[14]

Adjusting child welfare meant adjusting family welfare, for without knowledge of a child's home life and parents, it was believed, little could be done to bring about lasting change in her or his welfare. Increasingly, families were 'invited' into the welfare circle as government agencies recognised that they played a part in ensuring the welfare of their members. Some families sought out and demanded such invitations, or received them on their own terms; others, however, had little choice, and found that their 'invitations' came at a price.

CHAPTER 3

To train, rather than to punish: children's courts, supervision and residential institutions

Child welfare work after 1925 emphasised training and correction for all children who came into contact with the child welfare system, whether they had committed an offence, were neglected, or had a home life seen as likely to lead to future problems. The system of children's courts formalised under the Child Welfare Act 1925 provided an important structure for this role by acting as the conduit for much child welfare work. The expanding duties of child welfare officers and growing anxieties over juvenile delinquency brought more and more children into contact with the court system between 1925 and 1948. Despite the rhetoric of adjustment and welfare, courts were also punitive; the 'central dilemma' of balancing welfare and justice would continue to be faced in the courts for decades to come.[1] Some of this tension was played out between the judiciary and the Child Welfare Branch, as each attempted to control child welfare policies and practices.

Welfare first, justice second: the operation of children's courts

I said there is no justice
As they led me out of the door
And the judge said, 'This isn't a court of justice son
This is a court of law.'[2]

The children's courts established from 1925–6 were among the most far-reaching of the changes wrought under the Child Welfare Act. Newspapers throughout the country extolled their potential for beneficent reform. 'Excellent results' were anticipated from courts based on the assumption that the primary duty of the state towards delinquent and neglected children was one of guardianship and protection rather than punishment.[3] Politicians, public commentators, magistrates and child welfare officers all considered that the courts lifted New Zealand to the forefront of countries grappling with the complex issue of children's welfare, an opinion confirmed by the release of John Beck's favourable comparison of New Zealand with the North American system in 1927.

Almost 200 children's courts were gazetted, and more than twenty magistrates appointed to sit in them, during 1926. Despite the Branch's desire that these men should be carefully selected for their commitment to child welfare, all were existing magistrates whose duties were simply enlarged to include the new circuit. Six court associates, four of them women, had been appointed by the end of the year to assist in the four main centres. Justices of the peace were added to the list of those who could preside over children's courts, and at the end of 1927 the first women were so gazetted after serving 'apprenticeships' as associates.[4]

The official involvement of women in the court process marked a new step in New Zealand legal practice, one which followed the admission of a handful of women barristers. The appointment of women also confirmed a common perception that they had a special role to play in the care of children. All the women appointed as associates or justices had child welfare experience. One of the new justices of the peace was Sarah Jackson, who had been Matron at the Auckland Industrial School and District Agent for Auckland until her retirement in 1916. Nellie Ferner, who was appointed as an associate in 1926 and a justice the following year, had been involved in children's health and welfare movements for some years.[5]

Court associates or referees were established figures in United States juvenile courts, but in New Zealand few magistrates used them. A reluctance to call on the services of untrained officials may have accounted for this. Some associates were perceived as kindly do-gooders who took a benevolent interest in the child in court, but had little else to offer. *Truth* was colourful in its criticisms, vilifying associates as 'ecstatic spinsters who have never reared a child of their own'.[6] They nevertheless poured energy and commitment into their work. By late 1947, Annie McVicar had given 21 years of service since being appointed in the first group of associates in 1926. She was 79 years old and almost never missed a court sitting. The Superintendent of Child Welfare wondered how he could retire someone who had given so much time to the court; the Minister of Education sympathised and ordered her reappointment.[7]

As the channel for much of the work of the Branch, the children's courts heard a large number of cases. Even in their first year of operation more than 1600 passed through them. Between 1926 and 1948 they heard an annual average of 2400 cases, ranging up to 3076 in 1943. The numbers did not reach 2400 until the mid-1930s, after which they rose, but by 1948 had dropped back to 2000. The upper age limit for young people coming before the courts was raised from sixteen to seventeen years by an amendment to the Act in 1927, which caused a sudden increase in the number of cases.[8]

The Branch and the Justice Department did not regularly compile figures on the gender or racial composition of cases coming to court. Annual returns from some children's courts indicate that males substantially outnumbered females; visitors to children's courts remarked upon the 'strange absence of girl offenders'.[9] Maori children and adolescents increasingly appeared from the late 1930s as the general level of court appearances rose and as more Maori moved into urban areas. The Branch's annual reports from the early 1940s noted a growing 'problem' among Maori youth, and made unfavourable comparisons with offending among Pakeha adolescents. Whangarei officers noted that in 1940–1, Maori youths outnumbered Pakeha coming before the Northland children's courts by 2.5 to 1, although Maori were only about a quarter of the population of the area; two years earlier, East Coast courts had heard about three times as many Maori as Pakeha cases.[10]

Children's courts heard a mixture of charges against children and young people, and complaints under the Child Welfare Act. The latter, always a minority of cases, involved children or young people who were neglected, indigent, or delinquent, not under proper control, or living in a questionable environment. Most of the charges were for misdemeanours, or delinquent behaviour or offences. The first month of operation of the Christchurch children's court saw a procession of minor infractions, including cycling on the footpath, stealing apples, and being an indigent child. The very first case was brought by the police, who charged Ivan Mackay with cycling at night without a light. Policing cycling was clearly big business in Christchurch. By June 1926, only three months after its establishment, the court had purchased rubber stamps bearing the phrases 'cycling at night without light' and 'cycling on footpath', with which the registrar punched the court calendar rather than writing by hand.[11] Theft comprised by far the largest category of offences heard before the courts, making up well over half of all cases throughout the period. Delinquency and delinquent conduct – which were left undefined but encompassed 'cheekiness' and other 'bad behaviour' – was the next largest category. These two categories accounted for more than 80 per cent, and usually more than 90 per cent, of all cases heard in the courts between 1926 and 1948.

Christchurch magistrates were among the first to hear court cases involving children and young people separately from those involving adults, from 1905, and they were generally enthusiastic supporters of the children's courts established in 1926.
THE *PRESS* (CHRISTCHURCH) COLLECTION, ATL, G-40899-1/2

The pattern of court appearances differed markedly from that before 1925, when behavioural issues, destitution and neglect had made up the majority of cases. The reasons for this are unclear. From the late nineteenth century, New Zealand shared with other Western nations an increase in the number of arrests and court appearances for property offences, a phenomenon which some historians have attributed to rising standards of living. Perhaps New Zealand children and young people, like adults, actually committed more property offences, or were apprehended and convicted more frequently for those they did commit.[12] It is just as likely, however, that the new pattern reflected changing definitions of, and attitudes to, youthful behaviour. As Chapter One has shown, the reasons for children's committal to care could be very vague, with terms such as being 'uncontrollable' covering a multitude of behaviours, including petty thieving. 'Not under proper control' continued to be a category for committal, but may have become more focused on disruptive behaviour rather than theft. From the mid-1920s, the term 'juvenile delinquency' leapt to public attention, and as will be shown in the next section, this led to a more intense policing of youth behaviour in which a blind eye was not always turned to petty theft.

Children and young people came to the court through several channels. Police, as before, charged children with offences, or brought them to court for complaints made under the Act. The legislation also extended this last power to child welfare officers, who were able to investigate the circumstances of all cases coming before the court, whether or not they had brought the case. The opportunity to conduct inquiries and present a report to the court gave child welfare officers a role in all cases, whether they were offences, misdemeanours, or complaints under the Act. All court cases involving children thus became welfare matters.

Reconstituting as welfare issues the offending of children and young people enhanced considerably the responsibilities of child welfare officers, and to some extent diminished those of the police. Throughout the twentieth century, the police jurisdiction over children's welfare gradually diminished. The removal of infant life protection and then adoption inquiries from their duties were the first steps. The appointment of juvenile probation officers, who were drawn from the ranks of social service providers rather than police or justice officials, continued this process. The Child Welfare Act made police involvement in child welfare issues more confined. During the 1930s and 1940s, the police withdrew other welfare services, such as the collection of maintenance payments from parents who contributed towards the upkeep of children who were state wards, or from fathers in cases of ex-nuptial birth.

About half of the cases heard between 1925 and 1948 were passed to the jurisdiction of the Child Welfare Branch. Examination of those committed to care suggests a greater similarity to the pre-1925 pattern than is suggested by the number of court appearances alone. Girls were still more likely than boys to be committed to care on behavioural grounds, such as not being under proper control, and were more likely to be placed in a residential institution. But in marked contrast with the period before 1925, and in keeping with the aims of the legislation, magistrates often ordered non-institutional care. Discharge after admonition (with or without the payment of restitution) and supervision orders made up between half and two-thirds of all decisions, as the responsibility for children's welfare increasingly moved to the community. In virtually every year between 1925 and 1948, magistrates committed fewer than 600 children and young people to the care of the Superintendent of Child Welfare. Less than 300 of these normally remained in institutions at the end of the year; the remainder were boarded out or sent to private institutions.

Magistrates could also order corporal punishment if they considered this necessary, although few did, considering it to be 'out of harmony' with the 'proper methods' for dealing with young offenders. The birching ordered for the five members of Napier's 'Purple Mask Gang' for receiving stolen goods and possession of firearms aroused much debate. Some thought it the best treatment for boys who needed to be taught a 'short sharp lesson', but the Branch opposed the order, and the local child welfare officer endeavoured, unsuccessfully, to persuade the magistrate to change his mind. The Statutes Amendment Act 1936 abolished whipping as an option for cases heard in the children's courts, although magistrates could still allow a 'private whipping' under the terms of earlier legislation. The task fell to child welfare officers, and was sometimes administered with parents in attendance. Young Wiremu Orupe of Whangarei, who appeared in court in 1946 for inflicting cruelty to a horse, was strapped on his 'covered rearquarters' by the local child welfare officer in his father's presence.[13]

The emphasis on investigation and adjustment in children's courts distinguished them from other parts of the court system. As John Beck explained, children's courts were 'really courts of Equity', not criminal courts.[14] One or two magistrates expressed concern about this focus. Auckland's Wyvern Wilson pondered the question of whether the children's court were really a court at all, or 'merely an investigation by a Reformatory Committee'. Grave wrongs could arise, in his view, from the emphasis on investigation and adjustment, and he suggested that the regular rules of law be complied with.[15]

The distinctive nature of the children's court allowed legal procedures to differ substantially from those in other courts. The Child Welfare Act enabled the court to dispense with the need to hear and determine a charge. The court could, 'after taking into consideration the parentage of the child, its environment, history, education, mentality, disposition, and any other relevant matters', commit a child to the care of the Superintendent of Child Welfare.[16] Police and child welfare officers could present evidence, but magistrates were not compelled to take this into consideration when hearing a case. Parents had no right to appeal decisions, or to be privy to the contents of any report handed to the magistrate, and lawyers took little, if any, part in proceedings. Above all else, the child's personal history was important, and it was delineated through the process of investigation and presentation of reports and evidence to the courts. The focus on care for both those who had committed offences and those who had been offended against looked to the 'needs' of the child, whose 'deeds' assumed less importance in the formulation of a response. Under such a system magistrates could, and did, assume a powerful role; children and their parents were easily made ciphers as matters of justice took second place to those of welfare.

Appearing before the courts would have been daunting for many parents and children. Lester Butler's mother, clearly ill at ease when her son appeared in the Nelson children's court in 1932 for 'interfering' with sacks of grain, talked 'overmuch' in her state of 'nervous excitement'. The magistrate ordered supervision for Lester, 'for no reason that could be seen' except that Mrs Butler's conduct had annoyed him, suggested the local child welfare officer.[17] Magistrates often took the opportunity to lecture parents on their childrearing skills, and some, according to child welfare officers, could be very rude.[18] Maori parents and families attending courts with their children were often particularly disadvantaged. 'What chance of making any satisfactory plea had a frightened Maori woman when confronted by a magistrate, lawyer, Child Welfare Officer, police and social workers?', one Maori group wondered.[19] Some parents took an active role in court, and a few were ardent in attesting to their parenting skills. Mr and Mrs Batt of Invercargill told the local child welfare officer bringing a complaint that they would 'object most strenuously' to the proceedings, and considered employing counsel to assist them.[20] Such visible protest was rare, as most parents assumed a deferential attitude to the court and its legal trappings.

Children and young people, who did not perhaps hold the law or courts in the same regard as did their parents, expressed their attitudes openly. Child welfare officers and magistrates frequently wrote of 'cheeky' youngsters who exhibited an unseemly disregard for the court and its officers. 'I have known . . . proceedings to invoke mirth and contempt as soon as the offender gets outside', one magistrate claimed; 'hulking great boys and big girls come out of the Court giggling and laughing at it and treat it as a joke', another acknowledged. Some magistrates responded to such displays of disrespect by standing on their dignity and position, while others took a more flexible approach. New Plymouth's magistrate considered the children before him on a case by case basis, having an 'informal, fatherly way' with small children but being more assertive towards badly behaved youngsters.[21]

Child welfare officers sometimes saw magistrates as pompous and uncompromising. John Bartholomew of the Dunedin court, according to a local child welfare officer, had all the qualities which ought not to be possessed by a children's court magistrate, and none of those which were 'essential'. He displayed a 'rather obstinate manner', leading the officer to wonder, 'since . . . Magistrates are still a necessary evil, and will remain so in Children's Courts for some time to come, I should very much like to know if there is anything that can be done about appointing a man who has at least some spark of human sympathy and understanding in dealing with children'.[22] Other child welfare officers suggested that ordinary magistrates were not suited to the children's court: 'they are so steeped in legal formality and procedure that it is almost impossible for them to realise that such methods with children are not understood, are totally unnecessary and pernicious in effect in the long run'.[23]

Some magistrates – in marked opposition to child welfare officers and the philosophy of the Branch – retained the traditional court trappings, including uniformed police, to impress on children and young people the power of the law. John Salmon of the Wanganui children's court claimed that the room he used 'impresses [the child] no more than the dining room at home. It is less impressive than the schoolroom'. Courtrooms stripped of all their legal paraphernalia were ineffective, and incapable of inspiring respect in the children appearing before the bench; a 'proper court' was more likely to instil a suitable appreciation of law and justice 'than the bringing of an offender to a room with a few benevolent looking middle aged ladies and gentlemen and his being told that he is a naughty boy and that he is not to do it again.' Some magistrates believed that Maori were especially impressed by traditional court surroundings and procedures: 'unless they are sharply punished', Rotorua's children's court magistrate proclaimed, '[Maori children] and their parents regard the issue of the proceedings as a forensic victory to be boasted about in the kaingas.'[24]

Restrictions on publicity and on public attendance at the courts aroused disquiet about the secrecy of the proceedings, and the loss of legal rights thus incurred. The courts were frequently criticised for being 'Star Chambers' conducted beyond public view.[25] Newspapers claimed that this was contrary to the idea of 'British justice', and that the Act itself was nothing but a 'queer blend of American idealism, mixed with medieval tyranny, and the child regimentation system at present in vogue in Soviet Russia'.[26] Magistrates were also sometimes uneasy about the lack of publicity. The Justice Department surveyed magistrates on children's court matters in 1929; of the 26 who responded, fourteen allowed the press to remain in their courts, and sixteen maintained that name suppression should not be mandatory. Many considered that publicity, through either the presence of the press or the publication of case details, served a useful purpose. Shame for the action and ridicule from peers could have a beneficial effect on young minds, some maintained, with one suggesting that 'something like' the stocks should be assembled in school playgrounds to allow children to poke fun at those who were constrained in them.[27]

Other magistrates wanted to restrict markedly the number of people in court, and took a dogmatic approach to the presence of welfare groups. Although the Act allowed members of relevant social welfare organisations to be present during appropriate cases, magistrates interpreted the legislation differently. The

Auckland magistrate Ernest Cutten caused a furore in 1931 when he refused to allow representatives of the Society for the Protection of Women and Children into his court unless they had brought the case themselves; his decision stood until his retirement two years later.[28]

Administering children's courts and transforming them into sites of welfare proved to be more difficult than had been anticipated. Many of the early problems could be, and were, attributed to the newness of the legislation. Beck confirmed that there had been difficulties in simplifying court procedures and minimising publicity, and the Branch's report on the first year of the Act noted confusion over aspects of the court process.[29] The Education Department evidently considered that time and increased familiarity with the legislation would overcome the initial problems. During the first year of operation of the courts, Beck and other officials issued a steady stream of advice to both the police and the Department of Justice. Magisterial discretion in terms of publicity and police presence in courts was stressed, and the over-riding principle of abolishing ordinary court procedure was emphasised as part of the effort to make the children's courts agencies of protection and welfare.[30]

Courthouses and other premises were unprepared for such procedural innovation, and in some areas there was difficulty in finding suitable accommodation away from the adult court in which to hear cases. An Auckland magistrate claimed that the hurried arrangements there were both inconvenient and unsuitable; the new children's court was a hall in upper Queen Street. Despite the Act, some newspapers publicised details of cases. Charges were brought against the *Auckland Star* in late 1926 for reporting fully the proceedings of one case and publishing a photo of the child. Magistrates complained about the excessive number of petty cases coming before them, blaming lack of police discretion and implying that the ability of child welfare officers to bring complaints was flooding the courts with trivia.[31]

Some magistrates failed to give child welfare officers the opportunity to investigate cases or present reports on their findings. Others, uncertain of the legislation, followed earlier procedure and named the institution to which a child should be sent. Some were unsure of how to use Branch officers. Wanganui District staff protested vehemently when magistrate John Barton placed three boys in the custody of a Justice Department probation officer, rather than under the supervision of the Branch.[32] An Auckland magistrate's hearing of cases in the magistrate's court in 1927 and 1928 generated a frenzied exchange of tersely-worded letters between the Child Welfare Branch and the Department of Justice. The publication of the details of one of the cases only compounded the situation. The magistrate suggested, rather stridently, that if the Superintendent of Child Welfare wished to have the court conducted along the lines he wanted then he should have the entire system placed under the jurisdiction of the Education Department, 'for no Magistrate in the Dominion will accede to any dictation or influence from any quarter'.[33]

Magistrates, the press and the police all laboured under difficulties in the first year of the Act. According to the Branch's Napier staff, the legislation had taken local police by surprise: 'they are going about for most of the past week studying hard with the Act – a copy of which the Detective Sergeant stole from the court – and as they only have one copy between them, their studies will take most of the week'.[34] Neither the police nor magistrates seem to have been particularly well-briefed on the new procedures. Child welfare staff, on the other hand, were considerably better primed. During 1925 and 1926 Beck sent out memoranda and circulars to officers detailing the new duties and processes, and he went on the road with the Act in late 1926, visiting 21 centres and covering over 800 miles in two weeks to explain the legislation to staff.[35]

Beck had invested much time and effort in devising the legislation and getting it passed, and was determined that his staff would be ready to carry out its intention. The Child Welfare Branch, and its Superintendent in particular, considered the Act to be 'their' legislation. By the end of 1928 Beck claimed, somewhat prematurely as it turned out, that magistrates were endeavouring to carry out the spirit of the Act; it went without saying, it seems, that child welfare officers had been doing so all along.[36]

The early years of administrative difficulties set the tone for future relations between magistrates and child welfare officers. By the end of the 1920s it was evident that the operation of the children's courts was not proceeding as the Branch had hoped, even allowing for preliminary snags. Once-supportive newspapers and magistrates now condemned the court system, identifying its 'secrecy' as inimical to the spirit of justice. Magistrate Barton was vociferous in his criticisms, and his comments led the Minister of Justice to issue a questionnaire to magistrates seeking their opinions on the system. The magistrates supported the concept of the courts, but most tendered advice on how they could be improved, including by allowing more publicity and being held in more formal surroundings.[37]

Throughout the 1930s and 1940s, criticisms and complaints issued forth from all the groups involved in child welfare practice. Child welfare officers who continued to find that magistrates took little regard of their reports now blamed wilful magisterial disregard of appropriate procedures. In 1936, Beck alleged that Wyvern Wilson never read his officers' reports and ignored all the underlying principles of the legislation.[38] Magistrates, of course, did not have to take into account the reports of child welfare officers, a point which the Branch and its staff sometimes overlooked.

Such criticisms were symptomatic of a more general dissatisfaction within the Branch that children's courts magistrates were simply ordinary stipendiary magistrates rather than the specially selected group signalled by the Act. The Branch told the Justice Department that special justices and suitably qualified magistrates were needed to meet one of the basic tenets on which the courts were founded, but stipendiary magistrates continued to dominate them in the 1930s and 1940s. As one law officer noted, authorising all stipendiary magistrates to act in children's courts made the provisions of the Act little more than 'camouflage'; holding them away from the regular courts was the only distinctive feature of the system.[39] In 1945, McClune informed the Director of Education that he had still been unable to convince the Department of Justice to appoint specialist magistrates, although 80 special justices, including justices of the peace, were authorised to act in children's courts.[40]

Time and experience did little to bridge differences in what was, at its heart, a battle between professionals over the control of child welfare in the courts. Michael Lyons, who was a child welfare officer in Christchurch in the 1940s, recalled the intrinsic difficulties of children's court work: 'child welfare and the Court personnel looked across the table at each other, which was really an official and legal gulf, exchanging ideas in a language that the other party probably misunderstood'.[41] Contemporary commentators realised as much. As the draftsman preparing the amendment to the Act in 1927 noted, the Child Welfare Branch may have succeeded in pushing through its pioneering legislation, but it had failed to persuade either the police or the judiciary of the wisdom of the policies which were centred around the children's courts.[42]

Personal animosity led to some of the differences between magistrates and child welfare officers, and this became more evident once problems could no longer be attributed to 'teething troubles'. The children's courts forced magistrates to share their authority with both child welfare officers and court associates. This was a new experience for hitherto independent and unchallenged bastions of law, and at times they found it irksome. Child welfare officers and Branch officials became impatient with court officers who were unable or unwilling to embrace the new emphasis on welfare, and were reluctant to call on their expertise. Child welfare officers had been carving out for themselves a more defined niche in the social welfare area, and to have their status overlooked and their experience disregarded was vexing, particularly when the entire Act was constructed around the notions of investigation and adjustment. Some magistrates felt themselves to be put upon, with their own authority and status as professionals ignored. Following criticism of his methods from one child welfare officer, an Auckland magistrate declared that 'the Children's Court does not exist merely for the purpose of helping the Child Welfare Department to carry out a policy. If we wish to save a child from the result of that policy I do not doubt that in what seems to us an appropriate case we will still act as we think in the best interests of the child.'[43]

This sporadic dissension between the Branch and the judiciary hinted at the more fundamental tensions that surrounded child welfare issues during this period. The Child Welfare Branch frequently reiterated the concept of courts administering correction, adjustment and welfare rather than punishment and justice, a notion with which some magistrates disagreed.[44] Children's courts had to function on several levels, and it was perhaps inevitable that achieving balance between these would prove a challenge. All types of cases involving children and young people, whether they had offended or not, could be heard in the courts, but the emphasis was on the outcome, rather than the immediate reason for their attendance. This may have eroded some of the distinctions between dangerous and neglected children, but it also meant that responses to children sometimes had little relationship to why they had come to notice in the first place. The multifarious roles of the courts as agents of protection, support, aid, punishment and reformation would be sorely tested, particularly at times when one of the periodic alarms about youthful behaviour swept the country.

'Unsatisfactory social adjustment': inter-war and wartime juvenile delinquency

The expression 'juvenile delinquency' is historically contingent, and dependent on the social, political and economic contexts in which it is used. Actions and behaviours which one group or generation define as delinquency may not be regarded in the same way by others. Criminal actions such as petty theft or assault have usually been judged to be juvenile offending, but attitudes towards other forms of youthful conduct and behaviour have been more variable. The malicious ringing of doorbells, or 'giving cheek', may have led to committal to an industrial school in the late nineteenth century; 30 years later, these activities may not have been noticed, or if remarked upon, may have led to a brief period under the supervision of a child welfare officer. As several historians have argued, the concept of juvenile delinquency depends on a delineation of the behavioural norms that are expected of children.[45] High expectations for and condemnations of youthful behaviour were never far apart, as children were viewed both as hopes for the future and problems in the making.

The concept of juvenile delinquency also suggests a willingness by adults to reframe as problematic in others behaviours which they may have exhibited in their own youths. Each generation has commented adversely on the behaviour of its youth in a 'tradition of anguished regret for the past'. Naughty and disrespectful children were seldom found in the 'good old days' when youthful high spirits or misbehaviour was no more than 'good clean fun'. An historian of hooliganism has noted that 'the world may change, but somehow this vocabulary of complaints against declining standards and morals is immunised against change'.[46] The spurious notion that children were not as good or as dutiful as they 'used to be' played an important part in the articulation of anxieties over juvenile delinquency.

New Zealand shared a concern about youth (mis)conduct with other Western nations as increasing appearances before its children's courts 'proved' that juvenile delinquency was on the rise.[47] For the New Zealand public and the Child Welfare Branch, the concept encompassed a range of childhood and adolescent behaviour and activities, as well as various forms of criminal and petty offences. For the Wanganui Education Board, which commissioned an inquiry into child

The Auckland Headmasters' Association released a report in 1941 revealing the 'deplorable facts about the life and habits' of primary schoolchildren, who are depicted in this Minhinnick cartoon.
MINHINNICK/*NEW ZEALAND HERALD*

AN EVENING WITH THE YOUNGER SET

delinquency in the mid-1940s, the term was broad indeed: 'Child Delinquency is to be taken as such *continued breaches* of our civil, social and moral codes as to make the perpetrator a Real Behaviour Problem'. It was, in sum, a form of 'unsatisfactory social adjustment'.[48]

'New' forms of juvenile delinquency emerged during this period as new aspects of youth conduct and offending were seen as worrisome. Where larrikin 'pushes' had aroused consternation in the late nineteenth century, vandalism, youth gangs and joyriders – sometimes on bicycles – were the new malaise. Newspaper articles commented in detail on the activities of gangs of boys involved in theft and petty crime. Vandalism – often also attributed to gangs of youths – received considerable publicity, and during 1945 a Wellington City Anti-Vandalism Bill was introduced in Parliament in an attempt to stem a spate of fence-wrecking and manhole-cover smashing in Wellington and the Hutt Valley.[49] Some of the vandalism was very time-specific, as children targeted novelties and new inventions; during the 1930s, breaking insulators comprised a noticeable proportion of offences coming before the courts; in 1936/7 this was the fourth largest category of offence, with 122 cases.

As before, and indeed as would occur later, lack of parental control, poor parental example and iniquitous home conditions were identified as major causes of juvenile delinquency. The Wanganui Education Board's 1944 report noted that 'no cause was more frequently pressed upon the attention of the Committee than the failure of the parents to provide right home conditions, to discharge fully their responsibilities, to give adequate training, or to exercise proper control'. These failings were evidence of a lack of interest in children, which was also manifested by inadequate sex instruction, poor religious teaching, excessive pocket money, and irresponsible attitudes to their choices of companions and leisure activities.[50]

Child welfare officers frequently supported such environmentalist explanations, their faith in the reforming potential of preventive measures targeted at the home lending further weight to these conclusions. Officers lamented parental inability to instruct children suitably, and vilified those who allowed children to take charge in the home. Others castigated parents for taking insufficient interest in their children's well-being, condemning parental 'nagging', inconsistent treatment, and rejection. Parental slackness also contributed to an alleged new 'spirit' to be found among young New Zealanders. For some officers, a tendency to allow children's 'self-expression' free rein led only to delinquency and uncontrollable behaviour. According to George Brendon of the Wanganui office, 'self-expression may be an interesting theory, but is often objectionable in fact and does not work out at all well in adult life where obedience [is] important'. Other officers had a more generous attitude towards contemporary youth.

Dunedin child welfare officer Ewart Thorpe urged his colleagues to keep their faith in children, and to recognise that the modern child was really no different from that of the previous generation.[51]

The increasing use of psychology in general child welfare work is apparent in the explanations that were offered for juvenile delinquency. Child welfare officers attributed juvenile delinquency to socio-economic and 'socio-psychological' causes, such as traumatic family relationships and lack of familial affection.[52] They sent their clients to child guidance clinics, and increasingly used psychologists to help explain behaviour and map out treatment programmes. The Branch also used the work of the British psychologist Cyril Burt to explain juvenile delinquency. As part of a questionnaire on the effects of the cinema in the late 1920s, Beck sent all districts extracts from Burt's *The Young Delinquent* to assist officers with their interpretations.[53] Although psychological assessments became more important in New Zealand (as elsewhere) during this period, it is also clear that, as in other areas of child welfare where psychology was employed, this was often an alternative way of diagnosing familiar problems.[54] Many child welfare officers simply dressed up their tried and true diagnoses of family and child behaviour in more modern scientific parlance, and the degree to which they themselves understood the terminology is open to question.

Environmentalist explanations bolstered the emphasis on investigation and adjustment. Nine year old Con Edwards and three of his siblings were committed through the courts to the care of the Superintendent for not being under proper control. Investigation by child welfare officers found that after the death of their mother, their father had placed them with their maternal grandmother and two uncles. Their new home was 'very poor' and considerable 'immorality' occurred there; two uncles were charged with unnatural offences against Con.[55] Some officers, however, perhaps attached to other ways of working with children, decried the philosophy of adjustment of young offenders. Wanganui's George Brendon, whose reports to the Branch constituted a lament for days gone by, warned against it: 'We talk of adjustment now instead of punishment, which may be wise but the world classic case of adjustment failed badly – Mr Chamberlain's attempt to adjust that arch-criminal Mr Hitler'. Wicked nations cunningly watched New Zealand child welfare services – 'the Totallitarian countries have not allowed the opportunity to slip by', he warned ominously.[56]

Many child welfare officers were concerned by a lack of leisure facilities for youth. The apparent dearth of organised recreational pursuits in the community encouraged less wholesome activities, such as passing Saturday afternoons in stuffy, ill-ventilated picture theatres or congregating in gangs. Those giving evidence to the Wanganui Education Board's inquiry into delinquency urged the provision of structured leisure activities, noting the problems that could arise

Child welfare officers were divided over the effects on young minds of attendance at picture theatres. Christchurch's Globe Theatre, which closed in 1917, could seat more than 300 people, and as its sign suggests, showed films continuously throughout the day and evening.
STEFFANO WEBB COLLECTION, ATL, G-3991-1/1

from 'misdirected play' or aimless free time. Parents were advised in a circular letter from the Board that they should supervise their children's leisure, for 'it is during these periods . . . that "gangs" are formed, "dares" given and taken, and the emulation of the "tough guy" attempted.' The Board counselled that 'personal sacrifice on the part of the parent to ensure wise use of the child's leisure time will mean much to the child's future development as citizen and man.'[57]

Public commentators and newspapers also targeted the allegedly inimical effect of cinema and radio on young minds as a direct cause of juvenile delinquency – much as nineteenth-century opinion blamed cheap literature and today's commentators point to violent films and videos. Correspondents to newspapers and the Department of Education lamented the quality of films and demanded strict censorship. One worried parent urged that 'something' should be done about children at the cinema, and recommended that they be banned from viewing murder films, as many 'must be warped in their imaginations through the shocking films chosen'. Identifying as one cause of delinquency 'pernicious literature of [the] salacious and gangster type', a special committee of the Auckland Education Board called for the importation of 'suitable' pictures and reading matter for children.[58]

A few child welfare officers were also convinced of the deleterious role of the cinema. One regretted children's attraction to films that were full of 'pernicious nonsense'. The cinema had become the 'universal panacea' for youth at a loose end, and in his view, 'the most broad-minded persons could scarcely answer . . . in the affirmative – "Has the average film an uplifting influence even on the adult mind?" ' Another thought there were difficulties only when films did not appeal to the young theatregoers. Rotorua's child welfare officer found vandalism only after a 'heavy, adult drama' which did not hold the interest of boys. The likes of Hop-along Cassidy films were a different matter; these had particular appeal to Maori youth, apparently.[59]

On the whole, however, child welfare officers rarely agreed that the content of movies and radio serials or attendance at picture theatres caused juvenile delinquency. An informal survey among officers in 1927 supported Beck's contention that few cases of delinquency could be traced to the effect of movies. Auckland's John Cupit claimed that he was unable to recall a case in eight years in which the cinema had directly caused delinquency. Rather, he asserted that the picture theatre itself provided an agreeable venue at which gangs and delinquents could gather, and induced children to be on the streets at night.[60] Even after the introduction of talkies, and an expansion of the range and number of films, officers still accorded the cinema little role in producing delinquency, and in the late 1930s the Branch's annual reports claimed there was no 'substantial evidence' proving otherwise.[61] In the mid-1940s Whangarei's Lewis Anderson believed the detrimental effect of pictures to be so rare that he was prompted to report one relevant case: two youths, who were charged with breaking and entering and mischief, had left a note on the premises describing a recent film and pretending to be the actors. Anderson acknowledged that children liked 'plenty of action' in their chosen films, although he doubted whether film-makers such as 'Samuel Goldwyn, Wm Fox etc know how to distinguish between action and clap-trap'.[62]

Almost inevitably, some commentators saw the lenient treatment meted out by the children's courts as fostering a spirit of delinquency. As one judicial witness at the Wanganui Education Board's investigation noted, 'you can overdo the soft pedal'.[63] The abolition of corporal punishment for nearly all the offences that were dealt with in the children's courts aroused strident opposition in some quarters. In supporting the magistrate's decision to order the birching of all the members of the Purple Mask Gang, an editorial in the Christchurch *Press* claimed that the boys obviously needed a whipping; certainly this would be more beneficial than the alternative of supervision, which was likely 'to be borne with a sulphorous impatience damaging to a young disposition'.[64]

Both the Child Welfare Branch and individual child welfare officers were reluctant to ascribe juvenile delinquency to any one cause, and were not convinced that it was growing when only the annual fluctuations in the level of court appearances were used as a measure. Jim Ferguson attempted to analyse the causes of delinquency in the Invercargill area in the mid-1940s, but eventually declared his efforts to be fruitless. He had tried to distinguish in every case the social and individual factors which had contributed to delinquency, but noted that his analysis explained nothing. Its only use, he admitted, 'lies in the hint it gives of the utter complexity of conditions involved and the uselessness of the task of endeavouring to analyse yearly fluctuations'. The Branch argued that the depression of the 1930s had had little effect on the level of juvenile delinquency, and that the number of court appearances had scarcely changed during the 1930s.[65] While acknowledging the deleterious effects of the Second World War (the number of children's court appearances peaked in 1943/4), it interpreted this as a temporary departure from an otherwise slowly increasing level. A drop in the number of cases to the pre-depression level in 1947/8 seemed to confirm this judgment.[66]

The Second World War also had a short-term effect on public and Branch anxieties over juvenile delinquency. As in the First World War, the moral and social regulation of civilian life sometimes caused a hardening of attitudes. Some New Zealand historians have detected a wartime preoccupation with delinquency, and particularly with the 'aggressive sexuality' of young women which was seen to threaten the fragile wartime social order.[67] Church groups, welfare organisations and education boards all emphasised the negative effects of the war on adolescent behaviour. Absent fathers and working mothers led to the further weakening of already shaky parental control. Child welfare officers confirmed that the wartime 'excitement' was having a detrimental effect on adolescents, and was exacerbated by the abnormally high wages being earned by working youths. The Branch itself felt the impact of staff shortages and faced difficulties in attempting to keep delinquency in check.[68]

The presence of American servicemen in New Zealand from 1942 compounded the situation. Child welfare officers traced a spate of truanting in Manawatu and Horowhenua to the attractions of gambling and other money-making enterprises that were on offer in the nearby American camps. Boys in Foxton developed a lucrative trade ferrying in to camp various items required by troops who were unable to leave the compound. The news that one lad had collected £15 in a single weekend caused a major decline in school attendance the

American servicemen relaxing in the Hotel Cecil, Wellington in the 1940s (above). Child welfare officers were more familiar with other aspects of the presence of servicemen in and near New Zealand's main centres: young boys truanting to ferry goods into training camps, and young women having sexual relations with soldiers. Sometimes, such relations were more imagined than real. A New Plymouth schoolteacher intercepted this letter (right) written by one thirteen year old girl to another, and passed it on to child welfare officers. GORDON BURT COLLECTION, ATL, F-37119-1/2 & NATIONAL ARCHIVES, CW 1, 40/2/26

Darling Jean,

My pal Stan Strevo and I would like to meet you at the park on Saturday night somewhere about six o'clock. I am in the United States Marines and would like you to have a girl friend with you because we could have some (hotcha Bay). My name is Wayne Swenson. I am nineteen years of age and am going back to Palmerston North next week. I hear there is some nice bush in that park. I will give you a photo of myself. . . . P.S. I'll bring a packet of (F's). Not meaning may be either.

following week. In Wellington, children's exploitation of servicemen's desire for shoeshines led the council to ban the young entrepreneurs from the streets.[69]

Increasing juvenile delinquency among females especially was linked to wartime social change. Child welfare officers reported a marked increase in the number of young women being charged with morality offences, and attributed this to the presence of so many young men in the main centres that were close to training camps. Girls and young women were believed to flock to these centres, where, child welfare officers reported, they booked into hotels, consorted with and obtained liquor from servicemen.[70] The fact that some of the adolescent girls committed to the Branch's residential institution at the Burwood Home (formerly Te Oranga) had associated with American servicemen was regarded as a significant factor in their delinquency. Joan Andrews came to official notice when a youth centre reported that she was 'getting into trouble' with the soldiers at the camp near her home. Other young women at Burwood had been forced into prostitution with American servicemen by their mothers. 'Experiences with American Service men' was given as a reason for Miria Dewey's delinquent conduct when she was admitted in 1943 for being not under proper control after she had run away from her mother's house. Closer investigation revealed that Peggy Dewey, 'a most unsatisfactory mother' who was married to a Chinese market gardener, had forced her to have sex with American servicemen for money.[71]

The war affected the number of Maori children appearing before the courts, and by the early 1940s child welfare officers were speaking of Maori juvenile delinquency as a problem. This was especially so for young Maori women, whose allegedly lax moral attitudes were seen to lead them 'naturally' towards sexual delinquency. As the historian Philip Fleming has suggested, the anxiety over female sexual delinquency during the war was highly racialised, with young Maori women in the cities believed to be having a detrimental effect on Pakeha girls and young women.[72] To counter this, the Branch opened Fareham House, a residential institution specifically for Maori girls, so as to avoid housing them with Pakeha female sexual delinquents.

Wartime conditions accelerated the slow growth in contact between Maori and the courts. The increase in the number of Maori youths brought before the courts predated by some years the wartime drift of young Maori to cities in search of work that has often been seen as precipitating higher levels of Maori offending.[73] A perception of growing Maori juvenile delinquency was one consequence of the expansion of the network of child welfare and voluntary officers into the rural and outlying areas where most Maori resided. With few exceptions, most reports of Maori juvenile delinquency before the mid-1940s come from the rural districts of Northland, the East Coast and the central North

Fareham House, near Featherston, opened in 1944 as an institution for delinquent Maori girls and young women. Along with Maori language and culture, marching featured in the curriculum.
NATIONAL PUBLICITY STUDIOS PHOTOGRAPHIC COLLECTION, NATIONAL ARCHIVES, A46328

Island, all areas in which child welfare work was a new feature of government policy, and where Maori delinquency was 'discovered' as Maori health and housing became subject to closer inspection.

Child welfare officers suggested poor employment opportunities, and, by Pakeha standards, inadequate housing and living conditions, as primary causes of Maori youth delinquency. Yet there was also a recognition that adaptation to European cultural norms contributed to Maori social dislocation and juvenile delinquency. Child welfare officers and others believed that one way to overcome problems among Maori youth was to support traditional tribal structures and foster Maori responsibility for community welfare. Some child welfare officers attempted to work with the Maori welfare officers appointed following the passage of the Maori Social and Economic Advancement Act in 1945.[74]

Racial intolerance and ignorance of Maori customs among child welfare officers were also evident. Drunkenness, the 'misuse' of social security benefits, and 'laziness' were among the most common reasons given for Maori delinquency. An honorary child welfare officer in Shannon noted the poor living conditions of Maori at nearby Opiki, where families spent their 'enormous' wages on gambling and drinking; a Pukekohe officer claimed that Maori children lived in the 'filthiest of shacks', and that their 'only diversion is taxis, fish and chips and the cinema'.[75]

Some officers were aware of these perceptions in their communities, but did not share them. Lewis Anderson, who was to become Superintendent of Child Welfare, saw a 'great deal' of racial prejudice in Northland, where a colour bar operated against Maori in areas where Pakeha were a minority. He affirmed that those who proclaimed the prevalence of Maori 'laziness' were often those quickest to refuse jobs to Maori youths. He found few examples of heavy drinking among Maori, but suggested that if he gave evidence to that effect before the 1945 Liquor Licensing Commission, 'I can imagine the great numbers of irate pakeha Northlanders wrathfully proclaiming that the Child Welfare Officer did not know what he was talking about, that he did not look around, and that he was encouraging the Maoris in their lazy and drunken habits'.[76]

A close personal interest: court-ordered supervision

The emphasis in the Child Welfare Act on providing community-based care for as many children as possible facilitated the expansion after 1925 of probation, or 'court-ordered supervision', as it was renamed. The introduction of supervision for all types of children and young people, whether they had offended or not, symbolised the primacy of working with families to overcome child welfare problems. The 'friendly contact' and close personal interest that was the basis of supervision gave child welfare officers an entrance into family life and provided them with an opportunity to tackle the source of delinquency and other social ills: a maladjusted family environment. The chance to readjust that by focusing on children within their domestic circle furthered the family-centred policies which dominated social welfare during the second quarter of the twentieth century.

Magistrates placed, on average, almost 700 children and young people under supervision each year between 1926 and 1948, or between 30 and 40 per cent of cases brought before the courts, as Figure 3 indicates. As before, boys and young men made up the majority of orders, most of which lasted for between one and two years. The number of orders ranged from 412 in 1926/7 to 993 in 1943/4. Concern over juvenile delinquency had taken a sharper edge during the war, as magistrates seemed to respond to growing public alarm about the behaviour of young people: the 993 orders represented only 30 per cent of the cases before the courts, the lowest rate during the period.[77]

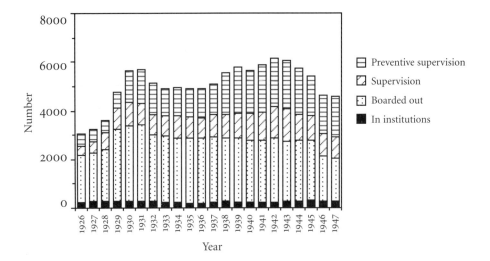

FIGURE 3   *Care options for children, 1926–1947*

Magistrates ordered supervision in all kinds of cases. Petty offences, not being under control, and complaints under the Child Welfare Act could all warrant it. If children posed a danger to the community, or their home circumstances were dangerous to them, magistrates could order their immediate committal and bypass supervision entirely. Serious offences and cases of sexual delinquency in young women were also more likely to lead to institutional care, as will be shown in the next section. The parameters of 'dangerousness' in children or their homes were vague, however; the decision between discharge, supervision and committal to an institution rested primarily on the circumstances of individual cases and the predilections of individual magistrates.

Many supervision orders were made for children charged with minor offences or whose conduct was becoming troublesome. During 1927, for example, the Timaru child welfare officer supervised boys who had committed theft or assault, were not under proper control, or had been charged with mischief. Some had their period of supervision extended when their behaviour was seen as not sufficiently improved. Twelve year old Jimmy O'Donnell committed theft during his twelve months of supervision and was sent to the Christchurch Probation Home before again coming under supervision. Abel South was under supervision for theft when he appeared in court again. His good behaviour during his first period of supervision led the court to order only another twelve-month term.[78]

Supervision could help ensure the protection or safety of a child. The on-going contact between child welfare officers and families which it afforded was

Cramped and unwholesome living conditions were believed to have a detrimental effect on family life and child welfare. These houses in Wellington's Tory Street were demolished in the 1920s to make way for factories. BRYANT AND MAY COLLECTION, ATL, G-26013-1/1

seen as a way of continuing to check on family welfare if the children were thought to be in danger of being neglected. The Paterson/Osgood family had been under loose observation for six years, with child welfare officers visiting them periodically. The father's unemployment had reduced the family to very straitened circumstances: the ten children were ill-clad, dirty and miserable-looking, and begged for pennies from passers-by. The magistrate visited the family himself before ordering the supervision of one of the children for five years – a very long term which effectively placed the entire family under observation.[79]

Young women whose behaviour threatened future illicit sexual activity could also be placed under supervision. 'Angela' was placed under the supervision of a Wellington child welfare officer while working at a hospital, but she proved 'most erratic' in her conduct, keeping late hours and being 'much sought after by boys and men'. In an attempt to control her conduct the child welfare officer arranged for her admission to a local institution; she gave the slip to her escort to the home, but was apprehended several days later and committed to the Girls' Training Centre at Burwood.[80]

Child welfare officers and magistrates were ambivalent about the value of supervision for Maori. A Gisborne child welfare officer argued in the mid-1930s that supervision of Maori youths was unsatisfactory, as all but a few saw it as a pardon and a licence to reoffend. Even though supervision was provided by an honorary child welfare officer whom local Maori respected, the officer suggested that a special set of laws was needed for 'this type of free-and-easy Maori'.[81] The essentially urban system of supervision was found wanting in the scattered rural districts where most Maori lived. In areas such as the East Coast, particularly around Ruatoria and Tikitiki, supervision and visiting were almost impossible as the nearest child welfare officer was stationed in Gisborne.[82] The Branch attempted to overcome problems in supervising Maori children by calling on the assistance of Native School teachers, local Maori groups and kaumatua. A reliance on traditional lines of Maori authority accorded with the Branch's policy of passing the practice of Maori child welfare back to the community. Although this was couched in terms of encouraging Maori self-reliance, and there was an awareness that some Maori took umbrage at Pakeha interference in community welfare, less salutary motives also played a part.[83] The Child Welfare Branch had insufficient staff and expertise to attend to rural Maori communities. This lack of resources, combined with the 'failure' of Maori children living in Pakeha child welfare institutions, forced the Education Department to foster alternative structures for addressing Maori child welfare needs.

The practice of supervision changed little after 1925, remaining similar in most respects to the system that had been established by the late 1910s. Following the court appearance, child welfare officers instructed both parents and children on the process of supervision. Officers recognised the need to probe the character of children if the adjustment and instruction were to be successful. Chatting with the children and their parents, winning their confidence and overcoming any barriers to communication were crucial. Aware that poor parental behaviour could lead to neglect and delinquency, officers stressed the importance of a strong parental example. This advice could be very gender-specific. One Hamilton officer encouraged fathers to understand their sons, to 'delve deep into the boy's soul to bring out the latent good that has probably been struggling for mastery', and to foster interest in the use of tools, healthy games and suitable reading matter.[84]

Supervision revolved around regular personal visits and correspondence. The latter had a special place in supervision, encouraging communication on an ongoing basis whether or not officers were personally visiting the home. The process of corresponding, rather than its content, was vital. 'I am writing to you to tell you that I have been a good boy and I have done everything that I have to do', Murray McLean informed Philip Goodwin, his child welfare officer, in 1939, five months into a two-year period of supervision. Murray went on to relate small but important details of his life: 'I have got a bike now and I go riding nearly every day we break up on Friday for our school holidays. I have not been over to the exhibition yet, but I am going over in the Christmas holidays with my mother. I think that this is all this time.' Perhaps to allay any suspicion that Murray was up to mischief, his mother also wrote to Goodwin: 'Just a few lines to let you know that Murray is being quite a good boy, he has been behaving himself like he should, he does everything that he is told to do.' For a child welfare officer, the correspondence was a way both to encourage the children and to deliver useful pieces of advice: 'When you next write to me I want you to write in ink as that is the way to correspond properly', Goodwin informed Murray.[85]

Officers visited children's homes periodically, the frequency determined at their discretion and by the size of their caseload. They also encouraged children to take part in activities and hobbies, in the belief that too much ill-spent leisure time led to delinquency. Enrolment in youth groups, such as the YMCA, religious clubs and sports teams awaited many of those placed under supervision. Physical education, that healthy outlet for high spirits, was favoured. Bracing physical exertion had long been supposed to be a fruitful training ground for citizenship, and physical jerks had formed an important part of the regime in the Education Department's industrial schools. Public concern about the welfare of the nation invested physical activity with a new meaning from the 1910s, as fit, healthy bodies became linked more explicitly with a healthy country. Less publicised, but equally important, was the supposed power of exercise to sublimate unhealthy sexual passions.[86] The establishment in 1937 of a Physical Welfare Branch of the Department of Internal Affairs signalled a new official commitment to the physical well-being and recreational needs of New Zealand's population. The Child Welfare Branch enlisted the services of physical welfare officers to devise and implement sporting and recreational regimes for adolescents. A scheme in Auckland in the 1940s placed 25 'troublesome lads' under the supervision of a physical welfare officer who, in cooperation with the local child welfare officer, arranged a 'corrective' sporting programme for the boys, who were taught basketball, gymnastics and boxing. To modern eyes the last-named may seem an unusual pastime for young men in court on 'serious charges', but contemporaries had faith in it. After three months, the scheme's supporters claimed, the boys had built up their physiques, their entire outlook had changed, and they were giving every indication that they would develop into useful citizens.[87] The reforming power of good literature was not ignored either. One child welfare officer encouraged his charges to join the local library, and eventually established his own to provide free (and suitable) reading matter.[88]

Voluntary organisations played an important part in supervision during the 1930s and 1940s, as they had earlier. The number of cases was sometimes too great for the Branch, which called on the services of selected groups for selected children: both small local groups such as the Community Sunshine Club, the Crichton Cobbers' Club, and St Christopher's Club, and the larger organisations of Roman Catholic and YMCA Big Brothers which catered only for boys. Using external assistance freed up Branch resources for other tasks. The extent of this assistance was realised most clearly during the Second World War, when the enlistment of YMCA Big Brothers left a significant gap in the Branch's supervision work.[89]

The Branch's preference was to rely on the YMCA Big Brothers. In the three years after the passage of the Child Welfare Act, the Big Brothers supervised more than 400 'Little Brothers', as their charges were known. Roman Catholic Big Brothers also operated during the 1930s, but the Branch sometimes found them to be both sectarian and irregular. Parents of children under Roman Catholic supervision periodically complained that the Sunday visits of Big Brothers were a device to enforce attendance at church. Unlike the Catholic Big Brothers, those in the YMCA were not clergy. The YMCA counselled great care in the selection of Big Brothers, recommending successful young businessmen or university students: 'the ordinary everyday young man with high ideals, a leader in sport and Big in every way is the type to choose for this work'. Despite the lofty ideals, some child welfare officers regarded Big Brothers as no more than kindly, enthusiastic amateurs. Nelson's child welfare officer was not convinced that the balance and tact necessary to influence young men and boys for the good could be found in the contemporary young man. He suggested that without intensive training courses for Big Brothers, their work would be no more than 'a haphazard attempt at something which can easily become unwieldy and almost worthless'.[90]

The system of Big Brother supervision was very similar to that of the Branch. Little Brothers were introduced to sporting and cultural activities, usually associated with the YMCA, encouraged to attend church and Sunday school, found employment if necessary, and given access to libraries. Unlike child welfare officers, each Big Brother had only a few Little Brothers to supervise, a fact which may have contributed to their success.[91] Big Brothers could spend a considerable amount of time with boys, and persevere if supervision started to break down. Christchurch Big Brother Lang found Robbie Cranford to be a 'high-spirited' boy who immediately broke his supervision agreement and ran off, leaving his mother a note explaining that he was going to sea as a cabin boy. The Big Brothers found Robbie stranded in Wellington, unable to obtain a berth, and

Many considered smoky billiard saloons (above) to be a source of moral contagion for the young. With the appointment of billiards champion Charlie Peek as Manager of the Boys' Training Farm in 1939, however, billiards became an acceptable activity in some child welfare circles – especially in boys' institutions such as Weraroa (left). TESLA STUDIOS COLLECTION, ATL, G-16661-1/1 & DEPARTMENT OF SOCIAL WELFARE returned him to Christchurch, where he was placed in work until he could be found a position in the Navy. Big Brother Lang had little doubt that Robbie had 'come to his senses' and was profiting by the guidance he was being given.[92]

Children's and families' reactions to supervision, whether by the Branch or Big Brothers, went largely unrecorded. Some officers claimed that they rarely met with parental opposition, and indeed the external supervision of a difficult child may have been welcomed by some parents.[93] Parents had little choice but to agree to court-ordered supervision, although they could, and sometimes did, request that a child be committed to the care of the state. Should parental cooperation not be forthcoming, the Child Welfare Act gave magistrates the authority to commit children to care, although the Branch preferred to nurture a more amicable relationship.

The Branch had considerable faith in the reformative and adjustment potential of supervision. Some magistrates and individual child welfare officers, however, viewed it as tolerance gone awry rather than measured, judicious treatment. Several of the magistrates surveyed about children's courts in the late 1920s suggested that punishment, rather than supervision, would best educate the young mind. Magistrate Luxton of Whangarei claimed that most of the children coming before the courts needed a shock, 'something that will create an impression on their minds'. Ruminating on times past, Wyvern Wilson reminded his colleagues that 'our forefathers were brought up under much sterner administration than the present with very good results'.[94]

The Branch was convinced of the success of supervision, although what this meant is difficult to define. Supervision saved some children and young people from future contact with the Branch, and enabled some to improve their circumstances. While others reoffended, they may well have done so without a period of supervision. Despite the visits and the letters, Murray McLean was given another two-year term of supervision for theft in 1942, and then a further year for theft in 1945. In 1947 he was arrested, along with his brothers, as part of a seven-member gang which had converted £18,000 worth of motor vehicles in Wellington. At that point, Murray's future became a matter for the Department of Justice.[95]

Murray's experiences may easily have come about in part as a result of supervision, as he and his family were drawn into the child welfare network. Once he was listed as a case, and supervision began, official interest in and intervention into the life of the McLean family increased. Visits from child welfare officers uncovered new 'problems', as in late 1940 when neighbours complained to the Branch that Mrs McLean left her children in the care of a fourteen year old during the day while she went out to work. Neither the girl nor her mother were efficient housekeepers, it seemed: the children were all shabby, poorly clothed and badly nourished. In a sense, the revelation and rectification of such additional problems was exactly what supervision was meant to accomplish.

From industrial schools to training centres: residential institutions

Child welfare policy after 1925 continued to move away from institutionalisation, as the Branch endeavoured to board out most state wards, leaving institutions to cope only with the most problematic children. The decision to commit was an option of last resort, ordered only when other methods had failed or were considered to be of no use. In keeping with the spirit of the legislation, admission to residential institutions became a comparatively minor feature of the child welfare system, numerically at least, as is shown in Figure 3 (p. 122). In all but one year between 1926 and 1948 there were fewer than 300 children in residences at any time, and they comprised less than 5 per cent of all children under observation from the 1930s. The late 1920s and the Second World War saw slight increases in the number of children in homes. This paralleled the greater interest in exploring the trend in juvenile delinquency in the 1940s; the increase in the late 1920s may have simply been a consequence of uncertainties in administering new legislation. Most residents remained in the institutions for less than two years before being released into the community, either to foster parents or back to their families.[96]

The Child Welfare Act dispensed with the term 'industrial school' in a deliberate break from past practices. Instead, it enabled the establishment of a variety of residences: receiving homes, probation homes, convalescent homes, training farms or schools, and other homes which would promote the general purposes of the Act. With the exception of convalescent homes, the Branch established institutions in all these categories.

As previously, receiving homes in the main centres took in children and young people on a short-term basis before their admission to another institution or placement with foster parents. Probation homes were also established in the main centres to give short periods of institutional care before supervision. In practice, the two types of residences provided separately for girls and boys. Girls and boys aged under ten were sent to receiving homes, while probation homes admitted boys for short periods. By the mid-1930s, child welfare officers referred to probation homes as 'boys' homes'; the term 'probation' had fallen out of use, and the institutions had become residences for boys only. Hostels for young working people were opened from the mid-1920s. In 1927, the Branch established a hostel for young women working in Wellington as a halfway house before discharge. Young women considered unsuitable for live-in domestic service were

Wellington Harbour, viewed from the balcony of the Girls' Hostel in Wadestown. NATIONAL
PUBLICITY STUDIOS PHOTOGRAPHIC COLLECTION, NATIONAL ARCHIVES, A45617

able to remain there provided they continued in their employment – usually in
shops or factories – and followed the hostel's rules. A similar institution for
young men was opened in Auckland in 1939/40, replacing an earlier YMCA
hostel.[97]

The residential institutions for boys at Otekaike and for girls at Richmond
continued to receive children who required special instruction. The 1924 Committee of Inquiry into Mental Defectives and Sexual Offenders had publicised the
question of the education of 'feeble-minded' children, and the Eugenics Board
established after the Committee reported furthered this interest. In 1929, the
Mental Hospitals Department opened the Templeton Farm School for children
considered unable to respond to the educational facilities offered in the Branch's
institutions. From then on, Otekaike and Richmond received school-age children
who could not be boarded out or attend regular schools. Both institutions now
took a mixture of school-age children and older pupils, some of whom had been
admitted through the courts because of delinquency.[98]

The training schools formed the core of the Branch's institutional services. Just as abandoning the term 'industrial schools' signalled a new direction in residential services, so too did the adoption of a new terminology. Training suggested instruction, re-education, and adjustment, with children and young people ceasing to be unruly and troublesome and becoming young citizens. The use of psychological testing and (intermittently) case clinics in the homes from the 1930s helped to map out training agendas. While the main institution for boys immediately took up the new term, being known as a 'training farm', the major institution for girls continued to be known as a 'home' until the mid-1940s. In 1944 its Principal, Kath Scotter, urged the adoption of the title of 'Girls' Training Centre'; 'Home' was out of step with the times, and carried a stigma of punishment, she considered.[99]

The existing institutions for boys and girls both underwent major changes between 1925 and 1948. Accommodation for delinquent girls and young women became a pressing problem in the mid-1920s. Following the closure of the Te Oranga Reformatory in 1918, the Branch relied on the former Caversham Industrial School for girls and young women. The poor state of the buildings, coupled with the lack of training facilities and public condemnation of the operation of this institution, led to its closure in 1926/7. Te Oranga reopened in 1928 as the Burwood Home for older delinquent girls; a junior section was added in 1942/3.[100] Wartime fears about the behaviour of young Maori women led in 1944 to the establishment of the first and only special institution for Maori. The Branch had debated the need for such an institution since the late 1930s, when it found that its efforts to recruit more Maori honorary child welfare officers and work with Maori communities were doing little to keep Maori children out of the courts. To counter this problem, the Branch purchased an old, rambling residence near Featherston in order to accommodate a small number of older Maori girls. Fareham House opened its doors in August 1944, and by March 1945 had received eighteen young Maori women.[101]

Few Maori had entered the Department's homes before the 1930s, partly because few had come into contact with the child welfare system, but also because the Branch consciously endeavoured to keep Maori children out of its institutions. The Branch acknowledged some of the pain and anguish which forcible separation from whanau could entail. As one child welfare inspector realised, the 'Maori girl does not take kindly to Institutional life, as they are home sick and crave to be with their own people'.[102] Maori groups which made their views known to the Branch reiterated such sentiments, and criticised the removal of Maori from their family groups. George Graham, representing Te Akarana Association, argued that any separation of Maori children from their locality and whanau was detrimental. He questioned the extent to which Maori youths were kept in contact with their kin groups and helped to retain competence in the Maori language.[103]

The central residential accommodation for boys at Weraroa also underwent a number of changes. From 1920 the Branch used an offshoot of Weraroa to accommodate school-age boys, keeping the older boys and those of working age at Weraroa. The Hokio Beach school, which was first used as a summer camp, rapidly developed into a permanent arrangement to alleviate overcrowding at Weraroa, and was gazetted as an institution in 1924. A reorganisation of the schools saw Hokio closed in 1936, but it reopened within a year after changes at Weraroa. Separating the younger from the older boys was presented as an 'incalculable good' for both groups, but particularly for the young ones, who could be bullied and picked on in the larger institution. Many of them were 'undersized' and 'below the average generally'. It was expected that the management difficulties which were endemic at Weraroa could be prevented at Hokio.[104]

The Branch assumed control of the Department of Agriculture's Central Development Farm near Weraroa in 1930, and added this to its institutional complex. The acquisition substantially enhanced the agricultural focus of the institution, which prided itself on its livestock-rearing and farming methods. Even with the addition of Hokio and the farm, the facilities at Weraroa were insufficient to cope with the growth in its population during the 1930s. The buildings were in dire need of repair, and a spate of abscondings put a spotlight on management difficulties. The Air Force commandeered Weraroa in 1939, and by 1940 its residents were split between Hokio Beach, the Central Development Farm, and a section of Weraroa. Perhaps not surprisingly, Manager Charlie Peek wondered how he could run the institution effectively under such conditions, particularly after he had been compelled to move the residents from Weraroa over a weekend to make way for the Air Force.[105] By 1941 new buildings had been erected and the institution was able to function fully once more.

Residential institutions were, in theory, reserved for 'special' cases, those 'failures' who would not respond to community-based care: the worst-behaved children, the most delinquent youngsters, the most serious offenders. In reality, these institutions continued to take the mix of children and young people that they had always received: young offenders, children from indigent homes, those who had been neglected, the persistently mischievous, and the sexually precocious.

Some children and young people were admitted to institutions only after they had 'failed' their supervision. Jimmy Heath, initially charged with theft, was placed on supervision for a short time before being sent to a Salvation Army Home. A further charge of theft led to his admission to Weraroa.[106] In this case the Branch tried other means before arranging for his admission, but sometimes it recommended immediate institutionalisation, or magistrates ordered committal straight away. This was particularly the case for girls and young women whose conduct was overtly sexual. Most of those admitted to Burwood during the 1940s were committed for not being under proper control, and admitted direct from court. Unlike the residents of institutions for boys and young men, few Burwood residents had committed an offence. Continuing a well-established pattern, most were admitted for living in an environment detrimental to their well-being or for indulging in questionable sexual conduct. Rona Hall was admitted direct to Burwood from court in 1943 after her mother had been warned about the excessive liberty she was granting her in allowing her to wander the streets 'at all hours of the night'. Others were admitted more to protect them from a poor family background than for any other reason. Maggie Hammond, whose mother had been well-known both to police and child welfare officers for many years, was admitted for living in a detrimental environment: an insanitary and condemned house in a swamp in Lower Hutt where her mother had attempted to prostitute her with a soldier.[107]

Committing offences, being delinquent and not being under proper control constituted the reasons for admission to an institution in the great majority of cases. Some children and young people were committed because of neglect, abuse, or the difficult conditions in which they lived. The Child Welfare Act also allowed for the immediate removal of children from poor surroundings, or if they were likely to be neglected, and their admission to an institution or other temporary home while a complaint under the Act was processed. While a few of these admissions were to Weraroa or Burwood, most children in this category went to receiving homes or boys' homes for a short period before being boarded out.

Some of these children had also been under supervision for a time while child welfare officers worked with the entire family to improve their living conditions. In 1930, for example, Palmerston North child welfare officers began to monitor the welfare of eight month old Mary Paterson, whose mother Irene, aged eighteen, had undergone a 'form of marriage' with a 47 year old man. Mary was neglected; she seldom received milk, and her mother did not 'seem to think a bath necessary'. Child welfare officers visited Mary's home over more than a decade, during which time she and several of her siblings were admitted to an orphanage. By the late 1930s, Mary was living with Irene and her de facto husband. She was committed to a receiving home along with six of her brothers and sisters in late 1942, and then boarded out when it was discovered that her 'stepfather' had sexually abused her.[108]

The Branch sometimes fell back on private assistance in finding institutional beds. It used selected homes if its own facilities were overcrowded, or, as it had before, if the training provided at a private institution was useful for specific groups of state wards. Convenience, rather than anything else, underpinned this policy, although admission to a private institution involved an implicit agreement that the Branch would abide by its rules.[109] From 1928, the Branch sent boys to Salvation Army homes throughout the country. Overcrowding at Weraroa in that year led to the transfer of eight of the residents to a Salvation Army home at Putaruru: the Branch paid the Army a maintenance fee, and required quarterly reports on the welfare of the residents. Maori children were sometimes sent to church or private institutions in preference to keeping them in state institutions. From 1941, the Branch sent selected Maori youths to the Presbyterian Boys' Farm at Te Whaiti, where they remained for periods of two years.[110]

Private institutions and orphanages had increased in number during the first part of the twentieth century, and by the mid-1920s, the 85 private institutions and orphanages in New Zealand housed more than 4000 children. The number of institutions remained stable between 1925 and 1948, although the number of children detained decreased; by the mid-1940s, there were fewer than 3000 children in 80 homes.[111] The Branch considered the initial growth in private provision to be due to a combination of parental irresponsibility and the increased activity of private social service and religious organisations. No doubt the gap in the institutional network created by the state's withdrawal facilitated the explosion in the number of private homes. Families in distress found their services invaluable in times of ill health or crises such as divorce. That many of the 'orphanages' housed children with a living parent who had placed the child there for a short period further illustrates their general role in community welfare.[112]

Greater use of the facilities of private groups led to attempts to assert greater control and direction over their child welfare work. As the Branch took from voluntary groups with one hand, it sought to regulate the types of services they could provide with the other. During the mid-1920s the Branch asserted its pre-eminent role as a child welfare provider by emphasising its authority over the management of private institutions, satisfying a long-desired aim in the process. An amendment to the Child Welfare Act in 1927 empowered the Branch to inspect and register all private institutions in which children resided. Beck had long viewed as dangerous private institutions' independence from state control and regulation. His first report as Superintendent of Child Welfare made explicit his intention to supervise the management of private institutions; he noted regretfully that the Child Welfare Act had not facilitated this.[113] With this authority came another opportunity for the Branch to emphasise the advantages of its own system of child welfare, and to encourage private groups to adopt it, particularly by boarding out children. In approving the registration of the All Saints' Children's Home in Palmerston North in 1929, Beck seized the opportunity to emphasise the benefits of the cottage home system and boarding

Agricultural work was an important part of vocational training in institutions for boys and young men. Here a resident of the Otekaike Special School for Boys feeds the eager Otekaike Princess.
NATIONAL PUBLICITY STUDIOS, DEPARTMENT OF SOCIAL WELFARE, A46107

out. He reminded the managers that the boarded-out child was far better equipped 'for the battle of life than a child who has been brought up in an institution where the tendency is to stifle initiative and to institutionalise'.[114]

Life in residential institutions revolved around a timetabled day of activities designed to build character and keep the residents quiet and busy: vocational instruction, primary or secondary education in the schools attached to the home, and a variety of recreational pursuits. The programmes were not too dissimilar in content from those of the earlier industrial schools. All of the larger institutions, such as Burwood, Hokio and Weraroa, had gymnasia, swimming pools and outdoor sporting areas. In marked contrast with the industrial school period, residents participated in the setting of institutional rules, within boundaries stipulated by the Branch. In 1947 Burwood introduced a Girls' Council, which produced a newsletter, 'Centre News', from 1948. Institutions also encouraged closer contact with the community, through sports teams, dances and other entertainments. From 1944 Burwood residents arranged an annual Christmas

From the 1940s, residents of the Girls' Training Centre at Burwood staged annual dances and tableaux (above). An emphasis on poise and graceful activities also formed part of the curriculum at the Richmond Special School for Girls (right).
NATIONAL PUBLICITY STUDIOS, DEPARTMENT OF SOCIAL WELFARE, A46066 & NATIONAL PUBLICITY STUDIOS PHOTOGRAPHIC COLLECTION, NATIONAL ARCHIVES, A45956

tableau, an event which gained a place on the Christchurch social calendar. After a spate of absconding from Weraroa in the 1930s, local people organised a visiting committee to foster interest in the home and its residents.[115]

Residents at Burwood and Fareham House received instruction in general household skills. The goal of Burwood (and Fareham), the Branch suggested, was to enable each girl to take her place in the community as a clean, honest, hard-working and self-respecting woman. In effect, this meant making the residents capable of managing their own homes. As Kath Scotter, the Principal of Burwood, explained, it was 'generally accepted' that all girls needed some training in domestic work if they were to become good wives and mothers. Most did not continue with their schoolwork after leaving Burwood, but went into factories, hospitals or dressmaking, where they found their training at the home particularly useful. Case files from the 1940s suggest that Burwood residents saw themselves in these careers only until marriage. Mavis Lilburn knew that she was good at housework, which would be her career choice; Rima Mahino 'giggled' when asked about her aspirations, and noted that while gardening was 'allright' she preferred housework to either that or farm work.[116]

Residents at Weraroa followed a similarly gendered pattern of vocational instruction, working primarily on the institution's farm but also in the various manual and technical workshops. The nature of the farming instruction came under particular criticism in the 1930s and early 1940s. According to one child welfare officer, the daily life of the residents was simply 'institutionalised farm labour, carried out under the "foremanship" of unscientific overseers'; he recommended that the instruction be reviewed and put on a proper scientific footing. Beck had visited Weraroa in the early 1930s and concluded that the boys and young men were not likely to benefit from their residence. The staff were too militaristic, and the senior staff lacked the 'special qualities' needed to control either their subordinates or the boys. Like Burnham before it, Weraroa had introduced cadet drill in lieu of physical education. 'A fig for your Cadet drill', child welfare officer John Cupit declared in condemning Weraroa as 'the last remnant of an obsolete system'. In his view it was 'the dust-bin into which is thrown all boys who are not amenable to Probation', and a place for young criminals 'in the post graduate stage'.[117] The employment of new staff, and in particular of skilled farm workers during the 1940s, improved the entire institution, the Branch believed.

The staffing problems at Weraroa were symptomatic of wider difficulties in the institutional system. Staff were untrained and forced to learn on the job, with the exception of those employed for their expertise in areas such as cookery and farming. Staff turnover was high, as many found it difficult to cope with the demands of the work. The women employed in the receiving homes found the constant influx of small children and babies very tiring. The Manager of the home at Miramar in Wellington demanded more staff; her women were working more than 70 hours a week.[118] The punishment returns from homes which frequently administered corporal punishment suggest the problems which some staff had in coping with their work and institutional life.

For children and young people, residential institutions meant the loss of liberty and removal from friends and family, no matter what type of training or staffing was provided. Residents had greater contact with their families than previously, through letters or periodic visits home, but the location of the two training homes prevented regular face-to-face contact between most children and their families. Children's thoughts on their confinement rarely entered institutional records directly; their responses are more readily discernible through their actions. Some found institutional life a relief from unhappy or abusive homes, and passed their stay in outward quiet. During an official visit to Otekaike in 1928, the visitors were awakened in the morning by a squad of boys, who were singing 'The More We Are Together the Happier We'll Be' and other

Gardening was one of the general household duties which residents of most institutions performed. Here the residents of Fareham House tend the grounds of the institution. NATIONAL PUBLICITY STUDIOS PHOTOGRAPHIC COLLECTION, NATIONAL ARCHIVES, A46329

popular songs while polishing the linoleum. Someone in the Education Department added a note in the margin of the file, asking 'was this stage-set?' We might well share this scepticism.[119] Others expressed their dissatisfaction or unhappiness with institutional life by absconding. Between January 1930 and June 1932, there were nearly 250 abscondings from Weraroa alone, and some of these boys and young men committed serious offences while at large. Neighbours blamed the inadequacy of discipline at the institution, and alleged that fear had become so widespread in the community that women were afraid to remain alone at night.[120] The Branch understood how difficult it was to manage open institutions by moral suasion rather than through locks and bars, and staffing changes and the reclassification of residents early in 1933 reduced some of the problems. By the outbreak of war, however, absconding from Weraroa was once more public news, with residents rioting and planning mass escapes.[121]

For children and young people who arrived at a residence in a distressed and traumatised state, their institutional stay could be a dismal torment. 'Angela' arrived at Burwood in late 1947 after an unhappy home life, sexual relationships

The need for self-sufficiency meant that residents had to help with all aspects of institutional work. Here residents of the Boys' Training Centre mend and iron clothing. DEPARTMENT OF SOCIAL WELFARE

with several men, and an attempted rape. She absconded four times during her first four months at the home. When her behaviour changed from 'noisy' and talkative to 'very quiet', staff suspected that something was amiss, particularly when she complained of feeling ill. Finally Angela admitted to swallowing a needle; a medical examination found that she had ingested fifteen.[122]

Parents' reactions to having their children removed were also seldom recorded. A few requested that the Branch take over the care of their child and arrange for committal to a home. Mrs Trethewey, who was separated from her husband and had three children, called on the Branch when her son Fred began stealing. Child welfare officers informed her that it was not necessary to have him committed to care to prevent him becoming a kleptomaniac, as she had believed.[123] Whether these parents wished to relinquish guardianship over their children was another matter. New Zealand parents may have shared the feelings of parents elsewhere at this time. An American study of the parental use of early twentieth-century juvenile courts suggests that parents saw the threat of admission to a home as a way of bolstering their own authority and perhaps giving their children a shock; few wanted to have their children removed entirely from their care.[124]

Some families protested vehemently when their children were committed. At times the Branch failed to disclose the intention to admit a child to an institution so as to avoid 'disagreeable scenes' with parents. Late in 1946 the Christchurch District Child Welfare Officer was reprimanded for resorting to subterfuge in order to admit a young boy to an institution. Neighbours had complained of the behaviour of Paul Crafar, whom they said was a nuisance and not under proper control. Officers told Mrs Crafar that Paul would be sent on a holiday; instead, he was admitted to a boy's home and then sent to board with foster parents. This practice cannot have been unique, as in mid-1948 the Branch circularised all district offices that secretive methods of achieving admissions to institutions should be avoided.[125]

As with other aspects of child welfare, the aim of both the courts and residential institutions went beyond the welfare of children to that of the wider community. Keeping children in a household or family unit was of pivotal importance, for the family was seen as the solution to child welfare problems. As Superintendent Charlie Peek noted, 'in the long run, if it preserves intact a family unit and at the same time avoids animosity, and the creation of long-standing grievances against authority, the quiet persuasive action is better'.[126] Yet children's welfare and community welfare were not necessarily synonymous; children's welfare was always perceived through a wider lens that encompassed adult and social needs, just as much as – or even more than – children's. Growing concerns about juvenile delinquency and youthful behaviour could override notions of children's welfare, as is suggested by the institutionalisation of 'oversexed' and 'uncontrollable' young women. The work of the courts and institutions placed in stark relief a tension between the issues of (children's) welfare and justice (for the community), a tension made more intense by the Branch's overt espousal of an ethos of welfare and protection. Balancing the two considerations was not easy, as was made explicit by the difficulties in the children's courts and other areas of training.

CHAPTER 4

'Saved to the State': preventive child welfare

Preventing children and adolescents needing further contact with the Child Welfare Branch was a central philosophy of child welfare by the later 1920s. Preventive child welfare policies, the 'adjustment of conditions in connection with homes and families that, if allowed to develop, would lead to destitution, delinquency, juvenile crime, vice, and to anti-social conduct generally', were one way to construct a new society.[1] Stressing the role positive social work in the present had in avoiding negative results in the future enabled the Branch to intervene in a variety of situations in the name of saving the child and, by extension, safeguarding the welfare of families and the nation. It was an enterprise which required assistance, however, and the Branch utilised community and family resources. In the process, the Child Welfare Branch became a general welfare department with responsibility for the welfare of all citizens, not just children.

'To prevent wastage in child-life': the development of preventive work

Josiah Hanan's special report of 1917 which delineated an agenda for change in the industrial school system also adumbrated an ethos of prevention. In a suitably military allusion, Hanan suggested that:

the industrial-school system might be called a Red Cross contingent picking up and attending to the socially wounded and maimed; but we should find out why there are so many wounded, and consider whether we cannot protect a child before, instead of helping him after he goes through the Criminal Court. Society has not made the best use of its powers until it seeks to forestall and prevent those damages which at present it seeks only to repair. It is a short-sighted policy to devote our attention to the punishment or even the reform of the criminal rather than to prevent the boy or girl from becoming a criminal.[2]

Along with other nations reeling from the effects of the First World War, New Zealand incorporated a self-consciously preventive aspect in its child welfare policies. Juvenile probation, of course, was a form of prevention, in that it was designed to keep children and young people out of institutions and out of further trouble; but preventing them going to court in the first place would be more desirable. From 1917, probation officers did not need a court order to supervise children whose actions had come to the attention of the police through either petty delinquency or 'mischievousness'.[3] The 1917 scheme was initially limited in scope, applying only in Auckland, and only to boys and young men. A few of the early cases were passed over to the Roman Catholic and YMCA Big Brothers as part of their general supervision work. Increasingly, however, preventive supervision, as it came to be known, assumed more importance in the Department's work. By the early 1920s it formed part of the core duties of all officers, not just the probation staff. Using the terms which would come to dominate the language of child welfare policy after 1925, Beck foresaw this work as the means of child welfare offices 'assuming the rôle of child-welfare bureaux of information and adjustment'.[4]

Although the Child Welfare Act made no reference to preventive work, the direction of policy and practice after 1925 made evident its centrality. The Act's emphasis on keeping children and young people out of institutions wherever possible offered a legislative rationale for prevention. In this respect, the permissiveness of the legislation enabled child welfare officers and the Branch as a whole to implement a range of policies, and was one reason why the Act remained in effect for so long. Officers regarded preventive policies as the focus of the Department's work with children and their families. Beck maintained that there was no more important social work than the reclamation of children who had the potential to swell the ranks of the country's prison inmates.[5]

The number of preventive supervision cases emphasised the importance of the preventive approach. In 1926, 398 children from 221 families were designated as preventive cases. As can be seen from Figure 3 (p. 122) this number grew to 1081 children in 1933/4, and reached a peak of 1978 in 1943/4 before dropping to 1645 by 1947/8. As a proportion of child welfare cases at the end of each year, preventive cases increased steadily from 7 per cent of the total in 1926 to more than 22 per cent in 1948. As a philosophy of welfare, prevention was now the dominant ethos.

Cases for preventive supervision came to the attention of the Branch by various means. Teachers, neighbours, local welfare organisations, religious groups, community agencies and the police all commonly referred cases, or suspicions about potential problems. Some were also referred by other government departments. The admission of one fifteen year old girl to hospital with venereal disease led to her inclusion on the Branch's preventive list following advice from the local medical officer of health. On investigating, the child welfare officer found that the girl and her mother were living in a dirty bedsit, and that the girl had recently had an accident at work. The mother, who was described as 'excitable', was 'terrified' of 'the welfare', as her four eldest children had been committed to care in 1914. The child welfare officer noted that her visit had given both mother and daughter a 'big fright', and believed that future visits would keep them 'up to the mark'.[6]

Parents themselves sometimes asked that their child be placed under preventive supervision. The widowed Mrs White rang her local office about her son Lawrence, demanding that the Branch take a 'preventive interest' in him: he refused to get a job, and spent much of his time in bed. The officers obliged, but held out little hope of progress: Mrs White had allowed Lawrence to become 'introspective', and by 'over-indulgence' and weak management encouraged his morbid preoccupation with his health. Mrs White may well have been concerned for her own safety at the hands of her physically strong son. Later reports described him as 'extremely vindictive' towards women, and at one stage he sent her a letter with the ominous opening line, 'Dear Bitch'; her letters, by contrast, were described as abject and cringing; she was almost 'grovelling' to her boy. Within a month of the Branch's involvement, Lawrence had been taken into custody for his truculent behaviour at home; he had broken windows and thrown items around the house. He was brandishing a rifle when the police arrived, and it took three officers to disarm him.[7]

Very rarely, children and young people themselves requested assistance. These cases could be clear cries for help, perhaps a final resort for unhappy children who could see no end to domestic problems. Early in 1947, fourteen year old Myrtle Hughes called the local child welfare office to say that she was scared of her mother. Rather than remain at home and endure physical and verbal abuse, she asked to be put in a child welfare home. Instead, the child welfare officer placed Myrtle under preventive supervision and arranged for her to board with a family.[8]

These cases, and others like them, suggest that the preventive supervision the Branch provided could be a tool with which families could disentangle complex and fraught relationships. Historians have noted that it was often the weaker members of families who approached welfare agencies for assistance, perhaps in the hope that an external intervention into their lives might tilt the balance of power in family dynamics in their direction – as often occurred.[9] As child welfare officers knew, some widows with adolescent sons were 'only too pleased' to call on them for assistance.[10] For women frightened of their stronger children, and children frightened of their parents, the local child welfare office could be an important source of support. The Branch did not always act, and when it did it was not always in their favour or as they wanted, but for those women and children who were assisted, its actions were sometimes of immeasurable value.

In keeping with the broad definition of preventive work, cases were placed under preventive supervision for delinquent behaviour, neglect, living in poor conditions and minor offences; children had to be 'problems' already, or have the potential to become problems in the future, to qualify as preventive cases. The freedom to place cases on the preventive list meant that child welfare officers did not have to take to the children's court complaints under the Child Welfare Act. Distinguishing between cases which should be kept in the community under preventive supervision and those which should be taken to the courts rested both on the individual circumstances and on the readiness of parents to cooperate with the Child Welfare Branch, which was, after all, acting beyond the letter of the law.

Preventive supervision cases reflected a wide spectrum of child and family situations, and offer a window into the lives, relationships and everyday problems of New Zealanders in the first half of the twentieth century. Complaints of truancy led to many children being placed on the preventive list. The teacher of thirteen year old John Poole informed the local child welfare officer of his continued absence from school. The Department knew his family well, as his mother had already been prosecuted several times for failing to send her children to school. The Child Welfare Branch took on John as a preventive case to induce him to overcome his truancy and improve his general behaviour.[11]

Cases of petty offending and minor theft could also be placed under supervision if the police were willing not to lay charges.[12] Warren Kane, who stole £15 from his widowed mother's boarders, was placed under preventive supervision in 1947. More serious cases of offending were sometimes put under supervision in the hope that intervention would remove the need for further punitive action. Wellington police referred Raymond Hastings to the local child welfare officer in early 1948 after he sexually assaulted two small boys. The child welfare officer hoped both to place Raymond in employment and 'readjust' his home life, which was believed to be contributing to his behaviour.

Preventive supervision was also used to monitor the well-being of children who had been abused, neglected or ill-treated, or whose parents were suspected of this. Dr Agnes Bennett informed Wellington child welfare officer Annie Tocker of a child who was seriously neglected in 1934, precipitating a relationship between the family and the Branch which lasted for at least seventeen years. Officers visited the family for two years until they felt compelled to take a complaint of neglect to the children's court.[13] The neighbours of three year old Jessie Ryan complained to child welfare officers that Mrs Ryan neglected the child. When the Branch investigated the case, they could find no grounds for committing the infant to a foster home. Instead, 'stern supervision' was arranged to enable the officers to take further action should it become necessary.

Being 'uncontrollable' was a frequent reason for placement on the preventive list, as it had earlier been a common cause of admission to industrial schools. Children who defied their parents, ran away from home, were disobedient or associated with doubtful characters could all be considered uncontrollable and therefore cases for preventive supervision. Classification as uncontrollable could be gender-specific and reflect contemporary anxieties over female sexuality. Betty Mabbett's association with sailors in the late 1940s led to her being classed as out of control and 'obviously' in need of a degree of official oversight. Equally undefined 'moodiness' or poor 'temperament' could also justify preventive supervision lest it become more pathological. Matthew Wentworth, for example, came under the Branch's notice in 1939 because of his 'sulky, delinquent tendencies'. The local child welfare officer took him on as a preventive case, established regular correspondence with him, and reported later that Matthew had come 'through' well and never appeared in the children's court.

Preventive child welfare policies broke down some of the boundaries created by the categorisation of children as delinquent or non-delinquent cases, and between children who were regarded as threats to society and those who were perceived as its victims. Any case could be taken on as preventive, as the above examples indicate, and it mattered little whether a child had been neglected or had committed an offence. Internationally, the abandonment of the distinction between the neglected and the delinquent child became a feature of child welfare policies after the First World War.[14] Blurring the boundaries between neglected and delinquent children by using preventive strategies could lead to a less punitive or different approach to children who had committed an offence, or whose behaviour warranted correction. Opaque boundaries also enabled child welfare officers to keep under surveillance those children who were not yet classed as problems, but had the potential to become so. Neglected children could be an incipient danger if they had family backgrounds which gave them the capacity for delinquency. In one sense, all the cases that came to attention were

The sedate merry-go-round held little moral danger for the young, but the more boisterous elements of amusement parks, such as the dodgem rides, were another matter, especially for young women. J. R. WALL COLLECTION, ATL, G-17772-1/2

problems to be solved, or they would not have been reported or uncovered. By treating some children as problems in the making, stringent and long-term intervention could be justified in the name of prevention.

The preventive policies applied to young women illustrated this approach most starkly. Association with 'undesirables', being 'uncontrollable', running away from home, or staying out late at night could lead them into future or further difficulty. Fourteen year old Esme Hawkins was placed on preventive supervision at the request of the police, who had found her frequenting dodgem rides. Esme had given no previous trouble and her parents were cooperative, but still the child welfare officer arranged to visit Esme every three months to check on her conduct.[15] The dividing line between taking such young women to court and placing them on preventive supervision in the community was thin indeed. As the cases of the Burwood residents outlined in the previous chapter suggest, it could take very little for these young women to come under the care of the Superintendent of Child Welfare.

If preventive supervision placed a premium on caring for children and young people in their family environment, it also placed considerable emphasis on improving that environment. Preventive policies were centred on a belief that home conditions were the primary cause of child neglect or incipient delinquency. Implementing such policies enabled the Branch to confront directly what it had long seen as the crux of child welfare problems. The development of preventive work followed from a diagnosis of inadequate parenting. Preventive supervision required that 'to build for the future a commencement should be made from the cradle with competent advice to parents during the child's early habit-forming years . . . . to ensure that the life of the child be directed in accordance with accepted standards of good conduct and morality.'[16] Parental education – or re-education – was the key to combating child abuse, neglect or delinquency; keeping families together, under surveillance and with preventive polices applied to the entire household through a focus on the child, was a means to accomplishing this.

Child welfare officers investigating the circumstances which had drawn cases to their attention were quick to find signs of parental neglect, inadequate home life, or quirky behaviour which could justify their intervention. An 'impatient, neurotic and over-emotional' mother and a father who had taken no part in the control of his son were the reasons supplied for one boy's poor behaviour. The parents themselves were described as 'fairly well adjusted', although the officer noted that the home environment had been 'unstable' for years.[17]

Placing children on the preventive list became a means of extending supervision over the whole family. Inquiries into the case of Esther Brown revealed her father to be a disciplinarian of the 'old school' and her stepmother to be unaffectionate. Between them they had the girl in a 'highly nervous state', but the child welfare officer was confident of righting the situation: 'I think that with a period of oversight these people may be brought to a better understanding of each other.'[18] In other cases, prevention enabled the monitoring of general family welfare rather than concentrating on the well-being of a child. Placing under supervision the six Smith children was considered to be a way of assisting their mother. The officer believed that oversight and advice would be helpful, as Mrs Smith, while very fond of the children, had little money and had kept them from school as they all had scabies. Sometimes entire families – parents and children – were placed under supervision, with the case being listed under the name of the parents. Parental neglect led to the Jones family of Wellington being placed on the preventive list in 1940; under the Branch's supervision for eighteen months, Mrs Jones 'improved vastly' in the care she took of her children.

The procedure for creating a preventive supervision case necessitated, in theory at least, a considerable amount of investigation and inquiry on the part of the child welfare officer, if she or he were to map out an adjustment programme that was likely to be successful. Child welfare officers had a strong, hands-on role both in recommending preventive supervision and in formulating its practice; the operation of preventive supervision may well have played a part in the increasing professionalisation of welfare work over this period. Officers made preliminary – and sometimes exhaustive – inquiries into potential cases, and if they believed that there were grounds for ongoing supervision, they would recommend that the case be added to the preventive 'list'. Officers would outline the details of the case: the actions and behaviour of the children at home, school or work; descriptions of their health and physique, perhaps along with a psychological profile, and of the family's circumstances in terms of siblings, housing, finances, parental conduct and employment. Officers would recommend when preventive supervision should proceed, how frequently visits should be made, and how long the supervision should last. They could also indicate the form that it would take, such as correspondence, visits, or contact with clubs and societies. Their position also gave them considerable power to judge the household and childrearing skills of families. A Wellington child welfare officer whose preventive list included the Wright family visited the home in 1941 to find Mrs Wright 'enjoying a good gossip over the fence'. Inside, the home was 'rather dirty'. Mrs Wright was, however, a 'simple sort of woman doing her best', and the child welfare officer made allowance for the fact that she had seven children and few conveniences.[19] Officers were evidently prepared to overlook 'poor housekeeping' so long as families were 'doing their best'.

The imperative of inquiry and monitoring emphasised the development of investigative skills and the ability to identify and carry out the most efficacious mode of treatment. Increasingly, during this period, child welfare officers used psychology to explain the characters of those under supervision. Departmental and other psychologists were called on to assess children under preventive supervision, and to assist in recommending the course that supervision should take.

McClune's annual report for 1945 illustrates the importance that psychology was assuming in the Branch's policies at mid-century. Preventive work could, he noted, be divided into two distinct methods: the 'psychological approach', and 'experience and experiment'. The 'useful adjustment' in children and their families that could be brought about through the psychological approach, as well as more child guidance clinics, would lead to a drop in the number appearing before children's courts. Any assertion that the utilisation of psychological services was symptomatic of a 'sentimental approach to the problem of the bad boy' could be dismissed. Psychology had 'proved its worth' in New Zealand and elsewhere, and was already leading to greater parental understanding of the 'real needs' of their children.[20]

Whether or not the use of psychological services had 'proved its worth' – presumably by preventing court appearances and further problems – is a moot point, for the Branch gave no indication of the success of its programme during the 1940s. What is clear is the extent to which psychological assessments and the use of psychological terms to describe welfare problems had become a regular part of the Branch's preventive work. Child welfare officers in centres such as Dunedin met weekly with the local psychological clinic in 1948 to discuss specific cases and general problems.[21] Officers could, if they thought it advisable, refer any preventive case for a psychological assessment. In early 1948 a Wellington officer formulated for Raymond Hastings a three-part preventive programme which included a psychological examination, placement in employment, and the provision of a satisfactory social life. The psychologist James Caughley diagnosed Hastings' problems as a combination of both hereditary and environmental factors, principally his being the child of elderly parents: 'the father plausible and quite unreliable, and the mother overwrought in her attempts to keep the family together by going out to work'.[22]

Child welfare officers incorporated aspects of psychology into their preventive work by using the terminology and indulging in amateur diagnosis. What some lacked in professional psychological skills and training, they made up for in enthusiasm. The Department's preventive supervision forms included a large space in which officers could note a child's psychological symptoms by indicating moods, ability to relate to others, propensity to violence, and so on; some filled up these spaces easily. Officers also made their own diagnoses after observation. Michael Hayes' officer described the ten year old as failing to progress satis-factorily through his 'emotional stages', and thus being unable to identify with his father at an appropriate age. June Forster's report for 1947 ascribed her enuresis as 'due probably to some serious psychological trouble at home'.[23]

As other historians have argued, however, psychological testing and the use of scientific terminology to describe children's problems did not necessarily have any effect on the actual practice of child welfare.[24] Scientific jargon could easily replace more established means of describing welfare issues; a 'bad' family background in the 1910s could become the 'mal-adjusted home' of the preventive case in the 1940s without any attempt at a more rigorous or systematic approach to solving the problem. Yet the influence of psychological assessments and terms should not be minimised. Describing old problems in new ways established a link between a child's home circumstances, background and mental state which facilitated alternative methods of treatment. It stressed the importance of ensuring a child's welfare in the home, marking the triumph of those who believed in the necessity of transforming environmental and family conditions as the prelude to more lasting change. As an historian of English child welfare has suggested, 'by 1940, social, medical and psychiatric knowledge of children was such that the mind–body unity in common with environmental and familial

Boxing was a corrective discipline for boys and young men under court-ordered and preventive supervision. These are contestants in the under-95lb division of the Wellesley College Annual Boxing Tournament, 1929. WELLESLEY COLLEGE COLLECTION, ATL, F-147278-1/2

influences gave children (and childhood) a greater sense of depth than at any other time during their history'.[25] Perhaps more significantly, the growing influence of psychology epitomised the emergence of a new group of experts in the field of child welfare in New Zealand. It was a group whose role would expand considerably in the 1950s in the face of new anxieties about juvenile delinquency. Regardless of how deeply psychological ideas penetrated the practice of preventive child welfare in New Zealand in the 1930s and 1940s, the use of assessments and the spread of scientific terminology illustrated the willingness of officers and the Branch to embrace new approaches to welfare problems. Research into aspects of child welfare assumed a heightened import-ance in the 1940s, and the Branch increasingly expected its officers to be conversant with the most recent trends in overseas policy and literature.[26]

The expansion of preventive work also led the Branch to call on private welfare groups for more assistance. The YMCA and Roman Catholic Big Brothers were the two major organisations involved, although other groups, such as TocH, were also included.[27] The actual number of preventive cases supervised by the Big Brothers is unclear, as the Child Welfare Branch did not always distinguish between cases passed over for court-ordered and for preventive supervision. The use of Big Brothers in certain aspects of preventive work was extensive, however. Linking children and adolescents with sports clubs and youth organisations was thought to be one of the more important features of preventive work. The Branch maintained that groups such as the YMCA imparted crucial skills to their members and the boys under their care, and that participation in their programmes was an important part of the 'proper development' of young people.[28] Indeed, ensuring more general adolescent participation in sport became a feature of the Branch's preventive work, as the lack of involvement in organised sports was deemed to be a cause of child welfare problems. The case histories that were compiled as part of preventive work provided space for child welfare officers to comment on children's sporting interests and hobbies. Officers attributed Warren Kane's drift into petty thieving in part to his lack of interest in sport; involving him in the local softball team was considered an important facet of his preventive programme.[29]

This utilisation of private welfare schemes was in marked contrast to the Department of Education's former stance towards voluntary endeavour. Beck had long opposed using all but a select group of voluntary agencies, but he signalled

The 1941 conference of child welfare officers. Director of Education Clarence Beeby is seated, with the Superintendent of Child Welfare, Jim McClune, on his right. Charlie Peek, the Superintendent from 1946, is standing fourth from left. BRIAN MANCHESTER

the new detente in his first report as Superintendent. Describing government and private systems of child welfare as 'adjacent zones of social service whose boundaries are undefined and whose tasks intermingle', he maintained that there should be a closer relationship between the two. Private groups, he noted, were in a position to enter 'undeveloped and experimental' areas of child welfare work, and in doing so, they should be able to rely on the advice and guidance of the more experienced state workers. This change of heart was due essentially to the increase in work that preventive policies entailed. As Beck noted, the Child Welfare Act had created such a workload that cases needed to be delegated and links made with outside organisations.[30]

Preventive work involved a greater use of honorary volunteer officers, especially when wartime staffing shortages and petrol restrictions affected the Branch's work. Superintendent Charlie Peek believed that the contribution of the honorary staff to the Branch's preventive programme was vital, especially because of the regular personal contact they were able to make with children.[31] The most extensive use of honorary officers and local social service groups was in Maori communities. In Northland, on the East Coast and in the central North Island, in particular, the Branch relied heavily on Maori honorary child welfare officers,

Maori living conditions came under official scrutiny as child welfare officers moved into rural districts from the later 1920s. MUSEUM OF NEW ZEALAND TE PAPA TONGAREWA, B.013749

Maori Councils and Maori welfare groups. Maori welfare officers, gazetted under the Maori Social and Economic Advancement Act 1945, also helped with the Branch's preventive schemes.

Maori had participated in child welfare matters since the mid-1920s. Representatives of groups such as Te Akarana Association sat in children's courts as delegates of welfare organisations, and gave advice on placing Maori children in Maori communities or with Maori foster families.[32] As child welfare operations were extended into outlying and rural districts – and aspects of Maori society came under the scrutiny of welfare officers – reliance on Maori assistance grew. A regional East Coast–Hawke's Bay tour by Jim McClune in 1940 led to the appointment of more Maori honorary welfare officers, and the establishment of links with local Maori committees.

This was part of a more general trend towards community participation in child welfare, and reflected the Branch's policy of passing to Maori limited responsibility for administering policies affecting Maori children. Since the late 1910s the Education Department had agreed in principle with the contention that aspects of the state's child welfare system did not support Maori interests: 'You may leave a native child among his own folk and he is likely to grow up a good Maori; but you cannot make a good Pakeha out of him.'[33] The Department's aim, not always adhered to in practice, was to keep Maori children in Maori communities, rather than placing them in institutions. Relying on Maori for assistance with preventive schemes expanded this notion. 'I am satisfied', McClune wrote, 'that the Maoris themselves must be given a large share in the responsibility of providing for the betterment of families – with assistance from government officials to back them up when required.' Closer contact between the Branch, the children concerned, local Maori liaison officers and District Maori Councils was identified as the key to ensuring 'reasonable conditions' for Maori youth.[34] Paternalism also played a part in fostering Maori participation in child welfare. Maori were to be 'helped' to recognise child welfare problems and respond to them in constructive ways – usually, those outlined by the Branch's officers. Following a visit to Ruatoria in 1940, McClune noted that 'we must not expect from the Maori too speedy an adjustment to our ways of thought and living and he needs for a long time yet a kindly lead from us.'[35]

More than the 'mere gift of money': child welfare and the needy families scheme

The emphasis on fostering child welfare by enhancing family welfare was manifested most explicitly in the needy families scheme. Begun in 1941 and administered primarily by the Child Welfare Branch, this scheme provided assistance to large or needy families whose children's well-being was endangered. The scheme was a highly targeted form of prevention. While preventive supervision could be arranged only where there was evidence, or at least suspicion, of neglect, delinquency, truancy or poor home conditions, the needy families scheme singled out a group which, by its composition or living situation rather than behaviour, was believed to pose problems for children's welfare. Intervening to change the conditions of this group was a means of averting family breakdown and social dislocation, and their attendant costs to the nation.

Increasing social services for New Zealanders during the twentieth century, and particularly from the late 1930s, had not stopped families or individuals falling through the sometimes large cracks in welfare provision. By the early 1940s there had long been a shortage of adequate and suitable housing in inner-city areas, as a national housing survey in 1937 confirmed. Maori housing was often the worst, and where it was overcrowded or decrepit there was a significant impact on Maori health; child welfare officers visiting rural Maori communities found 'deplorable conditions'. Commentators throughout the 1930s and 1940s linked poor housing with juvenile delinquency; overcrowded or unpleasant conditions forced children to take their leisure and find companionship on the streets.[36]

Despite the housing policies of the first Labour government and the growth in the number of state houses, a housing shortage remained, and was exacerbated during the Second World War. Large families found it particularly difficult to obtain adequate accommodation, partly because of the State Advances Corporation's reluctance to build big houses.[37] Child welfare officers reported on Wellington families living in cramped, unwholesome conditions that compromised the welfare of their children: the Davis family of parents and eight children was crushed into a caravan at Lower Hutt, and then into 'apartments' above a Petone shop; the Harker family of parents and twelve children, ten of whom lived at home and all of whom had been committed to the Branch's care between 1928 and 1935, used all five rooms in their house as sleeping quarters.[38]

The housing crisis and the potential problems it posed led the Minister of Housing to ask the State Advances Corporation to provide solutions. The Corporation estimated that there were 4000 families with more than eight children, and 35,000 with more than five. It asserted that housing these families was a 'national problem', and accordingly suggested that representatives from the Child Welfare Branch, the Social Security Department and the Corporation form a group to submit proposals for accommodating large families. The group had met within a week, and declared unanimously that assistance should be given to these families immediately, before their poor circumstances led their children to 'get out of hand'.[39]

The needy families scheme was designed, in part, to move families out of inadequate housing in rural areas (right) and cramped urban centres, such as this small Wellington residence (below). ATL, F-115895-1/2 & NATIONAL ARCHIVES NATIONAL PUBLICITY STUDIOS PHOTOGRAPHIC COLLECTION, ATL, F-10358-1/1

The interdepartmental group recommended a scheme to subsidise the rents of, or find new and suitable accommodation for, large families. Following referrals from either the State Advances Corporation or the Social Security Department, the Child Welfare Branch would inquire into all cases of large families needing assistance, and suggest a course of action. A committee comprising one representative from each of the Branch, the Corporation and the Social Security Department would then use the report to decide on the amount and type of assistance. This committee could hold over cases for further consideration, defer decisions, and order regular reviews of cases. If a rent subsidy or food vouchers were required, the Branch would pay it out of a special supplementary fund of £10,000 in the Education Department's vote. The group emphasised that assistance should be of a helpful and constructive character, and not a financial grant; it should be, Charlie Peek later reflected, more than the 'mere gift of money'.[40] This would be achieved in part by the Child Welfare Branch exercising guardianship over the children concerned, and in certain cases supervising the disbursement of the family benefit. 'Wherever possible', the group added, the family unit should be preserved intact.[41]

The scheme commenced in 1942, and although it was initially focused on providing for large families which were experiencing housing crises, it assumed the more generic title of 'needy families scheme'. The name reflected actual practice; it quickly developed into a broad system of social welfare which extended both the range of families targeted and the type of assistance given. Financial assistance, grants for food, clothing and bedding, budgetary advice and supplies of blankets were soon provided, in addition to rent subsidies and quicker access to state houses. The Child Welfare Branch took the lead in administering the scheme through its investigations and disbursements; in early 1948 it assumed sole responsibility for it, cementing its role as an important welfare service for the community.

The Branch was eager to be involved in the scheme, and later to extend its role. The Education Department viewed it as an intrinsic part of its preventive work, and readily approved this enhancement of the Branch's role; by the end of 1947 the scheme was funded directly by a special 'preventive work' vote in the Branch's estimates.[42] Keeping families together and saving children from becoming a further charge on the state were of paramount importance. One child welfare officer described the scheme as one of the most progressive advances in child welfare work he had encountered. Its influence for the good and for saving young lives was incalculable, and by improving the child's environment, the Branch would reach the source of many problems.[43]

The number of cases assisted climbed steadily throughout the 1940s. By mid-1943, after eighteen months of the scheme's operation, almost 300 families with

1730 children had been helped. The aid was divided fairly evenly between rental subsidies, grants, and the provision of houses. Three years later more than 900 families and more than 5000 children had been assisted. The committee had provided 296 rental subsidies and grants, another 68 rent subsidies alone, and 342 grants for food, bedding or furniture, and moved families into 382 houses. More than £30,000 had been spent during the four years of the scheme's operation.[44]

Compared with other areas of the welfare system, the expenditure on the needy families scheme was microscopic. An annual expenditure of less than £10,000, excluding the amount absorbed by the Child Welfare Branch in operating and personnel costs, was only a fraction of that spent on other areas of welfare. In 1947/8, when the Branch paid out less than £4000 worth of assistance, more than £20 million was spent on old-age pensions, superannuation and the family benefit. The significance of the scheme does not rest on its financial basis, however. The number of families helped, and the level of distress they were experiencing, illustrates some of the difficulties under which New Zealanders were living during the war years. Rationing and housing shortages took their toll, and despite the introduction of a range of benefits as part of Labour's housing policies from 1935 and in the social security package from 1938, sections of New Zealand society lived periodically or permanently in a distressed state. And for the Child Welfare Branch, the scheme extended markedly both the nature and the scope of its preventive work for children and their families.

Families came into the scheme through the Social Security Department or the State Advances Corporation, as well as the regular inquiries of child welfare officers. Frequent sickness among the seven McGowan children, for example, led the Branch to make further inquiries which revealed that the family lived in a house with 'deplorable' bedding and coverings, and was attempting to manage on an income sufficient only to pay for the rent and buy food.[45] The Branch sometimes sought possible cases from voluntary welfare groups, such as the Auckland branch of the Society for the Protection of Women and Children, which forwarded a list of families requiring housing assistance.[46]

Unlike other aspects of welfare provision, however, entitlement to this assistance was not enshrined in legislation, nor could families apply to be put on the scheme or have their case for assistance assessed. The committee which established the scheme requested that it be kept secret, or receive minimum publicity, lest it adversely affect other government policies. No doubt a desire to minimise the number of potential applicants contributed to the secrecy. McClune believed that the regular work of child welfare officers and staff from the other two agencies would uncover the most urgent cases, without any further publicity for a scheme which the Branch had insufficient personnel to run. Accordingly, no publicity was given at the time, and the scheme has received little attention since. The Branch complied with the request for discretion, making only scant mention of the assistance in annual reports, and then never by name. Its first public reference to this new aspect of its work, over three years after the inception of the scheme, noted cryptically that child welfare officers had 'made inquiries' into the 'living-conditions' of 300 families (1500 children), and in some cases had arranged for assistance to 'preserve the family unit'.[47]

A wide range of family circumstances was reflected in the cases. Neither the group which established the scheme, nor that which administered it, had provided firm parameters for deciding what actually constituted a needy family. Neither the number of children nor the marital situation of the parties concerned was stipulated. The absence of such criteria enabled a range of households and families to be considered for assistance, which suggests that welfare policies supported household arrangements other than the nuclear family.[48]

Many of the cases complied with the original intention to assist families with five or more children which needed housing immediately. The Dwyer family of Auckland, assisted in 1943, met all the requirements of the needy family. Mr and Mrs Dwyer and their eight children lived in an old, dilapidated house which had no modern domestic conveniences. There were neither electric lights nor hot water for washing, and the bathroom was so rundown that the children washed in the kitchen sink. All the children were ill, and medical officers confirmed that their surroundings were contributing to their health problems. The child welfare officer classed the case as urgent and recommended that the State Advances Corporation immediately expedite Mr Dwyer's application for a house.

Families with only one or two children could, if their circumstances warranted, be eligible for assistance. The Carnes family of Wellington was one example. After Mr Carnes entered a tuberculosis sanatorium in 1942, his wife struggled to pay the rent and provide food for her two children; assistance from the scheme took care of both food and housing costs. The undefined criteria for a needy family afforded support for women living in difficult circumstances. Women with husbands who failed to provide for their welfare could qualify for assistance, including those whose husbands drank or gambled away the family income. Single-parent families, which were usually headed by women, could also obtain relief. Widows with children were one group assisted on this basis: the widowed Agnes Frew received help with her rent and a clothing grant for her three children even though her accommodation was adequate. Women, and men, who had left their spouses or been deserted by them could also qualify. The James family received aid after Mrs James left her husband and children; the committee forwarded a grant for £20 to enable Mr James to clothe his children. After separating from her husband, who provided no assistance for her or her three children, Mrs Trethewey had managed to pay her debts; things became too much after a time, however, and the Branch authorised a subsidy of £15 to pay for rent, clothing and bedding. Geraldine White, an ex-state ward who had given birth to a child out of wedlock and who left her abusive husband, received a grant of £35 to cover food and clothing expenses.[49]

Maintaining the household unit – in whatever form – was an essential aspect of the scheme, as was indicated at the time of its establishment. Families which had been forced to separate could be granted a state house in order to reunite the family. One Dannevirke family was placed in a transit house until it could be found more permanent accommodation after it was discovered that the parents were considering placing their children for adoption. The family had transferred to Wellington, where they had been unable to find a house. For a year the husband lived in private board, the wife resided in the People's Palace, and the children lived in various homes. Child welfare officers were alert to signs that marital relations were deteriorating because of overcrowding. A family of three adults and six children living in a three-roomed bach in Auckland in 1948 may not have been in any financial difficulty, but their predicament made the provision of a house vital. The investigating officer reported that the relationship between wife and husband was becoming increasingly strained; unless something were done, 'it will soon mean a broken home'.[50]

Living in poor accommodation or having insufficient means to purchase the necessities of life did not automatically qualify families for assistance, however. The vague criteria for need could disadvantage a family by leaving their welfare to the caprice of the investigating officer. In a way that harked back to the work of charitable aid officers in the late nineteenth century, some child welfare officers commented in detail on the character of family members. An assessment was made of whether or not the family was attempting to help itself out of its situation, with a healthy display of self-help usually boosting their chances. Growing vegetables, making do, and seeking alternative sources of relief were indications that households were prepared to attend to their own welfare. The McGowan family maintained an 'excellent' vegetable garden, and Mrs McGowan was 'a good cook and knows how to handle her foodstuff wisely and to the best advantage'. Even families whose members could be seen as unrespectable or behaving inappropriately could gain assistance if they were endeavouring to improve their situation. A Greymouth woman whose husband was in prison in 1945 received temporary mortgage relief after she approached her local Mayor's Relief Fund. She had struggled to buy her own house, and kept up the mortgage payments to the best of her ability before needing assistance.

Conversely, families that were making little apparent effort could receive an unsupportive recommendation from the investigating officer. Untruthfulness

about finances, reluctance to improve a vegetable garden, or failure to part with
'luxury goods' could all count against an applicant. The Baker family of
Whangarei may have kept their own garden and poultry, and they were in
straitened financial circumstances and living in inadequate accommodation, but
the investigating officer commented adversely on their continued use of their
late-model Chrysler for shopping trips and motoring jaunts; the committee
declined to assist them. Refusing the offer of a house was a sure way to be taken
off the needy families list. The Taskers of Greymouth were removed after Mrs
Tasker declined a suitable house. The officer believed his actions vindicated when
it was later found that Mr Tasker had a drinking problem. In such cases, the
welfare of families and their children was left to others in the community.

The scheme invested child welfare officers with considerable power and
responsibility. As with other aspects of preventive work, the need for investigation and inquiry to map out a programme of adjustment placed a stress on
close and ongoing casework, in which an officer's judgment determined whether
or not assistance would be forthcoming.[51] Investigation could delve into all
areas of a family's life. Once a family had been targeted as eligible for relief,
officers prepared an 'exhaustive report' on its circumstances, including its
accommodation, income and expenditure, the condition of clothing, bedding
and food, the health of the children, details of savings and of other benefits the
family received.

The responsibilities of the officer did not end when a grant had been made or
new accommodation found. Although this was never enunciated as policy, the
scheme enabled child welfare officers to extend an informal preventive
supervision over the families and children. Once assistance had been provided
contact with child welfare officers was assured, as they checked periodically on
the family's welfare to ascertain when the assistance should cease. Intervention
in family life could take many forms. Officers could oversee the purchase of
items if families had been given a cash grant. Usually this involved an officer
accompanying the family while they did their shopping; wartime rationing and
shortages made this task doubly difficult. The very fact of contact with the
families inevitably led to extra work for officers, and the potential for their
greater involvement in family life through placing children in health camps,
arranging visits to doctors or clinics, or giving advice on domestic relations.[52]

It was, perhaps, inevitable that some needy families would turn into semi-
permanent preventive cases. The Tretheweys, first listed as a needy family in 1945,
remained in contact with the Branch for a decade, during which time the Branch
provided crucial support to enable Mrs Trethewey to keep her home and family
together. She frequently approached local officers for advice, for instance when
her son Fred began to steal money and small items. The Branch investigated the

family again in 1949 when Gwen, the youngest child, truanted while her mother was away in Auckland. Five years later child welfare officers were still visiting: Gwen continued to truant and Fred's earlier brushes with the law had led to his committal to Borstal.[53] The case exemplifies the double-edged consequences for families of having the Child Welfare Branch enter their lives.

The operation of this scheme, like other aspects of preventive policies, necessitated a close liaison between the Branch and families. Frequently, women were the first and ongoing point of contact, both for families and for the Branch. The scheme was in practice a predominantly female world of welfare provision and receipt. Women officers did most of the work, which added substantially to their sphere of duties. Male officers considered the investigation of needy families to be women's work, and claimed that it was inappropriate for men to conduct housing inquiries, or to be involved in cases concerning young children.[54] It was mothers who most often opened the doors to child welfare officers, answered their questions, discussed the welfare of their children, and listened to advice on household management and budgeting. Some may have welcomed the visits and found the assistance vital. But not all cheerfully greeted the arrival of a child welfare officer, and the enforced relationship could be onerous and intrusive. Investigations into household management and the domestic economy invariably involved a judgment on a woman's housewifely skills. Visits from child welfare officers were a visible sign to nosy neighbours that a family was under 'the Welfare', and the supervised and joint shopping expeditions must have been irksome to many women.

The scheme also meant that the Branch had to work closely with voluntary and local welfare groups. The Returned Servicemen's Association, Masonic Lodges, Mayors' Relief Funds, church social workers and hospital boards all received requests for grants, advice, or the supply of fuel, bedding, groceries or milk. Wellington child welfare officers assisted the Josephs after Mr Joseph had an accident and was unable to work. The family owed £8 for groceries and £6 for milk, and was behind with their hire purchase payments and two weeks in arrears with the rent. The Branch held the case over for further investigation, but arranged for the local hospital board to provide bedding and clothing, and issue regular supplies of groceries and milk. Of course, contact between the Branch and other welfare groups could trap families who were receiving assistance from a number of sources. The Baker family was found to be double-dipping by applying for a house when they were already being helped by their local Salvation Army and Happiness Club.[55]

Assistance from other groups also helped to keep down the costs of the scheme, and enabled the Branch to take a financially conservative approach. Expenditure always remained well within the budget, a pattern set in the first year of the scheme when McClune notified the Director of Education that the committee would not require all its budget. By the end of the 1947/8 financial year, during which the Branch had assumed sole responsibility for the programme, only £3427 had been spent of the allocated £6500.[56] Frequent checking and reassessment of cases kept down the cost, and the provision of additional government benefits could obviate the need for further assistance.

The needy families scheme enabled the Branch to expand the form and extent of its preventive policies outward from children to include families with children. The scheme thus spread the influence of the Branch into new sections of New Zealand society. Problems had only to be possibilities or vague indications for action to be initiated. Child abuse, neglect and delinquency were not the conditions which led to a family coming into the scheme; they existed only in the future as consequences of failing to intervene in the family's current situation. The Branch's role in the scheme constituted a unique blend of traditional philanthropic and modern welfare policies. Indeed the scheme itself occupied a mid-point between charity and state welfare in its odd mix of grants in kind and benefits. In some cases, the Branch itself administered in kind, dispensing blankets from supplies obtained specifically for the scheme.[57] As a broad system of relief for all types of families which had slipped through the fissures of social security, the scheme also epitomised the new focus on families and family welfare that now characterised New Zealand social policy. In theory, if not in practice, the scheme reflected the new aim of the 1930s of a welfare state for all, to be delivered in a variety of ways.

The state's big family: the significance of preventive child welfare policies

The pursuit of preventive policies was a major aspect of the practice of child welfare in New Zealand before the 1950s. The implications of this for the Branch were manifold, and would affect the nature of its work for years to come. Jim McClune used the significance of prevention to press for more staff, the development of research and statistical surveys, and the introduction of staff training.[58] The investigation and close casework carried out by child welfare officers laid the groundwork for the ongoing professionalisation of staff which would be a feature of the 1950s.

Preventive work was a fulfilment of the notion that the best environment for children was the home. Maintaining family relationships, and through these the wider society, was an essential feature of preventive work, and the needy families scheme represented the apogee of that principle. Family welfare increasingly came to dominate welfare policy during the 1930s, as in the social security schemes of the first Labour government. For the Child Welfare Branch, prevention was an ethos of achieving child welfare through family welfare, as New Zealand followed a broader international trend.[59]

In their focus on families and family welfare, preventive policies hinted at the triumph of the environmentalist interpretation of social problems. Family background was seen as crucial to children's welfare; maladjusted home conditions could precipitate drastic consequences. No longer was heredity or bad breeding considered to be the basis of a child's social ills, although it would be incorrect to suggest that such explanations disappeared entirely. Through pinpointing the material circumstances of a child's situation, in terms of inadequate home conditions, insufficient food or poor housing, there could, in fact, be a solution to child welfare problems.

The Branch's preventive child welfare work and attempts to secure family welfare displayed, at times, a flexibility in the notion of 'the family'. If a child were Maori, this could mean a Maori kin group. It was also not just ensuring the welfare of the nuclear family if children living with single mothers or, more rarely, fathers were cared for adequately. The definition of adequate care was the Branch's prerogative, and that extended by single women was frequently found to be wanting. Nevertheless, some areas of preventive child welfare work sought to support the single woman and her child. Officers working with single mothers helped them find employment, gave advice about placing children in foster homes, and instituted maintenance payments from putative fathers.[60] The Branch sometimes provided single mothers with a payment to enable them to maintain their children in their own home, rather than place them with a foster parent. In such circumstances, the Branch would commit the child to care, and then 'board out' the child to her or his mother at the regular rates of payment.[61] Responding to public criticism of such support, Minister of Education Gordon Coates argued that every effort should be made to keep mothers and children together; no child should be deprived of 'natural rights' because the parents had failed to observe the 'accepted moral codes'. Coates went on to defend the payments as one way to develop maternal instincts, which were the 'surest safeguard against future immorality'.[62]

The Branch's payments stood alongside other forms of financial assistance that were available to single mothers and ex-nuptial children under the Family Allowance Act 1926 and the Pensions Amendment Act 1936. Such legislation excluded illegitimate children from receiving any financial benefits, but also incorporated provisions which modified the exclusionary principles. These enabled the Pensions Department and later the Social Security Department to make payments for ex-nuptial children.[63] The existence of these payments, and those provided by the Child Welfare Branch, requires a modification of the

Some of the British children evacuated to New Zealand during the Second World War return home in 1945. NATIONAL ARCHIVES, CW 1, 40/2/116

notion that illegitimate children and single mothers received no state aid until the introduction of the domestic purposes benefit in 1973. The number assisted is not known, and may not have been large, but the facility to authorise support suggests that the state may have had a more flexible approach to supporting a variety of family structures than historians have allowed. It suggests too that women giving birth outside wedlock may not have been treated with as much disdain and condemnation as historians have assumed.[64]

In two-parent households, nevertheless, 'families' certainly implied both mothers *and* fathers. One of the features of preventive child welfare policies was to spotlight the role of both parents in promoting child and family welfare. The division of responsibility was gendered – fathers should be more responsible for discipline and mothers for affection – but both roles were seen as vital in a healthy family. Historians elsewhere have argued that the central focus in social policy was on the mother's role in child and family welfare, and this was clearly an aspect of social policy in New Zealand too, as the initiatives for promoting motherhood and educating women in its skills imply.[65] It was not until the emotional rather than the material circumstances of families were examined that the specific role of the mother in affecting child welfare came under observation in New Zealand.

Regardless of the emphasis on parenting, however, preventive child welfare policies could be, and were, employed sometimes to reformat family relationships. Actions which provided support to children and young people in difficult family circumstances, or to mothers concerned for their own well-being, could alter family dynamics and power structures. The historian Linda Gordon reminds us that families are not integers;[66] child welfare officers did not always perceive families this way either, as their flexibility towards different family forms and willingness to intervene to help change relationships show.

Preventive policies facilitated a greater degree of external intervention into family life. Parental cooperation was a vital prerequisite for preventive work, however superficial that cooperation may have been. The degree of parental

Child welfare officers often recognised the role that members of extended families could play in childcare. In the case of Maori, this could include kuia (below), while for Pakeha, it could include older family members (opposite). THELMA KENT COLLECTION, ATL, F-3347-1/4 & G. LESLIE ADKIN COLLECTION, MUSEUM OF NEW ZEALAND TE PAPA TONGAREWA, A.006406

choice was always circumscribed, and some parents and children may have found their choice to be between grudging cooperation and an appearance before the children's court. Not all the intervention was oppressive, or uninvited, although the extent of animosity or silent toleration of 'the Welfare' cannot be ignored. Intervention should not be conflated with the erosion of parental care or the functions of the family, as some have argued.[67] Periodic visits from a child welfare officer were not sufficient to supplant family autonomy or parental control, even if those visits were designed to give support to particular family members. A few minutes' advice on shopping from a child welfare officer to a harried mother may have had little long-term effect on the way she managed her home. Instead, preventive policies symbolised a faith in families' abilities to tend to their own welfare – under the guidance of officials of the state. Sometimes that guidance continued for years, as families and children became enmeshed in the network of welfare services. As cases in this chapter have shown, children went on to enter residential institutions despite – or even because of – supervision.

The entwining of family, state and community effort through preventive policies exemplifies the intersection of public, private and family effort in the

'mixed economy' of welfare.[68] The Child Welfare Branch, like other areas of state, had porous boundaries through which it reached to draw on family and community endeavour in working towards children's welfare during a period of expanding state initiatives in welfare.[69] The emphasis on preventive work had forced the Branch to soften its earlier harsh stance on voluntary child welfare schemes, and furthered its stated aim of attending to children's welfare within the context of the family.

PART III

Recording 'the history of social breakdown':

from child welfare to social welfare,

1948–1972

Introduction

A time of 'browns, greys, and army khaki' is how one historian has characterised inter-war and wartime New Zealand.[1] Economic depression and wartime controls generated a society well used to privation and caution. At war's end, a wave of optimism and expectancy swept New Zealand, as better times for all seemed achievable. And, to some extent, they were. The war-inspired economic booms continued into the 1950s, and with virtually full employment for more than twenty years, New Zealand enjoyed arguably its most sustained era of prosperity this century. The standard of living rose for many as more consumer goods came within their grasp, particularly as married women increasingly moved into the paid workforce, boosting the family income. Social policies buoyed incomes even further, with a universal family benefit and low-interest housing loans.

The population, like the economy, boomed. From 1.7 million at the end of the war, it had swelled to 2.9 million by 1972. Migration boosted the figures, but much of the increase was natural during the post-war baby boom: by the early 1960s, 34 per cent of the total population was aged under fifteen, compared with 27 per cent at the end of the war. Ex-nuptial births increased too, jumping from fewer than 2000 in 1948/9 to more than 9000 in 1971/2, a rise from less than 10 per cent to almost 20 per cent of all live births.[2] The growth of a youthful Maori population was pronounced, with half of all Maori aged under fifteen in the mid-1960s. Post-war society was also marked by the increasing urbanisation and suburbanisation of both Maori and Pakeha, and by an intensification of the surge of population to the north of the North Island. Sprawling and demographically homogeneous new housing suburbs became a feature of New Zealand's urban landscape.

The post-war quest for security has led some commentators to brand the 1950s as a dull and complacent prelude to the more diverse and swinging 1960s.[3] In the practice of child welfare work, as in many other areas of social life, a different pattern emerged; the 1950s are ripe for reassessment.[4] The story of mid-century child welfare policy and practice is one of responding to an ever-increasing range and number of demands in the wake of social change. The two chapters in Part III focus on key aspects of these responses. Chapter Five examines the effects on child welfare services of the perceived and actual increase in the level of juvenile delinquency. It traces the development of community-based prevention schemes and the changes in residential institutions, the number of which increased markedly. Chapter Six explores changes in foster care, and teases out the place of child welfare services in the fields of adoption and provision for ex-nuptial births. It also focuses on an emerging interest in child abuse and neglect.

Legislative and administrative changes in child welfare framed the period. The Child Welfare Amendment Act 1948 renamed the Branch as the Child Welfare Division. In April 1972, this joined with the Social Security Department in a 'forced marriage' to become the Department of Social Welfare.[5] Two superintendents guided the Division. Charlie Peek, Superintendent from 1946, had joined the Branch in 1939. He managed the Boys' Training Centre at Weraroa while both District Child Welfare Officer for Palmerston North and inspector at Head Office. Holding the three offices simultaneously was, he recalled, hard work, but not without its humour: 'In all communications among the three offices I was mostly communicating with myself. I made the proposals, I approved them. For the record I noted they were carried out and even commended any worthy effort. I always sent copies to my two other selves for their information.'[6] Following Peek's retirement in 1964, his deputy, Lewis Anderson, became Superintendent. Anderson had joined the staff in Hamilton in 1940 as a boys' welfare officer after gaining a law degree and working part-time as a teacher and sports broadcaster. From Hamilton he moved to Northland, before joining the Head Office staff in 1945.[7]

Numerically, the work of the Division exploded between 1948 and 1972. The number of court appearances leapt from fewer than 2000 in 1948/9 to 5000 in 1960/1 and more than 12,000 in 1971/2. The number of state wards – those in residential institutions or fostered out – rose from 3616 in the late 1940s to 5515 in 1971/2. The numbers under preventive supervision or supervision grew steadily from less than 4000 in 1948/9 to more than 10,000 in 1971/2. In all, the number of children and young people in regular contact with the Division swelled to more than 16,000 by the end of 1971. This does not include inquiries into adoptions and ex-nuptial births, which boomed during the 1960s, nor 'miscellaneous inquiries' which required no further action; the latter jumped from approximately 4500 in 1954, the first year on record, to almost 18,000 in 1972.[8] Taken together, these increases were far out of proportion to the growth in the juvenile population, which doubled between the late 1940s and early 1970s. Maori made up a disproportionate number of cases, particularly in youth offending and in court appearances. By 1971, Maori boys offended (or were apprehended) more than five times as frequently as Pakeha; the difference was even more marked for Maori girls, who were more than seven times as likely to offend or be apprehended.[9]

The Division's annual reports conveyed a mounting sense of dismay. 'One would reasonably be entitled to presume that, considering our high educational and health standard and our comparatively prosperous economy, delinquency and crime would be on the wane, or at the least, that any increase would lag behind the population increase', Lewis Anderson opined in 1965 as he recorded the highest ever annual number of children's court appearances. He, and others, spoke of social problems beyond the Division's control, which left 'no alternative' but for it to be an 'ambulance service'.[10] Child welfare officials referred darkly to problems which had become too big to handle. Mopping up, rather than adjustment, seemed to be the order of the day. Child welfare officer Aussie Malcolm captured the tenor of the period: 'We did not really have the power to effect change but only to record, for posterity, the history of social breakdown'.[11]

One response to this apparent loss of control was to establish more, and more varied, residential institutions. The Division administered seventeen institutions in 1948; there were twenty by 1972, five of which catered for long-term residents. Family homes, first introduced in 1954 as a mid-point between foster care and institutions, numbered 78 by 1972. The Division as a whole and institutions in particular relied increasingly on therapists and psychologists to discover the causes of delinquency, and to map out treatment programmes. The Girls' Training Centre at Burwood, which had introduced organised counselling and doctors' case conferences in 1943 and 1948 respectively, became a model for other institutions.[12] Faced with difficult residents, some institutions introduced drug therapy, administering tranquillisers to keep youngsters quiescent.[13]

The number of staff grew accordingly. The hundred or so field officers of 1948 had by the end of 1971 jumped to 291, assisted, as before, by more than 200 honorary officers. Including residential and clerical staff, the Division employed 1083 staff, over half of them women. Officers remained overworked and districts understaffed, however. Between 1957 and 1967 alone the number of the Division's cases and inquiries increased by 91 per cent, while its staffing increased by 46 per cent.[14] The publicity given to the Division as a consequence of various reports during the 1950s, and a heightened emphasis on preventive programmes, caused ever-increasing workloads, and contributed significantly to the stress under which officers worked:

> What is the strain I speak so glibly about? I have been threatened with physical violence, have been attacked by dogs, have witnessed distressing and hysterical outbursts by parents and children, have had a good old Irish curse put on me and my family, have been involved in a suicide, have been subjected to unpleasant Supreme Court cross examination, have been the subject of Ministerial enquiry, have been threatened with civil action for defamation of character, have been called at 6 a.m. to cope with a threatened suicide, have been called at midnight to protect children from an adult quarrel . . . and so I could go on.[15]

District officers petitioned frequently for increased staffing, often painting a picture of acute distress. Making suitable and adequate provision for the needs of the ever-enlarging city of Auckland was one area of major difficulty. The region had three district offices by 1966, but Anderson argued for an additional two to ease the strain on the Otahuhu and Auckland offices especially. A child welfare officer based at Otahuhu in the 1960s remembered working 'four nights a week, probably through to nine or ten at night . . . just doing office work . . . just doing catch-up work . . . and you'd also spend one day in the weekend working full-time in the office. . . . On a Saturday or a Sunday you could walk into Otahuhu Child Welfare and there would be almost the entire field staff working'.[16]

Women officers handled much of this greater workload. The traditional division between women's and men's duties broke down from the late 1960s, but women still carried much of the work, especially with changes to adoption legislation and the increasing number of ex-nuptial births. Wanganui's District Child Welfare Officer urgently requested more staff in 1962, as some parts of his district were sorely neglected, with only the bare necessities of work completed. His women officers were hard-pressed making inquiries into ex-nuptial births, notably in rural areas such as Taihape, where 'an astounding number of unmarried mothers go . . . to have their babies'. He informed Peek that the Division was 'grossly exploiting' its staff; he did not 'wish to be a party to it much longer'.[17]

In a lengthy report and plea for more staff in 1954, Wellington's District Child Welfare Officer graphically sketched the problems all districts were facing. He estimated that his officers spent eleven hours of their week writing up case notes, between five and six hours making visits to clients and other agencies, four or five hours fielding telephone inquiries, and five hours travelling. Children under supervision received about nine visits a year, each of fifteen minutes' duration: this amounted to little more than two hours annually, or (he calculated) five minutes a week.[18] Given such figures, it is not surprising that officers believed they could not meet the needs of children and community.

Both Peek and Anderson predicted a bleak future for child welfare work and social well-being if staff numbers were not increased and preventive work facilitated. An average 'case overload' of 44 per cent above the optimum number in the early 1970s meant that much statutory and preventive work was simply not done. Either the number of staff should be increased, Anderson suggested, or consideration should be given to dropping some of the functions which officers performed, such as the time-consuming inquiries into ex-nuptial births.[19]

An emphasis on staff training emerged. In the early 1940s the New Zealand Council for Educational Research discussed social work training with Victoria University College, and from 1950 that institution offered a two-year full-time course for a Diploma in Social Science. Within six years, more than twenty child welfare officers had gained the qualification, and around ten were graduating each year by 1972. Public service study awards allowed child welfare officers to take leave on full salary to gain the qualification, but in practice few were able to do so because of the high workloads. Former child welfare officers remember the course as of mixed utility: 'training helped me in getting a thorough understanding in the . . . factors that were significant in producing the difficulties children and young people encountered. . . . But I guess most of us felt that . . . [it] tended to be more appropriate for the person who might work more in a clinical setting'.[20] From the 1950s, social science cadetships and social work traineeships gave hands-on experience to young people interested in a social work career, through training placements within the Division.

In 1951 the Division also introduced in-house staff training schemes, which provided most of the training for residential staff from 1954, and for more junior field staff from 1955.[21] In 1963, following extensive discussions with the State Services Commission and the Social Science Advisory Committee, the Tiromoana Social Work Training Centre was set up in the grounds of Porirua Hospital. It provided a live-in training course for child welfare officers and other social workers; by 1971, more than 40 per cent of the Division's staff had taken it. The course sometimes added to the already excessive pressure on officers, and some districts were simply too busy to spare them for a month at a time.[22]

It was clear, though, that staff needed to be increasingly multi-skilled to cope with the variety of work. The 1950s and 1960s may have been the heyday of the welfare state and times of 'unsurpassed prosperity', but many New Zealand families, particularly Maori, still fell through the fissures of welfare provision.[23] The Child Welfare Division continued to be a general welfare agency catering to the spectrum of social need. Many of the Division's earlier functions remained. It still dispensed advice to those whose marriages had broken down, assisted with the management of family benefits, and continued the needy families scheme in a modified form. New duties were added: from 1948 the Division had responsibility for Polish and other refugee children, and from 1960 the task of registering and inspecting all children's day care centres. From the mid-1960s it offered an advisory service to private children's homes; this renewed spirit of cooperation was engendered by the growing difficulties in attending to children's welfare.[24]

From 1948, the Division also took a role in the child migrant scheme. Mooted as a system for New Zealanders to adopt children orphaned by the war, this developed into one of guardianship rather than adoption after it was found that there were actually few orphans available for resettlement outside Britain.[25] British parents who were having difficulty maintaining their children because of financial or housing problems could give them 'the best and happiest of circumstances' by sending them to New Zealand's 'less austere' environment. The Overseas League, which organised the scheme from the British end, assured parents that the 'happy assimilation' of their children would be safeguarded by New Zealand's 'ever-vigilant' Child Welfare Division. The Division selected suitable homes for the children, and maintained supervision until guardianship was transferred to the foster family, on average after about eleven months. In all, 550 children (118 girls and 432 boys) aged between five and eighteen arrived between 1948 and 1953.[26]

In practice the scheme did not live up to the ideals of its originators. Problems in selecting children, and inadequate reports on them from Britain, led to the scheme's restriction in 1953 to youths aged seventeen or eighteen. From 1951 there were complaints about ill-treatment and overwork, although the Division denied that there was any abuse of the children for their labour potential. The extent of its supervision is uncertain, however; one officer reported in 1962, when six children remained on the Division's books, that its oversight often did not extend beyond the original report on guardianship. Since the mid-1980s, former child migrants have spoken of abuse and exploitation, echoing the claims made by young migrants in the 1950s.[27]

Child life gained a new currency in post-war New Zealand as the wartime loss of life made population growth more important. As before, child welfare was best secured in the family and community, and the Division continued to emphasise the notion of child welfare through family welfare. Indeed, the balance between official and family power swung a little towards the latter after legislative amendments which allowed for appeals of court decisions (1960) and reviews of committal and supervision orders (1961). Attitudes to children and young people themselves were still ambiguous. The scare over juvenile delinquency revealed an adult society that was both fascinated with and repelled by teenage culture. 'Depraved' children were never far from their 'deprived' siblings, and they were frequently seen as both delinquents in need of control and victims in need of care.

CHAPTER 5

'That disagreeable term "teenagers"': juvenile delinquency and its prevention

In September 1954, the *Christchurch Star-Sun* reprinted an English depiction of New Zealand beneath the headline, 'The Ugly Things That Happen in a Lovely Land':

> This test tube baby of the welfare states has long been happy to be known to the world for its excellent dairy produce, thermal wonders, volcanoes, and above all, for its highly idealised athletes and Rugby footballers. It has bemused itself with the comforting idea that it is a place apart. It is eager to be seen as a nation of patient, industrious farmers, gazing from the saddle at sleek sheep, mustering in the distant hills, and clear-eyed youths and maidens playing their healthy games untainted by sin and sordidness. In its preoccupation it has tended to forget that its young people might show that they, too, are only human after all.[1]

The report referred to two events which dominated New Zealand news in mid-1954: the murder of Honora Parker by her teenaged daughter Pauline and friend Juliet Hulme, and the revelations of juvenile 'sexual immorality' in the Hutt Valley. Some viewed these episodes as evidence of a widespread malaise among the country's youth, portents for a nation devoid of self-discipline. For the Child Welfare Division, however, these and similar events were manifestations of juvenile behaviour which had always formed a part of New Zealand life. The publicity accorded juvenile delinquency in the mid-1950s thrust youthful behaviour into the limelight as never before. It was to be a relatively short-lived focus of attention, but juvenile delinquency, and the publicity surrounding it in the 1950s, provided much of the impetus for developments in the policy and practice of child welfare through to the early 1970s.

'We've made the headlines again with our old friend, sex': post-war juvenile delinquency

The advent of rock'n'roll and distinctive forms of entertainment, language and behaviour attest to the 'rise' of the teenager and the development of an adolescent culture in New Zealand from the 1950s.[2] Some youths were distinguished by a singular sartorial style which created an image of outrageous behaviour and attitudes. Clothing that was modelled on American film stars or based on a London-inspired revival of Edwardian dress became fashionable. Young men wore their hair longer, sported brightly-coloured clothing, and incorporated the 'Hollywood slouch' in their gait. Drape coats, zoot suits, blue jeans, stove-pipe trousers and vivid socks were favoured garments, and could make an immediate impression. 'I can remember the first pair of stove-pipe trousers in Lower Hutt', Bob Jones recalled: 'In a group of perhaps 50 or 100 kids we followed this fellow . . . down the street gazing in awe at stove-pipe trousers, pointing and laughing and mocking. . . . We were all wearing them, of course, a few years later, and another ten years passed and the public servants were wearing them.' Young women's fashion, in comparison, was less flamboyant: a casual, American look of tight black slacks or straight skirts, plain shirts, and low-heeled shoes – all worn with lipstick and abundant jewellery.[3]

'Teddy boys' and 'Teddy girls', 'bodgies' (male) and 'widgies' (female) were the interchangeable terms sometimes used to identify such adolescents in the 1950s, and these terms have endured as stereotypes of 1950s' youth. Those who rode motorbikes were dubbed 'milk-bar cowboys' – although one magistrate remarked wryly that 'the so-called "milk bar cowboy" has very little to do with milk, cows or even boys'. Their female companions, seldom motorbike riders themselves, were sometimes known as 'pillion pussies' or 'pillion pets'.[4] 'Speed-crazed youths' playing 'chicken' in old cars, and 'girl-toting teenagers on powerful motorbikes', were believed to mill around city centres and block footpaths. In the more florid accounts, they drove through the streets at high speed, with widgies clinging to their car bonnets or throwing underwear at passers-by.[5]

Adults were both fascinated with and appalled by what they saw in, and read into, the conduct of the young. Clothing, hairstyles and language were endlessly bewitching, and described with barely-concealed relish: children's court magis-

A Teddy boy and a gang member – in cartoonist Nevile Lodge's style – reflect on government plans to control their behaviour in 1958. COURTESY OF PAT LODGE

trate Stewart Hardy spoke of a young man appearing in his court 'wearing a lime-green three-quarter-length frock coat with a wide black wool edging, a bright pink shirt, a pastel pink cravat, trousers cut like riding breeches and made of fine black-and-white check serge, and emerald green "fluorescent" socks – and with his head shaven'.[6]

The behaviour of youth in the 1950s was not necessarily any 'worse', or any 'better', than that of earlier generations. Distinctive youth cultures occurred throughout New Zealand history, and were certainly not unique to the 1950s, but post-war society generated particular forms of adolescent life. The baby boom, Maori urbanisation and suburban expansion together created a visible pool of young New Zealanders. Higher standards of living brought a greater range of leisure pursuits within the grasp of more young people. Cars and motorbikes for travel, movies and music for entertainment, and milk-bars and coffee-bars for socialising walled off a section of culture which to adults remained arcane. Delinquency was a 'codeword' for an adolescent society of which adults disapproved or which they did not comprehend.[7]

'Juvenile delinquency' was a fluid term that was summoned into use to name and to castigate youthful behaviours. Sexual activity and the formation of gangs, both long-established, assumed greater importance as central components of these definitions. The gap between perceptions and 'reality' was large, however, and public consternation at youthful conduct emerged at a time when the number of those appearing before children's courts was declining; 'juvenile delinquency' had more to do with adult thoughts about social change and rebuilding a nation after a war than with adolescent 'misbehaviour'.

Events in the Hutt Valley in July 1954 brought together the various elements of the distinctive 1950s' youth culture and activities regarded as delinquent: the 'scandal that put the Hutt Valley on the map' has become arguably the quintessential episode in the history of juvenile delinquency in New Zealand.[8] An

The greater mobility of young people – by motorbike or car – led, some believed, to delinquent conduct. ATL, F-45136-1/2

admission to police by a member of a group of adolescents that she had led a 'depraved sexual life' exposed a nest of juvenile immorality.[9] Police inquiries revealed a 50-strong group whose members congregated around milk-bars, and had casual sexual relations. The storm of publicity which erupted induced the government to appoint a special committee to inquire into moral delinquency among the country's youth.

Headed by Oswald Mazengarb, after whom both the inquiry and its report have become known, the seven-member committee heard evidence from 145 witnesses and received 203 written submissions. Child Welfare Superintendent Charlie Peek, four child welfare officers, and the Manager of the Girls' Training Centre at Burwood were the only Division staff to be interviewed. Intent as it was on assuaging anxiety about the moral fibre of the nation's youth, the committee sought out the views of representatives of religious, social and youth groups rather than those of professionals with relevant expertise. The committee's composition reflected this bias, with only one member having a professional connection with juvenile delinquency. Only two were less than 45 years old; the youngest, at 39, represented, somewhat ludicrously, the views of youth. Hastily conceived, rigid in its interpretations of juvenile behaviour, and alarmist in its predictions, the inquiry and its report have been read as a knee-jerk, moralistic and exaggerated reaction to the activities of the young in 1950s' New Zealand.[10]

The circumstances surrounding the inquiry, the findings of the committee, and its report have formed the subject of a number of studies, and will not be covered here. As an episode in the history of child welfare practice and policy, the inquiry and its aftermath have received little attention. Despite the nature of its work and its status, the Division played a minimal role in the inquiry, and its welfare practice did not form a central part of either the inquiry or the report. Yet both the inquiry and its aftermath were pivotal events for child welfare work during the 1950s and 1960s. Criticisms of child welfare policy and the structure of the Division raised questions about the broad administration of child welfare and the role of preventive work. The publicity accorded juvenile delinquency had both a direct and an indirect impact on the Division. Its public profile was enhanced, with child welfare officers giving speeches on delinquency and its prevention. Rising consciousness about the activities of youth generated a new vigilance and a public willingness to perceive delinquency in adolescent behaviour; 'delinquency-spotting' added significantly to the Division's workload during the later 1950s .

Juvenile delinquency had been the focus of both departmental and public discussion during the early 1950s. The trial in 1953 of sixteen year old Anthony Gill and seventeen year old George Lacey for the wounding of a Palmerston North police officer raised the issue of teenage violence and the effects of popular entertainment after it was revealed that both adolescents were fans of comics, radio serials and gangster films. 'Crime waves' were reported across the country: in Southland, police uncovered a seven-member juvenile gang which admitted to 26 charges of breaking and entering and theft over an eighteen-month period; in Auckland, store police apprehended a hundred young shoplifters in one shop in a fortnight in 1951.[11]

The Mazengarb committee argued that the Hutt Valley events had some distinguishing and disturbing new features. The adolescents were younger, and some of them were already sexually experienced, with girls, rather than boys, taking the lead in initiating and encouraging sexual encounters. Many came from comfortable backgrounds, although their domestic arrangements were not always considered to be satisfactory. The activities were also organised, showing signs of gang influence. This 'new' pattern of juvenile immorality was 'uncertain in origin, insidious in growth, and has developed over a wide field', but the committee identified various causal factors. Child welfare officers supported some of the reasons suggested. Some explanations were general and time-honoured: excessive freedom for children, lack of parental interest in them, the decline of family values, the absence of religious instruction. Other explanations were specific to time and place. New housing suburbs such as those in the Hutt Valley lacked both a community spirit and the recreational and leisure amenities that would alleviate delinquent conduct. The combined effects of economic depression and then war had brought unwanted stress and insecurity to adolescent life. As one child welfare officer noted, 'war, continuing war and atom and hydrogen bomb hysteria' had furthered the breakdown of family life; 'it is only to be expected that the ordinary standards of morality and conduct must undergo some change when it is realised that since 1939 children have lived with war, violence, death, destruction, crime and sex continuously'.[12]

A few child welfare officers noted that the country's youth had more social and sexual freedom. According to some, adolescent activity no longer had such an ability to shock the wider public, as society had become more frank about sexual matters. Others supported the idea that adolescent girls took a more prominent role in sexual relationships than previously. Reporting in 1953 on the case of three young women who were 'jointly running a sort of outdoor brothel' around Ngapuna pa, a Rotorua child welfare officer suggested that girls were 'over-indulged' and sought sexual experiences as merely 'another form of stimulation'.[13] Kath Scotter, Manager of the Girls' Training Centre at Burwood, offered a more sensitive explanation for such occurrences. A number of young women at the institution were victims of sexual abuse and incest – a fact which never came up in their court appearances, she added. They had sex with men in a desire for affection, and would 'put up with' intercourse to have a fuss made of them.[14]

The indefinable complexities of modern life, with its stress on self-expression and individuality, were believed to contribute to the crisis of adolescence. Some commentators mourned the loss of 'the old ways' as modern delinquency reinforced a belief in the idyllic nature of former times. One school principal blamed the popularity of organised sports, which had removed the 'playing spirit' from games. Youths needed to keep themselves amused with simple and healthy pursuits: 'how many children today know those old games: whipping and spinning tops, making and flying kites, paper chase, hares and hounds, rotten egg, cappy, fly the garter, prisoner's base, toad in the hole, keeny seeny and blackball bee', he wondered.[15]

The pernicious effects of popular literature and entertainment were restated with a distinctive 1950s' flavour. The role of comics and other pulp fiction in fostering juvenile delinquency had already arisen in 1952, when an Inter-departmental Committee on the Control of Comics identified several 'objectionable features' of modern comics.[16] Distributors' and publishers' self-censorship after 1952 saw the removal of some comics from local shelves, but the issue remained topical in newspapers. Other forms of youth entertainment and activity were also investigated. In early 1954, Auckland child welfare officers surveyed adolescent use of slot machines on behalf of the Minister of Justice, who was considering their prohibition. They suggested that these were merely a 'craze' whose novelty would soon wear off.[17]

Continuing this denunciation of post-war youth culture, the Mazengarb committee condemned modern comics, notably those – 'basically designed for low-mentality adults' – with suggestive covers and titillating or violent story lines. They added radio serials, films, music, and advertising 'based on sex attraction, horror, and crime'.[18] Salaciousness and the seeds of dissent were read into other forms of literature and entertainment. The *Times* reminded its readers that many best-selling novels were noted for their 'luridness and unashamed' treatment of sexual matters. It criticised the New Zealand Broadcasting Service's presentation of the BBC's production of Chaucer's *Canterbury Tales* – a masterpiece, perhaps, 'but nevertheless one scarcely suitable for the ears or eyes of adolescents'.[19] Some child welfare officers agreed about the potentially harmful effects of comics and films, just as they had in the 1930s and 1940s. Timaru's officer believed there to be an excess of films depicting sex and violence. Too often, in his view, newspapers reported in breathless detail the minutiae of criminal cases and the peccadilloes of film stars, while 'love and marriage sanctity [were] smeared in the headlines'.[20]

The impact of psychological interpretations of social behaviour was also apparent in child welfare officers' assessments of youthful conduct. Arguments about the effects of poor environments were difficult to sustain in an era of

Salacious comics, along with films and peep shows, were among the amusements believed to be detrimentally affecting young minds in the 1950s and 1960s. R. J. SEARLE COLLECTION, ATL, P-AC0639-17-01

rising affluence; many of the adolescents came from families in comfortable circumstances. Instead, the emotional aspects of family life were emphasised, especially the importance of good family relationships. The separation of mother and child, broken homes, and 'abnormal' family life could all induce 'emotional disturbances' which might be acted out later as juvenile delinquency. This new emphasis was already evident in the pen portraits of juvenile delinquents that were constructed from the late 1940s, as the Division sought to perceive identifiable, and thus preventable, characteristics of delinquency. Using data from

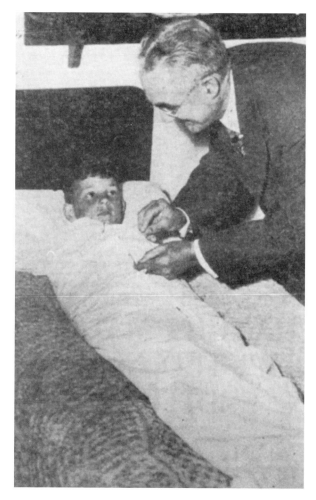

Pastor Eric Hare was one of several child delinquency experts to visit New Zealand in the 1950s. Here he demonstrates his method for controlling delinquent children: tightly wrapping them in a sheet and leaving them to cry.
CHRISTCHURCH STAR–SUN, CANTERBURY PUBLIC LIBRARY

court records for 1947 and 1949, for example, Wellington's District Child Welfare Officer profiled the 'average' juvenile delinquent: male, physically healthy, likely to come from a satisfactory physical environment in a suburban locality, but probably living in a difficult or unusual family relationship.[21]

Greater affluence and more choice of leisure pursuits were seen as contributing to delinquency, and as perhaps signs of unstable or inadequate home conditions. Mothers who 'worked' to increase their domestic comfort were particular targets, the Mazengarb committee finding that one third of the adolescents it was investigating came from homes in which the mother was in paid employment. The politician William Blair Tennent harked back to the traditional explanation of parental irresponsibility, but condemned mothers rather than fathers. In his view, the Hutt Valley episode had proved 'conclusively that mothers had not realised their responsibility'.[22]

The committee's recommendations addressed some of the perceived causes of juvenile delinquency: it advocated greater censorship of obscene and harmful publications, enhanced education of parents, and the provision of more leisure and recreational facilities in suburban areas. As a more long-term strategy, the committee suggested research into all aspects of juvenile delinquency. Religious, social and youth groups echoed these solutions, which they often framed in their own self-interest. The Association of Model Engineers, for instance, urged the committee to endorse the view that model making was a sensible means to combat juvenile delinquency, and recommended that it inform the government that the hobby should receive the widest practical assistance. Seizing upon the milk-bar cowboys' penchant for motorbikes, the Auckland Motor Cycle Club suggested that this interest be cultivated and channelled along the 'correct' lines.[23] The committee recognised that delinquency could not be 'cured' through organised leisure, for the 'pre-delinquent is not attracted by such forms of recreation or healthy pleasure', but suggestions along these lines abounded. The Minister of Police, Wilfred Fortune, favoured the extension of Police Boys' Clubs, the first of which had been set up some years earlier in Westport, while a Christchurch man endeavoured to start a boys' town movement modelled on Australian and American examples. The fact that some of the adolescents involved in the Hutt Valley events belonged to youth and sports clubs mattered little. Leisure clubs sprang up throughout the country, providing a place for youths to gather and listen to music while receiving a modicum of supervision. The Child Welfare Division's national survey of 42 youth clubs in 1957 found that all but three had been formed after the 1954 inquiry.[24]

The committee recognised the role of child welfare policies in curbing delinquency. Most of its points concerning the work of the Division were couched in the negative, focusing on the inadequacies of the Child Welfare Act, the shortcomings of children's courts, the dearth of qualified officers and the lack of preventive work; the committee recommended improvements in all these areas, along with the separation of the Division from the Department of Education.[25] Many of these criticisms were valid, and pointed to problems of which the Division was well aware. Perhaps more important than the committee's criticisms of administrative matters was its lack of awareness of the Division's work. The Division was a remedial institution, Peek informed the committee: 'it is not the custodian of the morals of the children of the community at all'. He and the other officers patiently explained their powers and responsibilities, and attempted to clarify the meaning of the supervisory and preventive services they offered. To charges that they did not act quickly enough to stop delinquency or abuse, they countered that 'we cannot just walk in and take the child – we have to get evidence and if we cannot get it, then we cannot take action'. The Division's representatives baulked at suggestions that magistrates be given powers of supervision or to act without recommendations from child welfare officers. Peek adamantly rejected amendments to the Act to boost magisterial authority. 'I could draw quite a lurid picture of what did happen in the days when the Magistrates had all the prerogatives', he noted. 'That was the day when they filled up our industrial schools by children who had in no sense deserved being put away.'[26]

Just as quickly as it had appointed the special committee, the government implemented in legislation some of its recommendations. The Child Welfare Amendment Act (No. 2) 1954 targeted the allegedly central role of girls and young women in fostering illicit relationships by creating the new category of 'delinquency' for all adolescents who committed indecent acts, or allowed them to be performed on them. The Indecent Publications Amendment Act 1954 attempted to control the proliferation of questionable publications through the creation of a register of distributors of printed matter, while the Police Offences Amendment Act 1954 made it an offence to supply contraceptives to those under sixteen, and for those younger than sixteen to possess them. In less hurried fashion, a Special Select Committee of Parliament sat periodically during 1954 and 1955 to reflect on the Mazengarb recommendations.[27]

These events spawned a wave of publicity in New Zealand and elsewhere. The Social Security Department distributed the Mazengarb report to all households receiving the family benefit, orphan's benefits and (where appropriate) war pensions. By March 1955, nearly 300,000 copies had been sent out.[28] Children's court magistrates as well as child welfare officers spoke at meetings, while newspapers carried editorials and reports on the issue for several months.[29] International newspapers fastened on the Hutt Valley episode, which followed hard on the heels of the publicity accorded the Parker–Hulme case. The events remained newsworthy for some time internationally: a 1957 issue of Sydney's *Sunday Telegraph* reflected on New Zealand's 'Dead End Kids' and reminded readers of the 'free-for-all child sex and petting parties' in Lower Hutt over recent years.[30]

Some dissenting voices were raised against both the recommendations of the committee and the subsequent government action. Contemporary observers used the unbalanced nature of the inquiry to question its findings. Wellington's 'Elected Committee of Citizens', comprising mainly educationalists, denounced its methods as unscientific and lacking the input of experts. Making a submission to the Special Select Committee, its representatives contended that the report was:

largely a compendium of well-intentioned (but often misleading) platitudes, emotionally couched; and more likely to dismay parents than to solve their problems. . . . It is not proper for statements of personal opinion, unsupported by evidence or full inquiry, and offering faint faith in New Zealand education to have been given the country-wide publicity that has happened in this case.[31]

The government's decision to introduce legislation almost immediately also generated disquiet. The *Christchurch Star–Sun,* branding the legislation as unduly rushed and plagued with shortcomings, noted that 'mature consideration . . . could present a finished job rather than the hurried patchwork'. The *Wanganui Chronicle* was more forthright: 'On the face of it it looks to be spineless, consistent with the customary technique once again of seeming to do something and yet committing the Government to no decision at all'.[32] The Special Select Committee heard a number of complaints. Booksellers claimed that they had not been consulted on the construction of a register for the distribution of literature, or the definition of an obscene publication. Public servants also took issue with some of the report's inaccurate statements concerning the activities of various official agencies.[33]

The Child Welfare Division was among these dissenting voices. The handful of officers questioned during the hearings had interpreted juvenile delinquency differently than had most other witnesses and the committee itself. They painted a broader picture of juvenile delinquency so as to place the Hutt Valley events in their proper context. Charlie Peek considered there to be little that was new in juvenile behaviour. In his view only the size of the group, and the influence of older adolescents on younger, distinguished the events from others that had gone before. While 'precocious and promiscuous girls' may have been involved, he did not concur with the committee's suggestion that a girl would become delinquent after transgressing the 'moral law' only once.[34]

A survey of child welfare officers indicated that they did not see as much juvenile delinquency as did others in the community. Of the eighteen district child welfare officers who responded to a request for information about juvenile immorality, only five believed that sexual misconduct among youths had increased, although many noted the difficulty of gaining reliable measurements of sexual activity. In contrast to stories of hordes of milk-bar cowboys, few child welfare officers remarked upon their presence.[35]

The behaviour evident in the Hutt Valley in 1954 had for some time made up part of the Division's portfolio of cases. During the early 1950s it had investigated a number of similar cases. In 1950, Auckland officer John Cupit inquired into four children who had been suspended from school for 'sexual misconduct'. He found this 'sordid and thoroughly unpleasant affair' to be little different from others with which teachers were regularly confronted.[36] Nor were such inquiries confined to large urban or suburban areas. Child welfare officers on the West Coast reported that a large number of children at Inangahua School were allegedly involved in sexual misbehaviour during 1953; two adolescent boys were brought before the children's court.[37]

A more serious case came to the Division's attention in 1952, when it investigated sexual misbehaviour among schoolchildren in the Hutt Valley suburbs of Naenae and Taita. The incidents came to light during the police prosecution of a man charged with sex offences against children. The Division's investigation, ordered by the court, indicated that his actions had affected many children, both directly and indirectly. Young girls whom he had indecently assaulted had gone on to become sexually involved with other adolescents. The central role of an adult in this inquiry distinguished it from the 1954 events, but there were striking similarities with the later Hutt Valley inquiry. As in 1954, adolescents were reported to be having sexual relations with each other in private

Children playing in Naenae streets in 1957. A string of inquiries into youth conduct in the area identified the need for more organised leisure activities. EVENING POST COLLECTION, ATL, C-11960

homes and open paddocks, and there were signs of a 'gang element'. Many had come from 'good' homes, were in their early teens, had not come to the Division's attention before, and had received little sex instruction from their parents. The child welfare officers concluded that 'what is called sexual misbehaviour' among children was not as uncommon as the public liked to think, but was in fact 'widespread' and in need of fuller investigation.[38]

The Hutt Valley had experienced two other surveys into the behaviour of local adolescents before 1954. Concerned parents had requested an official inquiry into allegations of juvenile immorality in 1951. A preparatory study by a local magistrate found insufficient grounds for such an inquiry, although it was claimed that parents had placed before him evidence of 'sexual looseness'.[39] Of more significance was the Hutt Valley Youth Survey. Representatives of government agencies, local bodies and voluntary organisations met in mid-1953 to consider whether the Hutt Valley suffered from an 'adolescent problem', and to suggest steps to combat this if it did. The detailed survey made by a sub-committee of eight members, two of whom were child welfare officers, indicated that juvenile delinquency in the area was 'excessive' in comparison with other centres, and occurred disproportionately in suburbs with a high proportion of state housing. Recommendations to overcome this problem included educational reform, the provision of home help for young mothers, more religious instruction and leisure facilities, and censorship. Well-researched and largely spurning moralistic interpretations, the survey and report stood in marked contrast to the government inquiry of the following year.[40]

Other cases of juvenile 'moral delinquency' surfaced during the 1954 inquiry. In early August, a fifteen year old Auckland youth sexually assaulted and murdered an eight year old boy. The youth had come to the Division's attention a year earlier after exhibiting 'immoral tendencies'. Officers had arranged for a psychological examination and vocational guidance but taken no further action, believing there to be no grounds on which they could bring him before the children's court. Questioned about this during the Mazengarb inquiry, District Child Welfare Officer Gordon Smith defended the decision. There were, he speculated, another 30 or 40 young adolescent men in Auckland who, 'under the right circumstances', would have committed a similar offence; without firm evidence, the Division was unable to act.[41] During the inquiry, Peek received a request from the chair of the school committee at Owenga on the Chatham Islands that he send an officer to investigate the morals of the local children.[42]

Rising levels of juvenile delinquency were common throughout the western world in the post-war years. The United States and Britain, in particular, experienced a marked upsurge in juvenile offending and a growth in the number of youth gangs during the 1950s.[43] The Division frequently pointed to the international character of juvenile delinquency in order to argue that the level and nature of New Zealand's delinquency was, comparatively speaking, unspectacular. Child welfare officers noted, for instance, that New Zealand's young offenders did not generally carry weapons or have drug problems, and that its juvenile gangs were not believed to be as dangerous as their overseas counterparts; New Zealand's Teddy boys, it was reported, did not follow the English custom of secreting razors in their caps.[44]

The general statistics on juvenile delinquency which the Division presented to the committee portrayed a less dramatic situation than the inquiry itself suggested. The great majority of children and young people did not get into trouble and appear before the children's court. Like many others at the time, the Mazengarb committee chose to focus on a short-term increase in the number of court appearances as proof of declining standards of youth, and by extension, New Zealand society. As Peek noted, 'everyone' seemed to think that youth was worse than fifteen years before, despite the fact that comparisons with the pre-war years were actually favourable.[45] The Division preferred to take a long-term view of delinquency, for the most part dismissing yearly fluctuations in the number of court appearances. Not until the annual changes were markedly out of proportion to the growth in the juvenile population did the Division consider them significant: substantial increases each year from the late 1960s, including an almost 30 per cent increase in 1970/1, prompted widespread and deep official disquiet.[46]

A long-term view of the statistics places the juvenile delinquency scare of the early 1950s in a broader context. Figure 4, which indicates the number of children's court appearances between 1948 and 1971, shows a steady increase which accelerated markedly from the mid-1960s.[47] Most came before the court for petty offences such as theft, or, until their removal from the children's courts in 1961, traffic offences. Breaches of the Child Welfare Act, such as being a neglected child, accounted for less than 20 per cent of appearances. The number of children in court for a second or subsequent misdemeanour climbed steadily, until by the early 1970s, more than 40 per cent of cases involved children who had appeared in court before. Juvenile delinquency remained a male phenomenon, despite the perception generated in 1954. In the later 1950s the Division estimated that for every girl appearing in court there were ten boys, half of whom were aged between fourteen and sixteen. Between the late 1940s and the early 1970s, between three and four times as many boys as girls made appearances in court, and boys dominated the figures for certain types of offending, such as traffic offences. In 1965, the Division noted that twelve out of every 100 boys then aged ten would be likely to appear in court before their seventeenth birthday.[48]

The Division did not collate separate figures for Maori and Pakeha court appearances, although Maori continued to appear in court in disproportionate

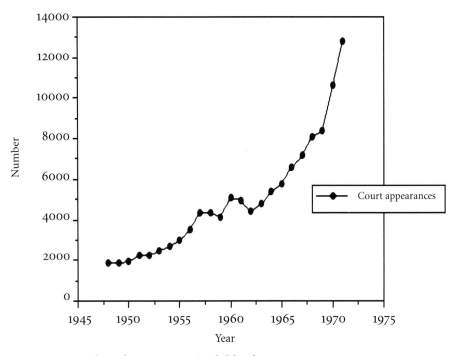

FIGURE 4 *Number of appearances in children's court, 1948–1971*

numbers. Sporadic reports indicated a steady growth in Maori juvenile delinquency, with Maori offending at three or four times the rate of Pakeha, particularly in the fifteen to twenty age group. These levels were sometimes even more disproportionate in areas with a high Maori population. The figures were sufficiently high for the Justice Department to undertake a special inquiry in 1953/4 which examined all Maori offending, including that of juveniles, an exercise it repeated less than ten years later. Although separate figures were again not gathered, Pacific Island children appeared in court in greater than proportionate numbers. The Division's researchers reported in 1968 that Pacific Island children appeared with more than four times the frequency of Pakeha children.[49]

Investigations into Maori delinquency formed little part of either the Mazengarb inquiry or the broader public consternation over juvenile delinquency in the 1950s. Child welfare officers identified Maori youths among the bodgies and widgies, but in the view of Auckland's District Child Welfare Officer, their participation went little further than adoption of the dress code. As Peek told the Mazengarb committee, Maori delinquency had reached a point where 'we cannot just blink our eyes' at the differences between Maori and Pakeha rates of offending. But the committee largely did just that, even though it noted that, at 10 per cent of the population, Maori were over-represented in comprising 28 per cent of appearances before children's courts in the previous year.[50]

Maori offending and over-representation in children's courts became of major concern in Maori communities. A number of Maori groups, such as the Maori Women's Welfare League, argued that Maori themselves were best suited to solving their delinquency problems. The President of Te Kotahitanga Tautaru informed Peek in 1948 that the Division's officers were not in a position to control delinquency among Maori girls, particularly those who boarded ships in the local port of New Plymouth. Supervision was needed at night and early in the morning, when paid child welfare officers might not be available.[51]

Maori groups had exercised limited responsibility over young Maori delinquents since 1945. The Maori Social and Economic Advancement Act of that year gave tribal committees a role in cooperating with the Education Department in the training of Maori children, a role which was extended to delinquent children. In areas where the tribal committees were strong, child welfare officers believed that there was little delinquency.[52] The committee at Ngararatunua, near Whangarei, for example, heard informal charges and complaints against young offenders in the area. In 1955 it fined fifteen year old Bert Hemi for throwing stones, and ordered him to leave the district for a period. Some child welfare officers questioned such authority, but the Division approved of it, and claimed that it was not the Division's function to undermine tribal committees or interpret the legislation for them.[53]

Child welfare officers saw the causes of Maori delinquency as largely distinct from those affecting Pakeha. Poor living conditions, the lack of employment and educational opportunities, and broken homes were all singled out as contributing factors. Social and economic dislocation arising from contact with Pakeha was also blamed, with some officers noting that Maori appeared to be 'caught between two influences – those which are fundamentally a part of his very fabric and those which are a part of modern civilisation'. Other officers, perhaps not delving as deeply into the more long-term reasons for delinquency, identified as causes excessive alcohol consumption and lazy parents.[54]

Rather than using the absolute number of court appearances as a guide to the level of juvenile delinquency, the Division relied on measurements which took account of changes in the juvenile population. These presented a less consistent pattern of juvenile delinquency than was implied by the absolute number of court appearances. Throughout the juvenile delinquency scare of the mid-1950s, the rate of appearances for offences was below the pre-war level, causing the Division to congratulate itself on what it saw as the benefits of its preventive policies.[55] The rate of court appearances for offences per 10,000 seven to seventeen year olds had declined from 84 in 1943/4 to 46 in 1949/50, but rose to 62 by 1954/5. The juvenile delinquency rates of the 1950s suggested to the Division that there had not been a marked deterioration in children's conduct, although the figures still gave cause for concern. As Charlie Peek pointed out as the anxiety over sexual immorality mounted during 1954, the Division owed it to the contemporary generation of children to offer 'some defence to the uninformed and sometimes irresponsible opinion being expressed'.[56]

Both the number and the rate of appearances before the children's court rose dramatically from the mid-1960s. The rate had reached 95 per 10,000 in 1966/7, and it soared thereafter. The Division compiled figures only for the population aged between ten and seventeen after 1969, and this made the growth appear even more pronounced: from 160 in 1968/9 the figure jumped to 231 in 1971.[57] The Division struggled to explain the increase, and took no comfort from the knowledge that other countries were experiencing a similar development. From the mid-1960s, its annual reports conveyed a growing sense of powerlessness in the face of a rapidly changing society. Superintendent Lewis Anderson was fond of pointing out the failings of modern adults and modern society; he saw juvenile delinquency as the price to be paid for an 'uninhibited freedom from moral standards'. Those who made a 'cult' of the rebellious and were anti-authoritarian could scarcely wonder, he suggested, when children and young people appeared in court. Alarmed by what he saw as the iniquitous influence of cult figures and musicians, Anderson warned of 'the colourful personalities who obviously exert some influence on our young people by causing them to equate immorality with honesty and frankness'. They were, to his mind, 'false prophets'.[58]

The rising number of appearances before the children's courts may have been a consequence of the disaffection of youth in the 1960s, when protests at aspects of adult society were mounting. More preventive work may also have brought greater numbers of young people to attention, and the Division certainly attributed some of the increase to greater police efficiency in detecting and reporting offences. The rise in the number of court appearances may have been a self-fulfilling prophecy: a belief that juvenile delinquency was out of control may have led the Division to adopt a harsher attitude towards youthful behaviour.

An emphasis on the 1954 inquiry can obscure, and indeed has obscured, a view of juvenile delinquency which places the events and the furore surrounding them in a broader context.[59] The Division contended with juvenile delinquency and people's fears about it on a daily basis. As with other issues of law, order and morality, public anxiety over juvenile delinquency waxed and waned. The wartime spectre of rising delinquency had largely subsided by the later 1940s, but the level was sufficiently high for child welfare officers to remain perturbed, and then become increasingly so, as New Zealand entered a period of political stability and economic growth. As the Mazengarb inquiry receded in popular memory from the mid-1960s, both the rate and number of court appearances increased – but largely without the brouhaha which had marked 1954 and 1955.

Juvenile sexual delinquency remained a smouldering issue for three or four years after the inquiry. Police in Palmerston North, Levin and Auckland all took groups of adolescents to court on charges of delinquency involving sexual activity.[60] The Hutt Valley, where locals and police were particularly alert to any signs of moral delinquency, also remained in the spotlight. Events came to a head once more in early 1958, when police concluded a six-week inquiry by taking to court 23 of the more than 40 adolescents they had interviewed concerning their sexual behaviour. Police and child welfare inquiries suggested that there had been a repetition of the events of four years earlier. The Division's investigating officer, Bruce Burton, identified the key role that had once again been played by adolescent girls. 'Unlovely, unattractive girls whose parents had failed or had been unable to teach them the compensating value of good dress and groomed appearance' had acted on the 'age old discovery' that there was 'at least one way of winning friends'. He noted, too, local conditions which he suggested made such events possible: 'the concentration of semi- and unskilled industrial jobs . . . should mean some concentration of sub-standard families'.[61]

The 1958 inquiry raised wider questions about the effects of this prolonged attention on juvenile delinquency. Neither Burton nor the Division's research unit considered the latest 'outbreak' to be anything unusual. Burton noted wryly that 'we, of the Lower Hutt Child Welfare District Office, don't mind our district being world news. . . . In 1954 Lower Hutt had "troubles" and here again in 1958 we've made the headlines again with our old friend, sex'. There was a more serious edge to his comment. Prolonged police inquiries had led to a spate of rumours in the area. The press 'sensed something juicy and commenced ferreting', with *Truth* apparently offering parents money for their 'story'. A teacher from another area asked Burton if it were true that 30 schoolgirls in the Hutt Valley were pregnant; he knew of another girl who had asked her teacher to provide her with a 'certificate of virtue'. The police inquiries were upsetting for both children and their parents; Burton concluded that the 'mass inquiry' had been harmful to children, whether or not they were implicated in the events. Some parents complained that they were unaware their children were being interviewed. The parents of one girl had their lawyer lodge a complaint over the police interviewing her for five hours to obtain two brief statements. All in all, the inquiry served as a reminder to the Division, and to the police, the officers suggested, to keep the issue of moral delinquency in perspective.[62]

As in a witch-hunt, public anxiety, once ignited, read immorality and mis-behaviour into an array of youthful activities. Parents framed concerns about their children's conduct in the context of sexual immorality, and child welfare officers used popular conceptions to explain their difficulties with troublesome youths. Jeff Gray, who was in and out of court, supervision and institutions for a number of years, bought a motorbike upon his release from the Boys' Training Centre. The child welfare officer predicted that Jeff would immediately identify with the local milk-bar cowboys; within six months he was part of a Newtown gang.[63]

Newspapers warned that juvenile misconduct was not confined to the Hutt Valley or even to New Zealand, although an internationally shared delinquency may have been cold comfort to anxious communities. 'Are you sure your children aren't moral delinquents?', the *Standard* asked parents, urging them to investigate their children's behaviour. Watch the 'odd clothing cults' – for these generally indicated a sense of sexual awareness – and do not be misled into assuming that officially-sponsored youth organisations were beyond 'undetected corruption', it advised its readers.[64] Milk-bar cowboys and larrikins appeared in many centres: in Dunedin, they congregated around the beaches but showed little interest in sex; in Auckland, they gathered in Queen Street and disturbed passers-by.[65]

Child welfare officers' court reports during 1955 and 1956 illustrated the enhanced public awareness of juvenile behaviour. As Peek pointed out in 1955, public interest and attitudes 'doubtless' affected rates of both notification and detection of children's offences. Campaigns by local bodies against such occurrences as vandalism could lead to a disproportionate increase in the figures.[66] Officers in Rotorua, Napier and Wellington all remarked upon the increased number of children appearing in court, some of them involved in gang behaviour or up on relatively trivial charges. Auckland experienced a record number of court appearances in 1955 and 1956, a fact which the District Child Welfare Officer attributed to heightened publicity and legislative changes concerning sexual misconduct. He also noted that a growing number of bodgies and widgies actively enjoyed the publicity which surrounded them. They had, in his view, an inflated sense of their own importance, and were distinguished by an 'emulation of sophisticated characters of screen and written fiction'. Even so, he argued – as did others – that the bodgie and widgie cults offered advantages to youths by allowing them an opportunity to work out their frustrations and 'childhood misfortune' – 'if only their standards of conduct were better founded', he hastened to add.[67]

The behaviour of bodgies and widgies, Teddy boys and milk-bar cowboys loomed large in the public imagination during the later 1950s, particularly following the violent killings of two Auckland teenagers involved in the 'bodgie cult'.[68] Christchurch milk-bar cowboys – 'self-styled charmers and their "pillion pets"' – made a 'swift invasion' of Timaru one weekend, while Hawke's Bay youths held a rock'n'roll party in a Hastings cemetery, and Napier was dubbed 'bodgie city'. In 1958 the Child Welfare Division conducted an inquiry into the actions of bodgies in the Hutt Valley's Manor Park following the arrest of a number of youths after disturbances on trains and vandalism at railway stations.[69]

These events, and others such as the four-part radio series *Youth Without Purpose*, broadcast in 1958, kept the issue before the public, and the 'bodgie cult' became the object of both popular and scholarly study. A. E. Manning's *The Bodgie: A Study in Abnormal Psychology* (1958), which traced the background of 30 Australian and New Zealand bodgies and widgies, concluded that their

To the amusement of many, Mabel Howard, the Minister in charge of the Welfare of Women and Children, met with bodgies and widgies in 1958 to ask them what they wanted out of life. CHRISTCHURCH STAR–SUN, CANTERBURY PUBLIC LIBRARY

behaviour was socially induced and that 'Society is the only possible agent of cure'. Official interest mounted too, particularly after Mabel Howard, the Minister in charge of Women and Children, sought out the views of bodgie leaders on the provision of leisure facilities for youth.[70]

Young people themselves featured in interviews in newspapers and on radio. The 1958 radio programme *The Rising Generation* featured a series of interviews with bodgies, Teddy boys and girls:

> A bodgie is a type to carry a knife and chains and things like that around and go round in gangs and get into fights or rumbles. You very seldom see a gang of bodgies in town, or anywhere about now. . . . we're just ordinary sensible jokers, or we try to be. But . . . I mean, we think as other human beings think, the jokers who wear square clothes as they call them, you have twenty-two inch cuffs and things. We think like them, we work like them only we wear different clothes to them, so we get called a bodgie. We're not really.[71]

'Ex-bodgie', interviewed in the *Evening Post* in the same year, was considerably less charitable to his former companions: 'To sum a bodgie up, he is nothing more than a teenager with a lot of big ideas centred around the underworld kings of America, and their tough, "I don't care" attitude is nothing but a sham. Bodgies are fakes, and deep inside, most of them know it.'[72]

Disruption of the 1960 Hastings Blossom Festival by groups of bodgies, teenagers and young adults generated one of the last major public outcries over youth behaviour in this period. Youth cultures in the 1960s fostered less alarm than previously, despite some violent episodes. Tensions between mods and rockers in Christchurch in 1966 spilled over into brawls and the shooting of eighteen year old rocker Les Thomas. Although the subsequent murder trial shocked 'prim Christchurch with its disclosures of youth gang crime and idle teenagers drinking, having sex and fighting', such events no longer had the power to harness public consternation.[73]

Child welfare officers, however, continued to investigate 'outbreaks' of juvenile delinquency throughout the 1960s, some of them involving considerably more adolescents than had the events leading to the Mazengarb inquiry. In 1964, police called child welfare officers to assist in an inquiry into sexual misbehaviour among adolescents in Grey Lynn and Panmure. Fifty-one young people appeared in the children's court as a result of police interviews with 400 children and parents. Despite the Division's fear that the events would receive undue publicity and be blown out of proportion – and *Truth* was shrill in its exposé of 'Pyjama games without pyjamas' – the inquiry and court appearances passed with little public comment.[74]

The repeated references to gang activity during the 1950s led the Division to initiate surveys into the conduct of gangs in 1958 and 1959. It appointed Alan Levett, formerly the Director of Dunedin's Kensington Youth Centre, as a boys' welfare officer-cum-researcher with a 'roving commission' to research gang activity in several 'troublesome' areas in Auckland. Levett's previous success in catering for bodgies, widgies and Teddy boys suggested that he would be able to mix with gang members, and his research methods bore this out. It was, he reflected, a '"follow your nose" procedure, indirect questioning and informal chat mixed with hamburgers and cheap coffee'.[75]

Levett reported on 41 juvenile gangs in Auckland which involved up to 700 members aged between twelve and 24. Most were not organised, but all shared an anti-authoritarian outlook. Their members came from families which lived in economically-straitened circumstances and had a high incidence of family breakdown. None of the gangs had been in existence for more than four years, and most had a membership of less than twenty. The Majestic Theatre gang was the exception, comprising between 40 and 100 members drawn from a range of loosely associated groups operating throughout the city. Others, such as the Kupe Street Boys, were localised and had only a handful of members. Most of the gangs were Pakeha. The Red Ram Rockers was the only predominantly Maori group Levett identified, and although he knew of gangs developed on purely racial lines, he believed that as a Pakeha he was not in a position to contact them. Males dominated the membership of gangs, although some had female members and others, such as the Ponsonby Kids, were primarily female-based. For the most part, gang activities centred on 'hanging around', drag-racing, drinking, fighting and sex.[76]

Consternation about gang activity also led, in 1958, to an interdepartmental committee to inquire into juvenile offending and possible solutions to it. Sam Barnett, the Secretary of Justice, initiated the committee in the wake of a spate of bodgie activity which the police had been unable to prevent. In his view, the time had come for the government to take control of juvenile gangs and show that 'the State still has supreme power within its borders, and that it will exercise that power'. He expected the bodgie cult to decline in popularity – for it was 'neither interesting nor satisfying' – but believed that more 'unpleasant' forms of association could take its place.[77] Comprising representatives from the Division, the Police, and the departments of Justice, Education and Maori Affairs, the committee met regularly from 1958, chaired by the Director of Education. A smaller working subcommittee, chaired by the Deputy-Superintendent of Child Welfare, took responsibility for devising a research programme through a research unit which was established in the Division in the same year.[78]

'This is here! – Not cosily far away', the Evening Post *told its readers in 1966 when it published these and other photographs of gang activities in New Zealand. The Auckland motorcycle gang Hell's Angels plays up in New Plymouth.*
JOHN McCOMBE

An attack on delinquency: prevention and diversion

The demand on child welfare services increased significantly following the 1954 inquiry. The Division capitalised on the sudden attention. In early 1956, it engaged publicist Tony Curnow to prepare radio programmes, newspaper articles and pamphlets explaining its work.[79] Lewis Anderson captured the essence of the transformation in 1966 when he commented on the 'marked change' in public attitudes to child welfare work over the previous twenty years. Whereas people had once paid only lip-service to child welfare officers, 'as though they were missionaries on furlough from some distant, little-known country', the publicity accorded juvenile delinquency meant that 'today Child Welfare is news'.[80]

The increased volume of preventive work posed considerable problems for the Division. According to Napier's District Child Welfare Officer:

Ten years ago the public used Child Welfare services only because they had to. . . . Now we are embarrassed by the number of people who consult us voluntarily on a miscellany of problems. . . . As we work with rather than for the client, each case demands a greater number of man hours than previously. You will agree that it takes much longer to show a person how to help himself.[81]

Officers were reluctant to take on more preventive cases because of pressures on their time. The Division's quarterly returns of preventive cases not visited during the mid-1950s highlighted the volume of work and lack of time among more prosaic difficulties: Northland's Mick Rewini had not been visited for some time because his home was accessible only by boat, while 53 inches of rain on the West Coast and six closures of the road had prevented officers calling on Ruth Knight in the autumn of 1958.[82]

The Division had always presented preventive child welfare policies as a shared community responsibility. Neither the Division nor the Branch before it had placed this joint effort on a formal footing, but called on other organisations as and when required. From the late 1950s, however, the Division and the police made a more formal and structured attempt to divert offenders away from the children's court. The Juvenile Crime Prevention Branch of the Police began in 1957, operating initially in Christchurch before being extended the following year. It was renamed the Juvenile Crime Prevention Section in 1959, and then the Youth Aid Section in 1969. Based loosely on a Liverpool scheme begun in 1949, New Zealand's diversion programme was designed to keep pre-delinquent and mildly delinquent adolescents under seventeen out of court. Specially-designated police officers investigated offences and complaints under the Child Welfare Act which normally came to police attention. Either on their own volition or after receiving advice from the Division, they decided on a course of action, which could be a police warning, preventive supervision from the Division or another social service agency, or, if necessary, prosecution.[83]

The Division welcomed the diversion scheme as both a complement to its own work and a means of removing trivial cases from the children's court. Peek and other senior officers participated in a series of meetings with the police to establish the scheme and clarify the spheres of responsibility of police and child welfare officers. Weekly meetings between the Division's staff and police officers encouraged cooperation and the sharing of information, and helped to avoid any overlap in the approach to cases.

The scheme expanded rapidly. In its first six months in Christchurch it dealt with 350 children, of whom 172 were subsequently prosecuted. Of those not taken to court, only six had come to police attention again within the year. The number of children diverted through the scheme grew steadily. In 1961/2 the Juvenile Crime Prevention Section handled almost 4000 cases, over half of which were disposed of with a police warning; a third of the cases were handed to the Child Welfare Division. In 1972, the Youth Aid Section dealt with 10,978 cases, 6956 of these by admonition. Youth Aid officers arranged for 333 adolescents to be placed under preventive supervision, handed 797 to the Division for general oversight, asked the Division to make a home visit to another 428, and passed 788 cases to it for referral to another agency; the remainder were sent on either to the children's court or directly to another agency. Replicating the pattern evident in children's courts, boys outnumbered girls by more than two to one. Offences rather than complaints dominated, reflecting the central role of the police in the system.[84]

The Juvenile Crime Prevention Section handled the full range of child welfare cases. The police found most of these in the course of their regular work, or as part of the special duties of the juvenile crime prevention officers. Plain-clothes officers patrolled Wellington streets looking for youngsters in trouble. Through these methods in 1959 they stumbled across two girls who were living in 'rather disreputable surroundings' without their parents' knowledge. Some parents approached the police directly to ask for assistance with their child, and Wellington police claimed that teenage girls regularly came into their office seeking advice.[85]

Other cases came to the scheme after other methods had 'failed'. Arthur Eru had had a chequered career by the time he became involved with the programme in 1960. Two years earlier he had broken into an ice-cream van and, with three other boys, consumed its contents. Although the child welfare officer recommended preventive supervision to keep Arthur and his nine siblings under notice while their father was unemployed, Arthur was sent to a foster home. He was unhappy and homesick there, and, caught stealing milk money, was passed to the local Juvenile Crime Prevention Section, which recommended prosecution, perhaps because of his earlier brushes with the law.[86]

There were a number of teething problems with the scheme, centred primarily around the division of responsibility for supervisory work. Some child welfare officers disliked the prospect of police acting as social workers and supervising cases which, they believed, should be handled by the Division. John O'Sullivan, in whose district the scheme was trialled, approached the arrangement with caution, welcoming it so long as the police did not do work that had traditionally fallen to the Division.[87] This did not happen in Christchurch, where a high degree of cooperation was maintained, but officers in other districts reported difficulties. In practice, the police did undertake some social service work. In the name of prevention, they patrolled the streets and found children in need of care. They had 'man to man' talks with young men, restricted the attendance at the pictures of others and introduced them to boys' clubs, and helped young women to find and keep jobs – all tasks performed by child welfare officers in the course of their regular work.[88] Other difficulties resulted from the varying knowledge which police had of the scheme; it seems there were tensions within the force over its practicality. According to Whangarei's District Child Welfare Officer, the scheme functioned poorly there because the police were neither committed nor interested. Outlying stations knew little of the scheme, and one refused to participate at all. A conference of police and child welfare officers called to discuss preventive work among juveniles in 1959 largely endorsed the scheme, but also noted the regional variation and duplication of responsibility.[89]

The scheme had a mixed impact on the Division's work. To some extent, it simply formalised an arrangement between police and the Division which already existed, and was certainly not a 'revolutionary development'.[90] Some child welfare officers found that cooperation with the police added substantially to their workload. Brian Manchester, who worked in the Wellington district office in the late 1960s, recalled the large number of cases that he and police sometimes had to discuss: 'I think the largest number of cases I had in one Youth Aid meeting was 168, and it was a weekly meeting. We got through them all, but it was about 7 o'clock in the evening by the time we finished – that was starting at 2'.[91]

The long-term success of the scheme in keeping children out of court is impossible to measure, for its development preceded by only a few years the dramatic rise in the number of cases heard in children's courts. While the Division noticed an initial decline in the number of young and first offenders appearing in court, the scheme's subsequent impact was hard to gauge, and in the end, the programme may have had the opposite effect from what was intended. The Division noted an 'almost staggering' increase in the number of Youth Aid cases from the late 1960s. Some of these cases would have been unlikely to come to notice before, as the scheme brought more children and young people into contact with police and child welfare officers. Diverting children from the court may have simply meant, in the end, diverting them to the Child Welfare Division or other social service agencies.

Strained to capacity: changes in residential institutions

The number of young people in residential institutions at the end of each year almost trebled between 1948 and 1972, outpacing the overall increase in the youth population. Two hundred and ninety young people lived in receiving homes, hostels or training centres at the end of 1947; by 1960 this number had grown to 360 and it increased rapidly thereafter – to 469 in 1965, 644 in 1970, and 718 by the end of 1972. The short-stay homes took a greater share of the residential population, over half from the late 1960s as the institutions became used for remand purposes.

Institutional staff commented on the changing nature of the residential population. According to some, the young people before the courts during the 1960s were more violent, used more alcohol, and were more likely to be part of a gang than previously.[92] Once admitted to the Division's institutions, they sometimes caused major problems. The Boys' Training Centre at Levin reported residents with a 'deep-rooted resentment' against all authority figures, and noted that the balance in the home was swinging towards such residents and away from more 'stable and reliable' ones. The admission of the sexually experienced or the sexually abused could have serious repercussions when they encouraged or forced others into sexual relationships. Burwood staff reported a serious case of sexual assault in early 1961; mutual and forced masturbation sessions at Otekaike in the early 1960s were traced back to one boy whose father had raped him. Burwood staff also found young women leaving windows ajar to allow their boyfriends to enter the institution at night. In 1959, the Principal reported that a group of eight young men entered the buildings up to three times a week to have sex with the residents.[93] The growing number of Maori admitted to institutions heightened racial hostility, and at Burwood Maori and Pakeha girls argued and fought with each other in what staff dubbed 'the Maori wars'.[94]

The separateness of the young Maori woman in the background of this photograph of the Wellington Girls' Hostel captures some of the racial divisions which became more evident in institutions from the 1950s. NATIONAL PUBLICITY STUDIOS, DEPARTMENT OF SOCIAL WELFARE, A45616

Child welfare officers and residential staff held that the adolescent girls now being admitted to institutions were more truculent and promiscuous than their predecessors. New Plymouth and Whangarei districts reported on the activities of the local 'ship girls' who frequented foreign vessels in port. Whangarei's officer considered the situation sufficiently dire in 1966 to ask staff of the shipping companies to ensure that no ship girls remained aboard vessels at night.[95] Girls who roamed the streets, associated with youths and became 'sex problems' formed a 'difficult group' in need of discipline, supervision and, in some cases, counselling. Psychologists at Burwood wrote of 'highly disturbed' residents, whom they believed fell into two groups: those influenced by gangs and cults who were prepared to injure others, and those with 'disordered personalities'.[96]

Such young women posed a danger to both themselves and others, destroying property and physically attacking staff and residents. During the 1950s, Burwood staff experienced an escalating number of physical attacks, and the Principal became so worried about the personal safety of her staff that she arranged for them to have judo lessons. This precaution had little effect against determined and disturbed young women. One resident attacked staff nine times in four months during 1959, secreting weapons in her room, or removing nails from doors to use as weapons. On one occasion, she fought with staff for two hours as they tried to remove her to hospital; on another, it took six staff and two ambulance drivers to restrain her and put her in an ambulance. Her activities influenced others, as staff found when they stumbled upon plans for a mass attack on them, and discovered weapons placed strategically around the institution.[97] Problems continued through the 1960s and into the 1970s. In 1966, Anderson reported that the riots at Mount Eden Prison in the previous year had had an 'epidemic effect' on most institutions, but particularly Kingslea (as Burwood was renamed in 1965), where 'every week or so' a resident started a 'rumble'. Nineteen residents were involved in one such 'rumble' in 1968 which became so serious that police had to be called in and four residents were taken into custody.[98]

Fareham House, the most severely affected institution, experienced major disturbances. Residents regularly absconded from the home, and ran riot on their return. Following a series of fracas in 1959 after the introduction of a ban on cigarette smoking and a policy of locking doors in the evening, the Division's Inspector, Lorna Hodder, moved in to 'sort out' the problems. She was horrified to discover that an 'unhealthy sex excitement' among the residents was stimulated by 'homosexual practices'. So widespread had these become, one staff member noted, that the girls were beginning to look 'quite mental'. Hodder removed several of the residents to foster homes, recommended that cubicles be built in the dormitories, and suggested that night lights be installed.[99]

Fareham House residents made forays on the building from the surrounding trees during one disturbance at the institution. NATIONAL PUBLICITY STUDIOS, DEPARTMENT OF SOCIAL WELFARE, A46321

The situation at Fareham deteriorated further, and at one stage the behaviour of the residents became so bad that the staff simply walked out. In 1965, a full-scale riot erupted after the Principal was run over by a car while trying to prevent some of the residents from absconding. Arthur Ricketts, who was called in to take charge, reported a state of chaos: girls armed with knives were 'swooping' on the building from among the trees while others hurled rocks and mattresses from the balcony; the Matron and staff hid in the broom cupboard while the residents were 'making sorties' through the premises, shouting 'We hate the staff' and 'We hate the Child Welfare'.[100]

Increasing numbers of residents, whether or not they were difficult, placed enormous strain on institutional resources. In 1955, Peek noted that there had been no expansion of institutional facilities for ten years, and as a result, there was an urgent need for extensions to the accommodation. The Division's major boys' institution at Levin was frequently full, with the Manager sometimes providing extra sleeping room in his own quarters. The growing population of the upper half of the North Island placed pressure on Auckland and Hamilton institutions. Hamilton officers relied on private homes or accommodated boys in the local police station in times of emergency. Institutions such as Burwood were full to capacity, and this added to the pressure on the short-term facilities. In the mid-1960s, the Centre ran a waiting list, and staff predicted that the situation would only worsen. Anderson noted in early 1971 that all the homes were 'strained to capacity'; admission figures for 1970 were 35.8 per cent higher than those for 1969. Staff were at their 'wits' end' to know where to place difficult children.[101]

Receiving homes and short-stay residences were among the institutions that were most disrupted. They were initially devised for the short-term care of younger children and older adolescent girls who did not require the more structured treatment provided at the Girls' Training Centre, but their function changed from the mid-1950s as they increasingly admitted those in need of such treatment. From the later 1960s, short-stay homes admitted young people on remand in greater numbers, which only added to their problems. Officers saw the residents as more difficult to manage than formerly, and as a result, secure facilities were added to the short-term institutions. The Principal of the Christchurch Girls' Home reported that one resident was amassing knives, razors and drill bits in preparation for a concerted attack on staff. She had already attacked a number of staff, claiming that the only pleasures she got out of life were from violence, alcohol and sex. The Principal recommended her transfer to Kingslea.[102] By 1972, as the difficulties facing institutions grew and their role was reassessed, the Division was considering constructing special remand homes along lines modelled in the United States and Britain.[103]

Residential staff also reported that receiving homes were being used for older delinquent girls who were considered unsuitable for placement in foster homes, or for whom there was insufficient space at the Training Centre. As a result, delinquent and non-delinquent girls mixed, abscondings from non-secure buildings were frequent, and the strain on staff led to an abnormally high turnover. In Hamilton, where 60 of the 90 residents during 1958 were older than fourteen, problems abounded. According to the District Child Welfare Officer, the older girls absconded after disseminating a 'precocious knowledge of sex experiences' to the younger.[104]

Auckland was the area most affected by the crisis in receiving homes and accommodation for girls and young women. Peek had recommended the establishment of a separate home for the older girls in 1955; three years later, he described the situation as 'fairly desperate', and noted that officers had been forced to use local convents and Mount Eden to accommodate extra or difficult residents.[105] New short-stay girls' homes in Auckland (1961) and Hamilton (1965) relieved some of the pressure on receiving homes, but the new institutions themselves were quickly overcrowded. Renaming the receiving homes as girls' homes in the later 1960s made little difference to the residential population, and despite the addition of secure facilities, difficulties continued.[106] A year after the change of name, the Division reported that young children of both sexes were still accommodated in the girls' homes. As a result, it constructed purpose-built girls' homes in Auckland and Hamilton, the first of which opened in late 1970. By 1972, the Division had two long-stay residences and seven short-stay homes for girls.

The Division also increased the amount of accommodation for boys and young men, who were by far the majority of the residential population. Problems in providing accommodation for younger boys had become a major issue as the residence at Hokio Beach became increasingly overcrowded. In 1971, the Division opened the Holdsworth School in Wanganui to accommodate boys aged between seven and thirteen. Henceforth Kohitere, as the Boys' Training Centre had been renamed in 1965, took in older boys on a long-term basis, while Hokio Beach accommodated those aged between eleven and fourteen. Five other boys' homes provided for boys of all ages on a short-term basis.

A number of residences tailored their programmes to the changing composition of the residential population. Hokio Beach School was one of several which catered for the growing Maori population in the Division's homes. In the late 1960s it introduced Maori language, history and culture into its curriculum, with the goal of encouraging residents to be 'true Maoris' rather than forcing them into a 'Pakeha mould'.[107] The desire to make appropriate provision for the Maori residents at Fareham House lay behind the appointment of Maori staff to the home. In the late 1950s, Kuini Te Tau was appointed to run Fareham. She emphasised the importance of Maori culture and language, and considered it vital to instruct the young women as Maori. 'Maoris are different', she recalled many years later, 'they have that aroha'. If the girls absconded, she would talk to them and 'have a real tangi' when they returned. Though Te Tau was known as 'Nana' by the residents, her methods could be abrupt. Following a spate of poor behaviour and swearing at the home in the early 1960s, she asserted control by slapping the girls 'good and hard'. Bad language was rarely heard afterwards, and was always followed by an apology, she claimed.[108]

The Division was less certain of the success of her methods. Lorna Hodder, who was called in to quell disturbances at the home in 1962, believed that Te Tau viewed Fareham – incorrectly – as a 'Maori Burwood'. Rather than imparting a knowledge of cooking and sewing, the training programme was inconsistent and 'flimsy' in all areas except Maori culture. Kuini Te Tau may have been 'kindly and sympathetic', but the Inspector did not believe her capable of running an institution: 'she deals with Maori girls as she knows best, by a mixture of

Traditional and gendered vocational training was prominent at Kingslea (above) and Kohitere (below) in the 1950s and 1960s. CANTERBURY MUSEUM, 8546 & DEPARTMENT OF SOCIAL WELFARE

emotional pleading, "please be good while I am away for the week-end", punishment by face-slapping and quite severe deprivation of privileges, and long discussions with girls . . . after which on some occasions "we all had a good cry together and everything was alright again – You know, the Maori way".' Hodder's comment was barbed, and meant as criticism, but it contained an element of truth. Te Tau's tenure was punctuated by difficulties, and in the end the Division decided that the only solution was to remove both staff and residents, and start again.[109]

Faced with residents who posed a danger to themselves and to staff, institutions increasingly used secure units. These differed from the punishment cells or rooms which some residences used or retained. Rather than being presented as punishment, admission to secure care or close custody could be reframed as a period of 'time-out'. Residents in secure care continued to receive educational and vocational instruction during the day, and some took their meals with the others. Those in Burwood's clinic, as its secure block was called, had staff constantly on duty, and senior staff slept in a bed-sitting room there.[110] Many of the institutions built new secure blocks or wings to provide time-out facilities for difficult residents, or to be used for 'acclimatisation' periods following admission.

By the 1950s, physical exercise for girls in residential institutions had become more active than in the past. NATIONAL PUBLICITY STUDIOS, DEPARTMENT OF SOCIAL WELFARE, A46071

Case conferences and group discussions became part of many residential institutions in the 1940s and 1950s. Here Kath Scotter presides over a group discussion at the Girls' Training Centre.
NATIONAL PUBLICITY STUDIOS, DEPARTMENT OF SOCIAL WELFARE, A46062

The erection of a medium-security block at the Boys' Training Centre from 1963 caused considerable consternation among the residents, to whom its function was clearly signalled by the protected windows. Staff anticipated that a major change in their approach to the residents would be necessitated by the ending of the centre's previously open nature. A small high-security block was added in the late 1960s.[111]

Despite an emphasis on 'time-out' and the positive aspects of time 'in secure', the units also served a punitive purpose and became a means of controlling a difficult residential population. Those who absconded sometimes spent several days in secure readjusting to institutional life, but no doubt feeling that they were being punished. Kohitere's annual report for 1970 noted 156 admissions to secure during the year; the institution had experienced a spate of fighting and bullying as rival gangs clashed.[112] Some homes admitted new residents to close custody rather than the open section, on the grounds that the resident's background and circumstances demanded it, or in the belief that a period in close custody would help a young person to settle in to institutional life. Hamilton's District Child

Psychologist R. Jeffrey applies a personality test to a Kohitere resident. NATIONAL PUBLICITY
STUDIOS, DEPARTMENT OF SOCIAL WELFARE, R301

Welfare Officer reported that this was common practice in the homes in the city,
a fact which he attributed to the inability of staff to control their residents.[113]

Other institutions increased the use of psychological or medical services for
difficult or disturbed residents. Burwood in particular employed these services
intensively as a way to 'drain off' and resolve violent emotions. Weekly meetings
of the residents with local physicians and psychologists, along with group
therapy, had become a core part of the treatment programme by the mid-1950s,
when a part-time psychiatrist joined the staff. The psychologist's report for 1966
indicated the extent of the assistance. He visited the home three times weekly,
and on other occasions as required. During the year he had conducted a total of
785 interviews with residents, compared with 524 in the previous year. Of the
67 residents he interviewed in 1966, four had between 21 and 30 sessions, ten
had between eleven and twenty, and another had ten sessions. Case conferences
also authorised the deployment of various medical services and the use of
prescription-only tranquillisers to calm disturbed residents. The young women
believed tranquillisers to be a way of keeping them quiescent, and referred to

them as 'peace pills'. Carol Arnott, who was transferred to prison in 1964, complained of her treatment at Burwood, where she claimed she had been heavily drugged 'merely for the sake of control'; her physician spoke scathingly of the 'disastrous trend' of putting every troublesome resident on a heavy dose of drugs.[114]

Regardless of the supposed benefits of medically-supervised drug therapy for difficult residents, or of the use of secure as a form of time-out, both practices attest to the Division's difficulties in responding both to the new demands on its resources and to the challenge of running open institutions. That residents reacted to the increasing controls with more and more indications of discontent is shown by the examples from Burwood and Fareham cited above. Parents, too, questioned the authority of institutions over the lives of their children. By the late 1960s the parent of a young woman detained in Fareham House had formed an Anti-Child Welfare Society to protest about treatment in institutions; young women in Fareham could be sent to the Porirua hospital for electroencephalo-graph tests that examined brainwaves so that appropriate treatment methods could be devised.[115] Anderson dismissed this group, and other critics, as 'silly people' and 'dangerous cranks', but their actions suggested a willingness to question the Division's authority and its handling of children's welfare.[116]

The growing level of juvenile delinquency from the 1960s led the Division to consider more fully than it had for some time the role its institutions played within broader child welfare policy. Its research suggested that the institutions did little to change the habits of those who were committed to them. A number of surveys of the training centres from the mid-1950s indicated a high 'failure' rate after discharge, with failure defined as continued contact with the Division, subsequent offending, or committal to another state institution. A follow-up survey of 36 adolescent girls discharged from Burwood in the mid-1950s showed that 42 per cent of them were faring well outside the institution: they had demonstrated no further delinquency, had not changed employment, and had had no conflicts sufficient to cause a change of abode or occupation. The remainder were classed as 'fair' or 'poor': they had appeared in court, had given birth to children out of wedlock, or were known to be sexually promiscuous.[117]

Surveys of residents discharged from the boys' institutions exhibited a greater degree of failure. Of 172 such boys who left the Training Centre at Levin during 1961 and 1962, only 14 per cent had not reoffended by 1967. More than 60 per cent had offended within a year of their discharge, with most committing property offences. Further information collected on those discharged during 1960/1 revealed that while ethnic background, legitimacy, age at first offence, type of offence, intelligence and length of stay all had little bearing on the failure rate, poor family circumstances may have been a contributing factor.[118]

These surveys employed different criteria for measuring male and female failure. For girls and young women, sexual activity out of wedlock was the primary yardstick for indicating failure. The researcher surveying the Burwood residents remarked upon this discrepancy in charting female and male success, and noted that the sex life of male residents was less likely to attract official attention; this reflected the 'dual standard of morality in our community'.[119]

By 1972 the complexion of institutions was very different from what it had been in 1948. Education and vocational training continued as before, but had been updated by the provision of wider career choices for boys and girls. Residents had greater contact with families and friends as home visits were introduced, more mail was allowed, and the length of time spent in residence lessened. Contact with neighbouring communities became far more frequent as institutions became more integrated into their surroundings. The growth in the number of residents, the altered make-up of the institutional population, and the more serious administrative difficulties, however, all pointed to environmental changes which the Child Welfare Division saw as increasingly unmanageable.

CHAPTER 6

'Deprived of a normal home life': ex-nuptial births, adoption, foster care, and child abuse

The treatment of delinquent children was one of the two main functions of the Child Welfare Division; the other, according to Superintendent Charlie Peek, was 'protecting the interests and advancing the welfare of children who face life under some handicap'.[1] These were children who had been 'deprived of a normal home life': they had been born out of wedlock, were placed for adoption, had been removed from their families and placed in foster care, or were the victims of abuse or neglect. The focus on delinquency throughout the 1950s had turned attention to the family life of children and kindled interest in the rights of children and parents. Links between family structure and delinquency were looked for, and found, as families became seen as the environment in which both delinquency and neglect occurred.

Sex and the single girl: inquiries into ex-nuptial births

Unwed motherhood was regarded as a social problem in twentieth-century New Zealand, and the welfare of the ex-nuptial child was a matter for both government and philanthropic attention. The articulation of this problem shifted during the course of the century, and this influenced the form and extent of services for single women and their children.[2] Perceptions of single mothers as fallen women in need of moral uplift, for example, lay behind the establishment of refuges and children's homes for babies 'disadvantaged' by their illegitimate status.[3] A heightened emphasis on the importance of child life and motherhood from the turn of the century generated new approaches to single mothers; the notion that all babies, whatever their status, contributed to a growing population led some welfare agencies and the government to encourage women to look after their children themselves rather than fostering them. A rise in the level of ex-nuptial births and less condemnatory attitudes to illegitimacy, symbolised by the abolition of legal distinctions between children born in and out of wedlock in 1969 and the consequent abandonment of the term 'illegitimacy' in favour of 'ex-nuptial', contributed to the introduction from 1973 of statutory benefits which gave support to sole parents.

Changing attitudes to ex-nuptial births were not a neat shift from harshly judgmental to grudgingly tolerant. As the American historian Regina Kunzel has argued, there were 'competing discourses of illegitimacy', and multiple under-standings of the single mother as 'innocent victim, sex delinquent, [or] unadjusted neurotic'.[4] Single mothers in New Zealand may have been the 'least deserving of women without male breadwinners', but that attitude did not necessarily preclude assistance to them, suggesting that there was a greater flexibility of attitudes than historians have allowed.[5]

The work of the Child Welfare Division and its predecessors paralleled these shifting social policies and coexisting attitudes. Inquiring into the condition of the ex-nuptial child was a statutory duty; giving assistance beyond ensuring that the welfare of the child could be maintained without resorting to the provisions of the Child Welfare Act was discretionary. The child, rather than the mother, was the focus of attention. Single mothers may have been pitied, but they were not entitled to assistance, or social security benefits.[6] Inquiries into ex-nuptial births could lead to a range of assistance to single mothers: finding them work and accommodation, instituting maintenance proceedings, and giving advice on childrearing. Such assistance was non-monetary, although child welfare officers developed ways of aiding women financially, such as 'fostering' their children with them and paying them board rates, and invoking the provisions of the Social Security Act 1938 to provide emergency and other benefits.

The proportion of ex-nuptial births to all Pakeha live births remained between 4 and 5 per cent from the turn of the century until the early 1960s. The inclusion of Maori ex-nuptial births in the statistics in 1962 boosted this figure to over 8 per cent, and from then on the proportion increased steadily to almost 15 per cent by 1972.[7] The Division did not collate separate figures for Maori and Pakeha, but a confidential report by the Government Statistician in the mid-1960s indicated that the Maori rate was higher. The practice of customary marriage influenced the level of Maori 'illegitimacy', although some officers gave more judgmental reasons for this: 'one could expect that a people emerging from backwardness would still have differing moral standards from those applying to groups having a longer history of civilised restraints, but I don't see what good can come of drawing attention to that', Lewis Anderson wrote in 1967.[8]

Rising ex-nuptial birth rates thrust the issue of the unmarried mother and her child into the news. Magazines and newspapers discussed the possible causes of the increase, and groups and organisations offered both expert and lay advice. *Out of Wedlock*, a two-part radio documentary, set out to discover why there seemed to be 'an increasing opportunity for pre-marital sexual relationships'. By 1968, Anderson and his staff had received an 'inordinate number' of requests to speak at meetings, and give papers and public addresses on the issue.[9]

The increasing number of ex-nuptial births suggested disturbing social trends, particularly when it was realised that the local rates exceeded those for Australia, England and Wales, and the United States.[10] The explanations offered were very similar to those advanced to account for juvenile delinquency. Anderson viewed ex-nuptial births as an inevitable consequence of a permissive society, and he predicted that the rate would only rise with the media's encouragement of 'trashy standards'. Others targeted New Zealand's social security system as 'encouraging' single women to have babies. Wellington physician Diana Mason considered that the provision of free maternity care and the payment of the sickness benefit to single mothers might be a contributing factor. Some commentators suggested that there was a new attitude to sexual activity, which was both more valued than previously and a more acceptable feature of unwed life.[11] As in earlier crises over the number of single mothers, the responsibility of women was also highlighted. This time, however, it was expressed as a consequence of social conditions rather than female immorality – just as explanations for juvenile delinquency had moved from the personal to the socio-economic and environmental. Even so, public commentators and divisional researchers alike still suggested as contributory factors the earlier maturity of girls, the decline of female 'frigidity', and the wearing of provocative dress by women.[12] Men's role remained a cipher, and their part in single parenthood continued largely to be unexplored.[13]

By the late 1960s, anxiety over ex-nuptial births prompted government departments to initiate further research into causes and solutions. An inter-departmental committee which met and reported in 1968 provided the basis for a more comprehensive study launched in April 1969 as the Committee for Research into Illegitimacy.[14] Led by Victoria University lecturer Jim Robb and including members of the Child Welfare Division, the committee initiated a descriptive study in order to construct a profile of the unmarried mother. In 1971 it prepared an extensive questionnaire in the hope of ascertaining the causes of illegitimacy, and put together a profile of the unmarried mother in the first months of pregnancy and immediately after the birth of the child.[15] Child welfare officers conducted the interviews as part of their work with single mothers. Hard-pressed as they were to complete their regular inquiries, some officers found it impossible to do the preliminary parts of the survey. In mid-1971, Anderson estimated that the main study would take between 50 and 100 weeks to complete.[16]

The Division's research unit cooperated with that of the Joint Committee on Young Offenders to make a more detailed study of possible causes and remedies. Many of its findings echoed general statements in the media, but the research units also commented on the greater value placed on sexual expression and the greater tolerance of premarital sex. It identified two possible solutions: a campaign to reduce premarital sex, and the promotion of increased use of contraceptives. Claiming the first idea to be ineffective and the second to be socially unacceptable, it suggested an alternative: take no action, and the rate of ex-nuptial births would eventually subside.[17]

A 'do-nothing' policy was in keeping with the Division's broader approach to reducing the number of ex-nuptial births. It offered few suggestions itself, and looked askance at the solutions appearing in newspapers and at public meetings. Referring to an *Evening Post* correspondent's recommendation that the Division do more to investigate the causes of ex-nuptial births, Anderson retorted that the writer 'should be nominated for the Nobel Prize or for this week's buttered biscuit' if he had any answers. Senior officers considered controlling the level of ex-nuptial births to be simply out of their power and beyond their responsibility. Along with delinquency, Anderson believed that single motherhood was a price that had to be paid for individual liberty. It was a moral issue, a problem for the individual and society, and not one against which the state either could or should legislate.[18]

For the Child Welfare Division, 'prevention' meant the prevention of problems concerning the children, rather than the prevention of illegitimacy itself. The welfare of the child, rather than the marital status of her or his parents, was the primary consideration. Peek claimed that the Division had never taken the 'arbitrary attitude' that couples living together without the 'benefit of marriage' were unsuitable parents. This was a rosy picture of official policy, as Peek himself considered that a woman living in a de facto relationship could not normally provide as satisfactory a home life as could a married couple. The experiences of unmarried mothers suggest that the Division's attitude was more 'arbitrary' than Peek implied.[19]

Nevertheless, the Division attempted to keep the single mother and her child together, particularly when the woman was reluctant to foster or adopt out her children. This may have been due to a lack of suitable alternatives, or to a belief

Taihape – where many single mothers came to give birth in the 1950s, according to child welfare officers in the district. NATIONAL ARCHIVES NATIONAL PUBLICITY STUDIOS PHOTOGRAPHIC COLLECTION, ATL, F-38952-1/2

that 'bad girls' should shoulder their own responsibilities. Yet it also indicates the emphasis on the importance of a home life for children, and the notion that a family was the most desirable situation in which to raise them. As one officer later reflected, 'sometimes the couples were living in a de facto marriage and I often felt we were invading . . . private lives'.[20] But a nuclear family arrangement, be it made up of birth, adoptive or foster parents, was not the Division's only definition of a suitable home, and it displayed a flexible approach towards household structures.

Until the mid-1960s, the Division followed a separate policy towards Maori single mothers and considered it impractical to have Maori ex-nuptial births in rural communities notified; the practice of customary marriage and the existence of tribal networks, it argued, guaranteed a baby's welfare. The Division asserted the importance of Maori responsibility for Maori welfare throughout the 1960s, stressing that women should look to their whanau networks for support. A reluctance to assist Maori communities no doubt contributed to such sentiments,

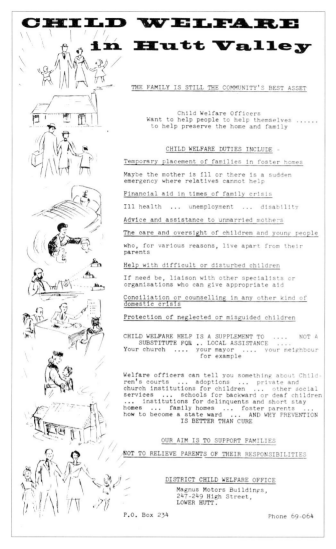

Advertising campaigns, such as this pamphlet from the Hutt Valley office, were designed to overcome public ignorance of the functions of the Child Welfare Division. NATIONAL ARCHIVES, CW 1, 8/9, PART 1

for the Division maintained that the investigation of Maori ex-nuptial births in urban areas certainly fell within the 'spirit' of its responsibilities. Only if a Maori woman were living 'more or less' as a Pakeha, or would receive no other assistance if she registered her child as a Maori, would the Division undertake inquiries.[21]

Infant life protection work fell markedly in significance as women explored other childcare options. Between 1949 and 1972, the number of babies and infants maintained in licensed foster homes fell from 832 to 452.[22] The Division had always found it difficult to obtain suitable homes, and fewer women may have been willing to foster young children for a pittance in prosperous times. For most of this period, more than half of the ex-nuptial babies whose circumstances the Division investigated lived with relatives, or with parents in de facto relationships or subsequent marriages, or stayed with their mothers.[23] The number remaining with their mothers fluctuated in line with changes in adoption. Of the 2311 ex-nuptial birth inquiries made in 1952/3, before the passage of the Adoption Act, 297 infants were placed for adoption while 932 stayed with the mother; ten years later, 1669 of the 4924 ex-nuptial babies investigated were placed for adoption and 1960 remained with the mother or parents. By 1971/2, when there were over 9000 ex-nuptial births and a record 3967 adoption orders, the Division reported that about 60 per cent of the babies stayed with their mothers or relatives.[24]

Social service agencies did not always know of the Division's role in offering advice and assistance to single mothers. They criticised the Division for not doing enough to influence the unmarried mother to adopt out her child. In Anderson's view, informing women of their options, rather than advising them whether or not to keep their baby, was the only fair practice, one which struck a balance between doing too much or too little for single mothers. Many women were also unaware of the Division's work, and had little idea of the type of support child welfare officers could give or the benefits that were available after a birth.[25] A few single mothers approached the Division personally seeking assistance, such as Gretchen Litwack, who requested help to find work and accommodation so that she could keep her child.[26] Asking for assistance, of course, meant opening up lives for investigation, possible judgment and the removal of the child. Women may have sought out or welcomed child welfare officers, and may have benefited from contact with them. But as others found in choosing to invite welfare agencies into their lives, this could be the beginning of a long relationship that might not work out as they had intended or wished.

The Division sought constantly, and unsuccessfully, during the 1960s to counter the belief that no assistance to single mothers was available. In 1964 it organised a conference to dispel the widespread notion that the unmarried mother received a 'bad deal' from government. Anderson wrote frequently to newspapers and organisations referring to the Division's responsibilities to single mothers. He criticised the publication of the works of 'colourfully irresponsible writers' at the expense of factual information about the 'steady work' of child welfare officers. New Zealand was doing a 'great deal' for the unmarried mother and her child, he confirmed.[27]

A 'great deal' was an exaggeration, as researchers pointed out at the time and have reiterated since.[28] The Division was the only government agency providing services for single mothers and their children, and the financial benefits it dispensed were discretionary rather than provided on a statutory basis. 'Entitlement' to assistance rested on the judgment of those who investigated the circumstances of mother and child. Casework was vital, as with other aspects of broadly preventive work. Some inquiries could be perfunctory: a quick knock on the door and a brief query about the welfare of the baby. But officers could delve into a woman's finances, background, relationships or work situation to assess whether or not the welfare of the baby could be maintained.

While the common assumption that there was no provision for single mothers and their children needs to be tempered in the light of the services provided by the Division, this does not minimise the problems that confronted single women with children, particularly those whose children remained with them. Women sometimes took extreme steps to hide their pregnancy from family and friends, moving town or even country to give birth. The shame of an ex-nuptial birth for some women had dire consequences and gave rise to scenes reminiscent of conditions facing unwed pregnant women in the nineteenth century. Whangarei's District Child Welfare Officer reported in 1953 the death of an ex-nuptial baby whose 30 year old mother had concealed her pregnancy from workmates at Paihia's Mon Desir Hotel. She gave birth on the lawn outside the hotel, cut the umbilical cord herself, and hid the placenta in a hedge. When the child died less than an hour later, she concealed the body in a rolled-up mattress under her bed.[29]

Maternity hospitals were often less than welcoming to unwed mothers, who could find their stay hedged around with regulations and conditions. The Division investigated the management of some hospitals in 1948 after receiving complaints over the regulations and work requirements placed on the women.[30] In 1960, child welfare officers were once more criticising facilities, particularly those in the Auckland area. The Motherhood of Man movement, Auckland's major private lay organisation providing assistance to single mothers and their children, came under a scrutiny which exacerbated its stormy progress through the post-war period and its tense relationship with the Division over adoption.[31] Some maternity hospitals and homes went to great lengths to hide women's single status, providing them with wedding rings and calling them 'Mrs'.

All the options facing single mothers were fraught with difficulties, and while there may have been both condemnatory and sympathetic attitudes towards single motherhood and ex-nuptial children, their position was never easy. As Anne Else has noted, 'unless genuine options exist, no "free decision" is possible'. Many of the women interviewed in her study of adoption considered they had little choice when it came to 'making a wise decision' about what was best for themselves and their children.[32] Child welfare officers commented on the lack of options for the 'unmarried or unsupported': 'she had few alternatives but to release her child for adoption. That was the greatest tragedy'.[33] Administering this option became a central part of child welfare work in the post-war years.

Making new families: the expansion of adoption services

The term 'adoption' encompasses a variety of arrangements for transferring, legally or by custom, the guardianship of a child from one group to another. Its form has changed over time and between cultures, but the type which assumed centrality in New Zealand, as elsewhere in the post-war years, was the legal adoption of a young baby by strangers, or 'closed stranger adoption'. Maori customary 'adoption', where children were raised by family members other than their birth parents, continued alongside both this and a complex arrangement for legal Maori adoptions. New Zealand's closed stranger adoption system is the subject of a number of contemporary and historical studies which offer detailed accounts of the adoption process.[34] This section focuses on the Division's adoption policies and practices before and after the passage of the pivotal Adoption Act 1955, and its part in the preparation of that legislation.

Before the Second World War, the proportion of legal adoptions was generally less than 3 per cent of all live births, and always well below 1000 orders a year. The war boosted these figures, and in 1944/5 the number of orders leapt to over 1000, a level above which they remained for all but one year from the 1950s to the 1970s. The number of orders increased most rapidly during the 1960s, rising from about 1800 in 1960/1 to reach its all-time high of almost 4000 in 1971/2, which represented more than 6 per cent of all live births.[35]

Contemporaries suggested several possible reasons for the rise. The Division had 'little doubt' that greater prosperity and improved standards of living were influential, although the connection was not made clear. In circular fashion, it claimed that adoption had become more widely known, more common and more acceptable, and that married couples spoke about it more frequently, presumably making it still more widely known, and so on. Anderson believed that there was no single answer, but suggested a combination of vague, unconfirmed possibilities: perhaps there were more childless marriages, perhaps there was a desire for a 'balanced' family, or a possibility that society was more 'humane . . . [and] more prepared to do something for children in need of care and protection'.[36]

Historians have placed the growth of adoption in the context of changing notions about the 'best environment' for children, to which could be added theories about the best types of relationships between parents, particularly mothers, and children. By the 1950s that environment was a 'permanent home with breadwinning father and stay-at-home mother'. Financial savings to the state, either while the child was still young or in the future, and a desire to break the 'vicious cycle of deviance' represented by ex-nuptial births, have also been suggested as important factors.[37] The Division's attitude towards single motherhood and other household forms suggests that the notion of the 'best environment' for children was never so rigid, but it too argued that adoption into a two-parent family afforded ex-nuptial children greater opportunities, and worked towards ensuring its popularity.

The extent of the Division's role in arranging adoptions changed substantially during the post-war years. It was always one of several agencies which matched adoptive parents with available babies. Religious and welfare organisations, and groups supplying services to unwed mothers, such as Auckland's Motherhood of Man, also arranged placements. Medical and legal professionals, as well as birth and adoptive parents themselves, placed children and sought adoption orders. The relative balance between these groups before the mid-1950s is very difficult to

The Salvation Army was among a number of groups which gave advice to single mothers considering adoption. Here Major Beatrice Palmer counsels a young woman. SALVATION ARMY ARCHIVES

assess. Sporadic returns from child welfare officers indicate that their role varied markedly between districts; in Dunedin during 1950–2, officers arranged 35 per cent of adoptions, while in Christchurch they were responsible for more than 70 per cent. Auckland, with its very active private groups, presented a different story: officers there had arranged only 3 per cent of all placements.[38] Regional differences remained after the passage of the Adoption Act in 1955, but the Division's overall share increased markedly, from 34 per cent of all placements in 1957 to over 70 per cent by the early 1970s. The Division considered that its nationwide coverage partially accounted for this increase, and it was probably correct.[39]

The passage of the Adoption Act 1955 (and subsequent amendments) and its administration formed the core of the Division's adoption work. The Act, an 'outstanding piece of social legislation' which placed New Zealand at the 'forefront' of English-speaking nations, overhauled the entire adoption system, and is still the major legislation applying to this area.[40] The Act clarified who could and who could not adopt children, gave Maori the right to adopt Pakeha children (a right which they had lost in 1909), prohibited the payment of fees, and closed access to adoption records. It introduced two separate court orders for adoption: an interim order (which could be dispensed with under certain conditions) made after the applicant's home had been inspected, and a final order made after the child had lived there for at least six months. The interim order was the more important, as it enabled adoptive parents to take a child into their home; final orders were dispatched very quickly if a favourable report was given. The Division was empowered to supervise or inspect the placements before each order, and the court was required to consider, but not necessarily to act on, any such reports. Birth mothers could not formally sign a consent to the adoption until the baby was ten days old, and they remained the legal guardians until the final order was made.

The issues of protection, clarification of roles and organisation lay behind the establishment early in 1952 of an interdepartmental committee to examine adoption practices. The Division was well-represented on the committee with three of the seven members, including Deputy-Superintendent Lewis Anderson, while the other members were drawn from the departments of Justice and Maori Affairs. The committee's report and recommendations, presented late in 1952, formed the basis of a Cabinet paper on adoption, and eventually of the Adoption Bill tabled in 1955.

The Division's representatives emphasised that unsatisfactory placements and a haphazard system made urgent the revision of the adoption laws. The Justice Department challenged this view and demanded proof of 'bad' adoptions; the Division then called on its officers to provide relevant examples.[41] Child welfare officers criticised, in tones reminiscent of the professional disagreements about the operation of children's courts, the loose and regionally varied procedure which magistrates' courts followed when considering adoption orders. Officers argued that magistrates paid too little or no heed to their reports, and that their recommendations were disregarded. Some questioned the very involvement of magistrates. Jim Ferguson of the Wellington district office suggested that a court, with its legal bias, was not the proper agency to decide whether or not an adoption order should be made. Other members of the legal fraternity were criticised. 'Most solicitors acting for the applicants are present at the hearing to earn their fee. . . . Many are not concerned as to whether it is in the child's interests or not', an Auckland officer claimed.[42]

The roles of private agencies and medical professionals also came under examination, and were generally found wanting. A Wanganui child welfare officer mentioned the placements arranged by doctors and matrons of maternity homes who ignored the necessity of inspecting prospective homes. 'When I have tried to explain to the applicants that their homes should have been passed I have been told that "This adoption has nothing to do with the Welfare. We got the baby from doctor. . ."'. Doctors and hospital matrons who failed to match 'types' – babies and adoptive parents – or neglected to inquire into the background of the birth mother or adoptive parents also created problems. One doctor visiting a single mother in the Waiouru Military Camp hospital allegedly told her, 'This is a nice baby. How about letting me place him for adoption'. The child welfare officer noted that 'absolutely nothing' was known of the mother's background, 'yet the doctor wanted to place this child in a very good adoptive home'.[43]

Officers also pinpointed the health, age or social condition of applicants as a problem. One cited the case of a 70 year old father and 50 year old mother who adopted an eight month old baby, while another suggested that single women should not be permitted to adopt, as this was an 'unnatural situation'. Some mentioned drunkenness or criminal convictions:

> Mrs Godwin had a conviction for being 'idle and disorderly'. This was un-beknown by her husband, however it was smoothed over, but judging by the state of her home, she hasn't improved much. We arrived at the home to find her flapping about in the greatest distress; the house in it's usual grubby muddle and the infant wallowing in dirty napkins and suffering from 'summer sickness'. This was not surprising considering that the day's supply of milk was standing uncovered on the window sill in the hot sunshine, partly curdled, and being used as a swimming pool by a portion of the dense fly population.[44]

That undue pressures were sometimes brought to bear on single mothers to place their children for adoption was also recognised. The Division's own role in

A grateful adoptive mother sent child welfare officers this photograph of her child, along with the accompanying poem, which she had modified.
NATIONAL ARCHIVES, ABNT, W4295

'A wish of Marney's', subtitled 'Wendy', dedicated by Marjorie

Deep down within my eager heart,
I wished a fervent prayer,
That I could have a Little Babe,
To guard and love and care.

And the Angels, understanding,
Just listened, and they smiled,
For midst hardship and sorrow,
They saw a Little Child.

And so they sent her to me,
A child with such appeal,
A little fragile cherub,
Who round my heart did steal.

A little tuft of silken hair,
Bedecked her small round head,
But, I heard the fairies whispering,
And *this* is what they said.

Some days her hair will be *quite* fair,
Some days it will look *dark*,
Some days 'twill look bright golden,
Just for a little lark.

Some days her eyes will be dark brown,
Some days a violet blue,
Sometimes a honey hazel,
When she looks so straight at you.

But best of all her 'Nature',
Will be surpassing sweet,
And so they made 'My Baby',
Fit for *anyone* to *eat.*

this was neither acknowledged nor discussed; its part was assumed to be uncomplicated, but as other scholars have shown, child welfare officers could also make hasty placements, or pressure women untowardly.[45] Officers decried the failure of some private groups to offer alternatives to single mothers when emphasising adoption above all else. Dunedin staff knew of young women who had changed their minds about their consent some months after they had signed the forms. This occurred mainly when a woman had been given insufficient time to make up her mind or was unaware of any alternative. The District Child Welfare Officer cited the example of one young woman whose doctor had hastily placed her baby for adoption after questioning her when she was coming out of the anaesthetic following the birth. The baby was moved to the Karitane Hospital, and after five months fretting for the child, whom she assumed to be still in the hospital, the young woman and her parents approached the Division for assistance when she received a request for her consent to adoption.[46]

Adoptions among Maori were generally outside the Division's jurisdiction, as they were the responsibility of the Maori Land Court, but child welfare officers nevertheless regarded some such cases as particularly fraught. Officers in Whangarei claimed that the Maori Land Court could act as haphazardly as other courts. Children were sometimes placed with known tuberculosis carriers, or in homes on which district nurses had compiled adverse reports. A Whangarei officer considered the situation to be 'so hopeless – the numbers are so terrific – that I hold my breath and hope that the Dis. Nurses will arrange hospitalization for infants if their condition falls too low'.[47]

All in all, officers concluded, 'a more efficient method of placement could be devised than the present one'.[48] The 1955 Act largely achieved this, in the Division's view, in that it provided for better consent provisions and greater 'protection' for all concerned in the process. Yet participation in the committee, the drafting of the bill, the submissions process, and discussions over the final form of the legislation was not easy for the Division. Despite its efforts and the problems it had demonstrated, it did not manage to enshrine all its aims in the final legislation.

One of the Division's primary goals had been to enforce a lengthy 'cooling off' period before a birth mother signed the consent forms and the child was placed for adoption. Following the English precedent, it considered six weeks to be ample. Even though other members of the committee maintained that this was too long and that consents and adoptions should be finalised quickly, the Division's recommendation was included in the final report on the grounds that the birth mother's power to consent should not be fettered.[49] Private agencies disagreed strongly. The Motherhood of Man stated that 'all persons engaged in adoption work will agree that it is in the best interests of the child that the bond between the natural parents and the child should be severed'. This was a view which others shared: 'because a few cases have had undesirable publicity, largely because of weak minded Natural parents who do not know their minds from one minute to another, all adoptions should not be hedged round with irritating regulations and delays', a Hamilton magistrate considered.[50] By the time of the final drafting of the legislation, the consent period had been whittled down to a maximum of ten days.

The committee and the submission process were sites in which departmental and agency interests were contested. While the representatives of the Department of Maori Affairs took, or were given, a back seat, those from the Division and the Justice Department engaged with each other in very real differences of value and interpretation. On one level, the differences stemmed from a struggle to control the adoption process. In Peek's view, the Justice Department was reluctant to 'see merit in any proposal which might restrict the Court's discretion by giving powers to an appropriate agency such as the Child Welfare Division'. Such reluctance swung both ways, however. Reports from child welfare officers and children's court magistrates revealed the tension that had existed between the two groups for many years. Magistrates spent too little time reading reports, made their decisions too quickly (in five minutes, according to Palmerston North staff), and paid too much attention to the applicant's lawyers; Auckland's District Child Welfare Officer suggested that it was the Justice Department, rather than the adoption laws, which needed to be overhauled. For their part, magistrates alleged a lack of 'intelligent' and correctly trained child welfare officers, inadequate reports, and officers with conflicting interests. Private groups claimed that they were being shut out of the process, and that they should have the same rights as the Division when it came to acting in the place of birth parents. They continued to campaign on this front, and argued for recognition of the expenses which they incurred in undertaking adoption work; a 1957 Amendment Act allowed them to collect agency fees from young women.[51]

Opposing perceptions of whose interests adoption should serve also contributed to differences between departments and agencies. For the Justice Department and private groups, the welfare of the child was the most important factor, but certainly not the only one; adopting parents were also entitled to consideration. The system should be designed to ensure only that a child was not allowed to go to an unsuitable home, Justice Department representatives suggested.[52] The Division, on the other hand, attempted to consider the rights of both the child and the birth mother. A six-week consent period would end the 'improper' practice of birth mothers signing irrevocable consents while in an 'abnormal state of health' a few days after a child's birth. As Anderson noted, the Adoption Bill needed to be balanced to ensure that birth parents were 'not unjustly treated because of an over-zealous desire to satisfy the present great demand for children for adoptions'.[53] The specific interests of the child who was being adopted received little direct attention in the discussion of opposing parental rights. This silence was, however, a feature of the entire process. For despite any implicit or explicit rhetoric of providing what was best for the children, adoption was seldom about their needs, but rather 'about adult beliefs and desires and dilemmas', as Anne Else has convincingly argued.[54]

The 1955 legislation afforded the Division a larger role in all aspects of the adoption process; in 1956, women officers reported that their workload had doubled.[55] The range of their responsibilities continued as before. Officers sought out applicants and children, often by issuing circulars to other districts, and received approaches from both applicants and birth mothers. Peek reported in 1950 that most adoptive parents found children through their own efforts, but as the decade continued, more looked to the Division for assistance. Staff frequently received calls from people in the hope of 'securing a child', and letters in the Division's files suggest that many may have come to see it as a first port of call. One applicant in 1958 had heard the rumours about teenage sexual activity in the Hutt Valley, and anticipated that there would soon be children to be adopted.[56]

For women who had not decided on adoption, however, the provision of information about the options, rather than advice on whether or not to choose adoption, was the Division's policy. As Anderson noted in 1960, 'we do not either encourage or discourage mothers to agree to an adoption'.[57] The practice could be very different, and many single mothers remembered that child welfare officers had encouraged adoption as the first choice.[58] Teresa Lawson's case file suggests that child welfare officers did more than provide information on her options when she became pregnant at sixteen. They discussed adoption with Teresa half-way through her pregnancy, and clearly hoped that she would agree to it. She did not, however, and at the request of her foster mother, child welfare officers visited her in hospital, ostensibly to discuss both sides of the issue. Instead, they informed Teresa that they would have to commit the baby to care (for reasons not recorded), and that they required her decision within two days. Clearly distressed, Teresa changed her mind about adoption several times in that period. Told of her final decision not to adopt, the Division decided to take the baby on a warrant and commit it to care; the following day, Teresa agreed to the adoption and the baby was placed out. For Teresa, though, this was not the end of the story. Within six months, child welfare officers reported that she had run away from home; her foster mother confirmed that she was still upset about the adoption.[59]

Child welfare officers themselves worked within the paucity of options which confronted single mothers. Mary Todd, who administered adoptions in Auckland during the 1950s and 1960s, acknowledged that:

there could have been some pressure . . . but it was pressure from society rather than pressure from the child welfare officers. . . . [However] a child welfare officer may have exerted some pressure, particularly . . . if she had what she termed 'nice applicants'. . . . By the time one met with a young woman, there had already been, more often than not, pressure exerted by family, pressure exerted in homes for unmarried mums.[60]

Giving advice rather than encouraging adoption was particularly the policy when, as happened quite rarely, married couples approached the Division requesting assistance in placing their children for adoption. A Christchurch officer was aghast at the breaching of an ultimate taboo when Mrs Wakefield wrote in 1953 asking for help in finding a home for her unborn child. She and her husband had four children, and they could not afford the expense of a new baby. Despite their using 'every contraceptive', their last two children 'just came along'. Mrs Wakefield's pregnancy was a difficult one, and poverty, ill-health, fatigue and an air of hopelessness rang through her letter. The officer informed her that the Division was never keen to see married couples contemplating adoption. Somewhat tactlessly, she reminded Mrs Wakefield that adoption meant depriving the child of its birth siblings and parents, and noted that the issue of birth control could be dealt with by putting her in touch with local 'specialists'.[61]

A year after its passage, the Division noted that the Adoption Act was generally achieving its purpose in facilitating more careful placement and supervision and greater security for both birth mothers and adoptive parents.[62] This was an over-optimistic prognosis, for beneath the rhetoric of success, problems remained. 'Breakdowns' in adoption occurred, with adoptive parents rejecting the children and birth mothers seeking the return of their babies. The Division continued to see placements by private agencies in which too much attention appeared to be given to the wishes of the applicant and too little to the interests of the child. Complaints about the treatment of mothers at Wellington's Alexandra Home in 1963 led the Division to investigate the institution's policy of charging women a £5 entrance fee and restricting their freedom unduly once they were in the home. While the complaints were dismissed, it is clear that the Division sought to keep private maternity homes and adoption agencies under a loose surveillance.[63]

The Division's generally optimistic appraisal also belied the administrative and human difficulties it faced. The sheer number of adoption orders meant that at times quality of welfare work was sacrificed in favour of quantity. Officers recalled superficial assessments of applicants: 'You just rushed in and rushed out, and that was it', Mary Todd remembered. Staff received little or no training in undertaking assessments, and based judgments on their own views about the best interests of birth mother and child. The pressure of work often told, too: 'One was doing 4, 5 or 6, on average, placements of children per week. There was just a surge of babies being born. It was a balancing act . . . trying to keep up and do the best one could . . . and literally just keeping the machinery going. . . . To the end of my days I will always have concerns for some'.[64] The lack of follow-up meant that officers had no knowledge of the 'success' of their placements. With the final orders, the child, birth mother and adoptive family all passed from the Division's view.

The major administrative challenges after 1955 were to satisfy all applications for adoption and to place all the children made available; demand and supply seldom matched. Until the mid-1960s, there was an excess of applicants over 'suitable' children. In 1958, 2000 unfilled applications were reported, with no indication that the number would fall, given the growing popularity of adoption. The Division also reported that long waiting lists deterred applicants, some of whom endeavoured to adopt children from overseas. It denied media reports of a shortage of applicants in the mid-1960s, but by then children did take longer to place than had been the case previously. The Division reported in 1969 that all available and suitable children had been placed. These terms, especially 'suitability', could be used very precisely. Adoptive parents preferred white baby girls; older children, baby boys, Maori, Pacific Island or 'mixed race' children were less popular and more difficult to place – although New Zealanders displayed little reluctance to adopt the 50 Hong Kong 'orphans' who were brought into the country in 1963. The Division maintained that no children ended up in its institutions or in children's homes after failing to be placed, although it did foster out unplaced children. Its consternation about a possible 'lowering of standards' in the selection of applicants suggests that the reality was somewhat different, and subsequent researchers have borne out this suspicion.[65]

The changes in adoption procedures also affected both customary and legal Maori adoptions. While customary adoption had been theoretically prohibited by legislation enacted in 1909, the practice continued.[66] The Division was well aware of this, as its work with Maori ex-nuptial births and fostering suggests. Legally, however, these adoptions were not binding; from 1909, all-Maori adoptions had to be approved by a judge of the Native Land Court. A tangle of restrictions surrounded Maori adoption until 1955: if both parents and the child were Maori, the adoption case would be heard in the Maori Land Court under the 1909 legislation; if the adopting parents were Pakeha and the child Maori, the Infants Act applied; a Maori/Pakeha couple could adopt a Maori child, but the case would be heard in the magistrate's court; Maori parents could not adopt Pakeha children. The sex of the child added further to the complexity: a Pakeha husband and Maori wife could only adopt a male Pakeha child, and a Maori husband and Pakeha wife a female Pakeha child.[67] A subtext of racially-based anxieties about intermarriage and the inheritance of property loomed large in these regulations.

The 1955 Act partially disentangled Maori legal adoption. On the inter-departmental committee, Maori Affairs representatives Charles Bennett and Jock McEwen argued for a revision of the grounds under which Maori could adopt. Their belief that Maori should be entitled legally to adopt on the same terms as Pakeha was incorporated in the final legislation, which removed the prohibitions on Maori adopting Pakeha children. Bennett and McEwen succeeded in clarifying the respective roles of child welfare officers and Maori welfare officers in assessing applicants and making reports. Henceforth, Maori welfare officers reported on the adoption of Maori children, and the orders were heard in the Maori Land Court.[68]

The division of labour did not always work well in practice. Some child welfare officers used the new arrangement to relinquish any role in Maori adoptions. Maori welfare officers, faced with new procedures, sometimes found it difficult to locate suitable placements and liaise with the Division. Female Maori welfare officers were 'few and far between' in some districts, and child welfare officers found their role continuing. Child welfare and Maori welfare officers worked cooperatively in most districts, however. Weekly conferences in areas such as Napier went some way towards easing the pressures of finding place-ments for both sets of officials.[69]

An attempt to standardise the adoption process by moving all Maori adoption hearings from the Maori Land Court to magistrates' courts from 1963 complicated matters further. Bennett and McEwen had earlier argued strenuously against this proposal, and predicted that it would lead to an increase in 'irregular' Maori adoptions.[70] Such 'standardisation' brought about the very problems which they had foreseen. After three years of the new system, McEwen reported that the number of Maori legal adoptions had fallen by 600. The Department's survey of 20,000 North Island Maori households indicated that between ten and twelve thousand children were living apart from their birth parents. Maori communities may have placed considerable emphasis on the centrality of kin and family networks and the importance of shared responsibility for children, but to McEwen and others, the implications of this were vast. He saw increased child neglect and delinquency resulting directly from children having no legal status in their own homes.[71]

The complexities and expense of using the Pakeha legal system were held accountable for the change, an analysis which ignored the extent and importance of Maori customary adoption. As McEwen had expected, Maori applicants distrusted the magistrate's court and the prospect of engaging solicitors. A circular sent to all court registrars in 1963 emphasised the necessity for providing assistance to Maori applicants, such as help with preparing the papers so that they did not have to use a solicitor. This had not always worked, with some magistrates disapproving and law societies protesting when the Department of Maori Affairs attempted to charge applicants a small fee for their legal services. Greater assistance rather than a return to the former practice was seen as the solution, but despite the criticisms voiced by such powerful groups as the New Zealand Maori Council and the Maori Women's Welfare League, the problems remained.[72]

The 'real basis' for children in care: changes in foster care

Fostering remained the most popular form of care open to the Division, and in comparison with other nations, New Zealand boarded out proportionately more state wards. The number in foster care increased from 1737 in 1948/9 to 2599 in 1971/2, and this group made up between 40 and 50 per cent of all children in care over the entire period. Children stayed in foster homes for anything from a few weeks to several years. Some, like Joan Marlows, spent a few months in a foster home to allow 'time-out' for both herself and her mother. Others, like Bessie Black, passed most of their childhood and adolescence in foster care. Unable to provide for her, Bessie's mother admitted her to the Wellington Salvation Army Home shortly after the birth, and she remained there for two years. By the time she married in 1955, Bessie had lived in several foster homes under the charge of the Division for nearly twenty years, presumably with little contact with her birth mother.[73]

The Division argued that in good foster homes, a child would 'develop naturally into a person with his own sense of worth in home, school and community'. Foster homes constituted the 'real basis' for children in care; foster parents were an 'integral part of the service' without whom the Division did not think it could manage effectively.[74] The expectations placed on foster parents were high. Ideally, they were stable, mature, 'balanced in outlook' and not 'put off' by small crises. The 'character' of foster mothers – as the main caregivers – was crucial. 'Preferably, a foster mother should have a generous and over-flowing nature; her affection for her children and foster children should be sensible and stable without being effusive. She should use plenty of commonsense when dealing with the children, know when to be firm and when to be lenient.'[75]

Actually locating ideal homes and paragons of womanhood was another matter. The perennial shortage of foster homes had become so normal by the post-war period that the Division never fully explored the possible reasons for

The new housing suburbs could be isolated for women without transport. Here the mobile Plunket van calls on mothers in the Mount Roskill area. NATIONAL ARCHIVES NATIONAL PUBLICITY STUDIOS PHOTOGRAPHIC COLLECTION, ATL, F-33855-1/2

the situation. It suggested that growing employment opportunities for women might lie behind the declining popularity of fostering.[76] Straitened facilities in institutions meant that children for whom residential training would be appropriate were placed out in board, a practice which imposed further strains on the foster home system. The popularity of adoption, and the notion of legal parents and guardians that went with it, may have placed a premium on binding relationships. In this environment, the possibility that children could be removed after parents gained the right to appeal against placement orders in 1961 may have rendered fostering a less attractive option than it had been previously.

The rate of payment for board, as ever, contributed to the difficulties in obtaining foster homes. The Division raised the amount several times in the post-war years, and added other payments: for pocket money, education and medical expenses, higher rates for difficult children, and graduated rates for older children. But it never examined the basis on which the general rate was calculated, and this always lagged behind increases in wages and benefits. The Division was reluctant to raise levels too high, lest 'mercenary motives' prompt families into fostering. Others shared this view, which had endured throughout the century and would continue for some years yet. Politicians supported an increase in the rates, but only to a level which would still ensure that foster parents did it for love. As one Member of Parliament noted in a debate about the issue in 1967, 'if the allowances were increased people might take foster children just for the monetary return, and the children would lack the affection that should be bestowed on them.'[77]

The Division tried in several ways to obtain new families. Some offices placed articles in newspapers describing the work and rewards of fostering. In 1960, the Timaru office inserted a piece in the local paper calling for people to board teenagers. 'Perfect substitute parents' were not required, 'as they expect perfect children and we have none', the office reflected. Some offices called on voluntary organisations to publicise the need for foster parents. A few displayed more imagination. The Lower Hutt office's advertisement reading, 'I am 10 years old. . . . I live in a boy's home. . . . please contact my Child Welfare Office', which appeared in a newspaper in 1969, drew an immediate reprimand from Anderson: 'this kind of nonsense must not occur. We are an adult mature service and should not stoop to deceptive misleading practices'.[78]

Foster homes were especially difficult to obtain for some groups of children. The Division's policy of boarding children with families of a similar religious faith or in the same ethnic group was sound in principle, but the practice could be different. Many districts experienced an ongoing shortage of homes for Roman Catholic children. In the late 1950s, 20 per cent of the children committed in Auckland were Roman Catholic and the need for appropriate homes was urgent. In the absence of Roman Catholic households willing to foster, the Division had to board children with Protestant families and arrange for regular visits from the parish priest.[79] The Division also experienced problems in fostering Pacific Island and Chinese children. Placing them with families of other ethnic groups was undesirable, but there was often little choice. As Anderson admitted, staff tried to do their best, but sometimes that was only 'second best'.[80] Such was the situation that confronted Wellington staff when Chinese-born Mr Yiw rang about the welfare of his daughter Cissie. She had been boarded with relatives following her mother's death, but Mr Yiw had removed her when he discovered that she had learnt to steal. Child welfare officers had considerable difficulty in locating a Chinese family. A placement with a European family broke down when officers discovered that the eldest son of the family was on probation and had got a sixteen year old pregnant; Cissie's relationship with a young man who had been involved in the 'Hutt Valley offences' led to her removal from another family. Other families refused to take her when they discovered she was Chinese, and a job at Woolworths fell through when the company's head office enforced its policy of employing only 'full Europeans'. Cissie was finally admitted to a Baptist hostel, where she remained until her marriage two years later.[81]

Fostering Maori children appropriately was the Division's biggest challenge. The lack of Maori foster homes was a frequent complaint, and staff constantly sought suitable new residences. Sometimes child welfare officers utilised Maori family networks when placing Maori children. Girlie Burrows and her siblings, who were committed to care when their mother was unable to look after them following her husband's death, were sent to board with their aunt and uncle.[82] Such kin placements were paid at less than the full board rate. Other Maori families and communities were used if they broke down or were not explored. Pita Wiki, who had been charged with theft and car conversion, stayed with an older brother for two years before being admitted to a boys' home and then the Boys' Training Centre. On his release, the Division arranged for him to work at the Maori Trust Station near Wairoa, where he was happy in a 'Mark Twain sort of way'. His year-long stay there was punctuated only by the consequences of his love of movies and dance: he was thrown out of a local cinema for 'rock-and-roll frenzies', and his welfare officer commented on Pita's 'immaturity in wearing flamboyant clothing and giving spontaneous public demonstrations of "rock and roll" dancing'.[83]

The Division increasingly relied on the assistance of Maori groups and welfare officers to obtain appropriate homes or establish whanau networks. Tribal committees sometimes kept lists of approved foster homes and maintained supervision over them. The Division's belief that iwi could ensure children's welfare meant that they sometimes took a hands-off approach when Maori children were fostered to families living under tribal supervision. The Department of Maori Affairs, aware that Maori children who were not boarded with Maori families were likely to be committed to an institution, provided an important link in obtaining suitable homes for Maori, searching for them and notifying the Division when it found them.[84]

Desirable as Maori foster homes were, the Division nevertheless inspected many of them closely, applying differing standards of approval or disapproval. Officers 'doubtful' about some Maori homes visited them more regularly. In 1957, for example, Lorna Hodder visited Mrs Whakaneke's New Plymouth foster home, where she found the children to be well cared for. Their sleeping arrangements were not up to 'European standards', however, as the children shared beds. She suggested that in future Mrs Whakaneke receive less than the full board rate. Some officers were able to look beyond their own cultural barriers

In some districts, storekeepers acted as agents for Maori families deemed unable to manage their family or social security benefits. NATIONAL ARCHIVES NATIONAL PUBLICITY STUDIOS PHOTOGRAPHIC COLLECTION, ATL, F-33742-1/2

and approve homes which were not up to the (undefined) 'European standards' benchmark. Kathleen Stewart's visit to the Whangarei District in 1950 took her to a house at Waiotemarama, where she found Mrs Cobham, her two foster children and eight other people living in or around a two-roomed 'shack'. It was clean inside, with rows of bottled jam and fruit on display. Stewart described the Cobhams as a 'respected Maori family' and had no intention of removing the children, although she did suggest that they should have their own room.[85]

Staff generally took a flexible attitude in matters of cleanliness, domestic order and home maintenance. As an article in the *Otago Daily Times* pointed out, the Division required a 'good standard of cleanliness', but would ignore a certain amount of superficial untidiness and select 'a modest home of grubby comfort' in preference to that of the 'over-fussy'. Mrs Nolan of Dunedin, an ex-ward herself, provided one such residence.[86] But officers were alert to signs of problems or disturbing behaviour. 'On both my visits [to Mrs Hogan's foster home] I have noted her made-up eyebrows, only because it is an odd and unusual feature amongst our general run of sensible and busy foster mothers, and the fact that she has talked and laughed non-stop', Lorna Hodder reported after a visit to the Masterton District in 1958. Mrs Sunderland's ideas on childrearing met with disapproval. Described as a 'crank' with an axe to grind, her experience as a social worker in India had convinced her that children should grow up in an 'Asian economic context'. The 'Asian diet' which this involved consisted entirely of soya beans, and proved so unpalatable to the foster child that he was caught scavenging food from his schoolmates. 'We cannot allow foster-parents to play fast and loose with State Wards', Peek thundered, removing the boy.[87]

But action did not always follow observation, and sometimes the Division removed children too late, or did not believe them when they complained of ill-treatment. Girlie Burrows experienced progressively more traumatic placements after being removed from her aunt's house following complaints that she had stolen money. The Division placed her with Mrs Hutton in Te Puna, but the placement proved short-lived when Girlie had sex with a male ward who also boarded there, as well as with several other young men who lived at the farm. Child welfare officers arranged for her removal to the Huriwai family at Te Teko, but within a few months Girlie reported that Mr Huriwai had kissed and touched her. Like other abused young women, she incurred some of the blame. 'Knowing her of old', the officer agreed that it was likely she had made Mr Huriwai's 'advances' easier. Girlie was removed, but only after Mr Huriwai admitted his actions.[88]

Fostering frequently, but not always, involved the severance of links with the birth family, particularly when children were removed from their homes at a young age. Tariana Taurima, who was fostered from the age of five, said that she did not want to return to her father when he requested this. The state had maintained Mr Taurima's eleven children, and he had taken little interest in any of them 'except when he thinks they may be of use'. Peek was blunt: Mr Taurima wanted his daughter to live with him so that she could do his housework.[89] The families of fostered children often experienced difficulty and sadness over the broken relationship. Parents wrote to the Department asking for the return of their children, or inquiring about their well-being, and sent photographs and messages to be passed on. Many of the letters during the 1950s were addressed personally to Hilda Ross or Mabel Howard, the Ministers in charge of the Child Welfare Division or of the Welfare of Women and Children. Perhaps mothers believed that they would get a more sympathetic hearing from a female Minister. Hilda Ross's replies, which she approved after they were drafted in the Division, suggest otherwise; she could be abrupt and sometimes taciturn towards parents who were upset about the removal of their children.

Letters from foster children to the Division were rare. Some later recorded their experiences; an example is Leigh Bonheur's *Hand Me Down: The Autobiography of an Illegitimate Child*, narrated by 'Doris'. 'What do you say when you meet a new mother and father for the first time, and you are seven?' Doris asked, 'What should I call them?' Doris described several placements, and the experience of being singled out as different. Overheard snippets of speech had ominous implications: 'as I went up the hall to my room, I heard my mother saying, "Something's got to be done about that child. I've had all I can stand of her."' The refrain, '"This afternoon you will have a new mummy and daddy"', echoes through the text.[90]

Fostered children sometimes expressed their views through their actions. Ian Billings, a thirteen year old British child migrant, had an unhappy time. Homesick and finding it difficult to adjust to a new life away from all family apart from his brother Ricky, Ian experienced numerous placements. Ian and Ricky were separated after some months, as they fought on the 'slightest pretext'. In the course of a year, Ian lived with five different families, each reporting that they could do nothing with him. He was described as very talkative, unresponsive and ungrateful, with a temperament characterised by 'traditional Scots dour stubbornness and meanness with money'. Ian finally settled with a Wellington family with whom he had a tempestuous relationship, quarrelling frequently with his foster mother and leaving home often. 'Mrs Sutton protests at him asking to return but she loves him like a son and is secretly proud that he likes his foster home sufficiently to want to go back', the child welfare officer reported. Ian remained with Mrs Sutton until he was discharged from the Division's oversight in 1955.[91]

Severance from their birth families may have been less traumatic for other children, for not all wanted to return to them. Burwood resident Sally Jackson, for example, asked the child welfare officer to board her well out of town so that she would not be near her 'difficult' mother. The officer agreed to this, but was aware that there could be repercussions.[92] When Mr Grundy requested the return of his son James, Peek refused, knowing what the young man thought of his father and home. 'Any parent who forces an unwilling boy in his late teens to accept without question the mode of life chosen for him by his parents is storing up trouble', Peek warned James's family.[93]

The Division's faith in family environments and belief that children should be with their parents led it to return some fostered children to their homes under questionable circumstances. Nita Januszkiewicz was returned home in 1951 even though her stepfather was known to be violent and was suspected of 'mercenary motives'. The Division knew that the trial return was liable to disruption, but it also recognised that its power to detain children when parents wanted them back

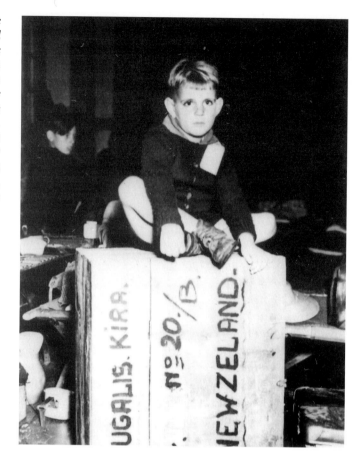

In 1948 the Child Welfare Division assumed responsibility for the Polish child refugees, such as this young boy, who had been sent to New Zealand during the Second World War.
NATIONAL ARCHIVES NATIONAL PUBLICITY STUDIOS PHOTOGRAPHIC COLLECTION, ATL, F-116910-1/2

was open to criticism. In 1950 it agreed to the trial return home of thirteen year old Emma Marner, whose five siblings had all at various times been under the control of the Division. Mrs Marner's living conditions were 'far from ideal', and she had a 'history of failure' in providing for her children. Nevertheless, as Anderson noted, she was Emma's mother, was fond of her, and 'sooner or later' had to be given the chance to reassume her natural rights of guardianship.[94] The Division's discretion over returning fostered children to their homes was curtailed when parents gained the right to an annual review of orders under the Child Welfare Amendment Act 1961. While few parents actually discharged this right, its existence could make foster care arrangements vulnerable.

The Division sometimes took the opportunity when returning children to their homes to castigate parents it saw as remiss in childrearing skills. When the two Symes children were returned to their mother after eight years in care, Hilda

Ross lectured Mrs Symes that she 'must have been freed from a great worry by the knowledge that, at no financial cost to yourself, the state was taking over your responsibility and obligations as a parent'. Mr Graham, receiving his two daughters on a trial placement, was told to be cooperative and appreciate the service he had been rendered: 'The State has had to maintain your children with little assistance from you, and the least you could do would be to be thankful for that', Peek informed him.[95]

'A close personal relationship allied to economy in operation': the development of family homes

If the Division experienced difficulties in obtaining foster homes for its wards, the task of acquiring accommodation for children with social, physical or mental disabilities was doubly hard. Children who were 'unsuited' to private homes but did not need to be confined in the Division's training institutions had always been difficult to place. Some required accommodation in between that available in short- and long-term institutions; others' needs fell between any form of institution and private foster homes. The Division had relied on 'special' foster homes, paying these parents slightly above the regular rate, or had reluctantly used institutional care. Special foster homes were not always available, and from the end of the 1940s they were difficult to obtain; areas such as Whangarei were in dire straits during the 1950s. Officers there, as elsewhere, had relied on special foster homes, but from April 1949 they had been unable to use any in the district. In 1951, when 63 temporary placements had to be made, they were compelled to use either the local hospital or their own premises.[96]

Such crises provoked the Division into searching for solutions. A 1952 survey of institutional facilities led to the notion of the 'family home' as an intermediate step before discharge: this would be a large house, purchased by the Division and run by a married couple who would care for several children at a special fostering rate. This idea built on precedents in England, where a form of family home with salaried foster parents had operated for some time.[97] The proposal received ministerial approval in late 1952. The first family home opened in Whangarei in 1954, and took in 100 children in its first year. Homes in Greymouth and Christchurch followed in 1955, and their number expanded rapidly, until by 1972 there were 78 homes throughout the country, each receiving an average of between 60 and 70 children a year.[98]

The purpose-built or redesigned homes had six or more bedrooms and were capable of holding twelve children in an emergency, but more suited to smaller numbers. The foster parents had the house rent-free, and were paid a fostering fee higher than the regular rate so that they could make a small profit. Sometimes selected from among the regular foster parents, they were expected to provide a genial, homely and well-maintained environment – a 'normal' family life, with the discipline appropriate for 'difficult' children. Unlike other foster parents, those running family homes had no say over the type of children they received. Foster fathers were expected to be in full-time paid employment, while the foster mothers ran the home. To allow them to devote as much time as possible to 'actual mothering', the homes were set up with a variety of labour-saving equipment, particularly washing and cooking facilities.[99]

The homes offered considerable advantages to the Division by allowing officers to select a particular site, home and foster parents, and to ensure a long-term placement if this was required. The homes were cost-effective too – always a high priority. By the late 1960s, the monthly cost of maintaining a child in a family home was $43.50, compared with $165.38 per child for a month of institutional care. All in all, the Division concluded, the homes were an 'undoubted success', and their establishment was touted as one of Peek's 'most progressive achievements'.[100] New Zealand's system rapidly became an international model. Throughout the 1950s and 1960s, the Division received many inquiries from social and child welfare authorities asking for further information and advice on how to develop a comparable system.[101]

Officers waxed lyrical about the impact of family homes on the services they could provide: the homes had 'transformed' the facilities available, and enabled staff to take a more positive approach when dealing with emergencies. They commented on the sense of family that developed in the homes, where children could feel less marked by the 'welfare stigma' of other arrangements. According to Jack Luckock, Otahuhu's District Child Welfare Officer, family homes provided 'almost indescribable relief and [have] given essential elasticity to our facilities and enabled us to place difficult children knowing that they will not be evicted at the first sign of trouble. . . . It is difficult to conceive or recall how we managed without them.'[102]

Staff knew that success depended on the foster parents themselves. Officers preferred down-to-earth folk who would not expect too much of the children; the 'rougher type of the working class seem to be best', one affirmed. Some, such as Mrs and Mr Croucher of Dunedin, devoted most of their time to the home and children. Lorna Hodder visited the family shortly before Easter 1963 and found them preparing for a holiday in Arrowtown. The Crouchers had run the home for four years, but Mrs Croucher showed 'no signs of wear and tear' or declining interest. They 'seem to be building their life and interests around this home', Hodder added. Others, particularly those who had not raised children of their own, were less successful. By 1968, of the 120 couples who had presided over family homes, 87 had resigned after a median term of 22 months. Clearly, there were some problems in the family home system and its administration, most of which the Division was well aware of and was attempting to ameliorate.[103]

The rate of board payments quickly became an issue. As early as 1957, Peek informed the Minister in charge of the Child Welfare Division, Hilda Ross, that the rates were insufficient, and that some foster parents had demanded higher levels. He supported this, noting that the special responsibilities placed on the parents meant that they were entitled to some financial reward. Initially, family home foster parents received 10s per week per child in addition to the basic rate. This was increased from 1957 to take account of the demands on these parents, and to enable them to pay the children pocket money, an expense which had not been incorporated in the initial system but was a part of regular foster payments. The provision of fees for special services, such as keeping a spare bed or admitting a child for a single night, improved the situation a little.[104]

In 1965, when the Division asked for expressions of 'frank opinion' on family homes, almost all the District Child Welfare Officers identified inadequate payment as a serious failing of the system. They described as 'illusory' the margin of profit that was supposedly built in; any profit was obtainable only by 'cheeseparing'. Others realised that making even a tiny profit was dependent on organising and business abilities, which they rarely identified as strengths of foster parents. Some believed that the Division was simply trading on foster parents' goodwill, expecting too much and paying too little. Whether the Division was entitled to rely on the parents' 'sense of vocation' seemed a 'matter of ethics rather than politics or administration', one senior officer commented. Anderson believed that the homes were better equipped than 95 per cent of those in the community, and that foster parents were on to a 'good thing'. 'I hope they are not encouraged to forget that', he added.[105] Rates were raised periodically during the 1960s, but remuneration would remain a vexed issue; foster parents were expected to be altruistic.

The question of payment was also raised with respect to meeting electricity bills. Officers in Whangarei reported that the high cost of electricity there caused undue strain; the family home foster mother received a 'very severe blow when the power bills come in'. Bills were paid on a one-off basis until the Division agreed to pay 75 per cent of all fuel and power costs from the mid-1960s.[106] Meeting bills was part of a broader philosophy of easing the burdens on foster parents, and particularly on the women who maintained the homes and could spend most of their days tending to the needs of the children. The Division prided itself on providing well-designed facilities which combined 'easy supervision' and the effective use of labour-saving devices. Suitable household appliances were seen as crucial, because it was believed their use would reduce

the amount of time women spent on housework.[107] Whangarei's District Child Welfare Officer saw proper appliances as extremely important. 'It is not beyond the bounds of possibility', he suggested, 'that the Family Home system could crash on this question alone'. Family home foster mothers sometimes had very specific requirements. The installation of new washing machines in 1959 generated much discussion between foster mothers and child welfare officers, with the merits and disadvantages of both these and driers analysed in minute detail. Some women preferred the new automatic machines, while others valued their trusted agitators; the Invercargill family home foster mother spurned both, choosing, rather heroically given southern winter conditions, to do all her washing by hand.[108]

The Division's aim to have fathers in paid work and mothers working full-time in the family home placed considerable strain on the women. Their responsibility to provide a comfortable home, and the expectations under which they lived and worked, made them the foundation of the family home system, as they were in so many other areas of child welfare work which relied on community and family participation. Some family home foster mothers were virtually housebound. A Whangarei child welfare officer reported that Mrs Dale was in urgent need of relief, as she had young twins of her own as well as a large number of children passing through the home. She knew few people in the town, and was too exhausted to go out in the evenings. At times, the district office minded the children while she shopped for her own family.[109]

Districts sometimes imposed additional demands on the women, admitting too many children or asking them to perform extra duties 'to the point of unreasonableness'. This was the case in both Whangarei and Rotorua in 1961, and the situation was so dire that the respective District Child Welfare Officers complained to Head Office. 'The constant movement . . . of diversified types of highly delinquent, sexually precocious, ill-mannered, untrained and unpleasant children, mixed with normal and lovable children makes for nothing more than strain on the foster parents', they argued. Foster mothers had been burdened with the care of 'dirty, smelly children' suffering from lice, venereal disease or vaginal discharges. Rotorua had had two sets of foster parents in four years, while five couples had been through the Whangarei home in six years.[110]

The provision of domestic assistance developed into a major issue for the Division and foster mothers. The Division had soon moved to arrange this; temporary housemaids had been employed from 1956. One officer's suggestion that the Division send out washing to laundries was not taken up, but the Division did enlist the help of voluntary agencies. Concerned at the possibly deleterious effects on both the children and the foster mothers of the latter's 'strain of continuous responsibility without relief', the Division authorised the temporary, and voluntary, services of church women to provide periodic respite. It also arranged for temporary assistance to be given to foster mothers. By 1962, the Division granted two weeks annual leave a year, one full weekend relief each month, and up to 24 hours of relief each week.[111]

A few of the foster mothers happily took advantage of this assistance. Rotorua's District Child Welfare Officer was perplexed at the amount of work performed by the relief worker at the local family home. When he asked whether it was appropriate that she did all the washing and ironing for the foster children, the parent's children, their son (who was in the army) and his friends, the response from Head Office was a firm 'No!': foster mothers who expected that level of assistance demonstrated 'stupidity, conceit, and almost total lack of perception or knowledge of personal relationships. If I was a D.C.W.O. she would either change her attitudes or else. . . .'[112]

The issues of relief and leave were closely linked to discussions about the kind of children that were placed. Some officers, evidently relieved at having a facility in their area, used the homes as dumping grounds for problem children. The District Child Welfare Officers from Whangarei and Rotorua decried the placement in family homes of all sorts of unpleasant and difficult children 'whom we know perfectly well should go straight to institutions'.[113] Foster parents sometimes protested about this. Joyce Gifford of Gisborne told her Member of Parliament that she had tried to create a family environment, but that this had been destroyed by the admission of adolescent boys and girls with 'promiscuous tendencies'. She and her husband now spent the 'greater part of each night' patrolling the corridors to ensure that each adolescent was in the right bed, although even this had failed to prevent sexual relations occurring between some of the youngsters.[114]

The young people themselves sometimes complained about the children with whom they were boarded, as well as about unsympathetic foster parents. The shortage of Maori family homes meant that some young Maori were placed in Pakeha homes and found the change of lifestyle very difficult. Arthur Eru was reported by other children to be unhappy in the family home to which he was admitted after running away from his Pakeha foster home, as he 'disliked' Pakeha and there were no other Maori children in residence; the Division arranged for his immediate admission to a Maori foster home.[115]

Force of circumstance, rather than a deliberate policy of utilising the family homes for the Division's most difficult cases, tended to dictate placements. Officers stressed the need to screen out disruptive elements, but the absence of suitable residential facilities compelled some districts to use family homes for difficult teenagers. Rotorua officers claimed to be at their wits' end in knowing where to place boys who had been in short-term institutions but were not a 'good bet' for private placement. They asked the Hamilton office to admit more to the boys' home there, 'otherwise we shall run our Family Home foster parents into the ground – or more so than at present'.[116]

Ongoing accommodation difficulties and the strains on family homes led to the development of specialised family homes for some state wards. Older children had always been difficult to place, and it was a truism in the Division that family home foster mothers had difficulty dealing with older adolescent girls. The Division boarded some young women privately or, as the least desirable solution, used boarding houses. In preference to utilising family homes for these adolescents, the Division established hostel-type family homes, the first of which opened on a trial basis in the Hutt Valley in 1962 and received girls who were working. By 1969 sixteen such hostels operated, four of them reserved for wards who had been discharged from institutions.[117] The Division also planned special-purpose family homes in which a group of siblings would live permanently, with the foster parents changing as required. This novel plan signalled a commitment to the well-being of children in a family group and the importance of sibling unity. The Department of Social Welfare put the plan into effect, and the first of these homes opened in 1972/3.[118]

Some specially designated foster homes continued to be used for children with special needs. Lois Murray of Addington, who had fostered children for more than twenty years by 1963, described her home as a 'last resort' for mentally disturbed children. Child welfare officers shared this view, noting that Mrs Murray had taken in children who would otherwise have been committed to institutions.[119] There would always be those who were difficult to place, who were potentially disruptive of family homes, or who had special needs. Keith Walker was such a child. The illegitimate child of an ex-Borstal inmate, six year old Keith and his brother had been committed in 1956 for being 'indigent'. By 1961, Keith had been in three foster homes, had four temporary placements, six periods in his own home and four placements in a receiving home, and lived in six different family homes. The Division's resources would never cater adequately for all of the children who were committed to its care.[120]

'The silence of these children engulfs us in its enormity': the rediscovery of child abuse

'Even more than with other sorts of family violence', the historian Linda Gordon writes, 'child abuse may appear outside of history. . . . The stubborn constancy of violence against children has tended to support ahistorical conceptions of the problem'.[121] The records of the Child Welfare Division and its predecessors reveal both the 'stubborn constancy' of child abuse in New Zealand, and the fact that the phenomenon has been shrouded by vacillations in public and official concern over its frequency and effects. From the late nineteenth century until the First World War, child abuse generated action in England, the United States, New Zealand and elsewhere. From then until the 1960s, there was an international hiatus in the public recognition of the abuse and ill-treatment of children. Child abuse was not 'discovered' in the 1960s, but 'rediscovered'. As the child welfare historian Harry Hendrick points out, '"abusing" parents are ever present and therefore, it is the definition of cruelty and abuse and public interest in the "problem" which is subject to rediscovery'.[122]

The scantness of historical research into child abuse in New Zealand makes the reasons for its rediscovery here in the 1960s a matter of speculation. A sudden upsurge of concern for the welfare of the battered child was perhaps the least important factor; 'it would be perverse to conclude that the "discovery" of abuse

had much to do with an uncluttered concern for the welfare of the child',
Hendrick reminds us.[123] New Zealand's growing attention to family welfare in the
inter-war and immediate post-war years glossed over child abuse and neglect; it
was the welfare of the whole family that was the primary issue. The focus on
delinquency in the 1950s turned attention to family life, as delinquency became
evidence of moral neglect or inadequate family support. Post-war reports on
English children had postulated that neglected children went on to become
delinquent, and New Zealand child welfare officers were aware of similar trends
here. The officials kept abreast of international research, and were well-versed in
the legislative means of overcoming abuse which were being adopted in the
United States. Local medical professionals also knew of initiatives overseas,
particularly the identification of a 'Battered Child (or Baby) Syndrome', which
physicians first discussed in the early 1960s. New Zealand medical practitioners
and paediatric radiologists took a central role in the dissemination of awareness
of the syndrome; staff at Wellington Hospital noted the large number of 'injury'
cases with a suspicion that was often confirmed when X-rays revealed earlier
healed fractures.[124]

New Zealand also picked up the new ethos that the child had rights as an
individual, with one scholar dubbing the 1970s as the era of 'children's
liberation'.[125] Legislation which removed disabilities against children, such as the
Status of Children Act 1969, which eroded distinctions between the rights of
those born in and out of wedlock, suggest a focus on the child *as* a child, rather
than as a member of a larger unit. The renewed emphasis on individualised
preventive work in the wake of the Mazengarb inquiry may have created a more
receptive climate of opinion, as children's actions were examined in greater detail
than previously. Changes in the Division's recording methods through the
introduction of a general 'information sheet' aided an explosion in the number of
'miscellaneous' cases being investigated and recorded, which led to more cases of
abuse being noted.

'Child abuse' in this chapter encompasses both physical abuse and neglect, the
two areas which were subsumed under the contemporary labels of 'cruelty' or 'ill-
treatment'.[126] There was little public or official discussion of the meaning of the
terms. Ill-treatment was assumed to be self-evident: people would recognise it
when they saw it. Child abuse covered the abuse of children of all ages, although
the term 'Battered Baby Syndrome' was used to refer to assaults on very young
infants. The rediscovery of sexual abuse, here as elsewhere, would come in the
1980s, although child welfare officers did report cases of children who had been
'interfered with' or 'molested'.

Charlie Peek's annual report for 1959 contained the Division's first extended
discussion of child abuse. He noted that investigating complaints of cruelty and

neglect occupied a substantial portion of the time of women officers; 1100 such complaints had been followed up that year.[127] The Division investigated the extent and causes of abuse seriously from the early 1960s. In 1962 its research unit began to collect information on all cases which came to the Division's attention or were reported in the newspapers. Four years later, the unit had amassed information on between 300 and 400 abusive families, and made a detailed analysis of 80 cases, most of whom were state wards. Because of the unsystematic nature of this research, a more extensive national survey was initiated in 1967. Officers working with child abuse cases were required to complete a 37-page questionnaire about the child and family. 'I can recall . . . filling out these rather large complex forms . . . and [I considered] they were a total . . . unnecessary thing to do because you had so much to do anyway', one child welfare officer remembered. The first year of the survey yielded reports on 363 cases which, as it took up to three hours to complete the form, represented a considerable amount of work.[128]

The Division began releasing the results of the survey in 1970.[129] A preliminary report in that year indicated that of the 363 cases reported in 1967, 210 definitely involved ill-treatment, the meaning of which was left undefined. The research unit suggested that approximately one in every 3000 children under the age of sixteen would come to the Division's attention because of abuse. In the final report these figures were revised; it was estimated that two or three per 10,000 children under sixteen experienced definite ill-treatment each year. In an unfortunate choice of words, these results were described as not 'particularly striking'. Even so, the research unit was aware that the actual incidence of abuse was probably much higher, given the lack of reporting and the disguising of abuse as regular childhood accidents. Child welfare officers recalled that the report downplayed the extent of abuse in the community. 'The words . . . were most unfortunate . . . some dismissive comment in relation to child abuse. . . . The number of times I had those words thrown at me [was] innumerable', Mary Todd later reflected.[130]

A further breakdown of the results indicated that almost half of the abused children were under five years of age. Young children experienced extreme beatings, while older children suffered harsh physical punishment. Females were more likely than males to be at risk, although young and adolescent boys tended to be subjected to repeated assaults. Of the abusers, 60 per cent were women. This bald numerical dominance masked significant factors. As scholars of family violence have suggested, the frequency of women's violence against children needs to be read in the light of the fact that they spend most time with children, especially those under five. Men are proportionately much more likely to abuse their children when the amount of time they spend in childcare is taken into account, some have argued. Nevertheless, child abuse is the only type of domestic violence in which women have played a prominent role.[131]

The survey indicated that children from some backgrounds and social groups were more likely to be abused than other children. Auckland provided a 'sizeable' percentage of the cases surveyed, and a large number of these came from within 1½ miles of the city centre. According to research officer Joan Fleming, this was consistent with overseas findings that 'the inner regions of a city tend to be characterised by a high incidence of all types of deviant behaviour'. Almost a quarter of the parents who abused their children had themselves come to the attention of the Division or its predecessors. Those born out of wedlock were more than three times as likely as legitimate children to suffer abuse. The reported rate of abuse of Maori children was six times that for Pakeha, while that of Pacific Island children was nine times as high. The Division saw these discrepancies as resulting from differing socio-economic levels and opportunities; diverse cultural attitudes to 'punishment' and 'abuse' were not considered. The fact that non-Pakeha families could come under more intense scrutiny may also have been a contributing factor.[132]

These results bore out more informal surveys, the impressions of child welfare officers, and general public perceptions of ill-treatment: that abusers were likely to come from disadvantaged backgrounds, to have previously come to the attention of social workers, and to be female and non-Pakeha.[133] These findings keyed into broader discussions about the social welfare of New Zealanders, and the growing awareness of the existence of a socially and racially constituted 'under-class'. The conclusions also seemed to support the notion that a poor environment would beget trans-generational social problems. Just as environmentalist interpretations had replaced earlier ideas about heredity being the cause of family and social problems, a psychological and sociological dimension dominated from the 1960s. Parents who abused their children were perceived as victims of childhood trauma. According to *Truth,* the real root of child abuse lay in the abuser's own childhood.[134] Depravation and deprivation were interconnected, forming a cycle which was difficult to rupture and a characterisation of families which could be hard to break down.

Many of the cases investigated by the Division displayed an inter-generational pattern. A request from Mrs Ritter in 1952 for the return of her three daughters, who had been removed because of ill-treatment and neglect, led to a search through case files which dated back to 1929, when Mrs Ritter had first come into contact with the Child Welfare Branch. Her father was described as a drunkard, her mother a 'deaf half-wit', and the home environment 'dreadful'. Mrs Ritter and her 'drunken waster' husband repeated this pattern of neglect with her own six children, five of whom were under the control of the Division. It was, Peek concluded, 'a sorry account of a complete failure as a mother'.[135] Officers also commented on the 'distressing' number of cases of ill-treatment of young Maori children who subsequently died by mothers who were 'girls' or state wards from homes in which they had experienced little stability or security.[136]

Child welfare officers reflected on the cycle of violence in the cases they attended:

> One little young mother I visited hadn't the energy to sort out her screaming toddlers when her 2½ year old snatched a piece of dried bread. She just sat, moved her head and shouted: 'Slosh him in the chops!' Her home was a shambles. She said she spent most of her life as a child in Nazareth House. . . . I often wondered what the children would grow up to be like, especially when they had inadequate parents and some lived a life of abuse and destruction with little or no love.[137]

As other scholars have suggested, and other examples in this history have shown, the 'cycle of violence' could sometimes be detected simply through families already being in the welfare system under loose supervision or suspicion.[138]

The focus on the sex of the abuser was intense, and in an era when the role of the mother in 'forming' the child was stressed, women's conduct came under scrutiny. Wellington Hospital reported that mothers formed the majority of abusers, and that abuse did not generally start until a baby was six months old. A 1965 Justice Department study also indicated that women played a predominant role, and that their abuse tended to be more 'vicious'; this was perhaps a startled reaction to the usually non-violent pattern of female offending. This study suggested that there were two sorts of female abusers: the young and 'inadequate' mother with a large family and no emotional support; and the 'tense perfectionist type' of mother.[139] Organisations such as the Plunket Society, recognising the problems facing young mothers, offered the Division the use of their Karitane Homes for women needing a period of rest who had begun to suffer from Battered Baby Syndrome.[140] Single motherhood, which was regarded as especially conducive to a range of child welfare problems, could also lead to child neglect and physical abuse. As historians such as Linda Gordon have pointed out, there has been an historical connection between single motherhood, child abuse and neglect. Gordon argues that these concepts have been 'mutually constructed'; neglect and abuse, just as much as single motherhood, represent the antithesis of a 'proper family life'.[141] It is perhaps no historical accident that in New Zealand, child abuse became a public and political issue at a time of rising levels of ex-nuptial births.

Investigating allegations of abuse and neglect was difficult and stressful work for all concerned, particularly as child welfare officers received no special training in the field. They had only informal advice and experience to guide them. 'Well, of course you had the [Child Welfare] manual, someone might tell you what to do, someone might go with you if you were lucky', Mary Todd recalled: 'you just literally boxed on, in blind ignorance really'.[142] Officers were not always alert to indications of abuse. This was particularly so for sexual abuse, which had not been openly acknowledged as a problem; without a vocabulary for constructing sexual abuse, officers could not pick up the warning signs. 'It wasn't in one's thinking', Mary Todd confirmed. Looking back with the knowledge gained from later sexual abuse work, child welfare officers could identify cases clearly: 'Adolescent girls, promiscuous, depressed, school failures, running away – it was all there. . . . I can still recall the fathers in the family doing the talking, and in fact acting as the link person between the child and child welfare. . . . It was all there to be seen and one did not see it.'[143] At other times, psychological diagnoses impeded the consideration of abuse as a possible cause of a child's behaviour. Deborah York's case file indicated that she had been sexually abused by her stepfather, but child welfare officers and psychologists searched elsewhere for explanations for her increasing defiance and overt sexual behaviour.[144]

Complaints about neglect and abuse came in from other social work agencies, police, relatives and neighbours. Child welfare officers made extensive use of these channels of information, although their own supervision of families also uncovered abusive situations. Many of the complaints were anonymous. Some were groundless, and motivated by personal spite. In 1953, for example, Wellington child welfare officers received an anonymous complaint that children were being 'thrashed' in homes in the inner-city area of Vivian, Jessie and Tory Streets. The allegation had no foundation; one of the women visited confirmed that the complainant was her sister, who had complained continually about the behaviour of the children and threatened to notify 'the Welfare' about local families.[145]

Witnesses to abuse could be reluctant to testify for fear of the consequences, which made any further action difficult. Peek believed, however, that simply registering and investigating a complaint was enough to correct some parents.[146] Some child welfare officers were less sanguine about the value of warnings. Wairoa's District Child Welfare Officer warned Danny Whaanga's parents that he would be closely watching the domestic situation, and might call to check on Danny's welfare at any time. 'Actually it is impossible for me to arrive there unexpectedly', he informed the Superintendent, for he had to contact the Whaanga family to ensure that the road to their property was passable.[147]

At times, families themselves requested help and attempted to use the powers of the Division or the children's court to improve their situations. Most of those who sought assistance were women, sometimes themselves victims of domestic violence, and their approach to the Division may have been a cry for help for themselves as well as their children.[148] Women wrote to the Division, or to Mabel Howard or Hilda Ross, expressing fears for their own and their children's safety and hoping that child welfare officers would arrive on the doorstep to intervene. In 1958, Avis Marten of Napier begged Howard for help in her domestic affairs. She was convinced that her husband was suffering from some form of mental illness, and was anxious about the safety of their thirteen year old son. The Minister arranged for an officer to visit and talk to the woman.[149]

Very rarely, the victims of child abuse broke the silence. After prolonged abuse, sixteen year old Ivy Tonk contacted her child welfare officer to report that her foster father, Mr Peters, had forced her to have sex with him. The sexual abuse was accompanied by additional physical violence, with Peters beating her and telling her that this was just a 'sample' of what she would get if she told anyone. Ivy was removed immediately and boarded elsewhere, with officers encouraging her to go to the police.[150] In 1961, when Lorna Hodder paid a regular supervisory visit to two boys who were boarding on a farm near Cambridge, they informed her that they were receiving regular 'hidings'. The home was in a state of disorder: there were unmade beds (at 4 p.m., Hodder noted), a stuffy atmosphere, food on the table, and flies everywhere. The foster father was in gaol, and the foster mother appeared strained, tired and overworked. Hodder ordered the boys' removal, as the home was 'no longer suitable'.[151]

Families known to have a history of abuse could be subjected to intensive supervision. When Auckland's private fostering agency, the Happiness Club, placed three year old Mavis Beard and her brother with the Turner family, child welfare officers visited them fortnightly. The Turners were well-known to the Division, having adopted two children and been investigated on two previous occasions for suspected ill-treatment. In this case, as in others, supervision was no insurance against trauma, serious injury, or even death. As Anderson noted with regard to the death of a child who was under supervision in 1964, the Division was not a clinical service; and he did not necessarily believe that the more time that was spent with a family, the better for the child.[152]

Although there was a policy of investigating all complaints immediately, the point at which abuse and neglect became sufficiently serious for the Division to remove the child was very unclear. The emphasis on maintaining families complicated decisions about when to take parents to court to obtain an order to remove a child, especially if they were making an effort to change. Here child welfare officers could be seriously disadvantaged by their lack of training. In the children's court, and especially when abuse was alleged, officers were required to present evidence and mount cases. Once parents gained the right to legal representation in the children's courts in the early 1960s, officers also had to be able to defend their position against counsel. Masterton District Child Welfare

Officer Brian Manchester believed that some officers did not take cases to court because they did not feel competent to prosecute them. Because they were faced with difficult court situations, Manchester provided his staff with guidelines on conducting prosecutions.[153]

Sometimes, prolonged neglect did provoke action. In 1966 the Christchurch children's court magistrate ordered the temporary committal of a family of eight children who were suffering from neglect. The parents were given three months to put their home and budget in order.[154] At other times, though, the Division trod carefully, aware that it was open to charges of disregarding parental rights. As Peek informed one officer, even brutal parents could evoke public sympathy by protesting about '"interference with the liberty of the subject" and "bureaucratic public servants riding rough-shod over a mother's love"'. Removing children from families was a last resort after all other methods had failed. Improvements in the domestic situation might be slow, but 'in the long run, if it preserves intact a family unit and at the same time avoids animosity, and the creation of long-standing grievances against authority, the quiet persuasive action is better'. 'Our primary aim', Peek added, 'and almost sole concern is for the welfare of the children but we must also ensure that justice is done, and appears plainly to be done, to all parties.'[155] Children's rights may have been on the rise, but they were tightly constrained within a wider family context.

'Experience' had shown that it was often best to leave children with their parents so as to enable the family to solve its own problems, under official oversight. 'Temporary setbacks', presumably continued abuse or neglect, could hamper a family's progress – for parents could not change their habits overnight, Peek noted. While the 'entire situation' was being improved, children could continue to suffer ill-treatment. Napier child welfare officers kept young Noel Rundle's family under supervision for some time after the children had been committed for being in indigent circumstances. Mrs Rundle suffered severely from post-natal depression, and on those occasions when she was 'mentally deranged', family life became very difficult for Noel and his siblings. The Division monitored the situation while waiting for circumstances to improve, and noted that its attempts to keep the family together had generated local criticism. In the end, the child welfare officer 'most reluctantly' came to the conclusion that 'we must sacrifice the family as a unit in order to salvage some of these children'. When Noel and his siblings were removed, Noel was found to be malnourished.[156]

Supervision continued in other cases, with officers 'working quietly and unobtrusively, and with gratifying success in many cases, for the rehabilitation of the whole family.'[157] Given the number of tragic occasions when 'gratifying success' was noticeably absent, it was not surprising that the Division was criticised for a lack of action in safeguarding children's welfare. Anderson took the brutally realistic view that no matter what staff did or how extensive their supervision or services were, children would still suffer or be killed at the hands of their parents or caregivers. He repeatedly pointed out that child welfare officers were 'not clairvoyant', that it was inevitable that children would be killed by their parents, and that there were abused children about whom the Division had no knowledge until it was too late.[158]

But there were times when a decision to remove a child from a family was delayed for too long. The suicide of young Andrew Rochester in 1952 caused considerable soul-searching within the Division. Andrew and his family had been under its oversight since 1947, when they were found living in unsuitable conditions. Registered as a needy family, they were assigned a state house, but complaints from the neighbours that Andrew was being beaten led to further supervision. The officers found no marks on Andrew, but his father admitted beating him with a strap and locking him in the wash-house during the night to 'discipline' him. The officers reprimanded Mr Rochester and encouraged Andrew to leave home. The fact that the parents always appeared to be 'making an effort', and that they were attached to all of their children, induced the Division to continue with supervision only. With the benefit of hindsight, officers admitted that it would have been better to have removed Andrew from the home. The death of Meri Te Paa in 1964 also led to an admission that 'things may have been different' had officers acted when they first learned of her physical abuse and neglect. Meri's death was a 'dreadful occurrence', but an 'occupational hazard', Anderson informed the distraught officer who had handled the case. No matter how expert they were, he noted, they could never be sure that foster parents or relatives would not 'give way' to impulse and do children 'serious damage'.[159]

Successfully altering parents' actions towards their children was a delicate and difficult task, involving as it did a rearrangement of domestic power relationships. Parents sometimes championed a claim to discipline or punish their child as they saw fit, and brooked little interference. The continued supervision of the Rochester children following Andrew's suicide displeased Mrs Rochester, who objected strenuously to the periodic visits of child welfare officers. Hilda Ross dismissed her objections, stating bluntly that they would continue to visit if they received reports that her children were uncared for: 'We would be failing in our duty if we didn't visit a home simply because the parents objected.'[160]

The new climate of opinion about cruelty to children induced calls for greater cooperation between groups to prevent abuse. Most notably, abuse became perceived as a medical issue, with medical intervention considered to be a means of prevention. Medical professionals did not dominate the public debate about and treatment of abuse in New Zealand as they did elsewhere, but the Division recognised them as a powerful lobby group. Throughout the later 1960s, Anderson encouraged medical officers who treated suspicious cases to notify the police or child welfare officers. The drafting of notes for a Child Welfare Bill during the 1960s provided the Division with an opportunity to make the reporting of child abuse by medical officers mandatory. The Division looked to the model of the United States where, by 1967, most states enforced mandatory reporting in some form. The Division knew that the issue was a delicate one for medical professionals, who saw compulsory notification as an infringement of the confidentiality of the relationship between doctor and patient. Medical practitioners also claimed that mandatory reporting would mean that they would see fewer cases of abuse, as parents who brought in children for treatment would no longer do so for fear of further inquiry. The Division tried to sidestep this problem by incorporating in the notes immunity from prosecution for professionals whose suspicions proved to be false.[161] Delays in introducing the legislation meant that nothing was done on this issue, but it refused to go away.

The roles played by the Child Welfare Division in responding to ex-nuptial births, changes in fostering, the waxing and waning of adoption, and child abuse signalled the beginning of a shift in policies towards children and families. While they were still held to be the best means of solving problems relating to children's welfare, families were also acknowledged as creating those problems in the first place. The work of child welfare officers provided them with a potent awareness of the tensions between family welfare and child welfare, parents' rights and children's rights. Officers recognised various family arrangements, and while upholding the nuclear family on the one hand, they also supported other household forms, so long as the welfare of children was safeguarded. Just how family arrangements ensured children's welfare became of crucial significance as the recognition of children as independent individuals grew from the beginning of the 1970s.

PART IV

Child-focused, family-centred:

changing philosophies and practices,

1972–1992

Introduction

The period from the early 1970s to the early 1990s encompassed a time of major change in New Zealand. Rising unemployment, growing inflation, and increasing government intervention in the economy characterised the 1970s; monetarist economic practices and enormous shifts in social policy marked the period from the mid-1980s which amounted to a 'revolution of the Right'.[1] The growing cost of providing welfare services and a new philosophy of 'user-pays' called into question the continued viability of extensive welfare support. The government's role in providing welfare services came up for debate in the face of a rising assertion of community, family and individual responsibility for people's well-being and a castigation of 'welfare dependency'. These discussions occurred within a context of social inequality and unrest. Some parts of the community enjoyed the fruits of change and a buoyant economy, but others experienced hardship, which was worsened by the structural disadvantages that could derive from race or region. These developments, debates and contexts affected both the policy and the practice of children's welfare, as the Department of Social Welfare was called on both to respond to high levels of need and to place limits on its role in welfare provision.

The 1970s and 1980s also saw an articulation of civil rights through the feminist movement and a Maori cultural and political renaissance. New Maori political groupings 'with no traditional mandate other than their sense of identity as Maori' critiqued racially-derived inequalities: Maori were disproportionately represented in crime statistics and unemployment figures, on welfare benefits, and as clients of child welfare services, and had a lower standard of living and greater ill-health than the Pakeha majority.[2] Using the Treaty of Waitangi as their mandate and guide, these groups highlighted both the racism in society and the institutional racism which bolstered government and social structures. With the Maori cultural resurgence came an assertion of rangatiratanga, and an emphasis on Maori management of Maori issues and resources, be these land, health, welfare or child welfare.

Children's rights came to prominence too, although never with the force of women's or Maori rights, or with an organised movement in support. Growing legal advocacy for children, the mention of children's rights in the 1973 *New Zealand Handbook of Civil Liberties*, and the 1979 International Year of the Child all suggested a new awareness of the child as an individual.[3] This recognition brought a questioning of the basis of the legal status of children, their place in family relationships, and their treatment in residential institutions and the child welfare system as a whole.

Important structural changes in child welfare services bracketed this period. The Child Welfare Division metamorphosed into the Social Work Section (later Division) of the Department of Social Welfare on 1 April 1972. Child welfare officers became social workers as the term 'child welfare' receded into history. A general welfare department had long been visualised, and had been planned since 1969 to incorporate all the social service functions which were spread over more than half a dozen government departments. In the end, only Social Security and Child Welfare merged – 'the only two that could be convinced', according to one contemporary observer.[4] The marriage of a large Department devoted to income maintenance and a relatively small Division dedicated to social work was a restless, and unequal, alliance. Ian McKay's first report as Director-General of Social Welfare in 1973 pointed to lingering dissatisfaction; 'old loyalties die hard', he commented.[5] The death throes of some 'old loyalties' were long and painful. Robin Wilson, who was transferred to the Hamilton office in the mid-1970s, remembered the atmosphere there as 'terrible': 'Hamilton had not changed since the '72 amalgamation. The social workers were still in the building they had been with their own boss . . . and the social security people were still in their building, and never the twain met, except when they were insulting each other'.[6]

The Department of Social Welfare restructured its services from the mid-1980s to respond to new user needs and priorities. Responsibility for the welfare of children and young persons was dispersed across several sections of the Department. The restructuring abolished the senior position of Assistant Director-General (Social Work), and removed a social work voice from the top of the departmental hierarchy. Generic regional managers were now responsible for all aspects of work, not just social work. In an era of massive change, some staff felt that social work issues took second place to income support matters: 'Social work became a poor relation. . . . Every spare dollar went into buying another computer or doing something for the benefits area', recalled one officer. By the late 1980s, some staff were becoming impatient about the continuing structural change, which they believed made their social work tasks more difficult. 'Difficult times' and 'a period of madness' are how some describe the climate.[7]

The Department of Social Welfare 'stumbled along somewhat uneasily' until it became 'literally unmanageable' by the late 1980s. Running a big organisation with discrete and complex functions was an onerous task, and the Department had problems in responding to the diverse demands placed on it.[8] In May 1992, it was segmented into three business units, which addressed distinct aspects of social service; the welfare of children and young people was once again the focus of a quasi-independent agency, the New Zealand Children and Young Persons Service. Robin Wilson, its first General Manager, argued that the separation was 'a chance to get the whole thing right. We were offering people the only opportunity they'd had in years to do a good job'. That it was an organisation specifically devoted to children's welfare was symbolised in the very name of the Service. As Wilson noted, 'our Service . . . was very focused', although he acknowledged that more prosaic reasons also dictated the new title: 'the legislation [we operated under] was the Children, Young Persons, and Their Families Act, and I copped a lot of flak over dropping the 'Families' bit [from the title of the Service]. . . . The reason was a very pragmatic one, actually, as it wouldn't fit on the top of the letterhead.'[9]

Social workers continued with many of the varied tasks of the earlier child welfare officers. These services included supervising foster care and family homes, adoption services, work with young offenders and the courts, residential services, preventive policies, and child abuse and other care and protection matters. Some services underwent considerable change. Work with young offenders and the administration of residential institutions, which is discussed in Chapter Seven, was a particular focus of departmental and public attention. Approaches to offending increasingly concentrated on the deeds, rather than the needs, of young offenders, reversing more than a century of child welfare practice. The emphasis of foster care and adoption work shifted as the Department explored new ways of working with families and acknowledged the rights of children and of birth families. Open adoption, and greater involvement of families in decisions affecting children, altered the face of these traditional areas of children's welfare. Together with policies towards child abuse, these developments are discussed in Chapter Eight.

Some long-standing child welfare duties disappeared. The introduction in 1973 of the domestic purposes benefit for single parents lessened some of the burden of raising a child single-handed, and reduced the need for services traditionally provided by child welfare officers. The Children and Young Persons Amendment Act 1983 formally removed the responsibility to investigate ex-nuptial births, much to the relief of social workers, who had performed these inquiries with growing reluctance and decreasing regularity.

Legislative changes framed the years between 1972 and 1992, and the ideologies enshrined in the legislation markedly affected the form of child welfare policy and practice. The Child Welfare Division had been preparing revisions to the Child Welfare Act since 1949. Protracted discussions and fruitless attempts to present the bill to the House dissipated the 'spirit of adventure' which Anderson and others initially had felt: 'I do have the rather depressing feeling that what we are arriving at is a fairly pedestrian piece of legislation', he sighed in the mid-1960s.[10] Contemporaries described the Children and Young Persons Act 1974 as a modest, 'workable, versatile and adequate piece of legislation' which clarified the points of 'doubt and procedure' in the 1925 Act.[11] Effective from April 1975, the Act distinguished between children and young persons, and mapped separate tracks for each group's movement through the social welfare system. A child, defined as under fourteen years of age, would no longer appear in court charged with committing an offence. Children were diverted from the court through children's boards, which could give warnings, order counselling, or recommend that a case be taken to court. Young persons, defined as aged between fourteen and seventeen years, would appear before the redesignated children and young persons court, which received new powers to order supervised community work. The Act gave a legislative basis to preventive work; the earlier absence of any mandate for preventive supervision had given rise to jests about 'illegal supervision'.[12] Henceforth, the Director-General of Social Welfare could undertake preventive programmes in the community and with families. Foster care also received a formal status that had only been implicit in the 1925 legislation. The Act addressed 'home alone' cases too, allowing action to be taken against parents who left small children in locked vehicles outside hotels or in parking lots, or for long periods at home without adequate supervision. In all, it emphasised community and parental responsibility for children's welfare.

The legislative review process culminating in the Children, Young Persons, and Their Families Act 1989 began in 1984, and went through working parties, reviews, submission processes and redraftings before the legislation came into effect in November 1989.[13] Described as 'the most advanced bit of social legislation of its time in the world', the Act radically transformed children's welfare services, and became a model for other countries.[14] Its principles were clear: to promote the well-being of children, young persons and their families in ways which were culturally appropriate, accessible and community-based, and which enabled parents and family groups to take charge of their child protection roles. The Act asserted the primacy of families, whanau and family groups in having and taking responsibility for the welfare of their members. Disruptions to families would henceforth be minimal; social workers would play the role of assistant, facilitator or coordinator. Children's rights as individuals within families were emphasised, with child and family viewed as inextricably bound together.

The legislation represented the triumph and realisation of the ideal of tending to children's welfare within family settings. The emphasis on empowering families and communities to take responsibility for children's well-being was expressed through the provisions for approval of, and powers of funding for, community- and iwi-based schemes. Enshrining community and family responsibility in the legislation recognised formally the relationship which had long sustained child welfare work. The Act also distinguished between issues of welfare and those of justice, or between those of care and protection and those of youth offending, as it differentiated between children as victims and children as threats. Family-based decision-making, in the form of family group conferences, a major innovation of the Act, became the dominant way of working with both groups.

Implementing the new way of working has been challenging, and the legislation has not been without its critics. Some have seen 'soft options' being taken towards abusive families and young offenders; others have pointed to the privatisation of public issues and the drawing of shutters on problematic family lives. Some social workers found it difficult to adjust to the new environment and their changed role: 'some have made the transition, some may never do so', commentators note. Funding the legislation adequately has been difficult in times of government retrenchment. Reductions in funding for youth justice have led some to question whether the vision has been fulfilled. The commitment to bicultural or multicultural modes of working and the recognition and funding of cultural programmes have also been questioned. Police officers have periodically been vocal in criticising the requirements of interviewing young offenders in the presence of an adult and making known to the offender her or his rights. Like others, they believe there to be too few options in working with adolescents who require custodial care.[15]

A 1992 ministerial review of the legislation identified these and other problems in the philosophy and practice of the Act. It acknowledged the innovative nature of the legislation, and emphasised that continuing to seek the objectives outlined in the Act was one of the best ways to combat cycles of violence, offending and abuse. Yet the review team also identified difficulties with family group conferences, problems in residential facilities, including the lack of secure facilities, and ongoing challenges in staff training. Care and protection issues came under particular scrutiny, the review team suggesting that children had in some ways been rendered more vulnerable by the legislation. The team made a series of recommendations, some of which the New Zealand Children and Young Persons Service has carried out. Those working in the area, however, note that implementing the Act has been and will continue to be a lengthy process: 'It will take us twenty years to implement it thoroughly – you virtually need to take a whole generation through it.'[16]

The legislation captured the spirit of the fundamental rethinking of children's welfare services that had occurred across the Department and in the wider community during the 1980s, validating processes such as family-based decision-making, which was already practised by some Social Welfare offices. Some areas, such as Otahuhu, assessed their cultural practices, appointed more Maori staff, and developed a greater awareness of the most appropriate ways of working with Maori and Pacific Island families and children.[17] Challenges from Maori to the way the Department delivered its services and provided for young Maori in care gathered in intensity from the late 1970s. The Act confronted this relationship head-on. The integration of Maori into departmental processes also lay behind the establishment of the Maatua Whangai programme in 1983. Run jointly by the departments of Maori Affairs and Social Welfare, which each provided specially designated Maatua Whangai social workers or mokai, the programme initially focused on obtaining more Maori foster parents. It quickly developed into a community-based preventive scheme for reabsorbing Maori youth into their whanau or iwi. A review in 1985 acknowledged that there had been problems arising from hasty implementation, without the correct underlying kaupapa of laying the scheme on a whakapapa-based concept of community. Refocusing the programme on strengthening whanau and iwi networks to enable them to take back their children moved it beyond its initial fostering role. In the first year of the new scheme, the Department of Social Welfare revised the criteria under which young Maori could be assisted: no longer were they required to be within the social welfare system. This marked a shift in the Department's work with Maatua Whangai and a withdrawal from any directive role, a role which passed initially to the Department of Maori Affairs and then to iwi themselves.

As the government moved to give greater recognition to the Treaty of Waitangi, it also became aware of the existence of institutional racism through-out its structures. The Department of Social Welfare was one of the first agencies to respond to Maori concerns over this issue, some of which emanated from staff, such as the Auckland-based Women's Anti-Racist Action Group. A series of hui addressed the anguish and anger many Maori felt over their treatment at the hands of welfare agencies, and in 1985 the Minister of Social Welfare appointed an advisory committee to report on welfare services for Maori. Chaired by the Tuhoe kaumatua John Rangihau, its report, *Puao-te-Ata-Tu*, was a landmark document which highlighted the connections between colonisation and Maori dependency on the state.[18] The report developed a new vision for the Department, one in which it would be accountable and responsible to Maori across the welfare spectrum. It also led directly to greater community involvement in the Department's work. During 1987 and 1988, the Department increased lay and Maori participation in its decision-making processes. A Social Welfare Commission, with five community and four departmental representatives, advised the Minister on the development of welfare policies. Local District Executive Committees attached to district offices each had seven community members and two departmental staff who monitored their work. Institution (later Residential) Management Committees, made up of community and iwi groups, oversaw the work of institutions. None of these groups lasted – they were disbanded in mid-1991 – but they symbolised an attempt to 'deprofessionalise' the administration of welfare.[19]

Increasing public discussion of children's rights, family rights, and the place of children within families contributed to the changes from the 1970s that culminated in the 1989 legislation. Adult assertion of children's rights placed the Department's residential homes under intense scrutiny from the late 1970s, and residential social workers became more attuned to the rights of children within institutions. Most important was a questioning of the appropriateness for children of judicial processes which effectively reduced their rights in the name of protecting their welfare.[20] Throughout the century, an emphasis on the needs or best interests of young offenders appearing before the courts had meant that offences were largely ignored as welfare agencies sought to discover and then to correct behaviour. Rising levels of court appearances and admissions to institutions indicated that a welfare approach to offending had failed, and perhaps even created further problems. Such an approach was increasingly regarded as intrusive and coercive, providing harmful rather than helpful intervention as remedies designed to protect children detrimentally affected their welfare and rights. Social workers acknowledged that young people in the Department's care drifted, caught in a professional limbo and receiving treatment for as long as the professionals thought necessary.[21] Making young people accountable for their offending rather than focusing on their social background to determine a course of intrusive welfare treatment, the concept at the heart of the youth justice provisions of the 1989 legislation, broke with the principles which had guided New Zealand child welfare work since the nineteenth century.

The 1989 Act embodied the wider thrust of government policies through the 1980s. The withdrawal of the state from social services occurred over several areas, and the welfare of children and young persons was no exception to this policy: family and community empowerment and responsibility were predicated on the state taking a back seat. The fostering of community and family initiatives redirected the Department, and then the Service, into an enabling role, and perhaps confined it even further as a referral agency or service purchaser. Emphasising the centrality of the family – however defined – as the nexus of care, protection, justice, welfare and responsibility was in keeping with contemporary social policy. Some of the imagery harked back to an imagined time in which families had taken full responsibility for their members – before 'the welfare state' and 'excessive' government intervention. 'Empowerment', rights-based language and policies, and the embracing of diverse cultural practices may have grown out of quests for equality and fairness, but they also coalesced in the late 1980s with New Right ideologies of individual responsibility and the rolling back of the state. In the discussions leading up to the legislation, such explicit claims were rarely made in the field of children's welfare, but for better or worse, this flavour of 1980s' social policy also inheres in the Act.[22]

Implementing the complex Children, Young Persons, and Their Families Act required a skilled cadre of staff. The training of social workers became increasingly important during the 1970s. The New Zealand Social Work Training Council, established in 1973, worked with the Department of Social Welfare to provide courses for new staff from 1974; universities offered degree courses in social work from the mid-1970s, followed by other tertiary institutions from the early 1980s.[23] Much training remained in-house or on-the-job, and the number of professionally qualified social workers remained low. From the mid-1980s, the Department recruited staff for the life skills and cultural perspectives that they could bring to the job. *Puao-te-Ata-Tu* challenged the Department to provide more Maori staff to match its client population, as well as calling for the implementation of greater cultural awareness in courses.

The dearth of professionally qualified, and adequately supported, social workers was highlighted by a much-publicised child abuse case in South Auckland in 1987. The subsequent inquiry exposed problems with departmental training and supervision, and led to further attempts to provide more professionally qualified staff and offer better training. From the late 1980s, the New Zealand Council for Education and Training in Social Services worked with the Department to devise new training courses and a staff accreditation system. Continuing concerns that less than a quarter of social workers had any tertiary qualification, and less than 10 per cent had a tertiary social work qualification, saw the issue of accreditation placed high on the agenda for the new Children and Young Persons Service in 1992.[24]

By 1992, the administration of children's welfare looked very different than it had twenty years before. Some of the changes were massive; some, like the closure of institutions from the mid-1980s, and the integration of foster parents into the decision-making circle, reversed practices of long duration. In other areas, 'traditional' policies and practices were extended and enshrined in legislation. The strategy of securing children's welfare by securing the welfare of their families, which had been evident since the 1920s, became official policy in the 1980s.

CHAPTER 7

'A new language':
youth justice and residential institutions

Defining and responding to youth offending were issues of critical importance to the Department of Social Welfare during the 1970s and 1980s. Diverting young people around the court system was a long-established aim of welfare workers. After 1972, the Department pursued this goal with greater vigour, and met with greater success. Alternatives to the formal court system and residential homes became wider, as the Department reacted to community-based initiatives and to the challenges raised through *Puao-te-Ata-Tu*. Changes in the composition of the residential population fuelled long-smouldering difficulties in institutions. By the late 1970s, residential services were in a state of crisis and subject to unprecedented public interest. The combination of problems within the institutions, the expansion of community schemes and the embracing of the notions of whanau and iwi led to a systematic rethinking of the Department's approach to matters of youth justice and residential institutions. The changes wrought from 1989 by the Children, Young Persons, and Their Families Act grew out of this reassessment, as the Department separated issues of justice from those of welfare, and developed a 'new language' of justice.[1]

'Sad, sad Thursday is children's day': youth offending and courts

Youth offending, especially among Maori and Pacific Islanders, persisted during the 1970s and 1980s. Property crimes and offences against the person remained

270

significant, but specific youth lifestyles also came under concerted public and departmental attention. Gang membership, solvent abuse and living on the streets were all considered as signs of deep-seated social problems and indicators of likely further offending.

Gang membership featured in the 1950s' alarm over youth behaviour, and continued to be an issue intermittently in the 1960s. A 1970 television documentary refuelled public anxiety and led to an investigation into juvenile gangs which reported in October of that year. The report noted that a high number of Maori and Pacific Islanders from the lower socio-economic groups in the main centres were joining gangs. Gang activity remained newsworthy throughout the 1970s, and in 1981 an Inter-departmental Committee on Gangs was established to discover why gangs formed and suggest possible solutions to the problems they caused.

Social workers, and particularly residential social workers, knew the negative side of gang life. Youths with gang affiliations comprised more than 80 per cent of those admitted to Auckland's Owairaka Boys' Home, where they created administrative and accommodation difficulties, not to mention violent incidents.[2] Some social workers recognised the important part that gangs could play in the life of a young person. Lainey Cowan, a social worker in Wellington in the early 1980s, worked with gangs which provided educational and cultural services to the young people who associated with them. Groups such as Black Power had members who liaised with Social Welfare – in the central Wellington chapter the two men were nicknamed 'The Wombles' – and could have 'quite an awareness of the place of culture':

> I remember . . . going to one of their inner-Wellington houses where a couple of 'my young people' had taken up residence. The sentry called out my arrival and the young people tried to call me in. . . . and formally welcomed me with speeches. . . . It was very impressive. . . . to see young people who wouldn't go to school, who were breaking the law and just being absolute terrors in every other part of their life, struggling to learn something that obviously had their total interest and commitment.

Cowan formalised contracts with Black Power to ensure that its junior members could receive instruction through the Correspondence School. But as she knew, 'the trouble was of course trying to tee-up the good things they were getting with the fact that it tended to lead them to break the law'.[3]

Membership of gangs was sometimes linked with solvent abuse and living on the streets. Alcohol and drug abuse had been issues for child welfare officers since the 1950s, but solvent abuse and its links with offending were phenomena of the

Gangs – centres of Maori culture, or lawbreakers? Social workers saw both sides of gang life for the young people under their care. EVENING POST

1980s. Social workers noted that youngsters 'high on substances' were responsible for a wave of offences in Auckland and Hamilton over the Christmas and New Year break of 1984/5, for example. In mid-1986, police estimated that there were up to 300 known chronic solvent abusers in Auckland, with fewer in Wellington, Christchurch and Invercargill; these were the tip of an iceberg.[4] Many solvent abusers lived on the streets, permanently or for short periods. 'Street kids' came under investigation in 1981, when a working party from the Select Committee on Violent Offending inquired into young people adrift from their homes. It estimated that there were 50 young people sleeping out in Wellington and up to 200 in Auckland, most of them Maori or Pacific Islanders with little education. Surveys among social workers in 1984 revealed considerably higher numbers: almost 700 living on the streets nationally, and over 1500 gathering there but not living out; these were purely 'guesstimates', according to the Director-General. They were often in poor health, and many were petty offenders with an anti-authoritarian attitude that was perhaps intensified by the police harassment and violence they experienced.[5]

This inquiry and its report spawned a flurry of publicity, mostly negative, about the street kid 'problem' in the mid-1980s. This reached its height with an inquiry into a Palmerston North gang in 1985. The 'Highbury Hoods' – 'a group of mates who named themselves after the hoods on their Swandri jackets', so it was claimed, rather than for the negative connotations associated with the term 'hoods' – was a 40-member group ranging in age from thirteen to eighteen. Its members gathered around suburban shops, sniffing glue, indulging in petty crime and vandalising the local businesses, or milled around The Square, Palmerston North's city centre. In mid-1985, the police claimed that the situation was 'explosive', and warned the public to keep out of The Square during weekends, when the Hoods moved in; the town was being 'held to ransom by a gang of juvenile glue-sniffing thugs', one newspaper blared. A local working party which interviewed the Hoods and their parents found considerable resentment against the police, social workers, and Maatua Whangai workers, all of whom were seen to have failed the predominantly Maori community. The provision of greater community resources was recommended, and the Department was urged to channel more funding into the hard-pressed Maatua Whangai programme.[6]

Solvent abuse and young people living rough remained issues into the 1990s, although social workers noted that both phenomena were on the decline and interpreted them as care and protection rather than justice issues.[7] In the main centres, the streets and abandoned warehouses and dwellings were homes for young people. In cities such as Wellington, inner-city malls were favoured areas for gatherings of street kids from the immediate area, and for gangs who travelled in from the suburbs. But youth offending in itself was no longer the problem it

The street-kid problem came to a head in the mid-1980s. Here a group occupy a disused schoolroom in Wellington's Aro Valley. EVENING POST

had been, statistically speaking, as the level of youth crime fell in comparison to that of other age groups in the 1990s.[8]

Social workers moved young people off the streets and into community programmes. In 1983, the government approved funding for organisations which provided accommodation for street kids. These houses operated under a variety of constraints; that run by Heather Hirama, who had four children of her own, took in up to six street kids when necessary – for $180 a week.[9] Social workers encouraged marae-based alternatives for street kids, such as holiday programmes, and in Otara, which had a large number of street kids, gained approval for emergency housing as well as salary subsidies for those people who took in street kids. Social workers, police and Maori Affairs officers in Whangarei cooperated to run outdoor pursuits camps for at-risk youths. The first camp, held in January 1978, offered a two-week adventure programme with three months of intensive follow-up; after two years, seven camps had been organised for 165 young people, of whom only fifteen were known to have reoffended. The success of the scheme led to the purchase of the surplus Ngararatunua School buildings as a base, and the extension of the programme to target at-risk school pupils through holiday activities or special one-day sessions.[10]

Glue-sniffing in Manners Mall, Wellington, in the late 1980s. By this time, social workers considered solvent abuse to be a care and protection matter rather than a justice issue.
EVENING POST

The operation and jurisdiction of the courts for young people remained a point of contention for social workers. The structure of this part of the court system underwent two major changes during the 1970s and 1980s. From 1975 the children and young persons court was reserved for offences committed by young people aged between fourteen and seventeen. The Children, Young Persons, and Their Families Act split the jurisdiction of courts for children and young people into welfare and justice sections. The family court gained jurisdiction over proceedings involving care and protection issues, while the youth court heard offences involving young people aged between fourteen and seventeen; children who committed offences were dealt with in the family court.

Despite the changing jurisdictions and functions of the courts, particularly after 1989, a general trend is discernible in the pattern of court appearances. Figure 5 depicts the annual number of court appearances between 1972 and 1992, and the growing importance of diversion. The number of appearances fluctuated between approximately 12,000 and 14,000 from 1972 until the mid-1980s, and then fell to around 9500 in 1987/8. The changes wrought under the 1989 legislation further reduced the number of appearances in court. Almost 600 cases were returned to the youth court for resolution in 1990, and 1081 in the following year; family courts had 198 cases returned to them in 1990, and 498 in 1991. Police played an important part by diverting more cases by issuing warnings and passing fewer on to the courts for resolution. In 1984, about 45 per cent of cases involving young people went to court; six years later, the proportion had fallen to about 10 per cent.[11]

The youths coming into contact with the youth justice system were still predominantly male, Maori, more than fifteen years old, and likely to be appearing for offences against the person. Three males appeared in court for

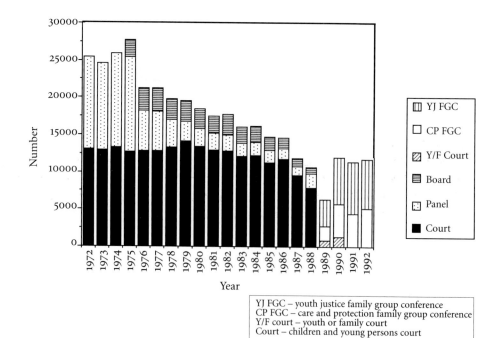

FIGURE 5   *Appearances before courts, Youth Aid panels, children's boards and family group conferences, 1972–1992*

*Some aspects of 1980s'
youth culture had as
much ability to shock
adult observers as that of
the 1950s.* EVENING POST

every female for most of this period, and although young women later featured
in greater numbers, they remained a minority. In 1986, the Department of Social
Welfare estimated that one in eight young males appeared in court before their
seventeenth birthday; for Maori, the ratio was almost one in three. By the early
1990s Maori were estimated to comprise half of all young people involved with
the youth justice system. The differences were more glaring on a regional or
district basis; Maori made up nearly all the cases in South Auckland, Rotorua, the
East Coast and Northland.[12]

In the last years of the children's courts, long-established administrative difficulties continued. The Auckland court was a 'shambles', with up to 100 people milling about waiting for their cases; a journalist attending the Otahuhu court in 1973 denounced its procedures and general atmosphere as a 'miserable drama' – 71 cases were heard in one day.[13] Few courts had the facilities to cope with the volume of cases in the 1960s. Mixing those involved with neglect or abuse and criminal cases in crowded waiting rooms reduced the privacy that was an essential component of courts for young people. One foster mother had to keep her distraught child at home for two days following a court appearance, so upset was the little girl at the things she had heard through being 'thrown' among some of the 'hard cases' attending court. While some courts separated complaint cases from offences, most could not. The scrambled procession of children and young people caused one newspaper to proclaim that 'sad, sad Thursday is children's day' at court.[14]

Distinguishing between children and young people, and reserving court appearances for the latter in most circumstances, lay at the core of the changes that were legislated for in 1974. By the early 1970s, the designation 'children's court' had for some time been a misnomer, given that most of those appearing in

A posed photograph of the Hamilton children's court in session in 1972, with police still appearing in uniform, despite the arguments of child welfare workers. WAIKATO TIMES

it were older adolescents. The change also emphasised that adolescents had a different status, somewhere between childhood and adulthood: 'It seems somewhat inappropriate to me', one magistrate noted, 'that a youth of 16½, with a Cassius Clay physique – this is true, I've had them in Children's Court – and who is earning $60 a week, should be required to appear in a court named "Children's Court"'.[15]

Children's courts were still similar to other courts in their surroundings and procedures. Many child welfare officers and social workers decried the attendance by police, formal language and strict procedures which governed some of them. While the Children and Young Persons Act did not overcome all of these problems, it was hoped that sittings would now be separated from the magistrate's court, but still held in rooms whose design and 'essential furnishings' encouraged the following of appropriate procedures. In the late 1970s, courts such as that at Papakura continued to resemble formal adult courts. Solicitors, uniformed police, traffic and probation officers all attended the sitting held in the magistrate's court, and social workers reported the magistrate to be 'totally unsympathetic' to suggestions that he hold it elsewhere and under less formal circumstances.[16]

The Children and Young Persons Act empowered courts to order preventive work, such as by directing young offenders to participate in planned recreational activities through sporting, educational or leisure clubs. This provision had little success. Even before the Act came into effect, social workers reported that there was scant interest among clubs and organisations. Clubs had 'no enthusiasm' for providing the service, and were reluctant to receive 'conscript members'. Social workers had their own doubts about the provision, arguing that sporting and recreational clubs were not established to do good for the delinquent and 'the unfortunate'; some simply regarded young offenders as 'unclubbable'.[17]

Of more, but still limited, success was the new provision for courts to order supervised community work. Organisations and community groups could specify the type of work to be done, and supervise it if necessary. The scheme's utility and success varied. Kaikohe and Moerewa had a broad programme which imparted a sense of skill and purpose to the young people involved, but this was the exception rather than the rule. A 1981 report on the Hamilton programme revealed considerable difficulties, particularly in finding suitable work. Gardening and 'cleaning up' predominated in most areas, but were hampered by a lack of equipment. Hamilton's equipment consisted of a first aid kit, a spade, a rake and a wheelbarrow – hardly sufficient for a team of workers – and social workers were compelled to borrow or hire gear. Organisations could also be reluctant to become involved. The Lions club in Morrinsville decided that they were not a law enforcement group and refused to participate; in the Hamilton area, only the

Salvation Army would cooperate. Expecting community groups to give freely of their time, and often their equipment, to supervise young people was unrealistic. 'In short', concluded one social worker, 'we feel that if the Department continues to try and do it on the cheap we may as well forget it'.[18]

The 1974 legislation introduced other changes that had long been advocated. The Act made it mandatory for magistrates to receive social workers' reports, and for the first time, made these reports available to the young person and their parents. Until then, one social worker recalled, 'we could make all sorts of . . . judgments and comments' about families, but once parents and their counsel had access to the reports social workers became more cautious in their statements about the social circumstances of clients.[19] Child welfare officers and social workers had long complained that their reports had gone unused, but the new provision was to be short-lived because of the time and effort that was required to provide them. A 1982 amendment to the legislation removed the requirement; henceforth, reports were to be compiled at magisterial request. In a reversal of positions, some magistrates disapproved of this step, while social workers found it beneficial in that it freed their time for more important tasks.[20]

The Act also provided for legal representation, or duty solicitors, for young people and their parents. The court associates provided for under the Child Welfare Act had rarely been successful, and few magistrates had used their services. Christchurch, the last district to use an associate, had not reappointed anyone to the position after 1961.[21] By the early 1970s, any legal representation a child or young person had was additional to rather than an integral part of the process. The legal assistance that was now provided varied in availability and quality. Not all of those appearing before the court could see a duty solicitor, as from 1981 this service was limited to those in police custody, on bail or charged with an imprisonable offence. Magistrates spoke disparagingly of the calibre of duty solicitors, with some recommending that they should have a special interest or qualification in working with young people – something which most magistrates themselves lacked. A pilot scheme using children's advocates in Auckland in 1984 also yielded mixed results. A report after six months suggested that the presence of advocates had actually increased the length of court sessions, and had not served young people's interests as well as had been hoped.[22]

Representation for Maori, and the general appropriateness of the court system for Maori, also came under examination. The Race Relations Conciliator's report on youth and the law in 1983 echoed sentiments about the inadequacy of representation. The Conciliator advocated training for all court personnel, and greater attention to the needs of young Maori people.[23] Some magistrates took up the challenge. From 1984, Otahuhu's Judge Ken Mason arranged for special mediators or Kai Tiaki to attend his court to support the young person and her

*Two young members of
Porirua East's drop-in centre
'Our Place', established in the
late 1980s to provide an
alternative to street culture.*
EVENING POST

or his family. This scheme was expanded into more general assistance to social
workers in supervising young people after court, as well as offering assistance in
court. The Volunteers in Person programme had trained 50 volunteers within a
year, and, according to social workers, played a vital role in the courts and
provided an important link between voluntary and official agencies.[24]

Despite the enduring difficulties in the court system, discussions about the
most appropriate form of court for young people featured very little in the
establishment of youth courts under the Children, Young Persons, and Their
Families Act. Attention focused more on the provisions for those who were not
going through the court process at all, and on the idea that care and protection
matters should go to the family court, rather than on the principle of a court for
young people per se.[25]

Under the 1989 legislation, the types of orders which courts could issue were markedly reduced. The usual orders of admonishment or fines remained, and courts increasingly turned to dismissal as an option: the proportion of all charges that were dismissed or withdrawn grew from 39 per cent before the Act to over 50 per cent in the years immediately following it.[26] The court's authority to make long-term orders, or orders which involved custodial sanctions, was circumscribed. If a case were very serious, and involved fifteen or sixteen year olds, the magistrate could send the case to the district court for resolution. Magistrates could still make an order for residential care (a 'supervision with residence' order), but this could not require more than three months in the Department's custody. In less serious cases, courts could make a 'supervision with activity' order, in terms of which a young person cooperated in a three-month period of structured supervision, such as by attending a community centre. Community work orders or supervision, both of which had time limitations, were other options in less serious cases. The Act required courts to consider various factors when making orders, including the attitude of the young person, their social background if this pertained to the offence, the family or whanau response to the offending, and any efforts by the young person to make reparation or apologise to the victim. No courts, however, could make an order before a family group conference had devised its own solutions. When families could not agree on the penalty for a young offender, the courts were still required to take their wishes into account when making an order.

The restriction on the types of orders which courts could grant, and the requirement that family group conferences be held prior to court proceedings and that the family's wishes be taken into account, altered the balance in matters of youth justice in favour of young people and their families. As one youth court magistrate noted, the change went beyond a shift from a welfare to a justice model of youth offending by bringing in a model of 'responsible reconciliation', a new paradigm of justice in terms of which judges realised that they no longer had the primary responsibility for dealing with youth. Unlike both the children's court and the children and young persons court, the youth court took into account the wishes of the young person and the family. Judges noted that only rarely did they decline to accept the decisions of family group conferences. They were also careful to explain the proceedings and their decisions to young people; before 1989, some had scant understanding of the outcomes of their case, reporting the court decision of 'admonished and discharged' as 'astonished and discharged'.[27]

The implementation of court orders also allowed for, and involved, more formal cooperation with community groups than had occurred previously. Social workers called on community and voluntary welfare groups to provide assistance with supervision, and this continued throughout the 1970s and 1980s in programmes for street kids and general preventive work. The 1989 legislation formalised a process of approving community groups, iwi authorities, and child and family support services, and made provision for the funding of approved organisations. Community groups now took the predominant role in supervision, with social workers or coordinators monitoring progress on the plans drawn up by the family group conferences. The 1989 legislation also provided for legal representation for young people, as well as for the appointment of lay advocates who could ensure that courts were aware of relevant cultural matters. Despite these provisions, some young people, particularly Maori, experienced the court system as an intimidating process or a Pakeha institution. Social workers have criticised how youth advocates are appointed, and claimed that there has been a blurring of perceptions of their role.[28] Such criticisms aside, the new structure of courts and the role assigned to families and young people within them stands in marked contrast to the period up to the late 1980s.

Alternatives to courts: children's boards, Youth Aid panels and family group conferences

The police Youth Aid scheme, formerly the Juvenile Crime Prevention Branch, offered an out-of-court system of youth justice. By the early 1970s, however, social workers were searching for a more effective alternative to courts. Many considered the Youth Aid process to be too prolonged and wasteful of both police and social workers' time. Under the scheme, police and social workers discussed cases, with the police making the final decision on the outcome. Former social worker Brian Manchester remembered the procedure as:

> pretty wasteful to have this meeting, all this deliberation, and then the files have to go back to the police and somebody else sits and looks through them and makes a decision independently. . . . My whole feeling was we needed some kind of youth aid board . . . in the statute, and that body could make the final decision.[29]

Giving such boards the power to make decisions about both outcome and follow-up would streamline the entire process. The draft Children and Young Persons legislation included a proposal for such youth boards which drew on South Australian models.[30]

The combined opposition of the Police, who feared a diminution of their powers, and the Department of Justice stymied the proposed youth boards. Instead, children's boards emerged from the 1974 legislation. These boards heard

In 1971 the Police and the departments of Social Welfare and Maori Affairs established J-teams – Joint teams – as a way of dealing with youth problems in the community. The teams, such as this Auckland J-team, visited schools, patrolled discos, and met young people on the streets. NATIONAL PUBLICITY STUDIOS PHOTOGRAPHIC COLLECTION, NATIONAL ARCHIVES, B4556

cases and complaints involving children aged up to fourteen and could, like the Youth Aid panels, refer cases to social workers. They could not, however, decide questions of guilt, a role which was reserved for the courts. The children's boards comprised a police officer, social worker, member of the Department of Maori Affairs, and a community representative. From 1977, the Secretary of Maori Affairs could nominate honorary community officers in place of Maori Affairs staff. Community representation was an afterthought: Brian Manchester, a member of the group which drafted the legislation, felt that there was a 'trade-off' with the Police rather than any attempt to involve community groups, and it was only after public submissions that lay representation was incorporated. The community representatives, who were appointed by the Minister of Social Welfare on the nomination of social workers, were drawn from local panels of residents which comprised women and men from community groups or with experience in working with children.[31]

Police Youth Aid workers organised a range of activities for young people, such as this Space Invaders contest in 1982. EVENING POST

Some social workers were critical of what they saw as a bland sameness in the panels. Christchurch social workers saw a trend, 'obvious' when the boards were first established, to nominate people like themselves: 'relatively well educated, very intelligent, comfortably-off people'. They identified an unwillingness to nominate folk from other backgrounds, or whose experience was closer to that of the child appearing before the board. Others complained of the gender and ethnic composition of boards, criticising the fact that some all-male boards heard cases involving child or sexual abuse.[32]

Children's boards received about 66 per cent of the cases that might have come to their notice, the Department estimated in the early 1980s. The number of cases they heard in any one year seldom rose above 3000, and declined over the period, falling to less than 1000 in their final year of existence. Of course, most of those who appeared before the children's courts were more than fourteen years old, so the boards were never likely to receive large numbers of cases. The police

Youth Aid system, which theoretically now only dealt with young persons under the 1974 Act, still received cases concerning children, the Department of Social Welfare suspected. Police in Otahuhu did their own preventive work and referred cases to agencies other than the boards. Police in rural districts sometimes dealt with offenders on the spot, and some country boards were largely inactive as a result. Social workers also believed that police sidestepped both the Youth Aid and board processes by simply arresting young people, detaining them overnight, and next day taking them to the court, which would order a period of remand. The number of court appearances, and the population of the Department's short-stay residences, were boosted in consequence.[33]

Social workers themselves did not always refer cases to boards, some considering them to be unable to add anything to their own efforts. 'I got the impression that there were plenty of cases . . . that were taken direct to the court without going to the children's board', Manchester acknowledged. 'It was quicker, and I suppose if the social workers had been asked for a rationale they would have simply said . . . there was nothing at that stage that the children's board could effectively do'. In some areas, social workers' reluctance to use the boards became a matter of concern. A 1980 seminar on children's boards emphasised that the Department should publicise the boards' role more to encourage social workers and police to use them. An evaluation of the 62 boards in 1982 revealed that social workers had a negative perception of them, and under-utilised them because of doubts about their effectiveness and their lack of legal powers. The Waitemata children's board heard 69 cases in 1984, only six of which were referred from the Department; social workers in Kaikohe bypassed the boards 'whenever possible'. An 'enduring tendency' to take cases directly to court was noted throughout the 1980s. The effectiveness of the boards was questionable too because of the limitations on their powers. Hawke's Bay police, for example, estimated that 52 per cent of the children who appeared before the board reoffended.[34]

Some boards did undertake the preventive role that had been visualised for them. The Papakura board went from strength to strength in the early 1980s, and decided to sit weekly rather than fortnightly. The board's 'non-social worker intensive response' considerably aided the understaffed local office, which would otherwise have taken either ineffective or no action.[35] In the 1970s, the Hutt Valley board visited children's homes and schools, and endeavoured to mend fragile family relationships. It visited and counselled Johnny Wetere's family for three months in 1975. Johnny's mother, who was described as a slight but very aggressive woman, maintained the family; her unemployed husband was a 'big man' who spoke to his children and wife with his fists. At the end of the supervision period, the board concluded that everything was fine. Mrs and Mr Wetere were both working and the house was tidy, and even though the entire family retained their 'anti-establishment attitude', the board reported itself pleased.[36]

Pervasive difficulties with both the concept and the practice of children's boards, and their declining use from 1982, forced the Department to reconsider their role. The working party set up to draft new legislation in 1984 targeted the boards as in need of change. The draft Children and Young Persons Bill 1986 suggested that they be replaced by youth assessment panels, comprising police, social workers and community representatives, which would decide on the management of a case after it had been through a screening panel. As with the earlier proposal for youth boards, the panels would act as the final decision-making body for both children and young people aged between ten and sixteen.

This proposal aroused considerable opposition, as indeed did the entire draft bill. Critics saw excessive bureaucracy and regulation, and insufficient community input. Rather than enhance the role of family and whanau, the proposed panels and bill were seen as likely to reduce further their participation. Some argued that the proposal was out of step with the increasing emphasis on justice approaches to youth offending. Like children's boards and Youth Aid panels, the proposed panels would widen the net of surveillance over young people. Although those involved in drafting the bill rejected charges that the proposed panels had a professional bias, when the entire bill was recast between 1986 and 1989 the replacements for children's boards were radically altered.[37]

The new concept of family group conferences which appeared in the Children, Young Persons, and Their Families Act 1989 legislated for youth justice (and care and protection issues) in an entirely different way. In introducing family group conferences, the Act picked up the various community- and family-based decision-making processes which were already occurring in social work practice. Partnership between families and the state was enshrined, with the balance now tipped towards families. The conferences gave families and family groups the first opportunity to respond to problems involving their young members: no proceedings could be taken against a young person until a family group conference had been convened. The conferences were a 'control mechanism on the power of the State'.[38] Youth justice coordinators, who were drawn from a range of backgrounds and did not necessarily have to be located within the Department of Social Welfare, acted as coordinators and advisors to conferences, liaising between conference and court, and reporting back to the court on progress with plans and decisions. They were responsible for ensuring that all who had an interest in each conference were invited to attend, including victims and the whanau members identified by Maatua Whangai officers or Maori social workers.

Both numerically and philosophically, family group conferences quickly became the central means of working with young offenders. In the first full year

The Children, Young Persons, and Their Families Act 1989 came in for considerable comment, especially from police who had to use a new procedure to interview young people. TOM SCOTT

of the Act's operation almost 6000 youth justice family group conferences were held, and the number rose to 6950 in 1992. Fewer than 300 of the nearly 6000 conferences in 1990/1 were referred back to the youth court for resolution.[39]

Families made a range of decisions which the youth court turned into the formal orders which were at its disposal. Families, rather than social workers or youth justice coordinators, had the responsibility of overseeing (and reporting on) any supervision with activity orders, either by doing this themselves or by nominating another person or agency. Activities involved such things as counselling, recreation, and work training. Apologies and reparation were important aspects of the decisions, and the Department of Social Welfare estimated that more than 70 per cent included these features. At times, families could be more punitive than the courts, and the Department noted that some wanted custodial sanctions in the belief that these were a harsher penalty than others.[40]

The legislation embodied a philosophy of restorative justice, with young people encouraged to make amends for their actions. Face to face encounters with the victims of offending, who were also able to attend the conferences, was considered to be a primary step in the restorative and accountability process. The participation of the victim in the conference was important, with some youth justice coordinators regarding the direct involvement of offender and victim as the crux of the youth justice system. The absence of victims from the process was seen as an opportunity for healing lost. Victims were asked to speak at conferences about their feelings and hurt; in responding to them, 'even the *most* inarticulate [young person] will admit to feeling "stink" '.[41]

Families surveyed on their reactions to the conferences reported that they felt more involved in decision-making, although some Maori families felt disempowered by the process. The more open environment of the conference was important for the young person, who was made a part of the process and given an understanding of the events, and many preferred these to the youth courts, in which they felt alienated. 'The court was more strict', one young person noted, 'at the FGC you are with your *whanau*'. Many young people found the presence of family and whanau comforting: 'I felt safe because my *whanau* were with me. I would have felt like stink if I had to face it on my own', one young person ventured. Often the location of a conference could make all the difference. For many Maori surveyed, holding the conference in their own homes or on their marae was vital for a successful resolution. Opening the conference with karakia, having kaumatua to chair it, and allowing full korero by all participants were important to the creation of an open and healing environment.[42]

Conferences could allow families and whanau to rebuild themselves and act in ways which the formal court process had traditionally excluded. 'The folklore of practice is full of really extraordinary happenings in family group conferences that can never have occurred in a court room, *would* never occur in a court room', social workers noted. Young Maori could find this a way of reconnecting with their culture and whanau, a way of gaining access to the language and to kaumatua. As one conference attendee affirmed, 'he [the offender] hadn't known Maori culture and now he will'.[43]

Some whanau and iwi groups approached conferences cautiously at first. As one Maatua Whangai officer pointed out in 1989, families viewed the process with suspicion simply because they were not used to having a pivotal role in the formal decision-making procedure.[44] Such reluctance and apprehension may explain the difficulties that some youth justice coordinators have experienced in gathering whanau members together for conferences. Other commentators suggested that the very strength of family group conferences – the empowerment of families – could be a weakness, with families taking on more than they could cope with. 'We're asking the [Maori] community an impossible task, and it's not a lack of willingness [on their part]', one former social worker noted. In the later 1980s, the concept of empowering whanau carried with it baggage from earlier efforts to utilise Maori resources before the community was ready: 'I went to meetings where the Maori community said, "You are using us, you are giving us the young people that aren't quite coming to your notice. You bloody keep the ones that have got as far as you, we can't handle them yet. We need to develop the skills and expertise to cope with them."'[45]

The complexity of the changes introduced in the 1989 legislation has led to some unevenness in the implementation of the new processes for youth justice, as the Department's own research has noted. Variations in practice from one district to another influenced how and when conferences proceeded, and whether or not victims attended. The 1992 ministerial review into the legislation urged the use of conference venues which were acceptable to both victims and families, and raised questions about lengthy delays in holding conferences. It noted the paucity of procedures for reviewing conference decisions, and claimed that some decisions were a 'laughing stock' in the community. The Commissioner for Children, who was appointed as a children's advocate under the Act, also highlighted practical problems during the early 1990s.[46]

The provision of funding for the conferences has been an issue, because of cuts in departmental budgets and the requirements of government financial accounting systems. With only about $150 to resource each conference and plan, youth justice coordinators and social workers have found it difficult to operate the conferences as they would wish. Poorer families, and particularly Maori and Pacific Island families, have struggled to attend conferences. Social workers and youth justice coordinators have not always been able to distance themselves from their traditional roles, either, with some continuing to steer the process. Some families reported that the conferences were still a Pakeha institution, and that only the shadow of the power had passed to them. Departmental staff, however, pointed to the difference that conferences had made: 'We're making progress. I heard . . . [someone] saying . . . only 40 per cent of family group conferences have victims in attendance. And I got up and I said "I think that's great, as four years ago there were none" . . . we'll just keep on with that, and it'll be 50, 60, 70 per cent as time goes on.'[47]

'Handicapped in almost every way conceivable against doing a reasonable job': residential care, 1972–1982

In 1973, Michael Lyons, a long-time child welfare officer and social worker, inspected the Christchurch Girls' Home. The conditions were, he noted in his report, 'deplorable', and he feared a tragedy would occur if replacement facilities were not found. Lyons concluded that the institution was 'handicapped in almost every way conceivable against doing a reasonable job'.[48] This characterisation could have been applied to many of the Department's residences. These 'handicaps', in terms of both the administration and physical condition of the institutions, had escalated over the 1960s and symbolised the entire residential service in the 1970s. They provide a backdrop against which to examine the management of the institutions. Residences were, in many respects, the public face of the Department's work.

The Department operated twenty institutions in 1972. Three catered for boys and young men on an extended basis: Kohitere took older boys and young men, and Hokio Beach and Holdsworth younger, pre-adolescent boys. Two facilities took in girls and young women on a long-term basis: Kingslea for older girls and young women, and Fareham House, which was initially for Maori but changed to a facility for pre-adolescent girls during the 1960s. There were seven girls' homes and five boys' homes in the main centres, complemented by two reception centres for assessment purposes, and a girls' hostel. The Department opened two further long-stay facilities: one at Weymouth in 1973 for older and more difficult girls, and Beck House, at Eskdale, in 1977 for disturbed pre-adolescent boys. Fareham House and Holdsworth closed as national institutions in 1981 and 1983 respectively. From 1982, national residences could admit young people directly without Head Office approval, a right which had been given to regional institutions in 1979. The Department continued to use the Education Department's special schools of Campbell Park (Otekaike) and Salisbury (Richmond) for boys and girls respectively who were in need of specialist care, but the number admitted to them by Social Welfare was declining.

The Department's short-stay facilities also underwent major changes. From the late 1960s, as was shown in Chapter Five, the Child Welfare Division struggled to cope with the increasing number of young people on remand who were being sent to its homes, and investigated the possibility of establishing remand homes. Instead, the Department opened new short-stay institutions which predominantly took in remand cases, and converted the girls' homes and boys' homes into similar regional facilities.[49] The two new girls' homes built in Hamilton and Auckland during the 1960s, as well as the boys' homes, assumed a remand function in addition to their role as assessment centres and short-stay facilities. Sixteen such facilities were in operation by 1981. By then, the Department also operated two specially-designated reception centres, which acted as a channel for very young children admitted to care. Three ten-bed 'group homes' for both boys and girls opened in Wanganui, Te Atatu and Christchurch from 1981, providing localised, small-scale facilities which enabled children to remain closer to their home communities, families and friends. By the early 1980s the Department ran a total of 26 institutions.

The number of young people in residences at the end of each year declined slightly during this period. At the end of 1972 the figure was 709, and it fell to 680 at the end of 1981. The number in short-term and remand facilities increased from 374 at the end of 1972 to a peak of 516 at the end of 1977. This posed major difficulties for the Department and placed institutions under 'heavy and continuous pressure'.[50] Particular strain was placed on Auckland facilities as the city received a growing proportion of all admissions. The former boys' home, renamed Owairaka, and the two girls' homes, Allendale and Bollard, were all hard-pressed throughout the 1970s. In 1976, the Department opened Wesleydale, a further facility for younger boys to relieve the overcrowding at Owairaka, which was receiving more than 1000 admissions annually, but this too was at once filled to capacity. National institutions, with the exception of that for pre-adolescent boys in Wanganui (Holdsworth) also experienced accommodation crises, with some running waiting lists.

A review of the facilities in Auckland and Hamilton in 1978 showed that they had a rapid throughput of residents, with many remaining for just a few days. The pressure to admit forced early discharges and created a 'revolving door' atmosphere. Bollard consistently had more residents than available beds; boys at Wesleydale slept on mattresses laid on the floor when there was insufficient bed space. Wesleydale's annual report for 1981 indicated that of the 307 admissions that year, 94 were for less than a week, 34 for one to two weeks, 45 for two to three weeks and 23 for between three weeks and a month. Institutions could fill very rapidly, and sometimes the Department used police cells as emergency accommodation. An inquiry in 1976 showed that more than 200 young people had spent time in police custody in each of the last three years, the majority of them Maori and Pacific Islanders.[51]

Changes in admission practices contributed to the growing turnover of residents. Increasingly, most admissions followed arrest by the police, the issuing of warrants, court remands, or from there being no other place available in which to hold young people at short notice – or no such place being sought. The 1978 review of the Auckland and Hamilton homes showed that police, rather than social workers, were the major source of admissions, reversing the pattern of twenty years earlier. The Department saw the figures as a sign that they had virtually lost control over admissions to their short-stay homes. Robin Wilson, the Regional Director for Auckland over some of this period, recalled that:

> the police vans literally used to come [to Owairaka] and they'd open the doors . . . and these big young men would tumble out. The police would have no papers for them often, wouldn't know who they were [as] they'd given false names. You

might get ten young people. You had no idea who they were, who their families were, only a vague idea of what their crimes were.[52]

The residential population was similar in broad outline to those appearing before the court: it was predominantly male and disproportionately Maori. Auckland's Cornwall Park Reception Centre noted that two-thirds of its admissions in 1981 were of Maori or Pacific Island children; Hokio had a similar proportion, and staff at Weymouth recall an even higher non-Pakeha represent-ation among the girls there. In the 1970s, as in the 1960s, the increasing admission of girls and young women requiring care and protection was remarked upon.[53] Girls always remained a minority of the institutional population, however, and in 1972 the Department maintained only 266 beds in girls' facilities compared with 385 in boys'.

Institutional staff reported more violent, difficult and severely traumatised residents. Some were very serious offenders whose presence affected the tone of the whole institution. In 1976, Owairaka's secure unit housed a young man charged with murder, another charged with attempted murder, one with a history of involvement in 'dramatic' cases, and another charged with using a knife as an offensive weapon. The austere secure facilities at Kohitere were inadequate for young men held on such charges. When two alleged murderers, both aged thirteen, became the Department's responsibility in 1977, grave doubts were expressed about its ability to house them.[54]

Disturbed or violent young people, some of whom had serious drug or alcohol problems or gang affiliations, added to the tension in institutions. Wesleydale received difficult and disturbed young boys who had been picked up off the streets for 'survival'-type offending or associating with gangs. The staff reported that these boys could be aggressive, and were not at all chary of being violent towards other residents and staff. Some institutions reported spates of glue-sniffing and its attendant problems, while others commented on bullying and brawls among residents, particularly if they were members of rival gangs. Some residences were threatened with raids by gangs intent on removing their children. Staff at Weymouth Girls' School remembered patrolling the grounds one evening after being warned of a raid to remove a young woman from secure care.[55]

Fareham House was in a 'parlous state' in the early 1970s because of its violent residents. An inspection visit in 1973 found a scene of destruction: there was 'broken furniture, ragged curtains, broken beds . . . and what can only be described as the astonishing state of the girls' bathroom and lavatory area where there were literally thousands of burn marks . . . from the stubbing out of cigarette butts'. Things had not improved by the end of the decade. Residents wrote letters to family and friends describing the institution as 'just a fucken hole' or stating less descriptively, 'I bloody hate it here', and relating their plans to abscond or worse: 'This time we aren't going to stop for anyone because we have had it here'. The Department believed that such letters were designed to upset the staff, but a 1979 riot at the home during which the residents set fire to the house suggests otherwise.[56]

The pressure of numbers, and the changing population of the homes, spilled over into other aspects of residential life. The rapid turnover of residents caused regional homes such as Owairaka to change their function and become remand centres instead of short-stay facilities. Staff saw Owairaka as a 'holding pen' and described their duties as more akin to prison work than social work practice.[57]

Short-stay institutions increasingly admitted young people directly to secure units in order to observe their behaviour and keep new arrivals separate from more settled residents. Weymouth admitted residents to the secure area as a matter of course in the later 1970s, holding them there for two weeks before their transfer to the open institution in the hope of reducing the rate of absconding from the home. Concern about absconding contributed to some of this reliance on secure admissions; Wesleydale had very high levels of absconding from the open parts of the home. Robin Wilson knew that 'escaping [from an open institution] was opening a window, getting out and walking out'.[58]

The lack of a middle ground between secure facilities and the open institution was detrimental to the programmes in both sections, officers argued. Reception and induction programmes conducted in 'outmoded' secure wings were acknowledged to be punitive and possibly anti-therapeutic in effect; the secure block at Kohitere was described as archaic and depressing. 'Mary', who was admitted directly to secure care in an Auckland home during this period, found the experience terrifying: 'I knew if I ever saw another cell again, I'd go really off the cliff, I'd go really stupid'.[59]

The growing number of short-stay residents, the sometimes excessive use of secure care, and heightened tension in the homes created an environment in which it could be difficult for staff to operate effectively. Residential social workers faced very real dilemmas in working in a social work model while also providing secure care for a minority of residents or controlling disruptive and disturbed young people.[60] This may have been even more the case once residential social workers were receiving specialist training and were encouraged to view their work as social work rather than custodial duties. The conditions in homes such as Owairaka contributed to and exacerbated the problems. When Robin Wilson visited Owairaka on a tour of inspection in the 1970s, he found an institution whose Principal Arthur Ricketts had developed 'survival strategies' to enable it to function smoothly. On the day Wilson visited, he saw a residence

A regular room at Kohitere (above) and the austere surroundings of the secure cell at the Boys' Home, Stanmore Road, Christchurch (below). DEPARTMENT OF SOCIAL WELFARE

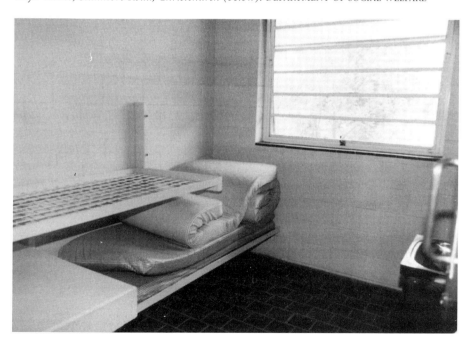

'built for 24 or something . . . but there were 80 young people, sleeping all over the place, not enough staff, so [Ricketts] used to bring his wife and his brother-in-law. . . . He was criticised for nepotism . . . [but] they were only there because no one else would damn well work there.' As Wilson reflected later, such staff poured considerable energy into their work without necessarily receiving wider support: 'They put up with being expected to do an impossible job. Nobody wanted to know, until things went wrong, and then everybody wanted to know.'[61]

High staff turnover and periodic tension between residential and field social workers added to the problems. Residential social workers sometimes believed that their counterparts in the field lacked appreciation of the role of the institutions. They were given insufficient information about the background of some of those who were admitted, and residents could arrive in a confused and frightened state, without any information about where they were going. Holdsworth's Principal described how 'children regularly reached [the home] in a state of utter confusion and disorientation, clutching a paper bag, or carton containing all their worldly goods.' The criticism went both ways, however. Lainey Cowan, a field social worker in Wellington, remembered that 'we often got bad vibes from them . . . . The residential social workers saw us as ineffectual. And we . . . never got reports off them. There was no feeling of working together then.'[62]

Many of the staff nevertheless put considerable effort into improving the lives and prospects of young people. During the 1970s, the Department expanded educational, vocational, recreational, counselling and treatment programmes, particularly for those in extended-care facilities. While these programmes were more varied than previously, the young men at homes such as Kohitere still maintained the surrounding property, and the young women at Kingslea continued with more traditional domestic-based instruction. Maori and Pacific Island culture and language also formed a part of some institutional regimes, although with a predominantly Pakeha staff, such programmes were the exception rather than the rule.[63]

Programmes to build the self-esteem and confidence of young people expanded into a structured practice. At Kingslea, residential social workers worked with the young women to develop personal qualities that would enable them to take greater responsibility in their lives. For the Principal, Marion Judge, Kingslea was a 'specialised boarding school' with 'nurturance' as its foundation. A 1977 inspection report described it as a 'caring institution' where staff sought to develop within the residents the 'inner controls' they needed to build their self-esteem.[64] Beck House instituted a comprehensive programme to modify the behaviour of its residents; staff worked intensively with the children to encourage them to see the consequences of their behaviour and change their actions. In 1974, the Department approved an Outward Bound scheme at Camp Peek, in the foothills of the Tararua Ranges, where young people undertook confidence courses. Many who experienced the camp saw it as a genuine attempt to help them. They were 'certainly no saints' when they left, and still stole food, but were more willing to own up when they did so, a report on the programme noted.[65]

Planned training and achievement programmes set by staff in conjunction with residents became an important part of institutional practice. In the mid-1970s, facilities such as Kohitere introduced training plans in which residents set short- and long-term goals. Other homes operated on more of a group basis; at Hokio, the residents were suspicious of individual counselling.[66] The short-term residences and those with predominantly remand cases found it more difficult to organise structured programmes. An inspection report on Wesleydale in 1981 noted that it was run too much on 'traditional lines', with a regimented system of giving orders to the residents. Maintaining discipline was difficult, and staff sometimes resorted to corporal punishment. The Inspector, aware that staff too wanted to see a more 'mellow and sensible' approach to the boys, advised the adoption of a more innovative and modern programme.[67] A shortage of expert professional help from psychologists could also be a problem for residences which were without constant access to counsellors. The Department's psychiatrist, reporting in mid-1980 on the variable quality of psychological services, saw a perpetuation of the 'old legacies of the past', with the role of psychologists remaining unclear and poorly defined, despite their potential for providing assistance.[68]

Institutional boundaries were now considerably more permeable than they had been, with many facilities forming links with the surrounding community. Janet Worfolk, who worked at several residences in the 1970s, remembers the bonds that were forged with local people and groups. At the Weymouth Girls' School, for example, sports and community groups practised in the residential gymnasium, with the proviso that at least one of the Weymouth children was involved. Staff who lived at the institution and had children in local schools maintained contact with the community, and the interaction between the residence and the surrounding population could be fruitful. Urban facilities such as the Miramar Girls' Home interacted with their neighbours, and local businesses showed their concern by donating goods for the residents.[69] Other homes drew in community agencies by encouraging them to take an interest in particular children and young people. The Cornwall Park Reception Centre utilised a network of voluntary 'aunts' and 'uncles' who took the young children on outings; Kingslea followed a similar practice, with 'foster families' allowing the girls and young women to experience a family environment.[70]

Perhaps the most important breach in the institutional walls was the enabling of greater contact with families. All the long-stay facilities had instituted home leave at holiday times by the mid-1970s. Some residential staff escorted children and young people home for the holidays, and used the opportunity to talk with their families about their progress and life in the residence. Field social workers also kept residents in closer contact with their parents and were involved in checking on holiday placements.[71]

Home leave was not always 'successful', and sometimes added to the stress that was being experienced by children and their families.[72] In part, this was due to a lack of work done with the families themselves. The goal of residential care over this period, as in earlier years, was behavioural change in the child or young person. Unlike supervision, which could focus on family circumstances, residential care occurred outside any family environment. When that environment was left untouched, or was uninvolved with residential training programmes, the chances for the successful 'rehabilitation' of the young person were reduced. One social worker remembered it as 'odd really' that the focus was only on the child, for 'rather than attempting to bring about change in the parental level . . . we attempted to bring about change in the kid, which was probably, in hindsight, the wrong approach'.[73] The expectation that behavioural changes made in the institutional environment would carry over into the home broke down in the 1980s, when the entire purpose of residential care was reexamined.

Contact with home could be minimal for some young people, by either their own 'choice' or that of their families. This could be particularly difficult at certain times of the year, especially Christmas, when isolation and loneliness were accentuated; Lewis Anderson noted that 47 per cent of the boys and young men at Kohitere had no communication with their parents over Christmas 1972.[74] Residential social workers knew that for some young people the institution provided the only secure environment and stable relationships they had experienced. Keeping in contact with families took on a heightened significance in such cases, and social workers at residences such as Kingslea endeavoured to maintain a loose supervision over young women after their discharge so as to monitor their reintegration into family life.[75]

The increasing rights of children in residential institutions were expressed in a variety of ways. The use of secure care in locked rooms had become an issue in the 1960s as institutions built or rebuilt their secure facilities. In 1974 the Department issued directions on the use of secure care which required that young people be supplied with daily showers and changes of clothes, that they be given access to reading material and recreation, that they experience no deprivation of food, and that regular visits be made to them.[76] Some institutions loosened the restrictions on children receiving mail, notably the practice of censoring outgoing mail and opening incoming correspondence. Two staff who had attended a Melbourne conference at which the rights of children in residential care were a major issue introduced the topic at a gathering of residential principals in 1976 – and met with a hostile reception. 'We weren't talking big things here. We were talking about elementary rights, like the right to have your mail delivered to you unopened, the right to have telephone calls. . . . Things that today we'd not even think twice about caused huge ructions'.[77] Censorship continued, buttressed by arguments which were 'all very altruistic and compassionate, but I believe they are essentially thinly-veiled rationalisations to justify a procedure which has the effect of protecting the institution from criticisms about its regime', Holdsworth's Principal informed the Director-General in 1979.[78] Not until after an inquiry into the Department's residences in 1982 were further active steps taken to increase residents' rights.

Despite the difficulties that faced well-intentioned staff, and the introduction of a variety of programmes, senior departmental officers considered that some aspects of institutional care were outmoded and needed to be changed. Compulsory rest periods at some homes and rules of silence at meal times were castigated as 'repressive, negative and authoritarian'; the employment of ex-servicemen in institutions was identified as unnecessary and potentially detrimental; making residents wear uniforms, using tranquillisers to quieten them, the lack of avenues for children to bring grievances and the continued censorship of mail were all targeted for review.[79]

The impetus to alter the residential environment received a sharp jolt in the late 1970s, when the Department's residences came under the public spotlight in a series of inquiries. The findings led to a rethinking of institutional care which dovetailed with the questions that had already been raised within the Department. The inquiries themselves, however, exposed some glaring problems and difficulties for residents and staff, and forced the Department to take a wider view of the place of residential care in providing for children's welfare.

In June 1978, the Auckland Committee on Racism and Discrimination (ACORD), Nga Tamatoa and Arohanui Inc. hosted an inquiry into allegations of cruel and inhuman punishment of young people in Auckland Social Welfare homes. 'We want the public to know the facts which Mr Walker [the Minister of Social Welfare] wants to hide', ACORD stated, referring to the Department's refusal to mount an inquiry. The complaints were focused on the treatment of residents at Owairaka, but also involved the Bollard Girls' Home and the Wesleydale Boys' Home. Former staff members, ex-residents and their families gave evidence that there was a 'threatening system' at the institutions, which were characterised as brutal, undignified, impersonal, and racist. 'Nothing short of restructuring the race and sex composition, administration and policy . . . is needed', ACORD concluded.[80]

The allegations and the inquiry sprang from New Zealand's emergent civil rights movement, which included new Maori groups and anti-racist organisations that targeted discriminatory policies in government and society, and highlighted the extent of institutional racism. The three groups involved in the initial allegations were all active in Maori issues, and ACORD had already sparked an inquiry into the use of police cells for young people on remand in 1976.

The allegations about institutional care generated intense public interest in the Department's residences. ACORD's inquiry came to the attention of the newly established Human Rights Commission, which investigated the alleged breaches of human rights and reported in September 1982. These and subsequent inquiries and reports were the first into homes for children and young people since the inquiry into the Te Oranga Reformatory 70 years earlier. Unlike that inquiry, however, those in the late 1970s and early 1980s contributed to the development of a climate of uncertainty about residential care.

ACORD's allegations centred on specific complaints: that young women were given compulsory and unnecessary examinations for venereal disease; that excessive and arbitrary forms of punishment were employed in the boys' homes, with secure cells used too frequently; that the forms of communication were impersonal; that the physical conditions in the homes were unhygienic; that they failed to address the cultural needs of their residents. ACORD charged the

Owairaka Boys' Home – the subject of controversy and inquiry in the late 1970s and early 1980s.
DEPARTMENT OF SOCIAL WELFARE

Department with violating several articles of the United Nations Covenant on Civil and Political Rights which New Zealand had ratified in 1978. According to the Human Rights Commission, the issues raised were 'certainly the most extensive representations yet made [in New Zealand] on a matter affecting human rights'.[81]

ACORD's 1978 inquiry and its aftermath provided former residents with an opportunity to talk about their experiences of institutional life. Many depicted a scenario that was at odds with the Department's view of how its institutions were run. Bad experiences were recollected with feeling, and few testified to any benefits they may have derived from their care, or referred to staff in positive terms. Former residents described 'abysmal and degrading conduct' in institutions. 'I don't remember anything good about the home', stated Phil O'Donnell, who was at Owairaka during his teenage years. 'I just looked forward to getting out. You were only there for the animals to give you a hard time.' 'They treat you better in prison', was Wayne Ace's recollection; 'If I had to live it all again, I'd end up committing suicide. I'd never go through it again.' Other former residents offered a different perspective on institutional care. New Plymouth's Mrs Kirkpatrick, who had lived in 21 foster homes and various institutions over a fifteen-year period, wrote that:

> the officers are very understanding, patient, and compassionate. . . . I was never neglected. I was better off than other children from normal homes. . . . If anything I have to thank the Social Welfare Department for the opportunities that I would not have had. . . . The officers are the only parents I acknowledge. I can still call on them today.[82]

Young women described painful and humiliating vaginal examinations to test them for venereal disease, which they referred to as a 'Mick Jagger'. Vanessa Allen claimed that she had been compelled to strip naked before staff on her admission to the Bollard Home, and had been watched while showering.[83] Former residents at Owairaka described a 'realm of silence' in which staff communicated by nodding rather than speaking to the boys. Arbitrary forms of discipline were recalled: physical exercise as punishment, boxing matches between residents to settle disputes, standing on lines or in specific areas – in 'Hitler's little half acre', according to one witness. The use of secure cells, and the conditions in them, came under scrutiny. Witnesses at both the ACORD and the Commission's inquiry stated that they had been detained in crowded secure cells, where they had to eat alongside toilet facilites. This practice contributed to charges of 'absolute monoculturalism' and ignorance of appropriate cultural and hygienic practices.[84]

The Commission's report confirmed that their procedures and practices raised serious questions about the residential facilities. It acknowledged that some of the alleged practices had occurred, including intense exercise as punishment, standing in line, and the use of stirrups on girls being tested for venereal disease, but stated that most had ceased by 1982. The report also emphasised that the staff were neither callous nor indifferent, but suggested that the Department's 'shutters to criticism' be lifted and its staff encouraged to utilise the assistance of community groups. There was a 'compelling need' for regulations governing secure care which should form part of a broader set of regulations concerning the appropriate treatment of young people in institutions, regulations which should take account of different racial heritages.[85]

ACORD's allegations and the Commission's report on them received a mixed response within the Department. Staff at the centre of the inquiry found the accusations hurtful, especially those like Arthur Ricketts, Owairaka's Principal, who had a long involvement in residential care and had worked in trying circumstances. Staff believed that their actions had been interpreted in the worst possible light and without regard for the difficulties they faced. Ricketts referred to the 'unscrupulous and appalling tactics used by ACORD', which he considered had not given either him or his staff a fair hearing. John Grant, the Director-General, considered the allegations to be 'most disturbing', but largely unsubstantiated, vague and difficult to check. The Minister of Social Welfare, Venn Young, echoed these sentiments and expressed his confidence in the quality of institutional care. The form of the Human Rights Commission's inquiry precipitated, in part, the Department's guarded response. Rather than providing its own evidence, the Department was invited only to respond to verbal and written questions, the latter numbering 240. It considered this unfair, particularly to staff who had no opportunity to defend themselves or offer another interpretation of events.[86]

On the release of the Commission's report, the government quickly appointed an independent observer to examine the Auckland institutions. Venn Young claimed that it was essential for the public to have confidence in the homes, and imperative for the integrity of residential staff that the grounds for the allegations be 'entirely dispelled'. The government appointed the 70 year old former Anglican Archbishop Allen Johnston to conduct the inquiry and report within six weeks; ACORD, which was still on the offensive, described him as 'another aging white male' as remote by culture and age from the residents of the homes as anyone could be.[87]

The Johnston report confirmed what the Department already knew: that there was overcrowding, direct admission to secure care, and disrupted social work programmes. Johnston found no evidence of the alleged punishments or disciplinary systems, but was aware that there had been 'occasional staff use of physical reprimand' in some homes. He emphasised the need for more instruction in Maoritanga, clear statements outlining the philosophy of care, a code of practice for institutions, and further investigation into secure care and short-term admissions.[88]

The various inquiries had a considerable impact on residential social workers. Staff at the Bollard Home were disappointed at what they perceived to be a lack of support from other offices, and noted that the inquiry and report seriously affected both themselves and their families, with some receiving abusive phone calls from members of the public. Many institutions reported that the Commission's findings dealt a 'devastating blow' to staff morale, and reflected on the 'over-reaction' to certain aspects of the report. Some offices had visits from parents who were concerned about the welfare of children in the Department's homes.[89] Mike Doolan, who was in charge of Kingslea at the time, recalled that he 'didn't know what to believe or not to believe about what was happening in Auckland, but [knew] quite strongly that that was not our approach here in Christchurch'. Nevertheless, the inquiries affected the entire residential service. Doolan confirmed that 'every residence was tarred with that same brush. And although the Commission's inquiry related to five Auckland residences, at the end of the day, no one ever really accepted that.'[90]

The ACORD complaints, the Commission's findings and to a lesser extent the Johnston report revealed that serious breaches of conduct had occurred in institutions. 'Some of it was pretty indefensible', Robin Wilson recalled, 'I guess the Department shouldn't have allowed it to happen. . . . With hindsight, a lot of what [ACORD] said was right'. By the time of the Commission's inquiry and the Johnston investigation, the Department had rectified some of the problems, such as the paucity of Maori and Pacific Island staff and the impersonal disciplinary systems, and had reviewed the regulations on the use of secure cells.[91]

The Department admitted to having arranged boxing matches between residents as a way to relieve tension. In early 1979, for example, the senior residential social worker at the Epuni Home reported supervising a fight between two residents. Peter Hatene and a group of residents had been 'annoying' Terry Ewing for several days, the social worker explained, and challenging him to fight. After attempting to resolve the situation in peaceful ways, the social worker decided that the 'best thing' would be to allow the two boys to fight in his presence. The fight led to Peter's admission to hospital with a broken nose; the rest of the residents, the social worker noted, experienced a 'change of attitude' towards Terry. The Department did not condone this sort of activity, and by the time of the Commission's report, even such isolated occurrences were a thing of the past.[92]

More common were excessive punishments, with some staff requiring residents to stand in line for long periods, or relying on strenuous exercise as a disciplinary measure. Mark Harrington, a resident at the Christchurch Boys' Home, complained of being beaten during a period of intense physical exercise that was administered as punishment for absconding. Under the supervision of the assistant housemaster, Mark had to jog and sprint around the gymnasium for twenty laps. After having a 'breather', he did 50 push-ups followed by more running. 'By this time Mark was starting to feel slightly exhausted', the housemaster reported with some understatement. The running continued, interspersed with hopping, until, completely fatigued, Mark refused to do any more. At that point, the housemaster threatened to 'kick him up the backside', a threat that was carried out when Mark told him to 'go ahead'. The whole situation, the Department's solicitor wrote, 'borders on the sadistic'.[93]

Such episodes were not common, but they were not necessarily exceptional either. Holdsworth's Principal affirmed in 1979 that 'all sorts of spontaneous and arbitrary' punishments had developed, including hard physical training and push-ups. One night attendant forced residents to run up and down the stairs as a disciplinary technique if they refused to settle down of an evening, and 'cruel and unusual' punishments still existed in the homes.[94] A 1981 report on the Wesleydale Boys' Home noted that three-day physical education sessions were used as punishment for absconding; if staff for supervision were unavailable, recalcitrant boys were compelled to stand 'on the line' facing a wall.[95]

Girls had undergone vaginal examinations for venereal disease in homes for a very long time, as the inquiry into the Te Oranga Reformatory in 1908 had indicated. Males were not tested; the assumption that young women were more sexually active and that sexual behaviour contributed to their admission remained. The Principal of the Bollard Girls' Home claimed that venereal disease examinations had not been compulsory, although all residents had been advised to have them. The physician's methods, however, had always been 'suspect' and open to criticism, most notably her use of foot stirrups, lack of a bedside manner, rough methods and failure to lubricate the speculum. The Principal was certain that the examination exposed the young women to a traumatic experience and was destructive rather than beneficial, particularly now that several sizes of speculum were available for use and it was known that only vaginal swabs were actually necessary. Her toleration of the physician's methods was not explained.[96]

It was clear, too, that ignorance of diverse cultural practices meant that the Department had a sometimes questionable grasp of the most appropriate way to approach Maori and Pacific Islanders who constituted the majority of the residential population. Forcing them to eat food in close proximity to toilet facilities in secure care symbolised this problem, but there were also other aspects, such as a lack of instruction in Maori culture in many of the homes. In one highly publicised incident at the Owairaka Boys' Home, a young Niuean boy's hair had been cut off because of hair lice, which denied him the money usually associated with the haircutting ceremony for young Niueans. The Pacific Islanders Council of New Zealand complained about government servants' ignorance of Pacific Island values, a deficiency the Minister of Social Welfare acknowledged freely and promised to remedy.[97]

These events and inquiries need to be set in the context of the broader problems that institutions faced, and placed alongside the attempts of staff to assist the young people in their care. Both the ACORD inquiry and the Commission's investigation, as well as the public statements about residential life, exposed in stark relief the difficulties that confronted institutions during the 1970s. The Johnston report raised serious questions about young people being admitted on remand and without prior warning. Johnston urged the Department to pay special attention to its role as a remand facility, recommending that it ask whether better use could be made of the institutions and the staff. In his view, the homes were in danger of becoming an 'uncomfortable appendage to the Welfare system, the place of last resort', with the staff reduced to a custodial role.[98]

The 1970s marked a turning point for residential social work. To some extent, the problems symbolised the passing of older ways of operating that had continued from the days of the Child Welfare Division. Robin Wilson described this approach as 'paternal. . . . We worked on the basis that you were right, parents' rights were negligible – what we said went'. The Department acknowledged that some of its staff 'could still be described as benevolent custodians and controllers' rather than social workers.[99] Arthur Ricketts of Owairaka pinpointed some of the issues at the principals' conference in 1982 when he reflected on the 'vulnerability' of residential social workers, who were berated by pressure groups and 'radical type social workers'.[100] These 'radical type social workers', some of whom had formal social work qualifications or had been trained in a different intellectual and social environment from their peers in the Child Welfare Division, and were imbued with the growing emphasis on children's rights, were to encourage a further reassessment of residential care in the 1980s and 1990s.

'The next ten years will not be dull': reassessing the role of residential care, 1982–1992

Speaking at the conference of residential principals in 1980, John Scott, the Director of Residential Services, informed his audience, with considerable prescience as it turned out, that 'the next ten years will not be dull'. Scott and many others had recognised that the 'climate of opinion' in New Zealand and throughout the Western world had turned against the provision of residential care for young people. Evaluation of the use of, and indeed the necessity for, institutions was imperative, he added. Director-General John Grant, speaking at the equivalent conference two years later, announced that residential care was at a crossroads; the time had come for change, and action was needed immediately.[101]

While Johnston conducted his investigation into the Auckland institutions in 1982, the Department formed its own internal review team to examine the role of institutions. Its report, 'New Horizons', agreed with most of Johnston's findings and recommendations. The Department responded quickly, limiting the use of secure care by admitting young people to open institutions whenever this was possible, providing special reception areas in some institutions, relaxing the censorship of mail, and beginning work on codes of practice. The 1982 principals' conference had already made a commitment to preparing a code of practice by early 1983, and the internal review team endorsed this goal. Some homes already used their own, but not until 1985 did the Department issue a national code. Regulations for institutional management were released in 1987, although some social workers had already adjusted their practices.[102]

The planning of programmes for young people in care was introduced in 1981 and extended to all residential homes in mid-1983, although a number of the long-stay residences had utilised such plans for some time. Residential social workers, like their counterparts in child protection, employed case conference methods in working with young people. The resident, and his or her parent if possible, discussed the proposed programme of care, negotiating and agreeing on a set procedure and system of review, and setting targets and responsibilities for both the resident and the social worker. Review panels, which comprised a senior social worker and a community representative, were entitled to comment on draft plans and monitor progress. In conjunction with the young person, residential social workers regularly reviewed the plans and goals.

The Department also provided an avenue for residents to air grievances, and developed closer links between the institutions and the community. It improved these procedures after the Human Rights Commission and the Johnston report outlined deficiencies in them. Visiting committees for all institutions were formed in 1978, not specifically in response to ACORD's allegations, as there had been provision for them since 1975. The committees were appointed by the Minister of Social Welfare on the recommendation of the Department, and could visit the homes to check on the well-being of residents and report any problems to the Director-General. Addressing the inaugural seminar for the committees, Bert Walker, the Minister of Social Welfare, noted that the institutions had been 'in the gun' of late, and that their staff were 'fed up with ill-informed griping which makes them appear like inhuman sadistic monsters whose sole pleasure in life is making life unbearable for captive youngsters'. He invited the committees to look into the homes as often as they wished and 'tell us what you see'. 'You don't look to me like the sort of people who are content to do nothing when you've been asked to do a job', he added.[103]

Welcome to Kohitere – *an orientation pamphlet produced for new residents which informed them of their rights and responsbilities.* DEPARTMENT OF SOCIAL WELFARE

Behaviour:

During the time you are at Kohitere, there may be an occasion when your behaviour is not acceptable and staff, along with you, will decide on a contract to change the un acceptable behaviour. The staff will be trying to do what is best for you. At no stage will we use physical force to punish you. Nor will we speak to you in a disrespectful way. I would hope that you too will behave in the same way when you speak to both staff and to your mates.

It may be necessary to use some physical force on you at some stage if you are hurting someone else or breaking something or possibly hurting yourself or to stop you from running away. You can help yourself by seeing that there is no need for staff to use physical force to control you.

Walker was wrong. The Human Rights Commission's report and the Johnston inquiry both revealed that visiting committees had done little to monitor residents' welfare, and had failed to report inappropriate conduct by staff. The committees had not worked properly, and some had not functioned at all. The composition of some committees had limited their objectivity: they included former social workers, and in one case, a committee member had two residential principals as neighbours. An over-abundance of 'middle-class professionals', too few Maori and Pacific Island members, and a predominance of men among the chairpeople were also identified.[104]

From 1982 the committees, which now had to have a member nominated by the Minister of Maori Affairs, and received allowances for their work, were required to visit the homes every three months and report annually. Their effectiveness remained limited, however. Very active committees, such as that at the Miramar Girls' Home, knew that their ability to be a watchdog for the rights of residents was circumscribed by the official nature of their appointment. To expect that 'by parading through the institution we can really come to terms with the girls' welfare is doubtful', this committee noted in 1984. Other committees also believed that they were in no position to effect meaningful change.[105] Residential staff did not always appreciate the role of an external committee, and residents themselves did not see its members as their advocates. 'There was no way [the residents] were going to talk to someone on a visit they would make once every three weeks for an hour', one staff member later reflected. 'How could kids see them as any separate part of the administration and organisation?'[106]

The committees stumbled along until 1987, when they were phased out and replaced by the Institution Management Committees suggested in *Puao-te-Ata-Tu*. These committees, made up of community and Maori representatives, had the responsibility of overseeing the types of services offered in institutions, but not to act as advocates for those in care or hear their grievances. Under the 1989 legislation, these committees became Residential Management Committees, with responsibilities to iwi and the community for ensuring that residences followed bicultural practices. By now, the Department had recognised the futility of expecting residents to take their grievances against institutional management to a group which was perceived as simply another arm of the organisation. The 1989 legislation provided instead for independent youth advocates to receive grievances and manage the grievance process.

The Department also reconsidered the holding of residents in secure care for extended periods. From 1983, principals had to review the use of secure care after 72 hours, and notify Head Office when young people had been detained in it for more than fourteen days. Secure care remained an important issue in the mid-

1980s, and continued to be debated until the 1989 legislation set rigid parameters for its use.

Secure care facilities came under pressure once again when the Department received fifteen and sixteen year olds who had previously been committed to penal institutions. The Criminal Justice Act 1985 passed to the Department a 'considerable burden of responsibility'; it was expected to result in 500 more admissions annually, and many of these young people would have spent time in penal institutions.[107] The Department was already experiencing a rise in the number of sixteen year olds entering the homes on secure custody orders. Between 1984 and 1985 the number of sixteen year olds admitted more than doubled, and the Department looked with alarm on the prospect of this trend continuing, particularly if the young people had previously been in prison. The Department may have received extra staff to help it cope, but the change created problems for the institutions. Overall, it reported an increase of 45 per cent in the number of sixteen year olds admitted, but only a 2 per cent rise in the number of fifteen year olds. Nearly 40 per cent of the two groups had previously come to the attention of the Justice Department, and the admissions had led to a 36 per cent increase in the number of serious offenders held, and a 60 per cent increase in those with chronic offending problems.[108]

During the 1980s, confinement in secure care was seen more clearly as an opportunity for intensive social work with residents, sometimes on a one-to-one basis. Some secure units symbolised the new focus with a change of title to 'special needs' unit. Janey Unuka remained in secure care at Kingslea for an extended period in late 1983 to allow staff to deflect her from her future goal of living with Black Power; Marama Paku, who was addicted to sniffing glue, was kept in secure care at Weymouth Residential Centre for ten weeks to prevent her absconding and obtaining solvents.[109]

Some residents asked to be kept in secure care so that they could prepare themselves to leave the institutions. Katerina Henare, who had absconded from Kingslea three times in as many months, asked to remain in secure care until her discharge, away from the open institution where she had made friends; Jolene Hampton wrote to Marion Judge, the Principal of Kingslea, asking to be kept away from the open residence in which she was subjected to taunts and put-downs: 'I don't feel I can cope with the pressure the girls are putting on me add I want to do some more work on assertiveness'. Staff were aware that residents sometimes used secure care to avoid their problems, and as a 'hiding place' if they did not want to have to cope with life in the wider residence.[110]

Even so, the punitive aspects of secure care could remain strong. The policy of preventing known absconders from leaving the open institution meant that some residents spent long periods in secure care, particularly if they threatened violence. Stewart Cooper, who was described as an 'absconding risk', had a history of using violence when doing so; on his admission to the boys' home in Hamilton he had immediately boasted that he could escape at any time by overpowering the staff.[111] A 1989 Human Rights Commission report found that there was excessive and unnecessary use of secure care. It noted that while some homes employed secure and special needs units positively, many used secure confinement as punishment. The report quoted staff who described their unit as 'not a therapeutic/special needs unit. It has four walls and a door that slams shut. It has the stark reality of a gaol'. Residents questioned about secure care viewed it as punishment, and suggested that it be dispensed with. The Commission estimated that 90 per cent of suicide attempts in residences occurred in secure care, a sobering illustration for the Department of its negative effects. The Commission recommended the adoption of policies which went beyond relying on secure care to cope with frequent absconders, and reminded the Department that its punitive use was contrary to its own regulations. There were no adequate grievance procedures; the Commission recommended the introduction of these, and the appointment of advocates attached to each institution. The report showed both how far the Department had gone towards erecting guidelines for institutional management, and how much more work it needed to do.[112]

The issues that arose over the use of secure care exemplified the Department's struggle to satisfy the competing demands that were placed on its residential service. Unlike other nations, New Zealand preferred open institutions which incorporated secure units, rather than maximum security facilities. The high walls around institutions had disappeared with John Beck's closure of the industrial schools, but as a result, absconding had occurred frequently. Residences laboured under a 'multiplicity of expectations, not all of them compatible', the Director-General noted in 1984. Some homes had long felt themselves to be under police and judicial pressure to hold young people in secure care. The publicity given to escapes from open institutions – 24 young people got away from three Auckland homes in one day in 1983 – attested to the public demand for tougher treatment for young offenders.[113]

The Department took major steps, sometimes with guidance from the Maori community, towards adopting a bicultural perspective and recognising and catering for the cultural make-up of the institutional population, particularly after the publication of *Puao-te-Ata-Tu* in 1986. Visiting the residences and seeing their tamariki there provided a sharp and painful reminder of the loss of young people from whanau for some Maori groups. Representatives from Te Arawa and Tuwharetoa who visited Bollard and Owairaka in 1985 were very disturbed by what they saw and resolved to become more fully involved with the Maatua Whangai programme.[114] As the first government department to be charged with

Institutions began to cater for their Maori residents from the 1980s. Here a Kingslea resident carves Maori pieces as well as wooden toys. DEPARTMENT OF SOCIAL WELFARE

institutional racism, and the first to attempt to ameliorate this problem, Social Welfare was embarking on a 'willing learning curve in its own way', as one social worker noted, in seeking to consult with and respond to the Maori community and Maori staff. At a conference on residences in 1986, the Director of Residential Services spoke of the negative consequences for Maori of institutionalisation. In his view, the Department needed to be guided by Maori and allow itself to stop some or even all of its current practices. Maatua Whangai itself grew in part out of the Johnston report, with officials from Social Welfare and Maori Affairs meeting shortly after the release of the report to discuss joint approaches to the treatment of young Maori in institutions.[115]

Institutions also developed more programmes for Maori residents, and employed more Maori staff and enabled them to work with residents in more appropriate ways. The Allendale Girls' Home, under the direction of a Maori principal and staff, introduced Maori forms of healing for the girls in care, many of whom had been sexually abused. In early 1988, the Department implemented a cultural enrichment programme which allowed young people to return to their tribal areas and develop an understanding of their cultural identity. The

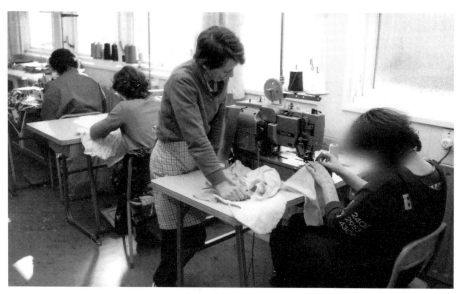

Gender-differentiated training in institutions, 1980s' style. Sewing at Kingslea (above) and military instruction for boys at the Army base in Waiouru (right). NATIONAL PUBLICITY STUDIOS PHOTOGRAPHIC COLLECTION, NATIONAL ARCHIVES, R18688 & DEPARTMENT OF SOCIAL WELFARE

disbursement of funds to iwi was difficult, but the programme put young Maori back into contact with their heritage. Social workers recalled young people travelling from Auckland residences to Taranaki marae for workshops which helped to impart a sense of tribal identity, and Maori staff and parents welcoming them back.[116]

The development of bicultural policies was seldom a smooth process. Regulations on the treatment of young people took little account of Maori and Pacific Island issues, despite submissions from Maori social workers. The Department was challenged to convince its staff and residents of the need to open themselves to the Maori community. Some staff were alarmed at *Puao-te-Ata-Tu*'s recommendations for management committees, believing that their positions were being undermined. The reactions ranged from 'plummeting morale' to 'cautious optimism', one staff member recalled. Few had anticipated the magnitude of the changes that emanated from *Puao-te-Ata-Tu*, with some interpreting it as a 'poor return' for their loyalty to the Department during the difficult years of the early 1980s. Some Pakeha residents took issue with the amount of Maori culture that now appeared in the homes. The visiting committee to the residential centre at Epuni knew that the Taha Maori programme had been a positive influence for Maori residents, but noted that many of the Pakeha there were fearful of the power that had been 'seemingly assumed' by Maori in the process, and felt lost and confused because they were unable, they believed, to express their own culture.[117]

The issues of biculturalism, difficulties relating to secure care, and an awareness of the need to limit residential facilities only to those who clearly required them coalesced into a plan to close institutions from the mid-1980s. An estimate of future accommodation requirements at the beginning of the 1980s had suggested that the Department could also expect a 10 per cent drop in the number of admissions during the decade resulting from a decline in the youth population.[118] Planning to close institutions began in earnest in 1986, and the number of children in residence dropped from more than 500 to fewer than 300 in only three years. The 1986 residential principals' conference recommended a programme of institutional closure and the diversion of the resources freed thereby to fund Maatua Whangai and implement the ideas of *Puao-te-Ata-Tu*. Mike Doolan described the conference:

> We went in with the position that change was inevitable, and that change was necessary . . . and it wasn't a question of *if* it would happen, it was *how* it was going to happen, and we were already picking up on the themes that were emerging from *Puao-te-Ata-Tu*. . . . So you can imagine the emotion, as people hassled these ideas against their own background. . . . But at the end, the conference resolved that it

would take some brave steps. . . . We laid out a process of systematic closure of residences to free up resources for *Puao-te-Ata-Tu* initiatives. . . . [John Rangihau] and John Grant were just staggered that a conference of residential administrators could . . . start writing themselves out of existence, and also accepting the notion that they were part of the problem rather than part of the solution.[119]

The conference resolved to close all homes for pre-adolescent children by the end of 1987, and to reorganise the remaining residences to release resources which could be used to fund alternative forms of locally-based care. A second phase of reorganisation of the residential services would see all institutional services provided either locally or regionally. Services would be flexible, and include non-residential options and outreach services. The concept of national training institutions would be phased out by 1990.[120]

These plans were implemented progressively from 1987. In that year, five institutions for pre-adolescent children were closed, freeing up almost $2.5 million for other uses. Other institutions were closed over the next two years, and by late 1989, the Department maintained only three residences in Auckland, two in Hamilton, two in the Wellington region, and two in the South Island. From a maximum of 26 institutions providing over 900 beds in 1979, the Department had reduced its capacity to nine with 300 beds in 1990. In keeping with the new policy of localisation and regionalisation, the institutions, most of which had become mixed-sex campuses, provided programmes for residents drawn from the area.

Most regions arranged alternative forms of care in the plans that were developed from 1987. Diversion policies, placements outside families, new programmes of providing special foster parents for difficult children in residence, and a range of supportive services to help parents keep their children at home all assisted in bringing down the number of admissions to the remaining residences. Home help schemes, parenting courses for families, and recreation programmes took up where residences left off. Some areas, such as New Plymouth, transformed family homes into family centres with residential social workers which worked towards the rehabilitation of the young person and the family rather than admitting the young person to care. 'By 1989', Mike Doolan recalled, 'we were able to close other institutions . . . because they were empty. And that was the amazing thing. By 1989 and 1990, places like the Auckland Boys' Home that had always had a waiting list, and was always crammed full, were nearly empty. . . . People stopped sending kids to these places'.[121]

During 1989 the average number of admissions to all institutions dropped from 202 per month to 75, and this led to a review of residential services in 1990. The review indicated that these services now provided three times the capacity that was required; the Department was spending $24 million annually to maintain institutions and property that it no longer needed. It found that the nine institutions provided a service that was inappropriate in the post-1989 environment. Kohitere, Kingslea and Weymouth simply reinforced the institutionalisation that the Department sought to avoid, even though they had reduced their bed capacity. The review emphasised the principles of the legislation, which had imposed strict limits on the use of secure care and circumscribed the time to be spent in residential care. It reiterated that residential facilities should maintain close contact with the community to enable young people to keep or re-establish their links with their families and whanau. 'Nineteen-ninety . . . signalled the end of the institutional history of the organisation', Mike Doolan stated. In that year the Department closed five more residences and reduced the number of beds by a further 200. The four remaining facilities – Weymouth, Epuni, Kingslea and Elliott St (Dunedin) – together provided 83 beds, twelve of which were for care and protection cases only, and 39 for secure care.[122]

While this may have marked the end of the Department's institutional history, the process had been a fraught one. The transfer to Maatua Whangai and *Puao-te-Ata-Tu* policies of the savings accruing from institutional closure was a slow process. Some of the initial savings went into financing *Puao-te-Ata-Tu* recommendations such as the District Executive Committees and the Social Welfare Commission, rather than providing alternative services. Maatua Whangai programmes had received almost $2 million by 1989, and regionally-based programmes of alternative care also absorbed some of the resources. The closures meant job losses for residential staff, whose numbers declined from approximately 600 in 1987 to around 300 in 1990. As a proportion of the Department's staff, the number of social workers fell from 22 per cent in 1984 to 14 per cent in 1992. Not surprisingly, morale could be low as staff faced up to an uncertain future; the 1990 review of services made many angry about the long process of change. A 1989 audit of the Auckland institutions noted that a pattern of 'learned helplessness' had been generated by the prolonged uncertainty about which homes would close, and when.[123]

Communities and residential staff sometimes protested at the loss of local facilities. There were claims that the decisions were driven by cost-cutting, that there were no alternatives to institutions, that insufficient time and money had been spent on developing them, and that communities were not ready to absorb the young people.[124] The Department knew that many of these claims had validity: according to one senior officer, 'in some ways I didn't think that was too bad a thing, because what we were looking for wasn't alternative programmes of professional intervention; we were looking for . . . kids to return to their family bases and for professionals and programmes to support those

Members of the Pacific Islands Youth Development Trust in 1991. The Trust was one of the cultural groups funded by the Department of Social Welfare under the Children, Young Persons, and Their Families Act to provide programmes for young offenders. EVENING POST

families. . . . The relative poverty of organisations was maybe a good thing . . . they weren't able to set up alternatives to state care that could have been just as exclusive'.[125] Some staff maintained that things went too far, too fast. Robin Wilson, who was in charge of the Auckland region in this period, and for a time Deputy Director-General, believed that too many institutions were closed, and for unsound reasons. 'In the time-honoured way we threw the baby out with the bath water', he later stated, 'but we were wrong. And we were left with not enough [homes].'[126]

While the institutions were closed independently of the Children, Young Persons, and Their Families Act, that legislation reinforced the emphasis on community-based care. The number admitted to institutions declined from 1295 individuals in 1989/90 to 655 in 1992/3.[127] The differentiation between welfare and justice matters meant that in any institution, keeping care and protection and youth justice cases apart was a priority; this was a reiteration of the principles enunciated in 1900, when the Department of Education sought to separate the 'worst' criminal children from younger and 'less-hardened' ones. The Act limited the type and the amount of residential care that could be ordered for both youth justice and care and protection cases. Youth courts could order up to three months' residential care with supervision. Care and protection residential care could only be ordered when young people were a danger to themselves or others. In practice, care and protection orders have only been for periods of up to three months.[128] When a young person's offence also contained a care and protection issue, the Department emphasised justice and first making the young person accountable for her or his actions.

The 1989 Act made funding available for community facilities to offer residential programmes which had been approved by the Department. Community, cultural and iwi groups seized this opportunity for a formal relationship with the Department, and social work staff speak of an 'explosion' of community-based schemes and programmes.[129] Approval for community residential programmes was subject to the provision of links with family groups and whanau, suitable personal development programmes, and adequate mechanisms to safeguard the residents' care and safety. The facilities were small and localised, taking in young people from the surrounding area with the primary aim of reintegrating them back into the community. They ranged from Christian-based groups to iwi services such as Napier's Nga Toko Rima Hinemanuhiri Trust, which provided care specifically for Ngati Kahungunu children admitted through private agencies and the Department. Placements could be for specialist day programmes only, such as those devoted to overcoming substance abuse, or could involve full-time residential care, such as that provided by the Dingwall Trust, which was based in Auckland.[130]

Organisations, iwi and cultural authorities, and individuals could all provide placements, although obtaining funding for them was not necessarily a straightforward matter. Placements could be with kin, with young people remaining in the custody of the family group. Non-kin placements were ideally with someone known to the family group, who was also known to and approved by the Department. In both these situations, the Department's role was to provide facilitation and assistance if required: the day-to-day responsibility for implementing and monitoring the care rested with the family group. In place of residential orders, the Department has encouraged the use of supervision with activity orders as a less restrictive option for both young people and their families.[131]

Some of the new programmes operated from former family homes which had become surplus to requirements. In the Hutt Valley, a team of families ran family homes to meet the short-term custody needs of the local community. Other family homes, such as that in Dunedin, became special youth justice residences, with placement criteria the same as those for other residences. The Dunedin

Youth Justice Whare was a family home which provided short-term care as an alternative to sending young people to Kingslea, and acted as the centre of the district's youth justice activities.[132]

The limited number of beds remaining in its own residences posed difficulties for the Department when demand outstripped supply or young people needed a form of care that was not available locally. Wellington youth justice coordinators reported the case of one young woman dependent on drugs, alcohol and solvents who was unwilling to seek treatment. With only Epuni available locally for residential stays of three months with supervision, the coordinators had her arrested on a minor charge and secured there to prevent her absconding while they set up programmes for her. As they informed the Director-General, such placement away from families may have been the only option when districts did not have the facilities that were required.[133] The Department also moved young people to residences in other areas, despite the importance that was placed on 'localisation' and ongoing contact with families. The availability of facilities, the need for specialist services, and problems with having rival gangs at one site could all influence a decision to move. At the end of 1992 the Department took steps to overcome such problems by increasing the number of youth justice beds by 30 per cent through additions at Weymouth and the opening of a short-term secure unit in Hamilton for young people from the surrounding district. With its facilities full and waiting lists in some areas, the Department noted that it required more specialist services to meet the varied needs of those entering its residences.[134]

Police, and some social workers, acknowledged that it could be difficult to get young people into the homes, with the result that repeat offenders were sometimes left at liberty. The 1992 ministerial review team highlighted the difficulties in providing appropriate care for at-risk young people, and criticised both the small number of available beds and the Department's 'last resort' policy. Residences could not always hold young people, and police and others complained about abscondings. Community care imposed a burden on groups that were not able to spare the time or resources to care for disturbed young people. Maori communities, in particular, could feel pressured to take young people even though they might not have the resources to cope with them. One Maori who made a submission to the 1992 review stated that 'we have some quite dangerous young people in our community, who have been placed back here by the Department, who are wandering around destroying whanau after whanau. And now the Department won't help us with them. They say they have empowered us!' The high barriers the Department erected for entering institutions had little relationship to what was really going on in the community, the review team suggested.[135]

The New Zealand Legionnaires Academy, based in South Auckland, was a privately-run organisation which offered residential care for serious offenders. The Department of Social Welfare sent young offenders to the Academy during 1991. NEWS MEDIA

The emphasis on non-residential care meant that the Department retained custody of only the most difficult young people. Some youth justice residences became more isolated from their communities, and the role of residential social workers more intensive. Groups have not been as actively involved in the daily life of the residences as they were until the early 1980s, although institutions such as Elliott St in Dunedin and Epuni have maintained active relationships with their surrounding communities. The smuggling of drugs and alcohol into the residences has also led to a reduction in the level of community contact. The location of the residences has meant that some families have found it difficult to visit their young members and have relied instead on toll calls, although some residences, such as that in Dunedin, have kept a flat for use by visiting families.[136]

The surrounding communities have not always been supportive of the change in the residential clientele, and this may lie behind community reluctance to take a greater interest in the young people. Long-standing facilities such as Weymouth have been the subject of community objections about the detention there of serious offenders. The Department's residences have always held such young people, but the previous abundance of residential options allowed them to be spread around the country and melded into the mixture of youth justice and care and protection cases. Since the passage of the Resource Management Act in 1991, the Department has become enmeshed in community politics through having to obtain resource consents for new or additional facilities. Convincing people that young offenders needed to be a part of their communities to foster their well-being and rehabilitation has not been an easy task, and it has been complicated by the serious nature of some of the offences for which the young people have been detained.[137]

As a social worker in Wellington in the 1980s, Lainey Cowan periodically travelled to Kohitere to visit young men from Wellington who had been admitted there:

> When we sat with our young people at lunch, we looked around and there were a lot of others crying – it's making me sad [now]. When I asked what was happening, [it] was that those young men came from more distant places and they had no contact, not only with their families, but not even the social workers who had sent them there. And . . . here we were kissing these young men in a Maori way, sitting down and talking with them and bringing greetings from other colleagues . . . and from their families . . . and all around us young men were weeping, not having had contact with their families or their social worker for sometimes months. . . . And it just reinforced my feelings . . . that although we didn't know what else to do with the young people – and we had precious little to offer – that removing them from everything was not . . . going to help them when they went back.[138]

Kohitere was one of the institutions to close in 1990. Problems with residences continued, but as Mike Doolan put it, 'what happened between 1986 and 1989 really broke the back of a significant industry'. He added, 'we will never go back to that. I'm quite convinced . . . [residences] are a thing of the past. And I think we are saying farewell to them in just the same way as the founders of the 1925 Act said goodbye to the industrial school.'[139]

CHAPTER 8

'Family solutions to family problems': care and protection matters

Issues surrounding adoption, single motherhood, family homes and, to a lesser extent, the rediscovery of child abuse had dominated the Child Welfare Division's 'non-delinquency' work during the 1950s and 1960s. After 1972 the emphasis shifted in care and protection issues, as these matters were designated. Falling levels of adoption and declining public anxiety about ex-nuptial births removed these matters from the forefront of child welfare work for most of the period. New developments in foster care and family homes and the exploding interest in child abuse became the focuses of social work with children and young people. A growing awareness first of children's rights and then of the importance of family well-being, which led to an emphasis on family and community responsibility for children's welfare, had a considerable impact on both the philosophy and the practice of child protection work. Recognition of the needs of Maori clients, and input from the Maori community, encouraged the Department of Social Welfare to examine closely how it worked with Maori. By the late 1980s, notions of social work accountability, along with the pivotal role accorded family and whanau, had tipped the balance of care and protection work away from professionals. 'Family solutions to family problems', an important philosophy of child welfare work for many years, became more significant as family decision-making assumed importance.[1]

Beyond 'Victorian charity': foster care and family homes

The Department of Social Welfare saw foster care and family homes as panaceas for children and young people who required care outside their family network. Foster care had long been the key resource for meeting the needs of those committed to government care, and the system had undergone few changes over the century. The advantages were legion. It was by far the cheapest form of care available: maintaining a child in a private foster home cost only about 10 per cent of the figure for institutional care, and in a family home about 20 per cent of this sum.[2] Administratively, foster care and family homes were simpler to operate than institutions: the homes were run as private residences, with official intervention limited to visits from social workers and as required for administrative and support purposes. Most importantly, the Department believed that foster care provided the most satisfactory form of care outside families. Foster care and family homes were manifestations of the strong ethos of family- and community-based approaches to children's welfare, with the family identified as the crucible for children's well-being.

The continued predominance of foster care in the 1970s and 1980s masked a reassessment of its philosophy and form. As in other countries, this reconsideration and the development of new policies occurred within the context of broader examinations of social policy, the rights of children and families, and the role of state agencies in private lives. A desire to reduce the number of children and young people coming into care, to restrict intervention into family circumstances, and to empower families and communities, drove such rethinking. The reassessment sought to reposition fostering in line with new ideologies and approaches to social welfare, rather than to remove it as an option from the spectrum of care opportunities. The system of fostering at board rates which relied on foster parents virtually donating their time, homes and privacy could no longer apply in the 1970s and 1980s; the reliance on 'Victorian charity' which had marked foster care had had its day.[3]

The New Zealand Foster Care Federation, which was established in 1976 as an umbrella group for a number of localised associations formed in the early 1970s, provided a forum for foster parents, including those in family homes, to air their concerns. The Federation eventually became the key agency with which the Department worked and consulted over all foster care matters. The conditions for fostering were a major issue for foster parents. Rates of pay had been a constant bugbear for both foster parents and the Department, with insistent calls for higher payment met with equally insistent refusals or at most small increases. The Department raised the boarding rates substantially in 1973, and doubled the amount of pocket money provided, but these increases met neither the rising costs of living nor the costs of maintaining foster homes. Until the 1980s the Department remained wedded to the idea that its payments should cover the cost of basic care only, with no financial recognition of the service provided by and burdens imposed on foster parents. Cabinet approved regular adjustments in the rates on the basis of the cost of living index, and then in 1978 authorised an annual review; the Department changed the level and frequency of clothing allowances, and in 1979 introduced an allowance for incidentals. But discontent simmered on, and in 1981 the Federation and the Department formed a working party to review the rates. This supported annual increases in line with the consumer price index, as well as more general five-yearly reviews, and an allowance to cover clothing and all actual and reasonable expenses associated with foster care. The changes were actioned in full by 1986; new allowances were paid to family home foster parents from 1983.[4]

Family homes posed particular issues in addition to more generic foster care matters. Many family home foster parents found it irksome and humiliating that their board rates left no margin for themselves. A Hamilton family home foster parent expressed the views of many. She was 'on duty' for 24 hours a day, seven days a week with no salary, even though she had been told that there would be a surplus left over from the board payments. Regular home help had been valuable, but had its subtle drawbacks: 'I am sick and tired of working alongside my home-help while she receives a good hourly rate plus holiday pay.'[5] More home help, after-hours assistance, tutoring, more babysitting hours and help with gardening were among the extra provisions that family home foster parents sought in 1981. The Department's agreement later that year to changes in the basis of payment to family home foster parents, along with greater provision for petrol and mileage costs to offset demands for departmentally-issued vehicles, alleviated some of the financial issues.[6]

The Child Welfare Division knew that unreasonable demands were sometimes placed on family home foster parents, who were expected to take in difficult children at short notice. John Grant, the Acting Director-General in 1981, expressed his concern at the 'unreasonably high levels' in family homes such as one at Takapuna which took in 70 young people over a fifteen-month period, causing problems for both the parents and the children. The 'overuse' of some of the homes raised questions about the quality of care, and Grant knew of two occasions that year when foster parents had administered excessive or inappropriate punishment. Other family home foster parents left or had their services dispensed with for similar reasons in 1982 and 1984. Family home foster parents called on the Department to develop a clear policy on the use of the homes, and the Department's 1984 Statement of Policy on Family Home Operations sought to clarify their role. Henceforth, family homes would provide only transitional and short-term placements, with the exception of special purpose and special use family homes, such as that at Masterton which provided a flatting situation for adolescents.[7]

The 'calibre', commitment and ability of foster parents in private and family homes was a significant element in the foster care relationship. Before the 1970s, few considered special training to be a prerequisite for foster parents. They were 'good, honest-to-God parents who have plenty of commonsense and maturity and good judgment, but training – no! That would be like asking the caterpillar to analyse how it walks. These people are naturals, and just do the job. They're warm, caring people!'[8] Foster and family home parents themselves, however, increasingly acknowledged the importance of training. The Christchurch Foster Parents' Association petitioned the Minister of Social Welfare to licence foster parents, and to provide instruction courses and information pamphlets. The Advisory Committee on Foster Care took up the call and recommended that attention be given to recruiting and preparing foster parents. Family home foster parents also identified the need for training, including 'pre-entry' or pre-selection instruction, such as spending time in a family home, and access to support groups and refresher training as required.[9]

Training and support were especially important for those involved in Intensive Foster Care Schemes. Based on overseas models and established in Auckland and Christchurch in 1979 with the assistance of the Foster Care Federation, these schemes provided for difficult or disturbed children who had little chance of 'success' in regular foster care. Described by the Federation, perhaps unfairly, as the only truly innovative scheme in which the Department was involved, Intensive Foster Care carefully matched children and foster parents, and provided the latter with comprehensive support. Following an extensive recruitment and selection process, foster parents attended training courses in various aspects of care under the guidance of specially-designated social workers. Support groups gave them ongoing advice and support, and restrictions on caseloads ensured that social workers could spend sufficient time with the families.[10]

Foster parents advocated the provision of special training for social workers. Concerned at the quality of social work support, foster parents and the Federation called for checks on social workers' caseloads. Criticisms about in-experienced social workers and a lack of departmental support were voiced throughout the Department's review of special purpose family homes in 1985, and had been raised more generally in the Advisory Committee on Foster Care in 1983/4. The Department supported some of these calls as part of its broader aim of providing training for social workers. It recognised that living in family homes for a short period would be a valuable learning experience for trainee

Visiting children and families at home remained an important part of social workers' duties in the 1970s. The Department of Social Welfare used this posed photograph to advertise social work as a career.
DEPARTMENT OF SOCIAL WELFARE

social workers, although the extent of this practice is uncertain. Surveys of foster parents and family home foster parents during the 1980s revealed that some simply wanted more frequent contact with their social worker; demands for increased training and more experienced case workers were made in this context.[11]

Foster parents and family home foster parents demanded more open relationships with social workers, and to be considered as part of the team working for the welfare of fostered children. The Foster Care Federation wrote in the late 1970s of 'clannishness' in the Department, which sometimes withheld information or failed to consult during the development of policies and proposals. For its part, the Department periodically found the Federation and foster parents difficult to approach. The Federation could be 'overdemanding here or there', one social worker confirmed, 'but they were really worth a lot'.[12]

Many foster parents resented their exclusion from the making of decisions about the future of the children for whom they cared. One described involvement with the Department as 'something like a horror story . . . a classic piece of bureaucratic bumbling and incompetence' during which frustrations and difficulties were regularly encountered.[13] Social workers recollected the frustrations:

> We treated our foster parents very badly in not giving them any stake in the situation. . . . they would be caring for a child to the best of their abilities, and suddenly the parents would . . . say, 'We can care for our daughter now'. . . . And the next thing the child would be going home on a trial basis to see how it made out. The foster parents would have done a lot of work and suddenly the child would be whipped away, and then perhaps that would fail and then there'd have to be another placement.[14]

Young residents of a Department of Social Welfare family home in Wellington in 1977. EVENING POST

The Foster Care Federation supported increased cooperation in its submission to the Advisory Committee on Foster Care in 1983. The Federation identified a lack of departmental support for placements as one reason why so many broke down; more flexibility from the Department, along with a willingness to support the entire foster family in its work, would go far in enhancing teamwork. The report of the Advisory Committee, which was issued in August 1984, echoed these sentiments, and outlined a goal of partnership, with social workers and foster parents both forming part of the team working for the welfare of the fostered child.[15]

During the 1980s, the Department moved a long way in developing such a partnership. The Statement of Policy on Family Home Operations in 1984 emphasised that foster parents were not claimants on the Department, but colleagues working in the same job, and should be treated as such when they made legitimate requests. The Department and social workers recognised that foster parents had important things to say about the children in their care, and that they should be consulted in any decisions over their future; they were, in effect, caseworkers too. By the late 1980s, senior officials were searching for ways to involve foster parents and the Federation even more, encouraging them to look outwards from the small, but important, daily issues of care to the bigger picture of the place of foster care in the entire welfare spectrum.[16]

However important issues such as rates and conditions were, they focused on administrative matters and spheres of responsibility rather than on the form of care itself. Internationally, and in the wake of an (adult) assertion of children's rights, disquiet emerged about the role of foster care as a long-term guarantor of the welfare of children. The weakening or severance of the link with birth families that was embodied in fostering was questioned. The generic family setting forming the cornerstone of fostering and non-institutional care was seen as insufficiently specific as the importance of bonds with birth families assumed prominence. A new focus on providing security for children and the need for permanence in their relationships with caregivers generated an anxiety about those in care who drifted from one short-term placement to another.[17] 'Discoveries' that children in care were sometimes abused also forced a rethinking of the value of fostering as a safe haven away from abusive birth families. From the mid-1970s, New Zealand shared in this growing reassessment of fostering, to which a local dimension was added with questioning of the appropriateness of out-of-family placements for Maori children. The Department's performance in foster care, perhaps to its surprise, now came under a community microscope.

Foster care received relatively little official attention until the late 1970s, as Ross Mackay noted in a 1981 study. 'No longer is it pronounced that fostering transforms children into "decent and useful citizens"; that the system is a source of great satisfaction to the Department, even that it is the best we can do', he asserted. Mackay's study revealed the impermanence of foster care. Children who were placed out over the five-year study period had an average of 6.5 placements each. The most common factor for children in care, he suggested, was instability in their home life, both before and during placement.[18]

Such figures prompted the Department to introduce planning programmes for children. A national planning system introduced for those in care from mid-1981 made social work more goal-oriented and aimed to reduce the extent to which children were allowed to 'drift' in care. The scheme incorporated plans and reviews in which all parties, including the birth family, participated. Plans were drawn up within three months of the child's entry into care, and reviewed after six months, and then again after twelve months by a special review panel of a departmental and a community representative. The report of the Advisory Committee on Foster Care further emphasised the need to plan for stable futures. The report stipulated the general principles that all children had the right to a secure place, preferably in a family unit, and that all children needed to feel secure and to belong, with an acknowledged past and a reasonably predictable future. The first consideration in any placement was to safeguard and promote the welfare of the child.[19]

A review of the planning programme in 1984 described it as potentially one of the Department's most significant actions, and one which would have a major impact on the way it operated. The programme was a significant forerunner of things to come, with its emphasis on moving children out of care and involving children, parents and foster parents. The attempt to reunite children with their birth families wherever possible reduced the number of children in care, which had been one of the aims of the process.[20] Equally important was the new relationship the Department forged with all members of the care nexus by recognising both foster parents and birth parents as significant partners.

For children and their families, the scheme meant greater participation in the decision-making process. Frankie Hanara, who was taken into care in 1980 following a complaint against his mother, was fostered with relatives for two or three years. The placement was stable, with Frankie excelling at school and in sporting and cultural areas. The care group agreed that long-term foster care would be best for Frankie, unless his mother's circumstances improved drastically.[21] The planning process also required social workers to work in different ways with different ethnic communities. For Maori and Pacific Island communities, planning meetings could bring together all members of a family, which was acknowledged to be the most appropriate way of working with these groups. In some cases, social workers from that ethnic group were also included, which was not always easy where there were few Maori or Pacific Island staff.[22]

Notwithstanding the value and importance of planning for the reintegration of children with their birth families, the Department realised that such planning sometimes had to be done with permanent placement in mind. Long-term fostering or adoption were possibilities when birth families were unable or unwilling to take their children back from foster care. A working party set up in mid-1984 explored the options for such cases, which included open adoptions, making foster parents legal guardians, and dispensing with parental consent for guardianship or adoption where appropriate.[23] The Department was reluctant to push for such measures, particularly when caregivers were unhappy with the prospect. Nor did it support the removal of a child from stable care to a home in which he or she might legally belong. Nevertheless, it espoused an ideology of permanent care, in terms of which children would be assured of continuity, stability and belonging as of right. It recognised that in most cases, that state would be realised in the birth family, whether within whanau, an extended family, or another culturally appropriate grouping.[24] This broad interpretation allowed children such as Rosie, Rhonda and Elizabeth Harper to find some security in their lives. All three had been sexually abused by their father, and the long-term prognosis for their return home was poor. Following a meeting with their whanau, the group decided that the children should go to live with an aunt in Auckland. The children's wish that the Department keep in close contact with them was satisfied through the vesting of interim guardianship in the Department, with plans that their aunt eventually become their guardian. If this turned out well, the Department would negotiate parental access to the children.[25]

While the reformulation of fostering occurred most significantly with respect to Maori children and young persons, the Department also acknowledged the importance of kin groupings for Pacific Island children. In the late 1980s, the So'otaga Programme assisted community groups to re-establish or maintain Samoan children with their aiga. In areas such as Otara, foster placements for Pacific Island and Maori children were little-used from the mid-1980s. The widespread presence of extended families in the immediate area, particularly in the case of Pacific Islanders, made placements with wider families more practicable than they were in other centres.[26] Social workers remember having fewer options when it came to placing Maori children; the shortage of Maori foster homes meant that 'we just had to go where we could'.[27] In the 1940s and 1950s the relatively few Maori children and young people coming into care could be placed with Maori families or passed back to tribal committees; the sheer numbers coming to notice from the 1970s made this impossible, and many had to be placed with Pakeha families.

The Maatua Whangai programme addressed this issue by aiming to reintegrate children into their whanau and iwi. Social workers designated as

Maatua Whangai officers or mokai worked with Maori Affairs staff to find foster homes and arrange and oversee placements. Within a few months of the scheme's inception, many Maori children had been referred to Maatua Whangai officers for placement. In June 1984, Maatua Whangai officers in seven districts had 241 Maori children referred to them for placement or family support.[28] Social workers involved in the programme regarded it as significant for the Maori community: 'It really turned foster care on its head, in terms of a conceptual framework for Maori. . . . To say [that] this should enrich the child, it should be something that young people are able to learn from and wear with pride, it should be a learning, not a degrading, shameful, abusing experience'.[29]

The review of Maatua Whangai in 1985 led to a reduced focus on finding Maori foster parents and placing children, and an increased emphasis on identifying whanau and iwi connections, and developing whakapapa. In 1985, the Department allocated funding to enable young people to be cared for in their own whanau and community after mokai had identified their affiliations. In 1987, the programme moved further in this direction by aiming to ensure that whanau and iwi had the necessary structures in place to enable them to take in children and young people.[30]

The Department had independently recruited more Maori foster parents before the introduction of Maatua Whangai. Social workers met in Rotorua in 1981 to debate the qualities that were needed in foster parents, and a subsequent working party visited marae to discuss the fostering of Maori children. Although they were phased out as Maatua Whangai came on stream, these efforts were important to the development of that scheme. The Department also entered into negotiations with the Orakei Marae Committee to erect a marae family home on the Hoani Waititi Memorial Marae. Zoning difficulties, and the opposition of the Department of Maori Affairs, perhaps on the grounds that this was essentially a Pakeha institution in a Maori setting, led to the abandonment of the proposal after four years of planning.[31]

Although it was ultimately unsuccessful in this attempt, the Department worked with Maatua Whangai officers and the Maori community to develop four family homes as special purpose family homes run by Maori management committees. These whanau support centres based in Auckland and Christchurch provided various services and took in a range of children and young people. Te Rau Marama, in Takapuna, drew extensively on rich community support for the sole foster parent based there, and the home became a centre for Maori and community activities. The establishment of these homes drew little from the principle of transferring resources to the Maori community – they had been classed as surplus to requirements rather than specially designated as whanau homes – but they were, nevertheless, an important development.[32]

In any cultural group, the separation of children from their families could be devastating. Mary Tepu wrote to the Minister of Social Welfare in 1988 expressing extreme anxiety about her young daughter, who had been taken into care after suffering prolonged physical and sexual abuse. Mrs Tepu had seen her daughter only once in the previous year, on Christmas Eve, and she was anguished at the tearing apart of her family.[33] Disrupting the link between children and their birth families had an added significance for Maori, who saw children and whanau as interlinked, with the well-being of one resting on that of the other.

Social workers knew that while children and young people might have problems in their family or whanau, when they were separated from that environment they felt their isolation and sense of family very keenly. Regardless of the quality of foster care, its very existence fractured a vital but fragile emotional tie, causing profound distress which young people sometimes expressed by running away. While aware that it was sometimes necessary to remove a child, the Department signalled its intention of placing greater importance on leaving a child in the birth family group, and working with that group to overcome difficulties. Without this, children were in danger of being deprived of a 'permanent family life' and their 'operative links to their biological families'.[34]

Young people questioned about their impressions of foster care voiced the hurt that fostering sometimes caused. Surveys of children and birth parents during the 1980s indicated that each group wanted to have more contact with the other during the period of care. Brian, a fifteen year old who had had 27 placements and attended nineteen different schools, had seen his birth family only once, and concluded that 'the relationship with my real parents now is zero, big zero'. His continued hope and desire was 'to be treated like one of the foster parents' children. . . . There was never a time when I felt that I was really at home.' Chris, who had entered the Department's care at two years of age along with the rest of his family, had lost all contact with his siblings and whanau. Fostered mainly with Pakeha families, he noted that 'There is a big cultural difference because you lose everything, your culture, and I just lost that and after that it didn't bother me. . . . I didn't really care.'[35]

The Department of Social Welfare only gradually recognised the potential for abuse and maltreatment to occur in foster homes. As has been shown in the previous chapters, child welfare officers had periodically reported on foster homes in which the children had been neglected or abused, or exploited for their labour. Such situations had been regarded as isolated aberrations committed by unsuitable foster parents. Growing awareness from the mid-1970s of the prevalence of abuse and neglect in a range of family and care situations, including departmental residences, made social workers more attuned to the potential for this to occur in foster care as well.

The extent of abuse in care was as difficult to calculate as that in other family situations. Social workers endeavoured to speak to fostered children alone, but most children were reluctant to speak up. One social worker reflected that 'the kids were dead scared to say anything', perhaps overawed by their situation. Some young people interviewed about foster care spoke vaguely of 'unpleasant memories' and of being treated 'unfairly'. A study of 136 young women in residential care in the mid-1980s indicated that 71 per cent of them had been sexually abused, about half after their committal to the Department's care. This survey, the first of its kind undertaken for the Department, was a formative experience for some social workers. 'Some of those young women had been on my caseload or on my team's caseload', one remembered. 'I'll never forget what awful, awful things had happened in our care. . . . Leaving horrible homes only to find themselves in another abusive situation, very often despite the best will in the world. . . . What can you do when you leave a young person in a home? You simply cannot be there for them.'[36]

Social worker Lainey Cowan retained vivid memories, which were still painful for her to relate after more than a decade, of one young woman's experiences in foster care and her life in subsequent years:

> She told me about being fed from rubbish bins . . . forced to eat under the table, being sexually abused in care. Field social workers would come, but never see her alone, so how could she talk? [She spoke] of being admitted to hospital, and the hospital . . . gently saying to Social Welfare, 'There seems to be some malnourishment and maltreatment'. So they moved her, but not to a situation that was any better. . . . She ended up in a Welfare home [in Wellington] hitting the streets, hitting Arohata, and at 25 being an utterly lost young person. . . . Tracking her life gave me a wish not to have too many more lives like that, or too many more people just wanting to die and feeling like there was no one for them anywhere, as all they'd had was a run of social workers and punitive, horrible foster homes.[37]

Foster parents' children experienced their own difficulties and trauma in the fostering relationship. The children of family home foster parents, especially, could feel deprived of parental affection, and resentful that foster children 'got away' with too much, such as breaking their toys or stealing favourite items. Foster parents noted with alarm the damage caused by some foster children. 'People taking on these children wouldn't be so hard to come by as the damage alone that some of them do [makes] you wonder if its all worth while', foster mother Mrs Morrison wrote to Ann Hercus, the Minister of Social Welfare; her husband needed two jobs to pay for the family and the house.[38]

Barnardo's increased its involvement in child and family care during the 1970s, and by the mid-1980s operated 31 family day care schemes and twelve childcare centres, such as this one in Christchurch. CANTERBURY MUSEUM, 15153

Happier tales balanced some of those of negative fostering experiences, both for those being fostered and for the foster families. Surveys of foster care in the 1980s indicated that many fostered young people felt satisfied with their foster families, and vice versa. Children often formed strong emotional bonds with their foster parents, especially if they had been with a family for some years and regarded the foster parents as Mum and Dad. Eru Murphy, who lived in a special purpose family home with his brothers and sisters, wrote warmly of his foster parents, Mr and Mrs Maaka. Being with his siblings was vital; he contrasted the 'true family atmosphere' of the home with his experience of placement in regular foster care, where he had been happy, but lonely without his family around him.[39]

The Department wrote in glowing terms about many foster parents, notably those who took in difficult children. Kuru Walters, who in 1988 was described as one of the most difficult boys in the southern region, lived in a Christchurch family home run by a man who did relief work as a residential social worker and was the only individual who had been able to make 'contact' with Kuru in the five years he had spent at Campbell Park and the year he had been the responsibility of the Department.[40] The Department frequently remarked on foster parents who fostered large numbers of children over many years with little complaint. Clarice Lilly was one of many women who fostered several generations of children, in her case more than 40 of them over 30 years.[41] Takapuna social workers referred to two valued foster mothers as 'The Aunts'. These women ran their home as a temporary and emergency fostering arrangement, taking in young babies, children who came into care at short notice, and those who needed special care. They carried out voluntary social work in Whangaparaoa, acted as emergency babysitters, and provided transport. One local social worker feared 'for the day they feel they need to give up fostering.'[42] Many foster parents lavished much love and care on those they fostered, and the abrupt return of children to their birth families could be devastating. Abigail Marshall, who was distraught when the young girl she had fostered for four years was returned to her birth mother, described the event as a 'depowering experience' that left her 'shocked and upset'.[43]

The Children, Young Persons, and Their Families Act 1989 enunciated a further reformulation of foster care. The primacy of care within the family group and the maintenance of bonds between child and family made untenable the notion of long-term fostering which had characterised foster care since the 1880s. The goal of keeping children within their families and family groups was explicit in the general objects and principles of the legislation. As if to give even greater weight to this emphasis, the term 'foster care' itself did not appear in the Act.

The new legislation clearly placed foster care, or 'out-of-family placements', on the care continuum, on which the first step was to keep the family together while any placement was considered. Placement with the immediate family was to be the first option explored. If this family was unable to offer care, or the child's well-being could be detrimentally affected by remaining within it, wider family group placements would be considered, including with hapu or iwi in the case of Maori children. Placement in a family-like setting, such as foster care or a family home, under approved caregivers living in the same locality as the immediate family, would only be investigated as an option after all kin networks had been explored.

Keeping children within their families or family groups required more intensive work in supporting families, either financially or through the provision of services. From 1989, the Department allocated specific funding to preserving families by offering support and assistance for them to build a safe and nurturing environment; special funding was available to ensure that Maori children could remain with their iwi if their immediate family was unable to maintain them. Families in danger of breaking down and having their children removed could make agreements with the Department under which they would receive support and assistance for three months. These family preservation services, which were renamed family/whanau agreements in mid-1991, could be either financial in nature or structured around social work services, not all of which would be provided by the Department. These services could include family therapy, individual therapy for specific family members, home- or marae-based support, tuition in parenting skills, budgetary advice, and time on a marae.[44]

As an option for families who could not, or would not, care for their children, out-of-family placements took a number of forms. As the Department told foster parents, it was no longer acceptable simply to sign children and young people over to out-of-family care. As with other aspects of the Act, the provision for such care was strictly time-limited, circumscribed, and based on a notion of partnership between foster parents, young people, the family group, and the Department.[45] Both short and longer-term care agreements could be arranged. Families needing respite from difficult or demanding children, or families in emergency situations, could make short-term temporary care agreements for up to 28 days. Ideally, such placements would be with members of the family or family group, but private carers or family homes could be used. Longer agreements would be made only after a family group conference, and only if there were substantial problems in providing care for children in the family situation. Periods of up to six months for children under seven years of age, and up to twelve months for older children could be arranged, but there had to be provision for continuing contact with the child's family.[46] All caregivers had to be assessed and approved by the Department, and there was provision for regular visiting, monitoring and review.

Increasingly, community-based organisations were officially brought into the care process, as voluntary workers, as sources of placements, and as caregivers themselves, with funding available for contracting their services, although this was not always easy to obtain. Some Maori found that the parameters under which funding was approved rested entirely with the Department, and others spoke of their difficulties in discovering the types of funding that were available.[47] As with other welfare practice in the 1990s, the withdrawal of direct government services was followed by a proliferation of non-governmental organisations stepping in to the breach. The use of such organisations reduced the Department's own pool of foster parents, and, to some extent, family homes. Rather than maintaining a list of foster parents, the Department once again sometimes placed advertisements which sought placements for specific children. More frequently, the Department, and later the Children and Young Persons Service, used the out-of-family placement services provided by groups such as Baptist Social Services, the Open Home Foundation, Methodist Social Services, and a wide range of local iwi groups and Maori Trust Boards. These groups provided their own foster parents, with the Department paying the cost of care.[48]

The Act also reassessed the role of family homes, turning them into out-of-family placements when other options were not available. A 1989 review of the homes indicated that many were underutilised now that fewer young people were entering care. The Department closed down and sold several; in 1992 there were 90 homes, compared with 150 a decade earlier. Under the new legislation, however, family homes were still to be utilised for family-based care, even though this was acknowledged to be the second-to-last placement option for children and young people, resorted to only after every other possibility with the exception of residential care had been explored.[49] Like foster care, the homes could be used both for temporary agreements and for longer-term care; their traditional function of providing shelter in emergencies and for difficult or hard-to-place children continued.

The new environment both changed the function of the homes and stipulated that the personnel working in them would be expected to display a commitment to biculturalism and to be highly skilled in working with children and families. Many districts used the family home facilities for new purposes, including as neutral venues in which to hold family group conferences or training programmes. Others passed the premises over to church and community groups; in Christchurch, for example, Methodist Social Services took over one of the homes. Several districts cooperated with community initiatives to enable homes to provide services to entire families by offering re-education in parenting skills or budgeting. Two family homes in Greymouth, for example, took in whole families which were having difficulties with parenting and managing alone, and provided them with instruction in hygiene, housekeeping, food preparation, and working with children. The Kimiora programme in New Plymouth admitted families for twelve days to teach them parenting skills, and followed this up with a three-month programme in the client family's home. Homes in other centres, such as Tokoroa, admitted children and young people for short periods while their families attended training and support programmes.[50] Achieving a 'mixed economy' of welfare, involving families, the community and the state, which had been the focus of so much twentieth-century welfare work, had finally become official policy.

Parents for children: changing adoption practices

Both the number and the form of adoptions changed during the 1970s and 1980s. More tolerant attitudes to single parenthood in the 1970s, and the availability of the domestic purposes benefit from 1973, made it easier for single mothers to keep their babies. More women chose to do this, leading to claims that there was a 'shortage' of babies available for adoption. The number of adoption orders declined, with the Department of Social Welfare involved in less than 1000 in most years during the 1980s. Fewer closed stranger adoptions occurred from the 1970s as more open adoptions became the norm, with birth and adoptive parents knowing about each other, and in some cases meeting and maintaining contact. Some adoptive and birth families met during the last few weeks of a pregnancy, discussing how the baby would be raised, or possible names.[51]

Perhaps in response to the wider emphasis on children's rights, departmental social workers recast adoption practices. They acknowledged that the earlier emphasis had been on meeting the needs of adoptive parents, on finding children for them rather than finding parents or cementing relationships for children in need.[52] A 1983 working party report on the organisation of adoption services

A social worker visits a recently-adopted child and her new mother in the early 1970s. Two decades earlier, such work was the domain of women child welfare officers. NATIONAL PUBLICITY STUDIOS PHOTOGRAPHIC COLLECTION, NATIONAL ARCHIVES, A97166

outlined a new philosophy. It defined the purpose of the Department's adoption service as finding parents for children, not vice versa. Social workers involved in the adoption area remarked on their changed views. Ann Corcoran, who had worked in adoption for 28 years by the mid-1980s, admitted to being embarrassed by earlier attitudes towards adoption, particularly towards birth mothers. Helping birth mothers to find the best home for their child was now considered to be the most appropriate option.[53]

The revision of the focus of adoption services led to marked shifts in practice. The Child Welfare Division had maintained a list of parents who wanted to adopt a child, and contacted the selected parents when an appropriate child came in. Refocusing adoption on finding parents for children made an extensive list of prospective parents redundant. Instead, the Department kept only a short list of couples wanting to adopt, and endeavoured to match these couples to the needs of the children who were available for adoption. In some cases, this could mean selective advertising to find the 'right' couple.[54] The Department increasingly provided a 'total adoption service' that was something like what had been suggested in 1955 when the Child Welfare Division sought to become more closely involved with all aspects of the adoption process. A total service would work intensively both before and after placement, and enable social workers to supervise the children for a period after the final adoption order had been made. Social workers estimated that the new approach required more time to be spent with both adoptive and birth families: ten hours pre-placement work with birth families, 25 hours pre-placement work with adoptive families, twelve hours arranging placements, and twelve hours supervising them. Providing such a service necessitated greater training for social workers, and from the mid-1970s, the Department offered seminars and training programmes for those involved in adoption work.[55]

Focusing on the needs of the children who were available for adoption turned departmental attention to finding permanent homes for those with special needs. Children who were not blond-haired, blue-eyed baby girls had traditionally been harder to place: those who were physically, emotionally or mentally disabled, more than one year old, or of a mixed racial heritage could be well down the list of 'desirable' children. The Department noted that it had 'never much' considered the needs of these children in its earlier attempts to provide adoptive parents with young babies. From the early 1980s, it expended considerable effort in finding permanent homes for children with special needs. In 1981, it established a Special Needs Unit in Auckland with a small group of social workers whose task was to place children already in care. Caseloads of between three and six children allowed social workers to provide intensive training for couples wanting to adopt special needs children. Within three years the unit had provided permanent homes for 28 children, all of whom received follow-up supervision.[56]

From the 1980s the Department of Social Welfare made particular efforts to find homes for special needs children – those with physical, emotional or mental disabilities – who had traditionally been difficult to place for adoption. Here a special needs child celebrates with his new family in 1988.
EVENING POST

During the early 1980s, the Department increased its role in the adoption of Maori children, with which it had had little involvement since the 1960s. An increase in other demands on Maori Affairs officers had led to a request in 1978 that the Department of Social Welfare take a greater role in finding homes for the 200 or so Maori children who were adopted annually. While they were helped by Maori Affairs officers, social workers largely took over the placement of Maori children, which they saw as a further opportunity to find homes for special needs children. The development of Maatua Whangai meant that Social Welfare's renewed role was relatively short-lived, as the Department of Maori Affairs responded to demands that it take a more proactive role in placing Maori children.[57]

The emphasis on addressing the needs of children in making adoption arrangements did not always meet with the approval of couples who were waiting to adopt. The Department's performance in administering adoptions came under fire from prospective adoptive couples unhappy about 'unreasonable' delays in obtaining children. Others believed that the Department was unsympathetic to their situation, and focused too little on their needs. In 1990 the Department appointed a review committee to examine adoption practices throughout the country. Although this committee found that there were regional variations of practice, it repeated the sentiments voiced throughout the 1980s that the Department's role was to meet the needs of children, not to provide a service to childless or infertile couples.[58]

Such couples found it easier and quicker to obtain a baby from overseas than to wait for a New Zealand child, particularly when there was a 'shortage' of babies available for adoption. New Zealand couples had travelled overseas to adopt children in the 1960s and 1970s, or had adopted 'orphans' from Hong Kong, South Vietnam or South America. In the later 1980s New Zealanders travelled to Eastern Europe in the wake of revelations about the conditions endured by babies and children in orphanages in countries such as Romania. As Anne Else noted in 1991, 'now any couple who can find at least $12,000, supply the Romanian authorities with an acceptable "home study" report by a "trained social worker", and locate an available child' would probably have the adoption recognised in New Zealand. Indeed, in July 1990 New Zealand recognised the validity of any adoption orders made in Romania. This situation did not last long, as the Romanian authorities placed a moratorium on international adoptions in June 1991.[59]

A major change to adoption policy and practice occurred with passage of the Adult Adoption Information Act 1985. The legislation enabled adopted people over twenty years of age to have access to their birth certificates, which informed them of their birth mother and sometimes their birth father. Birth mothers could, if they wished, veto access to this information. In recognition of the trauma which could accompany gaining knowledge of birth parents, the legislation also provided for counselling. Before the implementation of the legislation in 1986, social workers, agencies and independent counsellors gained approval to assist those who were seeking out their birth families. As one social worker noted, such counsellors would need to be highly skilled, as many adoptees who inquired about their birth families were likely to be disappointed by the nature of the information that their birth certificates contained.[60]

Within a year of the Act coming into force more than 10,000 people had used it, stretching the Department's resources to the full; by 1989, Anne Else estimates, about a quarter of those who had been adopted between 1944 and 1969 had sought information under the Act.[61] The Act allowed adopted people to piece together their lives, trace their histories, and perhaps gain answers to questions they had long wanted to ask. Jonathan Hunt, who presented the bill in Parliament,

Some New Zealand couples wanting to adopt children travelled to Romania in the 1990s. Two and a half year old Natalina is pictured here in 1990, eight weeks after her New Zealand adoptive mother collected her from a Romanian orphanage. EVENING POST

received many letters from grateful adoptees. 'God Bless you Mr Hunt', wrote one woman, who had been born in 1913 and adopted in the 1920s. Some adoptive families, and particularly adoptive mothers, felt threatened, fearing that they would 'lose' their children. The new rights of adopted people to gain access to their full histories did not impress some adoptive families. '[I] wonder what happened to our "Rights" as adoptive parents – apparently we have none', one woman wrote. Some birth mothers also found the prospect of meeting their children worrying, and feared having to tell their husbands about a pregnancy and adoption that had happened many years before.[62]

The changes in adoption policy and practice occurred independently of the other major changes in the delivery of child welfare services that took place in the late 1980s. The Children, Young Persons, and Their Families Act 1989 made very little mention of adoption, despite the fact that adoption entails the severance of the link with birth families, the maintenance of which is at the core of the legislation.[63] The Department of Social Welfare, and then the Children and Young Persons Service (through its Adoption Information and Services Unit) has maintained a role in adoptions under both the Adoption Act 1955 and the Adult Adoption Information Act 1985: it assesses placements, monitors adoptions made overseas, and facilitates access to information and support for adopted people.

Publicising the private nightmare: the policies and politics of child abuse

'I remembered the first child abuse case I had', recalled a social worker who was based in Auckland from the late 1970s, 'and thinking, "I know this is a big thing, but I don't know anything about it, and where do I find out?"'[64] Rectifying such situations by educating social workers about child abuse, and developing clear policies for dealing with cases, were significant aspects of child abuse work during the next decade and a half.

Interest in child abuse increased from the 1970s, despite the conclusions of a 1972 report which indicated that there was relatively little such abuse in the community. Internationally, child abuse was of growing concern, and New Zealand was influenced by overseas trends and developments, particularly the new emphasis on the rights of children as individuals. Openness to the possibility of child abuse in family situations distinguished the later 1970s from earlier periods, and social workers became more attuned to detecting indications of abuse. Assessing the level of child abuse in the community is always difficult, given that so much of it remains hidden from public view. The Department itself frequently combined figures for child abuse with other care and protection statistics or buried them under the heading of 'miscellaneous cases', the number of which increased dramatically during the 1970s. The number of child abuse and neglect investigations soared in the late 1980s, rising from 2131 in 1987/8 to more than 6500 the following year; in 1992, almost 11,000 notifications of abuse and neglect were recorded.[65]

Professional awareness of child abuse coalesced with a National Symposium on Child Abuse in Dunedin in 1979. This led to the formation of the National Advisory Committee for the Prevention of Child Abuse (NACPCA), which became fully operational in early 1981.[66] Chaired by David Geddis of the Plunket Society, and with representatives from the Department of Social Welfare and other agencies, the Advisory Committee was the most significant and influential group advising on child abuse policies until its disbandment in late 1989. It liaised very closely with the Department, although the relationship was not always amicable. The NACPCA was formed at a time when the media was picking up abuse stories, and the Committee itself generated further interest. The International Year of the Child in 1979, and its resulting committee, and the 1980 Telethon appeal for children also kept the issues of children's rights prominent.

He let me drive the car
but he was touching my private parts
and I guess and knew he went too far
at night he'd come to my bedside
then he'd whisper "Open Wide"
I used to do what I was told
even though I knew it was wrong.
I was so afraid to say no
because he was very strong,
this thing kept going on
for several years or so,
as I think about it now
I could sit and cry aloud
I feel so low
down humiliated and abused.
How was I to know
that it was wrong
he was older and
should have known better
but I guess it does take two to tango.

This poem, written by Kelly, who was raped by her uncle and adoptive father at the age of nine and committed for psychiatric treatment at thirteen, offers a glimpse into the pain and guilt lived by victims of child abuse. DEPARTMENT OF SOCIAL WELFARE

Newspapers carried stories of child abuse cases, and did much to raise public awareness. In early 1981, for example, Whangarei's *Northern Advocate* published reports on abuse cases which were accompanied by graphic photographs of abused children. These created considerable local interest and caused several people to call on voluntary agencies for advice. The newspaper had initially intended to run the stories on its women's pages, but instead announced them on the front page and included them in the news and features sections.[67]

Community groups and government agencies developed programmes to combat child abuse and referred cases to the Department of Social Welfare for action. 'Stranger danger' messages circulated to schoolchildren warned them of potentially dangerous situations. The recognition that child abuse was an aspect of family violence, and nearly always occurred within a family situation where the abuser was known to the child, led to a shift of emphasis to the broader notion of 'keeping safe'. Joint Police and Department of Education 'Keeping Ourselves Safe' programmes, which targeted primary schoolchildren, discussed which adult behaviours were appropriate and which were inappropriate, whatever the situation. The Family Violence Prevention Co-ordinating Committee, which was established in 1986, brought government and community family violence prevention schemes together under the umbrella of the Department of Social Welfare. In mid-1988, Michael Cullen, the Minister of Social Welfare, announced extensive funding for community initiatives to implement child abuse awareness programmes as part of the Department's broader efforts to increase community participation in welfare matters. The three-year funding programme enabled regions to appoint child abuse education advisors, provided funding to the New Zealand Child Abuse Prevention Society, and offered specific

The 1979 International Year of the Child aroused a range of responses. ERIC HEATH CARTOON, ATL, D-P144165-B

" WADJA MEAN DISCIPLINE EM ?— THIS IS THE YEAR OF THE CHILD! "

assistance to community and bicultural programmes, 26 of which had been established by late 1989.[68]

The sexual abuse of children came to public attention from the early 1980s. Quoting North American figures which estimated that one in ten boys and one in four girls had been sexually abused by the time they were fifteen years old, researchers suggested that New Zealand's levels were similar. The Otago Women's Health Survey, published in 1991, indicated that 20 per cent of the women questioned had been victims of sexual abuse in their youth. This 'last of the major social ills to come out of the national closet' quickly became the subject of both departmental and public attention.[69] In early 1986, the government appointed a committee, under the guidance of the NACPCA, to review sexual abuse and formulate recommendations for action. The committee's report, released in late 1988, stressed the importance of taking a multi-disciplinary team approach to working with sexual abuse cases, and emphasised the need for offender accountability and family reintegration.[70]

Research in residential institutions suggested that there was a very high incidence of sexual abuse among the girls and young women who were taken into care. The Principal of the girls' home at Allendale estimated in 1984 that four out of five girls she admitted had been sexually abused, and in the following year, a counsellor at Kingslea gave a similar estimate of between 75 and 80 per cent of admissions. Departmental research on a sample of fifteen year old girls in care which was released in 1987 indicated that 71 per cent of admissions had been sexually abused, either before entering care or under the Department's jurisdiction in foster homes, family homes, or institutions.[71] In 1984, after two years of negotiations with women in the community, Auckland social workers presented the Department with a proposal to establish a residential facility for sexually abused women and young girls. The facility would be a departmentally-funded, women-only space based on the principles of aroha and belief in the testimony of the young residents, and accountable to a collective of community representatives. By the time the facility became operational, residential care was 'on the way out', in the words of one of the home's advocates, and the residence was to have only a short life.[72] Social workers instead worked in special sexual abuse teams. Auckland's team combined staff from the Auckland district office with local police and members of the voluntary HELP foundation, and another team began work from the Hamilton Girls' Home in 1986.[73]

During the 1980s, the British and North American multi-disciplinary team approach to overcoming child abuse gained widespread currency in New Zealand. Multi-disciplinary teams, often known as child protection teams, combined the skills of police, social workers, medical professionals, social workers and lawyers to give expert advice to case workers. The Paediatric

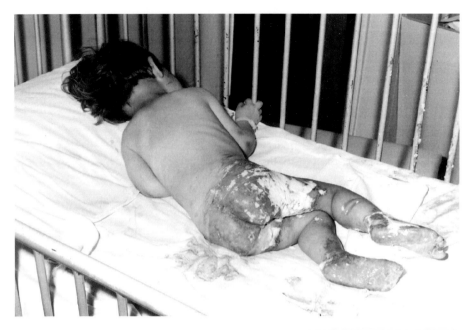

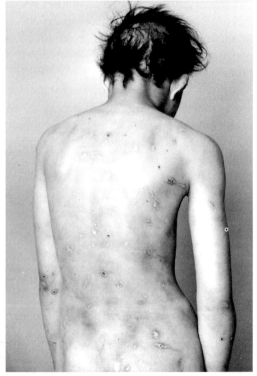

Images of child abuse began appearing in newspapers from the early 1980s. They ranged from graphic photographs from police files (above and right) to the quiet menace of more stylised impressions (opposite).
NEW ZEALAND POLICE &
EVENING POST

Department of the Dunedin Public Hospital began such work in 1975, with medical staff and representatives from the Police and the Department of Social Welfare advising on cases which came to notice.[74] Within a few years of the establishment of this and other teams, the Department of Social Welfare implemented a new policy on child abuse. In conjunction with other government agencies, it formulated in 1978 preparatory guidelines for the processing of child abuse cases, and then established a pilot multi-disciplinary child abuse project to trial the guidelines and assemble a register of abuse cases. Based in Hamilton, the trial project began in early 1980, drawing together a departmental social worker, police, paediatricians and representatives of voluntary groups. By the end of its first year, the team had worked on 53 cases referred from other groups, half of them concerning children younger than five years of age. A lack of publicity meant that many groups and medical practitioners did not refer cases, and the project had a strained relationship with some voluntary agencies.[75]

The Hamilton team was the first child abuse team to which the Department provided a social worker and funding. While other teams worked without such services, the Department's social workers were assisting more than 30 teams by the late 1980s. By 1987, there were five fully resourced teams, based in Otara,

South Auckland, Hamilton, Christchurch and Dunedin. The South Auckland team received 67 referrals in its first six months of operation, in contrast with 45 in Dunedin and 53 in Hamilton over their first year. The large number of cases referred to the South Auckland team led to its split, with a team formed specifically for Otara in early 1985 – this received 101 referrals in its first year. The teams functioned in different ways. Some, such as the South Auckland team based at Otara, involved the child's family as far as possible. Teams in Panmure and Lower Hutt in the later 1980s developed a system of strongly family-based decision-making in working with the family and kin group to resolve care and protection issues. This 'child-focused but family-based' operation was a blueprint for the Department's adoption of this principle in care and protection matters.[76]

Advocates of the multi-disciplinary approach pointed to the deaths of abused children who had been left to drift by uncoordinated professional efforts. The Department concluded that its procedures needed to be improved after the death of three year old Maggie Pulakula in Taumarunui in 1984. Social workers had liaised with the local Plunket nurse, but they had acted largely in isolation, without legal advice and without arranging for full medical treatment, particularly X-rays, to check for signs of abuse.[77] The multi-disciplinary approach could ensure that there was a coordinated system of working with child abuse, but the teams had varying success in implementing this. 'In my view', stated Mary Todd, who oversaw the establishment of some of the teams, 'considerable strides were made. . . . It increased communication, it increased knowledge, it increased the depth of thinking, it shared the problem'. But as Anne Caton, a member of the South Auckland team, recalled, the quality of the work so often depended on the quality and commitment of its members, and their willingness to work together. Her team 'had the pick of Auckland [professionals]. . . . We had the most wonderful team of people. . . . who just knew their stuff'.[78]

Disputes, sometimes serious, emerged between team members, between the Department and its social workers, between the teams and other social workers, and between members and other agencies. The multi-disciplinary environment accentuated inter-agency differences, and perhaps difficulties inherent in child abuse work also intensified problems. A report from the South Auckland child protection team in 1986 referred to tension between the team and the Department, and suggested that despite its stated commitment, the latter was unwilling to work in a team environment and seek the advice of other professionals. Social workers from the Hamilton team reported a periodic lack of cooperation from some groups, with agencies such as Parentline referring very few cases. A number of groups and individuals believed that the Department should play no or little part in the teams, citing its alleged ineffectiveness in taking action on the problem. Indeed, the very establishment of a multi-

Sexual abuse counsellors and social workers used anatomically-correct dolls to help suspected child abuse victims explain what had happened to them.
EVENING POST

disciplinary model with its origins in medical practice rested on a belief that social workers were unable to cope with such cases because of either too much work or too little experience. With a degree of foresight, one social worker suggested that child abuse was becoming a political football to be kicked around between agencies, and that in the end, the abused child would be the loser.[79]

Recognition of the warning signs of child abuse was dependent on clear indications of what constituted abuse. Defining abuse, and noting its presenting signs, were not easy matters. The question of establishing what abuse was, and knowing when to take action to prevent its escalation, recurred from the late 1970s and continued to be asked through to the 1990s as both the NACPCA and the Department developed practice guidelines to assist social workers and multi-disciplinary teams. In 1978 an officials committee defined abuse as non-accidental injury or serious neglect of an emotional or physical nature, and ruled that cases should be referred to child abuse teams only if abuse was proven or at least strongly suspected. Within two years, the committee refined its definition to apply to children and young people who were subject to obvious physical injury, sexual abuse, emotional impairment or extensive neglect. In practice, detecting 'obvious' abuse was difficult, given that so much was not obvious, as social workers found when trying to implement the committee's guidelines; the Hamilton child abuse project quickly amended the criterion to 'suspected' abuse.[80]

The NACPCA also prepared guidelines for social workers and multi-disciplinary teams. During 1986, the Committee convened working parties to establish guidelines for investigating and managing sexual abuse cases. Based largely on the practice of the Dunedin child protection team, these were released in October 1986. Some social workers found the guidelines useful, but they needed adaptation to take into account the varied facilities available in specific areas.[81] The Committee's proposals for cooperation between police and social workers emphasised the need for training for all staff that would enable them to recognise the signs of abuse and respond appropriately, with due regard for the cultural and family circumstances of all concerned.[82] Police and the Department focused first on the training aspects of the guidelines, arguing that providing adequate staff training was the crucial first step in working with abuse. Sporadic in-house and specialist training was carried out over the next two years, and in mid-1988 the Department agreed to adopt the guidelines. Issued in late 1988, these included a new focus on strengthening the ability of families to keep children safe by using family/whanau decision-making processes whenever possible.[83]

The question of whether there should be mandatory reporting of suspected child abuse proved to be the most vexed aspect of child abuse policy, with firm opinions expressed by professionals and voluntary groups alike. When Lewis Anderson first raised the idea of mandatory reporting in the 1960s, there was loud opposition from medical practitioners. The idea gained currency during the 1970s, and was taken up by the NACPCA, the Department of Social Welfare and other agencies in the 1980s.

Submissions on the child abuse policies contained in the draft bills and working party reports of the mid-1980s offered mixed views about the merits of mandatory reporting, and raised serious questions about the extent of government involvement in family life, and the power of professionals. The supporters of mandatory reporting outlined its advantages. Its adoption would be a clear and unequivocal statement that abuse was unacceptable, and make explicit the government's duty to protect children. Reporting all cases to the Department of Social Welfare would centralise notifications and ensure that people knew whom to contact about abuse. The requirement to report abuse would also remove any uncertainty people might have about whether or not they should do so. Mary Todd, a member of the team which drafted the 1986 proposals, noted that 'there are difficulties with mandatory reporting, where . . .

you get a great upsurge in numbers, therefore you have to have the resources to really handle that. . . . But my argument was always, "So what?" If it in fact eases or facilitates . . . the means whereby people feel they can bring cases to notice, then get on and do it!'[84]

Those who argued against mandatory reporting presented an equally compelling list of disadvantages. Citing international examples, some noted that mandatory reporting did not assist people in deciding what constituted abuse, and that rather than ending the dilemma of whether or not to report, it made more potent the problem of determining whether abuse had occurred. Compulsion to report could engender a community climate of suspicion, or an increase in malicious reporting which could reduce the services available to genuine cases. The centralisation of notification was questionable, too, at a time when the Department was broadening the base of its delivery of welfare. Mandatory reporting could disempower communities by removing the filtering processes which they and professionals went through in trying to determine whether or not abuse had occurred. Some saw mandatory reporting as an intrusion on family rights, and predicted dire consequences if it were enacted. 'Parents must be free to bring up, to teach and to chastise their children in accordance with God-given principles and not at the dictate of the State', one correspondent informed the Minister of Social Welfare; 'high moral standards' were all that was needed, another suggested, noting that mandatory reporting would turn New Zealand into a 'totalitarian State', comparable only to Nazi Germany with its protective custody and selective breeding programmes. The Royal New Zealand Council of General Practitioners noted astutely that the presence of child abuse revealed broader problems which involved the entire family unit, and that mandatory reporting would make it more difficult to work with the whole family. The breaching of confidentiality and the rupturing of the doctor/patient relationship would be other negative consequences of the introduction of mandatory reporting.[85]

Transforming the guidelines, the recommendations on mandatory reporting, and the multi-disciplinary team approach into legislation became an important issue from the mid-1980s. In 1983, David Geddis of the NACPCA and the Auckland academic and lawyer Pauline Tapp drew up a Child Protection Bill which codified the policy and practice that had guided some of the child protection teams over the previous few years. The bill provided for mandatory reporting, the establishment of multi-disciplinary child protection teams in all districts, and for time-limited interventions into family life that would not be more harmful than was the abusive situation. Parents would be notified as soon as a report was received, they would be entitled to be represented at any case conference, and the child would be separated from the family only if she or he had been or was likely to be harmed. Parents would have a right to continued contact with a child who had been removed unless this was specifically prohibited by a court order. The Department took up many of these points in drafting its own legislative revisions from 1984, with the 1986 draft Children and Young Persons Bill providing for mandatory reporting, child protection teams, and professionally-based screening panels which would decide on plans of action.[86]

The need for thorough guidelines and adequate social work training was dramatically illustrated in 1987, when a two year old South Auckland girl died as a result of injuries inflicted by her mother, even though both the child and her family were under the supervision of a network of departmental social workers and other agencies. A departmental inquiry uncovered practice shortcomings: there had been insufficient supervision of staff and decisions, and too many different staff working on the case who had failed to communicate with each other. In all, the Department had not taken the primary responsibility for ensuring that the child's case had been fully assessed.[87]

The implications for child abuse policies led the Department to commission an independent review to inquire into both this case and the adequacy of child protection measures more generally. Its report, 'Dangerous Situations', which was released in early 1988, outlined a causal web linking inappropriate front-line social work decisions with inadequate back-up and support and the lack of training of the social work professionals involved. Rather than cooperating with external agencies and the extended family, the Department did not trust the abilities of other professionals and community groups. Its responses to the extended family showed that it had not acted in a culturally sensitive manner, despite the departmental commitment to *Puao-te-Ata-Tu*. Because the case had been interpreted through the medical model of child abuse, in terms of which the perpetrator was considered to be sick and in need of treatment, attention had been deflected from the child, who had been left at considerable risk. The review team recognised that the events had occurred within a wider context of departmental change. Like all staff in 1987, child protection workers were uncertain of their status as the Department restructured and refocused its work. The report recommended several solutions: an extensive review of the training and supervision of social workers; the development of partnerships with community and other professional agencies; better policies and practices on appropriate cultural methods of working; improved monitoring of staff; the recognition of multi-disciplinary practices in legislation. The review also urged the Department to incorporate in child abuse work the slogan, 'The child must be made safe, now', and to develop mechanisms that would allow this to happen.[88]

Both the case and the findings of the review had significant ramifications for child abuse policy, and created widespread consternation in the Department, particularly among the staff most closely associated with the case, who felt that their integrity was in question.[89] Within days of receiving the report, the Minister of Social Welfare, Michael Cullen, announced a substantial increase in government funding for child abuse prevention and protection. The Department accepted most of the report's recommendations, arranging for better and more intensive training of social workers, greater consultation with Maori and Pacific Island groups, and the appointment of more Maori and Pacific Island staff. It accepted the criticisms of the medical model of approaching child abuse, and agreed with the team's recommendation to use situational analysis and review the entire family situation. It acknowledged the importance of the philosophy of 'making the child safe, now', and agreed to incorporate this concept in all training and manuals. In practice, the social workers who developed new child abuse policies modified the slogan to take account of the practicalities that front-line staff faced, and to ameliorate potentially harmful interventions into family life. Rather than stating that 'The child must be made safe, now', policies and guidelines issued from the later 1980s encouraged social workers to ask the question, 'Is the child safe now?', and proceed from there.[90]

By the time that 'Dangerous Situations' came out, the Department had already reconsidered its position on two of the policies which had underpinned its child abuse work for most of the 1980s. The 'Review of the Children and Young Persons Bill' which was released in December 1987 substantially recast the 1986 proposals after extensive consultation and a major reconsideration of policies. Taking on board concerns about the monocultural nature of the earlier bill and its over-emphasis on the role of professionals, the review team recommended that the strong decision-making role that had been envisaged for child protection teams be reduced to that of giving advice, and not embodied in the legislation. It recommended dropping the proposal for mandatory reporting, concluding that its introduction would not improve the well-being of children, and could, in fact, be detrimental to it. Overseas examples of mandatory reporting, the working party claimed, showed that it led to an over-reporting of 'grey areas', cases where abuse may or may not have occurred; already stretched social services would only be extended further. More significantly, families would be afraid to seek medical treatment for injured children if they knew that agencies would automatically report suspected cases of abuse. The working party favoured greater education about child abuse, and voluntary reporting, with protection for those who made the notification. The Department supported both recommendations, and mandatory reporting and child protection teams both disappeared from the final draft which became the Children, Young Persons, and Their Families Act 1989.[91]

Some groups and individuals were dismayed by this decision. The National Council of Women and the Maori Women's Welfare League stressed the need for mandatory reporting and child protection teams, and urged the Department to reconsider its stance and prepare new legislation. Police argued that the victims of abuse were often too young to tell of their suffering, and that in such circumstances, mandatory reporting was invaluable.[92] Social workers who had long advocated the deleted provisions felt that the Department had gone back on its policies. '[The Department] did an about face on all issues in the end, it did an about face essentially on multi-disciplinary child protection teams, and it did an about face on mandatory reporting', claimed Mary Todd, who had supported both provisions during the 1980s.[93] Others welcomed the decisions not to introduce mandatory reporting and to reduce the professional focus of the teams involved in child protection work. Various child protection teams had already diluted the involvement of professionals by including families in case conferences. The submissions that had been received from social workers on mandatory reporting, the professional focus of some child protection teams, and proposals for screening and resolution panels during the mid-1980s showed that front-line staff held various opinions on these issues.[94]

The Department's position on mandatory reporting and child protection teams should be read within the wider context of policies to ensure the integrity of the family group. During the 1970s and the early 1980s, child abuse policies and practices were structured by the philosophy of children's rights. These rights were exemplified in the 'paramountcy principle', which held that the welfare of the child should be both the first and the paramount consideration when decisions about a child's well-being were being made. The Children and Young Persons Act 1974 had signalled the adoption of this principle, and amending legislation in 1983 had taken it further by emphasising the child's right to a regular and permanent family life. A growing awareness that adherence to this principle could actually disrupt family ties led to its gradual modification. As in other areas of welfare policy, due consideration was now to be given to the relative harm that could be caused if a child was removed from a family situation. The 1986 draft legislation embodied a balance between the rights of the child and the rights of the child in the family group.[95] For many, though, the 1986 proposals had swung too far in the direction of children's rights and the role of professionals, and isolated children within their family networks. Claims of monoculturalism and a lack of faith in the ability of families to make their own decisions drove the process of legislative revision after 1986. Extensive consultation with Maori and Pacific Island groups led to a new 'crystallisation' of the paramountcy principle which identified child and family as linked; the interests of one could not be considered without reference to the other.[96]

The conclusions and recommendations of the 1987 working party posed a major challenge to the paramountcy principle. The working party's report argued that adherence to this principle demonstrated insensitivity to Maori and Pacific Island conceptions of family well-being. Even though other reports, such as *Puao-te-Ata-Tu,* had noted that it was the practice, rather than the principle itself, that was problematic, the working party concluded that there should be a presumption in favour of the family and whanau. Only when these groups were unable to ensure the well-being of their members should thought be given to finding solutions outside that context.[97] While some in the community expressed anxiety about this shift in interpretation, the Department of Social Welfare supported the new direction that was eventually spelt out in the Children, Young Persons, and Their Families Act 1989. As departmental staff note, however, the shift in favour of family integrity did not necessarily imply a minimisation of children's welfare, but could enhance this by working with children through their family structures.[98] Changing approaches to overcoming and dealing with child abuse were contained within the broader issues of empowering families and reducing the extent of official intervention in family life.

The thrust of child abuse policies and practices since 1989 has been to provide families and communities with the skills to identify abuse, and then to deal with it in ways which ensure that the child is safe and which keep the ruptures to normal family and community life to the minimum level necessary. In practice, this has meant working with families to overcome and amend abusive situations, providing funding for child abuse education programmes, and offering information and access to counselling services. Upon being notified of suspected child abuse, social workers are required to investigate after consulting with their local care and protection resource panel. The members of panels are nominated by the Department of Social Welfare from lists compiled by community and professional groups. Ideally, the panels were to include both lay and professional members, and Maori, Pacific Islanders and Pakeha; in practice, they have been community-based, with only sporadic professional representation. The legislation required social workers, or police if they had been notified of abuse, to consult with all panel members, either separately or as a panel, before deciding on any plan of investigation. Social workers and police could still obtain place of safety warrants to remove children if they had reasonable grounds for suspecting that their well-being or safety was being impaired by remaining at home.

Busy social workers have not always found the requirement to consult to be practical, particularly between 1989 and 1992 when the number of notifications of child abuse increased dramatically – and without mandatory reporting – to more than 10,000 in 1992, approximately five times as many as five years earlier.[99] Consultation is time-consuming, and the practical barriers to getting the members of a panel together deterred some social workers from fulfilling all the consultative requirements. A 1992 report by the Office of the Commissioner for

Children on the operation of the panels expressed sympathy for social workers, noting the 'major challenge' which consulting on all cases presented. Panel members were also aware of the difficulties that faced busy social workers. In 1991, a member of a Porirua panel resigned, claiming that it was 'wrong-headed' to require front-line social workers to consult before proceeding with an investigation.[100]

Sometimes, however, social workers did not consult because they had little faith in the panel process. A review of district office services in the South Island in early 1991 revealed that, 'without exception', every social work team recommended that the panels be dispensed with, regarding them as an expensive option which hindered their work. Some social work teams believed that panel members needed more awareness of the legislation and of child abuse work to function better. Panel members could accept this, but also knew that at times they were merely rubber-stamping social workers' decisions. The 1992 review of the legislation identified wide variations in practice around the country, ranging from social workers who stated that 'Resource Panels play a full part in our casework management programme' to those who baldly asserted that 'we do not need anybody from outside keeping an eye on us'.[101]

In late 1991, the Department described panels as an 'undeveloped area' which would need considerably more proactive development to function properly. Budgetary constraints which hampered the work of the panels, compromising 'vital aspects' of the care and protection process, had a major effect on their operation. The Takapuna panel had been compelled to restrict the hours and number of its meetings, potentially limiting its functions.[102] Although the legislation entitled panels to undertake funded community education and preventive work, cutbacks across the Department meant that not all could actually do this. By 1992 some panels had published pamphlets and begun education programmes in schools and the community, but most had not been able to do so.

Family group conferences for child abuse cases functioned more smoothly than did the care and protection resource panels. Social workers who identified children in need of care and protection were required to pass the case over to a care and protection coordinator who, in turn, convened a family group conference to formulate a course of action. Families had the same range of options open to them as they did with other care and protection issues; these included agreements that the child would be placed in the care of the extended family for a period, or receive intensive counselling or other assistance.

An evaluation of care and protection family group conferences in 1991 indicated that there had been teething problems as social workers and families adjusted to the new ways of working. Coordinators noted that abuse, and sexual abuse in particular, could be a very difficult issue to work through in a family group conference setting. The attendance at the conference of both the child victim and the adult offender posed powerful challenges for all. One coordinator believed that the subject of sexual abuse was difficult to approach when the family was unsupportive of or blamed the child. 'All too often', and across all cultures, families protected their men to the detriment of the women and children, some coordinators claimed.[103]

The legislative review team focused on this aspect of care and protection work, particularly as it related to working with child abuse. The review cited family group conferences in which, it believed, the interests of parents had overridden those of the child. The team asserted that social workers refused to acknowledge that there was any potential conflict between parents and children in care and protection matters. The risk that children could suffer when social workers acted to support the integrity of the family rather than the well-being of the child led the team to state emphatically that 'never before in New Zealand child protection legislation has the need been greater for a strong statement in support of the interests of children and young persons.'[104] Here the review team identified the fundamental tension in late twentieth-century child protection work: the location of children's rights within the sphere of family integrity. Balancing these issues has been a challenge in New Zealand, as it has elsewhere, and one which has exposed the ongoing issues involved in working to ensure that both children and families are protected.[105]

On the whole, however, family group conferences have allowed families to talk through their problems and seek ways of safeguarding the rights of children, with the professionals working in the background. The availability of funding for groups, such as the more than $500,000 provided to Parentline in 1990/1, has led to the creation of a greater range and number of community programmes on which social workers and families can draw. Family focus programmes, schemes with Maori and Pacific Island families, and projects to build parenting skills have all been developed thanks to this and other funding.[106]

Public interest in child and sexual abuse has remained high in spite of a backlash against allegations of abuse from the late 1980s. Despite evidence that 'hundreds' of children were abused for every man who was falsely accused, the few cases of incorrect allegations generated widespread interest.[107] The English 'Cleveland Affair' of 1987/8 in which social workers and child abuse workers incorrectly accused parents of child abuse had repercussions in New Zealand. A number of correspondents to the Department based their opposition to mandatory reporting on the risk of incorrect allegations being made, and cited the Cleveland affair as proof of what could go wrong. A local version of the English Parents Against Injustice (PAIN) claimed to have 130 members by the end

The backlash against sexual abuse allegations. TOM SCOTT

of 1989. Founded by a man who maintained he had been incorrectly accused of the sexual abuse of his de facto wife's daughter, PAIN demanded a ministerial inquiry into New Zealand's 'sexual abuse industry'.[108]

'False allegations' gained more exposure in 1989 when Michael Cullen, the Minister of Social Welfare, ordered an independent review of the case of a man who stated that his family had fallen apart after departmental social workers wrongly accused him of sexual abuse. Ken Mason's report acknowledged that the social workers had acted in ways that had not been justified by the evidence before them, and recommended that the Department make an apology to the man concerned and pay his court and other costs.[109] Such instances exemplified the dilemmas and ethical issues inherent in child abuse work, problems which the improved training of social workers could only ever partially remedy. Identifying cases of abuse was always difficult, and doing so exposed complex power relationships in families and family groups. The evidential basis for abuse so often rests on the word of the child at the centre of the inquiry. Witnesses to sexual abuse are rare or, if they are the mother of the child, can themselves be too traumatised by violence to come forward. Some commentators believed that social workers removed children from families unnecessarily or too quickly, or that they failed to consult adequately with family and community support networks; others argued that social workers were too slow to take action, and that abuse had escalated and children died as a consequence. The 'backlash' against abuse investigations occurred within the broader context of a reassessment of the role of professionals; child abuse investigations were caught up with late-1980s' critiques of the sometimes intrusive role of professionals in family life.[110]

The rising level of notifications and investigations since the late 1980s indicates that child abuse remains a frequent occurrence in the community, and also that communities and families have been increasingly willing to report cases. Well-publicised and distressing cases have kept child abuse to the fore: that of three year old Delcelia Witika, who lived amidst a 'rising tide of unimaginable violence', and was sexually abused and beaten to death by her mother's de facto husband in 1991; the inquiry into the alleged sexual abuse of children at and the role and function of Christchurch Hospital's Ward 24 in 1989; the Christchurch Civic Creche case in 1992/3.[111] Social workers have not always felt fully supported in their work, and their discontent has kept child abuse services to the forefront within the Department as well. Meetings in various centres in late 1991 discussed

By the early 1990s, the Department of Social Welfare's handling of child abuse cases had come under the public spotlight. MALCOLM WALKER CARTOON, ATL, D-P024001-H

the hard work that was put in by social workers in what they saw as an unstable organisational environment which provided them with little professional supervision or support.[112]

Questions surrounding child safety, making the welfare of the child paramount, and the mandatory reporting of child abuse also remained current issues. In the early 1990s the Department was accused of leaving children in abusive situations rather than removing them for their own safety.[113] Explaining to the Minister of Social Welfare why one young girl had been allowed to remain with her father, who had been imprisoned for sexual abuse, Robin Wilson, the Deputy Director-General of Social Welfare, noted that staff needed to find a balance between being responsible to all parties and considering the potential harm that could come from any actions. The challenge of the legislation was for social workers to 'work creatively with the tension between these two critical needs'. In the case at the centre of the episode, social workers were uncertain about the girl's father: 'I instinctively do not trust him and neither does my fellow social worker', one reported. They had, however, set up mechanisms to monitor the welfare of the girl, and assisted her mother to keep her daughter in her own home rather than send her to her father. In this case, as in all others, Wilson suggested, the 'absolute protection' of a child was not practicable: emphasising the paramount importance of the welfare of the child 'does not mean that children will be saved from physical harm at all costs. This is too narrow a view of children's needs, and has been found to carry too high a cost.'[114]

The legislative review team, which was concerned by what it interpreted as the minimisation of children's rights by social workers in favour of maintaining family integrity, recommended the reinstatement of the principle that the rights of the child were paramount as a primary means of securing children's safety and safeguarding their rights. According to some departmental staff, 'the professional lobby who didn't like the Children, Young Persons, and Their Families Act actually focused their opposition around the loss of this word paramountcy'. Although social work staff argued that the notion of paramountcy was inherent in the legislation, the Department agreed to an amendment in 1994 which reinserted the word itself. Where the original Act stipulated that 'the welfare and interests of the child or young person shall be the deciding factor' in administering the legislation, the 1994 Amendment Act was more specific: 'In all matters relating to the administration . . . of this Act . . . the welfare and interests of the child or young person shall be the first and paramount consideration'.[115]

The legislative review team also expressed grave concern at the growth in the number of child abuse investigations. Many of the submissions to the review had called for the introduction of mandatory reporting. While acknowledging that this was an 'emotionally charged' issue which could cause difficulties in respect to professional confidentiality, the review team nevertheless recommended its introduction. Even though mandatory reporting could intrude upon the rights of the family – and 'the privacy of the family should be intruded upon only as a last resort' – the team concluded that in cases where children's lives were at stake, such an intrusion was a 'small price to pay'. David Geddis starkly presented his view of the alternative: 'the reality is that without intervention some children will be killed or severely harmed and it is hard to see how a family has "won" if through "keeping" the child they subsequently have to face the desolate situation arising from having killed a child'.[116]

The Department did not agree to the introduction of mandatory reporting, noting that further consultation on the subject was required. Financial considerations, which had not been the main factor in the decision to drop proposals for mandatory reporting in 1988, now loomed larger in view of the new funding systems and tight budgetary constraints under which the Department worked. Its attitude towards mandatory reporting left the review team with the 'impression' that policy-makers were more concerned about 'scarce resources' and workloads than about investigating cases.[117]

Treasury-driven budgetary constraints certainly played their part, as the Department had to adhere to the Public Finance Act 1989 as well as working to maintain children's welfare. 'Funding is so tied to the Act,' stated Robin Wilson, the first General Manager of the Children and Young Persons Service. 'I'll say this, and I don't know that anyone will actually believe it, but I swear to you it's true: that the Treasury actually suggested to us, because we couldn't manage with our budget, that we should actually do fewer child abuse investigations . . . that's just unbelievable!' Social workers sometimes conducted investigations for which they had not received funding. 'We were unable to set those sort of priorities', Wilson continued, 'and so people just kept on doing them without the funding'.[118]

Social workers have always experienced difficulty in striking a balance between children's well-being and the integrity of the family, in deciding when to take action and when to step back and leave the family to devise its own solutions. Cases such as the death of Craig Manukau in 1992 have underlined the challenges and tragedies of working in the difficult area of child abuse. 'To be a social worker with the Children and Young Persons Service is a daunting task', the Commissioner for Children concluded after reviewing the handling of this case. This is a comment that could apply to all aspects of social work with children and young people: 'There always will be . . . death, despair and pain until society changes, and [social workers are] hard-pushed to be involved in changing society.'[119]

Conclusion

In 1996, the New Zealand Children and Young Persons Service took one further symbolic step in its journey towards a child-focused, family-centred mode of welfare provision for children and young people: it became the Children, Young Persons, and Their Families Service, thereby completing the philosophical shift that had been captured in the 1989 legislation. In its brief existence, the Service has faced considerable challenges in providing welfare services for children and young people.

Physical and sexual abuse, neglect and behavioural difficulties still form part of the lives of many children and young people, and more notifications are made every year. Offending, sometimes in ways that are more violent than they were in the past, brings young people into contact with youth justice services. The rising level of youth suicide poses a new and disturbing problem to be understood and countered. These issues have continued to be dealt with through family and community processes working in conjunction with social workers and coordinators. The ongoing political reassessment of the place of government in all welfare provision, and the withdrawal of government agencies from the central decision-making role in the area of children's welfare, have opened the door to more community-based initiatives across the spectrum of welfare provision. Families now take a more dominant role in decisions about their children's welfare than they did in the past; both they and policy-makers advocate family-based care and community responsibility for children's welfare.

Difficulties in achieving and maintaining child-focused, family-centred philosophy and practice persist, often in a climate of tight financial discipline and close community attention. The Service sometimes struggles to provide residential beds for young people in communities which demand protection, but do not want a local residential facility. The deaths of children who were under the supervision of the Service have exposed the abiding dilemmas in child protection work, but also pointed to enduring problems in implementing the spirit and the principles of the 1989 legislation. Training and staff competencies programmes, which were begun in earnest in 1992, have fallen behind schedule. Biculturalism and culturally appropriate ways of working with children and their family networks are ideals but not always realities, as the Service has been slow to fund iwi authorities as social service providers. These issues have been intensified in, and contributed to, an organisation which has experienced cycles of review, restructuring, and reform.[1]

Balancing the roles of the government, communities and families has become more difficult in the 1990s. Putting into practice the philosophy of the government passing greater power and responsibility to communities and families has sometimes been hampered by a lack of community and family resources. Community and iwi groups have not always felt integrated into the new modes of working, and sometimes find funding difficult to obtain; many families find themselves without the resources to cope adequately with the central role in children's welfare that is now accorded them. Serious budgetary constraints, and potential conflict between the provisions of the Public Finance Act and the Children, Young Persons, and Their Families Act are very real issues within the government agencies which deliver welfare services to children. The need to work within the new fiscal climate also has ramifications for how the state delivers child welfare services to communities and families, and influences the extent of those services. In the child abuse area, these considerations have raised the threshold at which the Service will take on a case, and left 'lesser' cases to community groups. 'I hope we never get to the stage when we say, "Has this child got one bruise? Oh no, we're not interested in that, we're only interested in three bruises"', one social worker said. He went on: 'but I'd like to say that social workers and their managers are exercising these judgments daily in a high-pressure environment'.[2]

The maintenance of children's and families' welfare takes place in a public spotlight that was hitherto not turned onto child welfare work in New Zealand. Children's welfare services, and the performance of the Service, are newsworthy topics. Stories about children left in abusive situations, youth crime sprees, and the inadequacy of residential facilities occur frequently in the media; politicians allege poor work practices and criticise decisions; reviews of work practices and policies outline the problems arising from financial stringencies, heavy caseloads, and the ongoing challenges of working with the new legislation. The big news stories of children's welfare are nearly all negative ones; positive stories about children's lives being turned around tend to circulate within families, in community groups, and within the Service, rather than in the public arena.

With the exception of this intense media and public interest, and the new forms of financial constraints, most of the challenges facing the New Zealand Children, Young Persons, and Their Families Service are not new; they differ from the challenges of the earlier years of the twentieth century in degree rather than kind. The best methods of overcoming child abuse and neglect, the best ways to respond to young offenders, the most appropriate methods for working with Maori and Pacific Island groups, and the most suitable forms of out-of-family care have all been subjects for negotiation throughout the century. This history may have recorded the stubborn persistence of child welfare problems, but it has also revealed that there has been constant review and reassessment of the methods used to overcome such problems.

Some of the reassessments have been enormous in their scope. Residential care, once a mainstay of child welfare, is now clearly an option of last resort. Children requiring care and protection now follow a different path through the welfare system than do young offenders, as contemporaries try to differentiate between children as victims and children as dangers to society and themselves. The provision made for children in the justice system has moved from the general to the specific, as child welfare cases were shifted from the magistrate's court to the children's court and then to the youth court and the family court. The care of children born out of wedlock is no longer the pressing social issue that it once was, and the adopting out of ex-nuptial babies is no longer a first resort. Foster care is still a component of child welfare provision, but it has given ground to the use of family and kin networks. Preventive policies, and the supervision of children and young people in their homes, have increased in importance over the course of the century.

Developments in policy and practice both built upon and influenced changing attitudes towards children. Early twentieth-century perceptions of children as the basis of New Zealand's future developed into a recognition of children as individuals in their own right. The place of children within families is the dominant social work ideology of the 1990s, as families claim responsibility to make decisions about the welfare of their members. There are tensions in this most recent articulation of children's status, for unless children's rights are only to coincide with wider interests, protecting children must sometimes mean impinging on the autonomy of the family.[3]

Successive child welfare administrations pictured themselves as alternatives to family care, and forged relationships with children, and often with their families, which could last for many years. Especially since the 1980s, the government has drawn back from this position. Maori desires for self-determination and the culturally appropriate provision of welfare services, as well as community demands for greater responsibility in providing for children, have been influential in a reformulation of the state's approach to child welfare. The spectre of 'welfare dependency', the rising costs of providing welfare services and a refocusing of the government's role in all social services have also affected the state's attitude to child welfare. 'The state cannot be a family for a child', Robin Wilson informed the Minister of Social Welfare in 1991, summing up the massive shift which had occurred in the government's view of its role in providing child welfare services.[4] Such changes form part of the shifting balance between state, community and family care in the mixed economy of welfare.

As I have argued throughout this history, the sustaining philosophy of child welfare has been the safeguarding and enhancing of children's welfare by providing family care. Running through all of the reformulations and shifts during the twentieth century has been the central importance of the family environment as the foundation of children's welfare. Some features of 'family' have changed, as the current preference for birth families and family groups rather than out-of-family care demonstrates. Others have been more constant, and successive government child welfare agencies have worked to ensure children's welfare within a variety of family forms, including extended families and whanau, and sole-parent families, in addition to nuclear families. The importance of family-based care has sometimes been honoured more in the breach than in the observance, and at other times welfare assistance in family life has created as well as remedied damage. Yet the goal of achieving child welfare through family welfare is visible across twentieth-century child welfare policies and practices, even if we may not agree with some of its specific manifestations.

Child welfare practices and policies have encompassed many features: punishment and control, welfare and justice, assistance and observation, empowerment and self-awareness, ideas of children as victims and as threats. The balance between these features has fluctuated over time, as each generation has devised child welfare schemes to meet its particular needs. The provision of welfare for children and young people is tightly embedded in its social, economic, political and cultural context; it sometimes helped to shape that context, and at other times was shaped by it. But the fact that there have been both changing and constant features in twentieth-century child welfare philosophies and practices does not lead to a conclusion that previous welfare services have been 'bad', or that contemporary ones are 'reformed'. Successive ways of administering child welfare have been simply threads in the story of welfare, each adding to what has gone before in the belief that, this time, the direction is the right one.

NOTES

ABBREVIATIONS

BWO   Boys' Welfare Officer
CWO   Child Welfare Officer
DCWO   District Child Welfare Officer
RSW   Residential Social Worker
SCWO   Senior Child Welfare Officer
SM   Stipendiary Magistrate
SRSW   Senior Residential Social Worker
SSW   Senior Social Worker
SW   Social Worker

Introduction

1 Case file, ABNT, W4295. I have used substitute names for all children and families in contact with child welfare agencies after 1925. These names retain a sense of the ethnic identity of the originals.

2 For a discussion of the different strands of testimony contained in case records, see Linda Gordon, *Heroes of Their Own Lives: The Politics and History of Family Violence*, London, Virago, 1989, pp. 12–19; Regina Kunzel, *Fallen Women, Problem Girls: Unmarried Mothers and the Professionalization of Social Work, 1890–1945*, New Haven, Yale University Press, 1993, pp. 6–8, 102–14, and 'Pulp Fictions and Problem Girls: Reading and Rewriting Single Pregnancy in the Postwar United States', *American Historical Review*, vol. 100, no. 5, 1995, pp. 1465–87.

3 The organisational structure of the various agencies, and the development of a social work profession, constitute a part of this history only where these factors influence child welfare services.

4 Robert van Krieken, *Children and the State: Social Control and the Formation of Australian Child Welfare*, Sydney, Allen and Unwin, 1991, p. 2.

5 Discussions of the constructions of childhood since before the twentieth century can be found in Philippe Ariès, *Centuries of Childhood: A Social History of Family Life*, New York, Vintage Books, 1962; Roger Cooter (ed.), *In the Name of the Child: Health and Welfare, 1880–1940*, London, Routledge, 1992; John Gillis, *Youth and History: Tradition and Change in European Age Relations 1770–Present*, New York and London, Academic Press, 1974; Diana Gittins, 'Disentangling the History of Childhood', *Gender and History*, vol. 1, no. 3, 1989, pp. 342–9; Harry Hendrick, *Child Welfare: England 1872–1989*, London, Routledge, 1994, pp. 19–37; Harry Hendrick, 'Constructions and Reconstructions of British Childhood: An Interpretative Survey, 1800 to the Present', in Alison James and Alan Prout (eds), *Constructing and Reconstructing Childhood: Contemporary Issues in the Sociological Study of Childhood*, London, Falmer Press, 1990, pp. 35–59; Ludmilla Jordanova, 'Children in History: Concepts of Nature and Society', in Geoffrey Scarre (ed.), *Children, Parents and Politics*, Cambridge, Cambridge University Press, 1989, pp. 3–24; Ludmilla Jordanova, 'Fantasy and History in the Study of Childhood', *Free Associations*, 2, 1985, pp. 110–22; Dugald McDonald, 'Children and Young Persons in New Zealand Society', in Peggy Koopman-Boyden (ed.), *Families in New Zealand Society*, Wellington, Methuen,

1978, pp. 44–56; Carolyn Steedman, *Strange Dislocations: Childhood and the Idea of Human Interiority 1780–1930*, London, Virago, 1995; Viviana Zelizer, *Pricing the Priceless Child. The Changing Social Value of Children*, New York, Basic Books, 1985.

6   The fullest elaboration of the victims/threats paradigm is in Hendrick, *Child Welfare*, pp. 1–15. See also Mary Louise Adams, 'Youth, Corruptibility, and English-Canadian Postwar Campaigns Against Indecency, 1948–1955', *Journal of the History of Sexuality*, vol. 6, no. 1, 1995, pp. 89–117; Bob Bessant, 'Children and Youth in Australia 1860s–1930s', in Bob Bessant (ed.), *Mother State and Her Little Ones: Children and Youth in Australia 1860s–1930s*, Melbourne, Centre for Youth and Community Studies, 1987, pp. 7–30; James Gilbert, *A Cycle of Outrage: America's Reaction to the Juvenile Delinquent in the 1950s*, New York and Oxford, Oxford University Press, 1986, *passim*; Gillis, *Youth and History*, pp. 182–3; Susan Tiffin, *In Whose Best Interest? Child Welfare Reform in the Progressive Era*, Westport, Connecticut, Greenwood Press, 1982, pp. 9–10 (who presents the argument in terms of social order and social justice).

7   Good discussions of why families sought out child welfare assistance can be found in Gordon, *Heroes of Their Own Lives*, *passim*; Kunzel, 'Pulp Fictions and Problem Girls', *passim*; Mary E. Odem, *Delinquent Daughters: Protecting and Policing Adolescent Female Sexuality in the United States, 1885–1920*, Chapel Hill, University of North Carolina Press, 1995, pp. 158–88; van Krieken, *Children and the State*, pp. 26–30.

8   For a New Zealand study of the work of one voluntary group in the broad area of children's welfare, see Margaret Tennant, *Children's Health, the Nation's Wealth: A History of Children's Health Camps*, Wellington, Bridget Williams Books and Historical Branch, Department of Internal Affairs, 1994.

9   On the mixed economy of welfare, see Jane Lewis, 'Family Provision of Health and Welfare in the Mixed Economy of Care in the Late Nineteenth and Twentieth Centuries', *Social History of Medicine*, vol. 8, no. 1, 1995, pp. 1–16, and 'The Boundary Between Voluntary and Statutory Social Service in the Late Nineteenth and Early Twentieth Centuries', *Historical Journal*, vol. 39, no. 1, 1996, pp. 155–77. A large body of literature has developed internationally around the state/community/family nexus of welfare provision. Much of this has derived from feminist examinations of the welfare state which seek to explain the role of feminist professionals and philanthropic workers in building welfare systems. For recent feminist and other interpretations, see David T. Beito, 'Mutual Aid, State Welfare, and Organized Charity: Fraternal Societies and the "Deserving" and "Undeserving" Poor, 1900–1930', *Journal of Policy History*, vol. 5, no. 4, 1993, pp. 419–34; Miriam Cohen and Michael Hanagan, 'The Politics of Gender and the Making of the Welfare State, 1900–1940: A Comparative Perspective', *Journal of Social History*, vol. 24, no. 3, 1991, pp. 469–84; Linda Gordon, *Pitied But Not Entitled: Single Mothers and the History of Welfare*, New York, The Free Press, 1994; Linda Gordon (ed.), *Women, the State, and Welfare*, Madison, University of Wisconsin Press, 1990; Seth Koven and Sonya Michel (eds), *Mothers of a New World: Maternalist Politics and the Origins of Welfare States*, New York and London, Routledge, 1993; Seth Koven and Sonya Michel, 'Gender and the Origins of the Welfare State', *Radical History Review*, 43, 1989, pp. 112–19; Seth Koven and Sonya Michel, 'Womanly Duties: Maternalist Politics and the Origins of Welfare States in France, Germany, Great Britain, and the United States, 1880–1920', *American Historical Review*, vol. 95, no. 4, 1990, pp. 1076–1108; Kunzel, *Fallen Women*, *passim*; Molly Ladd-Taylor, *Mother-Work: Women, Child Welfare, and the State, 1890–1930*, Urbana and Chicago, University of Illinois Press, 1994; Jane Lewis, 'Gender, the Family and Women's Agency in the Building of "Welfare States": The British Case', *Social History*, vol. 19, no. 1, 1994, pp. 37–55; Jane Lewis, *The Politics of Motherhood: Child and Maternal Welfare in England, 1900–1939*, London/Montreal, Croom Helm/McGill–Queen's University Press, 1980; Susan Pedersen, 'Gender, Welfare and Citizenship in Britain During the Great War', *American Historical Review*, vol. 95, no. 4, 1990, pp. 983–1006; Ellen Ross, 'Good and Bad Mothers: Lady Philanthropists and London Housewives Before World War One', in Dorothy O. Helly and Susan M. Reverby (eds), *Gendered Domains: Rethinking Public and Private in Women's History*, Ithaca, Cornell University Press, 1992, pp. 199–216; Wendy Sarvasy, 'Beyond the Difference versus Equality Policy Debate: Postsuffrage Feminism, Citizenship, and the Quest for a Feminist Welfare State', *Signs: Journal of Women in Culture and Society*, vol. 17, no. 2, 1992, pp. 329–62; Margaret Weir, Ann Shola Orloff and Theda Skocpol (eds), *The Politics of Social*

Policy in the United States, Princeton, Princeton University Press, 1988.

10 The role of the state in the delivery of welfare services has been under discussion internationally thanks to scholars who seek to 'bring the state back in' to policy history. For an example of this type of approach, see Theda Skocpol, *Protecting Soldiers and Mothers: The Political Origins of Social Policy in the United States*, Cambridge, Belknap Press of Harvard University Press, 1992. Critics of this approach point out its manifold shortcomings, emphasising, for example, the participation in policy of groups throughout society, the key role of the family as a welfare provider, and diffuse concepts of power which see it located and played out in diverse social groupings. A useful debate on the merits of each approach is Linda Gordon and Theda Skocpol, 'Gender, State and Society: A Debate with Theda Skocpol', *Contention*, vol. 2, no. 3, 1993, pp. 139–89. The discussions of welfare cited in footnote 9 largely demonstrate a non-polity-centred interpretation.

11 For example, see Hendrick, *Child Welfare*, pp. 1–2; Jane Lewis, 'Anxieties About the Family and the Relationships Between Parents, Children and the State in Twentieth-century England', in Martin Richards and Paul Light (eds), *Children of Social Worlds: Development in a Social Context*, Cambridge, Harvard University Press, 1986, p. 50.

12 Hendrick, *Child Welfare*, p. 211.

13 Late 1980s child welfare policy is discussed in Hendrick, *Child Welfare*, pp. 272–88; Tim Hacsi, 'From Indenture to Family Foster Care: A Brief History of Child Placing', in Eve P. Smith and Lisa A. Merkel-Holguín (eds), *A History of Child Welfare*, New Brunswick, Transaction Publishers, 1996, pp. 155–73; Rebecca Hegar and Maria Scannapieco, 'From Family Duty to Family Policy: The Evolution of Kinship Care', in ibid., pp. 193–209; Terry Irving, David Maunders and Geoff Sherington, *Youth in Australia: Policy Administration and Politics. A History Since World War II*, Melbourne, Macmillan Education, 1995, pp. 259ff.

14 David Thomson, 'Society and Social Welfare', in Colin Davis and Peter Lineham (eds), *The Future of the Past: Themes in New Zealand History*, Palmerston North, History Department, Massey University, 1991, p. 101. Child welfare forms part of wider welfare history in only a few New Zealand studies, replicating a pattern elsewhere in which child welfare historiography is separate from other welfare historiography. For other discussions of child welfare in New Zealand, see McDonald, 'Children and Young Persons in New Zealand Society', *passim*; W. H. Oliver, 'The Origins and Growth of the Welfare State', in A. D. Trlin (ed.), *Social Welfare and New Zealand Society*, Wellington, Methuen, 1977, pp. 1–28, and 'Social Policy in New Zealand: An Historical Overview', *The April Report. New Zealand Today: Report of the Royal Commission on Social Policy*, vol. 1, Wellington, 1988, pp. 21–30; Tennant, *Children's Health, the Nation's Wealth*, *passim*, and *Paupers and Providers: Charitable Aid in New Zealand*, Wellington, Allen and Unwin/Historical Branch, Department of Internal Affairs, 1989.

PART I **Introduction**

1 *AJHR*, 1901, E-3, p. 3; John Beck, Memoirs, p. 7, CW 1, 8/22; *AJHR*, 1917, E-1A, *passim*.

2 The birth rate dropped by more than 30 per cent between 1878 and 1901, and average family size fell from 6.5 live births in 1880 to 3.3 in 1913. Erik Olssen and Andrée Lévesque, 'Towards a History of the European Family in New Zealand', in Koopman-Boyden (ed.), *Families in New Zealand Society*, Table 1.2, p. 16; C. James O'Neill, 'Fertility: Past, Present, and Future', in R. J. Warwick Neville and C. James O'Neill (eds), *The Population of New Zealand: Interdisciplinary Perspectives*, Auckland, Longman Paul, 1979, pp. 126–30.

3 Discussions of a range of state welfare and health provision can be found in Linda Bryder (ed.), *A Healthy Country: Essays on the Social History of Medicine in New Zealand*, Wellington, Bridget Williams Books, 1991; Derek A. Dow, *Safeguarding the Public Health: A History of the New Zealand Department of Health*, Wellington, Victoria University Press in association with the Ministry of Health and with the assistance of the Historical Branch, Department of Internal Affairs, 1995; W. H. Oliver, '100 Years of the Welfare State', in Atholl Anderson et al., *Towards 1990: Seven Leading Historians Examine Significant Aspects of New Zealand History*, Wellington, GP Books, 1989, pp. 82–90, 'Origins and Growth of the Welfare State', pp. 1–28, 'Social Policy in New Zealand', pp. 21–30, 'Social Welfare: Social Justice or Social Efficiency?', *New Zealand Journal of History*, vol. 13, no. 1, 1979, pp. 3–23;

Tennant, *Paupers and Providers*.

4   The science of eugenics in New Zealand, unlike in some other nations, placed considerable emphasis on the environmental as well as the hereditary aspects of racial health. For fuller examinations of the impact of eugenics on New Zealand social policy over this period, see Philip Fleming, 'Eugenics in New Zealand, 1900–1940', MA thesis, Massey University, 1981; Tennant, *Children's Health*, pp. 18–25.

5   Tennant, *Children's Health*, p. 17, and *Paupers and Providers*, pp. 143, 200.

6   Hendrick, 'Constructions and Reconstructions', p. 36.

7   In Hendrick's periodisation of childhood in Britain since the eighteenth century, the 'welfare child' perception developed in tandem with the construction of the 'psycho-medical child', Hendrick, 'Constructions and Reconstructions', pp. 47–50.

8   Zelizer, *Pricing the Priceless Child*, p. 3.

9   For surveys of the emergence of child protection work, see LeRoy Ashby, *Saving the Waifs: Reformers and Dependent Children, 1890–1917*, Philadelphia, Temple University Press, 1984; George Behlmer, *Child Abuse and Moral Reform in England, 1870–1908*, Stanford, Stanford University Press, 1982; essays in Bessant (ed.), *Mother State and Her Little Ones*; essays in Cooter (ed.), *In the Name of the Child*; Tove Stang Dahl, *Child Welfare and Social Defence*, Oslo, Norwegian University Press, 1985; Gillis, *Youth and History*; Gordon, *Heroes of Their Own Lives*; Anthony Platt, *The Child Savers: The Invention of Delinquency*, 2nd edition, Chicago, University of Chicago Press, 1977; Tiffin, *In Whose Best Interest?*; van Krieken, *Children and the State*.

10   For more on the construction of juvenile delinquency, see Gillis, *Youth and History*, pp. 170ff; Margaret May, 'Innocence and Experience: The Evolution of the Concept of Juvenile Delinquency in the Mid-nineteenth Century', *Victorian Studies*, vol. 17, no. 1, 1973, pp. 7–29.

11   McDonald, 'Children and Young Persons', pp. 47–9.

12   Jeanine Graham, 'Child Employment in New Zealand', *New Zealand Journal of History*, vol. 21, no. 1, 1987, pp. 62–78. See also Erik Olssen, 'Towards a New Society', in Geoffrey W. Rice (ed.), *The Oxford History of New Zealand*, 2nd edition, Auckland, Oxford University Press, 1992, pp. 260–8.

13   For further discussion of these groups, see Raewyn Dalziel, *Focus on the Family: The Auckland Home and Family Society 1893–1993*, Auckland, Home and Family Society, 1993; Scott Gallacher, '"Publishing Our Own Dishonour": The Criminalisation of Incest in New Zealand and the Judicial Response', BA (Hons) long essay, University of Otago, 1993; V. M. Kerr, 'The Society for the Protection of Women and Children in Auckland, 1917–1947', MA research essay, University of Auckland, 1992; F. J. MacCuish, 'The Society for the Protection of Women and Children, 1893–1916', MA research essay, University of Auckland, 1983.

14   McDonald, 'Children and Young Persons', pp. 44–56, and 'The Governing of Children: Social Policy for Children and Young Persons in New Zealand, 1840–1982', PhD thesis, University of Canterbury, 1988.

15   For more on the nineteenth-century industrial school system, see Jan Beagle, 'Children of the State: A Study of the New Zealand Industrial School System 1880–1925', MA thesis, University of Auckland, 1974; Bronwyn Dalley, 'From Demi-mondes to Slaveys: A Study of the Te Oranga Reformatory for Delinquent Women, 1900–1918', MA thesis, Massey University, 1987, pp. 13–36.

16   Gillis, *Youth and History*, pp. 98–132.

17   P. A. Gregory, 'Saving the Children in New Zealand: A Study of Social Attitudes Towards Larrikinism in the Later Nineteenth Century', BA (Hons) research essay, Massey University, 1975.

18   For more on this, see Brian Dickey, *Rations, Residence, Resources: A History of Social Welfare in South Australia Since 1836*, South Australia, Wakefield Press, 1986; Leonora Ritter, 'Boarding-Out in New South Wales and South Australia: Adoption, Adaptation or Innovation?', *Journal of the Royal Australian Historical Society*, vol. 64, no. 2, 1978, pp. 120–6.

19   Beagle, 'Children of the State', Tables 5.1 and 5.2, following p. 181.

20   For a fuller discussion of Hogben, see Bert Roth, *George Hogben: A Biography*, Wellington, New Zealand Council for Educational Research, 1952.

21   *AJHR*, 1900, E-3, 1925, E-4.

22   C. E. Peek, 'A Superintendent Looks Back', *New Zealand Social Worker*, vol. 5, no. 4, 1969, p. 19.

CHAPTER 1 **Control, reformation and protection: the basis of child welfare**

1 Roth, *George Hogben*, p. 89.

2 *AJHR*, 1900, E-3B, *passim*. Police inquiries into the running of the orphanage indicated that a number of the young boys had been indecently assaulted by one of the Marist Brothers, P 10/1, Stoke Industrial School.

3 Inspection report, T. Walker, 7 Dec 1903, Pope to Hogben, 8 Dec 1903, Evidence of William Robert Byrnes, 25 Nov 1904, in Inspection report, R. Pope, 9 Dec 1904, Walker to Secretary of Education, 23 Mar 1908, Inspection report, R. Pope, 31 Mar 1908, Inspection report, T. Walker, 20 Jul 1908, Gibbes to Minister of Education, 11 Mar 1916, CW 1, 40/3/39.

4 *AJHR*, 1906, E-3, p. 2.

5 Despite a belief that feeble-minded girls posed a greater threat than boys due to their stronger 'immoral' tendencies, plans for a girls' institution did not reach fruition until 1916, delayed perhaps both by difficulties in obtaining staff and by financial considerations.

6 The numbers are of those residents in institutions or boarded out on 31 December each year. *AJHR*, 1902–8, E-3, 1909–17, E-4.

7 Dalley, 'From Demi-mondes to Slaveys', p. 115.

8 *AJHR*, E-4, 1913, pp. 8, 18, 1916, p. 2.

9 For more on this in other areas of policy and in general, see Bronwyn Dalley, '"Making Bricks Without Straw": Feminism and Prison Reform in New Zealand, 1896–1925', *Women's Studies Journal*, vol. 9, no. 2, 1993, pp. 30–50, and 'Prisons Without Men: The Development of a Separate Women's Prison in New Zealand', *New Zealand Journal of History*, vol. 27, no. 1, 1993, pp. 43–53; Fleming, 'Eugenics ', *passim*.

10 *Evening Star*, 15 Dec 1909, CW 1, 6/12.

11 *New Zealand Times*, 16 Dec 1909, CW 1, 6/12.

12 Those committed for a punishable offence, such as theft or minor assaults, comprised about one quarter of committals for the whole of this period. *AJHR*, 1902, E-3, pp. 6–7, 1916, E-4, p. 8.

13 See Dalley, 'From Demi-mondes to Slaveys', pp. 111–17; Bronwyn Dalley, 'Women's Imprisonment in New Zealand, 1880–1920', PhD thesis, University of Otago, 1992, pp. 76–83; Kunzel, *Fallen Women*, *passim*; Odem, *Delinquent Daughters, passim*; Joan Sangster, 'Incarcerating "Bad Girls": The Regulation of Sexuality Through the Female Refuges Act in Ontario, 1920–1945', *Journal of the History of Sexuality*, vol. 7, no. 2, 1996, pp. 239–75; Steven Schlossman and Stephanie Wallach, 'The Crime of Precocious Sexuality: Female Juvenile Delinquency in the Progressive Era', *Harvard Educational Review*, vol. 48, no. 1, 1978, pp. 65–94.

14 Odem, *Delinquent Daughters*, pp. 158, 188. A large literature has developed about the extent to which welfare systems, and child welfare practices more specifically, reflected the aspirations of the state and bourgeois society to control and shape working-class life. Historical debate was particularly strong during the 1970s and 1980s, in the wake of the 'new' social history. Examples include essays in Bessant (ed.), *Mother State and Her Little Ones*; Jacques Donzelot, *The Policing of Families: Welfare versus the State*, London, Hutchinson, 1980; Christopher Lasch, *Haven in a Heartless World: The Family Besieged*, New York, Basic Books, 1977; Platt, *The Child Savers*. Among useful critiques of the social control thesis in welfare and child welfare are Linda Gordon, 'Child Abuse, Gender, and the Myth of Family Independence: A Historical Critique', *Child Welfare*, vol. 64, no. 3, 1985, pp. 213–24; Gordon, *Heroes of Their Own Lives, passim*; F. M. L. Thompson, 'Social Control in Victorian Britain', *Economic History Review*, vol. 34, no. 2, 1981, pp. 189–208; van Krieken, *Children and the State*, pp. 13–42, 133–45; Robert van Krieken, 'The Poverty of Social Control: Explaining Power in the Historical Sociology of the Welfare State', *Sociological Review*, vol. 39, no. 1, 1991, pp. 1–25. Historians now seldom debate the social control thesis. Influenced by post-structuralist explanations of the diffuseness of power in society, scholars refer to a process of negotiation and contestation between parties to welfare relationships; for one such example, see Odem, *Delinquent Daughters, passim*.

15 Mrs McAlaster to Burnham School, 1 Sep 1916, Mrs Jensen to Secretary of Education, 6 Sep 1916, Mrs Sampson to Secretary of Education, nd [Feb 1916], CW 1, 40/14/24; AADW 1110/5b.

16 Tennant, *Paupers and Providers*, pp. 103–25, and 'Welfare Organisations', in Anne Else (ed.), *Women Together: A History of Women's Organisations in New Zealand/ Nga Ropu Wahine o te Motu*,

Wellington, Daphne Brasell Associates Press and Historical Branch, Department of Internal Affairs, 1993, pp. 109–19, for elsewhere, see Gordon, *Heroes of Their Own Lives*, *passim*; Odem, *Delinquent Daughters*, pp. 167ff.

17 *Press*, 17 Aug 1909, CW 1, 40/4/13.
18 G. Benstead to Secretary of Education, 29 Sep 1915, CW 1, 40/19/41; see also S. Bardsley, 'The Functions of an Institution: The Otekaike Special School for Boys 1908–1950', BA (Hons) long essay, University of Otago, 1991, *passim*.
19 *AJHR*, 1908, H-21, p. 112.
20 Dalley, 'From Demi-mondes to Slaveys', pp. 71–96.
21 Sarah Jackson to Assistant Secretary of Education, 6 Apr 1905, C. F. Scale to E. Gibbes, 8 Oct 1906, 'Notes to guide boys who are at service', CW 1, 40/22/4.
22 Masters to Director of Education, 5 Feb 1917, Walker to Gibbes, 31 May 1913, CW 1, 40/25.
23 Notes of interviews, 9 Sep 1915, CW 1, 40/3/16.
24 Gibbes to Petremant, 12 Oct 1908, Petremant to Gibbes, 22 Aug 1908, CW 1, 40/4/11; Pope to Hogben, 17 Jul 1909, Gibbes to Petremant, 23 Jul 1909, WEL 9/3/3, part 1.
25 Gibbes to Petremant, 12 Oct 1908, CW 1, 40/4/11; *AJHR*, 1908, H-21, *passim*.
26 *AJHR*, 1908, H-21, p. ii.
27 Walker to Gibbes, 19 Mar, 24 May 1906, CW 1, 40/4/13; Pope to Gibbes, 11 Oct 1912, CW 1, 40/28/5.
28 Anna Cox to Gibbes, 19 May, 29 Aug 1911, Report of Jessie Maddison (medical officer), 25 Nov 1910, 3 Jun 1911, CW 1, 19/14.
29 Meeting of the Industrial School Board of Advice, 12 Sep 1902, George Burlinson, Manager, Caversham, to Gibbes, 18 Sep 1902, CW 1, 41/19, part 1.
30 Beagle, 'Children of the State', p. 112.
31 Pope to Gibbes, 6 Dec 1915, Gibbes to W. Anderson, 7 Dec 1915, CW 1, 40/5.
32 Walker to Gibbes, 14 Aug 1908, Petremant to Gibbes, 22 Aug 1908, Gibbes to Petremant, 12 Oct 1908, CW 1, 40/4/11.
33 For example, see Beryl Hughes, 'The Enquiry into the Te Oranga Girls' Home, 1908', *Women's Studies Journal*, vol. 4, no. 1, 1988, pp. 27–38.
34 John A. Lee, *Delinquent Days*, Auckland, Collins, 1967, pp. 5–25.
35 For example, see *AJHR*, 1908, H-21, pp. 5, 7, 8, 16, 20–1, 57–70.
36 Lee, *Delinquent Days*, p. 24.
37 The expansion of private children's homes is discussed in Tennant, *Paupers and Providers*, pp. 137–43.
38 Ibid., p. 133; Gibbes to Hanan, 22 Nov 1915, Hanan to Gibbes, 11 Dec 1915, CW 1, 3/5/1; Pope to Hogben, 4 Feb 1908, CW 1, 40/6/11.
39 Hogben to Minister of Education, 8 Jan 1908, CW 1, 40/1/11.
40 Hogben to Minister of Education, 9 Jan 1906, CW 1, 5/1/5, part 1.
41 Gibbes to Reverend Holbrooke, 29 Jun 1911, CW 1, 40/3/34.
42 Scales to Gibbes, 24 Mar 1914, CW 1, 40/6/42.
43 Tennant, *Paupers and Providers*, p. 200.
44 Holbrooke to Minister of Education, 19 Sep 1924, CW 1, 3/5/1, part 1.
45 Pope to Hogben, 4 Feb 1908, CW 1, 40/6/11.
46 Gibbes to Minister of Education, 30 Aug, 1 Oct 1915, CW 1, 41/17/3.
47 Benstead to Gibbes, 14 May 1912, CW 1, 40/6/1.
48 For more on this, see Tennant, *Paupers and Providers*, pp. 127–43.
49 Tiffin, *In Whose Best Interest?*, pp. 216ff.
50 *NZPD*, 1905, vol. 133, p. 158, 1906, vol. 137, p. 283.
51 *NZPD*, 1906, vol. 137, p. 175.
52 For more on this, see Victor Bailey, *Delinquency and Citizenship: Reclaiming the Young Offender, 1914–1948*, Oxford, Clarendon Press, 1987, pp. 7–30; Gillis, *Youth and History*, pp. 156–83.
53 Such attempts to 'protect' children and young people from the world of adults actually served to circumscribe their social and political rights. In time, the system of youth justice symbolised in children's courts became reconceptualised as a problem, rather than as a remedy, for children's

welfare. This is discussed further in Chapter Seven; see also Estelle Freedman, *Maternal Justice: Miriam Van Waters and the Female Reform Tradition*, Chicago, University of Chicago Press, 1996, pp. 77–90; Gillis, *Youth and History*, p. 142; McDonald, 'The Governing of Children', pp. 139–41.

54   See William Reece's discussion of the need to expand the courts in the direction of those in the United States, *AJHR*, 1909, E-11, p. 2.

55   Pope to Hogben, 20 May 1912, 'Juvenile Delinquency', nd [Financial statement, 1912], CW 1, 40/10A.

56   Widdowson to Under-Secretary of Justice, 15 Dec 1912, CW 1, 40/10A. Axelsen's probation service had a more sinister side – it was revealed in the 1920s that he had for many years systematically sexually abused the boys assigned to his care. See *Otago Daily Times*, 27 May 1922. Thanks to Peter Boston for this reference.

57   *Evening Post*, 6 Dec 1912, CW 1, 40/10A.

58   Pope to Gibbes, 12 Nov, Gibbes to F. S. Shell, 23 Nov, Gibbes to all industrial schools and reformatories, 23 Nov 1912, CW 1, 40/10A.

59   Beck to Pope, 25 Mar 1915, CW 1, 40/10A.

60   Shell to Secretary of Education, 20 Aug 1915, CW 1, 40/10A.

61   Beck to Pope, 25 Mar, Secretary of Education to Shell, 7 May, Shell to Secretary of Education, 24 Aug 1915, CW 1, 40/10A.

62   Tennant, *Paupers and Providers*, p. 138.

63   For a fuller discussion of the evolution and development of the system in Australia, see Brian Dickey, 'The Evolution of Care for Destitute Children in New South Wales, 1875–1901', *Journal of Australian Studies*, 4, 1979, pp. 38–57; Michael Horsburgh, 'Child Care in New South Wales in 1890', *Australian Social Work*, vol. 30, no. 3, 1977, pp. 21–40; John Ramsland, *Children of the Back Lanes: Destitute and Neglected Children in Colonial New South Wales*, Sydney, University of New South Wales Press, 1986; Ritter, 'Boarding-out in New South Wales', pp. 120–6.

64   *AJHR*, 1881, E-6, p. 1.

65   The total committed to care includes those resident in institutions, those in service positions, and those boarded out at the end of the year. *AJHR*, 1903, E-3, p. 7, 1917, E-4, p. 8.

66   *New Zealand Gazette*, 16 Jun 1902, pp. 1303–4.

67   E. Cunnington, Letter to Editor, *Lyttelton Times*, 29 Mar 1911, CW 1, 40/1/13.

68   Report on Public Conference on Boarding Out, *Press*, 7 May 1907, Mrs Lissaman to Minister of Education, 5 Mar 1908, WCTU, Christchurch, to Minister of Education, 25 May 1907, CW 1, 40/1/13.

69   *AJHR*, 1909, E-4, pp. 24–34.

70   Dick to John Beck, 4 Oct 1916, Dick to Secretary of Education, 22 Mar 1916, CW 1, 40/25/21.

71   *AJHR*, 1909, E-4, pp. 24–34.

72   *New Zealand Official Year-book*, 1903, pp. 465–7.

73   Gibbes to Hogben, 2 Oct 1912, CW 1, 40/25/21.

74   Dick to Director of Education, 5 Oct 1916, Mrs Payne to Ella Dick, 28 Jun, 22 Sep 1916, CW 1, 40/25/1.

75   Scale to Gibbes, 29 Mar 1915, CW 1, 40/25/21.

76   J. Hanan, memo to staff, 4 Apr 1916, Dick to Director of Education, 22 Aug 1916, CW 1, 40/25/21.

77   Pope to Secretary of Education, 18 Jun 1903, CW 1, 40/4/9.

78   George Behlmer, 'Deadly Motherhood: Infanticide and Medical Opinion in Mid-Victorian England', *Journal of the History of Medicine and Allied Sciences*, 34, 1979, pp. 403–27. For a discussion of baby-farming in New Zealand, see Lynley Hood, *Minnie Dean: Her Life and Crimes*, Auckland, Penguin, 1994, *passim*.

79   Arthur Hume, Commissioner of Police, to Minister of Justice, 31 Aug 1893, J 40, 93/598.

80   Infant Life Protection Act 1896.

81   *NZPD*, 1907, vol. 140, p. 630.

82   Ibid., p. 199.

83   Ibid., pp. 780, 785; *Lyttelton Times*, 9 Sep 1907, Pope to Gibbes, 30 Aug 1907, CW 1, 40/8.

84   *NZPD*, 1907, vol. 140, p. 783.

85   Dick to Gibbes, 10 Jun 1910, CW 1, 40/8/12.

86   A consolidation of statutes in 1908 saw the Infant life Protection Act absorbed into the Infants Act

1908, which became the governing legislation for this aspect of the Education Department's work. The Department preferred to continue using the expression 'infant life protection', although this was not mentioned in the consolidated legislation.

87   *New Zealand Gazette*, 19 Dec 1907, p. 3553.

88   'Feeding of Infants', 'Notes for Guidance of Foster-parents', Apr 1909, CW 1, 40/8/28.

89   4 Feb 1908, BAAA 1959/1b.

90   Petremant to Gibbes, 29 Jan 1908, CW 1, 40/8/12A.

91   Statement of Mrs Truby King to George Fowlds, 11 Mar 1910, CW 1, 40/6/9.

92   Pope to Mrs Hosking, Society for the Promotion of the Health of Women and Children, Dunedin, 24 Jan 1908, CW 1, 40/1/13.

93   Amy Carr, President, Royal New Zealand Society for the Health of Women and Children, to Minister of Education, 23 Mar 1910, CW 1, 40/8/28.

94   Report of deputation to Minister of Education, 5 Jun 1914, Pope to Hogben, 8 Jul 1914, CW 1, 40/1/13.

95   Truby King to Gibbes, 18 Jul 1914, Gibbes to Maude Kempton, District Agent, Dunedin, 17 Aug 1914, Jane Ralston, District Agent, Dunedin, to Director of Education, 10 May 1927, CW 1, 40/8/28.

96   Report on Public Conference on Boarding Out, *Press*, 7 May 1907, CW 1, 40/1/13.

97   *Press*, 30 Dec 1910, CW 1, 40/1/13.

98   Dick to Gibbes, 10 Jun 1910, CW 1, 40/8/12.

99   *AJHR*, 1910, E-4, pp. 28–9.

100   'Report on Invercargill', 7 Feb 1908, CW 1, 40/8/12A.

101   *AJHR*, 1910, E-4, p. 26.

102   Ibid., p. 28.

103   Mrs Johnstone, Wellington, to Director of Education, John Kiernander to District Agent, Wellington, 1 Dec 1916, CW 1, 40/8/13.

104   14 May 1910, BAAA 1959/1b; Jackson to Gibbes, 11 Mar 1913, CW 1, 40/8/12.

105   18 Jan 1909, 18 May 1910, BAAA 1959/1b.

106   Janet Hercock, Superintendent, St Mary's Home, Otahuhu, *Auckland Star*, 18 Aug 1910, Jackson to Secretary of Education, 25 Sep 1914, CW 1, 40/6/43. Jessie Munro, *The Story of Suzanne Aubert*, Auckland, Auckland University Press/Bridget Williams Books, 1996, pp. 302–38, relates the story from the perspective of Mother Aubert.

107   Tennant, for example, comments on the lack of assistance to single mothers because of fear that this would be endorsing immorality. Tennant, *Paupers and Providers*, p. 120.

108   Ibid., p. 113.

109   *New Zealand Herald*, 4 Sep 1907, CW 1, 40/8/14.

110   Jackson to Secretary of Education, 26 Feb 1915, CW 1, 40/6/43.

111   *AJHR*, 1910, E-4, p. 27.

112   Ibid., 1916, pp. 11–12.

113   17 Jul 1909, BAAA 1959/1b.

114   nd, BAAA 1962/1a.

115   AADW 1110/13b.

116   Maori 'legal' adoption followed a distinct pattern. Maori concepts of kin and family emphasised the sharing of responsibility for childrearing, and placing children in the care of adults other than their birth parents was common. The legal standing of this practice seemed tenuous to Pakeha administrators, and in 1909 the Native Land Act required that Maori adoptions be given legal status through the Native Land Court. 'Customary' Maori adoption – atawhai, taurima and whangai – continued, nevertheless. For more on this, see Anne Else, *A Question of Adoption: Closed Stranger Adoption in New Zealand 1944–1974*, Wellington, Bridget Williams Books, 1991, pp. 172–96; Joan Metge, *New Growth From Old: The Whanau in the Modern World*, Wellington, Victoria University Press, 1995, pp. 210-57; *Puao-te-Ata-Tu*, Report of the Ministerial Advisory Committee on a Maori Perspective for the Department of Social Welfare, Wellington, 1986, *passim*. Maori adoption is discussed further in Chapter Six.

117   Pope to Secretary of Education, 17 Aug 1906, CW 1, 40/31.

118   A. F. Wright to Pope, 4 Feb 1908, CW 1, 40/31.

119   *AJHR*, 1909, E-4, pp. 39–40; List of unsatisfactory adoption cases known to Department, nd [1908], CW 1, 40/31.

120   List of unsatisfactory adoption cases known to Department, nd [1908], CW 1, 40/31.

121   Report of meeting, 24 Mar 1905, qMS-1562.

122   nd, BAAA 1962/1a.

CHAPTER 2   **Towards the Child Welfare Act 1925**

1   *AJHR*, 1916, 1917, E-1A, p. 1.

2   Ibid., 1917, pp. 1, 3.

3   Ibid., pp. 5–6.

4   Deborah Dwork, *War is Good for Babies and Other Young Children: A History of the Infant and Child Welfare Movement in England 1898–1918*, London, Tavistock, 1987. Discussions about the pivotal role of the First World War in social policy include Cynthia R. Abeele, '"The Infant Soldier": The Great War and the Medical Campaign for Child Welfare', *Canadian Bulletin of Medical History*, 5, 1988, pp. 99–119; David F. Crew, 'German Socialism, the State, and Family Policy, 1918–33', *Continuity and Change*, vol. 1, no. 2, 1986, pp. 235–63; Anna Davin, 'Imperialism and Motherhood', *History Workshop Journal*, 5, 1978, p. 43; Lewis, *The Politics of Motherhood*, pp. 16ff; Geoffrey Pearson, *Hooligan: A History of Respectable Fears*, London, Macmillan, 1983, pp. 43–6; Ross, 'Good and Bad Mothers', pp. 200–1; Richard A. Soloway, 'Eugenics and Pronatalism in Wartime Britain', in Richard Wall and Jay Winter (eds), *The Upheaval of War: Family, Work and Welfare in Europe, 1914–1918*, Cambridge, Cambridge University Press, 1988, pp. 369–88; Cathy Urwin and Elaine Sharland, 'From Bodies to Minds in Childcare Literature: Advice to Parents in Interwar Britain', in Cooter (ed.), *In the Name of the Child*, pp. 188–9.

5   Official Register, E 16/1; Beck, Memoirs, pp. 1–3, CW 1, 8/22.

6   Beck, Memoirs, p. 5, CW 1, 8/22.

7   Beck had been in charge of the section since the latter part of 1916. His appointment was confirmed in May 1917.

8   The Department's reluctance to increase the rate of payment during the war no doubt contributed to the declining use of boarding out. Gibbes to Caughley, 19 Jun 1916, CW 1, 40/25/21; Caughley to Manager, Burnham, 31 May 1917, CW 1, 40/1/19.

9   Beck to Anderson, 8 May 1917, CW 1, 40/1/19.

10   Beck, Memoirs, p. 7, CW 1, 8/22.

11   *AJHR*, 1917, E-1A, p. 6.

12   *AJHR*, 1918, E-4, p. 6.

13   Beck, Memoirs, p. 5, CW 1, 8/22.

14   Beck to Caughley, 12 Jun 1917, Beck to Anderson, 16 Oct 1918, CW 1, 40/1/19; *AJHR*, 1916–26, E-4.

15   Beck, Memoirs, pp. 10–12, CW 1, 8/22; Beck to Anderson, 5 Apr 1918, CW 1, 40/1/19.

16   Beck to Anderson, 28 Aug 1918, CW 1, 6/12/2.

17   *AJHR*, 1920, E-4, p. 14.

18   Beck to Anderson, 12 Jan 1917, CW 1, 40/10A.

19   Beck, Memoirs, p. 5, CW 1, 8/22.

20   Pope to Anderson, 23 Nov 1916, CW 1, 40/1A; Unsourced press clipping, nd [Jun 1917], CW 1, 40/1/19.

21   Howard Ellis to Minister of Education, 14 Jun 1920, Beck to Minister of Education, 19 Jul 1920, Mrs Spicer, Auckland Receiving Home, to Caughley, 1 Mar 1921, CW 1, 3/6/9.

22   Beck to Caughley, 12 Jun 1917, CW 1, 40/1/19; *AJHR*, 1917, E-1A, pp. 5–11.

23   Beck to Caughley, 9 Oct 1917, CW 1, 40/1/19.

24   Beck, Memoirs, p. 14, CW 1, 8/22; Beck to Anderson, 17 Dec 1917, CW 1, 40/1/19.

25   Manager, Boys' Training Farm, Weraroa, to Anderson, 16 Jun 1919, CW 1, 40/22/8.

26   Hanan's comments, 19 Dec 1917, Anderson to Caughley, 9 Mar 1917, CW 1, 40/1/19.

27   Beck to Anderson, 12 Feb 1917, Beck to Caughley, 10 Oct 1917, Caughley to Anderson, 19 Nov 1917, CW 1, 40/1/19; Beck, Memoirs, pp. 15–16, CW 1, 8/22.

28 Beck, Memoirs, p. 15, CW 1, 8/22.
29 *AJHR*, 1919, E-4, p. 5.
30 Beck, Memoirs, p. 16, CW 1, 8/22; for more on the closure of Te Oranga, see Dalley, 'From Demi mondes to Slaveys', pp. 34–6.
31 For example, *Press*, 28 Mar 1923, cited in Fleming, 'Eugenics', p. 35.
32 Beck to Anderson, 12 Jan 1917, CW 1, 40/10A.
33 *AJHR*, 1917, E-1A, p. 7.
34 Beck to Anderson, 12 Jan 1917, CW 1, 40/10A; *New Zealand Herald*, 26 Oct 1925, CW 1, 40/10/63.
35 *New Zealand Gazette*, 2 May 1918, p. 1712, 9 May 1918, p. 1776; Caughley to Commissioner of Police, Wellington, 27 Apr 1918, CW 1, 40/1/19.
36 See Shell to Gibbes, 3 Mar 1913, Beck to Caughley, 24 Aug 1916, CW 1, 40/10A.
37 *AJHR*, 1924, E-4, p. 4.
38 Ibid., 1925, p. 5.
39 P. Goodwin, Juvenile Probation Officer, Hamilton, to Anderson, 18 Dec 1925, CW 1, 40/10/63.
40 Shell to Anderson, 15 Feb 1919, CW 1, 40/37/5; *AJHR*, 1920, E-4, p. 5; Beck to Anderson, 16 Oct 1918, CW 1, 40/1/19.
41 Beck to Royal Danish Consulate, New South Wales, 22 Apr 1925, CW 1, 40/1/35.
42 Beck, report, 8 Jan 1919, CW 1, 40/8/32; *AJHR*, 1925, E-4, p. 6.
43 *AJHR*, 1924, E-4, p. 7.
44 Mr Brasted, Secretary of YMCA, report on Big Brothers, 4 Sep 1925, CW 1, 8/14/2.
45 *AJHR*, 1918, E-4, p. 2; Beck to Anderson, 16 Oct 1918, CW 1, 40/1/19; Beck, report, 8 Jan 1919, CW 1, 40/8/32; *AJHR*, 1920, E-4, p. 12.
46 Pope to Anderson, 23 Nov 1916, CW 1, 40/1A.
47 *New Zealand Herald*, 2 Oct 1919, CW 1, 3/6/9.
48 *New Zealand Truth*, 27 Jan 1923, CW 1, 40/26/9.
49 *AJHR*, 1925, E-4, p. 5.
50 Ibid., 1920, p. 13.
51 Beck to Caughley, 13 May 1920, CW 1, 40/1/35.
52 *AJHR*, 1922, E-4, p. 4.
53 Beck to Anderson, 8 May 1917, Beck to Caughley, 12 Jun 1917, CW 1, 40/1/19; *AJHR*, 1917, E-1A, pp. 8–9.
54 Beck to Caughley, 12 Jun 1917, CW 1, 40/1/19; *AJHR*, 1920, E-4, p. 13.
55 Beck, Memoirs, p. 29, CW 1, 8/22.
56 Charlie Peek, Superintendent of Child Welfare, to Secretary of Justice, 10 Jul 1963, CW 1, 4/5/6.
57 Beck, Memoirs, pp. 25–7, CW 1, 8/22.
58 *AJHR*, 1920, E-4, pp. 13–17; Beck, Memoirs, p. 25, CW 1, 8/22; *AJHR*, 1920, E-4, p. 13.
59 Report of meeting, 27 May 1921, qMS-1566.
60 Community Sunshine Association, *The Call of the Child*, nd [1933], p. 1.
61 Report of deputation to Minister of Education from Auckland Community Welfare Council, 13 Feb 1929, CW 1, 40/1/35; Beck, Memoirs, p. 25, CW 1, 8/22; Tunks to Minister of Education, 6 May 1931, CW 1, 40/1/63.
62 Beck to Anderson, 8 May 1917, 16 Oct 1918, CW 1, 40/1/19.
63 Beck to Anderson, 8 May 1917, CW 1, 40/1/19, 23 Jun 1917, CW 1, 6/12/2.
64 *AJHR*, 1918, E-4, p. 2.
65 Zelizer, *Pricing the Priceless Child*, pp. 57–8.
66 *NZPD*, 1919, vol. 185, pp. 635–6; Zelizer, *Pricing the Priceless Child*, p. 80.
67 *AJHR*, 1920, E-4, p. 15.
68 Beck to Anderson, 8 May 1917, CW 1, 40/1/19.
69 Caughley to Caversham Industrial School, 27 Apr 1918, CW 1, 6/12/2.
70 *NZPD*, 1925, vol. 206, p. 677.
71 Beck, report, 8 Jan 1919, CW 1, 40/8/32.
72 Ibid.
73 *AJHR*, 1920, E-4, p. 14.

74 Ibid., p. 13.
75 Caughley to Minister of Education, 30 Jan 1919, CW 1, 40/8/32.
76 *NZPD*, 1925, vol. 206, p. 677.

PART II **Introduction**

1 Elizabeth Clapp, 'Welfare and the Role of Women: The Juvenile Court Movement', *Journal of American Studies*, vol. 28, no. 3, 1994, pp. 359–83; Freedman, *Maternal Justice*, pp. 77ff. The issue of women referees aroused considerable discussion in Parliament during debates on the Child Welfare Bill in 1925. Submissions from women's groups had indicated that they would have preferred to see a greater role for women associates in cases involving girls; see *NZPD*, 1925, vol. 206, pp. 583–7, 671–82, vol. 208, pp. 564–9.
2 *AJHR*, 1927, E-4, p. 1.
3 John Beck, *Child Welfare in the United States of America and Canada: Report of a Visit of the Superintendent, Child Welfare Branch, Education Department*, Special Reports on Educational Subjects, no. 15, Wellington, 1927, pp. 21–3, Hist/2. The Minister of Education noted in 1926 that there was 'not the least possibility' of forming a separate department, despite the demands of some staff, Minister of Education to Director of Education, 12 Nov 1926, CW 1, 40/1/35.
4 This was one of New Zealand's departures from the methods used in the United States and Britain, where courts ordered preventive work, McClune to Director of Education, 5 Oct 1945, CW 1, 41/41/1.
5 *AJHR*, E-4, 1937, p. 3, 1939, p. 7.
6 J. McClune, notes prepared for October conference, 18 Aug 1944, CW 1, 40/1/51; Report on female child welfare officers for the consultative committee, [Mar 1945], E 1, 19/28/38A.
7 'Child welfare officer' was the term used in reports to the courts.
8 Beck, *Child Welfare*, pp. 23–4; *AJHR*, 1937, E-4, p. 2.
9 *AJHR*, 1926–48, E-4; *Census of New Zealand*, 1926, 1945.
10 Hendrick, *Child Welfare*, pp. 179–87, discusses similar developments in the English context.
11 For example, see evidence of Dr Clark, School Medical Officer, Napier, p. 13, Evidence of Claire Wylie, Headmistress, Otekaike, p. 347, H 3/13.
12 See pp. 36–8, 152, 167, 181–6, 243, 286, H 3/13.
13 Beck, *Child Welfare*, pp. 9–10, 14, 24.
14 McClune to Director of Education, 8 Nov 1943, CW 1, 40/14/27; [Beck], Note for child guidance clinics, 16 Dec 1936, CW 1, 40/1/71; C. E. Beeby, *The Biography of an Idea: Beeby on Education*, Wellington, New Zealand Council for Educational Research, 1992, pp. 61–82, 150; Memo, 10 Nov 1947, CW 1, 40/42/1.

CHAPTER 3 **To train, rather than to punish: children's courts, supervision and residential institutions**

1 Hendrick, *Child Welfare*, p. 179.
2 Billy Bragg, 'Rotting on Remand', *Workers Playtime*, Festival Records, 1988, track 6.
3 *Dominion*, 27, 29 Mar 1926, *Ashburton Guardian*, 21 Apr 1926, *Manawatu Evening Standard*, 23 Apr 1926, CW 1, 40/50/8.
4 Beck to all child welfare officers, 31 Mar 1926, CW 1, 40/50/8; Director of Education to Minister of Education, 21 Jun 1927, CW 1, 40/4; *New Zealand Gazette*, 15 Apr 1926, pp. 1031–4, 20 May 1926, p. 1338, 17 Jun 1926, pp. 1653, 1656, 15 Dec 1927, p. 3698.
5 Bronwyn Dalley, 'Sarah Elizabeth Jackson', in *The Dictionary of New Zealand Biography*, vol. 3, 1901–1920, Auckland, Auckland University Press with Bridget Williams Books/Department of Internal Affairs, 1996, pp. 245–6; Community Sunshine Association, *The Call of the Child*, pp. 2–3.
6 *Truth*, 12 Jun 1935, CW 1, 40/50/4.
7 Peek to Minister of Education, 14 Nov 1947, Minister of Education to Peek, 15 Dec 1947, CW 1, 4/12/1.
8 *AJHR*, 1926–48, E-4.
9 *Otago Daily Times*, 5 Jun 1926, CW 1, 40/50/8.
10 *AJHR*, E-4, 1944, p. 3, 1945, p. 4; Raymond Ferner, SM, Whangarei, to D. McCarroll, BWO, Whangarei, 21 May 1941, Burton's notes and verbal comments on Ferner's letter, nd, CW 1, 40/25/26.

11 CH 132/252.
12 For a discussion on property offences and levels of prosperity, and the use of criminal statistics, see V. A. C. Gatrell and T. B. Hadden, 'Criminal Statistics and Their Interpretation', in E. A. Wrigley (ed.), *Nineteenth-century Society: Essays in the Use of Quantitative Methods for the Study of Social Data*, Cambridge, Cambridge University Press, 1972, pp. 336–92.
13 See CW 1, 40/50/34. Whipping and flogging were distinguished under the Crimes Act 1908: flogging, up to 50 strokes with the cat-o'-nine-tails, could be administered to those over sixteen; whipping, up to 25 strokes with a rod or birch, was reserved for those under sixteen.
14 Beck to Tom Vivian, Auckland, 8 Oct 1924, CW 1, 6/12/2.
15 Wyvern Wilson, SM, to Minister of Justice, 16 Feb 1929, J 1, 18/6/1.
16 Child Welfare Act 1925, sec. 31.
17 BWO, Nelson, to Beck, 15 Sep 1932, CW 1, 40/50/4.
18 J. Ferguson, BWO, Dunedin, to McClune, 5 Feb 1945, CW 1, 2/9/25, part 1.
19 George Graham to Minister of Education, 1 Nov 1930, *Sun*, 16 Jul 1930, CW 1, 40/25/26.
20 J. McCarroll to Beck, 19 Apr 1926, CW 1, 40/50/8.
21 S. Paterson, SM, to Minister of Justice, 8 Mar 1929, ?, SM, Auckland, to Minister of Justice, 25 Mar 1929, R. Tate, SM, New Plymouth, to Minister of Justice, 19 Feb 1929, J 1, 18/6/1.
22 Ferguson to McClune, 23 Apr 1945, CW 1, 40/50/4, 5 Feb 1945, CW 1, 2/9/25, part 1.
23 J. Cupit to Beck, 13 Oct 1936, J 1, 18/6/2.
24 J. Salmon, SM, to Minister of Justice, 23 Feb 1929, Paterson to Minister of Justice, 8 Mar 1929, J 1, 18/6/1.
25 See, for example, *Auckland Star*, 6 Mar 1935, CW 1, 4/12/9, part 1.
26 *Truth*, 12 Jun 1935, CW 1, 40/50/4.
27 See the responses in J 1, 18/6/1.
28 J. Bryce, Secretary, Society for the Protection of Women and Children, to Minister of Justice, 15 Sep 1931, C. Taylor, Crown Solicitor, to Under-Secretary of Justice, 23 Oct 1931, John Cobbe, Minister of Justice, to SPWC, 30 Oct and 30 Dec 1931, E. Cutten to SPWC, 13 Nov 1931, Under-Secretary of Justice to Wyvern Wilson, 25 May 1933, Wilson to Under-Secretary of Justice, 27 May 1933, *Auckland Star*, 2 Jun 1933, J 1, 18/6/2.
29 Beck, *Child Welfare*, p. 31; *AJHR*, 1927, E-4, pp. 9–10.
30 Minister of Education to Minister of Justice, 10 Jun 1926, CW 1, 40/50/11.
31 Cutten to Under-Secretary of Justice, 26 Mar 1927, J 1, 18/6/1; *Dominion*, 5 Jul 1926, CW 1, 40/50/8; Cutten to Beck, 6 Dec 1926, CW 1, 40/50/4.
32 M. Gibb, BWO, Hawera, to Beck, 10 Nov 1927, CW 1, 40/50/13.
33 *Sun*, 14 Jun 1927, Cupit to Beck, 15 Jun 1927, CW 1, 40/50/11; Beck to Under-Secretary of Justice, 4 Feb 1928, Cutten to Under-Secretary of Justice, 29 Feb 1928, J 1, 18/6/2.
34 G. Young, Probation Officer, Napier, to Director of Education, 17 Apr 1926, CW 1, 40/50/4.
35 Director of Education to Public Service Commissioner, 10 Nov 1926, CW 1, 40/50/4.
36 *AJHR*, 1928, E-4, p. 2.
37 Christchurch *Star*, 20 Dec 1928, Thomas Wilford, Minister of Justice, to Stipendiary Magistrates, 7 Feb 1929, J 1, 18/6/1.
38 See letters from child welfare officers in CW 1, 40/50/37; Beck to Director of Education, 18 Apr 1936, CW 1, 4/12/9, part 1.
39 Cupit to Beck, 13 Oct 1936, Beck to Under-Secretary of Justice, 22 Oct 1936, J 1, 18/6/2; Director of Education to Minister of Education, 27 May, 14 Jun 1927, J. Christie, Law Drafting Office, to Attorney-General, 8 Jun 1927, J 1, 18/6/1.
40 McClune to Director of Education, 5 Oct 1945, CW 1, 40/50/11.
41 M. Lyons, 'Children's Courts in the 1940s', *New Zealand Social Worker*, vol. 6, no. 1, 1970, p. 15.
42 Christie to Attorney-General, 8 Jun 1927, J 1, 18/6/1.
43 W. McKean, SM, to Under-Secretary of Justice, 24 May 1940, J 1, 1940/41/1, bundle 64.
44 *AJHR*, E-4, 1928, p. 2, 1946, p. 10.
45 For more on this, see John Gillis, 'The Evolution of Juvenile Delinquency in England 1890–1914', *Past and Present*, 67, 1975, pp. 96–216, *Youth and History, passim*; Hendrick, *Child Welfare*, pp. 27–9; May,

'Innocence and Experience', pp. 7–29.

46   Pearson, *Hooligan*, pp. 7, 48.

47   See Gillis, *Youth and History, passim*; Pearson, *Hooligan*, pp. 43ff.

48   Wanganui Education Board, Report on Character Training and Citizenship, nd [1944], p. 15, CW 1, 40/55B; Department of Education, 'New Zealand Child and Youth Welfare and Social Services', 1949, p. 23.

49   See CW 1, 4/16/9.

50   Wanganui Education Board, Report, pp. 21–4, CW 1, 40/55B.

51   See various reports to children's courts, Ferguson to Senior Magistrate, Wellington, 30 Apr 1947, G. Brendon, BWO, Wanganui, to Magistrate, Wanganui Children's Court, 9 Apr 1941, E. Thorpe, BWO, Dunedin, report, 23 Apr 1947, CW 1, 40/50/40.

52   For example, see Ferguson to Presiding Magistrate, Invercargill Children's Court, 18 Apr 1945, pp. 4–6, Ferguson to Senior Magistrate, Wellington Children's Court, 30 Apr 1947, CW 1, 40/50/40.

53   Beck to Cupit, 7 Nov 1927, CW 1, 4/19/2, part 1.

54   For a discussion of Britain, see Hendrick, *Child Welfare*, pp. 177–8; for Australia, see van Krieken, *Children and the State*, pp. 119–29.

55   Director of Education to Minister of Education, 19 Oct 1939, CW 1, 40/25/8.

56   Brendon to Magistrate, Wanganui Children's Court, 9 Apr 1941, CW 1, 40/50/40.

57   Wanganui Education Board, Report, pp. 67–8, 'Circular letter to Parents on Child Welfare', [Apr 1943], CW 1, 40/55B.

58   K. Tannahill, Takapuna, to Minister of Education, 8 Jun 1940, CW 1, 4/19/2, part 1; V. Campbell, Chair, Auckland Education Board, to Peter Fraser, 16 Apr 1943, CW 1, 40/55B.

59   Brendon to Magistrate, Wanganui Children's Court, 9 Apr 1941, 13 Apr 1943, CW 1, 40/50/40; Evidence of Brendon to Wanganui Education Board, Report, p. 57, CW 1, 40/55B; G. Gilling, BWO, Rotorua, to McClune, 14 Sep 1945, CW 1, 4/16/9.

60   Cupit to Beck, 9 Nov 1927, CW 1, 4/19/2, part 1.

61   *AJHR*, 1939, E-4, p. 7.

62   Lewis Anderson, DCWO, Whangarei, to McClune, 14 Jun 1946, CW 1, 4/19/2, part 1.

63   H. P. Lawry, SM, Evidence to Wanganui Education Board, Report, p. 48, CW 1, 40/55B.

64   *Press*, 5 Sep 1936, CW 1, 40/50/34.

65   Ferguson to Presiding Magistrate, Invercargill Children's Court, 18 Apr 1945, CW 1, 40/50/40.

66   *AJHR*, 1946, E-4, p.12.

67   Philip J. Fleming, '"Shadow Over New Zealand": The Response to Venereal Disease in New Zealand, 1910–1945', PhD thesis, Massey University, 1989, pp. 95–7, 176–86.

68   See reports by Thorpe, 14 Apr 1941, and P. Goodwin, 15 May 1941, CW 1, 40/50/40; McClune to Director of Education, 5 Oct 1945, CW 1, 40/55/2.

69   Gilling to McClune, 16 Mar 1943, H. L. Hunt, BWO, Palmerston North, to McClune, 20 Oct 1943, CW 1, 4/16/3, part 1; Jock Phillips with Ellen Ellis, *Brief Encounter: American Forces and the New Zealand People 1942–1945*, Wellington, Historical Branch, Department of Internal Affairs, 1992, p. 47.

70   McClune to Under-Secretary of Justice, 4 Mar 1943, J 1, 21/2/34, part 1; Annie Tocker, 'Recollections From 1926', and Lorna Hodder, 'Recollections From 1940', *New Zealand Social Worker*, vol. 5, no. 4, 1969, pp. 23, 29; *Evening Post*, 18 Sep 1945, CW 1, 40/2/124A.

71   CW 1, 40/29/32.

72   Fleming, '"Shadow Over New Zealand"', p. 186.

73   Michael King, 'Between Two Worlds', in Rice (ed.), *Oxford History of New Zealand*, p. 305.

74   *AJHR*, 1945, E-4, p. 4; 'Delinquent Maori Youth and Employment', 31 Jul 1941, Beck to Director of Education, 23 Sep 1936, CW 1, 40/25/26; Wanganui Education Board, Report, pp. 40–1, CW 1, 40/55B; McClune, Notes on visit to Napier, Gisborne and East Coast, Mar 1940, CW 1, 19/52; Beck to Gilmour, DCWO, Gisborne, 28 Mar 1935, CW 1, 4/13; CW 1, 40/50/40.

75   D. Campbell, Honorary Child Welfare Officer, Shannon, to CWO, Palmerston North, 20 Dec 1944, CW 1, 4/16/3, part 1; H. Giles, BWO, Auckland, to DCWO, Auckland, 20 Oct 1943, CW 1, 4/15/5.

76   Anderson to McClune, 2 Apr 1945, CW 1, 40/2/124.

77   *AJHR*, 1925–48, E-4.

78   W. Cumming, BWO, Timaru, to Beck, 26 Oct 1927, CW 1, 40/50/12.

79   Case file, ABNT, W4295.

80   V. B. Newman, 'The Burwood Girls' Training Centre', fifth year preventive medicine thesis, University of Otago, 1952, pp. 11–16.

81   Gilmour to Magistrate, Gisborne Children's Court, 3 Jun 1936, CW 1, 40/50/24; Gilmour to Beck, 1 Mar 1935, CW 1, 4/13.

82   Beck to Director of Education, 23 Sep 1936, CW 1, 40/25/26.

83   Thorpe to Magistrate, Hamilton Children's Court, 6 Jul 1938, CW 1, 40/50/24.

84   Goodwin to Director of Education, 18 December 1925, CW 1, 40/10/63.

85   Case file, ABNT, W4295.

86   For more on fit bodies, see Tennant, *Children's Health*, pp. 13–61. On sexuality, see R. P. Neuman, 'Masturbation, Madness, and the Modern Concepts of Childhood and Adolescence', *Journal of Social History*, vol. 8, no. 1, 1976, pp. 1–27, and David Walker, 'Continence for a Nation: Seminal Loss and National Vigour', *Labour History*, no. 48, 1985, pp. 1–14.

87   J. Heenan to McClune, 6 Sep 1940, *Dominion*, 7 Oct 1940, CW 1, 40/1/72.

88   Goodwin to magistrates and associates, Wellington Children's Court, 2 May 1930, CW 1, 40/50/24.

89   J. Lock, BWO, Dunedin, to Magistrate, Dunedin Children's Court, 27 Apr 1942, CW 1, 40/50/40.

90   *AJHR*, 1928, E-4, p. 6; Cupit to Beck, 23 Sep 1926, Secretary YMCA, report on Big Brothers, 4 Sep 1925, CW 1, 8/14/2; D. McKee Wright, BWO, Nelson, to Beck, 20 Jan 1930, CW 1, 40/50/12.

91   The YMCA's 'failure' rate was 5 per cent in 1926. This was significantly better than that of the Branch, but may well have reflected the fact that it was the 'easier' cases which were passed on to voluntary groups. Falconer to Minister of Education, 24 Nov 1926, CW 1, 40/1/45.

92   R. A. Kenner, YMCA, Christchurch, to Beck, 8 Oct 1926, CW 1, 40/10/63.

93   Cumming to Beck, 11 Aug 1930, CW 1, 40/50/12.

94   Replies from magistrates, 1929, J 1, 18/6/1.

95   Material in this and the next paragraph is from the case file in ABNT, W4295.

96   The figures are as at 31 March each year. *AJHR*, 1927–48, E-4.

97   Ibid., 1928, p. 8, 1940, p. 3; Circular, 17 Mar 1927, CW 1, 40/15/42.

98   Beck to Director of Education, 8 May 1929, Minutes of Eugenics Board, 23 Jul 1929, Director of Education to Minister of Education, 26 Jul 1929, CW 1, 40/5/5; Bardsley, 'The Functions of an Institution', pp. 38ff; CW 1, 2/6/30, part 1.

99   K. Scotter, Principal, Burwood, to McClune, 24 Nov 1944, CW 1, 41/37/10.

100 Beck to Director of Education, 27 Jan 1925, 2 Jun, 12 Jul 1926, CW 1, 41/37/1; Scotter to McClune, 24 Nov 1944, CW 1, 41/37/10; *AJHR*, 1943, E-4, p. 1.

101 *AJHR*, 1945, E-4, p. 3.

102 M. Hamilton to McClune, 30 Jun 1939, CW 1, 40/25/26.

103 *Sun*, 16 Jul 1930, Graham to Minister of Education, 1 Nov, 11 Dec 1930, 9 Mar 1931, ibid.

104 Beck to Director of Education, 26 Jul 1927, CW 1, 7/90/1, part 1; Beck to Acting-Director of Education, 10 Dec 1935, CW 1, 40/15/43; McClune's report, 10 Jun 1937, ? to Minister of Education, 2 Apr 1938, Note for file, 2 Jul 1938, E 2, 1943/8b.

105 Peek to McClune, 13 Dec 1939, Director of Education to Chair, Building Co-ordination Committee, Wellington, 18 Jan 1940, E 2, 1943/8b; Peek, 'A Superintendent Looks Back', p. 15.

106 Cumming to Beck, 26 Oct 1927, CW 1, 40/50/12.

107 CW 1, 40/29/32.

108 Case file, ABNT, W4295.

109 Director of Education to Minister of Education, 2 May 1934, 4 Jul 1945, CW 1, 3/5/1; Peek to all child welfare officers, 26 Feb 1948, CW 1, 40/51/1.

110 Beck to Director of Education, 16 Apr 1928, Beck to Lt-Col. Horne, Wellington, 18 Apr 1928, CW 1, 40/51/1; Revd J. Currie, Te Whaiti, to CWO, Gisborne, 25 Nov 1941, McClune to CWO, Gisborne, 9 Mar 1942, CW 1, 40/25/26.

111 *AJHR*, 1946, E-4, p. 8.

112 See the report on the Dunkley Home in Dunedin, which took in children during the 1930s, *Evening*

Star, 12 Jan 1931, CW 1, 40/6/59. Beck reported in 1927 that more than 87 per cent of the children in orphanages had at least one living parent, *AJHR*, 1927, E-4, p. 8.

113   *AJHR*, 1926, E-4, p. 4.

114   Beck to Revd Fancourt, Palmerston North, 22 Aug 1929, CW 1, 5/1/33, part 1.

115   Scotter, annual report for year ended 31/12/70, WEL 9/53/4, part 3; Minister of Education to P. Goldsmith, 14 Nov 1932, WEL 9/50, part 1.

116   Notes on Burwood, nd [1926–8], Notes on girls' home, Burwood, May 1938, Scotter to Peek, 25 Feb 1948, CW 1, 40/1/47; CW 1, 40/29/32.

117   J. S. Cupit, 'Wera Roa. Its shortcomings', nd [1939], Beck to Director of Education, 14 Mar 1933, WEL 9/50, part 1.

118   K. Masters to Beck, 26 May 1936, 8 Jul 1937, CW 1, 19/9/19.

119   Alfred Cowles to Director of Education, 8 Aug 1928, CW 1, 40/4/29.

120   Acting Manager, Weraroa, to Beck, 27 Jun 1932, *Otaki Mail*, 5 Sep 1932, Director of Education to Minister of Education, 30 Jan 1933, CW 1, 40/22/8.

121   W. Cumming, Weraroa, to McClune, 14 Mar 1939, Manager, Weraroa, to McClune, 29 May 1939, CW 1, 8/16; *NZPD*, 1939, vol. 254, p. 833; Peek, 'A Superintendent Looks Back', p. 16.

122   Newman, 'The Burwood Girls' Training Centre', pp. 11–16.

123   Case file, ABNT, W4295.

124   Odem, *Delinquent Daughters*, pp. 176ff.

125   Peek to Mabel Howard, Minister in charge of the Child Welfare Division, 29 Jun 1948, Circular, 9 Jul 1948, CW 1, 40/1/72.

126   Peek to Mabel Howard, 3 Nov 1948, CW 1, 2/10/2, part 1.

CHAPTER 4   'Saved to the State': preventive child welfare

1   *AJHR*, 1929, E-4, p. 4.

2   *AJHR*, 1917, E-1A, p. 2.

3   Ibid., p. 7.

4   *AJHR*, 1925, E-4, p. 5.

5   Beck to ?, nd, incomplete, CW 1, 40/50/4.

6   This and the following cases are drawn from CW 1, 40/47/25, unless otherwise indicated.

7   Child welfare officers also had reason to fear for their safety. Now employed on a farm near Napier, Lawrence claimed that he would not be content until he had 'fixed' the child welfare officer and could see the blood 'flow and flow and flow'. His employers caught him attempting to strangle one of their children, and confirmed that he was 'sadistic', enjoying making youngsters suffer and, like some young boys, gaining pleasure out of torturing insects. He was finally admitted to Weraroa, where staff reported that he did well and noted a growing mutual affection with his mother. Case file, ABNT, W4295.

8   Case file, ABNT, W4295.

9   Gordon, 'Child Abuse', pp. 219–20, and 'Family Violence, Feminism, and Social Control', in Gordon (ed.), *Women, the State, and Welfare*, pp. 191–3.

10   Brendon to Beck, 17 Jun 1929, CW 1, 4/13/1.

11   This and the following cases are drawn from CW 1, 40/47/25, unless otherwise indicated.

12   Different styles of policing throughout the country influenced whether or not the police decided to prosecute. Rural and suburban police sometimes tended to avoid dealing with youths formally, but police discretion over whether or not to prosecute could be more circumscribed in the city. Rather than prosecuting, police sometimes administered their own 'rough justice' to young males, as well as passing cases to the Child Welfare Branch. Graeme Dunstall to Bronwyn Dalley, 28 Feb 1997, personal communication.

13   Case file, ABNT, W4295.

14   Bailey, *Delinquency and Citizenship*, p. 16.

15   Case history, CW 1, 40/47/25.

16   *AJHR*, 1944, E-4, p. 5.

17 This and the following cases, unless otherwise stated, are drawn from CW 1, 40/47/25.

18 Case file, ABNT, W4295.

19 Ibid.

20 *AJHR*, 1945, E-4, p. 7.

21 Thorpe to DCWO, Christchurch, 2 Sep 1948, CW 1, 4/14/1.

22 Case history, CW 1, 40/47/25.

23 Case histories, ibid.

24 Robert van Krieken, 'State Bureaucracy and Social Science: Child Welfare in New South Wales, 1915–1940', *Labour History*, no. 58, 1990, pp. 19–20.

25 Hendrick, *Child Welfare*, p. 5. For more on the expansion of psychological advice literature and the use of psychology in child welfare, see Denise Riley, *War in the Nursery: Theories of the Child and Mother*, London, Virago, 1983, *passim*; Hendrick, *Child Welfare*, pp. 149–76; Urwin and Sharland, 'From Bodies to Minds', pp. 174–99.

26 *AJHR*, 1939, E-4, p. 3.

27 Cupit to Beck, 8 Jun 1937, John McLean to Young, 15 Jun 1938, Young to Superintendent of Child Welfare, 17 Jun 1938, CW 1, 8/14/2.

28 Director of Education to J. Tyler, President, YMCA, 10 Nov 1939, CW 1, 41/39.

29 Case history, CW 1, 40/47/25.

30 *AJHR*, 1927, E-4, p. 9; Beck to ?, nd, CW 1, 40/50/4.

31 *AJHR*, 1946, E-4, p. 2.

32 See CW 1, 40/25/26.

33 Te Akarana Association, quoted in *Sun*, 16 Jul 1930, CW 1, 40/25/26.

34 *AJHR*, 1944, E-4, p. 3.

35 McClune, notes on visit to Napier, Gisborne and East Coast, Mar 1940, CW 1, 19/52.

36 Young to McClune, 26 Sep 1940, CW 1, 40/25/26; see 'Housing and Social Problems: A Report to the Mayor and Councillors of Invercargill', Mar 1946, CW 1, 2/9/26, part 1.

37 Gael Ferguson, *Building the New Zealand Dream*, Palmerston North, Dunmore Press with the assistance of the Historical Branch, Department of Internal Affairs, 1994, p. 172.

38 Goodwin to McClune, 8 Aug 1941, CW 1, 4/7, part 1.

39 T. N. Smallwood, Joint Manager, State Advances Corporation, to Director of Education, 7 Aug 1941, Bernard Ashwin, Secretary of Treasury, to Minister of Housing, 12 Aug 1941, CW 1, 4/7, part 1.

40 Peek to Hilda Ross, Minister for the Welfare of Women and Children, 1 Feb 1952, CW 1, 4/7, part 2.

41 Ashwin to Minister of Housing, 12 Aug 1941, CW 1, 4/7, part 1; Peek to Director of Education, 16 Jun 1947, CW 1, 4/7, part 2.

42 Director of Education to Minister of Education, 21 Oct 1941, Director of Education to Peek, 10 Jul 1947, CW 1, 4/7, part 2.

43 Thorpe to McClune, 20 Mar 1942, CW 1, 4/7, part 1.

44 McClune, statement of action taken to 5 Aug 1943, Peek's report on assistance to needy families to 31 Mar 1946, CW 1, 4/7, part 1.

45 Unless otherwise stated, these cases are drawn from the needy families files: CW 1, 4/7, parts 1 and 2, and CW 1, 40/2/94.

46 K. Stewart, CWO, Auckland, to McClune, 27 Aug 1943, CW 1, 4/7, part 1.

47 Peek to Director of Education, 16 Jun 1947, McClune to all child welfare officers, 19 Dec 1941, CW 1, 4/7, part 2; McClune, statement of action taken to 5 Aug 1943, CW 1, 4/7, part 1; *AJHR*, 1944, E-4, p. 5.

48 For a contrasting view that welfare supported nuclear family arrangements, see Linda Bryder, '"A Social Laboratory": New Zealand and Social Welfare, 1840–1990', *British Review of New Zealand Studies*, 3, 1991, pp. 37–48.

49 Case file, ABNT, W4295; CW 1, 4/7/4.

50 Needy family cases, E 2, 1950/25b.

51 Linda Gordon argues that a needs-based welfare system flourished as social work became increasingly professionalised, particularly through casework. The operation of the needy families scheme provides an example of this in the New Zealand context. Gordon, *Pitied But Not Entitled*, p. 162.

52 Report on female child welfare officers for the consultative committee, 1945, E 1, 19/28/38A.

53 Case file, ABNT, W4295.

54 K. Stewart, Inspector of Child Welfare, to Peek, 17 Mar 1947, CW 1, 40/4/56.

55 CW 1, 40/2/94.

56 McClune to Director of Education, 30 Jun 1942, CW 1, 4/7, part 1; *AJHR*, 1948, B-7, p. 227.

57 McClune to DCWO, Napier, 10 Feb 1943, CW 1, 4/7, part 1.

58 McClune to Director of Education, 1 Jun 1939, CW 1, 40/1/72.

59 See Joyce Antler and Stephen Antler, 'From Child Rescue to Family Protection: The Evolution of the Child Protection Movement in the United States', *Children and Youth Services Review*, 1, 1979, p. 192; Crew, 'German Socialism', pp. 238–40; Gordon, *Heroes of Their Own Lives*, pp. 72–4; Hendrick, *Child Welfare*, p. 171; Margo Horn, 'The Moral Message of Child Guidance 1925–1945', *Journal of Social History*, vol. 18, no. 1, 1984, pp. 26–34; Lewis, 'Anxieties About the Family', pp. 40–50; Neil Sutherland, *Children in English-Canadian Society: Framing the Twentieth-century Consensus*, Toronto, University of Toronto Press, 1976, pp. 128–30; Tiffin, *In Whose Best Interest?*, pp. 110–16.

60 Beck to all district agents, 11 Aug 1926, CW 1, 4/6/1.

61 Beck to all child welfare officers, 31 Mar 1926, CW 1, 4/5.

62 Gordon Coates to Mr Carleton, Auckland, 6 Nov 1928, CW 1, 40/1/35.

63 Commissioner of Pensions to Director of Education, 17 Oct 1938, CW 1, 4/6, part 1.

64 See, for example, Ann Beaglehole, *Benefiting Women: Income Support for Women, 1893–1993*, Wellington, Social Policy Agency, 1993, p. 29.

65 For good discussions of policies targeted towards mothers, see Davin, 'Imperialism and Motherhood', pp. 9–66; Ladd-Taylor, *Mother-Work, passim*; Lewis, *The Politics of Motherhood, passim*.

66 Gordon, 'Child Abuse', p. 219.

67 In the New Zealand context, see Olssen, 'Towards a New Society', in Rice (ed.), *Oxford History of New Zealand*, pp. 262–8.

68 Jane Lewis argues for the existence of the 'mixed economy of welfare' most strongly in 'Gender, the Family and Women's Agency', pp. 37–55, and 'Family Provision', pp. 1–16. For a recent New Zealand study which examines the relationship between voluntary welfare organisations and the state, see Tennant, *Children's Health, passim*.

69 Koven and Michel, 'Gender and the Origins of the Welfare State', p. 113.

PART III **Introduction**

1 Redmer Yska, *All Shook Up: The Flash Bodgie and the Rise of the New Zealand Teenager in the Fifties*, Auckland, Penguin, 1993, p. 38.

2 *AJHR*, 1949–72, E-4.

3 'The period between 1951 and 1967 was the most conservative in New Zealand history, in every sphere of life', notes Tom Brooking in *Milestones: Turning Points in New Zealand History*, Lower Hutt, Mills, 1988, p. 183; Helen May comments on post-war New Zealand's 'paradigm of order and conformity' in *Minding Children, Managing Men: Conflict and Compromise in the Lives of Postwar Pakeha Women*, Wellington, Bridget Williams Books, 1992, p. 70.

4 For an analysis of youth culture in this period, see Yska, *All Shook Up, passim*. Studies examining the flowering of literary, artistic and musical culture, as well as those exploring an urban Maori renaissance, also suggest different interpretations of the period.

5 P. Avery Jack and J. H. Robb, 'Social Welfare Policies: Development and Patterns Since 1945', in Trlin (ed.), *Social Welfare and New Zealand Society*, p. 35.

6 Peek, 'A Superintendent Looks Back', pp. 15–18; *AJHR*, 1964, E-4, p. 4.

7 *Dominion*, 28 Oct 1967, CW 1, 8/9/1, part 1.

8 *AJHR*, 1949–72, E-4.

9 In 1945 there were 571,082 persons aged nineteen or younger, and in 1971 1,170,412; *Juvenile Crime in New Zealand*, Wellington, Department of Social Welfare, 1973, pp. 13–17.

10 *AJHR*, 1965, E-4, p. 5; Anderson, 'Child Welfare in 1971', report to meeting of Directors-General, 1 Mar 1971, p. 12, annotated copy in possession of Brian Manchester.

11 In Dugald McDonald (ed.), *Working for the Welfare: Stories by Staff of the Former Child Welfare Division*, Christchurch, Social Work Press, 1994, p. 14.

12 Kathleen Ford, annual report for year ended 31/12/70, WEL 9/53/4, part 3.

13 Ford to Anderson, 1 Apr 1964, WEL 9/53/2.

14 Anderson, report on district office facilities, 31 Jan 1969, CW 1, 2/10/10, part 5.

15 B. C. Burton, DCWO, Napier, to Peek, 13 Jul 1956, CW 1, 2/10/10, part 1.

16 Mary Todd, interviewed by Bronwyn Dalley, 25 Jun 1996, tape 1.

17 D. McKee Wright, DCWO, Wanganui, to Peek, 9 Apr 1962, CW 1, 2/10/10, part 3.

18 On the basis of the figures given, the weekly average was actually 2.6 minutes. J. Ferguson, DCWO, Wellington, to Peek, 24 Dec 1954, CW 1, 2/10/10, part 1.

19 Anderson to Minister in charge of Child Welfare Division, 26 Jul 1971, CW 1, 2/10/10, part 6.

20 B. M. Manchester, 'Some Further Comments on the Development of Social Work Training in New Zealand', Nov 1995, pp. 1–2; Brian Manchester, interviewed by Bronwyn Dalley, 20 Jun 1996, tape 2.

21 *AJHR*, E-4, 1954, p. 15, 1955, p. 5.

22 Ibid., 1971, p. 20; Brian Manchester, 'Notes on Some Developments in Social Work Training in New Zealand', Nov 1995, pp. 2–3.

23 Graeme Dunstall, 'The Social Pattern', in Rice (ed.), *Oxford History of New Zealand*, p. 451.

24 *AJHR*, 1965, E-4, p. 19.

25 Children also travelled to Canada and Australia under a similar child migration scheme. See Philip Bean and Joy Melville, *Lost Children of the Empire: The Untold Story of Britain's Child Migrants*, London, Unwin Hyman, 1989. Minister of External Affairs to New Zealand High Commissioner, London, 14 Dec 1944, High Commissioner, London, to Minister of External Affairs, 4 Jan 1945, Peek to Mabel Howard, 4 Feb 1948, CW 1, 40/57.

26 'The New Zealand Government Child Migration Scheme', nd, Overseas League, London, *Southern Cross*, 14 Mar 1951, *Dominion*, 15 Mar 1951, 1 Mar 1952, CW 1, 4/8/5; Peek to Director, Department of Employment and Labour, 1 Nov 1951, British Migrant Children report, 31 Mar 1954, [Peek?] to Ferguson, 2 Oct 1962, CW 1, 4/8, part 1; *AJHR*, 1954, E-4, p. 9.

27 In June 1953 *Truth* carried the headline, 'Immigrant Says He was Treated Like a Child Slave', an account from a sixteen year old youth who stated that his North Island farming foster family had mistreated him while putting on a good show for the visits of the child welfare officer, CW 1, 4/8/5.

CHAPTER 5 **'That disagreeable term "teenagers"': juvenile delinquency and its prevention**

1 Reprinted from London's *News Chronicle*, 26 Sep 1954, in *Christchurch Star–Sun*, 27 Sep 1954, CW 1, 4/19, part 1.

2 Yska, *All Shook Up,* is the best examination of teenage culture in 1950s' New Zealand; the rise of rock'n'roll is explored in Roger Watkins, *Hostage to the Beat: The Auckland Scene 1955–70*, Auckland, Penguin, 1995. For a contemporary discussion, see A. E. Manning, *The Bodgie: A Study in Abnormal Psychology*, Wellington, A. H. and A. W. Reed, 1958. There are a large number of works focusing on the rise of the teenager in other societies. Some of the better examples include Adams, 'Youth, Corruptibility'; Wini Breines, *Young, White and Miserable: Growing Up Female in the Fifties*, Boston, Beacon Press, 1992; Gilbert, *A Cycle of Outrage*; Gillis, *Youth and History*; Pearson, *Hooligan*.

3 *Christchurch Star-Sun*, 2 Apr 1956, CW 1, 4/19/1, part 2; Bob Jones, in 'The Mazengarb Report', *Spectrum* Documentary, Radio New Zealand, no. 731. A fuller discussion of teenage dress in the 1950s can be found in Yska, *All Shook Up*, pp. 171–6.

4 Magistrate Harlow in *Dominion*, 4 Aug 1954, CW 1, 4/19/5.

5 *Press*, 26 Aug 1957, CW 1, 4/19, part 2; *Christchurch Star-Sun*, 24 Aug 1955, CW 1, 4/19/1, part 2; *Taranaki Herald*, 5 Jun 1957, CW 1, 4/19, part 3.

6 S. Hardy, SM, quoted in *Bay of Plenty Times*, 20 Aug 1958, CW 1, 4/19, part 3.

7 Gilbert, *A Cycle of Outrage*, pp. 13–15; for discussions of juvenile delinquency elsewhere, see Adams, 'Youth, Corruptibility', *passim*; Pearson, *Hooligan*, pp. 7–43; Simonetta Piccone Stella, '"Rebels Without a Cause": Male Youth in Italy Around 1960', *History Workshop Journal*, 38, 1994, pp. 157–78; Jon Stratton, 'Bodgies and Widgies: Youth Cultures in the 1950s', *Journal of Australian Studies*, 15, 1984,

pp. 10–24.

8 In 'The Mazengarb Report'.

9 Report of Senior Sergeant Le Fort, Petone Police Station, to Chair, Special Committee, 31 Jul 1954, MS-Papers 2384/7.

10 See Julie Glamuzina and Alison Laurie, *Parker and Hulme: A Lesbian View*, Auckland, New Women's Press, 1991, pp. 58–60; Bernadette Lavelle, '"Youth Without Purpose": Juvenile Delinquency in New Zealand in the 1950s', MA thesis, University of Otago, 1990; Maureen Molloy, 'Science, Myth and the Adolescent Female: The Mazengarb Report, the Parker–Hulme Trial, and the Adoption Act of 1955', *Women's Studies Journal*, vol. 9, no. 1, 1993, pp. 1–25; Roy Shuker and Roger Openshaw with Janet Soler, *Youth, Media and Moral Panic in New Zealand: From Hooligans to Video Nasties*, Palmerston North, Education Department, Massey University, Delta Research Monograph no. 11, 1990; Janet Soler, '"Drifting Towards Moral Chaos": The 1954 Mazengarb Report – A Moral Panic Over "Juvenile Delinquency"', MPhil thesis, Massey University, 1988; Michael Stace, 'Legal Form and Moral Phenomena: A Study of Two Events', Doctor of Jurisprudence thesis, York University, 1980; Yska, *All Shook Up*, pp. 58–84. A full account can also be found in the Report of the Special Committee on Moral Delinquency in Children and Adolescents, *AJHR*, 1954, H-47; the submissions to the committee are in MS-Papers 2384. Most secondary analyses place the inquiry in the context of a society in the midst of a 'moral panic' over youthful behaviour and other nonconformist activity. The motivations for this differ: Shuker and Openshaw with Soler (*Youth, Media and Moral Panic*) and Soler ('"Drifting Towards Moral Chaos"') view it as a media-inspired and media-led crisis which fed a receptive audience of conservative Christians and moral campaigners; Stace ('Legal Form') plays down the role of the media, instead examining the inquiry and report as an attempt by a society with an attachment to the past to shape morality through legal processes; Molloy ('Science, Myth') views the inquiry as part of a broader international anxiety about adolescent female sexuality and motherhood.

11 *Manawatu Evening Standard*, 19 Dec 1952, CW 1, 8/9/1, part 2; *Taranaki Herald*, 24 Nov 1952, *Thames Star*, 4 Dec 1952, *Manawatu Daily Times*, 13 Feb 1953, *Dominion*, 13 Feb 1953, CW 1, 4/19/1, part 1; *Auckland Star*, 14 Sep 1951, *Southland News*, 19 Feb 1954, CW 1, 4/19/1, part 1.

12 *AJHR*, 1954, H-47, p. 21; J. Medcalf, DCWO, Timaru, to Peek, 30 Jul 1954, and other responses, CW 1, 4/19/4, part 1.

13 E. Naylor, SCWO, Rotorua, to Peek, 30 Jul 1954, CW 1, 4/19/4, part 1.

14 Kath Scotter, Principal, Burwood, evidence to the special committee, 1 Sep 1954, MS-Papers 2384/3.

15 *Taranaki Daily News*, 25 Aug 1954, CW 1, 4/19, part 1.

16 Revised proposals of Inter-departmental Committee on the Control of Comics, nd [1952], CW 1, 13/2/7, part 1; Yska, *All Shook Up*, pp. 87–106, contains a detailed discussion of the reactions to all forms of printed matter that were considered objectionable.

17 Secretary of Justice to Peek, 9 Mar 1954, G. Smith, DCWO, Auckland, to Peek, 18 Mar 1954, CW 1, 4/19/3.

18 *AJHR*, 1954, H-47, pp. 21–7.

19 *Times*, 14 Jul 1954, CW 1, 4/19/1, part 1.

20 Medcalf to Peek, 30 Jul 1954, CW 1, 4/19/4, part 1.

21 J. Ferguson, Wellington, annual report to magistrates, nd [1949], CW 1, 4/12/3, part 1.

22 *Evening Post*, 15 Jul 1954, CW 1, 4/19, part 1.

23 Submission from F. Ford, Chair, New Zealand Association of Model Engineers, 10 Sep 1954, MS-Papers 2384/7; *Otago Daily Times*, 27 Aug 1954, *New Zealand Herald*, 20 Jan 1955, CW 1, 4/19, part 1.

24 *AJHR*, 1954, H-47, p. 35; *Dominion*, 13 Oct 1954, John McKenzie to Child Welfare Division, 29 Oct 1954, CW 1, 4/19, part 1; Survey of Youth Clubs, SS 8/10/11, part 1.

25 *AJHR*, 1954, H-47, pp. 54–63.

26 Peek to special committee, 6 Aug 1954, MS-Papers 2384/1.

27 *AJHR*, 1955, I-15.

28 New Zealand Post Office circular memo, 21 Oct 1954, E. Halstead, Minister of Social Security, to Minister of Education, 11 Mar 1955, SS 7/7/17.

29 Shuker and Openshaw with Soler, *Youth, Media and Moral Panic*, pp. 19–30, argue that media – and

thus other – interest subsided after mid-October 1954. While interest in the issue fell somewhat from later 1954, particularly in comparison with the flood of reports earlier, juvenile immorality and delinquency more generally remained newsworthy throughout the following year. The Child Welfare Division's comprehensive set of newspaper clippings on juvenile delinquency in the mid-1950s attest to a more long-term media interest in the topic than Shuker et al. have allowed. See CW 1, 4/19, parts 1 and 2, 4/19/1, parts 1 and 2, 4/19/4, part 1, 4/19/5.

30 In *Taranaki Herald*, 5 Jun 1957, CW 1, 4/19, part 3.

31 *Evening Post*, 3 Nov 1954, CW 1, 4/19/5; Elected Committee of Citizens (Wellington), Submission to Select Committee, 28 Feb 1955, Le 1/1955/6, Submissions.

32 *Christchurch Star–Sun*, 29 Sep 1954, *Wanganui Chronicle*, 30 Sep 1954, CW 1, 4/19, part 1.

33 See Le 1/1955/6, Submissions; Le 1/1955/6, Juvenile Delinquency Committee.

34 C. E. Peek's evidence to the special committee, 3 Aug 1954, MS-Papers 2384/1.

35 Responses to survey, Jul–Aug 1954, CW 1, 4/19/4, part 1. Timaru's officer was the only one to note the behaviour of milk-bar cowboys.

36 J. Cupit, DCWO, Auckland, to Secretary, Education Board, nd [May 1950], CW 1, 4/16/7.

37 L. Macartney, DCWO, Greymouth, to Peek, 30 Jul 1954, CW 1, 4/19/4, part 1.

38 Report of G. Smidt and L. Uttley, Wellington, nd [Mar 1952], CW 1, 4/16/7.

39 *Christchurch Star–Sun*, 15 Jul 1954, *New Zealand Herald*, 15 Jul 1954, CW 1, 4/19/5.

40 'Report of the Hutt Valley Youth Survey', CW 1, 4/19/4, part 1. For a fuller examination of both the survey and a comparison with the 1954 inquiry, see Soler, '"Drifting Towards Moral Chaos"', pp. 44–70.

41 *Auckland Star*, 4 Nov 1954, CW 1, 4/19, part 1; Gordon Smith, DCWO, Auckland, to the special committee, 7 Sep 1954, MS-Papers 2384/4.

42 Peter Kamo, Chair, Owenga School Committee, Chatham Islands, to Peek, 10 Aug 1954, CW 1, 4/16/7. Peek arranged for an inspector of schools to visit the area.

43 For more, see Bailey, *Delinquency and Citizenship*, pp. 300ff; Robert Bremner (ed.), *Children and Youth in America: A Documentary History*, vol. 3, 1933–1973, Cambridge, Harvard University Press, 1974, pp. 1004, 1048ff; Gillis, *Youth and History*, pp. 186ff; Hendrick, *Child Welfare*, pp. 222ff; Pearson, *Hooligan*, chapters 1 and 2.

44 See *AJHR*, E-4, 1955, p. 6, 1958, p. 3, 1965, p. 5, 1969, p. 6; M. Lyons, DCWO, Hamilton, to Presiding Magistrate, Children's Court, Jun 1955, CW 1, 4/12/3, part 3; J. Medcalf, DCWO, Timaru, to Peek, 30 Jul 1954, CW 1, 4/19/4, part 1; *Evening Post*, 26 May 1955, CW 1, 4/19/1, part 2.

45 Peek to the special committee, 3 and 6 Aug 1954, MS-Papers 2384/1.

46 See *AJHR*, 1969–72, E-4.

47 The figures are for the number of cases heard during the year ending on either 31 March or 31 December, depending on how the Division collated the figures, *AJHR*, 1948–73, E-4. Children's court appearances represent only one segment of juvenile delinquency – those cases considered sufficiently serious to warrant court action. They do not provide any indication of the number of cases handled out of court, nor, of course, of the number of children who committed offences but were not detected. The number of court appearances also should be used with a degree of caution because the Child Welfare Division changed its recording methods a number of times during this period, making it difficult to devise a standardised long-term measure: from 1949 cases were counted only if a charge had been proved; traffic offences were removed from the children's court in 1961; figures from 1963 on refer to the calendar year rather than the year ending 31 March.

48 'Preliminary facts and comparisons from study of returns of Children's Court appearances', nd, SS 8/10/7, part 1; *AJHR*, 1965, E-4, p. 5.

49 Juvenile court appearances, 1953–54, SS 8/10, part 1; 'A Limited Study comparing Maoris and non-Maoris appearing in the Children's Court in 1960', report of Joint Committee on Young Offenders, 17 Jun 1963, J 1, 21/2/46, part 2; 'Preliminary facts and comparisons', nd, SS 8/10/7, part 1; Peek to Secretary of Maori Affairs, 28 Apr 1961, *New Zealand Herald*, 8 Jan 1964, *Wanganui Herald*, 20 Dec 1965, CW 1, 4/15/3; Lyons, annual report on children's court, 20 Jul 1956, CW 1, 4/12/3, part 3; S. Barnett, Secretary of Justice, to Director of Education, 14 Jun 1957, Ferguson, note for file, 1 Aug 1958, Research Officer, Department of Maori Affairs, to Ferguson, 4 Nov 1958, SS 8/10/8, part 1; Anderson to Minister in

charge of Child Welfare Division, 15 Jan 1970, CW 1, 4/19, part 4.

50　Lyons to Presiding Magistrate, Auckland Children's Court, 25 Jul 1956, CW 1, 4/12/3, part 3; Peek to special committee, 2 Sep 1954, MS-Papers 2384/3; *AJHR*, 1954, H-47, p. 16.

51　A. Witten-Hannah, Honorary CWO and President, Te Kotahitanga Tautaru, New Plymouth, to Peek, 9 Mar 1958, CW 1, 4/12/10; Minister of Education to Ralph Love, Secretary, Maori Women's Welfare League, 15 Jul 1952, CW 1, 4/12/6; Love to Minister of Education, 10 Sep 1952, CW 1, 4/15/3.

52　R. Walton, DCWO, Rotorua, to Magistrate, Children's Court, 9 Jul 1957, CW 1, 4/12/3, part 4.

53　A. Rounthwaite, DCWO, Whangarei, note for file, 29 Mar 1955, Anderson, note for file, 18 Apr 1955, CW 1, 4/15/3.

54　D. Reilly, DCWO, Hamilton, to Peek, 25 Aug 1950, CW 1, 4/16, part 1; Rounthwaite to J. Herd, SM, 1 Apr 1952, CW 1, 4/12/3, part 2; K. Stewart, visit to Masterton district, 18–20 Jan 1954, CW 1, 2/6/27, part 2; F. Hallett, DCWO, Taumarunui, to Peek, 30 Oct 1957, CW 1, 4/7/5; 'Recent Research into Crime amongst Maoris', Joint Committee on Young Offenders, 3 Dec 1962, SS 8/10/9, part 5; Lorna Hodder's report on Gisborne district, Jun 1963, CW 1, 2/6/27; 'A Limited Study comparing Maoris and non-Maoris', 17 Jun 1963, J 1, 21/2/46, part 2; L. Uttley, DCWO, Whangarei, to Peek, 8 Oct 1963, SS 20/2/4W.

55　*AJHR*, 1949, E-4, p. 8; Anderson, quoted in *Dominion*, 27 Aug 1954, CW 1, 4/19, part 1.

56　Peek to Director of Education, 31 Aug 1954, SS 8/10, part 1.

57　*AJHR*, 1955–72, E-4.

58　*AJHR*, E-4, 1967, pp. 4–5, 1969, p. 6.

59　Very few works which examine juvenile delinquency in the 1950s expand the discussion to consider other forms of delinquency in the decade, or other scares over it. Soler, '"Drifting Towards Moral Chaos"', investigates the 1953 Hutt Valley survey into juvenile delinquency, while Yska, *All Shook Up*, analyses the events surrounding the trial of Frederick Foster, the 'jukebox killer', in Auckland in 1955. Considering juvenile delinquency in a wider context also suggests a need to reassess the dominant interpretation of the 1950s' events as evidence of a moral panic at the activities of youthful folk devils. The reaction to the Hutt Valley episode was perhaps extreme, but it is certainly more explicable when seen through a wider lens.

60　*Manawatu Daily Times*, 14 Dec 1954, *Levin Chronicle*, 22 Apr 1955, *Auckland Star*, 25 May 1955, CW 1, 4/19/1, part 2.

61　*Dominion* clipping, nd [May 1957], CW 1, 4/19/1, part 2; *Hutt News*, 23 Apr 1958, *Evening Post*, 13, 14 Jun 1958, *Dominion*, 14 Jun 1958, CW 1, 4/19, part 3; B. Burton, DCWO, Lower Hutt, to Anderson, 15 May, 5, 26 Jun 1958, CW 1, 4/19/7.

62　B. C. Burton, 'The Hutt Valley Court Cases', *Child Welfare Head Office Newsletter*, vol. 2, no. 6, 1958, Burton to Anderson, 26 Jun 1958, CW 1, 4/19/7; *Evening Post*, 13 Jun 1958, CW 1, 4/19, part 3; Research unit's report on sexual misbehaviour in the Hutt Valley, nd, SS 8/10/9, part 1.

63　Case file, ABNT, W4295.

64　*Bay of Plenty Times*, 13 Jul 1954, *Standard*, 21 Jul 1954, CW 1, 4/19/1, part 1.

65　*Otago Daily Times*, 15 Jul 1954, CW 1, 4/19/1, part 1; *New Zealand Herald*, 19 Jan 1955, CW 1, 4/19, part 1.

66　*AJHR*, 1955, E-4, pp. 28–9.

67　See annual reports on children's courts, especially Lyons to Presiding Magistrate, 25 Jul 1956, *Auckland Star*, 4 Jul 1955, CW 1, 4/12/3, part 3.

68　Yska, *All Shook Up*, pp. 176–94.

69　*Timaru Herald*, 6 May 1957, *Hawke's Bay Herald–Tribune*, 15 Apr 1958, CW 1, 4/19, part 3; J. Green to Chair, Joint Committee on Young Offenders, 29 Jul 1958, Green, Head of Research Unit, 'Report No. 2 on Group Anti-social Activity, Manor Park July 1958, Featherston, 25 April 1958', 18 Aug 1958, SS 8/10/9, part 1.

70　*New Zealand Listener*, 8 Aug 1958, CW 1, 4/19/6. For more on the series, see Lavelle, '"Youth Without Purpose"', *passim*; Manning, *The Bodgie, passim*; *New Zealand Herald*, 11 Mar 1958, CW 1, 4/19, part 2.

71　*In Their Own Words: From the Sound Archives of Radio New Zealand*, compiled by Stephen Barnett and Jim Sullivan, Wellington, GP Books in association with Radio New Zealand Sound Archives, 1988, pp. 78–83.

72　*Evening Post*, 13, 31 Mar 1958, CW 1, 4/19, part 2.

73 'Mods Killed Lightning', *Social End Product*, vol. 1, no. 1, 1995, pp. 34–5.

74 'Sexual misconduct among school children in Auckland', 20 Oct 1964, SS 20/2/3, vol. 1; CW 1, 4/19/4, part 2.

75 Director of Education to Minister of Education, 24 Mar 1958, CW 1, 2/10/10, part 1; A. E. Levett, BWO, to DCWO, Auckland, 18 Nov 1959, SS 8/10/11, part 1.

76 Levett's study excluded areas which he noted were likely to contain gangs – Otahuhu, Papatoetoe, Glen Innes, Tamaki, Panmure, Penrose and the entire North Shore, A. E. Levett, 'Gangs in Auckland', Feb 1959, SS 8/10/11, part 1.

77 Barnett to Minister of Police, 12 Feb 1958, SS 8/10/9, part 1.

78 Director-General of Education to ?, 11 Mar 1966, SS 20/1, vol. 2; Director of Education to Minister of Education, 30 Apr 1959, J 1, 21/2/46, part 1.

79 A. Curnow to Peek, 16 Mar 1956, Circular to all DCWOs, 16 Apr 1956, CW 1, 8/9, part 1.

80 *AJHR*, 1966, E-4, p. 7.

81 Burton to Peek, 13 Jul 1956, CW 1, 2/10/10, part 1.

82 See reports in CW 1, 2/18/2, part 1.

83 For a full discussion of the scheme, see Brian Mooney, 'The History and Development of the Youth Aid Section of the New Zealand Police', Dip. Criminology dissertation, University of Auckland, 1971, and John Seymour, 'Dealing with Young Offenders', PhD thesis, University of Auckland, 1975; Liverpool City Police, *Juvenile Liaison Officers: A New Police Approach to the Prevention of Juvenile Crime*, Liverpool, 1953, pp. 2–7, J 1, 21/2/34, part 1.

84 Director of Education to Minister of Education, 1 Aug 1958, CW 1, 8/8/6; *AJHR*, E-4, 1962, p. 11, 1972, pp. 10–11.

85 *Dominion*, 8 Mar 1959, P 1, 1/1/220; *Dominion*, 10 Apr 1962, CW 1, 8/8/6.

86 Case file, ABNT, W4295.

87 O'Sullivan to Peek, 5 Mar, 21 Jul 1958, CW 1, 8/8/6.

88 *Dominion*, 8 Mar 1959, P 1, 1/1/220; *Dominion*, 10 Apr 1962, CW 1, 8/8/6.

89 A lengthy report on the scheme in Christchurch in 1959 indicated considerable disagreement about it among police, and specifically a lack of cooperation between the Section's officers and other staff. 'Report on Enquiries and Impressions about J.C.P.B. in Christchurch', 10 Feb 1959, 'Report of conference on preventive work amongst juveniles held at Police Headquarters, Wellington on 5 and 6 August 1959', CW 1, 8/8/7; Uttley to Peek, 23 Feb 1960, CW 1, 8/8/6.

90 O'Sullivan to Peek, 7 Feb 1958, CW 1, 8/8/6.

91 Brian Manchester, interviewed by Bronwyn Dalley, 20 Jun 1996, tape 4.

92 Anon to Director-General, Department of Social Welfare, nd [Jul 1972], CW 1, 13/2/8, part 4; Peek to Director of Education, 28 Sep 1956, CW 1, 2/10, part 2; *New Zealand Herald*, 22 Apr 1970, CW 1, 8/8/1, part 1; Report of the committee investigating juvenile gangs, 9 Oct 1970, 'Youth Gangs in Auckland', Feb 1971, SS 8/10/9, part 9; *AJHR*, 1972, E-4, p. 20.

93 Elsie Feist, note for file, 4 Jan 1961, Ford to Superintendent, 20 Jan 1959, WEL 9/53, part 2; Det Sgt R. C. Anderson, Auckland, to DCWO, Auckland, 19 Jun 1962, D. O'Connor, Principal, Otekaike, to Superintendent, 25 Jun 1962, CW 1, 4/19/4, part 1.

94 Boys' Training Centre, Levin, annual reports for 1963, 1968, WEL 9/50/4, part 1; Ford to Peek, 20 Feb 1962, S. Slater to J. Ferguson, 18 Apr 1962, WEL 9/53, part 2.

95 Uttley to Anderson, 20 Apr 1966, CW 1, 4/19/4, part 2. For the views of ship girls themselves, see Jan Jordan, *Working Girls: Women in the New Zealand Sex Industry Talk to Jan Jordan*, Auckland, Penguin, 1991, pp. 150–5.

96 Psychologists, Burwood, to Superintendent, 15 Oct 1956, WEL 9/53.

97 Prof. H. Field to Peek, Ford to Peek, 21 Jul 1959, WEL 9/53, part 2.

98 Anderson to Director-General of Education, 15 Apr 1966, WEL 9/53, part 3; Ford to DCWO, Christchurch, 11 Apr 1968, WEL 9/0/3.

99 Visit, Sep 1959, CW 1, 2/6/27, part 4.

100 Fareham House, annual report, 16 Apr 1962, WEL 9/52/4; A. Ricketts to Anderson, 2 Nov 1965, WEL 9/52, part 2.

101 Peek to Director of Education, 8 Jun 1955, CW 1, 2/10/10, part 1; Anderson to Minister in charge of Child Welfare Division, 21 Jun 1965, CW 1, 2/10/10, part 4; Anderson to Bruce Kildey, Principal, Fareham, 5 Feb 1971, WEL 9/52/4.

102 Principal, Christchurch Girls' Home, to Assistant Director-General of Social Welfare, 22 Aug 1972, WEL 9/0/3.

103 *AJHR*, E-4, 1965, p. 27, 1968, p. 25, 1972, p. 22; Ferguson to Director-General of Education, 30 Jun 1971, CW 1, 13/2/8, part 4; Dennis Reilly to Minister in charge of Child Welfare Division, 29 Jan 1971, CW 1, 2/10/10, part 6.

104 Rounthwaite to Peek, 19 Nov 1958, CW 1, 2/10/2, part 1; C. Ellis, Assistant-Director, to Minister of Education, 9 Mar 1959, CW 1, 7/50/3; Rounthwaite to Peek, 19 Nov 1958, 17 Mar 1959, CW 1, 3/3/9.

105 Peek to Director of Education, 8 Jun 1955, 28 Jan 1958, CW 1, 2/10/10, part 1.

106 Peek to Minister in charge of Child Welfare Division, 15 Jan 1965, CW 1, 2/10/10, part 4.

107 *Wanganui Herald*, 11 Jul 1970, WEL 9/51, part 2.

108 Quoted in Penny Ehrhardt with Ann Beaglehole, *Women and Welfare Work, 1893–1993*, Wellington, Department of Social Welfare with the assistance of the Historical Branch, Department of Internal Affairs, 1993, p. 42; Hodder's report on visits to Fareham, Jun–Jul 1962, CW 1, 2/6/27, part 4; Fareham House, annual report, 16 Apr 1962, WEL 9/52/4.

109 Hodder's report on visits to Fareham, Jun–Jul 1962, CW 1, 2/6/27, part 4.

110 *Weekly News*, 2 May 1956, WEL 9/53; Reilly, note for file, 27 Oct 1967, WEL 9/50/3.

111 Boys' Training Centre, annual report for 1963, WEL 9/50/4, part 1.

112 Kohitere, annual report for 1970, WEL 9/50/4, part 1.

113 Rounthwaite to Anderson, 4 Nov 1970, CW 1, 2/16.

114 Scotter to Peek, 9 Jan 1957, WEL 9/53; Scotter to Peek, 30 Apr 1952, CW 1, 4/14/1; M. H. Aiken to Anderson, 25 Jan 1967, Extract from Dr McLachlin's report, nd, Ford to Anderson, 1 Apr 1964, WEL 9/53/2.

115 Anderson to Dr D. Clouston, Porirua, 1 Apr 1969, CW 1, 2/10/2, part 3.

116 Anderson to Minister in charge of Child Welfare Division, 18 Feb 1969, CW 1, 13/12/2.

117 Follow-up of girls discharged from Burwood 1/8/55–1/6/57, CW 1, 3/18/2, part 1.

118 Follow-up of Kohitere discharges, 25 Aug 1967 and part 2, nd, D. P. O'Neill, 'Follow-up of Kohitere admissions', 10 Aug 1967 and 19 Aug 1968, CW 1, 3/18/2, part 2. A complex study of discharges from all boys' homes over three months in March 1967 indicated, against the general pattern, a 70 per cent success rate for long-term institutions. The methods used to reach this conclusion are not clear from the report, which examined only a small number of residents and did not provide the more long-term perspective used in other surveys. See 'Discharges from Boys' Homes March–May 1967', CW 1, 3/18, part 2.

119 Follow-up of girls, CW 1, 3/18/2, part 1.

CHAPTER 6 **'Deprived of a normal home life': ex-nuptial births, adoption, foster care, and child abuse**

1 *AJHR*, 1955, E-4, p. 7.

2 For more on single motherhood and responses to it, see Gordon, *Heroes of Their Own Lives*, pp. 82–115; Gordon, *Pitied But Not Entitled*, *passim*; Linda Gordon, 'Single Mothers and Child Neglect, 1880–1920', *American Quarterly*, vol. 37, no. 2, 1985, pp. 173–92; Kunzel, *Fallen Women, passim*. For New Zealand, see Tennant, *Paupers and Providers*, pp. 112–20, and 'Maternity and Morality: Homes for Single Mothers 1890–1930', *Women's Studies Journal*, vol. 2, no. 1, 1985, pp. 28–49.

3 Tennant, 'Maternity and Morality', p. 40.

4 Kunzel, *Fallen Women*, p. 5.

5 See, for example, Beaglehole, *Benefiting Women*, p. 29.

6 Gordon's *Pitied But Not Entitled* explores this issue fully in the North American context.

7 The percentage of ex-nuptial births fell during the depression of the 1930s; it rose during the Second World War to a peak of 6.01 per cent in 1944, the highest level before 1962. K. Griffith, *Adoption: Procedure, Documentation, Statistics. New Zealand 1881–1981*, Wellington, 1981, p. A2.

8 J. Robson, Secretary of Justice, to Directors-General of Health and Education and Government

Statistician, 31 Oct 1966, Robson to Minister of Justice, 23 Nov 1967, J 1, 18/4/40, part 1; Anderson to Pat Whelan, Principal, Hawera High School, 1 Feb 1967, CW 1, 4/6, part 3.

9 Review of *Out of Wedlock*, *New Zealand Listener*, 7 Aug 1964, CW 1, 4/6, part 2; Anderson to General-Manager, State Advances Corporation, 15 May 1968, CW 1, 4/6, part 3.

10 Interdepartmental report on ex-nuptial births, P 1, 1/1/349.

11 Anderson, quoted in *Hawke's Bay Herald–Tribune*, 8 Nov 1967, Anderson to Duncan McKay, Minister in charge of Child Welfare Division, 25 Mar 1968, Christchurch *Star*, 19 Feb 1966, and other clippings, CW 1, 4/6, part 3; Anderson, quoted in *Dominion*, 8 Nov 1967, CW 1, 8/9/1, part 1; *Dominion*, 22 Jun 1965, CW 1, 4/6, part 2; J. A'Court, Registrar-General, to Secretary of Justice, 22 Jun 1965, J 1, 18/4/7, part 2.

12 A'Court to Secretary of Justice, 22 Jun 1965, J 1, 18/4/7, part 2; Joint Committee Research Unit, 'Illegitimacy: some notes on the increase in illegitimacy over recent years and some speculations on what has caused it', Mar 1969, P 1, 1/1/349.

13 For more on this and with respect to adoption, see Else, *A Question of Adoption*, pp. 14–22. A conference on adoption in 1968 discussed the idea of providing support to fathers of ex-nuptial children, who it was recognised sometimes felt guilty and confused about the pregnancy and birth. Without such support men could continue to assume that their values about 'sexual freedom' were acceptable, that young women could raise children alone, and that premarital sex involved no risks. Little seems to have come of the discussion. See 'Conference on Adoption, Illegitimate Birth Enquiries and Fostering', Child Welfare Division, Department of Education, 1968, pp. 3–4.

14 See Committee for study of ex-nuptial births, 'Report of sub-committee', 7 Aug 1968, CW 1, 4/6, part 3.

15 Proposal for an interview study of mothers of illegitimate children, J 1, 18/4/7, part 3.

16 Anderson to Duncan McKay, 26 Jul 1971, CW 1, 2/10/10, part 6.

17 Joint Committee Research Unit, 'Illegitimacy', Mar 1969, P 1, 1/1/349.

18 The comment appears as a handwritten note on the bottom of an official letter, Anderson to Editor, *Evening Post*, 17 Nov 1967, Anderson quoted in *Hawke's Bay Herald–Tribune*, 8 Nov 1967, Anderson to Duncan McKay, 25 Mar 1968, CW 1, 4/6, part 3; *AJHR*, 1969, E-4, p. 6.

19 Peek to DCWO, Christchurch, 10 Nov 1949, CW 1, 2/10, part 1; see Else, *A Question of Adoption*, pp. 1–47; May, *Minding Children*, pp. 260–5.

20 Muriel Bowden, quoted in McDonald (ed.), *Working for the Welfare*, p. 18.

21 Memo to all CWOs, 5 Aug 1949, CW 1, 4/6, part 1; Peek to Registrar Births, Deaths and Marriages, Chatham Islands, 9 Aug 1951, CW 1, 4/6/1.

22 *AJHR*, 1949–72, E-4.

23 Here the New Zealand figures differ from those elsewhere. In Victoria, for example, some 70 per cent of ex-nuptial babies were adopted between 1940 and 1975, Shurlee Swain with Renate Howe, *Single Mothers and Their Children: Disposal, Punishment and Survival in Australia*, Melbourne, Cambridge University Press, 1995, p. 146.

24 Griffith, *Adoption*, pp. A2, A3; *AJHR*, E-4, 1953, p. 8, 1963, p. 7, 1972, p. 7. While some of the babies may have subsequently been maintained in foster homes or placed for adoption, most adoptions were of babies less than a year old.

25 Report of panel discussion held on 23 Sep 1960, CW 1, 4/6, part 2; Anderson to Duncan McKay, 15 Jun 1967, CW 1, 4/6, part 3; Else, *A Question of Adoption*, pp. 42–4; H. L. Bockett, Director of Employment, Department of Labour, to Peek, 3 Jun 1948, CW 1, 40/57/2.

26 F. Hallett, DCWO, New Plymouth, to Peek, 25 May 1959, Hallett to DCWOs, Napier, Wellington and Gisborne, 10 Aug 1959, CW 1, 4/5, part 2.

27 Anderson to Duncan McKay, 16 Feb 1964, J 1, 18/6/28; Memo to all CWOs, 22 May 1968, Anderson to General Manager, State Advances Corporation, 15 May 1968, CW 1, 4/6, part 3.

28 See Society for Research on Women in New Zealand, *The Unmarried Mother: Problems Involved in Keeping Her Child*, Wellington, SROW, 1970, *passim*; Report on panel discussion, 23 Sep 1960, CW 1, 4/6, part 2.

29 A. Rounthwaite, DCWO, Whangarei, to Peek, 12 May 1953, CW 1, 4/5/3, part 1.

30 Bockett to Peek, 3 Jun 1948, A. Tocker, CWO, Wellington, to Peek, 21 Jul 1948, note for file, 11 Aug 1948,

H. Burnett, CWO, Christchurch, to Peek, 23 Aug 1948, CW 1, 40/57/2.

31   Peek to DCWO, Auckland, 3 Oct 1960, M. Chalcraft, CWO, Auckland, to DCWO, Auckland, 19 Oct 1960, CW 1, 4/6, part 2. A discussion of the movement and various inquiries into it can be found in Anne Else, '"The Need is Ever Present": The Motherhood of Man Movement and Stranger Adoption in New Zealand', in Barbara Brookes, Charlotte Macdonald and Margaret Tennant (eds), *Women in History 2*, Wellington, Bridget Williams Books, 1992, pp. 225–53. Else, *A Question of Adoption, passim*, discusses in detail the problems facing unwed women.

32   Else, *A Question of Adoption*, p. 37.

33   Kath Beattie, quoted in McDonald (ed.), *Working for the Welfare*, p. 21.

34   See Else, *A Question of Adoption*; see also Griffith, *Adoption, passim*.

35   *AJHR*, 1944–72, E-4.

36   Ibid., 1959, p. 7; L. G. Anderson, 'Chosen Children', *New Zealand Parent and Child*, vol. 1, no. 4, 1953, p. 19.

37   Else, *A Question of Adoption*, p. 25.

38   R. Henry Donaldson, DCWO, Dunedin, to Peek, 30 Apr 1952, F. L. Kennedy, ADCWO, Timaru, to Peek, 1 May 1952, D. Tresidder, SCWO, Auckland, to Peek, 30 Apr 1952, Placements for Adoption by CWOs, nd, CW 1, 2/12/2.

39   Griffith, *Adoption*, p. A4; *AJHR*, 1968, E-4, p. 11.

40   *AJHR*, 1956, E-4, p. 6.

41   Memo to all SCWOs, 6 May 1952, CW 1, 2/12/1.

42   J. Ferguson, DCWO, Wellington, to Peek, 7 May 1951, Tresidder to Peek, 12 May 1952, CW 1, 2/12/2.

43   Feist to Peek, 19 May 1952, H. Hunt, DCWO, Palmerston North, to Peek, 19 May 1952, CW 1, 2/12/2.

44   E. Naylor to Anderson, 8 May 1952, Tressider to Peek, 12 May 1952, D. McKee Wright, DCWO, Wanganui, to Peek, 30 May 1952, CW 1, 2/12/2.

45   Else, *A Question of Adoption*, provides numerous accounts of mothers' and applicants' subsequent feelings towards the actions of child welfare officers at the time of placement.

46   DCWO, Christchurch, to Peek, 21 May 1952, Donaldson to Peek, 21 May 1952, CW 1, 2/12/2.

47   J. Maud, SCWO, Whangarei, to Anderson, 20 May 1952, CW 1, 2/12/2.

48   Donaldson to Peek, 21 May 1952, CW 1, 2/12/2.

49   Attorney-General, memo to Cabinet, 12 Aug 1953, CW 1, 2/12/2.

50   Submission by Motherhood of Man Movement, nd, Catholic Social Services comments on Adoption Bill, 17 Aug 1955, S. Paterson, SM, Hamilton, to Assistant Secretary of Justice, 23 Aug 1955, J 1, 18/20/18, part 1.

51   Peek to Hilda Ross, 20 Mar 1953, and replies to Peek from Hunt, Tresidder, Ferguson, May 1952, CW 1, 2/12/2; see J 1, 18/20/21, parts 1 and 2.

52   Statement from Justice Department representatives on proposed adoption procedure, 5 May 1952, J 1, 18/20/18, part 1.

53   Peek to Law Drafting Office, 23 Feb 1955, Anderson to Hilda Ross, 24 Aug 1955, J 1, 18/20/18, part 1.

54   Else, *A Question of Adoption*, p. xiii.

55   Peek to Director of Education, 28 Sep 1956, CW 1, 2/10, part 2.

56   Peek to Hilda Ross, 17 Feb 1950, and other letters in CW 1, 4/4/1, part 1; Hilda Ross to Mr Moohan, MP, 27 Sep 1954, CW 1, 2/10/2, part 1; James Cran, Okato, to Anderson, 12 Jun 1958, CW 1, 4/4/1, part 4.

57   Anderson, note on report of panel discussion held on 23 Sep, 10 Nov 1960, CW 1, 4/6, part 2.

58   For accounts of these, see Else, *A Question of Adoption*, pp. 23–47.

59   Case file, ABNT, W4295.

60   Todd interview, 25 Jun 1996, tape 1.

61   Mrs W___ to H. Campbell, SCWO, Christchurch, 11 Feb 1953, Campbell to W___, 12 Feb 1953, CW 1, 4/4/6.

62   *AJHR*, 1956, E-4, p. 6.

63   Private Secretary, Minister of Education, to Chair, Social Security Commission, 25 Jun 1963, J. H. Lucas, DCWO, Wellington, to Peek, 2 Jul 1963, CW 1, 4/5/8.

64   Todd interview, 25 Jun 1996, tapes 1, 2.

65   *AJHR*, E-4, 1958, p. 14, 1965, pp. 6–8, 1968, p. 7. Else discusses possible reasons for these changes in *A*

Question of Adoption, pp. 159–71.

66 For a discussion of this, see Metge, *New Growth From Old*, pp. 210–57.

67 Berkeley Dallard, Under-Secretary of Justice, to Minister of Justice, 23 Mar 1948, J 1, 18/20/17, part 1.

68 Views of Department of Maori Affairs, prepared for interdepartmental committee meeting, 19 Jun 1952, J 1, 18/20/18, part 1.

69 Hodder, visit to Whangarei, Feb 1957, CW 1, 2/6/27, part 3; Hodder, visit to Napier, Jun 1963, CW 1, 2/6/27, part 5; A. Bulmer, CWO, to Anderson, nd, CW 1, 4/15, part 2.

70 Views of Department of Maori Affairs, 19 Jun 1952, J 1, 18/20/18, part 1.

71 J. McEwen, Secretary of Maori Affairs, to Secretary of Justice, 7 Jun 1966, J 1, 18/20/21, part 3.

72 Circular to all Registrars, 29 Mar 1963, McEwen to Secretary of Justice, 7 Jun 1966, J 1, 18/20/21, part 3.

73 Case files, ABNT, W4295.

74 *AJHR*, E-4, 1955, p. 20, 1968, p. 23.

75 *AJHR*, 1955, E-4, p. 21; quoted in *Otago Daily Times*, 3 Sep 1957, CW 1, 4/19, part 2.

76 *AJHR*, 1971, E-4, p. 18.

77 *NZPD*, 1968, vol. 357, pp. 1959–61.

78 J. Medcalf, DCWO, Timaru, to Peek, 15 Jun 1960, CW 1, 8/9, part 2; Anderson to DCWO, Lower Hutt, 27 May 1969, CW 1, 8/9, part 3.

79 Lyons to Peek, 7 Jul 1959, CW 1, 8/9, part 1.

80 Anderson to Mr Haigh, Auckland, 3 Jul 1964, CW 1, 2/10, part 3.

81 Case file, ABNT, W4295.

82 Case file, ibid.

83 Case file, ibid.

84 Secretary of Justice to Under-Secretary of Maori Affairs, 30 Apr 1957, and reply, 30 Apr 1957, J 1, 18/20/9; Under-Secretary of Maori Affairs to Controller of Maori Affairs, 15 Jun 1950, MA 36/11, part 1.

85 Hodder, visit to New Plymouth, Aug 1957, CW 1, 2/6/27, part 3; Stewart, visit to Whangarei, 14 Mar 1950, CW 1, 2/6/27, part 1.

86 *Otago Daily Times*, 3 Sep 1957, CW 1, 4/19, part 2; Hodder, visit to Dunedin, Feb 1958, CW 1, 2/6/27, part 3.

87 Hodder, visit to Masterton, Mar 1958, CW 1, 2/6/27, part 3; Peek to Norman Shelton, 20 Mar 1961, CW 1, 3/1/6.

88 Case file, ABNT, W4295.

89 Peek to E. Ongley, Wellington, 13 Jun 1952, CW 1, 3/4/1.

90 Leigh Bonheur, *Hand Me Down: The Autobiography of an Illegitimate Child*, Sydney, Ure Smith, 1971, *passim*.

91 Case file, ABNT, W4295.

92 Hodder, visit to Burwood, Oct 1958, CW 1, 2/6/27, part 4.

93 Peek to Mr G___, Auckland, 17 Jun 1952, CW 1, 3/4/1.

94 Peek to Hilda Ross, 20 Sep 1951, CW 1, 2/10, part 1; Anderson to Hilda Ross, 7 Dec 1950, CW 1, 3/4/1.

95 Hilda Ross to Mrs F. S___, Onehunga, 27 Apr 1951, CW 1, 3/4/1; Peek to Mr T. G___, Morrinsville, 31 Mar 1950, CW 1, 2/10, part 1.

96 Director of Education to Minister of Education, 17 Oct 1952, CW 1, 7/30, part 1.

97 Peek to Minister of Education, 15 Jul 1959, CW 1, 13/2/8, part 1.

98 Peek, 'Child Welfare Division need for Family Homes', 15 Jul 1959, CW 1, 2/10/10, part 2; *AJHR*, 1954–72, E-4.

99 Peek to Miss L. Pablo, Social Welfare Office, Manila, 26 Jul 1956, CW 1, 7/30, part 1; Peek to Director of Education, 8 Jun 1955, CW 1, 2/10/10, part 1.

100 M. Dwyer to D. Reilly, 26 Sep 1968, CW 1, 7/30/1, part 1; Notes on Child Welfare services for Minister, nd, CW 1, 2/10/10, part 1; *AJHR*, 1964, E-4, p. 4.

101 See letter from Sandra Bendayan, Department of Public Welfare, Massachusetts, 5 Nov 1968, CW 1, 7/30/1, part 2; and various letters in CW 1, 7/30, parts 2 and 3.

102 D. Gibb, DCWO, Greymouth, to Anderson, 2 Jun 1965, Rounthwaite to Anderson, 3 Jun 1965, K. Watson, DCWO, Rotorua, to Anderson, 3 Jun 1965, J. Luckock, DCWO, Otahuhu, to Anderson, 2 Jun

1965, CW 1, 7/30/1, part 2.

103   B. Baker, DCWO, Paeroa, to Anderson, 21 Jun 1965, CW 1, 7/30/1, part 2; Hodder, visit to Dunedin, Apr 1963, CW 1, 2/6/27, part 5; Uttley and Watson to Peek, 29 Mar 1961, CW 1, 7/30/1, part 1; 'Family Home system as it operates in New Zealand', 1968, CW 1, 7/30, part 3.

104   Peek to Hilda Ross, 28 Mar 1957, CW 1, 7/30, part 1; Peek to all DCWOs, 22 Aug 1957, CW 1, 3/1/8.

105   Luckock to Anderson, 2 Jun 1965, J. Hancock, DCWO, Taumarunui, to Anderson, 3 Jun 1965, Review of Family Home system, nd, Anderson, note on file, 7 Jul 1965, CW 1, 7/30/1, part 2.

106   Uttley to Peek, 8 Apr 1959, CW 1, 7/30, part 1; Minutes of Special Meeting, 5 Oct 1966, CW 1, 7/30/1, part 2.

107   'Family Home system as it operates in New Zealand', 1968, CW 1, 7/30, part 3; Draft briefing for Family Home Child Welfare Division, Jan 1968, CW 1, 7/30/1, part 2. Historians have shown that this was not, in fact, the case: women spent more time on childcare, and new appliances encouraged higher standards of cleanliness, and consequently more work. For a New Zealand study, see Jean-Marie O'Donnell, '"Electric Servants" and the Science of Housework: Changing Patterns of Domestic Work, 1935–1956', in Brookes, Macdonald and Tennant (eds), *Women in History 2*, pp. 168–83.

108   Uttley to Peek, 8 Apr 1959, CW 1, 7/30, part 1.

109   Maud to ADCWO, Whangarei, 4 Aug 1961, CW 1, 7/30/1, part 1.

110   Gibb to Anderson, 2 Jun 1965, Circular memo, 28 Jul 1967, CW 1, 7/30/1, part 2, Uttley and Watson to Peek, 29 Mar 1961, CW 1, 7/30/1, part 1.

111   Luckock to Anderson, 2 Jun 1965, Baker to Anderson, 21 Jun 1965, CW 1, 7/30/1, part 2; Peek to Mr D. Sinclair, Department of Reformatory Institutions, Toronto, 12 Apr 1962, CW 1, 7/30, part 2.

112   Peek to Pablo, 26 Jul 1956, Uttley to Peek, 8 Apr 1959, Circular, 12 Jan 1959, CW 1, 7/30, part 1.

113   Uttley and Watson to Peek, 29 Mar 1961, CW 1, 7/30/1, part 1.

114   J___ G___ to Esme Tombleson, 7 Oct 1964, CW 1, 7/30, part 2.

115   'No Home for Mary', *Spectrum* Documentary, Radio New Zealand, nos 259, 260; Case file, ABNT, W4295.

116   P. Walsh, SBWO, Rotorua, to DCWO, 29 Sep 1965, N. Josephs, Rotorua, to Anderson, 27 Sep 1968, D. Reilly to DCWO, Rotorua, 7 Oct 1968, CW 1, 7/30, part 3; *AJHR*, 1970, E-4, p. 27.

117   Reilly to DCWOs, Christchurch, Hamilton, Paeroa, Lower Hutt, 10 Apr 1969, CW 1, 7/30/1, part 2; Reilly to Peek, 5 Aug 1963, Anderson to Duncan McKay, 1 Apr 1964, CW 1, 7/30, part 2; *AJHR*, E-4, 1962, p. 26, 1969, pp. 27, 29.

118   *AJHR*, E-12, 1973, p.51.

119   L___ M___ to Mr Connelly, MP, 12 Aug 1963, C. Hudd, CWO, to DCWO, Christchurch, 22 Aug 1963, CW 1, 3/1/6/3.

120   Hodder, visit to Hamilton, Oct 1961, CW 1, 2/6/27, part 4.

121   Gordon, *Heroes of Their Own Lives*, p. 171.

122   Hendrick, *Child Welfare*, p. 242.

123   Ibid., p. 256.

124   Ibid., pp. 214–31; *Dominion*, 18 Sep 1969, CW 1, 4/16/3, part 5.

125   McDonald, 'Children and Young Persons', pp. 51–3, and also May, *Minding Children*, pp. 310–14.

126   A study of abuse published in 1972 distinguished between abuse and neglect, considering the latter to be less serious; cases involving neglect only were discarded from the sample collected. David Ferguson, Joan Fleming and David O'Neill, *Child Abuse in New Zealand: A Report on a Nationwide Survey of the Physical Ill-treatment of Children in New Zealand*, Research Section, Department of Social Welfare, 1972, pp. 16–36.

127   *AJHR*, 1959, E-4, p. 13.

128   Memo to all CWOs, 4 Nov 1966, CW 1, 4/16/3, part 4; Anderson, Report on District Office facilities and increase in field staff establishment, 31 Jan 1969, CW 1, 2/10/10, part 5; Todd interview, 25 Jun 1996, tape 2.

129   Unless otherwise indicated, the material in this and the next two paragraphs comes from 'Child Abuse in New Zealand', [1971], 'Child Abuse in New Zealand' (Abstract), [1972], SS 8/10/21, part 2.

130   Todd interview, 25 Jun 1996, tape 2.

131   Gordon, *Heroes of Their Own Lives*, pp. 173–4.

132 Joan Fleming to Lady Ferguson Family Counselling Service, Auckland, 9 Mar 1970, Minister of Social Welfare to Minister of Maori Affairs, 16 May 1972, SS 8/10/21, part 2.

133 Quoted in *New Zealand Herald*, 8 Jul 1967, CW 1, 4/16/3, part 4.

134 *Truth*, 1 Sep 1965, CW 1, 4/16/3, part 3.

135 Peek to Hilda Ross, 29 Jul 1952, CW 1, 3/4/1.

136 Extract from report, 15–19 Aug 1966, CW 1, 4/15, part 2.

137 Ruth Paton, quoted in McDonald (ed.), *Working for the Welfare*, p. 25. Nazareth House was a privately-run children's home.

138 Gordon, *Heroes of Their Own Lives*, p. 172.

139 *Dominion*, 18 Sep 1969, CW 1, 4/16/3, part 5; *Auckland Star*, 1 Mar 1965, CW 1, 4/16/3, part 3.

140 Secretary, Plunket Society, to Anderson, 28 Sep 1966, CW 1, 4/16/3, part 4.

141 Gordon, *Heroes of Their Own Lives*, pp. 82–203, and 'Single Mothers and Child Neglect', pp. 173–92.

142 Todd interview, 25 Jun 1996, tape 2.

143 Ibid.

144 Case file, ABNT, W4295.

145 J. Guy, CWO, Wellington, to DCWO, Wellington, 6 Jan 1953, CW 1, 4/16, part 1. For a fuller discussion of the factors behind reporting child abuse, see Gordon, *Heroes of Their Own Lives*, pp. 168–203.

146 *AJHR*, 1959, E-4, p. 13.

147 P. S. Bygate, DCWO, Wairoa, to Anderson, 2 Mar 1964, CW 1, 4/16/3, part 3.

148 Linda Gordon's work on child abuse and family violence in the United States discusses battered women's approaches to welfare agencies as a way of getting help for themselves and their children. See Gordon, 'Child Abuse', *passim*.

149 A___ M___ to Mabel Howard, 9 Jun 1958, CW 1, 4/16, part 1.

150 Note for file, 31 Mar 1953, CW 1, 4/12/5.

151 Hodder, visit to Hamilton, Oct 1961, CW 1, 2/6/27, part 4.

152 S. Stanton, DCWO, Takapuna, to Anderson, 13 Aug 1967, Anderson to DCWO, Otahuhu, 24 Jul 1964, CW 1, 4/5/3, part 2.

153 Manchester interview, 20 Jun 1996, tape 2.

154 *Press*, 2 Apr 1966, CW 1, 4/16/3, part 4.

155 Peek to Mabel Howard, 3 Nov 1948, CW 1, 2/10/2, part 1.

156 Case file, ABNT, W4295.

157 *AJHR*, 1959, E-4, p. 13.

158 Anderson, quoted in *Evening Post*, 13 May 1964, Anderson to Mrs Gordon, Federation of New Zealand Housewives, 13 Jul 1964, CW 1, 4/16/3, part 4.

159 N. K. Collins, CWO, Wellington, to DCWO, 14 Oct 1952, Ferguson to Peek, 14 Oct 1952, CW 1, 4/7/3; Anderson to DCWO, Otahuhu, 24 Jul 1964, CW 1, 4/5/3, part 2.

160 Hilda Ross to Mrs R___, 20 Oct 1952, CW 1, 4/7/3.

161 Anderson to Gordon, 13 Jul 1964, CW 1, 2/10, part 3; Anderson to Duncan McKay, 1 Nov 1966, Anderson to Director-General, Social Welfare Department, Melbourne, CW 1, 4/16/3, part 4; *Christchurch Star*, 6 Aug 1968, CW 1, 4/19, part 4.

PART IV **Introduction**

1 Keith Sinclair, 'Hard Times', in Keith Sinclair (ed.), *Oxford Illustrated History of New Zealand*, Auckland, Oxford University Press, 1990, p. 362.

2 Ranginui J. Walker, 'Maori People Since 1950', in Rice (ed.), *Oxford History of New Zealand*, pp. 510–19.

3 See McDonald, 'The Governing of Children', pp. 311ff. For a more general discussion of children's rights, see Hendrick, *Child Welfare*, pp. 272ff.

4 Dennis Reilly, interviewed by Bruce Asher, 13 Jun 1985, tape 1.

5 For a discussion of opposition to the merger, see New Zealand Association of Social Workers (Inc.), *Social Welfare at the Crossroads: Report on Social Welfare in New Zealand*, Wellington, New Zealand Association of Social Workers, 1971, *passim*; *AJHR*, 1973, E-12, p. 7.

6 Robin Wilson, interviewed by Bronwyn Dalley, 13 Jun 1996, tape 1.

7 Ibid.; Robin Wilson to Jock Phillips, 17 Jan 1997, personal communication; Anne Caton to Bronwyn Dalley, 17 Jan 1997, personal communication; Anne Caton, interviewed by Bronwyn Dalley, 19 Jul 1996, tape 3.

8 Manchester interview, 20 Jun 1996, tape 4; Wilson interview, 13 Jun 1996, tape 1; 'DSW into the 1990s: The "Blueprint". Report of the Department of Social Welfare Organisation Review', Department of Social Welfare, Oct 1991, pp. 6–8.

9 'The Blue Print', Update 4, nd, ITS 1/6/4, part 2; Wilson interview, 13 Jun 1996, tape 2.

10 Anderson to Director-General, Social Welfare Department, Melbourne, 11 Aug 1967, CW 1, 4/16/3, part 4; Patricia Webb to Secretary of Justice, 31 Oct 1963, Anderson to Duncan McKay, 19 Feb 1964, J 1, 18/6/28; Anderson to Director of Education, 5 Apr 1965, CW 1, 13/12/12.

11 I. J. D. McKay, Director-General of Social Welfare, to Minister of Social Welfare, 6 Nov 1973, CW 1, 4/12/4.

12 McDonald, 'The Governing of Children', p. 209.

13 The process of redrafting the legislation and the series of public discussions and submissions form a separate story in themselves. Versions of the events can be found in M. P. Doolan, 'Youth Justice: Legislation and Practice', in B. J. Brown and F. W. M. McElrea (eds), *The Youth Court in New Zealand: A New Model of Justice – Four Papers*, Auckland, Legal Research Foundation, 1993, pp. 18–19, and Pauline Tapp, David Geddis and Nicola Taylor, 'Protecting the Family', in Mark Henaghan and Bill Atkin (eds), *Family Law Policy in New Zealand*, Auckland, Oxford University Press, 1992, pp. 168–209.

14 Wilson interview, 13 Jun 1996, tapes 2, 3.

15 Liz Beddoe, 'Editorial', *Social Work Review*, vol. 3, no. 3, 1990; John Bradley, 'The Resolve to Devolve: Maori and Social Services', *Social Work Now: The Practice Journal of the New Zealand Children and Young Persons Service*, 1, 1995, pp. 29–35; Gabrielle Maxwell, 'Funding Youth Justice 1990–1994', *Children: A Newsletter from the Office of the Commissioner for Children*, 15, 1994, pp. 7–8; Gabrielle Maxwell, 'Rights and Responsibilities: Youth Justice', in *Rights and Responsibilities: Papers From the International Year of the Family Symposium on Rights and Responsibilities of the Family held in Wellington 14 to 16 October 1994*, Wellington, International Year of the Family Committee in association with the Office of the Commissioner for Children, 1995, pp. 61–9; Joan Metge and Donna Durie-Hall, 'Kua Tutu te Puehu, Kia Mau: Maori Aspirations and Family Law', in Henaghan and Atkin (eds), *Family Law Policy in New Zealand*, pp. 76–9; Teresa Olsen, Gabrielle Maxwell and Allison Morris, 'Maori and Youth Justice in New Zealand', in Kayleen Hazelhurst (ed.), *Popular Justice and Community Regeneration: Pathways of Indigenous Reform*, Westport, Connecticut, Praeger, 1995, pp. 45–65; P. F. Tapp, 'Family Group Conferences and the Children, Young Persons and Their Families Act 1989: An Ineffective Statute?', *New Zealand Recent Law Review*, 1990, pp. 82–8.

16 'Review of the Children, Young Persons, and Their Families Act 1989', Report of the Ministerial Review Team to the Minister of Social Welfare, Hon. Jenny Shipley, Feb 1992, *passim*; Mike Doolan, interviewed by Bronwyn Dalley, 24 Jun 1996, tape 4.

17 Practice Paper: Family Decision-making and Child Protection, 22 Feb 1989, Department of Social Welfare, Circular memo 1989/34; Greg Putland, interviewed by Bronwyn Dalley, 19 Feb 1997, tape 2.

18 For more on this, see Danny Keenan, '*Puao-te-Ata-Tu*: A Brief History and Reflection', *Social Work Review*, vol. 7, no. 1, 1995, pp. 11, 29.

19 The Department noted that several problems with the groups had led to the decision to disband them: they were an expensive way to obtain community input, and they restricted wider community access to knowledge of the Department's policies and practices, *AJHR*, 1991, E-12, pp. 52–4.

20 For discussions of the move from welfare to justice for young offenders, see M. P. Doolan, 'From Welfare to Justice: Towards New Social Work Practice with Young Offenders – An Overseas Study Tour Report', Department of Social Welfare, nd [1988], *passim*; Doolan, 'Youth Justice', *passim*; Hendrick, *Child Welfare*, pp. 272–88; Irving, Maunders and Sherington, *Youth in Australia*, pp. 259–64.

21 Mike Doolan in 'Youth Justice', *Children, Young Persons, and Their Families Act 1989*, Programme One, videotape, Department of Social Welfare, 1989; B. Manchester, 'Planning for Children in Care', Planning for Children in Care Consultative Group meeting, Nov 1984, SWK 3/10/1, part 1.

22 See Gabrielle Maxwell and Allison Morris, *Family, Victims and Culture: Youth Justice in New Zealand*,

Wellington, Social Policy Agency and Institute of Criminology, 1993, pp. 2–11.

23 Manchester, 'Notes on Some Developments in Social Work Training', pp. 4–7.

24 Figures taken from *Evening Post*, 12 Jul 1991, F&C 2/4/2, part 2.

CHAPTER 7 'A new language': youth justice and residential institutions

1 Doolan, 'Youth Justice', in Brown and McElrea (eds), *The Youth Court in New Zealand*, p. 28.

2 D. Tucker, C. Howie and A. Ricketts, Owairaka, Notes for Committee on Gangs, 14 Apr 1981, B. Manchester to Secretary, Committee on Gangs, SWK 11/17, part 1.

3 Manchester to Secretary, Committee on Gangs, 23 Apr 1981, SWK 11/17, part 1; Lainey Cowan, interviewed by Bronwyn Dalley, 23 Jul 1996, tape 1.

4 Discussion Paper, Juvenile Delinquency in Auckland, nd [1982], SWK 10/7/1; Althea Vercoe, Assistant-Director (Social Work), Hamilton, to Director, Hamilton, 16 Jan 1985, SWK 11/20, part 2; K. Thompson, Commissioner of Police, to Director-General, Department of Social Welfare, 9 Jun 1986, SWK 11/20, part 4.

5 Draft Report of the Working Party on Absconding Teenage and Sub-teenage Children, nd [Nov 1981], ADM 4/2/23/6; Minutes of Cabinet Committee Meeting on Family and Social Affairs, 28 Apr 1983, ADM 4/2/23/7, part 2; 'Report of the Working Party on Unsupervised Young People (Street Kids)', Feb 1983, ADM 4/2/23/7, part 1; John Grant to Minister of Social Welfare, 13 Jun 1984, SWK 11/20, part 2.

6 *Dominion*, 19 Jun 1985, *New Zealand Listener*, 3 Aug 1985, Report of the Working Party into Young People in the Highbury area of Palmerston North, Aug 1985, SWK 11/20, part 3.

7 Department of Social Welfare submission to Justice and Law Reform Committee, 15 Aug 1990, Y&C 1/1/1, part 6.

8 Gabrielle Maxwell and Allison Morris, 'What Do We Know About Youth Crime?', paper presented to the Youth Justice: The Vision conference, Victoria University of Wellington, Oct 1996.

9 Street Kids House Parent Programme – Guidelines for Voluntary Organisations, Sep 1983, L. O'Reilly, Investigating Officer, Office of the Ombudsman, Interview with Mrs Heather Hirama, 17 Mar 1983, Manchester to Director, Manukau, 21 Dec 1983, SWK 11/20, part 1.

10 R. Ketko to Divisional Director, Social Work Operations, 9 Oct 1979, E. Te Moananui, Director, Whangarei, to Ketko, 11 Sep 1980, 'Outdoor Education Youth Activities: A Brief Outline', nd, M. Doolan to L. Mundell, Assistant Director, Community Development, 2 Nov 1984, SWK 10/1, part 1.

11 Gabrielle Maxwell and Allison Morris, 'Juvenile Crime and the Children, Young Persons and their Families Act 1989', in Office of the Commissioner for Children, *An Appraisal of the First Year of the Children, Young Persons and their Families Act 1989*, Wellington, Office of the Commissioner for Children, 1991, pp. 24–30.

12 Olsen, Maxwell and Morris, 'Maori and Youth Justice', pp. 49–50; Maxwell and Morris, *Family, Victims and Culture*, p. 134; Statistics Section, 'Statistics on Violent Offending by Young Persons', Jul 1978, WEL 13/0; Human Rights Commission, *The Use of Secure Care and Related Issues in Social Welfare Institutions*, Wellington, Human Rights Commission, 1989, p. 43; *AJHR*, E-12, 1973, p. 46, 1986, p. 7; Guy Powles, 'Children and Young Persons on Remand in Penal Institutions', 5 Apr 1977, WEL 10/1; 'Juvenile Offending in New Zealand', Sep 1977, ADM 4/2/9, part 2; Donald Woolford, Statistics Unit, to Ann Corcoran, 6 Sep 1982, SWK 4/5/2; *Puao-te-Ata-Tu*, p. 17.

13 Selwyn Stanton for Director, Auckland, to Director-General, 24 Mar 1975, ADM 14/1/6; *8 O'Clock*, 14 Apr 1973, CW 1, 4/12, part 2.

14 Beryl Davey to Minister of Justice, 2 Jul 1972, A. Bulmer for Director-General to ?, 7 Aug 1972, *Waikato Times*, 17 Jun 1972, CW 1, 4/12, part 2.

15 K. Richardson, SM, Otahuhu, quoted in *Auckland Star*, 26 Jun 1971, CW 1, 4/12, part 2.

16 Children and Young Persons Bill, Explanatory notes, nd, private papers, Brian Manchester; B. Maher, Area Welfare Officer, to Director, Papakura, 3 Jul 1979, ADM 25/22/10.

17 J. Luckock, Assistant-Director (Social Work), to Director, Otahuhu, 29 May 1974, Director, Whangarei, to Director-General, 24 May 1974, ADM 25/22/3C.

18 C. Waggott, SSW, Kaikohe, to Director-General, 15 Sep 1981, SWK 2/4/1, part 1; S. Young, for Assistant Director, Hamilton, to Director-General, 16 Oct 1981, Otahuhu–Manukau Community Work Review,

Jun 1981, SWK 2/4/1, part 1.

19 Putland interview, 19 Feb 1997, tape 2.

20 Circular, 1 Sep 1980, E. Zander to Assistant Director-General (Social Work), 4 Feb 1981, R. Jones, Gisborne, to Director-General, 24 Mar 1983, SWK 2/7/2, part 1; Circular, 29 Jun 1983, SWK 2/7/2, part 2.

21 Anderson to Minister of Social Welfare, 29 May 1973, ADM 24/22/74, part 1.

22 P. Chatterton to Director, Auckland, 30 Jan 1985, SWK 2/7/5.

23 Minutes of meeting of Auckland Sub-Committee of Officials Committee of Cabinet, 10 Mar 1983, M. Moriarty, Treasury, to Minister of Finance, 23 Aug 1984; E. Te R. Tauroa, 'Report of Advisory Committee on Youth and Law in our Multicultural Society', Race Relations Conciliator's Office, Feb 1983, pp. 78, 107, 170ff.

24 Ken Mason, Otahuhu District Court, to Alan Thomson, Otahuhu, 21 May 1985, Manchester to Director, Otahuhu, 17 Jun 1985, *Zealandia*, 15 and 22 Jun 1986, SWK 2/7/0.

25 Submission, Christchurch social workers, 8 Mar 1985, ADM 24/22/84/3, part 2; Submission, New Zealand Association of Social Workers (Inc.), nd, ADM 24/22/84/3, part 4.

26 Gabrielle Maxwell and Allison Morris, 'Research on Family Group Conferences with Young Offenders in New Zealand', in Joe Hudson, Allison Morris, Gabrielle Maxwell and Burt Galaway (eds), *Family Group Conferences: Perspectives on Policy and Practice*, Annandale/New York, The Federation Press/Willow Tree Press, 1996, p. 92.

27 See F. W. M. McElrea, 'A New Model of Justice', in Brown and McElrea (eds), *The Youth Court in New Zealand*, pp. 3–14; Trish Stewart, 'The Youth Justice Co-ordinator's Role: A Personal Perspective of the New Legislation in Action', in Brown and McElrea (eds), *The Youth Court in New Zealand*, p. 45.

28 Maxwell and Morris, *Families, Victims and Culture*, pp. 160–3; Margie Michael, 'Youth Advocates: Seeing Justice to be Done?', *Social Work Now: The Practice Journal of the New Zealand Children and Young Persons Service*, 2, 1995, pp. 13–15.

29 Manchester interview, 20 Jun 1996, tape 4.

30 Children and Young Persons Bill, Explanatory notes, nd, private papers, Brian Manchester; J. Lucas (for Director-General) to Minister of Social Welfare, 24 Aug 1973, ADM 24/22/74, part 1. For a discussion of the South Australian system, see Irving, Maunders and Sherington, *Youth in Australia*, pp. 141ff.

31 Manchester interview, 20 Jun 1996, tape 4; Submission, Social Council, Mar 1974, ADM 25/22/10, part 4; Submission, 6A Incorporated, nd, Submission, New Zealand Association of Social Workers (Inc.), Feb 1974, Submission, Auckland Committee on Racism and Discrimination, Feb 1974, ADM 24/22/74A, part 1; Department of Maori Affairs, Head Office memo, 2 Jan 1978, W. Herewini (for Secretary of Maori Affairs) to Director-General, 20 Dec 1978, SWK 2/1/5.

32 Director, Christchurch, to Assistant-Director (Social Work), 26 Jun 1984, SWK 2/1/3, part 5; Ailsa Bailey, Timaru, to Michael Cullen, 12 Jul 1988, SWK 2/1/3, part 7.

33 Francis Luketina, 'Some Statistics on Cases Heard by Children's Boards in 1982', Research Division, Department of Social Welfare, Apr 1984; Evaluating children's boards, Minutes of Meeting, 23 Feb 1981, SWK 2/1/6; N. Helleur, SW, Wanganui, to Director, 22 Oct 1980, SWK 2/1/2; Brian Manchester to Bronwyn Dalley, 5 Feb 1997, personal communication.

34 Seminar on children's boards, 1977, MA 1, 36/11/3/10, part 2; Manchester interview, 27 Jun 1996, tape 5; R. Letham, SSW, Dunedin, to Director-General, 15 Sep 1980, Children's boards, 1980, seminar report, Minutes of meeting, Napier, 31 Jul 1980, SWK 2/1/2; Evaluation unit 1982, 22 Jul 1982, Waitemata children's board, report for 1984, SWK 2/1/1; Proposed changes to the Children and Young Persons legislation, nd, SWK 4/7, part 3.

35 Assistant-Director, Papakura, to Director-General, 17 Dec 1980, SWK 2/1/3, part 2A.

36 Minutes of children's board, 24 Sep 1975, 3, 29 May 1976, MA 1, 36/11/3/10, part 1.

37 See submissions in ADM 24/22/84/3, part 5; Submission, ACORD, Apr 1985, ADM 24/22/84/2, part 8; Manchester interview, 27 Jun 1996, tape 6.

38 John Grant, 'The Family Group Conference within the Children, Young Persons, and Their Families Act', paper presented to the Australian Social Welfare Administrators conference, Melbourne, 15–17 Oct 1990, F&C 2/4/6, part 1.

39 The number of youth justice family group conferences declined to 6559 in 1992/3, rose to 7083 in 1994, and fell to 6935 'outcomes' in fiscal 1995, *AJHR*, 1992–5, E-12.

40 Alan Nixon to Minister of Social Welfare, 21 Feb 1992, Y&C 1/1/1, part 6; McElrea, 'A New Model of Justice', p. 4.

41 Stewart, 'The Youth Justice Co-ordinator's Role', pp. 43–8.

42 Human Rights Commission, *Who Cares For the Kids? A Study of Children and Young People in Out of Family Care*, Wellington, Human Rights Commission, 1992, pp. 168–70; Maxwell and Morris, *Families, Victims and Culture*, pp. 113–29; Olsen, Maxwell and Morris, 'Maori and Youth Justice', pp. 53–60.

43 Doolan interview, 24 Jun 1996, tape 4; Olsen, Maxwell and Morris, 'Maori and Youth Justice', p. 58.

44 Ossie Peri, in 'Youth Justice', *Children, Young Persons, and Their Families Act*, videotape.

45 'Review of the Children, Young Persons, and Their Families Act', p. 46; Cowan interview, 24 Jul 1996, tape 6.

46 'Review of the Children, Young Persons, and Their Families Act', *passim*; Ian Hassall and Gabrielle Maxwell, 'The Family Group Conference: A New Statutory Way of Resolving Care, Protection and Justice Matters Affecting Children', in Office of the Commissioner for Children, *An Appraisal of the First Year of the Children, Young Persons and their Families Act 1989*, pp. 1–13.

47 Department of Social Welfare Submission to Review of the Children, Young Persons, and Their Families Act, 7 Oct 1991, Y&C 1/1/1, part 5; 'Review of the Children, Young Persons, and Their Families Act', pp. 20–48; Maxwell, 'Funding Youth Justice', p. 7; John Angus, National Director, Children, Young Persons and their Families Unit, to Director-General, 8 Feb 1992, F&C 4/1/1/1, part 3; Maxwell and Morris, *Families, Victims and Culture*, pp. 83, 91, 102, 191; Olsen, Maxwell and Morris, 'Maori and Youth Justice', pp. 57–9; Doolan interview, 24 Jun 1996, tape 4.

48 M. Lyons, Director, Christchurch, to Director-General, 26 Apr 1973, WEL 10/1.

49 The Department of Social Welfare suggested that opposition from local communities to the establishment of remand homes in their midst swayed the Division's decision not to proceed with remand centres, Review of Residential Facilities – Auckland and Hamilton regions, nd, WEL 9/0/4.

50 1980/81 Works Programme: Vote: Social Welfare, Jun 1982, SWK 9/0, part 1.

51 Manchester interview, 27 Jun 1996, tape 6; Review of Residential Facilities, nd, WEL 9/0/4; Director, Auckland, to Director-General, 29 Mar 1976, T. Waetford, Principal, Wesleydale, to Director, Auckland, 8 March 1977, WEL 9/1/6; Waetford to Regional Director, 24 Feb 1982 and 12 Jan 1984, SWK 9/1/5/1; ACORD, 'Children in Prison: Where's the Justice? Who's the Criminal?', Mar 1976, WEL 5/5, part 3, Director-General to Minister of Social Welfare, 12 Apr 1973, Guy Powles, Draft report, 'Children and Young Persons on Remand in Penal Institutions', 5 Apr 1977, WEL 10/1.

52 Review of Residential Facilities, nd, WEL 9/0/4; Wilson interview, 13 Jun 1996, tape 3.

53 R. B. Marsden, Acting Principal, Cornwall Park, to Regional Manager, Auckland, 26 Feb 1982, SWK 9/1/4/1; Doolan interview, 24 Jun 1996, tape 1; Janet Worfolk, interviewed by Bronwyn Dalley, 10 Mar 1997, tape 1; *AJHR*, 1979, E-12, p. 43, noted that most of the girls admitted were care and protection cases.

54 Principal, Owairaka, to Director, Auckland, 19 May 1976, WEL 9/1/6; Children and Young Persons requiring long-term institutional treatment – Background Paper, 1977, ADM 4/2/28, part 1; Minutes of Quarterly Residential Care Review Meeting, 12 Aug 1981, SWK 9/0, part 1.

55 Note for file, 29 Jul 1981, SWK 9/1/5/1; N. Stevens, Wesleydale Boys' Home, Report, nd [Feb 1984], SWK 9/1/5; Kohitere, annual review, 24 Jan 1980, WEL 9/50/4, part 2; [comments on Hokio], nd [1981], SWK 7/2/5; Worfolk, interview, 10 Mar 1997, tape 1.

56 Francis Waitohi to Fofaga, nd, Lucy to James and others, nd, J. Scott to J. Lucas, 26 Feb 1979, WEL 9/52, part 3.

57 Review of Residential Facilities, nd, WEL 9/0/4; G. Comber, Director, Regional Residential Services, to Regional Director, Auckland, 24 Aug 1983, SWK 9/1/5; Principal, Owairaka, to Director, Auckland, 19 May 1976, WEL 9/1/6.

58 Mary Todd, 'Assessment and comparison of the training programmes at Kingslea and Weymouth', 1977, SWK 7/2/1; Wilson interview, 13 Jun 1996, tape 3.

59 J. C. Watson, 'The Current Use of Secure Facilities Within Department of Social Welfare Institutions',

paper presented at New Zealand Psychological Society annual conference, Aug 1978, *passim*; Principal, Kohitere, to Director-General, 23 Nov 1973, WEL 9/50, part 3; 'No Home for Mary', *Spectrum* Documentary, no. 260.

60 Stanton to J. Lucas, 23 Dec 1982, ADM 4/2/28, part 1.

61 Wilson interview, 13 Jun 1996, tape 3; Wilson to Phillips, 17 Jan 1997.

62 Holdsworth School, annual report, 1977, WEL 9/54; Doolan, Principal, Holdsworth, to Director-General, 6 Aug 1979, ADM 25/22/24, part 2; Cowan interview, 23 Jul 1996, tape 1.

63 Inspection report on Hokio, 21–26 Sep 1981, SWK 7/2/5.

64 Marion Judge, 'An approach to treatment', 1976, WEL 9/53, part 4; Todd, 'Assessment and comparison of the training programmes', SWK 7/2/1.

65 Francis Luketina, 'Assessment of Camp Peek Pilot Scheme', Jun 1978, WEL 9/57, part 1.

66 Annual review, 1976, WEL 9/50/4, part 2; [Comments on Hokio], nd [1981], Inspection report on Hokio, 21–26 Sep 1981, SWK 7/2/5.

67 Note for file, 29 Jul 1981, SWK 9/1/5/1.

68 A. Frazer, 'Psychological Services in DSW institutions', 19 Aug 1980, SWK 6/0/6.

69 Worfolk interview, 10 Mar 1997, tape 1.

70 L. Johnston, Cornwall Park Reception Centre, Annual report, 1982, SWK 9/1/4/1; Judge to Assistant-Director (Social Work), 31 Jul 1978, WEL 9/53, part 4.

71 Worfolk interview, 10 Mar 1997, tape 1; Putland interview, 19 Feb 1997, tape 1.

72 *AJHR*, 1976, E-12, p. 43; Putland interview, 19 Feb 1997, tape 1.

73 Putland interview, 19 Feb 1997, tape 1.

74 *AJHR*, 1973, E-12, p. 50.

75 Judge to Assistant-Director (Social Work), 31 Jul 1978, WEL 9/53, part 4.

76 Reilly to all directors and principals, 16 Jul 1974, SWK 7/2/4.

77 Doolan interview, 24 Jun 1996, tape 1.

78 Doolan to Director-General, 6 Aug 1979, ADM 25/22/24, part 2.

79 Anderson to Mr Nattrass, 1 Oct 1974, WEL 9/0, part 1, 'Report of the Human Rights Commission on Representations by the Auckland Committee on Racism and Discrimination. Children and Young Persons Homes Administered by the Department of Social Welfare', Human Rights Commission, Sep 1982, p. 133.

80 'Social Welfare Children's Homes: Report on an Inquiry Held on June 11 1978', Auckland Committee on Racism and Discrimination, 1978, *passim*.

81 'Report of the Human Rights Commission', *passim*.

82 A. M. J. Egan, *Press*, 3 Sep 1982, Phil O'Donnell in *Taranaki Daily News*, 6 Sep 1982, Wayne Ace in *Northern Advocate*, 6 Sep 1982, Mrs C. M. J. Kirkpatrick in *Taranaki Daily News*, 10 Sep 1982, SWK 9/0, part 1.

83 Zita Arnich, ACORD, to Human Rights Commission, 21 Mar 1979, O&D 311/1, part 1; 'Running Away from Home', *Broadsheet*, Jun 1983, pp. 12–13.

84 'Social Welfare Children's Homes', ACORD, pp. 11–13; 'Report of the Human Rights Commission', pp. 23–41, 123–5.

85 'Report of the Human Rights Commission', pp. 71–86, 127–33.

86 Arthur Ricketts, 'Some thoughts for the Principals' Conference, 1982', Minutes of 1982 Principals' Conference, SWK 9/0/2, part 1; Grant to Minister of Social Welfare, 1 Sep 1982, Ministerial press statement, 1 Sep 1982, SWK 9/0, part 1; S. Callahan to Office Solicitor, 30 Jul 1979, Rodney Hooker, Office Solicitor, to Manchester, 1 Feb 1980, O&D 311/1, part 1; Wilson interview, 13 Jun 1996, tape 3.

87 Ministerial press statement, 1 Sep 1982, *Auckland Star*, 13 Sep 1982, SWK 9/0, part 1.

88 'Report of Committee to Report to the Minister of Social Welfare on the Current Practices and Procedures Followed in Institutions of the Department of Social Welfare in Auckland', Oct 1982.

89 Kevin Woods, Bollard Girls' Home, Comments on HRC report, Minutes of 1982 Principals' Conference, SWK 9/0/2, part 1; Report of the Visiting Committee, Miramar Girls' Home, Mar 1983, SWK 2/2/2/17; Peter Boshier, Miramar Girls' Home Visiting Committee, to Director-General, 9 Sep 1982, V. Dobson, Director, Tauranga, to Director-General, 13 Sep 1982, O&D 311/1, part 2.

90   Doolan interview, 24 Jun 1996, tape 1; Judge, 'An approach to treatment', WEL 9/53, part 4; *Wanganui Herald*, 11 Jul 1970, WEL 9/51, part 2; Inspection report on Hokio Beach School, 21–26 Sep 1981, SWK 7/2/5.

91   Wilson interview, 13 Jun 1996, tape 3; Human Rights Commission Report, DSW initial comments, nd, SWK 9/0, part 1.

92   Campbell, SRSW, Epuni, to Principal, Epuni, 10 Jan 1979, T. Ball (for Director-General) to Director, Lower Hutt, 30 Jan 1979, WEL 9/22/1, part 2.

93   Report, H. Williams, Assistant Housemaster, 28 Nov 1978, Maurice Gavin, Office Solicitor, to Director-General, 22 Dec 1978, WEL 9/2/2, part 1.

94   Doolan, Holdsworth, to Director-General, 6 Aug 1979, ADM 25/22/24, part 2.

95   Note for file, 29 Jul 1981, SWK 9/1/5/1.

96   K. Woods, Principal, Bollard Home, to Director, Auckland, 26 Feb 1979, WEL 9/1/4.

97   Erolini Ala'ilima-Etevahi to Minister of Social Welfare, 29 Sep 1975, Norman King, Minister of Social Welfare, to Ala'ilima-Etevahi, 15 Oct 1975, WEL 9/1/1, part 1. The government launched an inquiry into the treatment of the Niuean youth; see *AJHR*, 1977, E-25.

98   'Report of Committee to Report to Minister of Social Welfare', pp. 43–6.

99   Wilson interview, 13 Jun 1996, tape 3; 'New Horizons: A Review of the Residential Services of the Department of Social Welfare', Department of Social Welfare, Oct 1982, p. 18.

100 Ricketts, 'Some thoughts', Minutes of 1982 Principals' Conference, SWK 9/0/2, part 1.

101 Notes of Principals' Conference, Jun 1980, 1982, SWK 9/0/2, part 1.

102 Manchester to Regional Director, 26 Nov 1982, SWK 9/1/5; Minister of Social Welfare, press statement, 25 Feb 1983, SWK 10/13, part 1; John Scott to all principals and directors, 9 Nov 1982, SWK 9/0, part 1; 'New Horizons', *passim*; Circular memo, 14 Mar 1983, O&D 311/1, part 2; P. Woulfe, Principal, Kohitere, to Legal Section, DSW, 28 Aug 1986, SWK 9/0/12, part 2.

103 Address to visiting committees seminar, 10 Aug 1978, ADM 25/22/24, part 2.

104 Scott to Divisional Director, Social Work, 23 Jun 1981, SWK 2/2/3, part 1; Clifford Robb to Director-General, 7 Aug 1978, Scott to Lucas, 5 Oct 1979, ADM 25/22/24, part 3; D. Hutchinson, Senior Residential Advisory Officer, to Director, Residential Services, 1 Feb 1985, SWK 2/2/3, part 3.

105 Report of Visiting Committee, Miramar Girls' Home, nd [Jun 1984], SWK 2/2/4, part 1; Owairaka Visiting Committee to Minister of Social Welfare, 7 Nov 1986, SWK 2/2/2/6.

106 Doolan interview, 24 Jun 1996, tape 1.

107 Minutes of Residential Care Review, 5 Nov 1985, SWK 9/0, part 3; Robyn Bailey, 'Implications of Criminal Justice Act 1985 for Department of Social Welfare Residential Institutions – Issue Paper', Sep 1986, SWK 9/0/2, part 2.

108 Aidan McLean, Principal, Epuni, to Director, Lower Hutt, 10 Mar 1986, Doolan to Secretary, State Services Commission, 18 Nov 1986, SWK 9/0/20.

109 Doolan, Principal, Kingslea, to Director-General, 28 Oct and 25 Nov 1983, Hostel 4 Proposal, Weymouth, 6 May 1983, SWK 2/12/1, part 1.

110 Judge to Director-General, 31 Jul 1984, J_ H_ to Judge, 31 Jul 1984, SWK 13/92; Worfolk interview, 10 Mar 1997, tape 1.

111 J. Love, RSW, to Principal, Hamilton Boys' Home, 2 May 1987, SWK 1/9/3.

112 Human Rights Commission, *The Use of Secure Care*, *passim*; Doolan to Director-General, 3 Jul 1989, Y&C 1/2/12.

113 John Grant, Address to Principals' Conference, 1984, SWK 9/0/2, part 2; G. Comber, Regional Residential Services, to Director-General, 29 Jun 1983, *Auckland Star*, 30 Jun 1983, SWK 3/4/1; Doolan to Regional Director, Auckland, 19 Dec 1984, SWK 9/0/5; A. Whitmore, Director, Kohitere, to Directors, 29 Mar 1989, Y&C 1/2/11/4; Note for file, Jul 1982, SWK 9/0/5; *New Zealand Herald*, 11 May 1987, SWK 1/9/2; G__ D__, Kohitere, to S__ D__, 11 Nov 1983, SWK 9/0/12, part 7.

114 D. A. Whata, chair, Hui o Te Arawa me Tuwharetoa, to Minister of Police, 24 May 1985, SWK 11/9.

115 Cowan interview, 23 Jun 1996, tape 4; Doolan, 'Issues for consideration by the conference on residential services', 1986, SWK 9/0/2, part 2; Notes of meeting between Department of Social Welfare and Department of Maori Affairs, 3 Dec 1982, SWK 10/13, part 1.

116 Doolan to directors and principals, 24 Feb 1988, Circular, 2 Mar 1988, M. Quinlivan to Jocelyn Quinnel, 22 Aug 1988, SWK 9/0/23; Cowan interview, 23 Jun 1996, tape 4; Mt Roskill Reception Office social workers to Minister of Social Welfare, Dec 1986, SWK 1/9/2.

117 *New Zealand Herald*, 1 Nov 1986, Ann Hercus to John Antonio, 22 Dec 1986, SWK 1/9/2; Doolan to Deputy Director-General, 4 Sep 1986, SWK 9/0, part 3; Patrick O'Hagan to Minister of Social Welfare, 16 Jul 1987, SWK 2/2/2/16.

118 1980/81 Works Programme: Vote: Social Welfare, Jun 1982, SWK 9/0, part 1; Raoul Ketko, 'Issue Paper on Maori Perspective Implementation', 23 Sep 1986, SWK 9/0, part 3.

119 Doolan interview, 24 Jun 1996, tape 3.

120 Youth and Employment Circular, 23 Feb 1988, SWK 9/0/3, part 3; Doolan to Social Welfare Commission, 8 Feb 1989, Y&C 1/2/1; *AJHR*, 1987, E-12, pp. 32–8.

121 Youth and Employment Circular, 23 Feb 1988, Robin Wilson to Director-General, 9 Mar 1989, SWK 9/0/3, part 3; Outreach Review, as at 31 Jan 1989, Y&C 1/2/11/6; Regional Director, Southern, to Director-General, 29 Oct 1987, SWK 1/9/6; Doolan to Social Welfare Commission, 8 Feb 1989, Y&C 1/2/1; Worfolk interview, 10 Mar 1997, tape 2; Doolan interview, 24 Jun 1996, tape 3.

122 Doolan interview, 24 Jun 1996, tape 3; 'Review of Residential Services: Executive Summary and Recommendations', Department of Social Welfare, 1990, *passim*; Director-General to all staff, 9 May 1990, Unnumbered memo.

123 Geoffrey R. Pearman, 'The Pursuit of Organisational Legitimacy: Organising Social Work Services in the Department of Social Welfare 1984–1994', MA thesis, University of Canterbury, 1995, pp. 30–1; C. Grant, Audit Manager, to Chief Auditor, DSW, 25 Jul 1989, Y&C 1/2/11/2.

124 See SWK 1/9/2 and 1/9/3 for reactions to closures.

125 Doolan interview, 24 Jun 1996, tape 3.

126 Wilson interview, 13 Jun 1996, tape 4.

127 The figures are for admissions over the year, rather than the number in residence at the end of the year. There were 79 young people in the Department's residences at the end of 1991, Human Rights Commission, *Who Cares for the Kids?*, p. 6.

128 Worfolk interview, 10 Mar 1997, tape 2.

129 Putland interview, 19 Feb 1997, tape 3; Worfolk interview, 10 Mar 1997, tape 2.

130 Human Rights Commission, *Who Cares for the Kids?*, *passim*.

131 Faith Denny, Children, Young Persons and their Families Unit, to Alan Nixon, nd [1991], Y&C 1/2/3, part 2.

132 Circular memo 1991/164.

133 Gordon McFayden, youth justice co-ordinator, to Director-General, 7 Mar 1990, Y&C 1/1/1, part 3.

134 *AJHR*, 1993, E-12, pp. 42, 44; Worfolk interview, 10 Mar 1997, tape 2.

135 'Review of the Children, Young Persons, and Their Families Act 1989', pp. 79–84.

136 Worfolk interview, 10 Mar 1997, tape 2.

137 Robin Wilson, 'Address to Residential Care Seminar', in 'New Beginnings/Ara Hou: Working Towards Excellence in Residential Care Practice', seminar papers presented at a residential care seminar, Christchurch, 28–30 Jul 1993, p. 4, discusses some of the problems with the siting of institutions.

138 Cowan interview, 23 Jul 1996, tape 1.

139 Doolan interview, 24 Jun 1996, tape 3.

CHAPTER 8 **'Family solutions to family problems': care and protection matters**

1 'Review of the Children, Young Persons, and Their Families Act', p. 4.

2 New policy proposals for 1983/84, Manchester to Director-General, 31 Jan 1983, SWK 4/1, part 1.

3 Jane Thomson, 'Ninety Years of Foster Care', paper presented to New Zealand Foster Care Federation Conference, 1976, O&D 123/-, part 2.

4 Interim paper from Working Party on Foster Board Rates and Allowances, Nov 1983, SWK 4/7, part 3; Manchester to Minister of Social Welfare, 22 May 1986, SWK 4/7, part 4; *AJHR*, 1983, E-12, p. 31.

5 Notes from Collins Rd Family Home, Hamilton, nd, SWK FH 1/1, part 1.

6 New Zealand Foster Care Federation, 'Report on Family Homes', 1981, Notes of meeting to discuss

Family Homes Review, 19 Aug 1981, SWK FH 1/3, part 2.

7   Visit to Takapuna Office, nd [1979?], WEL 8/2/7; Circular memo, 23 Oct 1981, SWK FH 1/1, part 1; F&C 4/6/11/5, part 1; Circular memo, 3 Dec 1984, SWK FH 1/1, part 1.

8   Manchester interview, 27 Jun 1996, tape 6.

9   Foster Parents' Association, Recommendations to Minister of Social Welfare, nd [1974], O&D 123/-, part 1; 'Foster Care – Report to the Minister of Social Welfare', Advisory Committee on Foster Care, Aug 1984, SWK 4/7, part 3; New Zealand Foster Care Federation, 'Report on Family Homes', 1981, Review of Family Homes, May 1981, SWK FH 1/3, part 2; Ann Corcoran, note for file, 1 May 1981, 'Family Homes Review', Department of Social Welfare, 1981.

10   Bobby Duncan, New Zealand Foster Care Federation, to Minister of Social Welfare, 3 Jun 1981, SWK 4/3, part 1; Corcoran, Notes as to stage of planning for foster care scheme, nd [Nov 1979], Corcoran to Director-General, 20 Dec 1979 and 21 May 1980, WEL 10/5; Mary Todd, 'Departmental Evaluation of Intensive Foster Care Scheme in Auckland and Christchurch', nd, WEL 10/6/2.

11   Foster Parents' Association, Recommendations to the Minister of Social Welfare, nd [1974], O&D 123/-, part 1; Assistant Director-General to B. Duncan, Chairperson, New Zealand Foster Care Federation, 10 Nov 1981, O&D 123/-, part 5; Herbert Matheson to Minister of Social Welfare, 8 Sep 1987, SWK 4/1, part 4; Circular memo, 9 Sep 1982, SWK FH 1/1/1, part 2; Corcoran, note for file, 1 May 1981, 'Family Homes Review'; Ross Mackay, 'The Views of Foster Children and their Natural Families on Two Fostering Systems Operated by the Department of Social Welfare: The Intensive Foster Care Scheme and Conventional Foster Care', Research Section, Department of Social Welfare, Nov 1984, pp. 26–7; Dan Jones and Vanessa Meiklen, 'Family Home Foster Parents: A Case Study', MA research paper, Victoria University of Wellington, 1988, pp. 48–9.

12   Chairman's annual report, New Zealand Foster Care Federation, May 1979, O&D 123/-, part 4; Manchester interview, 27 Jun 1996, tape 6.

13   R. Yarrow to Caucus Committee on Social Welfare, 10 Jun 1980, WEL 14/0.

14   Manchester interview, 27 Jun 1996, tape 6.

15   New Zealand Foster Care Federation, Submission to Advisory Committee, 2 Nov 1983, SWK 4/7, part 1; 'Foster Care – A Report to the Minister of Social Welfare', Advisory Committee on Foster Care, Aug 1984, M. Craig, New Zealand Foster Care Federation, to Ann Hercus, 18 Aug 1984, Advisory Committee on Foster Care Minority Report, SWK 4/7, part 3.

16   Circular memo, 3 Dec 1984, SWK FH 1/1, part 1; Dickens, Topic notes, SWK 4/5/3, part 2.

17   Hendrick, *Child Welfare*, pp. 241, 272–4.

18   Ross Mackay, 'Children in Foster Care: An Examination of the Case Histories of a Sample of Children in Care, With a Particular Emphasis on Placements of Children in Foster Homes', Research Section, Department of Social Welfare, 1981, pp. 8, 59–81.

19   'Foster Care – A Report to the Minister of Social Welfare', SWK 4/7, part 3.

20   Circular memo, 29 Aug 1984, Brian Manchester, 'Planning for Children in Care', nd [1984], SWK 3/10/1, part 1.

21   V. Manarangi, 'Planning for Children in Care – Comments', Rotorua, nd [Sep 1984], SWK 3/10/1, part 2.

22   *Planning for Children and Young Persons in Care*, videotape, Department of Social Welfare, 1985.

23   Manchester, 'View of departmental policy on long-term fostering, permanent guardianship and permanency planning', 6 Sep 1983, Report of Working Party, May 1985, SWK 3/3/3.

24   J. Callon (for Director-General) to Regional Director, 2 Oct 1986, Minutes of workshop on planning for future projects, 8–9 Sep 1988, SWK 3/10/6.

25   Mrs W. Penhearow, SSW, Gisborne, to Assistant Director, Casework Services, 8 Sep 1987, SWK 3/10/6/3.

26   Putland interview, 19 Feb 1997, tape 3.

27   Cowan interview, 24 Jul 1996, tape 6.

28   Maatua Whangai Statistical Summary, Jun 1984, SWK 10/13, part 3.

29   Cowan interview, 23 Jul 1996, tape 3.

30   Circular, Feb 1987, SWK 10/12, part 6.

31   A. Vercoe to Corcoran, 29 Sep 1982, SWK 4/5/2; Corcoran to all Maatua Whangai officers, 28 Sep 1983,

SWK 4/1, part 2; Selwyn Stanton, Social Work and Residential Services, to Director-General, 16 Jul 1979, J. Scott, Director, Residential Services, to Acting Director-General, 29 Jun 1981, Stanton to Director-General, 26 Jan 1983, Peter Sharples to Minister of Social Welfare, 26 Aug 1983, SWK 9/0/7.

32 Anne Frizelle to Director, Residential Services, 11 Apr 1986, Frizelle, 'Summary of district reports on progress of whanau support homes', 4 Jul 1986, SWK FH 1/1, part 1.

33 M___ T___ to Minister of Social Welfare, 15 Feb 1988, Michael Cullen to Mrs T___, 19 May 1988, F&C 4/1/11/2.

34 *AJHR*, 1988, E-12, p. 48.

35 Mackay, 'The Views of Foster Children', pp. 18–22; Lynne Whitney, Bryony Walker and Jane von Dadelszen, 'Experiencing Foster Care: The Views of Children, Natural Family and Foster Parents', Research Section, Department of Social Welfare, nd [1988], pp. 6–10; Julia Macaskill Duffin, 'Growing Up Fostered: Four Young People Present an Indepth View of How it Feels to be "Nobody's Child"', Office of Child Care Studies, Department of Social Welfare, 1985, pp. 6–7, 10–11, 24–30.

36 Putland interview, 19 Feb 1997, tape 1; Duffin, 'Growing Up Fostered', *passim*; Jane von Dadelszen, 'Sexual Abuse Study: An Examination of the Histories of Sexual Abuse Among Girls Currently in the Care of the Department of Social Welfare', Research Report Series no. 7, Department of Social Welfare, 1987, pp. 142–4; Cowan interview, 23 Jul 1996, tape 4.

37 Cowan interview, 23 Jul 1996, tape 2.

38 *Preparation for Fostering – Effects on Your Children*, videotape, Department of Social Welfare, 1985; Mrs D. M___ to Ann Hercus, nd [Jan 1985], SWK 4/1, part 3.

39 Mackay, 'The Views of Foster Children', *passim*; Whitney et al., 'Experiencing Foster Care', *passim*; E___ M___, on behalf of siblings in the special purpose family home of Mr and Mrs M___, nd [1982], SWK FH 1/2.

40 Bill Jang, RSW, Christchurch Boys' Home, to Principal, Christchurch Boys' Home, 3 Feb 1988, F&C 4/1/11/6, part 1.

41 Christchurch *Star*, 24 Sep 1983, SWK 4/1/5.

42 Margaret Bruce, SW, to Director-General, 18 May 1981, SWK 3/1/3.

43 A___ M___ to Corcoran, 21 Mar 1987, SWK 4/1, part 4.

44 Circular memo 1991/172; Resource Paper: the concept of family and using court orders to provide care for children and young persons, Circular memo 1991/38; Family/whanau agreements, Resource Paper, Sep 1991, F&C 2/3/6/1.

45 Newsletter for Families and Caregivers, no. 2, 'What Sort of Things are Going to Change?', Circular memo 1989/129.

46 Newsletter for families and caregivers, no. 3, 'From Here to There', Circular memo 1989/129; Draft guidelines on care arrangements, Circular memo 1989/189.

47 Human Rights Commission, *Who Cares for the Kids?*, pp. 104–8.

48 Putland interview, 19 Feb 1997, tape 3.

49 Resource Paper: the use of family homes for care and protection purposes, Circular memo 1992/36.

50 Resource Paper: alternative uses of family homes and different approaches to local care/custody needs, 14 Aug 1991, Circular memo 1991/164.

51 A. Ellis, SW, Palmerston North, to Assistant-Director (Social Work), 2 Mar 1977, WEL 8/2/3.

52 R. Burt, Training Officer, to Chief Education and Training Officer, Department of Social Welfare, 10 Mar 1976, WEL 8/2/5.

53 'Report of the working party on the organisation of adoption services, Sep 1982–Jul 1983', SWK 5/1/6, part 2; *Dominion Sunday Times*, 17 May 1987, Corcoran to Divisional Director, Social Work (Operations), 29 Jul 1985, SWK 5/1/0, part 3.

54 Corcoran to Divisional Director, 29 Jul 1985, SWK 5/1/0, part 3; 'Report of the working party on the organisation of adoption services', SWK 5/1/6, part 2.

55 [Elspeth Zander], Submission for increase in social work staff to provide a quality adoption service, nd [1984], SWK 5/6/2; Burt to Chief Education Officer, 10 Mar 1976, WEL 8/2/5.

56 Corcoran to Director-General, 30 Jan 1980, SWK 5/1/0, part 1; Submission for increase in social work staff, SWK 5/6/2; Review of first year's work of the adoption of children with special needs unit, 21 Apr

1982, SWK 5/1/4, part 2.

57 A. Delamere, Department of Maori Affairs, to Director-General of Social Welfare, 8 Dec 1980, WEL 8/1/0, part 6; Corcoran, notes on meeting at Maori Affairs re adoption, nd [1979], WEL 8/1/0, part 5; Departmental working party on reorganisation of adoption services, 16 Sep 1982, SWK 5/1/6, part 1; Corcoran to Director, Social Welfare Services, 2 Jul 1985, SWK 5/2/1.

58 See 'Adoption Practices Review Committee: Report to the Minister of Social Welfare', Wellington, Aug 1990.

59 Else, *A Question of Adoption*, pp. 204–5; *AJHR*, 1991, E-12, p. 15.

60 Corcoran to Director-General, 17 Jun 1986, SWK 5/7/1.

61 *AJHR*, 1987, E-12, p. 33; Else, *A Question of Adoption*, pp. 197–8.

62 Letters in SWK 5/7/1 and SWK 5/7/4.

63 For further comments on this issue, see Else, *A Question of Adoption*, pp. 199–201.

64 Caton interview, 19 Jul 1996, tape 1.

65 *AJHR*, E-12, 1988, p. 50, 1989, p. 39, 1993, p. 37.

66 Minutes of first meeting of Advisory Committee, 15 Apr 1981, ADM 4/2/38/2.

67 The Telethon appeal funded a child abuse project in Dunedin in early 1981, Todd to Assistant Director-General, 16 Dec 1982, SWK 10/3/3; *Northern Advocate*, 12–16 Jan 1981, J. Feeney (for Director, Whangarei) to Director-General, 11 Feb 1981, SWK 10/3/2, part 1.

68 News release, 8 Jun 1988, F&C 2/2/2/1; Circular memo, 1989/128; Circular memo, 1990/150.

69 *Auckland Star*, 27 Mar 1984, SWK 11/13, part 3; Max Abbott, 'Preface', in Max Abbott (ed.), *Child Abuse Prevention in New Zealand: The Edited Proceedings of the National Symposium on Child Abuse Prevention, Palmerston North, 9–11 November 1982*, [Wellington], Mental Health Foundation of New Zealand, 1983, p. i.

70 'A Private or Public Nightmare? Report of the Advisory Committee on the Investigation, Detection and Prosecution of Offences Against Children', Oct 1988, pp. 8–22.

71 Franz Kney, Counsellor, Kingslea, to Todd, 12 Aug 1985, SWK 11/3/2; von Dadelszen, 'Sexual Abuse Study', pp. 1, 142. Sexual abuse by other residents in departmental homes had been noted periodically, and the Department sought by a range of measures to isolate young people who behaved in sexually inappropriate ways towards fellow residents. Abuse by staff at the residences was more difficult to identify, as the children and young people were reluctant to speak up. For the experiences of one young man who was abused in a departmental residence, see Rob Sinclair, *All God's Children*, British Columbia, Sinclair International Publishing, 1993.

72 Proposal for a facility for sexually-abused girls and young women in the Auckland region, Jun 1984, SWK 11/30; Cowan interview, 23 Jul 1996, tape 4.

73 J. Frost, Cornwall Park Reception Centre, to Todd, 15 Aug 1985, Maureen Mildon-Miebach, Hamilton Girls' Home, to Todd, 12 Sep 1986, SWK 11/13/2.

74 Mary Todd and Nicola Taylor, 'Child Protection Teams Overview Report', Oct 1987, SWK 10/3, part 2.

75 Manchester to Director-General, 18 Jun 1979, Manchester to Secretary, Inter-Departmental Committee on Health, Education and Social Welfare, 22 Feb 1980, WEL 13/1, part 1; Wilson interview, 13 Jun 1996, tape 3; Roger Down, 'Twelve-month evaluation of Child Abuse Project', nd [1981], SWK 10/3/2, part 1.

76 *AJHR*, 1988, E-12, p. 50; Todd to Director, Social Work Development, 26 Jan 1984, SWK 10/3/3; Report for 1985 for the South Auckland Child Protection Team (Otara), SWK 10/3/4; Caton interview, 19 Jul 1996, tape 2; Practice Paper: Family decision-making and child protection, Circular memo 1989/34.

77 A. Mitchell (for Director-General) to Minister of Social Welfare, nd, Maurice Gavin, Office Solicitor, to Director-General, 26 Sep 1984, Notes from Plunket Nurse, 6 Sep 1983, H. Quivooy, SSW, Taumarunui, to Director-General, 3 Oct 1984, Circular memo, Jan 1985, SWK 11/13, part 3.

78 Todd interview, 25 Jun 1996, tape 3; Caton interview, 19 Jul 1996, tape 1.

79 Todd to Manchester, 16 Mar 1984, SWK 11/13, part 2; Jan Wilson, Child Protection Team, to Todd, 2 Dec 1986, SWK 10/3/4; Wilson, Director, Hamilton, to Director-General, 7 Apr 1981, Roger Down, 'Report of visit to Christchurch Department of Social Welfare and Dunedin Child Abuse Project, 9–12 Nov 1981', SWK 10/3/2, part 1; L. Booth to Director, Hamilton, nd [Jan 1986], SWK 10/3/2, part 2; Anne

Caton, 'The Recent Development of Child Protection Legislation in New Zealand: An Illustration of Martin Rein's Analysis of Programme Implementation', SOWK 531 essay, Victoria University of Wellington, nd [1987], pp. 1–3.

80 Director-General to Chair, Inter-Departmental Committee on Health, Education and Social Welfare, 9 Oct 1980, Manchester to Secretary, Inter-Departmental Committee on Health, Education and Social Welfare, 22 Feb 1980, WEL 13/1, part 1; Six and Nine Monthly Report on Child Abuse Pilot Project, Hamilton, Aug and Nov 1980, WEL 13/1, part 2.

81 Kate Casey, Sexual Abuse Team, Mangere Office, to Minister of Police, 14 Apr 1987, SWK 11/13/2; Pad Grainer, Programmes Director, to Minister of Social Welfare, 7 Nov 1988, ADM 4/2/53, part 2; Caton, 'The Recent Development of Child Protection Legislation', pp. 4–5.

82 Police and Department of Social Welfare Investigative Procedures and Liaison, Paper One in Appendix One – Guidelines for the Investigation and Management of Child Sexual Abuse, in 'A Private or Public Nightmare?'

83 Caton and Grainer to Child Protection Teams, 6 Sep 1988, Caton to Child Protection Teams, 7 Mar 1989, SWK 10/3, part 3; Grainer to Minister of Social Welfare, 7 Nov 1988, ADM 4/2/53, part 2; Caton, 'Summary of Report on Child Protection Services, Northland region, Jan 1988', 'Report of the Working Party working on child abuse training for primary health care professionals', Feb 1988, SWK 11/13, part 4.

84 Jacky Renouf to Minister of Social Welfare, 22 Apr 1984, SWK 11/13, part 4; Todd interview, 25 Jun 1996, tape 3.

85 Michael Cullen to Jocelyn Fish, National Council of Women, 26 Jan 1989, CYP&F 5/5; Post-election briefing papers: critical issues, nd [1980], F&C 2/3/1, part 2; Renouf, National Director, Families in Special Circumstances, to Minister of Social Welfare, 22 Apr 1988, SWK 11/13, part 4; Anne Caton to Bronwyn Dalley, 6 Mar 1997, personal communication; Mary Head, Lower Hutt, to Minister of Social Welfare, 26 Aug 1988, Marianne Hanak to Minister of Social Welfare, 19 Jul 1988, CYP&F 5/5; Submission, M. Herbert, Royal New Zealand Council of General Practitioners, 2 Sep 1983, ADM 4/2/38, part 2.

86 David Geddis to Director-General, 23 May 1983, SWK 11/13, part 2; Director-General to Minister of Social Welfare, 10 Apr 1984, ADM 24/22/84/1, part 1.

87 Director-General to Minister of Social Welfare, 24 Jul 1987, Otahuhu District Court, Legal submissions, nd, New Zealand Police Job Sheet, Detective-Sergeant A. J. Lovelock, 23 Jul 1987, Mary Todd, 'Supplementary Report on A___ L___', 19 Aug 1987, SWK 11/13/4, part 1.

88 'Dangerous Situations: The Report of the Independent Inquiry Team Reporting on the Circumstances of the Death of a Child', Mar 1988, *passim*; Director-General to Minister of Social Welfare, 17 May 1988, SWK 11/13/4, part 2.

89 D. Bush, Social Worker, Pukekohe, to Independent Inquiry Team, 17 Jun 1988, P. Lafferty, Area Welfare Officer, Pukekohe, to Director, Papakura, 31 May 1988, SWK 11/13/4, part 2.

90 Minister of Social Welfare, news release, 8 Jun 1988, F&C 2/2/1/1; Director-General to Minister of Social Welfare, 17 May 1988, SWK 11/13/4, part 2; Caton to Dalley, 6 Mar 1997.

91 Renouf to Minister of Social Welfare, 22 Apr 1988, SWK 11/13, part 4; Director-General to Chair, Parliamentary Select Committee, Social Services, 25 May 1988, CYP&F 4/2; 'Review of the Children and Young Persons Bill', Report of the Working Party on the Children and Young Persons Bill, Department of Social Welfare, Dec 1987.

92 Fish to Minister of Social Welfare, 15 Dec 1988, CYP&F 5/5; Minister of Police to Minister of Social Welfare, 21 Feb 1989, ADM 24/54/1, part 3.

93 Todd interview, 25 Jun 1996, tape 3.

94 Report for 1985 for the South Auckland child protection team (Otara), SWK 10/3/4; Points from DSW consultations, nd [1984], ADM 24/22/84/2, part 2; see the various submissions in ADM 24/22/84/3, parts 2–6; O. Wanders, Data analysis, 7 May 1985, ADM 24/22/86/2, part 9.

95 'A Guide to the Children and Young Persons Legislation', Department of Social Welfare, Dec 1986, *passim*.

96 Dickens, Topic notes, 3 May 1988, SWK 4/5/3, part 2.

97 *Puao-te-Ata-Tu*, p. 29; 'Review of the Children and Young Persons Bill', p. 24.

98 Doolan interview, 24 Jun 1996, tape 4; Putland interview, 19 Feb 1997, tape 3

99 *AJHR*, 1993, E-12, p. 37.

100 'Care and Protection Resource Panels', A Report from the Office of the Commissioner for Children, 1992, pp. 7–8; John McArthur to Brian Hay, Assistant-Director, Social Services, Porirua, 7 Mar 1991, F&C 2/4/4, part 2.

101 John Wallis, Senior Advisor, Social Services, to Andrew Lagzdins, Children, Young Persons and their Families Unit, 25 Mar 1991, F&C 2/4/4, part 2; Report from fono for care and protection resource panels of Department of Social Welfare Eastern operations region, 21 Mar 1991, Veronique Vervoort, Children, Young Persons and their Families Unit, to Director-General, 28 Nov 1991, F&C 2/4/4, part 3; 'Review of the Children, Young Persons, and Their Families Act', pp. 50–9.

102 Report from fono, 21 Mar 1991, Alan Nixon to Vervoort, 23 Apr 1991, Vervoort to Director-General, 28 Nov 1991, F&C 2/4/4, part 3; Ian Hassall, Commissioner for Children, to Director-General, 11 Mar 1991, F&C 2/4/4, part 2.

103 Karen Paterson and Michael Harvey, *An Evaluation of the Organisation and Operation of Care and Protection Family Group Conferences*, Wellington, Evaluation Unit, Department of Social Welfare, 1991, pp. 59–60; Caton to assistant-directors and area welfare officers, 2 Jul 1990, Unnumbered memo; Circular memo 1991/132.

104 'Review of the Children, Young Persons, and Their Families Act', pp. 8–12.

105 See Robert Dingwall and John Eekelaar, 'Rethinking Child Protection', in Michael D. A. Freeman (ed.), *The State, the Law and the Family: Critical Perspectives*, London/New York, Tavistock/Sweet and Maxwell, 1984, pp. 93–114, and Hendrick, *Child Welfare*, pp. 272ff, for fuller discussions of these issues.

106 John Angus to Minister of Social Welfare, 14 May 1991, F&C 2/2/1, part 3.

107 Caton, 'Summary of Report on Child Protection services, Northland region, Jan 1988', SWK 11/13, part 4; *New Zealand Herald*, 12 Jul 1989, F&C 2/2/2/1; Michael Watt in 'A Family Affair', *Frontline* Documentary, Television New Zealand, 1992.

108 Mrs S. Keenan, Secretary, Family Forum, to Minister of Social Welfare, 14 Jul 1988, CYP&F 5/5; *Auckland Star*, 22 Oct 1988, F&C 2/2/1/1; Newztel Log: *EyeWitness News*, Television One, 10 Mar 1989, F&C 2/2/2/1.

109 Ken Mason, 'Report on Inquiry into _____ and Review of the Case of ____, to Michael Cullen, Minister of Social Welfare, 12 May 1989', F&C 2/2/2/1.

110 *Press*, 15 Jul 1989, *New Zealand Herald*, 22 Jul 1989, F&C 2/2/1/1; Hendrick, *Child Welfare*, pp. 270ff.

111 'Silent Tears', *One Network News Special*, Television New Zealand, 1991.

112 Result of meetings in Rotorua, Wellington, Auckland and Christchurch Nov 1991, F&C 2/2/2, part 4; Beverly Keall, Principal Social Worker, to Wilson, 26 Apr 1991, F&C 2/2/1, part 4.

113 *Dominion Sunday Times*, 16 Jun 1991, F&C 2/4/2, part 4.

114 Carol Hood, Acting SSW, Rangiora, to Director, New Lynn, 7 Jan 1991, Wilson to Minister of Social Welfare, 19 Mar 1991, F&C 2/4/2, part 4.

115 'Review of the Children, Young Persons, and Their Families Act', pp. 8–12; Doolan interview, 24 Jun 1996, tape 4; Children, Young Persons, and Their Families Act 1989, sec. 6; Children, Young Persons, and Their Families Amendment Act 1994, sec. 3.

116 In 'Review of the Children, Young Persons, and Their Families Act', pp. 13–18.

117 *AJHR*, 1992, E-12, p. 14; 'Review of the Children, Young Persons, and Their Families Act', p. 13.

118 Wilson interview, 13 Jun 1996, tape 3.

119 Ian Hassall, 'Report to the Minister of Social Welfare on the New Zealand Children and Young Persons Service's Review of Practice in Relation to Craig Manukau and his Family', Office of the Commissioner for Children, 7 Oct 1993, p. 6; Cowan interview, 24 Jul 1996, tape 6.

Conclusion

1 On the funding of iwi, see Bradley, 'The Resolve to Devolve', pp. 31–5. For a discussion of some of the reviews, see Leon Fulcher and Frank Ainsworth, 'Child Welfare Abandoned? The Ideology and Economics of Contemporary Service Reform in New Zealand', *Social Work Review*, vol. 6, no. 3, 1994,

pp. 7–13; Pearman, 'The Pursuit of Organisational Legitimacy', *passim*.

2   Putland interview, 19 Feb 1997, tape 3.

3   Dingwall and Eekelaar, in 'Rethinking Child Protection', discuss the tension between children's and family rights, suggesting that locating children's rights within families is not so much an articulation of rights as a political theory about the proper relationship between parents and children. Hendrick, in *Child Welfare*, pp. 272ff, also considers this tension.

4   Wilson to Minister of Social Welfare, 19 Mar 1991, F&C 2/4/2, part 4.

BIBLIOGRAPHY

Unpublished

Archives and manuscripts
Alexander Turnbull Library
New Zealand Society for the Protection of Home and Family (Wellington)
    qMS-1561–1567, Minutebooks, 1901–25
Special Committee on Moral Delinquency, MS-Papers-2384
    2384/1 Hearings, 3–10 Aug 1954
    2384/2 Hearings 10–15 Aug 1954
    2384/3 Hearings 30 Aug–7 Sep 1954
    2384/4 Hearings 7–13 Sep 1954
    2384/5 Correspondence relating to work of the Committee, Oct 1953–Sep 1954
    2384/6–8 Submissions, 1954
    2384/9 Reports and memoranda considered by Special Committee, 1954
    2384/10 Memoranda, notes and articles, 1953–54
    2384/11 Printed material, 1954
    2384/12 Printed material, 1944–54
St Mary's Home Committee, Minutes and History, MS-Papers-3820

Manchester, Brian, Private papers, Waikanae

National Archives, Auckland
AADW Auckland Police District Headquarters
    Series 1110 Police reports
BAAA Department of Education, Northern Regional Office
    1959/1a Visits to children's homes, 1901–7
    1959/1b Visits to children's home, 1908–10
    1960/1a Reports on institutions, 1909–14
    1962/1a Children not formally under control, 1908–16

National Archives, Christchurch
CH8 Department of Education, Van Asch College
    8/9 Report of the Proceedings of the Conference of District Child Welfare Officers to discuss a new
        Child Welfare Bill, 1964
    8/15 Photograph album, 1913–22
CH90 Department of Education, Southern Regional Office, Christchurch
    37/1/47 Separation of Child Welfare Division from the Department of Education, part I, 1970–4
CH132 Christchurch Magistrate, Court Records
    132/252 Christchurch Children's Court, Criminal Record Book, Apr 1926–Mar 1928
CH 232 Department of Education, Southern Regional Office, Residual Management Unit

36/1/25/2, part 1 Kingslea School
36/1/25/4, part 1 Christchurch Boys' Home School
CH 378 Kingslea Girls' Home
378/483 Ex-girls case notes, 1968

National Archives, Wellington
Child Welfare (CW)
Series 1
2/6/14 Audit Inspectors, general
2/6/27, parts 1–5 Visits, reports of lady inspectors
2/6/28 Reports by Inspector M. Lyons
2/6/31 Schools for the Deaf, Sumner and Kelston
2/9/5 Office procedure and organisation, state of work reports
2/9/6, parts 1, 2 Office procedure and organisation, accounting procedure and instructions
2/9/8 Whangarei District Office
2/9/9, parts 1, 2 Administration, Auckland
2/9/10, parts 1, 2 Hamilton District Office
2/9/11, parts 1, 2 Administration, Rotorua
2/9/12, parts 1, 2 Administration, Gisborne
2/9/13, parts 1, 2 Administration, Napier
2/9/14, parts 1, 2 New Plymouth District Office
2/9/15, parts 1, 2 Wanganui District Office
2/9/16, parts 1, 2 Palmerston North District Office
2/9/17, parts 1, 2 Masterton District Office
2/9/18, parts 1, 2 Wellington District Office
2/9/21, part 1 Nelson District Office
2/9/22, parts 1, 2 Greymouth District Office
2/9/24, parts 1, 2 Timaru District Office
2/9/25, parts 1, 2 Dunedin District Office
2/9/26, parts 1, 2 Invercargill District Office
2/10, parts 1–3 Administration policy systems, general
2/10/2, parts 1–4 Criticisms of policy decisions
2/10/10, parts 1–6 Policy systems, extension of child welfare facilities
2/11/4 Maintenance, minor capital works programmes
2/12/2 Inter-departmental committee on adoptions
2/12/3 Organisation and methods committee
2/16, part 2 Punishment, general
2/16/11, part 2 Punishment returns, Christchurch Boys' Home
2/16/13 Punishment returns, Dunedin Boys' Home
2/16/18, part 2 Punishment returns, Kohitere and Hokio Beach
2/18/2, parts 1, 2 Administration returns, children not visited
2/18/6, parts 2, 3 Annual returns of children's institutions
2/18/16, parts 1–5 Annual returns, children under legal and preventive supervision
2/18/17, part 1 Annual returns, reasons for children placed under preventive supervision
2/18/28 Returns, case loads male and female officers
2/18/43, part 1 Returns, volume of work, district offices
3/1/6/1 Foster homes, suggestions for improvement in care of foster children
3/1/6/2 Foster homes, foster parent R. W. Anderson
3/1/6/3 Foster homes, foster parent Mrs Louise Miles
3/1/8 Ministerial approval of rates payment
3/2/2 Unsatisfactory employers
3/2/3 Unsatisfactory employers, under-rate workers

3/2/4 Unsatisfactory employers, apprenticeships
3/2/12 Inmates from Special School for Boys, Otekaike
3/3/3 Admissions to and placements from the four private institutions
3/3/9 Institutional needs, adolescent girls
3/4/1 Placement with parents or relatives, general correspondence
3/5/1, parts 1, 2 Capitation payments
3/6/9 Vocational training
3/10 General (breaches, censorship etc)
3/12/2 Dietary scales, institutions
3/12/4 Supplies of medicines, surgical appliances
3/12/7 Treatment of enuresis
4/1/1 Blind children, admissions, terms of payment
4/1/2 Travel arrangements and concessions
4/1/3 Maintenance claims
4/2/7 Compulsory admission of deaf children to the schools for the deaf, difficulties met with
4/3 Mentally defective children, general, including admission to special schools, special class leavers,
      work experience scheme
4/3/5 After care and finding suitable positions for ex-inmates
4/4/1, parts 1–5 Adoptions, applications for children
4/4/5 Consent to adoption given by Superintendent pursuant to section 15, Statutes Amendment Act
      1951
4/4/6 Adoption orders varied and discharged
4/5, parts 1, 2 Infant life protection, general
4/5/1 Exemption
4/5/2 Licences revoked
4/5/3, parts 1, 2 Deaths in foster homes (and children awaiting adoption)
4/5/6 Breaches of Act (prosecutions etc)
4/5/8 Alexandra Home, Wellington, placing of children from, with a view to adoption
4/5/11 Cases reported needing assistance etc after hospital treatment
4/6, part 1 Illegitimate births, general
4/6, part 2 Unmarried mothers, policy and general
4/6, part 3 Unmarried both parents
4/6/1 Notifications, births and deaths
4/7, parts 1, 2 Needy families, general
4/7/1, parts 1, 2 Housing assistance
4/7/2 Assistance from Social Security Department
4/7/3 General correspondence
4/7/4 Assistance, summary of cases
4/7/5 Problem families, housing
4/8, parts 1, 2 Immigrant children, general
4/8/4, part 1 Refugee children, general
4/8/5 Extracts from newspapers
4/8/9 Cases of misrepresentation
4/9 Polish children, policy and organisation, administration of grants
4/9/8 Polish children, matters relating to welfare
4/10 Industrial awards and labour legislation, general
4/10/1, parts 1, 2 Employment of child labour, street trading
4/12, parts 1, 2 Children's courts, general
4/12/1 Appointment of associates
4/12/3, parts 1–5 Annual reports to magistrates
4/12/4 Publications of proceedings
4/12/5 Recommendations, general

4/12/6 Court reports, general
4/12/7 Court accommodation
4/12/9, parts 1, 2 Decisions and directions of magistrates
4/12/10 Establishment
4/12/11 Procedure
4/12/12, part 1 Appointment of special magistrates
4/12/13 Serving of copies of orders on parents or guardians
4/13 Supervision, general
4/13/1 Preventive, general
4/14/1 Clinics
4/14/2 Intelligence tests
4/14/4 Psychological etc on play therapy
4/15, parts 1, 2 Maori welfare, general
4/15/2 Adoptions
4/15/3 Delinquency
4/15/4 Illegitimate births
4/15/5 Problems, Pukekohe district
4/16, part 1 Miscellaneous cases investigated by child welfare officers, general
4/16/3, parts 1–5 Reports of truancy, ill-treatment, neglect
4/16/7 Reports on misconduct at schools
4/16/9, parts 1, 2 Vandalism
4/16/10, parts 1, 2 Requests from solicitors and others for reports by child welfare officers
4/16/11 Eviction cases
4/16/12 Cruelty to animals
4/17 Clothing, general
4/18 Holiday homes, miscellaneous
4/19, parts 1–4 Juvenile delinquency, suggested causal factors and remedial measures, newspaper clippings
4/19/1, parts 1–3 Newspaper clippings
4/19/2, parts 1, 2 Effect of the cinema on child welfare
4/19/3 Slot game machines
4/19/4, parts 1, 2 Sexual misconduct
4/19/5 Hutt Valley inquiry, newspaper clippings
4/19/6 Bodgies and widgies
4/19/7 Investigation, Taita
5/1/5, parts 1, 2 The Orphan Home, Papatoetoe, Auckland
5/1/25, parts 1, 2 St Hilda's Home, Waipawa, Hawkes Bay
5/1/33, parts 1, 2 All Saints Children's Home, Palmerston North
5/1/44, parts 1, 2 St Mary's Home, Karori, Wellington
5/1/59, parts 1, 2 Presbyterian Boys' and Girls' Home, Christchurch
5/1/75, parts 1, 2 Private institutions, registration, general
5/1/79, parts 1, 2 Inspections of private institutions, general
5/2/5 Reports on individual cases
5/2/12 Centres closed or application withdrawn
6/12 Industrial Schools Act, proposed amendment
6/12/2 Industrial school legislation
6/70/1 Campbell Park School for Boys, Otekaike, management and general
6/71/1, parts 1, 2 Salisbury Girls' School, Richmond, management, work experience, general
7/29/1 Administration and management policy
7/30, parts 1–3 Establishment of family homes
7/30/1, parts 1, 2 Family homes, administration, management, policy
7/50/3 Auckland Girls' Home, building, maintenance, alterations
8/7, parts 1, 2 Maintenance of state wards, general

8/8/6 Adjustment of cases between Child Welfare, Police including JCPS

8/8/7 JCPS reports of the schemes and records being kept by Child Welfare districts

8/9, parts 1–3 Publicity, general

8/9/1, parts 1, 2 Newspaper cuttings, talks by field staff

8/11 Social Security, general

8/11/3 Family benefits

8/14/2 Big Brother movement, general

8/14/6 Happiness Club, Wellington

8/14/7 Catholic Youth movement

8/14/8 Scout movement

8/14/11 New Zealand Howard League

8/14/12 Children's Club, general

8/14/15 Voluntary help in child welfare institutions

8/18 Restitution payments, general

8/18/1 Claims against state wards

8/20/9 Cooperation with social service agencies in New Zealand, Kensington Youth Club

8/22 Memoirs and obituary of John Beck

13/2/3 Annual report (administrative) of Child Welfare Division

13/2/7, parts 1, 2 Comics, control of salacious literature, effect of

13/2/8, parts 1–4 Cabinet instructions, parliamentary papers, questions and answers, drafts for minister's speeches

3/12/12 Speech from the Throne

19/8/2 Staff, Hokio Beach School

19/14 Staff, Receiving Home, Christchurch, general questions

19/19 Staff, Boys' Home, Christchurch, general

19/20, part 2 Staff, Boys' Home, Auckland, general

19/25/41 Staff, Child Welfare Office, Auckland, general

19/25/49 Staff, Child Welfare Office, Napier, general

19/25/54 Staff, Child Welfare Office, Greymouth, general

19/37/2 B89 Training of social workers

19/48 Staff, Receiving Home, Auckland, general

19/52 Staff, Receiving Home, Napier, general

19/63 B89 Staff, Receiving Home, Hamilton, general, question and field staff

19/69 Staff, Girls' Hostel, Wellington, general

19/70/1, part 1 Staff, Girls' Home, Burwood, general

19/78 Staff, Fareham House, Featherston, general

26/1/18 Secondary education: general secondary and technical education for inmates under child welfare supervision

29/72/5 Miscellaneous, correspondence with League of Nations

38/19/8 Child Welfare Act 1925, forms

40/1 Industrial schools system, cost of

40/1A Special and industrial schools system, general

40/1/1 Proposal that government should assume control of destitute children

40/1/7 Mr Reece's report on industrial school and reformatory system outside New Zealand

40/1/11 Private industrial schools, system and general

40/1/13 Special schools system, boarding out children

40/1/19 Proposed reforms in industrial schools system

40/1/23, parts 1, 2 Child welfare system, deaf children, general

40/1/24 Supervision of all illegitimate children

40/1/35 Child welfare system, general

40/1/42 Boarding out, criticism by Mrs L. M. Diamond of Dargaville and subsequent reports re her house

40/1/45 Big Brother movement, government assistance to YMCA

40/1/47 Girls' Home, Burwood, purpose of home and general scheme of training

40/1/51 Information asked for about child welfare system

40/1/62 Records to be kept by matron of institutions

40/1/63 Complaint by Mrs M. B. Saljack [sic] and others re child welfare system in Auckland

40/1/66 Request that headquarters in Taranaki be transferred from Hawera to New Plymouth

40/1/69 Child welfare system, general, complaint by Mr Dakin

40/1/70 Admission to and placing out of inmates from St Joseph's, Waikowhai

40/1/71 Child guidance clinics

40/1/72 Child welfare system, general

40/1/73 Maori consorting with Chinese and other Asiatics

40/1/83 Question of committal or dealing with children whose parent is on military service

40/1/89 Information asked for

40/1/95 Enquiry into alleged ill-treatment of state wards by Miss P. M. Kidd

40/2/10 Estate of late T. Brown, Dunedin, Sumner School for Deaf

40/2/11 Report of Inspector Mrs Gyfford Moore

40/2/14 Special industrial schools, miscellaneous correspondence

40/2/20 Report of child welfare officers re complaints of children at certain public schools

40/2/26 Sale of contraceptives

40/2/48 British children being brought to New Zealand, newspaper extracts

40/2/50 British children, applications for, general correspondence, Auckland district

40/2/58 British children, applications for, Wellington district

40/2/66 British children, general correspondence

40/2/84 British children, education

40/2/88 British children, proposed remission of contributions to foster parents

40/2/92 War evacuees from Pacific Islands

40/2/94 Assistance to needy families, reports and decisions of special committee

40/2/101 Department assisting with placement of cured lepers from Makogai passing through New Zealand

40/2/102 Assistance to needy families, reports and decisions of special committee

40/2/107, part 2 Child welfare reports on female applicants

40/2/116 British children, return to United Kingdom, general correspondence

40/2/119 Provision for pregnant WAAFs and WRNs and children

40/2/123 Objectionable features of radio

40/2/124 Liquor Licensing Commission

40/3/3 Management of Boys' Training Farm, Weraroa

40/3/9 Burnham Commission of Enquiry

40/3/16 Te Oranga Home, Sir E. W. Gibbes' report on criticisms

40/3/30 Manager, St Vincent de Paul's, Dunedin

40/3/34 Management, St Mary's Industrial School, Auckland

40/3/36 Recognition of St Joseph's Orphanage as private industrial school

40/3/39 Management, St Mary's, Nelson

40/3/44A Management, Burnham Industrial School

40/4 Inspection of industrial schools, general

40/4/4 Inspection, St Mary's, Nelson

40/4/5 Inspection, Nelson Boys' Training Farm

40/4/8 Inspection, Wellington Receiving Home

40/4/9 Inspection, St Vincent de Paul's School

40/4/10 Inspection, Te Oranga Home for Girls

40/4/11 Inspection, Caversham

40/4/12 Inspection, Christchurch Receiving Home

40/4/13 Inspection, Burnham Industrial School

40/4/56 Child welfare reports and lady inspectors
40/5 Feeble-minded children, general
40/5/5 Mental Defectives Act 1911, amendment
40/5/9 Care and control of feeble-minded, replies to circular of 1 May 1924. Also special report of Committee of Enquiry re Mental Defectives and Sexual Offenders
40/6/1 Special and industrial schools, orphanages and other institutions, Lorne Farm, Makarewa
40/6/2 Children's Convalescent Home, New Brighton
40/6/7 Victoria Memorial Home, Invercargill
40/6/9 Karitane Home, Dunedin
40/6/11 Presbyterian Orphanage, Anderson's Bay and Nisbet Home for Girls, Anderson's Bay, Dunedin
40/6/16 Mission House of the Order of the Good Shepherd, Auckland
40/6/22 Methodist Orphanage, Epworth, Auckland
40/6/25 Salvation Army Boys' Home, Island Bay, now at Wallaceville
40/6/29 Costley Training Institute
40/6/32 Salvation Army Home, Middlemarch
40/6/35 Dilworth Institute, Auckland
40/6/40A Complaint by C. V. Nattrass re treatment of his children, Presbyterian Orphanage, Berhampore
40/6/42 Materoa Home Creche, Gisborne
40/6/43 St Vincent de Paul Foundling Home, Epsom, Auckland
40/6/44 St Mary's Home, Napier
40/6/50 G. Benstead's private school for feebleminded, Timaru
40/6/56 St Anne's Home for Girls, Christchurch
40/6/57 Mrs M. M. Kirk's temporary home for infants in case of sickness
40/6/59 Dunkley Children's Home, Inc., Dunedin
40/6/63 Mansell Bebbington Home, New Plymouth, proposed pioneer settlement for children from United Kingdom
40/6/65 Presbyterian Maori Mission Home, Whakatane
40/6/73 Establishment of convalescent or nursing home for feeble-minded children
40/6/111 Crompton Nurseries, New Plymouth
40/6/116 Establishment of day nursery, Auckland
40/6/120 Day nursery, Wellington, re assistance for additions etc
40/7/3 Jubilee Institute for the Blind, training
40/8 Infant Life Protection, transfer of control
40/8/3 Infant Life Protection, general instructions
40/8/12 Infant Life Protection, general system
40/8/12A Infant Life Protection, inauguration of system
40/8/13 Infant Life Protection system
40/8/14 Infant Life Protection, criticisms
40/8/28 Infant Life Protection, feeding and care of infants
40/8/32 Infant Life Protection, suggested scheme for systematizing the work
40/8/37 Infant Life Protection, health and medical attendance
40/8/39 Infant Life Protection, Plunket training, Karitane, for nurses under Education Department
40/8/58 Case of Miss Sylvia Lynn, who borrowed baby from St Mary's Home, Napier, ostensibly for adoption, but really to falsify affiliation and maintenance orders
40/10A Probation system
40/10/1 Boys on probation
40/10/63 Probation system
40/12/3 Children suffering from venereal diseases committed to industrial schools
40/12/8 Health, self-abuse and circumcision
40/12/61 Social Security benefits, report on Maori beneficiaries, Gisborne
40/14/24 Proposed admissions to industrial schools
40/14/27 Admission to special schools

40/14/28 Admissions to special schools, cases of children whose parents are recent arrivals
40/14/29 Committal of infants whose mothers are serving a term of reformative detention
40/15/4 Transfer of girls from St Mary's, Auckland to Mt Magdala in preference to Te Oranga Home
40/15/20 Transfer of inmates, general correspondence
40/15/42 Transfer of inmates, opening of Burwood Home
40/15/43 Transfer of boys from Weraroa to Special School for Boys, Otekaike
40/17 Special schools, maintenance, funeral
40/17/10 Child welfare, maintenance
40/17/17 Maintenance of children in industrial schools: rates increased from 10/- to £1/10/-
40/17/24 Maintenance, child welfare
40/17/25 Recoveries of payment in cases of children admitted to homes where parents are not paying for their maintenance
40/19/5 Physical instruction, Weraroa
40/19/15 Religious instruction, Otekaike
40/19/25 Instructions to inmates, Otekaike
40/19/41 Basket and strawberry boxmaking, Otekaike
40/19/45 Physical training, Otekaike
40/22/4 Notes to guide boys at service
40/22/8 Child welfare absconders
40/23/7 Punishments, St Vincent de Paul, Dunedin
40/23/23 Punishments, Napier Receiving Home
40/23/24 Punishments, Nelson
40/24A Inmates' earnings, general
40/24/35 Creation of a fund to assist deserving boys by each contributing amount appropriate to establish a boy in some vocation
40/25 Licensing
40/25/8 Licensing, boarding out
40/25/12 Service conflict with Arbitration Court awards
40/25/20 Licensing of inmates to friends, visits
40/25/21 Boarding-out system
40/25/22 Boarding-out system
40/25/26 Placing Maori children
40/25/35 Limitation of numbers in foster homes
40/25/48 Licensing, placing of girls in Salem House, Auckland
40/25/47 Licensing, general conditions of service, rates and wages
40/25/52 Licensing, application for increased boarding rate
40/26/1 Inmates sentenced to imprisonment
40/26/9 Communication between inmates and their friends
40/28/5 Recreation, Otekaike
40/28/10 Recreation, Burwood
40/29/32 Reports on inmates, case histories of girls at Burwood
40/31 Adoption, general
40/31/9 Adoption, general
40/31/20 Adoption, child welfare officers reporting to magistrates on all adoptions
40/31/28 Adoption, application by Mrs Dowse for cancellation of order for her daughter, Elvira Frederickson
40/31/37 Adoption, general
40/31/48 Native Land Court, Rotorua, case of Ellen Lowe, Honi Ira Shrimpton
40/32/1 Treatment and provision for epileptics
40/37/5 Probation statistics
40/41/7 Office arrangements outside offices
40/42/1 Libraries

40/47/25 Preventive cases, Wellington
40/48/1 Street labour and employment of children
40/48/2 Street trading and employment of child labour, work outside school hours, boarded-out children
40/50 Child Welfare Act 1925, regulations
40/50A Child Welfare Act, 1902 regulations
40/50/4 Child Welfare Act 1925, establishment of children's courts
40/50/6 Child Welfare Act 1925, inmates' earnings
40/50/8 Child Welfare Act 1925, miscellaneous correspondence re inauguration of new system
40/50/9 Child Welfare Act 1925, interpretations and legal decisions
40/50/11 Child Welfare Act 1925, children's courts
40/50/12 Reports furnished for courts
40/50/13 Procedure in children's courts for young offenders
40/50/24 Child Welfare Act 1925, periodical reports on working of children's courts
40/50/34 Powers of children's courts to order a whipping
40/50/37 Convictions in children's courts
40/50/40 Periodical reports on workings of children's courts
40/51/1 Placing of certain children in orphanages and private homes, payment Salvation Army homes
40/55A Juvenile delinquency, extracts from papers
40/55B Juvenile delinquency, correspondence
40/55/1 Juvenile delinquency
40/55/2 Juvenile delinquency, report by Mrs Philipp
40/57 Immigration, general
40/57/2 Immigration, assistance and advice to unmarried mothers
41/1/2 Farming operations
41/6/3 Proposed institution in North Island for feebleminded
41/17/3 Property, buildings, etc, destruction of first division building by fire
41/19, parts 1, 2 Caversham, buildings and site
41/19A, part 2 Caversham, buildings and site
41/21/24 Special School for Boys, Otekaike, buildings and site
41/22 Christchurch Boys' Home, establishment, property, buildings
41/23 Wellington Boys' Home, property, buildings
41/25 Auckland Boys' Home, establishment, property
41/25/2 Auckland Boys' Home, small farming
41/26/1 Auckland Boys' Home, buildings
41/26/2 Receiving Home, Auckland, furniture and fittings
41/27/1 Wanganui Receiving Home, buildings, site
41/29 Napier Receiving Home, buildings, site
41/34 Palmerston North Receiving Home, buildings, site
41/35 Invercargill Receiving Home, establishment
41/37/10 Burwood, official name
41/39 Auckland Boys' Hostel, property
41/41/1 Remand homes, establishment of, correspondence
41/43 North Island School for Deaf, property, proposed site
51/1/4 Special classes for backward children, general
Series 10
10/4 Nominal roll of licensed foster parents, 1908
10/5 Nominal roll of licensed foster parents, 1909
Series 11
11/1 Proposed admissions
Series 15
15/2 List of past inmates discharged
15/9 Burnham Inquiry

Department of Education (E)
Series 1
    E 1 19/28/38a Child welfare officers, salaries
Series 2
    E 2 1932/2c Supervision of native children
    E 2 1942/7b Boys' Training Farm Weraroa
    E 2 1943/8b Boys' Training Farm Weraroa, buildings and site
    E 2 1950/25b Needy families, housing requirements
Series 12
    Personal Files: W. J. Anderson, J. Caughley F. K. de Castro
Series 16
    Official Register

Department of Health (H)
    H 3/13 Committee of Enquiry into Mental Defectives and Sexual Offenders (transcript of evidence)
Series 1
    8987 45/1 Venereal Diseases, preparation of pamphlets
    B.83 130/1/1 Social Hygiene Act, Venereal Diseases Committee, general
    B.83 130/1/2 Venereal Diseases Committee, evidence

Department of Internal Affairs (IA)
Series 1
    173/1, parts 1–3 War evacuation of children refugees from England
    173/1/1 War evacuation of children refugees from England
    173/2 War evacuation from England, offers of accommodation

Department of Justice (J, JC)
Series 1
    18/6/1, parts 1, 2 Suggested amendments, Child Welfare Amendment Bill 1961
    18/6/2 Children's Court, Auckland
    18/6/3 Establishment of Children's Court at Tokomaru Bay
    18/20/18, part 1 Adoption Act 1955
    18/20/21, parts 1, 2 Adoption regulations
    21/2/34, parts 1–3 Committee of Inquiry into Juvenile Delinquency (Morals Committee)
    21/2/36 Interdepartmental committee set up to coordinate government social welfare activities, general
        file
    21/2/46, parts 1, 2 Joint Committee on Young Offenders
    1933/41/1, bundle 13 Child Welfare Act, establishment of children's courts
    1938/41/2, bundle 58 Child Welfare Act 1925, Section 32
    1940/41/1, bundle 64 Practice of adjourning children in custody by Children's Court, Auckland
    W2304, 18/4/7, parts 2, 3 Inquiry as to Illegitimacy Act
    W2304, 18/4/40, part 1 Illegitimacy, general inquiries
    W2304, 18/6/1, part 3 Child Welfare Act and matters pertaining to, suggested amendment
    W2304, 18/6/8, part 1 Children's Court procedure
    W2304, 18/6/12, part 1 Children's Court procedure
    W2304, 18/6/17, part 1 Justices of the Peace authorised to exercise jurisdiction in children's courts,
        magistrates, right of appeal
    W2304, 18/20/9 Minister of Maori Affairs, guardianship order
    W2304, 18/20/17, part 1 Consents taken by registrar of court
    W2304, 18/20/19 Infants Act (adoption fees), rules, 1937
    W2304, 18/20/21, parts 3, 4 Rules relating to the adoption of children
    W2304, 18/22/24, part 1 Youth juries

Series 40
> 93/598 Re Baby Farms
> JC 18/10/6 For amendment of the Crimes Act

Legislative Council (Le)
> 1/1921/173 Preliminary report by Director of Education on his visit to Australia
> 1/1925/4 Education Committee
> 1/1955/6 Juvenile Delinquency Committee
> 1/1955/6 Correspondence, report, summaries, miscellaneous
> 1/1955/6 Submissions etc

Department of Maori Affairs (MA)
Series 1
> 36/11, parts 1, 2 Children's welfare
> 36/11/3/10, parts 1, 2 Children's board, Hutt Valley

Police (P)
Series 1
> 1/1/220 Preventive work among juveniles by Police
> 1/1/229 Children's courts, Police procedure
> 1/1/349 Committee on Illegitimacy
Series 10
> 10/1 Stoke Industrial School

Social Security Department (SS)
Series 7
> 7/6/18 Motherhood of Man movement
> 7/7/17 Special committee on moral delinquency
> 7/7/22, parts 1, 2 Coordination of government welfare administration
> 33/1/3 Research administration, Social Work amalgamation
> W2363 Joint Committee on Young Offenders, research 1976
Series 8
> 8/10, parts 1, 2 Surveys and reports, incidence rate of juvenile delinquency in New Zealand
> 8/10/1 Case histories
> 8/10/3, part 1 Research thesis
> 8/10/7, part 1 Juvenile delinquency research group
> 8/10/8, parts 1, 2 Interdepartmental Committee on Maori Crime
> 8/10/9, parts 1–9 Joint Committee on Young Offenders,
> 8/10/11, part 1 Adolescent group activities in Auckland
> 8/10/13 Report of the special committee on moral delinquency in children and adolescents and matters arising therefrom
> 8/10/21, part 2 Ill-treatment survey, 1967
Series 20
> 20/1, vols 1, 2 Research
> 20/2/3, vols 1–4 Material circulated other than minutes and agenda
> 20/2/4W Workshop of the Joint Committee of Young Offenders

Department of Social Welfare, Child Welfare Division
> ABNT W4295 Case files

Department of Social Welfare, Corporate Records, Wellington
HIST/2 Historical Papers, Child Welfare, Legislation, 1887–1964
   John Beck, *Child Welfare in the United States of America and Canada: Report of a Visit of the Superintendent, Child Welfare Branch, Education Department*, Special Reports on Educational Subjects, no. 15, Education Department, 1927
HIST/10 Historical Papers, Miscellaneous, Documents and Photographs
   Mr J. Hercock, Reminiscences
Circular memoranda, 1989–92
Unnumbered memoranda, 1989–92
Administration (ADM)
   4/2/5 Research into illegitimacy
   4/2/9, parts 1, 2 Interdepartmental Committee, young offenders
   4/2/23/6 Working Party on Absconding Teenage and Sub-teenage Children
   4/2/23/7, parts 1, 2 Sub-committee on Young Offenders of the Officials Committee on Family and Social Policy
   4/2/28, parts 1, 2 Inter-departmental committee, secure institutional treatment
   4/2/33/3 Health, Education and Welfare Standing Committee on Services for Disturbed Children
   4/2/38, part 2 National Advisory Committee on the Prevention of Child Abuse
   4/2/38/1, part 1 National Advisory Committee on the Prevention of Child Abuse, meetings
   4/2/38/2 National Advisory Committee on the Prevention of Child Abuse, agenda and minutes
   4/2/42, parts 1, 5, 6 Advisory Committee on Maori and Island Youth
   4/2/42/1 Advisory Committee on Maori and Island Youth, Rotorua pilot project
   4/2/51, part 3 Ministerial Advisory Committee on a Maori Perspective in the Department of Social Welfare
   4/2/53, parts 1, 2 Advisory Committee on the Investigation, Detection and Prosecution of Offences against Children
   8/3 Social Work Division investigation, foster homes
   14/1/6 Policy decisions, Children and Young Persons Court
   24/18/80/1 Adult Adoption Information Bill, submissions to Statutes Revision Committee
   24/18/82 Adult Adoption Information Bill
   24/18/84 Adult Adoption Information Bill 1984
   24/18/85, part 2 Adult Adoption Information Act, general correspondence, policy
   24/22/74 Children and Young Persons Act 1974
   24/22/74A, parts 1–4 Children and Young Persons Act 1974, submissions
   24/22/77 Children and Young Persons Amendment Bill 1977
   24/22/80 Children and Young Persons Amendment Bill 1980
   24/22/81 Children and Young Persons Amendment Bill 1981
   24/22/82 Children and Young Persons Amendment Bill
   24/22/83, parts 1, 2 Children and Young Persons Amendment Bill 1983
   24/22/83/1, part 1 Revision of Children and Young Persons Regulations 1983
   24/22/84 Children and Young Persons Amendment Bill 1984
   24/22/84/1, parts 1, 2 Children and Young Persons Amendment Bill 1984, revision
   24/22/84/2, parts 1, 2 Working Party to review the Children and Young Persons Act
   24/22/84/3, parts 1–9 Revision of Children and Young Persons Act 1974, submissions on public discussion paper
   24/22/85, parts 1, 2 Revision of Children and Young Persons Act 1974, general correspondence
   24/22/86/2, parts 8, 9 Children and Young Persons Act 1989, submissions, legal section
   24/30/25, parts 1–4 Child Welfare Act 1925 and amendments
   24/54/1, parts 1–3 Children, Young Persons, and Their Families Act
   25/22/3B Children's boards, Hamilton to New Plymouth
   25/22/3C Children's boards, Otahuhu to Whangarei
   25/22/10, parts 1–5 Children and Young Persons Court, procedure

25/22/24, parts 1–3 Children and Young Persons Act, visiting committees
Children, Young Persons and Their Families (CYP&F)
    4/2 Drafting instructions
    5/5 Ministerials/questions in Parliament
Families and Children (F&C)
    2/2/1, parts 3, 4 Children needing protection, child abuse and neglect
    2/2/1/1 Child abuse and neglect: media reports, general
    2/2/2, parts 1–4 Children needing protection, sexual abuse
    2/2/2/1 Children needing protection, sexual abuse, media reports
    2/2/4 Independent inquiry
    2/3/1, parts 1, 2 Families needing support: family welfare, general
    2/3/5/1 Grant funding programme, policy
    2/3/6/1 Family/whanau agreement policy
    2/4/2, parts 1–6 Care and protection under the Children and Young Persons Act, general
    2/4/3, part 1 Care and protection under the Children and Young Persons Act, ministerials and
       correspondence
    2/4/4, parts 1–3 Care and protection resource panels
    2/4/6, parts 1–3 Care and protection under the Children and Young Persons Act, the family group
       conference
    4/1/11/2 Regional services/projects: Case clearing house, South-West Auckland region
    4/1/11/6, parts 1, 2 Regional services/projects: Case clearing house, Southern region
    4/2/2/1, part 3 Placement and funding policy, general
    4/2/4/3, part 1 Children under care orders and agreements, Maori children
    4/6/11/4 Regional services/projects, Central North
    4/6/11/5, part 1 Regional services, North and South Islands
Information Technology Services Bureau (ITS)
    1/6/4, part 2 Restructuring, general
Organisations and Departments (O&D)
    19/- , parts 1–4 New Zealand Society for the Protection of Home and Family, general
    62/7, parts 1–5 International Year of the Child 1979
    62/7/1 International Year of the Child 1979, publicity, press clippings
    62/7/5, parts 1–4 Committee for Children
    93/1/2 Police Department, social work liaison, custody of inmates
    93/2/2 Police Department Youth Aid Section, adjustment of cases and general
    98/- Boystown Police and Citizens Club Inc
    123/-, parts 1–8 New Zealand Foster Care Federation, correspondence
    311/1, parts 1, 2 Human Rights Commission inquiries, ACORD
    559/-, parts 1, 2 Children's Commissioner Office, establishment and general
Social Work (SWK)
    1/6/9 Administration institutions, general, Southern region
    1/9/2 Administration institutions, general, South-West Auckland
    1/9/3 Administration institutions, general, Central Northern region
    1/9/4, parts 1, 2 Administration institutions, general, Central region
    1/9/5 Administration institutions, general, Central South region
    2/1/1 Children's boards: policy
    2/1/2 Children's boards: correspondence
    2/1/3, parts 1, 2A, 5, 7 Children's boards: appointments to panel of residents
    2/1/5 Children's boards: appointments by Secretary for Maori Affairs
    2/1/6 Children's boards: evaluation of children's boards
    2/2/1 Visiting committees: policy, management and general correspondence
    2/2/2/4 Visiting committees: Hokio
    2/2/2/5 Visiting committees: Kingslea

2/2/2/6 Visiting committees: Owairaka Boys' Home
2/2/2/7 Visiting committees: Allendale Girls' Home, correspondence and appointments in the interim
2/2/2/15 Visiting committees: Arbor House
2/2/2/16 Visiting committees: Epuni Boys' Home
2/2/2/17 Visiting committees: Miramar Girls' Home
2/2/2/20 Visiting committees: Dunedin Girls' Home
2/2/3, parts 1, 3 Visiting committees: triennial appointments
2/2/4, parts 1, 2 Visiting committees: annual report
2/4/1, part 1 Community work scheme
2/7/0 Children and Young Persons Court: general
2/7/2, parts 1, 2 Children and Young Persons Court: social workers' report, general
2/7/4 Children and Young Persons Court: decisions and directions of judges
2/7/5 Children and Young Persons Court: legal supervision, general
2/7/7, parts 1, 2 Children and Young Persons Court: young persons held in custody, policy
2/7/8 Children and Young Persons Court: duty solicitor scheme
2/7/10 Children and Young Persons Court: night sittings
2/10/1 Ex-nuptial births, unmarried mothers
2/12/1, part 1 Requests and decisions for extended secure care
3/1/0 Children and young persons in care: general
3/1/2, part 1 Board payments and pocket money: rates
3/1/3 Board payments: special rates
3/3/3 Working party placements for children in care of Director-General
3/4/1 Absconders, general
3/6/4 Admissions: national and regional institutions, policy and general
3/10/1, parts 1, 2 Planning for children in care: policy
3/10/6 Planning for children in care: Permanency Planning Task Force, general
3/10/6/1 Permanency Planning Task Force, Christchurch
3/10/6/3 Planning for children in care: Permanency Planning Task Force, Central North
4/1, parts 1–4 Foster care policy and practice
4/1/3 Foster Care Week
4/1/5 100 years of foster care (1983)
4/3, part 1 Intensive foster care scheme (departmental): policy and general
4/5 Foster parent recruitment and training
4/5/1 Foster parent training: R. Prasad pack
4/5/2 Recruitment of Maori foster parents: Rotorua Working Party
4/5/3, parts 1, 2 New Zealand Foster Care conferences
4/7, parts 1–4 Advisory Committee on Foster Care
5/1/0, parts 1–3 Adoptions: policy
5/1/4 Adoption of children in care
5/1/6, parts 1, 2 Reorganisation of adoption services: working party 1982
5/2/1 Adoption orders and legal decisions
5/2/3 Visits to districts
5/3/2 Babies available for adoption: Catholic Social Services, Christchurch
5/6/2 Staffing for reorganised Adoption Service and Special Needs Units
5/7/1, part 1 Adult Adoption Information Act: independent counsellors and social work staff
5/7/4, parts 1–3 Adult adoptions: general correspondence
6/0/6 Specialist services, general: residential services, general
6/0/9, part 2 Family work practices: working party
7/0/2 Annual reports of social work inspections
7/2/1 Social work inspections, Weymouth
7/2/2 Social work inspections, Holdsworth
7/2/4 Social work inspections, Kohitere

7/2/5 Social work inspections, Hokio
7/2/6 Social work inspections, Fareham
7/4/0/2 Visits to and reports on districts, activity reports to Director-General's meetings
8/0 Social Work Volunteer Scheme, policy and general
8/0/2 Social Work Volunteer Scheme, monitoring and evaluation
9/0, parts 1–4 Residential services, policy and general
9/0/1, parts 1, 2 Assessment and remand facilities: general/policy
9/0/2, parts 1, 2 Principals and Assistant Principals conferences
9/0/3, parts 1–3 National and regional institutions: schools in institutions, general
9/0/5 Violent and aggressive acts by children and young persons in residence
9/0/6 Review of Residential Facilities: Auckland and Hamilton region
9/0/7 Marae Homes, policy
9/0/9, parts 1, 2 1982 Review of Departmental Institutions
9/0/12, parts 1–3 Basic rights and legal safeguards in institutions, policy and regulations
9/0/20 Criminal Justice Act, effect on institutions
9/0/23 Cultural Environment Programme, Department of Social Welfare institutions
9/1/4 Cornwall Park Reception Centre, general
9/1/4/1 Cornwall Park Reception Centre, annual report
9/1/5 Wesleydale Boys' Home, general
9/1/5/1 Wesleydale Boys' Home, annual report
9/2/2/1 Intermediate treatment facility, Christchurch
9/3/3 Dunedin, Review of Residential Services
9/17/1 Palmerston North Girls' Home, general
9/19/1 Arbor House (Greytown Reception Centre), general
9/19/2 Adolescent Support Centre, Kibblewhite Rd, Masterton, policy
9/52 Fareham House, general
9/54 Holdsworth, general
10/1, part 1 Whangarei Youth Development Project
10/2, part 1 Red Cross Home-maker Service, policy
10/3, parts 1–3 Child abuse projects, general
10/3/2, parts 1–3 Child abuse pilot project, Hamilton
10/3/3 Child abuse, South Auckland (Mangere)
10/3/4 Child abuse pilot project, South Auckland (Otara)
10/3/5 Projects/pilot schemes, Child Protection Team, Christchurch
10/7/0 Community Care Scheme, policy
10/7/1 Community Care Unit, South Auckland
10/7/2 Cornwall Park Reception Centre
10/13, parts 1–7 Maatua Whangai, policy and general
11/2, part 1 Social work with families
11/9 Maori welfare
11/13, parts 1–5 Ill-treatment, neglect, child abuse
11/13/2 Sexual abuse
11/13/4, parts 1, 2 Independent inquiry into the death of a child in South Auckland 1987/1988
11/17, parts 1, 2 Social work with the young offender
11/18 J-teams, policy
11/19 Crisis intervention, crisis care
11/20, parts 1–4 Runaway children and adolescents
11/30 Family home for sexually abused girls
13/90 Casework correspondence, Kohitere
13/92 Casework correspondence, Kingslea
13/93 Casework correspondence, Weymouth
13/94 Casework correspondence, Beck House

FH 1/1, parts 1, 2 General purpose family homes, policy
FH 1/1/1, part 2 General purpose family homes, administration and management
FH 1/1/5 Family Home Foster Parent Association
FH 1/2 Special purpose family homes, policy
FH 1/3, parts 1–3 General purpose family homes, Family Homes Review
Welfare (WEL)
5/5, parts 1–3 Juvenile crime in New Zealand, correspondence
6/1/1, parts 1, 2 Children's homes, policy
8/1/0, parts 1–7 Adoptions, case work policy
8/2/3 Administration, Adoption Review 1976
8/2/5 Adoption seminar 1976, reports
8/2/7 Adoptions, administration, visits to districts, arrangements and reports
9/0, parts 1, 2 National institution management, general
9/0/3 Violent and aggressive acts by state wards
9/0/4 Review of residential facilities, Auckland and Hamilton
9/1/1, parts 1, 2 Owairaka Boys' Home, Auckland
9/1/2 Allendale Girls' Home, Auckland, general
9/1/4 Bollard Girls' Home, Auckland, general
9/1/5 Cornwall Park Reception Centre, Market Rd, Epsom, Auckland
9/1/6 Wesleydale Boys' Home, Mt Roskill, Auckland
9/2/2, parts 1, 2 Christchurch Boys' Home, Stanmore St, Richmond
9/2/3 Strathmore Girls' Home, Ferry Rd, Christchurch
9/3/3, parts 1, 2 Dunedin Boys' Home, Lookout Point, Dunedin
9/3/4 Dunedin Girls' Home, Elliott St, Andersons Bay
9/4/2 Wellington Girls' Home, Camperdown Rd, Miramar
9/8/2 Hamilton Boys' Home, Mt View Rd
9/8/3 Hamilton Girls' Home, Rey St
9/17/1 Palmerston North Girls' Home, Margaret St
9/22/1, parts 1, 2 Epuni Boys' Home, Riverside Drive
9/50, parts 1, 2 Kohitere C. D. Farm Rd, Levin
9/50/3 Kohitere, Levin, recreation, general
9/50/4, parts 1, 2 Kohitere, Levin, annual reports
9/51 parts 1, 2 Hokio Beach School, general
9/52, parts 1–3 Fareham House, Underhill St, Featherston
9/52/4 Fareham House, annual reports
9/53, parts 1–4 Kingslea, Horseshoe Rd, Shirley, Christchurch
9/53/2 Kingslea, Christchurch, health, medical and dental
9/53/4, part 3 Kingslea, Christchurch, annual report
9/54 Holdsworth School, St Johns Hill, Wanganui
9/56 Beck House, Napier
9/57, part 1 Camp Peek
10/1 Young persons held in custody
10/6 Intensive Foster Care Scheme, policy
10/6/2 Intensive Foster Care Scheme, evaluation material
13/0 Violence in families
13/1, parts 1, 2 Child abuse, developmental project
14/0 Foster care policy and practice
Youth and community (Y&C)
1/1/1, parts 1–6 Young offenders programmes, legislation and policy
1/1/3 Young offenders programmes, general correspondence
1/1/8 Young offenders programmes, diversionary programmes for young offenders
1/2/1 Department residential services and alternatives to residential care

1/2/1, parts 1–3 Departmental residential services and alternatives to residential care, legislation and policy

1/2/3, parts 1, 2 General correspondence

1/2/11/2 Residential and Alternative Care Services Management Plan Steering Committee, South-West Auckland region

1/2/11/4 Residential and Alternative Care Services Management Plan Steering Committee, Central region

1/2/11/6 Residential and Alternative Care Services Management Plan Steering Committee, Southern region

1/2/12 Residential services, secure care

1/2/13 Alternatives to residential care

1/2/16/1 Weymouth Residential Centre

1/2/16/2 Epuni Youth Centre

1/2/16/3 Kingslea Resource Centre

1/2/16/4 Dunedin Resource Centre

Reports

'Adoption Practices Review Committee: Report to the Minister of Social Welfare', Wellington, Aug 1990

'Background Paper Prepared by the Department of Social Welfare on Trends in Illegitimacy, Adoption and Related Matters', for the Royal Commission to Enquire into and Report upon Contraception, Sterilisation and Abortion, Sep 1975, Department of Social Welfare Library

Beckingham, Barbara, 'What Shall I Do? Influences on the Decision of Unmarried Mothers to Keep their Babies or Offer them for Adoption', Auckland, Society for Research on Women, May 1977

'Care and Protection Resource Panels', A Report from the Office of the Commissioner for Children, 1992

Caton, Anne, 'The Recent Development of Child Protection Legislation in New Zealand: An Illustration of Martin Rein's Analysis of Programme Implementation', SOWK 531 essay, Victoria University of Wellington, nd [1987], copy in author's possession

'Church Social Services: A Report of an Inquiry into Child Care Services', Oct 1977, Department of Social Welfare Library

'Conference on Adoption, Illegitimate Birth Enquiries and Fostering', Child Welfare Division, Department of Education, 1968, Department of Social Welfare Library

'Dangerous Situations: The Report of the Independent Inquiry Team Reporting on the Circumstances of the Death of a Child', Mar 1988, Department of Social Welfare Library

Dobson, Valerie E., 'The Working Years', nd [1994], Department of Social Welfare Library

Doolan, M. P., 'From Welfare to Justice: Towards New Social Work Practice with Young Offenders – An Overseas Study Tour Report', Department of Social Welfare, nd [1988]

'DSW into the 1990s: The "Blueprint". Report of the Department of Social Welfare Organisation Review', Department of Social Welfare, Oct 1991

Duffin, Julia Macaskill, 'Growing Up Fostered: Four Young People Present an Indepth View of How it Feels to be "Nobody's Child"', Office of Child Care Studies, Department of Social Welfare, 1985

'Family Homes Review', Department of Social Welfare, 1981

'A Guide to the Children and Young Persons Legislation', Department of Social Welfare, Dec 1986

Hassall, Ian, 'Report to the Minister of Social Welfare on the New Zealand Children and Young Persons Service's Review of Practice in Relation to Craig Manukau and his Family', Office of the Commissioner for Children, 7 Oct 1993

'Interdepartmental Report on Ex-nuptial Births', nd [1969?], Department of Social Welfare Library

Jack, Avery, 'Delinquency Among Girls', Jun 1959, Department of Social Welfare Library

Luketina, Francis, 'Some Statistics on Cases Heard by Children's Boards in 1982', Research Division, Department of Social Welfare, Apr 1984

'Maatua Whangai: A Community Initiative', Secretariat Report, Aug 1986, Department of Social Welfare Library

Mackay, Ross, 'Children in Foster Care: An Examination of the Case Histories of a Sample of Children in

Care, with a Particular Emphasis on Placements of Children in Foster Homes', Research Section, Department of Social Welfare, 1981

Mackay, Ross, 'The Views of Foster Children and their Natural Families on Two Fostering Systems Operated by the Department of Social Welfare: The Intensive Foster Care Scheme and Conventional Foster Care', Research Section, Department of Social Welfare, Nov 1984

Manchester, B. M., 'Some Further Comments on the Development of Social Work Training in New Zealand', Nov 1995, copy in author's possession

Manchester, Brian, 'Notes on Some Developments in Social Work Training in New Zealand', Nov 1995, copy in author's possession

Maxwell, Gabrielle, and Allison Morris, 'What Do We Know About Youth Crime?', paper presented to Youth Justice: The Vision conference, Victoria University of Wellington, Oct 1996

'New Beginnings/Ara Hou: Working Towards Excellence in Residential Care Practice', seminar papers presented at a residential care seminar, Christchurch, 28–30 Jul 1993, Department of Social Welfare Library

'New Horizons: A Review of the Residential Services of the Department of Social Welfare', Department of Social Welfare, Oct 1982

'New Zealand Child and Youth Welfare and Social Services', Department of Education, 1949, Department of Social Welfare Library

'Notes for Guidance on Child Psychotherapy Services within the Department of Social Welfare', Department of Social Welfare, Sep 1979

'A Private or Public Nightmare? Report of the Advisory Committee on the Investigation, Detection and Prosecution of Offences Against Children', Oct 1988

'A Proposal for a Family and Community Welfare Act', submission prepared by a working party of Lower Hutt Department of Social Welfare Social Workers in response to the Public Discussion Paper on the Review of the Children and Young Persons Legislation, Mar 1985, Department of Social Welfare Library

'Proposed Children and Young Persons Legislation: Explanatory Notes and Draft Bill', Department of Social Welfare, Sep 1985

Renouf, J., G. Robb and P. Wells, 'Children, Young Persons and their Families Act 1989: Report on its First Year of Operation', Department of Social Welfare, Nov 1990

'Report of Committee to Report to the Minister of Social Welfare on the Current Practices and Procedures followed in Institutions of the Department of Social Welfare in Auckland' [Johnston report], Oct 1982

'Report of E. G. Heggie on his Inquiry into Certain Happenings relating to the Child Joshua Steel', nd [1983], Department of Social Welfare Library

'Report of the Human Rights Commission on Representations by the Auckland Committee on Racism and Discrimination. Children and Young Persons Homes Administered by the Department of Social Welfare', Human Rights Commission, Sep 1982

'Report on Residential Care: Prepared for the Minister of Social Welfare, the New Zealand Council of Christian Social Services and the Director-General of Social Welfare', Child Care Coordinating Committee, May 1982, Department of Social Welfare Library

'Report to the Minister of Social Welfare on the Review of the Resourcing of the Community and Social Services of the Department of Social Welfare', Department of Social Welfare, Aug 1989

'Review of Residential Services: Executive Summary and Recommendations', Department of Social Welfare, 1990

'Review of Special Purpose Family Homes', Residential Services, Department of Social Welfare, Nov 1985

'Review of the Children and Young Persons Bill', Report of the Working Party on the Children and Young Persons Bill, Department of Social Welfare, Dec 1987

'Review of the Children, Young Persons, and Their Families Act 1989', Report of the Ministerial Review Team to the Minister of Social Welfare, Hon. Jenny Shipley, Feb 1992

'Review of the Social Work Division', Report of a Working Party, Department of Social Welfare, Dec 1982

Rolfe, J. N., and M. P. Doolan, 'Review of Schools and Teaching Services in Department of Social Welfare Homes', Department of Social Welfare, 1981

Smith, Fergus, 'Kingslea Resource Centre: Fostering and Family Home Services Proposed Strategy to April

1st 1991', Mar 1989, Department of Social Welfare Library

'Social Welfare Children's Homes: Report on an Inquiry held on June 11 1978', Auckland Committee on Racism and Discrimination, 1978

'Social Welfare Services: The Way Ahead', Report of a Ministerial Task Force on Social Welfare Services, Jul 1987, Department of Social Welfare Library

'Support Services for the Survivors of Sexual Abuse: Phase Two Report', Report of the Interdepartmental Working Party on the Funding of Sexual Abuse Services, Dec 1989, Department of Social Welfare Library

Tauroa, E. Te R., 'Report of Advisory Committee on Youth and Law in our Multicultural Society', Race Relations Conciliator's Office, Feb 1983

von Dadelszen, Jane, 'Sexual Abuse Study: An Examination of the Histories of Sexual Abuse Among Girls Currently in the Care of the Department of Social Welfare', Research Report Series no. 7, Department of Social Welfare, 1987

Watson, J. C., 'The Current Use of Secure Facilities Within Department of Social Welfare Institutions', paper presented at New Zealand Psychological Society annual conference, Aug 1978, Department of Social Welfare Library

'What is Legal Supervision? A Report based on a Survey of Social Workers', Social Programme Evaluation Unit, Department of Social Welfare, 1983

Whitney, Lynne, Bryony Walker and Jane von Dadelszen, 'Experiencing Foster Care: The Views of Children, Natural Family and Foster Parents', Research Section, Department of Social Welfare, nd [1988]

Theses

Bardsley, S., 'The Functions of an Institution: The Otekaike Special School for Boys 1908–1950', BA (Hons) long essay, University of Otago, 1991

Barretta-Herman, Angeline, 'The Restructuring of the Department of Social Welfare and Implications for Social Work Practice, 1986–1988', PhD thesis, Massey University, 1990

Beagle, Jan, 'Children of the State: A Study of the New Zealand Industrial School System 1880–1925', MA thesis, University of Auckland, 1974

Carryer, Basil G., 'The Duty of the State', MEd thesis, University of Waikato, 1990

Cox, R. W., 'The Provision made in New Zealand by the State for the Welfare of Delinquent and Dependent Children', fifth year preventive medicine thesis, University of Otago, 1947

Dalley, Bronwyn, 'From Demi-mondes to Slaveys: A Study of the Te Oranga Reformatory for Delinquent Women, 1900–1918', MA thesis, Massey University, 1987

Dalley, Bronwyn, 'Women's Imprisonment in New Zealand, 1880–1920', PhD thesis, University of Otago, 1992

Fleming, Philip, 'Eugenics in New Zealand, 1900–1940', MA thesis, Massey University, 1981

Fleming, Philip J., '"Shadow Over New Zealand": The Response to Venereal Disease in New Zealand, 1910–1945', PhD thesis, Massey University, 1989

Gallacher, Scott, '"Publishing Our Own Dishonour": The Criminalisation of Incest in New Zealand and the Judicial Response', BA (Hons) long essay, University of Otago, 1993

Gregory, P. A., 'Saving the Children in New Zealand: A Study of Social Attitudes Towards Larrikinism in the Later Nineteenth Century', BA (Hons) research essay, Massey University, 1975

Griffiths, Shelley, 'Feminism and the Ideology of Motherhood in New Zealand, 1896–1930', MA thesis, University of Otago, 1984

Jones, Dan, and Vanessa Meiklen, 'Family Home Foster Parents: A Case Study', MA research paper, Victoria University of Wellington, 1988

Kerr, V. M., 'The Society for the Protection of Women and Children in Auckland, 1917–1947', MA research essay, University of Auckland, 1992

Lavelle, Bernadette, '"Youth Without Purpose": Juvenile Delinquency in New Zealand in the 1950s', MA thesis, University of Otago, 1990

MacCuish, F. J., 'The Society for the Protection of Women and Children, 1893–1916', MA research essay, University of Auckland, 1983

McDonald, Dugald, 'Perceptions of Residential Child Care in New Zealand', MA thesis, Massey University, 1976

McDonald, Dugald J., 'The Governing of Children: Social Policy for Children and Young Persons in New Zealand, 1840–1982', PhD thesis, University of Canterbury, 1988

Mooney, Brian, 'The History and Development of the Youth Aid Section of the New Zealand Police', Dip. Criminology dissertation, University of Auckland, 1971

Newman, V. B., 'The Burwood Girls' Training Centre', fifth year preventive medicine thesis, University of Otago, 1952

Parcell, K. V., 'The 1922 Committee of Inquiry into Venereal Disease in New Zealand', MA research essay, University of Auckland, 1990

Paxton, C. T., 'Childhood in New Zealand, 1862–1921: Child Labour and the Gradual Popular Acceptance of Primary School Attendance', MA research essay, University of Auckland, 1987

Pearman, Geoffrey R., 'The Pursuit of Organisational Legitimacy: Organising Social Work Services in the Department of Social Welfare 1984–1994', MA thesis, University of Canterbury, 1995

Prasad, Rajendra, 'Success and Failure in Foster Care in Auckland, New Zealand', MA thesis, University of Auckland, 1975

Seymour, John, 'Dealing with Young Offenders', PhD thesis, University of Auckland, 1975

Slater, M. A., 'The Joint Team: A Descriptive Study', MA thesis, Victoria University of Wellington, 1975

Soler, Janet, '"Drifting Towards Moral Chaos": The 1954 Mazengarb Report – A Moral Panic Over "Juvenile Delinquency"', MPhil thesis, Massey University, 1988

Somerville, Alan, 'Moominapappa Got Away: The State and Child Welfare in New Zealand 1925–1930', BA (Hons) long essay, University of Otago, 1982

Stace, Michael, 'Legal Form and Moral Phenomena: A Study of Two Events', Doctor of Jurisprudence thesis, York University, 1980

Strang, Justin, 'Welfare in Transition: Reform's Income Support Policy, 1912–1938', MA thesis, Victoria University of Wellington, 1992

Thompson, Shayleen, '"The Keepers of Happiness": European Psychiatry and the Insane in New Zealand, 1911 to 1950', MA thesis, University of Auckland, 1992

Interviews
Anne Caton, interviewed by Bronwyn Dalley, 19 Jul 1996
Lainey Cowan, interviewed by Bronwyn Dalley, 23, 24 Jul 1996
Mike Doolan, interviewed by Bronwyn Dalley, 24 Jun 1996
Elsie Feist, interviewed by Bruce Asher, 26 Aug 1985
Jack Luckock, interviewed by Bruce Asher, 5 Oct 1984
Brian Manchester, interviewed by Bronwyn Dalley, 20, 27 Jun 1996
Charlie Peek, with Aileen Peek, interviewed by Bruce Asher, 31 Jan 1985
Greg Putland, interviewed by Bronwyn Dalley, 19 Feb 1997
Dennis Reilly, interviewed by Bruce Asher, 13 Jun 1985
Mary Todd, interviewed by Bronwyn Dalley, 25 Jun 1996
Charles Watson, interviewed by Bruce Asher, 27 Aug 1985
Robin Wilson, interviewed by Bronwyn Dalley, 13, 24 Jun 1996
Janet Worfolk, interviewed by Bronwyn Dalley, 10 Mar 1997

Personal communications
Anne Caton to Bronwyn Dalley, 17 Jan, 6 Mar 1997
Lainey Cowan to Bronwyn Dalley, 3 Dec 1996
Graeme Dunstall to Bronwyn Dalley, 28 Feb 1997
Brian Manchester to Bronwyn Dalley, 5 Feb 1997
Robin Wilson to Jock Phillips, 17 Jan 1997

Published

Official publications

Appendix to the Journals of the House of Representatives (*AJHR*)

    B-7, 1948, Estimates of the Expenditure of the Government of New Zealand

    E-1, 1959, Report of the Minister of Education

    E-1A, 1916, Educational Progress (Memorandum by the Minister of Education Dealing with some Phases of Educational Progress and Reviewing Existing Conditions in the Light of National Requirements)

    E-1A, 1917, Industrial-School System (Memorandum by the Minister of Education, Hon. J. A. Hanan)

    E-2, 1962, Report of the Commission on Education in New Zealand

    E-3, 1900–8, Education: Industrial Schools

    E-3B, 1900, Report of Royal Commission on Stoke Industrial School, Nelson

    E-3B, 1906, Education: Burnham Industrial School. Report of Commissioner

    E-4, 1909–18, Education: Special Schools, and Infant Life Protection

    E-4, 1919, Education: Children's Welfare and Special Schools

    E-4, 1920–5, Education: State Care of Children, Special Schools, and Infant Life Protection

    E-4, 1926–57, Child Welfare, State Care of Children, Special Schools, and Infant Life Protection

    E-4, 1958–66, Report on Child Welfare, State Care of Children, Special Schools and Infant Life Protection

    E-4, 1967–72, Report on the Work of the Child Welfare Division

    E-6, 1881, Education: The Boarding-out of Industrial School Children

    E-11, 1909, Report on Reformatory Work in England, Germany and America

    E-12, 1973–95, Report of the Department of Social Welfare

    E-25, 1977, Report of the Commission of Inquiry into the case of a Niuean Boy

    H-2, 1978, Report of the Royal Commission on Courts

    H-21, 1908, Education: Te Oranga Home. Report of Commission, together with Minutes of Evidence and Exhibits

    H-47, 1954, Report of the Special Committee on Moral Delinquency in Children and Adolescents

    I-12, 1964, Report of the Public Expenditure Committee

    I-15, 1955, Report of the Juvenile Delinquency Committee

New Zealand Official Yearbook, 1902–96

New Zealand Parliamentary Debates (*NZPD*), 1902–92

Statutes of New Zealand, 1882–1994

Articles and books

Abbott, Max (ed.), *Child Abuse Prevention in New Zealand: The Edited Proceedings of the National Symposium on Child Abuse Prevention, Palmerston North, 9–11 November 1982*, [Wellington], Mental Health Foundation of New Zealand, 1983

Abeele, Cynthia R., '"The Infant Soldier": The Great War and the Medical Campaign for Child Welfare', *Canadian Bulletin of Medical History*, 5, 1988, pp. 99–119

Adams, Mary Louise, 'Youth, Corruptibility, and English-Canadian Postwar Campaigns Against Indecency, 1948–1955', *Journal of the History of Sexuality*, vol. 6, no. 1, 1995, pp. 89–117

Allen, Ann Taylor, 'Gardens of Children, Gardens of God: Kindergartens and Day-care Centres in Nineteenth-century Germany', *Journal of Social History*, vol. 19, no. 3, 1986, pp. 433–50

Allen, Ann Taylor, 'Mothers of the New Generation: Adele Schreiber, Helene Stöcker, and the Evolution of a German Idea of Motherhood, 1900–1914', *Signs: Journal of Women in Culture and Society*, vol. 10, no. 3, 1985, pp. 418–38

Allen, Ann Taylor, 'Spiritual Motherhood: German Feminists and the Kindergarten Movement, 1848–1911', *History of Education Quarterly*, 22, 1982, pp. 319–40

Anderson, Lewis, 'Adoptions by Maori Applicants', *New Zealand Child Welfare Division Newsletter*, vol. 2, no. 29, 1968, pp. 9–13

Anderson, L. G., 'Chosen Children', *New Zealand Parent and Child*, vol. 1, no. 4, 1953, pp. 19–20, 41–2

Angus, John, 'The Act: One Year On', *Social Work Review*, vol. 3, no. 3, 1990, pp. 5–6

Antler, Joyce, and Stephen Antler, 'From Child Rescue to Family Protection: The Evolution of the Child Protection Movement in the United States', *Children and Youth Services Review*, 1, 1979, pp. 177–204

Apple, Rima D., 'Constructing Mothers: Scientific Motherhood in the Nineteenth and Twentieth Centuries', *Social History of Medicine*, vol. 8, no. 2, 1995, pp. 161–78

Ariès, Philippe, *Centuries of Childhood: A Social History of Family Life*, New York, Vintage Books, 1962

Arnold, Rollo, 'The Country Child in Later Victorian New Zealand', *Comment*, 15, 1982, pp. 22–7

Ashby, LeRoy, *Saving the Waifs: Reformers and Dependent Children, 1890–1917*, Philadelphia, Temple University Press, 1984

Atkin, W. R., 'The Courts and Child Protection: Aspects of the Children, Young Persons, and Their Families Act 1989', *Victoria University of Wellington Law Review*, vol. 20, no. 4, 1990, pp. 319–32

Bailey, Victor, *Delinquency and Citizenship: Reclaiming the Young Offender, 1914–1948*, Oxford, Clarendon Press, 1987

Baldwin, Peter, 'The Welfare State for Historians: A Review Article', *Comparative Studies in Society and History*, 34, 1992, pp. 695–707

Barbalet, Margaret, *Far From a Low Gutter Girl: The Forgotten World of State Wards, South Australia, 1887–1940*, Melbourne, Oxford University Press, 1983

Barbour, Ann, 'Family Group Conferences: Context and Consequences', *Social Work Review*, vol. 3, no. 4, 1991, pp. 16–21

Beaglehole, Ann, *Benefiting Women: Income Support for Women, 1893–1993*, Wellington, Social Policy Agency, 1993

Bean, Philip, and Joy Melville, *Lost Children of the Empire: The Untold Story of Britain's Child Migrants*, London, Unwin Hyman, 1989

Beck, John, 'The Development of the Child Welfare System', *New Zealand Child Welfare Workers' Bulletin*, vol. 3, no. 4, 1954, pp. 87–91

Beddoe, Liz, 'Editorial', *Social Work Review*, vol. 3, no. 3, 1990

Beeby, C. E., *The Biography of an Idea: Beeby on Education*, Wellington, New Zealand Council for Educational Research, 1992

Behlmer, George K., *Child Abuse and Moral Reform in England, 1870–1908*, Stanford, Stanford University Press, 1982

Behlmer, George K., 'Deadly Motherhood: Infanticide and Medical Opinion in Mid-Victorian England', *Journal of the History of Medicine and Allied Sciences*, 34, 1979, pp. 403–27

Beito, David T., 'Mutual Aid, State Welfare, and Organized Charity: Fraternal Societies and the "Deserving" and "Undeserving" Poor, 1900–1930', *Journal of Policy History*, vol. 5, no. 4, 1993, pp. 419–34

Bellingham, Bruce, 'The "Unspeakable Blessing": Street Children, Reform Rhetoric, and Misery in Early Industrial Capitalism', *Politics and Society*, 12, 1983, pp. 303–30

Bessant, Bob (ed.), *Mother State and Her Little Ones: Children and Youth in Australia 1860s–1930s*, Melbourne, Centre for Youth and Community Studies, 1987

Binney, Judith, Judith Bassett and Erik Olssen, *The People and the Land/Te Tangata me te Whenua: An Illustrated History of New Zealand, 1880–1920*, Wellington, Allen and Unwin, 1990

Blackburn, Sheila, 'How Useful are Feminist Theories of the Welfare State?', *Women's History Review*, vol. 4, no. 3, 1995, pp. 369–94

Boli-Bennett, John, and John Meyer, 'The Ideology of Childhood and the State: Rules Distinguishing Children in National Constitutions, 1870–1970', *American Sociological Review*, vol. 43, no. 5, 1978, pp. 797–812

Bonheur, Leigh, *Hand Me Down: The Autobiography of an Illegitimate Child*, Sydney, Ure Smith, 1971

Bradley, John, 'The Resolve to Devolve: Maori and Social Services', *Social Work Now: The Practice Journal of the New Zealand Children and Young Persons Service*, 1, 1995, pp. 29–35

Bragg, Billy, 'Rotting on Remand', *Workers Playtime*, Festival Records, 1988, track 6

Breines, Wini, *Young, White and Miserable: Growing Up Female in the Fifties*, Boston, Beacon Press, 1992

Breines, Wini, and Linda Gordon, 'The New Scholarship on Family Violence', *Signs: Journal of Women in Culture and Society*, vol. 8, no. 3, 1983, pp. 490–531

Bremner, Robert H. (ed.), *Children and Youth in America: A Documentary History*, vol. 3, 1933–1973, Cambridge, Harvard Unversity Press, 1974

Bremner, Robert, 'Other People's Children', *Journal of Social History*, vol. 16, no. 3, 1983, pp. 83–103

Brenzel, Barbara M., *Daughters of the State: A Social Portrait of the First Reform School for Girls in North America, 1856–1905*, Cambridge, Massachusetts Institute of Technology Press, 1983

Brookes, Barbara, 'A Weakness for Strong Subjects: The Women's Movement and Sexuality', *New Zealand Journal of History*, vol. 27, no. 2, 1993, pp. 140–56

Brookes, Barbara, Charlotte Macdonald and Margaret Tennant (eds), *Women in History 2*, Wellington, Bridget Williams Books, 1992

Brooking, Tom, *Milestones: Turning Points in New Zealand History*, Lower Hutt, Mills, 1988

Brown, B. J., and F. W. M. McElrea (eds), *The Youth Court in New Zealand: A New Model of Justice – Four Papers*, Auckland, Legal Research Foundation, 1993

Brumberg, Joan, '"Ruined" Girls: Changing Community Responses to Illegitimacy in Upstate New York, 1890–1920', *Journal of Social History*, vol. 18, no. 2, 1984, pp. 247–72

Bryder, Linda, '"A Social Laboratory": New Zealand and Social Welfare, 1840–1990', *British Review of New Zealand Studies*, 3, 1991, pp. 37–48

Bryder, Linda (ed.), *A Healthy Country: Essays on the Social History of Medicine in New Zealand*, Wellington, Bridget Williams Books, 1991

Bullen, John, 'J. J. Kelso and the "New" Child-savers: The Genesis of the Children's Aid Movement in Ontario', *Ontario History*, vol. 82, no. 2, 1990, pp. 107–28

Cale, Michelle, 'Girls and the Perception of Sexual Danger in the Victorian Reformatory System', *History*, vol. 78, no. 253, 1993, pp. 201–17

Carmichael, Gordon A., 'From Floating Brothels to Suburban Semi-respectability: Two Centuries of Non-marital Pregnancy in Australia', *Journal of Family History*, vol. 21, no. 3, 1996, pp. 281–315

Castles, Francis G., *The Working Class and Welfare: Reflections of the Political Development of the Welfare State in Australia and New Zealand, 1890–1980*, Wellington, Allen and Unwin/Port Nicholson Press, 1985

Chambers, Clarke A., 'Toward a Redefinition of Welfare History', *Journal of American History*, vol. 73, no. 2, 1986, pp. 407–33

Chapman, Terry L., '"Till Death Do Us Part": Wife Beating in Alberta, 1905–1920', *Alberta History*, vol. 36, no. 4, 1988, pp. 13–22

Clapp, Elizabeth, 'Welfare and the Role of Women: The Juvenile Court Movement', *Journal of American Studies*, vol. 28, no. 3, 1994, pp. 359–83

Cleaver, Neil, 'Another Arm of the Bureaucracy?', *Social Work Now: The Practice Journal of the New Zealand Children and Young Persons Service*, 1, 1995, pp. 7–10

Cohen, Miriam, and Michael Hanagan, 'The Politics of Gender and the Making of the Welfare State, 1900–1940: A Comparative Perspective', *Journal of Social History*, vol. 24, no. 3, 1991, pp. 469–84

Collins, Nancy, 'Adoption', *New Zealand Social Worker*, vol. 2, no. 2, 1966, pp. 71–9

Comacchio, Cynthia, 'Another Brick in the Wall: Toward a History of the Welfare State in Canada', *Left History*, vol. 1, no. 1, 1993, pp. 103–8

Community Sunshine Association, *The Call of the Child*, nd [1933]

Connolly, Marie, 'An Act of Empowerment: The Children, Young Persons and their Families Act (1989)', *British Journal of Social Work*, 24, 1994, pp. 87–100

Cooter, Roger (ed.), *In the Name of the Child: Health and Welfare, 1880–1940*, London, Routledge, 1992

Crew, David F., 'German Socialism, the State and Family Policy, 1918–33', *Continuity and Change*, vol. 1, no. 2, 1986, pp. 235–63

Cule, John, and Terry Turner (eds), *Child Care Through the Centuries*, Cardiff, British Society for the History of Medicine, 1986

Cupit, J. S., 'Child Welfare Work in New Zealand before 1925. II – The Industrial Schools', *New Zealand Child Welfare Workers' Bulletin*, vol. 1, no. 3, 1951, pp. 8–9

Cupit, J. S., 'Child Welfare Work in New Zealand before 1925. III – Old Burnham', *New Zealand Child*

Welfare Workers' Bulletin, vol. 1. no. 5, 1951, pp. 9–10

Dahl, Tove Stang, *Child Welfare and Social Defence*, Oslo, Norwegian University Press, 1985

Dalley, Bronwyn, '"Making Bricks Without Straw": Feminism and Prison Reform in New Zealand, 1896–1925', *Women's Studies Journal*, vol. 9, no. 2, 1993, pp. 30–50

Dalley, Bronwyn, 'Prisons Without Men: The Development of a Separate Women's Prison in New Zealand', *New Zealand Journal of History*, vol. 27, no. 1, 1993, pp. 43–53

Dalziel, Raewyn, *Focus on the Family: The Auckland Home and Family Society 1893–1993*, Auckland, Home and Family Society, 1993

Davidson, Alexander, *Two Models of Welfare: The Origins and Development of the Welfare State in Sweden and New Zealand 1888–1988*, Stockholm, Almquist and Wiksell, 1989

Davin, Anna, 'Imperialism and Motherhood', *History Workshop Journal*, 5, 1978, pp. 9–66

Demos, John, and Virginia Demos, 'Adolescence in Historical Perspective', *Journal of Marriage and the Family*, 31, 1969, pp. 632–8

Dickey, Brian, 'Care for Deprived, Neglected and Delinquent Children in New South Wales, 1901–1915', *Journal of the Royal Australian Historical Society*, vol. 63, no. 3, 1977, pp. 167–83

Dickey, Brian, 'The Evolution of Care for Destitute Children in New South Wales, 1875–1901', *Journal of Australian Studies*, 4, 1979, pp. 38–57

Dickey, Brian, *Rations, Residence, Resources: A History of Social Welfare in South Australia Since 1836*, South Australia, Wakefield Press, 1986

The Dictionary of New Zealand Biography, vol. 3, 1901–1920, Auckland, Auckland University Press with Bridget Williams Books/Department of Internal Affairs, 1996

Dingwall, R., J. M. Eekelaar, and T. Murray, 'Childhood as a Social Problem: A Survey of the History of Legal Regulation', *Journal of Law and Society*, vol. 11, no. 2, 1984, pp. 207–32

Dingwall, Robert, and John Eekelaar, 'Rethinking Child Protection', in Michael D. A. Freeman (ed.), *The State, the Law and the Family: Critical Perspectives*, London/New York, Tavistock/Sweet and Maxwell, 1984, pp. 93–114

Doll, Eugene E., 'Before the Big Time: Early History of the Training School at Vineland, 1888 to 1949', *American Journal of Mental Retardation*, vol. 93, no. 1, 1988, pp. 1–15

Donovan, James M., 'Combatting the Sexual Abuse of Children in France, 1825–1913', *Criminal Justice History*, 15, 1994, pp. 59–93

Donzelot, Jacques, *The Policing of Families: Welfare versus the State*, London, Hutchinson, 1980

Dow, Derek A., *Safeguarding the Public Health: A History of the New Zealand Department of Health*, Wellington, Victoria University Press in association with the Ministry of Health and with the assistance of the Historical Branch, Department of Internal Affairs, 1995

Downs, Susan Whitelaw, and Michael W. Sherraden, 'The Orphan Asylum in the Nineteenth Century', *Social Service Review*, 57, 1983, pp. 272–90

Dwork, Deborah, *War is Good for Babies and Other Young Children: A History of the Infant Life and Child Welfare Movement in England 1898–1918*, London, Tavistock, 1987

Dyhouse, Carol, *Girls Growing Up in Late Victorian and Edwardian England*, London, Routledge and Kegan Paul, 1981

Dyhouse, Carol, 'Working-class Mothers and Infant Mortality in England, 1895–1914', *Journal of Social History*, vol. 12, no. 2, 1978, pp. 248–62

Ehrhardt, Penny, with Ann Beaglehole, *Women and Welfare Work, 1893–1993*, Wellington, Department of Social Welfare with the assistance of the Historical Branch, Department of Internal Affairs, 1993

Else, Anne, 'Legal Fictions: Women and New Zealand Law on Adoption and Assisted Reproductive Technologies', *Australian Feminist Law Journal*, 5, 1995, pp. 65–79

Else, Anne, *A Question of Adoption: Closed Stranger Adoption in New Zealand 1944–1974*, Wellington, Bridget Williams Books, 1991

Else, Anne (ed.), *Women Together: A History of Women's Organisations in New Zealand/Nga Ropu Wahine o te Motu*, Wellington, Daphne Brasell Associates Press and Historical Branch, Department of Internal Affairs, 1993

Ende, Aurel, 'Battering and Neglect: Children in Germany, 1860–1978', *Journal of Psychohistory*, 7, 1979, pp.

249–79

Ferguson, David, Joan Fleming and David O'Neill, *Child Abuse in New Zealand: A Report on a Nationwide Survey of the Physical Ill-treatment of Children in New Zealand*, Research Section, Department of Social Welfare, 1972

Ferguson, Gael, *Building the New Zealand Dream*, Palmerston North, Dunmore Press with the assistance of the Historical Branch, Department of Internal Affairs, 1994

Fildes, Valerie, Lara Marks and Hilary Marland (eds), *Women and Children First: International Maternal and Infant Welfare 1870–1945*, London and New York, Routledge, 1992

Finch, Lynette, *The Classing Gaze: Sexuality, Class and Surveillance*, Sydney, Allen and Unwin, 1993

Fox, Richard, 'Beyond "Social Control": Institutions and Disorder in Bourgeois Society', *History of Education Quarterly*, vol. 16, no. 2, 1976, pp. 203–7

Fraser, Nancy, 'Women, Welfare and the Politics of Need Interpretation', *Hypatia*, vol. 2, no. 1, 1987, pp. 103–21

Fraser, Nancy, and Linda Gordon, 'Contract versus Charity: Why is there no Social Citizenship in the United States?', *Socialist Review*, 22, 1992, pp. 45–67

Fraser, Nancy, and Linda Gordon, 'A Genealogy of Dependency: Tracing a Keyword of the US Welfare State', *Signs: Journal of Women in Culture and Society*, vol. 19, no. 2, 1994, pp. 309–36

Freedman, Estelle B., *Maternal Justice: Miriam Van Waters and the Female Reform Tradition*, Chicago, University of Chicago Press, 1996

Fulcher, Leon, and Frank Ainsworth, 'Child Welfare Abandoned? The Ideology and Economics of Contemporary Service Reform in New Zealand', *Social Work Review*, vol. 6, no. 3, 1994, pp. 2–13

Garton, Stephen, 'Sound Minds and Healthy Bodies: Reconsidering Eugenics in Australia, 1914–1940', *Australian Historical Studies*, vol. 26, no. 103, 1994, pp. 163–81

Gatrell, V. A. C., and T. B. Hadden, 'Criminal Statistics and their Interpretation', in E. A. Wrigley (ed.), *Nineteenth-century Society: Essays in the Use of Quantitative Methods for the Study of Social Data*, Cambridge, Cambridge University Press, 1972, pp. 336–92

Geddis, David, 'A Critical Analysis of the Family Group Conference', *Family Law Bulletin*, 3, 1993, pp. 141–4

Geddis, David, 'New Developments Concerning Child Abuse', *New Zealand Medical Journal*, 27 Jun 1984, pp. 403–4

Gerstenberger, Heide, 'The Poor and the Respectable Worker: On the Introduction of Social Insurance in Germany', *Labour History*, no. 48, 1985, pp. 69–85

Gilbert, James, *A Cycle of Outrage: America's Reaction to the Juvenile Delinquent in the 1950s*, New York and Oxford, Oxford University Press, 1986

Gillis, John, *Youth and History: Tradition and Change in European Age Relations 1770–Present*, New York and London, Academic Press, 1974

Gillis, John R., 'The Evolution of Juvenile Delinquency in England 1890–1914', *Past and Present*, 67, 1975, pp. 96–126

Gittins, Diana, 'Disentangling the History of Childhood', *Gender and History*, vol. 1, no. 3, 1989, pp. 342–9

Glamuzina, Julie, and Alison Laurie, *Parker and Hulme: A Lesbian View*, Auckland, New Women's Press, 1991

Gordon, Linda, 'Black and White Visions of Welfare: Women's Welfare Activism, 1890–1945', *Journal of American History*, vol. 78, no. 2, 1991, pp. 559–90

Gordon, Linda, 'Child Abuse, Gender, and the Myth of Family Independence: A Historical Critique', *Child Welfare*, vol. 64, no. 3, 1985, pp. 213–24

Gordon, Linda, *Heroes of Their Own Lives: The Politics and History of Family Violence*, London, Virago, 1989

Gordon, Linda, *Pitied But Not Entitled: Single Mothers and the History of Welfare*, New York, The Free Press, 1994

Gordon, Linda, 'Single Mothers and Child Neglect, 1880–1920', *American Quarterly*, vol. 37, no. 2, 1985, pp. 173–92

Gordon, Linda, 'Social Insurance and Public Assistance: The Influence of Gender in Welfare Thought in the United States, 1890–1935', *American Historical Review*, vol. 97, no. 1, 1992, pp. 19–54

Gordon, Linda, 'What does Welfare Regulate?', *Social Research*, vol. 5, no. 4, 1988, pp. 609–30

Gordon, Linda (ed.), *Women, the State, and Welfare*, Madison, University of Wisconsin Press, 1990

Gordon, Linda, and Sara McLanahan, 'Single Parenthood in 1900', *Journal of Family History*, vol. 16, no. 2, 1991, pp. 97–116

Gordon, Linda, and Theda Skocpol, 'Gender, State and Society: A Debate with Theda Skocpol', *Contention*, vol. 2, no. 3, 1993, pp. 139–89

Graham, Jeanine, 'Child Employment in New Zealand', *New Zealand Journal of History*, vol. 21, no. 1, 1987, pp. 62–78

Griffith, K. C., *Adoption: Procedure, Documentation, Statistics. New Zealand 1881–1981*, Wellington, 1981

Hartman, Mary S., 'Child-abuse and Self-abuse: Two Victorian Cases', *History of Childhood Quarterly*, vol. 2, no. 2, 1974, pp. 221–48

Havill, S. J., and D. R. Mitchell (eds), *Issues in New Zealand Special Education*, Auckland, Hodder and Stoughton, 1972

Hawes, Joseph M., 'The Strange History of Female Adolescence in the United States', *Journal of Psychohistory*, vol. 13, no. 1, 1985, pp. 51–63

Helly, Dorothy O., and Susan M. Reverby (eds), *Gendered Domains: Rethinking Public and Private in Women's History*, Ithaca, Cornell University Press, 1992

Henaghan, Mark, and Bill Atkin (eds), *Family Law Policy in New Zealand*, Auckland, Oxford University Press, 1992

Hendrick, Harry, *Child Welfare: England 1872–1989*, London, Routledge, 1994

Hendrick, Harry, 'Constructions and Reconstructions of British Childhood: An Interpretive Survey, 1800 to the Present', in Alison James and Alan Prout (eds), *Constructing and Reconstructing Childhood: Contemporary Issues in the Sociological Study of Childhood*, London, Falmer Press, 1990, pp. 35–59

Heywood, Colin, *Childhood in Nineteenth-century France: Work, Health and Education among the 'Classes Populaires'*, Cambridge, Cambridge University Press, 1988

Heywood, Colin, 'On Learning Gender Roles during Childhood in Nineteenth-century France', *French History*, vol. 5, no. 4, 1991, pp. 451–66

Hilton, Matthew, '"Tabs", "Fags" and the "Boy Labour Problem" in Late Victorian and Edwardian Britain', *Journal of Social History*, vol. 28, no. 3, 1995, pp. 587–607

Hodder, Lorna, 'Recollections From 1940', *New Zealand Social Worker*, vol. 5, no. 4, 1969, pp. 27–9

Hollis, Patricia (ed.), *Pressure From Without in Early Victorian England*, London, Edward Arnold, 1974

Hood, Lynley, *Minnie Dean: Her Life and Crimes*, Auckland, Penguin, 1994

Hooper, Carol-Ann, 'Rethinking the Politics of Child Abuse', *Social History of Medicine*, 2, 1989, pp. 356–64

Horn, Margo, 'The Moral Message of Child Guidance 1925–1945', *Journal of Social History*, vol. 18, no. 1, 1984, pp. 25–36

Horsburgh, Michael, 'Child Care in New South Wales in 1890', *Australian Social Work*, vol. 30, no. 3, 1977, pp. 21–40

Horsburgh, Michael, 'Her Father's Daughter: Florence Davenport-Hill, 1829–1919', *International Social Work*, vol. 26, no. 4, 1981, pp. 1–13

Houston, Susan E., 'The "Waifs and Strays" of a Late Victorian City: Juvenile Delinquents in Toronto', in Joy Parr (ed.), *Childhood and Family in Canadian History*, Ontario, McClelland and Stewart, 1982, pp. 129–42

Howard, Christopher, 'Sowing the Seeds of "Welfare": The Transformation of Mothers' Pensions, 1900–1940', *Journal of Policy History*, vol. 4, no. 2, 1992, pp. 188–227

Hudson, Joe, Allison Morris, Gabrielle Maxwell and Burt Galaway (eds), *Family Group Conferences: Perspectives on Policy and Practice*, Annandale/New York, The Federation Press/Willow Tree Press, 1996

Hughes, Beryl, 'The Enquiry into the Te Oranga Girls' Home, 1908', *Women's Studies Journal*, vol. 4, no. 1, 1988, pp. 27–38

Human Rights Commission, *The Use of Secure Care and Related Issues in Social Welfare Institutions*, Wellington, Human Rights Commission, 1989

Human Rights Commission, *Who Cares for the Kids? A Study of Children and Young People in Out of Family Care*, Wellington, Human Rights Commission, 1992

Hunt, Marion, 'Women and Childsaving: St Louis Children's Hospital 1879–1979', *Missouri Historical*

Society Bulletin, vol. 36. no. 2, 1980, pp. 65–79

Husbands, Paul, 'Poverty in Freeman's Bay 1886–1913', *New Zealand Journal of History*, vol. 28, no. 1, 1994, pp. 3–21

Ignatieff, Michael, *The Needs of Strangers*, London, Chatto and Windus, 1984

In Their Own Words: From the Sound Archives of Radio New Zealand, compiled by Stephen Barnett and Jim Sullivan, Wellington, GP Books in association with Radio New Zealand Sound Archives, 1988

Irving, Terry, David Maunders and Geoff Sherington, *Youth in Australia: Policy Administration and Politics. A History Since World War II*, Melbourne, Macmillan Education, 1995

Jenson, Jane, 'Gender and Reproduction: Or, Babies and the State', *Studies in Political Economy*, 20, 1986, pp. 9–46

Johnson, Iain, and David Geddis, 'Child Abuse and Neglect: Reform of the Law', *New Zealand Medical Journal*, 13 Jun 1984, pp. 367–70

Johnson, Richard, 'Educational Policy and Social Control in Early Victorian England', *Past and Present*, 49, 1970, pp. 96–119

Jones, Kathleen, 'Sentiment and Science: The Late Nineteenth Century Pediatrician as Mother's Advisor', *Journal of Social History*, vol. 17, no. 1, 1983, pp. 79–96

Jordan, Jan, *Working Girls: Women in the New Zealand Sex Industry Talk to Jan Jordan*, Auckland, Penguin, 1991

Jordanova, Ludmilla, 'Children in History: Concepts of Nature and Society', in Geoffrey Scarre (ed.), *Children, Parents and Politics*, Cambridge, Cambridge University Press, 1989, pp. 3–24

Jordanova, Ludmilla, 'Conceptualizing Childhood in the Eighteenth Century: The Problem of Child Labour', *British Journal for Eighteenth-Century Studies*, 10, 1987, pp. 188–99

Jordanova, Ludmilla, 'Fantasy and History in the Study of Childhood', *Free Associations*, 2, 1985, pp. 110–22

Juvenile Crime in New Zealand, Wellington, Department of Social Welfare, 1973

Katz, Michael B., *Poverty and Policy in American History*, New York, Academic Press, 1983

Keenan, Danny, '*Puao-te-Ata-Tu*: A Brief History and Reflection', *Social Work Review*, vol. 7, no. 1, 1995, pp. 11, 29

Kendrick, June, 'The British Children: Wartime Evacuees in New Zealand', *New Zealand Social Worker*, vol. 3, no. 1, 1979, pp. 3–5

Kett, Joseph F., 'Adolescence and Youth in Nineteenth-century America', *Journal of Interdisciplinary History*, vol. 2, no. 2, 1971, pp. 283–98

Kidd, Alan J., 'Philanthropy and the "Social History Paradigm"', *Social History*, vol. 21, no. 2, 1996, pp. 180–92

Koopman-Boyden, Peggy (ed.), *Families in New Zealand Society*, Wellington, Methuen, 1978

Koven, Seth, 'Remembering and Dismemberment: Crippled Children, Wounded Soldiers, and the Great War in Great Britain', *American Historical Review*, vol. 99, no. 4, 1994, pp. 1167–1202

Koven, Seth, and Sonya Michel, 'Gender and the Origins of the Welfare State', *Radical History Review*, 43, 1989, pp. 112–19

Koven, Seth, and Sonya Michel, 'Womanly Duties: Maternalist Politics and the Origins of Welfare States in France, Germany, Great Britain, and the United States, 1880–1920', *American Historical Review*, vol. 95, no. 4, 1990, pp. 1076–1108

Koven, Seth, and Sonya Michel (eds), *Mothers of a New World: Maternalist Politics and the Origins of Welfare States*, New York and London, Routledge, 1993

Kudlien, Fridolf, 'The German Response to the Birth-rate Problem during the Third Reich', *Continuity and Change*, vol. 5, no. 2, 1990, pp. 225–47

Kunzel, Regina, *Fallen Women, Problem Girls: Unmarried Mothers and the Professionalization of Social Work, 1890–1945*, New Haven, Yale University Press, 1993

Kunzel, Regina, 'Pulp Fictions and Problem Girls: Reading and Rewriting Single Pregnancy in the Postwar United States', *American Historical Review*, vol. 100, no. 5, 1995, pp. 1465–87

Ladd-Taylor, Molly, *Mother-Work: Women, Child Welfare, and the State, 1890–1930*, Urbana and Chicago, University of Illinois Press, 1994

Lasch, Christopher, *Haven in a Heartless World: The Family Besieged*, New York, Basic Books, 1977

Lassonde, Stephen, 'Learning and Earning: Schooling, Juvenile Employment, and the Early Life Course in Late Nineteenth-century New Haven', *Journal of Social History*, vol. 29, no. 4, 1996, pp. 839–70

Lee, John A., *Delinquent Days*, Auckland, Collins, 1967

Lee, John A., 'Guest Editorial', *New Zealand Social Worker*, vol. 5, no. 4, 1969, pp. 3–5

Leff, Mark H., 'Consensus for Reform: The Mothers' Pension Movement in the Progressive Era', *Social Service Review*, 47, 1973, pp. 397–417

Lewis, Jane, 'Anxieties About the Family and the Relationships Between Parents, Children and the State in Twentieth-century England', in Martin Richards and Paul Light (eds), *Children of Social Worlds: Development in a Social Context*, Cambridge, Harvard University Press, 1986, pp. 31–54

Lewis, Jane, 'The Boundary Between Voluntary and Statutory Social Service in the Late Nineteenth and Early Twentieth Centuries', *Historical Journal*, vol. 39, no. 1, 1996, pp. 155–77

Lewis, Jane, 'Family Provision of Health and Welfare in the Mixed Economy of Care in the Late Nineteenth and Twentieth Centuries', *Social History of Medicine*, vol. 8, no. 1, 1995, pp. 1–16

Lewis, Jane, 'Gender, the Family and Women's Agency in the Building of "Welfare States": The British Case', *Social History*, vol. 19, no. 1, 1994, pp. 37–55

Lewis, Jane, *The Politics of Motherhood: Child and Maternal Welfare in England, 1900–1939*, London/Montreal, Croom Helm/McGill–Queen's University Press, 1980

Lilienthal, Georg, 'The Illegitimacy Question in Germany, 1900–1945: Areas of Tension in Social and Population Policy', *Continuity and Change*, vol. 5, no. 2, 1990, pp. 249–81

Lindenmeyer, Kriste, 'The U. S. Children's Bureau and Infant Mortality in the Progressive Era', *Journal of Education*, vol. 177, no. 3, 1995, pp. 57–69

Lunbeck, Elizabeth, '"A New Generation of Women": Progressive Psychiatrists and the Hypersexual Female', *Feminist Studies*, vol. 13, no. 3, 1987, pp. 513–43

Luckin, Bill, 'Towards a Social History of Institutionalization', *Social History*, vol. 8, no. 1, 1983, pp. 87–94

Lyons, M., 'Children's Courts in the 1940s', *New Zealand Social Worker*, vol. 6, no. 1, 1970, pp. 15–19

Macleod, David, 'Act Your Age: Boyhood, Adolescence, and the Rise of the Boy Scouts of America', *Journal of Social History*, vol. 16, no. 2, 1982, pp. 3–20

McDonald, D. J., 'The Anatomy of a Semi-Profession: Residential Child Care', *New Zealand Social Work*, vol. 1, no. 1, 1977, pp. 5–8

McDonald, Dugald (ed.), *Working for the Welfare: Stories by Staff of the Former Child Welfare Division*, Christchurch, Social Work Press, 1994

McDougall, Mary Lynn, 'Protecting Infants: The French Campaign for Maternity Leaves, 1890s–1913', *French Historical Studies*, vol. 13, no. 1, 1983, pp. 79–105

Mahood, Linda, and Barbara Littlewood, 'The "Vicious" Girl and the "Street-corner" Boy: Sexuality and the Gendered Delinquent in the Scottish Child-saving Movement, 1850–1940', *Journal of the History of Sexuality*, vol. 4, no. 4, 1994, pp. 549–78

Manning, A. E., *The Bodgie: A Study in Abnormal Psychology*, Wellington, A. H. and A. W. Reed, 1958

Maxwell, Gabrielle, 'Funding Youth Justice 1990–1994', *Children: A Newsletter from the Office of the Commissioner for Children*, 15, 1994, pp. 7–8

Maxwell, Gabrielle, and Allison Morris, *Family, Victims and Culture: Youth Justice in New Zealand*, Wellington, Social Policy Agency and Institute of Criminology, 1993

May, Helen, *Minding Children, Managing Men: Conflict and Compromise in the Lives of Postwar Pakeha Women*, Wellington, Bridget Williams Books, 1992

May, Margaret, 'Innocence and Experience: The Evolution of the Concept of Juvenile Delinquency in the Mid-nineteenth Century', *Victorian Studies*, vol. 17, no. 1, 1973, pp. 7–29

Meckel, Richard Alan, 'Childhood and the Historians: A Review Essay', *Journal of Family History*, vol. 9, no. 4, 1984, pp. 415–24

Metge, Joan, *New Growth From Old: The Whanau in the Modern World*, Wellington, Victoria University Press, 1995

Michael, Margie, 'Youth Advocates: Seeing Justice to be Done?', *Social Work Now: The Practice Journal of the New Zealand Children and Young Persons Service*, 2, 1995, pp. 13–15

Michel, Sonya, 'American Women and the Discourse of the Democratic Family in World War II', in

Margaret Randolph Higonnet, Jane Jenson, Sonya Michel and Margaret Collins Weitz (eds), *Behind the Lines: Gender and the Two World Wars*, New Haven, Yale University Press, 1987, pp. 154–67

Mirams, Doris Meares, *Orphanages Without Orphans*, Timaru, 1949

'Mods Killed Lightning', *Social End Product*, vol. 1, no. 1, 1995, pp. 34–5

Moeller, Robert G., 'The State of Women's Welfare in European Welfare States', *Social History*, vol. 19, no. 3, 1994, pp. 385–93

Molloy, Maureen, 'Science, Myth and the Adolescent Female: The Mazengarb Report, the Parker-Hulme Trial, and the Adoption Act of 1955', *Women's Studies Journal*, vol. 9, no. 1, 1993, pp. 1–25

Morris, Allison, and Warren Young, *Juvenile Justice in New Zealand: Policy and Practice*, Wellington, Study Series no. 1, Institute of Criminology, 1987

Mumm, Susan, '"Not Worse than Other Girls": The Convent-based Rehabilitation of Fallen Women in Victorian Britain', *Journal of Social History*, vol. 29, no. 3, 1996, pp. 527–46

Munford Robyn, and Mary Nash (eds), *Social Work in Action*, Palmerston North, Dunmore Press, 1994

Munro, Jessie, *The Story of Suzanne Aubert*, Auckland, Auckland University Press/Bridget Williams Books, 1996

Neuman, R. P., 'Masturbation, Madness, and the Modern Concepts of Childhood and Adolescence', *Journal of Social History*, vol. 8, no. 1, 1976, pp. 1–27

Neustadter, Roger, 'The Politics of Growing Up: The Status of Childhood in Modern Social Thought', *Current Perspectives in Social Theory*, 9, 1989, pp. 199–221

New Zealand Association of Social Workers (Inc.), *Social Welfare at the Crossroads: Report on Social Welfare in New Zealand*, Wellington, New Zealand Association of Social Workers, 1971

Oakley, Ann, 'Eugenics, Social Medicine and the Career of Richard Titmuss in Britain 1935–50', *British Journal of Sociology*, vol. 42, no. 2, 1991, pp. 165–94

Odem, Mary E., *Delinquent Daughters: Protecting and Policing Adolescent Female Sexuality in the United States, 1885–1920*, Chapel Hill, University of North Carolina Press, 1995

Odem, Mary, 'Single Mothers, Delinquent Daughters, and the Juvenile Court in Early 20th Century Los Angeles', *Journal of Social History*, vol. 25, no. 1, 1991, pp. 27–43

Odem, Mary E., and Steven Shlossman, 'Guardians of Virtue: The Juvenile Court and Female Delinquency in Early 20th Century Los Angeles', *Crime and Delinquency*, vol. 37, no. 2, 1991, pp. 186–203

O'Donnell, Sandra, 'The Care of Dependent African-American Children in Chicago: The Struggle Between Black Self-help and Professionalism', *Journal of Social History*, vol. 27, no. 4, 1994, pp. 763–76

Offen, Karen, 'Depopulation, Nationalism and Feminism in Fin-de-siècle France', *American Historical Review*, vol. 89, no. 3, 1984, pp. 648–76

Office of the Commissioner for Children, *An Appraisal of the First Year of the Children, Young Persons and their Families Act 1989*, Wellington, Office of the Commissioner for Children, 1991

Oliver, W. H., '100 Years of the Welfare State', in Atholl Anderson et al, *Towards 1990: Seven Leading Historians Examine Significant Aspects of New Zealand History*, Wellington, GP Books, 1989, pp. 82–90

Oliver, W. H., 'Social Policy in New Zealand: An Historical Overview', *The April Report. New Zealand Today: Report of the Royal Commission on Social Policy*, vol. 1, Wellington, 1988, pp. 21–30

Oliver, W. H., 'Social Welfare: Social Justice or Social Efficiency?', *New Zealand Journal of History*, vol. 13, no. 1, 1979, pp. 3–23

Olsen, Teresa, Gabrielle Maxwell and Allison Morris, 'Maori and Youth Justice in New Zealand', in Kayleen Hazelhurst (ed.), *Popular Justice and Community Regeneration: Pathways of Indigenous Reform*, Westport, Connecticut, Praeger, 1995, pp. 45–65

O'Neill, C. James, 'Fertility: Past, Present, and Future', in R. J. Warwick Neville and C. James O'Neill (eds), *The Population of New Zealand: Interdisciplinary Perspectives*, Auckland, Longman Paul, 1979, pp. 125–49

Openshaw, Roger, Greg Lee and Howard Lee, *Challenging the Myths: Rethinking New Zealand's Educational History*, Palmerston North, Dunmore Press, 1993

Orloff, Ann Shola, 'Gender in Early U. S. Social Policy', *Journal of Policy History*, vol. 3, no. 3, 1991, pp. 249–81

Page, Dorothy, *The National Council of Women: A Centennial History*, Auckland, Auckland University Press/Bridget Williams Books with the National Council of Women, 1996

Pateman, Carole, 'The Patriarchal Welfare State', in Linda McDowell and Rosemary Pringle (eds), *Defining Women: Social Institutions and Gender Divisions*, Cambridge, Polity Press, 1992, pp. 223–45

Paterson, Karen, and Michael Harvey, *An Evaluation of the Organisation and Operation of Care and Protection Family Group Conferences*, Wellington, Evaluation Unit, Department of Social Welfare, 1991

Pearson, Geoffrey, *Hooligan: A History of Respectable Fears*, London, Macmillan, 1983

Pedersen, Susan, 'Gender, Welfare and Citizenship in Britain During the Great War', *American Historical Review*, vol. 95, no. 4, 1990, pp. 983–1006

Peek, C. E., 'A Superintendent Looks Back', *New Zealand Social Worker*, vol. 5, no. 4, 1969, pp. 15–19

Pfohl, Stephen J., 'The "Discovery" of Child Abuse', *Social Problems*, 24, 1977, pp. 310–23

Philipp, Ernst, and Robin Philipp, 'Specialists in Juvenile Delinquency', *New Zealand Medical Journal*, 13 Jun 1984, pp. 370–2

Phillips, Jock, with Ellen Ellis, *Brief Encounter: American Forces and the New Zealand People 1942–1945*, Wellington, Historical Branch, Department of Internal Affairs, 1992

Piven, Frances Fox, and Richard Cloward, 'Welfare Doesn't Shore up Traditional Family Roles: A Reply to Linda Gordon', *Social Research*, vol. 55, no. 4, 1988, pp. 631–47

Platt, Anthony M., *The Child Savers: The Invention of Delinquency*, 2nd edition, Chicago, University of Chicago Press, 1977

Plumb, J. H., 'The New World of Children in Eighteenth-century England', *Past and Present*, 67, 1975, pp. 64–95

Porter, Dorothy, '"Enemies of the Race": Biologism, Environmentalism and Public Health in Edwardian England', *Victorian Studies*, vol. 34, no. 2, 1991, pp. 159–78

Potts, Patricia, 'Medicine, Morals and Mental Deficiency: The Contribution of Doctors to the Development of Special Education in England', *Oxford Review of Education*, vol. 9, no. 3, 1983, pp. 181–96

Puao-te-Ata-Tu, Report of the Ministerial Advisory Committee on a Maori Perspective for the Department of Social Welfare, Wellington, 1986

Ramsland, John, 'An Anatomy of a Nineteenth-century Child-saving Institution', *Journal of the Royal Australian Historical Society*, 70, 1984, pp. 194–209

Ramsland, John, *Children of the Back Lanes: Destitute and Neglected Children in Colonial New South Wales*, Sydney, University of New South Wales Press, 1986

Redhead, Steve, *The End-of-the-century Party: Youth and Pop Towards 2000*, Manchester, Manchester University Press, 1990

Rice, Geoffrey, *Black November: The 1918 Influenza Epidemic in New Zealand*, Wellington, Allen and Unwin/Historical Branch, Department of Internal Affairs, 1988

Rice, Geoffrey W. (ed.), *The Oxford History of New Zealand*, 2nd edition, Auckland, Oxford University Press, 1992

Richards, Raymond, *Closing the Door to Destitution: The Shaping of the Social Security Acts of the United States and New Zealand*, Philadelphia, Pennsylvania State University Press, 1994

Rights and Responsibilities: Papers from the International Year of the Family Symposium on Rights and Responsibilities of the Family held in Wellington 14 to 16 October 1994, Wellington, International Year of the Family Committee in association with the Office of the Commissioner for Children, 1995

Riley, Denise, *War in the Nursery: Theories of the Child and Mother*, London, Virago, 1983

Ritter, Leonora, 'Boarding-out in New South Wales and South Australia: Adoption, Adaptation or Innovation?', *Journal of the Royal Australian Historical Society*, vol. 64, no. 2, 1978, pp. 120–6

Robb, George, 'The Way of All Flesh: Degeneration, Eugenics, and the Gospel of Free Love', *Journal of the History of Sexuality*, vol. 6, no. 4, 1996, pp. 589–603

Rooke, Patricia T., and R. L. Schnell, *Discarding the Asylum: From Child Rescue to the Welfare State in English-Canada (1800–1950)*, Lanham, University Press of America, 1983

Rosenthal, Marguerite, 'The Children's Bureau and the Juvenile Court: Delinquency Policy, 1912–1940', *Social Service Review*, 60, 1986, pp. 303–18

Roth, Bert, *George Hogben: A Biography*, Wellington, New Zealand Council for Educational Research, 1952

Rotundo, E. Anthony, 'Boy Culture: Middle-class Boyhood in Nineteenth-century America', in Mark C. Carnes and Clyde Griffen (eds), *Meanings for Manhood: Constructions of Masculinity in Victorian*

America, Chicago, University of Chicago Press, 1990, pp. 15–36

'Running Away from Home', *Broadsheet*, Jun 1983, pp. 12–15

Sangster, Joan, 'Incarcerating "Bad Girls": The Regulation of Sexuality Through the Female Refuges Act in Ontario, 1920–1945', *Journal of the History of Sexuality*, vol. 7, no. 2, 1996, pp. 239–75

Sarvasy, Wendy, 'Beyond the Difference versus Equality Policy Debate: Postsuffrage Feminism, Citizenship, and the Quest for a Feminist Welfare State', *Signs: Journal of Women in Culture and Society*, vol. 17, no. 2, 1992, pp. 329–62

Schlossman, Steven L., 'Philanthropy and the Gospel of Child Development', *History of Education Quarterly*, 21, 1981, pp. 275–99

Schlossman, Steven, and Stephanie Wallach, 'The Crime of Precocious Female Sexuality: Female Juvenile Delinquency in the Progressive Era', *Harvard Educational Review*, vol. 48, no. 1, 1978, pp. 65–94

Schnell, R. L., 'Childhood as Ideology: A Reinterpretation of the Common School', *British Journal of Educational Studies*, vol. 28, no. 1, 1979, pp. 7–28

Searle, G. R., *The Quest for National Efficiency: A Study in British Politics and Political Thought, 1899–1914*, Berkeley, University of California Press, 1971

Sedlak, Michael W., 'Young Women and the City: Adolescent Deviance and the Transformation of Educational Policy, 1870–1960', *History of Education Quarterly*, 23, 1983, pp. 1–28

Sedlak, Michael W., 'Youth Policy and Young Women, 1870–1972', *Social Service Review*, 56, 1982, pp. 448–64

Shiman, Lilian Lewis, 'The Band of Hope Movement: Respectable Recreation for Working-class Children', *Victorian Studies*, vol. 17, no. 1, 1973, pp. 49–74

Shuker, Roy, and Roger Openshaw with Janet Soler, *Youth, Media and Moral Panic in New Zealand: From Hooligans to Video Nasties*, Palmerston North, Education Department, Massey University, Delta Research Monograph no. 11, 1990

Simmons, Harvey G., 'Explaining Social Policy: The English Mental Deficiency Act of 1913', *Journal of Social History*, vol. 11, no. 3, 1978, pp. 387–403

Sinclair, Keith, *A History of New Zealand*, revised edition, Auckland, Penguin, 1980

Sinclair, Keith (ed.), *Oxford Illustrated History of New Zealand*, Auckland, Oxford University Press, 1990

Sinclair, Rob, *All God's Children*, British Columbia, Sinclair International Publishing, 1993

Sklar, Kathryn Kish, 'Hull House in the 1890s: A Community of Women Reformers', *Signs: Journal of Women in Culture and Society*, vol. 10, no. 4, 1985, pp. 638–77

Skocpol, Theda, *Protecting Soldiers and Mothers: The Political Origins of Social Policy in the United States*, Cambridge, Belknap Press of Harvard University Press, 1992

Smith, Eve P., and Lisa A. Merkel-Holguín (eds), *A History of Child Welfare*, New Brunswick, Transaction Publishers, 1996

Smith, F. B., *The People's Health 1830–1910*, London, Croom Helm, 1979

Smith, Pam, 'Moving Beyond the Ambulance', *Social Work Now: The Practice Journal of the New Zealand Children and Young Persons Service*, 2, 1995, pp. 31–3

Society for Research on Women in New Zealand, *The Unmarried Mother: Problems Involved in Keeping Her Child*, Wellington, SROW, 1970

Stansell, Christine, 'Women, Children and the Uses of the Streets: Class and Gender Conflict in New York City, 1850–1860', *Feminist Studies*, vol. 8, no. 2, 1982, pp. 309–35

Stearns, Peter N., and Timothy Haggerty, 'The Role of Fear: Transitions in American Emotional Standards for Children, 1850–1950', *American Historical Review*, vol. 96, no. 1, 1991, pp. 63–94

Steedman, Carolyn, *Strange Dislocations: Childhood and the Idea of Human Interiority 1780–1930*, London, Virago, 1995

Stella, Simonetta Piccone, '"Rebels Without a Cause": Male Youth in Italy Around 1960', *History Workshop Journal*, 38, 1994, pp. 157–78

Stewart, Graham, 'Power to the Community', *Social Work Now: The Practice Journal of the New Zealand Children and Young Persons Service*, 4, 1996, pp. 15–18

Stewart, Kathleen, 'Recollections From 1930', *New Zealand Social Worker*, vol. 5, no. 4, 1969, p. 25

Strange, Carolyn, 'From Modern Babylon to a City Upon a Hill: The Toronto Social Survey Commission of 1915 and the Search for Sexual Order in the City', in Roger Hall, William Westfall and Laurel Sefton

MacDowell (eds), *Patterns of the Past: Interpreting Ontario's History*, Toronto, Dundern Press, 1988, pp. 255–77

Stratton, Jon, 'Bodgies and Widgies: Youth Cultures in the 1950s', *Journal of Australian Studies*, 15, 1984, pp. 10–24

Summerfield, Penelope, 'Women, Work and Welfare: A Study of Child Care and Shopping in Britain in the Second World War', *Journal of Social History*, vol. 17, no. 2, 1983, pp. 249–69

Sutherland, Neil, *Children in English-Canadian Society: Framing the Twentieth-century Consensus*, Toronto, University of Toronto Press, 1976

Sutherland, Neil, '"Everyone Seemed Happy in Those Days": The Culture of Childhood in Vancouver Between the 1920s and the 1960s', *History of Education Review*, vol. 15, no. 2, 1986, pp. 37–51

Swain, Shurlee, with Renate Howe, *Single Mothers and Their Children: Disposal, Punishment and Survival in Australia*, Melbourne, Cambridge University Press, 1995

Synott, Anthony, 'Little Angels, Little Devils: A Sociology of Children', *Canadian Review of Sociology and Anthropology*, vol. 20, no. 1, 1983, pp. 79–95

Tapp, P. F., 'Family Group Conferences and the Children, Young Persons and Their Families Act 1989: An Ineffective Statute?', *New Zealand Recent Law Review*, 1990, pp. 82–8

Tennant, Margaret, *Children's Health, the Nation's Wealth: A History of Children's Health Camps*, Wellington, Bridget Williams Books and Historical Branch, Department of Internal Affairs, 1994

Tennant, Margaret, 'Maternity and Morality: Homes for Single Mothers 1890–1930', *Women's Studies Journal*, vol. 2, no. 1, 1985, pp. 28–49

Tennant, Margaret, *Paupers and Providers: Charitable Aid in New Zealand*, Wellington, Allen and Unwin/Historical Branch, Department of Internal Affairs, 1989

Thane, Pat, 'The Working Class and State "Welfare" in Britain, 1880–1914', *Historical Journal*, vol. 27, no. 4, 1984, pp. 877–900

Thavenet, Dennis, 'Tending their Flock: Diet, Hygiene and Health for 19th Century Reformatory Children', *Michigan Historical Review*, 15, 1989, pp. 23–46

Thompson, F. M. L., 'Social Control in Victorian Britain', *Economic History Review*, vol. 34, no. 2, 1981, pp. 189–208

Thompson, Paul, 'The War with Adults', *Oral History*, 3, 1975, pp. 29–38

Thomson, David, 'Society and Social Welfare', in Colin Davis and Peter Lineham (eds), *The Future of the Past: Themes in New Zealand History*, Palmerston North, History Department, Massey University, 1991, pp. 98–120

Thomson, David, 'Welfare and the Historians', in Lloyd Bonfield, Richard M. Smith and Keith Wrightson (eds), *The World We Have Gained*, Oxford, Blackwells, 1986, pp. 355–78

Tiffin, Susan, *In Whose Best Interest? Child Welfare Reform in the Progressive Era*, Westport, Connecticut, Greenwood Press, 1982

Te Timatanga Tatau Tatau: Early Stories from the Founding Members of the Maori Women's Welfare League, Wellington, Maori Women's Welfare League and Bridget Williams Books, 1993

Tinkler, Penny, 'Sexuality and Citizenship: The State and Girls' Leisure Provision in England, 1939–45', *Women's History Review*, vol. 4, no. 2, 1995, pp. 193–217

Tocker, Annie, 'Recollections From 1926', *New Zealand Social Worker*, vol. 5, no. 4, 1969, pp. 21–3

Toynbee, Claire, *Her Work and His: Family, Kin and Community in New Zealand 1900–1930*, Wellington, Victoria University Press, 1995

Trlin, A. D. (ed.), *Social Welfare and New Zealand Society*, Wellington, Methuen, 1977

Tropea, Joseph L., 'Bureaucratic Order and Special Children: Urban Schools, 1890s–1940s', *History of Education Quarterly*, vol. 27, no. 1, 1987, pp. 29–53

Turtle, Alison M., 'The Short-lived Appointment of the First New South Wales Government Psychologist, Dr Lorna Hodgkinson', *Australian Historical Studies*, 101, 1993, pp. 569–88

Vandepol, Ann, 'Dependent Children, Child Custody, and the Mothers' Pensions: The Transformation of State-family Relations in the Early 20th Century', *Social Problems*, vol. 29, no. 3, 1982, pp. 221–35

van Krieken, Robert, *Children and the State: Social Control and the Formation of Australian Child Welfare*, Sydney, Allen and Unwin, 1991 van Krieken, Robert, 'The Poverty of Social Control: Explaining Power in the Historical Sociology of the Welfare State', *Sociological Review*, vol. 39, no. 1, 1991, pp. 1- 25

van Krieken, Robert, 'Social Theory and Child Welfare: Beyond Social Control', *Theory and Society*, 15, 1986, pp. 401–29

van Krieken, Robert, 'State Bureaucracy and Social Science: Child Welfare in New South Wales, 1915–1940', *Labour History*, no. 58, 1990, pp. 17–35

van Krieken, Robert, 'Towards "Good and Useful Men and Women": The State and Childhood in Sydney, 1840–1890', *Australian Historical Studies*, 23, 1989, pp. 405–25

Vigne, Thea, 'Parents and Children 1890–1918: Distance and Dependence', *Oral History*, 3, 1975, pp. 6–11

Walker, David, 'Continence for a Nation: Seminal Loss and National Vigour', *Labour History*, no. 48, 1985, pp. 1–14

Wall, Richard, and Jay Winter (eds), *The Upheaval of War: Family, Work and Welfare in Europe, 1914–1918*, Cambridge, Cambridge University Press, 1988

Walvin, James, *A Child's World: A Social History of English Childhood 1800–1914*, Harmondsworth, Penguin, 1982

Watkins, Roger, *Hostage to the Beat: The Auckland Scene 1955–70*, Auckland, Penguin, 1995

Weir, Margaret, Ann Shola Orloff and Theda Skocpol (eds), *The Politics of Social Policy in the United States*, Princeton, Princeton University Press, 1988

Williamson, Noeline, '"Hymns, Songs and Blackguard Verses": Life in the Industrial and Reformatory School for Girls in New South Wales. Part I – 1867 to 1887', *Journal of the Royal Australian Historical Society*, 64, 1982, pp. 375–87

Wilson, Adrian, 'The Infancy of the History of Childhood: An Appraisal of Philippe Ariès', *History and Theory*, 19, 1980, pp. 132–53

Wilson, Stephen, 'The Myth of Motherhood Myth: The Historical View of European Child-rearing', *Social History*, vol. 9, no. 2, 1984, pp. 181–98

Wimshurst, K., 'Child Labour and School Attendance in South Australia 1890–1915', *Historical Studies*, 19, 1981, pp. 388–411

Wood, Beth, 'Care and Protection Resource Panels', *Children: A Newsletter from the Office of the Commissioner for Children*, 18, 1995, pp. 13–14

Yska, Redmer, *All Shook Up: The Flash Bodgie and the Rise of the New Zealand Teenager in the Fifties*, Auckland, Penguin, 1993

Zelizer, Viviana, *Pricing the Priceless Child: The Changing Social Value of Children*, New York, Basic Books, 1985

Oral Sources

'The Mazengarb Report', *Spectrum* Documentary, Radio New Zealand, no. 731

'No Home for Mary', *Spectrum* Documentary, Radio New Zealand, nos 259, 260

'Two Wellington Childhoods', *Spectrum* Documentary, Radio New Zealand, no. 012

Videos

'Care and Protection', *Children, Young Persons, and Their Families Act 1989*, Programme Two, Department of Social Welfare, nd

'A Family Affair', *Frontline* Documentary, Television New Zealand, 1992

Kingi's Story, Morrow Productions in association with Television New Zealand, 1981

Planning for Children and Young Persons in Care, Department of Social Welfare, 1985

Preparation for Fostering – Effects on Your Children, Department of Social Welfare, 1985

'Silent Tears', *One Network News Special*, Television New Zealand, 1991

'Under Duress?', *60 Minutes*, TV3, 1993

'Youth Justice', *Children, Young Persons, and Their Families Act 1989*, Programme One, Department of Social Welfare, 1989

INDEX